Israel:
Its Politics and Philosophy

AN ANNOTATED READER

Edited by

ISRAEL T. NAAMANI
*Professor and Chairman,
Department of Political Science,
University of Louisville*

DAVID RUDAVSKY
*Professor and Head,
Institute of Hebrew Studies,
New York University*

ABRAHAM I. KATSH
*President,
Dropsie University*

BEHRMAN HOUSE, INC.
Publishers • New York

Revised edition © 1974
© Copyright 1971 by Israel T. Naamani,
David Rudavsky, Abraham I. Katsh.
All rights reserved.

Library of Congress Cataloging in Publication Data
Naamani, Israel T   comp.
  Israel: its politics and philosophy.
  Published in 1971 in Tel Aviv under title: Israel through the eyes of its leaders.
  1. Israel—Addresses, essays, lectures. I. Rudavsky, David, joint comp. II. Katsh, Abraham Isaac, 1908-   joint comp. III. Title.
DS126.5.N22 1973   915.694'05'08   73-15645
ISBN 0-87441-249-8

Manufactured in the United States of America

PREFACE TO THE 1974 EDITION

An Israeli military victory quivered on the west bank of the Suez Canal and on the road to Damascus late in October 1973. The victory was denied. There was uncertain glory in the datelines, abruptly stopped late in January 1974, in soldiers' letters received by Israeli parents, wives, and sweethearts from "the Land of Goshen." Israel is no longer in Africa. There are those who assert that Israeli feats in the Yom Kippur War were more brilliant than even those of 1967. Yet Israel's aura has been dimmed.

The Introduction to this book, in its earlier edition, points out, however, on Page xi: "The solutions faced by Israel even before 1973-74 are not Sinaic or millennial." In the same paragraph the editors add: "Quite ambiguously, Israel often has been described as a miracle. In more mundane terms, the State is the result of *preparedness* that met opportunity." (Italics by the editors.)

The massive hangover still experienced by Israelis in the spring of 1974 will naturally disappear because of the essentially strong anatomy of the State. The editors of this book may sound a bit immodest when they say that this volume (which, incidentally, sold out in its hardcover edition) captured the very essence of the State through the living testimonies of its founders and leaders—the utterances that they, *not the editors,* felt are the most pertinent. Thus the significance of their statements, put together in this book, would seem to increase as history goes on.

The singular concession to time that we all must make is purely chronological. Wherever needed the following paragraphs update very briefly the biographical sketches of some of the participants in the volume.

Yigal Allon is still in search of his destiny. The Yom Kippur War, however, did not diminish his political stature.

Shulamit Aloni's time has come. "A consistent non-conformist" she rose to great political influence in 1974. Having split from the Labor Party, mostly because of Golda Meir, she organized the Civil Rights Party. An agnostic, a feminist, a consumer advocate, she will be heard—and often— in and out of government.

Uri Avnery, because of "in-fighting" with his left-wing comrades and the current eclipse of the "Semitic Idea," lost his seat in Parliament. Thus, at the moment, his political tones are subdued.

Menahem Begin is now the leader of *Likud* ("Unity"), a strange collection of parties, factions, and individuals, mostly right-wing but also a scattering of left-wing elements who believe in "maximal" Israel. The *Likud* was put together by a relatively young general, "Arik" Sharon, in 1973. Hence Begin still has the roar, but he lost much of the echo.

Yitzhak Ben-Aharon was forced to "volunteer" his resignation in November of 1973 from the Secretary Generalship of the *Histadrut* (General Federation of Labor). His ideology is unswerving, but not his future.

Moshe Dayan as Defense Minister during the Yom Kippur War was blamed for the initial Israeli setbacks. He was also castigated for his party's losses in the elections of 1973. Yet he was probably the strongest personality in the country in the early months of 1974. The reason seems to be that while he was still a member of the Labor Party (and Alignment), with the left-wing "doves" snapping at him, he was not far, ideologically, from the *Likud*. Moderate and labor "hawks" plus a grudging *Likud* thus gave him a broad base of acceptibility. Also, one should not forget—and many have— that in *1971* Dayan suggested roughly the format of the Sinai disengagement. Dr. Henry Kissinger remembered.

Abba Eban is still a stranger in his own country. Among the most gifted diplomats in the world, speaking Hebrew and a dozen or more other languages, he still cannot and does not speak to his people.

Arie Eliav, feeling the need for more formal education, completed his doctoral work at the University of Tel Aviv. He is one of the minority voices in the Labor Party advocating the greatest possible accommodation with the Arabs. He is imaginative and popular with practically all factions in the country.

David Horowitz has retired from his post as Governor of the Bank of Israel.

Golda Meir, the amazing synthesis of a "sceptered lady" and "a Jewish mother," may have committed in October of 1973 her gravest mistake or her noblest achievement.

Shmuel Mikunis may have lost some of his political clout in the Communist Party of Israel (*Maki*), but he certainly maintained his ideological virtue in 1974. A crazy quilt of Israel communists and new-left elements combined and sidetracked Mikunis to create *Moked*. The leadership was vested in Meir Payil, the sole elected member of Parliament from the new group (whereas in some of the former Parliaments two were elected from *Maki*).

Yitzhak Nissim has retired from the Chief Rabbinate of Israel.

Shimon Peres, a protege of Ben-Gurion, is considered by some as the most capable statesman in Israel, but he is overshadowed by his charismatic friend, Dayan.

Yitzhak Rabin has returned to Israel from his ambassadorship in Washington, where he has distinguished himself both as a diplomat and as an administrator. Elected to the 1973 Knesset, he is a "comer" in Israeli politics.

Moshe Shamir, although ideologically a socialist, associated himself in 1973 with *Likud,* a rightist bloc, but only in the matter of "maximal" Israel, he claimed.

Zalman Shazar has retired from the Presidency of Israel.

Shmuel Tamir, leader of the Free Center, joined *Likud,* essentially a conservative group with aspirations for "Israel in its historic boundaries."

Tawfiq Toubi (and Meir Wilner) of *Rakah,* the New Communist Party (Moscow-oriented), have made many gains in the December 1973, elections for Parliament. Some of it was at the expense of *Maki-Moked,* the Israel oriented communists. Mostly, though, it was due to the Arab vote in Nazareth and in other Arab towns and villages.

Yisrael Yeshayahu was elected earlier and then reelected in 1974 as Speaker of the Parliament.

David Ben-Gurion, André Chouraqui, Levi Eshkol, Hayim Hazaz, Aryeh Pincus, and Yitzhak Tabenkin are no longer living.

THE EDITORS

TABLE OF CONTENTS

List of Contributors

Introduction

I. Pangs of Rebirth

DAVID BEN-GURION, Statement to the Anglo-American Committee of Inquiry, March 19, 1946 — 3
ZALMAN SHAZAR, Horrors of a Final Battle — 23
GOLDA MEIR, The Zionist Purpose — 31
LEVI ESHKOL, The Initial Step — 41
BENJAMIN AKZIN, Introduction to a Project of a Constitution for the State of Israel — 47

II. Vessels of Tested Culture

JACOB L. TALMON, Uniqueness and Universality of Jewish History — 55
SAMUEL HUGO BERGMAN, The Phenomenon of Israel — 75
ERNST A. SIMON, Valid and Invalid Quoting from the Scriptures — 91
ELIEZER LIVNEH, Values and Society in Israel — 101
MOSHE SILBERG, The Purity of Judgment in the Hebrew Code — 113
MOSHE SHAMIR, The Hard Way — 131

III. Mosaic Theophany and Mosaic Secularism

NATHAN ROTENSTREICH, Secularism and Religion in Israel — 145
YISRAEL YESHAYAHU, The Status of Religion in the State of Israel and Among the Jews of Israel — 169
SHULAMIT ALONI, The Absurdity of Religious Legislation; Comments on Marriage Laws in Israel — 181
ZURIEL ADMONIT, One Poem and Its Meaning — 197
YITZHAK NISSIM, Religion and the Jewish State — 203

IV. Social Messianism and Unyielding Realities

YIGAL ALLON, The Essence of Democracy — 213
YITZHAK TABENKIN, The Kibbutz in an Era of Change — 225
ARYEH L. PINCUS, The Crux of the Problem—Immigration — 233
SHIMON PERES, Jacob's New Ladder — 237
ISRAEL GOLDSTEIN, Israel's Dilemma and Imperative — 247
HAYIM HAZAZ, An Interview, by Raphael Bashan — 253

V. Molding a Nation—Ingathering of Exiles and Ingathering of Problems

ANDRE N. CHOURAQUI, Between East and West	265
NISSIM REJWAN, The Communal Front	283
MOSHE DAVIS, Teaching American Jewish History in Israel	293
YITZHAK RABIN, The People and Its Army	305

VI. Securing the Future

MENAHEM BEGIN, An Address at the Herut Party Convention, May, 1968	315
URI AVNERY, The Mistake of Columbus; The Federation of Palestine	331
TAWFIQ TOUBI, An Address at the World Peace Council, June, 1968	347
SHMUEL MIKUNIS, In the Battle for Peace	353
SHMUEL TAMIR, After the Victory—Dangers and Prospects	369
ARIE ELIAV, Israel and Palestinians	375
DAVID HOROWITZ, The Economics of Israel	381
ABBA EBAN, An Address at the General Assembly of the U.N., June, 1967	387
MOSHE DAYAN, Jewish-Arab Coexistence	409
YITZHAK BEN-AHARON, The Just Society in Israel	427

LIST OF CONTRIBUTORS

ADMONIT, ZURIEL—writer, editor, leader of young religionists (Hakibbutz Hadati)
AKZIN, BENJAMIN—professor of political science; former dean, law faculty, Hebrew University
ALLON, YIGAL—Deputy Prime Minister; Minister of Education and Culture
ALONI, SHULAMIT—former member of Knesset; leader of anti-clericalists
AVNERY, URI—member of Knesset; editor of *Haolam Hazeh*; advocate of Israeli-Arab bi-nationalism
BEGIN, MENAHEM—cabinet member; leader of *Herut* party (ultra-nationalist)
BEN-AHARON, YITZHAK—ideologist of labor movement; secretary, General Federation of Labor
BEN-GURION, DAVID—former Prime Minister of Israel
BERGMAN, SAMUEL HUGO—professor of philosophy (emeritus), Hebrew University; pacifist
CHOURAQUI, ANDRE—one-time Deputy Mayor of Jerusalem; leader of North African Jewry
DAVIS, MOSHE—Director, Institute of Contemporary Jewry, Hebrew University
DAYAN, MOSHE—former Chief-of-Staff; Defense Minister of Israel
EBAN, ABBA—former Israeli ambassador to Washington; Foreign Minister of Israel
ELIAV, ARIE—former Secretary-General, Labor Party of Israel *(Avodah)*; director of development projects
ESHKOL, LEVI—late Prime Minister of Israel
GOLDSTEIN, ISRAEL—former President, Keren Hayesod-United Jewish Appeal; General-Zionist leader
HAZAZ, HAYIM—eminent novelist and social thinker
HOROWITZ, DAVID—former Governor of Bank of Israel
LIVNEH, ELIEZER—noted essayist and sociologist
MEIR, GOLDA—Prime Minister of Israel
MIKUNIS, SHMUEL—Secretary-General, Communist Party of Israel
NISSIM, YITZHAK—Chief Rabbi of Israel
PERES, SHIMON—Minister of Communications
PINCUS, ARYEH L.—Chairman, Jewish Agency for Israel
RABIN, YITZHAK—Israel's ambassador to Washington; Chief-of-Staff during the Six Day War
REJWAN, NISSIM—editor of Arab-language newspapers; journalist; sociologist
ROTENSTREICH, NATHAN—former Rector, Hebrew University
SHAMIR, MOSHE—noted novelist and publicist
SHAZAR, ZALMAN—President of Israel
SILBERG, MOSHE—former Deputy Chief Justice, Supreme Court
SIMON, ERNST A.—professor of education; proponent of Israel-Arab bi-nationalism

TABENKIN, YITZHAK—ideologist of labor movement; leader of *Hakibbutz Hameuhad*
TALMON, JACOB L.—noted historian; taught at Hebrew, Harvard and Oxford Universities; pacifist
TAMIR, SHMUEL—leader of right-wing, ultra-nationalist *Hamerkaz Hahofshi* Party
TOUBI, TAWFIQ—member Politburo, the New Communist Party of Israel
YESHAYAHU, YISRAEL—former Minister of Posts and Telegraph; spokesman of Oriental Jews

INTRODUCTION

Rarely has a people been so willing and so able to serve history as the Jews. Arnold J. Toynbee who persisted in his notion of the "fossilization" of Judaism —acting like the proverbial man who said, "My mind is made up; don't confuse me with facts"—must have been very piqued when in the span of one year, 1966–1967, the Jews won both the Nobel Prize for Literature and a Napoleonic victory.

Quite ambiguously, Israel often has been described as a miracle. In more mundane terms, the State is the result of preparedness that met opportunity. The Jews have been drawn together throughout history under the relentless compulsion of events beyond their control, yet Israel's future is at least as manipulative as it is ordained. The messianic accents echoing in many pages of this book are matched by physical staying-power and the imperatives of expedience. The problems Israel has faced and is facing are multifarious. The solutions were not and are not always Sinaic or millennial. The purpose of this volume is to see the present and the future of Israel through the eyes of its leaders in every walk of its life.

The editorship of an anthology or reader is ordinarily a work of presumption. Despite the very best and unbiased of intentions, the contents of such a book are a reflection of the tastes as well as the subconscious preferences of the compilers. Happily this is not altogether the case in this project. The uniqueness of this undertaking lies in the fact that the editors, instead of choosing the material themselves, asked the contributors to make their own selections— what *they*, the participants, thought were their most pertinent utterances with regard to the past, the present, and the potential of Israel. Consequently, this is not a collection of replies to an *enquete*. It is, nevertheless, an indication by the participants, in their chosen manner, of the role they, or the groups they represent, play in the retention or modification of Israel's socio-economic, ethno-religious and politico-behaviorist values.

If there is an element of subjectivity in this book, it is in the choice of contributors. The editors have, to the best of their knowledge, selected the generally recognized, representative and accepted spokesmen of their respective movements or groups.

The editors wrote to 42 personalities—leaders in government, philosophers, heads of religious movements, freethinkers, party ideologists, social workers, military men, pacifists, representatives of ethnic groups, economists, political scientists and belletrists—who together mirror the views of all the elements in Israeli society. Of the 42, three ignored the request to participate in the anthology even after follow-up reminders; three indicated inability to take time out for the project; 36 replied in the affirmative; and 33 actually furnished the compilers with their essays, summations of several of their works, or the sources from which to cull their articles, speeches or book-chapters. In 3 instances the editors themselves selected essays or speeches and requested permission to use them.

All the personalities quoted in this book were alive at the time the project got under way. One of them, Levi Eshkol, the Prime Minister who died in office early in 1969, shortly before his death instructed his staff to forward his essay to the compendium. Another, Yitzhak Tabenkin, died in 1971.

Some articles in the anthology fit into any section of the book or can stand alone. There is a bit of overlapping and repetition, but this was anticipated by the compilers, who did not wish to tamper with the material. (In a number of instances they were explicitly enjoined by the authors not to alter either the language or the length of the contributions.) In several cases the editors would have preferred other selections by the writers—essays or speeches which in the opinion of the compilers were more representative of their authors or had greater merit. But this is the particular significance of the book—it presents the material as the participants desired (with the three aforementioned exceptions where acquiescence instead of preference was expressed).

There is a brief biographical sketch and evaluative introduction of each contributor, which includes the main currents of his thinking, his leadership role and the area of his specific competence.

Shoshana Perla translated from the Hebrew the essays by Zalman Shazar, Levi Eshkol, Yigal Allon, Moshe Silberg, Hayim Hazaz, Yitzhak Tabenkin, Shimon Peres, Ernst A. Simon, Shmuel Tamir, Yisrael Yeshayahu, Zuriel Admonit and Shulamit Aloni (the portion entitled "The Absurdity of Religious Legislation"). Menahem Begin's speech was rendered into English by members of his staff; Moshe Shamir's contribution was translated by *Uzy Nystar,* Chief Rabbi Nissim's essay by *Mendel Kaufman,* and S. H. Bergman's work by *Moses Hadas.*

What impressions does a study of this compendium awaken? The following views are the compilers'; the readers may or may not share them. We submit these "thoughts" as "theses" for reflection.

One may discern here:

An ideological transformation in Israel, the apparent fading away of the old doctrinal socialism of Mapai (the non-Marxist plurality party, until it merged with other workers' factions, after the Six Day War of 1967, to form *Mifleget Avodah Yisraelit,* the Labor Party of Israel, and its replacement by seemingly more empirical schemata).

The challenge of secularism and reformism to theological fundamentalism and the ensuing ethno-religious concepts.

The self-assertion of the Jewish immigrants from the Middle East and North

Africa—at times by the sheer power of numbers—for a place in the Israeli sun, and the concomitant desire by the "establishment" to meet the socio-cultural needs of the newcomers, but inability to do so effectively or speedily. The strange phenomenon of a conflict between the "Old Generation" and the "Middle-Aged Generations"—with the "Young Generation" as an amused observer—in contrast to the struggle or gap between the "Old Generation" and the "Young Generation" in the United States and Europe.

The simultaneous accommodation of various ideological views and the balancing out of kibbutz collectivism on the one hand, and concessions to capital investors on the other; also the paralleling of cooperative projects with private enterprise, thus avoiding the tragic mistake of new, "developing" countries: There is *no single* economic *system* or *undertaking* so enveloping as to pose catastrophic risks for Israel.

A poor land, Israel's greatest natural resources lie in the brains and energy of her people, yet the political leadership (not the military) in and out of government acts more by intuition than by scientific planning, more by bureaucratic traditionalism than by technological skills.

On the international problem—war and peace with the Arabs—Israel is as divided on this issue as the United States was in the late 1960's and in 1970 on Vietnam.

Although most Israelis want to be "like unto all nations", they are really in quest of a unique identity. They walk with the sand of Sinai in their sandals.

—*The Editors*

1
Pangs of Rebirth

DAVID BEN-GURION
ZALMAN SHAZAR
GOLDA MEIR
LEVI ESHKOL
BENJAMIN AKZIN

DAVID BEN-GURION

David Ben-Gurion was born in Plonsk, Poland (then part of Russia) in 1886, and settled in Palestine in 1906. On his arrival in the new land he worked in various agricultural settlements and set out, with the help of others, to organize a Jewish labor movement, serving later, in 1921-35, as the chief executive officer of the newly formed, powerful Histadrut (General Federation of Jewish Labor). Feeling the need for more systematic education, Ben-Gurion spent two years, 1912-14, studying law in Constantinople. When he came back to Palestine he was expelled by the Turkish authorities. From 1915 to 1918 he lived in the United States where he was active in organizing the Jewish Legion (under British command), returning to Palestine as a soldier.

Ben-Gurion's dynamic personality eventually brought him the chairmanship of the Jewish Agency for Palestine, in 1935-48. In 1942 he formulated the "Biltmore Program" for the establishment of Palestine as "a Jewish Commonwealth integrated in the structure of the new democratic world." It was his forceful leadership that was largely instrumental in Israel's declaration of independence on May 14, 1948. He served as his country's first Prime-Minister and Minister for Defense until 1953. Ben-Gurion then retired to Sdeh Boker in the Negev desert to meditate and to study Greek and Buddhist thought, coming back as Minister of Defense in 1955 and again as Prime Minister from 1956 to 1963.

A non-Marxist socialist, Ben-Gurion developed ideological and personal differences between himself and his colleagues in the government and in the ruling Mapai Party. Ben-Gurion insisted on reforming the country's electoral system, shifting the emphasis from East European to West European democratic processes, reducing the number of political parties, removing the Old Guard in the Mapai and in the Histadrut, who, he felt, could not administer a young democracy in the second half of the 20th century. When the Old Guard resisted its leader, Ben-Gurion in 1965, formed a new party, *Rafi*, Notwithstanding the popularity, admiration and reverence in which he was held, his new political effort failed. Ben-Gurion retired again to his beloved Sdeh Boker.

Relentless activist, scouring moralizer, prophetic, mythogenic, Ben-Gurion is perhaps best described by one of his former disciples, Abba Eban. "Ben-Gurion's natural bend did not lie in international statesmanship . . . . His genius lay rather in the capacity to animate the national will and to create solid and entrenched Israeli facts which in their turn, would pull a decisive weight on the international scale. He was an immensely galvanizing force, sending out sparks of vitality in all directions."

The Anglo-American Committee of Inquiry, to whom Ben-Gurion presented the the following statement, consisted of six Britons and six Americans, who examined the situation in Palestine and who visited the concentration camps in Europe in 1946. It was to make recommendations to the British government, then administering Palestine, whether to allow or deny entry into Palestine to 100,000 Jewish refugees. This presentation, perhaps more than any other statement by Ben-Gurion—except the Declaration of Independence—captured the hearts of the Jews in what was at the time Palestine.

Statement to the Anglo-American Committee of Inquiry, March 19, 1946

by DAVID BEN-GURION

MR. CHAIRMAN AND GENTLEMEN, I fully realize that you have been on this inquiry for more than two months and you have already had a good deal of evidence, orally and in writing, and I cannot presume to tell you new things entirely. The reason for my statement is that up till now you have had only the view of Jews from abroad looking to this country. I will try to present to you the case as seen by those in their own country; by those who are no longer American, British, Russian, Polish, German Jews, but just Jews.

I want first of all to tell you that there was considerable discussion whether to appear before the Commission or not, both here and in America, and many reasons are given for not cooperating. It was said that the appointment of the Commission was in practice a means of putting off the request of the President of the United States for an immediate admission of 100,000 refugees from Germany. It was said that the setting up of this Commission was a means of silencing the voice of the Labor Party in England for the immediate repeal of the White Paper.[1] It was said that the statement made by the Secretary of State for Foreign Affairs, Mr. Bevin, pre-judged many conclusions of the Commission. It was said that anyway the policy of the Mandatory power would not be determined by the findings of the Commission on facts and figures, or by considerations of justice, but on considerations of political expediency, and it was especially urged that the only result of this inquiry would be the prolongation of the agony and sufferings of hundreds of thousands of Jewish victims of the Nazis, who meanwhile would be condemned to stay in that hell.

We decided otherwise, not because we thought all these objections were entirely without foundation, but first of all we thought that whatever might be the intention of those who set up this Commission, the Commission itself was in no way responsible for it or for the results. We appreciate the fact that distinguished personalities from Great Britain and America have undertaken this complicated and not too pleasant inquiry, have left their home and work and are engaged in finding out what is the truth of this complicated problem,

---

[1] The White Paper of 1939 was issued by the British government and stated that 75,000 Jews would be allowed to enter Palestine over a period of five years, to 1944, after which Jewish immigration would depend on Arab consent. (Eds.)

and we therefore considered it our moral duty to help as far as we could to ascertain the truth and justice of the case. On behalf of our community I invite you to see how we are living and what we are doing, and you will be welcome everywhere.

THE JEWISH PEOPLE IN PALESTINE AS OF RIGHT

Sir, our case it seems to us is simple and compelling, and it rests on two elementary principles: one, that we Jews are just like other human beings, entitled to the same rights as every human being in the world, and we Jewish people are just like any other people, entitled to the same equality of treatment as any free and independent people in the world. The second principle is: this always has been, and will remain our country. We are here as of right. We are not here on the strength of the Balfour Declaration[2] or the Palestine Mandate.[3] We were here long, long before. I myself was here before. Many thousands were here before me, and our people were here for centuries and millenia before that. It is the Mandatory power that is here—legally speaking—on the strength of that Mandate. Our case, and I think you have just seen many such cases in Europe, is like that of the Jews who were forcibly expelled from their homes, which were then given to somebody else. These homes changed hands, and then after the Nazi defeat some Jewish owners came back and found their houses occupied. In many cases they were not allowed to return to their houses. To make it more exact, I shall put it this way. It is a large building, the building of our family, say 50 rooms. We were expelled from that house, our family was scattered, somebody else took it away and again it changed hands many times, and then we had to come back and we found some five rooms occupied by other people, the other rooms destroyed and uninhabitable from neglect. We said to these occupants, "We do not want to remove you; please stay where you are; we are going back into the uninhabitable rooms; we will repair them." And we did repair some of them and settled there. Then some other members of our family come back, and they want to repair some other uninhabitable rooms; but then these occupants say, "No, we are here, we do not want you. We do not live in these rooms, they are no good for any human beings, but we do not want you to repair them, to make them better." And again we do not say to them, "Leave, the house is ours." We say, "You may stay, though you have only been here since yesterday. We are even willing to help you to repair your rooms too, if you like; if not, you can do it yourselves." In the neighborhood are many big buildings, half empty; we do not say to them, "Please move over to that other big building." No, we say, "Please

---

[2] The Balfour Declaration was issued by the British government on November 2, 1917, favoring the establishment of a Jewish national home in Palestine, without prejudicing the civil and religious rights of the existing non-Jewish communities in the country. (Eds.)
[3] The Palestine Mandate was part of a plan by the League of Nations in the 1920's to prepare various areas in the Middle East for eventual independence. Great Britain was entrusted with the administration of Palestine. (Eds.)

stay here; we shall be good neighbors." This is our case; it is simple and compelling.

I realize the intellectual difficulty of our case. There are practical difficulties, but now I am talking of the intellectual difficulty of understanding our case because it is unique. There is no precedent, there is no example in the world's history of this problem of the Jews and their country. There is no example or precedent of such a people. It is a people, and it is not. There is no precedent for the history of the Jewish people and there is no parallel to the fate of this country, no precedent for the special significance this country has for us. There is no parallel to the relations between our people and this country, a country they do not live in. It is unique. People usually think in analogies, and when they are faced with a new phenomenon, they prefer to deny the existence of what they cannot understand. But it remains a fact nevertheless. You have the unique case of the homeless Jewish people and their historic country.

I have read a great deal of the evidence given to you in America and in England. I saw the real difficulty you had of getting at it. What is this Jewish people? Is it a people? Are they not citizens of Poland, Russia, America, and England? Did we not treat them as brothers and as co-citizens? And people say it sincerely, and I have the greatest admiration for the people saying it, because they really think the Jew is like themselves. There is a Jewish people and there is a problem. The Jews have been torn away from this country for many centuries, the greater part of them, and still it is their country. But it is not empty. There are people here, part of them have been here for many centuries—a great part of them also newcomers, but a part of them for many centuries. From afar it is not easy to get really at the core of the problem. But I believe when you see things here, it will become a little easier to understand.

What I am going to do is simply to tell you what we Jews in our own country are like, who we are, what we are doing, what we are aiming at. Why are we here, for what purpose are we here? Perhaps this will explain things.

WHY JEWS COME TO PALESTINE

There are now some 600,000 here, more than one-third born in this country, some of them living here for many centuries. Their number used to be much greater, and they were found in many villages in Galilee. But the majority were destroyed, and only a remnant remained, in the village of Pekiin (in Arabic: Bukea). But the majority of us were not born in this country; I am one of them. We came from all parts of the world, from all countries, and we came not only from countries where Jews were persecuted physically, exterminated, repressed, as in Nazi Germany, Poland, the Yemen, Morocco, Czarist Russia, Persia, Fascist Italy. Many of us came from free countries where Jews were treated like citizens, where there was no persecution, from England, from the United States of America, Canada, the Argentine, from pre-war Germany, Imperial Germany, from Soviet Russia, France, Egypt and other countries. Why did they come? They did not come only because they were persecuted. What is the common denominator which brought all these people, whether from Nazi Germany or from England, whether from Yemen or from Egypt? That is what I want to tell you.

ESCAPE FROM DEPENDENCE AND DISCRIMINATION

The first thing which brought them over, all of them, was to escape from dependence and discrimination. I do not mean from anti-Semitism. There was a great deal of talk in your Commission about anti-Semitism and many of our people were asked to explain why it exists. It is not for us to explain. It's your baby, it is a Christian baby. It is for you Gentiles to explain why it exists. Perhaps it would be necessary to set up a Jewish Commission to make an inquiry of the Gentiles, or perhaps a joint Jewish-Gentile Commission, one chairman Jewish, one chairman Gentile, to make an inquiry among leaders of the church, teachers, educators, journalists, political parties as to what this disease is, what is the reason for it in the Gentile world. To me it seems it is part of a larger phenomenon which does not concern only Jews, a general human phenomenon. Wherever you have two groups, one a strong group, powerful, and the other weak and helpless, there is bound to be mischief. The strong group will always take advantage of the weaker group, rightly or wrongly. You cannot expect of human beings, human nature being what it is, people having power over other people, that they should not sometimes—not always, not necessarily always—abuse it. But I am not concerned with anti-Semitism, it is not our business. I am concerned with the question why Jews have come to this country, and have come not only from other countries where they were physically persecuted. They came because they felt it was unendurable that they should be at the mercy of others. Sometimes the others are excellent people, but not always, and there is discrimination—not necessarily legal, or political or economic—sometimes merely a moral discrimination, and they did not like it. As human beings with human dignity, they do not like it, and they do not see how they can change the whole world, so they decided to return to their own country and be masters of their own destiny.

I want to give you one example of moral discrimination. Gentlemen, I do not know in Europe a more tolerant, a more liberal, a more fair-minded people than the English people in their own country; perhaps the Scandinavian peoples are also like that; I do not know them as well as I do the British, although I do not think anyone can claim that except the British themselves, if even they can. There was recently in the House of Lords, one of the noblest institutions in the world, whatever one thinks of it on democratic principles, there was a debate on the Jewish problem. I think only in England could you have such a debate, a debate on the Jewish problem. It was on 7th December 1945, and in that debate the Archbishop of York in very strong language condemned anti-Semitism as un-Christian. Coming from His Grace it means a lot, un-Christian. He also expressed deep concern over the sufferings of the Jewish people. It may not help us very much practically, but we appreciate it very deeply as a moral help. He then began talking about the Jewish attacks on or criticism of the policy of His Majesty's Government in Palestine, meaning the White Paper policy of 1939, and the attacks being made by Jews on both sides of the Atlantic, and he said these significant words: "It (meaning this criticism) is being resented and may easily lead to a most dangerous reaction." Well, Jews are not the only people who are criticizing or attacking the White Paper policy. In 1939, the White Paper policy was described, not by a Jew, but an Englishman, a pure Englishman, a Gentile, as "a mortal blow to the Jewish people." The name of the Englishman, Gentlemen, is Winston Churchill. We agree with his description. It was and is a mortal blow.

Well, Gentlemen, when a people receives a mortal blow from somebody, would anybody ask them to lie down and take it silently—a mortal blow? Would anybody resent this criticism, this attack on that mortal blow? This was said by Mr. Churchill in 1939 when our people in Europe were still alive. Since then tens of thousands of human beings, of babies—after all, Jewish babies are also babies—have met their death because of that policy. Because of that policy they could not be saved. Not all of them found their death because of it, but tens of thousands could have been saved and were not, because of that policy. Is it surprising that we as human beings should criticize or attack this policy? I am sure His Grace understands that. He is a great personality, he knows the mind of his people, and he said that this may lead to a most dangerous reaction. This is what I call moral discrimination. We receive a mortal blow; we must be silent. If not, it may lead to a dangerous reaction. Where? Not in Poland, but in that most liberal and tolerant country—I say it with the greatest respect—England. Why this discrimination? There were many Jews who submitted; there were some Jews who refused. And that is what brought them over here. There they were at the mercy of nice people, but nice people may sometimes become very nasty, when they have the power and are dealing with a minority.

THE JEWS CHOSE TO REMAIN JEWISH

Why is there this discrimination? As I see it, it is for two reasons; because we happen to be different from others, and because we happen to be a minority. We are not the only ones who are different from others. In truth we are not different at all, because difference is a term of relativity. If there were only one person in the world he would not be different. We are what we are. Others are different, but, as they see us, we are different. But we are what we are and we like to be what we are. Is it a crime? Cannot a man be what he is? Cannot a people be what they are? I know on the continent they consider British people very different, and they are, but no Britisher will think he is different. He is just what he is, but to continental people he looks different. We happen to be different because other people are different. For that our people suffer. The English people do not suffer because they are different. On the contrary, it is a great compliment, it is a great strength. They have their own individuality

Statement to the Anglo-American Committee, March 19, 1946

and people are brought to respect it. But with us, not only are we different, we are in a minority. We are at the mercy of others, and when they don't like our being different they can do us harm. Our position becomes very precarious when our "difference" is disliked, and from time to time we are asked to renounce what we are, either our being a people or our religion or our country or our language. Certain Jews did renounce, not all, but some of us do and did. In the course of your inquiry, I think you met some of those people. But the Jewish people as a whole stick to their Jewishness, whether other people like it or not. One of the characteristic forms of our "differentness" is that we, the Jewish people, have always been ready to defy superior material power when asked by this superior material power to renounce spiritual values that are dear to us and that are a part of us. And we pay the price, sometimes a very high price, because we stick to our spiritual values.

It is a long, long story. It goes back 2,300 years to when the world became Hellenized, when Egypt, Syria, Persia became Hellenized. Judea did not submit to that "superior" culture—and it was in many respects a superior culture—but the Jews preferred to be just what they were and they suffered. Then it became unendurable. They revolted, they fought and they were victorious. There was another clash when Rome became the dominant power and we were asked to accept the divinity of the Caesars, and we refused. The most powerful rulers of the world, they were above all the people, recognized as divine persons in the whole Roman Empire, but not by us; and we suffered and fought, and this time we were defeated, but only materially, not spiritually. We defied that superior material power. Then it happened again with the rise of Christianity. I must be careful now in speaking to Christians. The whole of Europe was converted to Christianity, many voluntarily, many by force; we refused. We perhaps had more to do with the new religion than other peoples; St. Paul was a Jew. Nevertheless, we refused and we paid the price. We are still paying it, a very high price. I have read the evidence given before you by some Christian missionaries and sensed traces of that old hatred. The story was repeated again with the rise of another great religion in the East, a religion to which almost the entire East was converted, either voluntarily or by force. Again we refused and had to suffer. But here I prefer to be entirely silent.

The French Revolution asked us to renounce our being a people. Some Jews did it. The Jewish people refused.

And now the last phase—what was done to us in this war. I am not going to speak about that—what has happened in the last few years is unspeakable. Why should I burden you with Jewish feelings? It happened to us, not to anybody else. I will tell you only one feeling which I had, one of the feelings which I had when I knew the whole story of what happened to us: I felt that at least I and my children are happy that we belong to a people that is slaughtered and not to those who slaughter us and not to those who look on us indifferently. I know many Christians in France, in Holland, in Belgium and other countries risked their lives to save a Jew or Jewish baby. We shall never forget that, never. But what were other people doing? Not the Nazis in Europe, they are outside the pale of humanity, I am not discussing them. There was a conspiracy of silence in the entire world. When millions of Jews suffered death and when we tried to tell the world of this horror, the answer was: It is Jewish atrocity propaganda, it is press propaganda of the Jews. And I asked myself, "Would I behave like that if a million Gentile babies were slaughtered in Europe?"

Just imagine for a moment that a British fighting division was captured by the Japanese, an entire division was slaughtered after being taken prisoners of war, and only one platoon remained alive. Then the war ends and America gets the concentration camp where this platoon was in captivity, and prevents them from going back to England for some reason. Can you imagine the feelings of every Englishman in the world? Can you imagine our feelings when this Jewish remnant is being held, after the war is over and Europe is liberated, when they want to get out and they cannot get to their home, to our country? Is it not their home, the national home of the Jewish people, and are they not Jews? Why is this happening? Here is a people bleeding to death; a few remnants remain. Why are they being tortured? It is torture. Not physical torture, no. I saw them there, being well treated, very well—physically—in the American and the British camps. I have not seen the Russian camps. I have not seen the French camps. But it is torture—there is such a thing as spiritual torture. Not only they are being tortured. Everyone of us in this country is, because we are here for their sake. They are our blood, they are our brothers. Many of them are our brothers literally, but all of them are our brothers because they suffered for the same crime that we are guilty of, for being Jews. Why are we being tortured? Why are attempts being made to lock up that unfortunate remnant of Polish Jewry, some 30,000 Jews remaining out of three millions, who are still being massacred every day in Poland? Why are attempts being made to lock them up there and not let them out? They are human beings.

Why this discrimination in your Christian world? Why cannot we save ourselves, why cannot we escape from this dependence, this being at the mercy of others?

LOVE OF ZION

That is one reason why ten, thirty, fifty years ago, Jews came over here, to get rid of this bitter dependence and all the discrimination involved in it. There you may have one reason why we want to get back here. And there is another reason. It is love of Zion, a deep passionate love, strong as death, the love of Zion. There is no parallel to that in all human history. It is unique, but it is a fact; you will see it here. There are 600,000 of us here because of that deep, undying love of Zion.

In evidence given to you in America, an American Arab, I believe it was John Hassan, said there was never a Palestine as a political and geographical entity; and another American Arab, a great Arabic historian, Dr. Hitti, went even further and said, and I am quoting him, "There is no such thing as Palestine in history, absolutely not." And I agree with him. (That is not the only thing

Statement to the Anglo-American Committee, March 19, 1946

on which I agree with Arabs.) I agree with him entirely; there is no such thing in history as Palestine, absolutely, but when Dr. Hitti speaks of history he means Arabic history. He is a specialist in Arabic history and he knows his business. In Arabic history there is no such thing as Palestine. Arabic history was made in Arabia, in Persia, and in Spain and North Africa. You will not find Palestine in that history, nor was Arabic history made in Palestine. There is not, however, only Arabic history; there is world history and Jewish history and in that history there is a country by the name of Judea, or as we call it, Eretz Yisrael, the Land of Israel. We have called it Israel since the days of Joshua the son of Nun. There was such a country in history, there was and it is still there. It is a little country, a very little country, but that little country made a very deep impression on world history and on our history. This country made us a people; our people made this country. No other people in the world made this country; this country made no other people in the world. Now again we are beginning to make this country and again this country is beginning to make us. It is unique, but it is a fact. This country came into world history through many wars, fought for its sake by Egyptians, Babylonians, Assyrians, Persians, Greeks, Romans, Byzantines and others, but it was not these wars that gained it its place. It gained its own place in history. Our country won its place in world history as not many other countries have done, even bigger and richer countries, for one reason only: because our people created here, perhaps a limited, but a very great civilization, which became the heritage of the whole of humanity. This country shaped our people, the Jewish people, to make it what it has been from then until today; a very exclusive people on one side and a universal people on the other; very national and very international. Exclusive in its internal life and its attachment to its history, to its national and religious tradition; very universal in its religious, social and ethical ideas. We were told that there is one God in the entire world, that there is unity of the human race because every human being was created in the image of God, that there ought to be and will be universal brotherhood and social justice, peace between peoples. Those were our ideas, this was our culture; and this was what won this country its place in world history. We created here a book, many books; many were lost, many remained only in translations, but a considerable number, some twenty-four, remain in their original language, Hebrew, the same language, Mr. Chairman, in which I am thinking now when I am talking to you in English, and which the Jews in this country are speaking now. We went into exile, we took that book with us and in that book, which was more to us than a book—it was ourselves, we took with us our country in our hearts, in our soul. There is such a thing as a soul, as well as a body, and these three—the land, the book, and the people—are one for us forever. It is an indissoluble bond. There is no material power which can dissolve it except by destroying us physically.

The distinguished British Chairman of this Commission quoted something from a book by Sir Ronald Storrs and another gentleman, whose name I don't remember, to define our rights in this country. Sir, our rights and our attachment and our significance in this country you will find in a book, in one book alone. That book is binding upon us, and only that book. It is binding on us. Whether or not it is on anyone else is not for me to say—I know many Christian people who believe it is binding upon them too—but it is binding upon us. You cannot conceive of our people without this book, neither in the far-away past nor in the present, just as you cannot conceive of our people within this country, in the past, present or future.

Somebody has told you in evidence, "All this is merely attachment to a mystical Zion, not to this concrete Zion." But now you will see 600,000 living human beings whom the love of Zion has brought over and kept here. They are attached to the living Zion. It has also for them a great and deep spiritual significance.

Then we are asked this question, which seems a very commonplace question: When the Arabs conquered Spain, didn't they create there a magnificent civilization? They did. They created a magnificent civilization in Spain and then they were driven out. Can they claim Spain for the Arabs? Have they a right to Spain? I know of no other objection which proves our case so forcibly as this one, and I am taking it up. Is there a single Arab in the entire world who dreams about Spain? Is there an Arab in Iraq or in Egypt or anywhere else who knows the rivers and mountains of Spain better than he knows his own country? Is there an Arab in the world who will give his money to Spain? What is Spain to him? What does he care about Spain? Is there a single Arab in the world who loves Spain? And is there a people other than the Jews that loves this country? There are many peoples who want to conquer and possess all kinds of countries as well as this one—not because of love for this country, but because they want power. This love is peculiar to our people alone, and you will find it among the Jewish people wherever they are, not only in countries of oppression like Germany and the Yemen, but also in free countries like England and Canada. Here are Jews who have been away for centuries, some of them many centuries, some of them thousands of years, like the Jews in Yemen. They have always carried Zion in their hearts, and they came back, and came back with love. In no other country in the world will you find people loving their country as the Jews love this country.

In the first world war thousands of Jewish boys from America, from the United States of America, came over as volunteers to fight for the liberation of this country in a Jewish Legion in the British Army, in the Royal Fusiliers. I must deny the stories of Arab troops taking part at that time in the liberation of Palestine. I happened to be in America then and I had the privilege of taking part in that, and I too, was a volunteer in the British Army and served under Allenby here in the 39th Battalion of the Royal Fusiliers. I know what happened then in Palestine. (I may not know what happened in Hejaz.) There were Semitic soldiers who fought in Allenby's army for the liberation of this country, many thousands. All these Semites were Jews. The Palestine Arabs fought on the other side, in the Turkish army, and I don't blame them. It was their right and perhaps their duty. What brought over these thousands of American Jewish

Statement to the Anglo-American Committee, March 19, 1946

boys with the consent and blessing of the President of the United States of America, the late Woodrow Wilson? What brought them over if not the love of Zion? Perhaps it can hardly be explained, but it is there.

Another thing, and it has been mentioned to you: Jews tried to settle on the land in many other countries. It was tried in Russia. Czars Alexander and Nicolai I tried to settle Jews on the land. The Soviet Government has tried to settle Jews on the land—and it is a powerful government. Jews tried settling in Argentina; Jews tried to settle in the United States of America. It failed. It succeeded here. There was no love for the land there; there was love for the land here. Much as I love this country, I must tell you that Argentina is a much richer and more fertile country than this is. America certainly is more fertile, and so is Russia. And they failed there, they succeeded here. It is because of love of Zion.

What is the source of this love? A man can change many things, even his religion, even his wife, even his name. There is one thing which a man cannot change, his parents. There is no means of changing that. The parents of our people are this country. It is unique, but there it is.

More than 300 years ago a ship by the name of *Mayflower* left Plymouth for the New World. It was a great event in American and English history. I wonder how many Englishmen or how many Americans know exactly the date when that ship left Plymouth, how many people were on that ship, and what was the kind of bread those people ate when they left Plymouth.

Well, more than 3,300 years ago the Jews left Egypt. It was more than 3,000 years before the Mayflower, and every Jew in the world knows exactly the date when we left. It was on the 15th day of Nissan. The bread they ate was matzoth. Up till today all the Jews throughout the world, in America, in Russia, on the 15th of Nissan eat the same matzoth, and tell the story of the exile in Egypt; they tell what happened, all the sufferings that happened to the Jews since they went into exile. They finish with these two sentences: "This year we are slaves; next year we shall be free. This year we are here; next year we shall be in the Land of Israel."

THE URGE FOR JEWISH INDEPENDENCE

There was a third reason why we came, and this is the crux of the problem. We came here with an urge for Jewish independence, what you call a Jewish state. I want to explain to you, since this is the center of the entire program, what is meant by that. When some people abroad talk about the State, it means power, it means domination. I want to tell you what it means to us when we speak of the Jewish State.

We came here to be free Jews. I mean free Jews in the full sense of these two words, 100 per cent free and 100 per cent Jews, which we couldn't be anywhere else. We couldn't be Jews in the full sense, we couldn't be free, in any country in the world; and we believe we are entitled to be Jews, to live a full Jewish life as an Englishman lives an English life and an American lives an American life;

to be free from fear and dependence, not to be objects of pity and sympathy, of philanthropy and justice, at the mercy of others. We believe we are entitled to that as human beings and as a people.

We here are the freest Jews in the world. Not in a legal sense. On the contrary, here we are deprived even of equality before the law. We are living under a most arbitrary regime. I know no other regime in the entire world as arbitrary as the regime of the White Paper Administration. The White Paper discriminates against us in land legislation and denies us the elementary right to the soil and freedom to settle in all parts of the country. In spite of all that, we here are the freest Jews in the world. Freedom begins at home, it begins in the human mind and the human spirit, and we are free men, and here we are building our Jewish freedom, more so than all the other Jews in the entire world. Why? Why do we feel freer than any other Jews? Because we are self-made Jews, made by our country, making our country. We are a Jewish community which is, in fact, a Jewish commonwealth in the making.

RETURN TO THE SOIL

I will tell you in a few words how we are making it. When we say "Jewish independence" or a "Jewish State" we mean Jewish country, Jewish soil; we mean Jewish labor, we mean Jewish economy, Jewish agriculture, Jewish industry, Jewish sea. We mean Jewish language, schools, culture. We mean Jewish safety, security, independence, complete independence, as for any other free people.

I will begin from the foundation. You heard already from Dr. Hitti that there is no such thing as Palestine, absolutely not. We are not coming to Palestine; we are coming to a country which we are re-creating. Building a state means for us in the first place a return to the soil. We found hundreds of Arab villages, Moslem and Christian. We didn't take them away; we didn't settle there. Not a single Jew settled in all these villages. We established hundreds of new Jewish villages on new soil. We didn't produce soil, it is made by God, but what nature left to people is not enough, they must work. We didn't merely buy the land, we re-created the land. We did that in rocky hills like Motza, of which you will find a description in the Royal Commission's report. In the swamps of Hadera, hundreds of Jews died of malaria, and they refused to leave that place until it was made healthy, because of the love of Zion, because of the need to create their own soil. We did it on the sand dunes of Rishon-le-Zion. With our toil, our sweat, and with our love and devotion, we are re-making the soil to enable us to settle there, not at the expense of anybody else.

Now you are here and you may visit, you are cordially invited to visit these villages. You will find the land reclaimed by our own toil. It was uncultivable, it was certainly uncultivated. We made it cultivable and we cultivated it. Land for us is not an object of trade, to be bought and sold. We considered it for the whole world, as the foundation for humanity; everything comes from there. It is a sacred trust to human beings. We shouldn't spoil it. We shouldn't neglect it. We should fertilize it, keep it up. This is what we are trying to do to the best of our ability. We did not entirely fail in our endeavors, although we have been living in towns for many centuries, and we are told there is a law, this time not a legal law but a scientific law, a scientific law that people go from the country to the town, but not from the town to the country. We didn't submit to that law because it was contrary to our existence, because we believed we had to go back to the land. We went back from the town to the country, and while we go against that law, I hope you will agree it is not illegal. We did it and we will continue to do it. Building a state means for us in the first place a return to the soil.

You heard the evidence of a representative of an Arab state about this country, that more than 60 per cent of this country is uncultivable. It is certainly uncultivated. These lands which from the Arab point of view are uninhabitable and uncultivable, we want to make cultivable, perhaps all of them, perhaps part of them, I don't know. We will make an effort. Is it a crime to make this effort?

RETURN TO LABOR

A Jewish state means for us a return to labor, to manual work. We don't consider manual work a curse, or a bitter necessity, not even as a means of making a living. We consider it as a high human function, as the basis of human life, the most dignified thing in the life of the human being, and which ought to be free, creative. Men ought to be proud of it. Our boys and girls, middle-class boys and girls, are encouraged before they finish high school to go out and work on the land, and if they cannot find land, to work somewhere else. The Jewish commonwealth means Jewish labor. You cannot buy a commonwealth; you cannot conquer a commonwealth. You have to create it by your own work. We are trying to do it, and you will find Jews working here in trades which were closed to them everywhere else in the entire world, in fields and factories, in quarries, everywhere.

By Jewish commonwealth we mean Jewish economy, Jewish agriculture, industry, seafaring trades, fishing. Independence means first of all reliance on yourself, creating your own economy and your own culture. We don't want to say that this is our country because we conquered it, but because we made it. We re-made it; we created it. That is what we are trying to do, and you will see it wherever you go. You cannot have a Jewish commonwealth without a great, continuous, constructive effort on land, on sea, in fields and factories.

REVIVAL OF JEWISH CULTURE

A Jewish commonwealth means Jewish culture and Jewish language. If you had come here, not now, but 40 years ago and I had told you that we were going to revive the Hebrew language and make it a spoken language, a language of work and trades and industry, of schools, universities, science and art, you would have said we were mad, it couldn't be done, it is a dead language, it is an old language, it hasn't got all the modern words. Well, it was done, and those Jews came from America and England and Canada and Russia and Persia and Yemen, with all their many languages, and they now speak Hebrew. We have educated their children in Hebrew, and this is now the mother-tongue of our children and of our grandchildren.

We don't believe that men live by bread alone, and we are creating a new Jewish society and we are trying to base it on high intellectual, scientific, cultural and artistic values. There are two Hebrew theatres in this country. There is a Palestine orchestra; there is an opera; there are scientific institutes. I wonder whether anywhere else so many books are being published, original and translated, taking into consideration the size of our population. We happen to be a people who have practiced universal education for 2,500 years, and we had all these needs and we satisfied them in our own language.

JEWISH SECURITY

A Jewish state means Jewish security. If there is one thing a Jew lacks everywhere, it is security; even in countries where he seems secure, he lacks the feeling of security. Why? Because even if he is safe, he has not provided for his safety himself. Somebody else provides for his security. Well, we want to provide for our own security, and we have been doing it from the beginning of our return, for the last 60 to 70 years. I came to Palestine 40 years ago and I went to work in Sedjera, a little village in Galilee. I had never before been a worker and never before a farmer, and I had to learn two things at once, to hold a plough in my hands and a rifle. I had to provide for my security, for the security of the village, and I went to work in the fields of Sedjera with a rifle on my shoulders. We had a special organization to keep watch, called "Hashomer". There were very few Jewish villages, and they were attacked from time to time by our Arab neighbors. When I stood watch in the long nights in Sedjera and looked at the skies, I understood the full meaning of that magnificent verse in the book of Psalms, that the heavens tell the glory of God, because I never saw such glorious skies at night as when I was a watchman.

We also tried to make friends with our neighbors. It wasn't easy. I don't know what their reasons were for attacking us. They sometimes attacked each other too, but us a little more frequently, and we had to stand watch. They have a great contempt for people who are afraid, and they looked upon Jews as weaklings, "tenderfeet." They learned to know we were not like that, that we could take care of ourselves, and they respected us; and we made an effort to win their friendship, and in many cases we succeeded, and we are making this effort all the time in all our settlements to maintain the best human relations with our neighbors the Arabs. Even if sometimes they attack us we don't remember. We want to remember the good things, not the bad. But we had to

Statement to the Anglo-American Committee, March 19, 1946

provide for our own security because we came here to take care of ourselves. We never gave up our defense weapons, we always sought to keep our arms unstained and they were never used in our hands for aggression against anybody, only for our protection.

THE JEWISH STATE

We are trying to build up a new society, a free society based on justice, human justice, and based on the highest human intellectual and moral endeavor. If you have time to visit out agricultural settlements, you will find some of that spirit there. In order to be able to live according to our own wishes, without external interference and coercion, we want independence. That means a Jewish state. We can't conceive of being independent and being ruled by somebody else. We are building a Jewish state for two reasons. One is in order to enable us, those Jews who are already in this country, to live our own lives, and the other is to help the solution of the tragic problem, the great tragic historic problem of the Jewish people in the world. Because, Sir, only a Jewish state will be able to build a Jewish National Home without hindrance. We need a Jewish state in order to continue building the National Home for the Jewish people, for those Jews abroad who for one reason or another will need, even if their fate is death, to come out here just as we came out here, and only the Jewish state can do it.

We began building the Jewish National Home under the Turkish regime. I am not going to describe all that. We continued it under the British Mandate, and I am not going to describe the British Mandate nor to make any complaints. But we learned from experience, I wouldn't say bitter experience, that no foreign administration, even of the best friends of the Jews and of the National Home, is able to fulfill that function of building up a National Home for the Jewish people and bringing to this country those Jews who want and have a right to come to it; is able to develop the country, is able to raise the general level for the benefit of all the people and those who have to come. It is the most difficult function, and it requires from the people undertaking it a full identification with the aims and purposes of the immigrants and the people of the country; this work requires love, devotion, and immediate connection with those for whom it is being done, and even from the best of peoples—and the British are not the worst—you cannot expect such identification and such devotion as is required to build up a Jewish National Home. This can be done only by Jews. Not that we are more able than the British. Ah, no. I know what the British people have done in many countries, in Canada and New Zealand and Australia and others, but they have done it for themselves. Even then I am afraid that some English people in America some 150 years ago revolted against the British administration. They made war on them. It was their own people. They thought that this administration coming from London—I don't know whether at that time it was Whitehall or not, but coming from London—could not satisfy the needs of the English settlers in America, and they made war on King George III. Well, really it would be too much to expect that what they couldn't do for their own kin in America they would be able to do for the Jews. In this country the task of the colonial administration is not the normal task of maintaining law and order. It is a dynamic function; it is a constructive function, a creative one which is beset with great difficulties, requiring initiative, imagination, and drive.

We know the difficulties. Perhaps we are not more difficult than anybody else. They are our own difficulties, and require not only knowledge but something more. It requires devotion and love. We have the urge and the need and we can overcome the difficulties. Not every woman, even when she is just and fair, can bring up a child, but you can trust every child to its mother. Only the Jews can build for themselves. Therefore we ask that the Jewish Agency, which means the Jewish people themselves, be authorized to conduct this business of immigration. They know the needs of the Jews and their abilities and the possibilities, and they will do it. The Agency, in accordance with Paragraph II of the Mandate, should be enabled to develop the country to the maximum in agriculture and industry, on land and sea, for the benefit of all the people here, Jews and Arabs. Only the Jews are able to do it.

Our ultimate aim is not a majority, Sir. A majority is not a solution of our problem. The number of non-Jews in Palestine has nothing to do with the number of Jews who need to return to Palestine, or with the number of people Palestine can absorb economically when fully developed. It isn't the numerical proportion between ourselves and the number of non-Jews in Palestine. This is an accidental thing. The number of Jews who need to come back is much, much bigger. The majority is a stage, a very important one but not final. You need that merely to establish the commonwealth efficiently, but then the State will have to continue building up the National Home, settle new Jews as the country is more and more developed, until the problem of the Jewish people is finally solved.

The Jewish state will have two functions; one, the function to care for the welfare of the people of this country, all of them, without any difference between Jews, Arabs or others; to care for their security, to work for their welfare and to raise them higher and higher economically, socially and intellectually. The other function is to continue building a National Home.

THE ARABS

We will have to treat our Arab and other non-Jewish neighbors on the basis of absolute equality, as if they were Jews, but make every effort to see that they preserve their Arab characteristics, their language, their Arab culture, their Arab religion, their Arab way of life. We shall have to exert every effort to make all the citizens of the country equal civilly, socially, economically, politically, intellectually, and gradually raise the standard of life of everyone, Jews and others.

We are not afraid of the present tragic conflict between us and the Arabs.

Statement to the Anglo-American Committee, March 19, 1946

It is a passing thing. We are an old people and we have seen many, many changes in the world, small and big, and we never accept a position, if it is bad, as something final; it will change and it will improve. I know that the Arabs, at least some of them, don't want us to return and I understand it. I merely am convinced that their opposition is futile, but it is natural. We will return, and there will be understanding between us and the Arabs.

In the course of your inquiry you heard two reasons given against the Jewish state by representatives of our neighbors. One was given, I believe, in London by the Chairman of the Syrian Chamber of Deputies, Faris Bey al-Khoury. I believe it was Dr. Aydelotte who asked him, "Why are you afraid of having this little Jewish state? Is this a threat to the security of the big Arab states and of the Arab people?" And this is what he answered: "Yes, a state like that is small in its place, but it would depend upon 15 or 16 millions of rich, qualified, able people outside, who would always help in everything. It will be sufficiently strong to threaten peace and security." Then in Cairo another representative of the Arab states said just the opposite. "You cannot have a Jewish state. We will destroy it." Something like that. I haven't got the actual words. "We will destroy it. It would have to depend on British bayonets." I think both arguments are not very serious. I don't attach great importance either to the threat or to the fear, both are without foundation. As to the threat, we will take care of ourselves. We did it when we were few; I could tell you many, many stories from 60 years ago and 40 years ago and 20 years ago. Perhaps you heard about Tel Hai.[4] I am not going to take up your time now. We will take care of ourselves. Still less is there any foundation for fear that the Jewish state will threaten the mighty Arab nations, some 40 million or more, with their big and numerous states. I have more respect, more faith in the Arab than I find in that answer by that gentleman. The Arabs, too, will take care of themselves. There is nothing to be feared and there is nothing to be threatened, and we certainly will not be affected either by threats or by fear.

There is now tension, perhaps a little more, between us and the Arabs. It is very unfortunate, but it is a passing thing. It is not a danger. We will come together and help each other, just as numbers of Jews and Arabs are helping each other now, as in the past. I believe we need each other. We have something to offer each other as equals, only as equals. We are not going to be "schutz-juden" here, Jews protected by the British or the Americans or the United Nations' Organization, just as the Arabs don't want to be "schutz-Arabs" nor does anybody else. We are not going to rely on the Arabs for protection, or the British or Americans. We are going to be independent as a free and equal people.

No people in the world can stand alone, neither a small people nor even big powers. There is interdependence. We shall be no more independent than

---

[4] Tel Hai is a national shrine. Joseph Trumpeldor and seven of his followers fell in the defense of the settlement against Arabs in 1920. (Eds.)

Belgium, Sweden, Switzerland or Norway. Norway is the best example for us in many ways. They have something in common with us here, on the human, the social side. There will be not only peace between us and the Arabs, there will be an alliance between us and the Arabs; there will be not only interdependence, but close friendship and cooperation. It is a historical necessity, just as the Jewish state is a historical necessity and will come to pass. It is a moral, political and economic necessity.

We are here as of right. We will not renounce Zion and Jewish independence, as we never renounced our religion and our nationality, whatever the price may be, and we will not renounce a Jewish commonwealth. Just as I am convinced there will be a Jewish commonwealth, so I am convinced there will be not only an alliance, but peace and friendship—permanent, true friendship.

It was Mr. Crossman who asked a Jewish witness in London a rather difficult question: "If you had the choice of getting 100,000 refugees from Germany to Palestine or giving up the Jewish state, which would you choose?" That gentleman couldn't answer that question for his personal reasons. I want to answer it. It is my belief that every human being is a means in himself, who has ideals which he cherishes. I will not sacrifice another fellow human being, even for the dearest of my own ideals. I am entitled to sacrifice only myself. I may only ask another fellow human being to do what I am willing to do myself, but it is for him to decide. I will sacrifice nobody else for my ideal. The question of Mr. Crossman should have been put to the 100,000 refugees in Germany. They are there, and you know how anxiously they are waiting to go home. If you asked whether they are willing to buy the certificates to Palestine, as you call it, by renouncing Jewish independence and a Jewish commonwealth, I know what their reply would be. As is the Jewish habit, I shall answer your question with another question. I hope you will allow me to do it.

Suppose Hitler had in his hands 100,000 English prisoners, and he told Mr. Churchill, "Either you give me the British Navy or we will slaughter all these 100,000 Englishmen." If you asked Mr. Churchill this question, can anyone doubt his reply? He would know he could rely on the hundred thousand Englishmen to answer for themselves. Wouldn't they gladly die rather than buy their lives at the cost of the British Navy?

I was in England, Sir, in the darkest hour of this war, when France collapsed, when there was a real danger of invasion, when there was almost no British Army in England except the famous few with their planes; I was there in the blitz when Nazi planes were raining fire and death on London every night and the British people took it. I saw the common people in the underground. I saw the taxi drivers; I saw the workers. They were not afraid. Many of them were bombed and were killed. But I saw people for whom their country and their freedom is dearer than their life.

Why do you think and have reason to suppose that we are different from you in this respect? To us too there are things dearer than our lives, and we love life. The Jewish religion was never an ascetic religion, we don't despise life, we cherish life. The life of every Jew is of the greatest value to us, even if what happened to us in this war had not happened. We are not going to renounce our independence, even if we have to pay the supreme price, and there are hundreds of thousands of Jews, Mr. Crossman, both in this country and abroad, who will give up their lives, if necessary, for Jewish independence—for Zion.

Now, Sir, for one minute or two I want to say a few words to the Arabs who are here and to those who are not here. What I want to say to them is this:

The conflict between us today is the most tragic, for it is in a way a family conflict. But it will not last long. We shall carry out the work of our regeneration even if the obstacles in our path increase, for it is a matter of life and death to us. We are returning to our country as of right. It is your wish that this land, too, should be Arab. Perhaps it is a natural desire. Many of you prefer a poor Arab country to a prosperous Jewish country. That does you honor, but we are not strangers to this land. It always has been and remains forever a historic homeland. History has decreed that we should return to our country and re-establish here the Jewish state, and the Jewish state will be established. Many of you know it as well as we do.

In the name of the Jewish people, I say to you: Even though you are still opposing us, we want you to know that you have not throughout the entire world a more loyal and useful friend than the Jewish people. We will build our country on the foundation of Jewish justice, brotherhood and peace. The closer and more quickly we draw together, the better it will be both for us and for you. The Jewish people and the Arab people need each other in the fashioning of their future as free peoples in this part of the world.

We are convinced, with the arrival of the Jewish state on the one hand and independent Arab unity on the other, we shall be able to cooperate closely in a spirit of mutual aid, in a true covenant of brothers and equals.

ZALMAN SHAZAR

Zalman Shazar was born in Mir, Russia, in 1889. He first visited Palestine in 1911. In 1924 he settled permanently in the country. Since then he has held many important offices in the socio-political and cultural life of the Jewish community having served as: an editor of *Davar* (the daily published by the *Histadrut,* the General Federation of Jewish Labor), a member of *Knesset* (parliament), head of the Jewish Agency's Department of Education and Culture in the Diaspora, Minister of Education, and since 1963, President of Israel.

A non-controversial figure, he did much to unify the various labor factions before and after the establishment of the State of Israel. As so many of the elder statesmen in the country, he, too, is a synthesis of Jewish traditional, Orthodox-Hasidic, small-town upbringing and of secular European culture (the Universities of Berlin, Freiburg, Strasbourg).

As he is a gifted orator and a master of Hebrew style, his utterances in speech and in writing, carry messianic overtones. His socialism is rooted in Amos and Isaiah, not in Marx and Kautsky. His ardor is not that of a bleeding liberal, but of an exultant *hasid.* Shazar, universally beloved by the rank and file of labor, is also esteemed by the Orthodox Jews in and out of Israel and by Yiddish secularists and socialists in the United States.

Following are excerpts from a speech delivered by Shazar on June 18, 1948, the first post-independence meeting of the *Mapai* Party Council. In 1969 Mapai merged with other workers' groups to form a new and larger party, *Mifleget Avodah Yisraelit,* usually referred to as *Avodah.*

Horrors of a Final Battle

by ZALMAN SHAZAR

As though to deepen and substantiate our awareness of the magnitude of those days, there appeared along with the magnitude also its everlasting companion, terror. Unimpeded they came, all the symbolic terrors, all the "horrors of a final battle." From all sides they streamed, the foes, the adversaries, the arch-enemies. Yet scarcely any breach was revealed in the ranks of our people. Notwithstanding the quarrels and differences among themselves, our nation rallied as one man, beyond all imagination, around the miracle of independence.

Externally, however, we were completely surrounded. States and armies were upon us, rulers and would-be rulers. Tenfold stronger, and even more, were our antagonists in numbers. Concealed behind them were the masters of intrigue, while over all towered the mighty power which had decided to "smite the feeble", in order to frustrate our striving toward freedom. Our country was in flames. Like young eagles swooping down from their youthful nests, our sons and brothers leapt to repulse the attack. This first generation of our redemption was thus transformed into a generation of heroic fighters, a generation of war zealots. Have we not sensed that from their sublimely courageous assault, pure forces, invisible to the naked eye, were bursting forth miraculously, forces long dormant in the treasure-house of past generations, which the fierce thirst of a pioneering generation awakened to new life? They will not be defeated by the intrigues of evanescent powers nor by the riots of blindly incited mobs!

MOUNT MORIAH

This month of battles-for-Israel, a month of bloody fighting over the signing of our magnificently won independence, an entire month which seemed as one endless day of sacrifice, this month transformed the whole Land of Israel into one vast Mount Moriah, and the hundreds who are being sacrificed upon it, — our brothers, sons, students, friends, the superlative best of all we have cherished throughout our creative years, the first-fruits of our blessing, for which we have been praying and yearning—we are now offering up on the altar every day and every night.

In silence each of us will remember in his innermost heart his own dear ones, while all of us together recall those whom we bore and brought up and offered up as sacrifices. (Several minutes of silence). With brotherly admiration for their heroism and with boundless sorrow for their grief we come to console our fellow-members, the parents who have lost the sons they loved so much, the mothers who saw their beloved children leaving never to return, the sweethearts and widows whose young mates are gone forever, some of whom are mere girls whom time had not even allowed to marry their young men. Our entire party, our whole nation, are mourning with them, are blessed by their devotion and courage, and sanctified by their dauntless spirit. Silent we all stand before Mt. Moriah, deeply afflicted because the sacrifices have not yet ended but profoundly convinced that from the midst of it, ascending like a flame to the uppermost heaven, stretches the hope of the now emergent State of Israel.

"FROM THE DAYS OF ZERUBBABEL [1]"

Our movement—which during our generation cultivated this hope as well as the people to fight for its realization, which gave expression to this yearning and mobilized the forces needed to defend it, and which moreover removed from its rank the non-believers and their leaders and lifted them up together with itself to sublime faith in Israel—this movement, the members of whose Council are assembled here today, is naturally enough stirred and affected not only by the achievements which have been attained, but also by the historic missions which have been placed on its shoulders for present and future implementation and which had not even entered our minds in the years when we were building the movement.

The day following the proclamation [of the State] I was asked to quote a verse. I responded with lines from the well-known poem by Bialik which were that day echoing in my mind:

> "Since Zerubbabel's day
> Have our hands not built
> Ought as magnificent
> As this, or as great."

But fearing I might perhaps have exaggerated, I meditated deeply on the matter, and then I understood the tremendous difference between the undertaking of Zerubbabel's time and the undertaking incumbent on our generation today. Inherent in these differences lie our movement's primary objectives from now on. I shall not weary you with detailed analogies but will only point out two lines which are also fundamental guidelines for our future work.

At the time of Zerubbabel's return, the primary task was to weave anew the threads of independence which had been broken—only recently. There were aged men among those returning to Zion who still bore in their hearts memories

---

[1] Zerubbabel was a descendant of King David who returned from the Babylonian exile in the sixth century B.C. to help rebuild a Jewish political and religious entity in Palestine. (Eds.)

of their people's independence, cherished from their childhood days. For the exile then had lasted "seventy years." Now the duration of our exile totals nearly seventy generations! If we are correct in assuming, as we were once taught, that from a historical standpoint a generation equals thirty years, then on the Ninth of Ab[2] of this year about sixty-three generations will have passed since our life of independence in our motherland was severed. In the course of sixty-three generations we were weaned away from the life of a free nation; we developed substitutes-for-independence and the features of a people-in-alien-surroundings, as well as the complexes of a nation-in-exile and ways of living that were not living. Now we must train ourselves anew for the life of a free people, for the life of state-discipline, of a nation that knows how to manifest its independence and how to unite around the manifestations of its independence. Independence is not merely a matter of official approval, or of international recognition. It is an external frame whose entire value consists of the fact that inside it the bowed soul of the nation grows erect, that inside it the nation releases the sun from the bonds which have held it fast and opens wide the door to the free development of its spirit, language, and creativity; its arts, faculties and talents in all spheres of its social, spiritual and military life, of revealed or concealed nature. To arouse these slumbering forces and adapt them to our new life we must have a master educator, a collective educator, an educator capable of defending, protecting, uniting and advancing. For this we need a *movement* of the builders-of-the-State, of those who establish, fortify and advance it step by step.

THE STATE AND THE INGATHERING OF THE EXILES

In the days of the *Yissud Ha-Ma'aleh,* Establishing the Return, there was essentially only one period of mass immigration from Babylonia. Once the Jewish State was established, immigration did not persist; the Jews of the Dispersion remained in their diasporas. Today however we are impelled first of all to create a *tremendous impetus for continuous immigration into the State* by means of a genuine and methodical ingathering of the exiles. As soon as we shall have liberated our country from those who would infiltrate and destroy it, our people will take the keys of immigration into its own hands and unlock gate after gate to all the revealed and concealed treasures in the land, for all our dispersed Jews who yearn for the motherland. *Let all those come who are not able or not willing to stay in the Diaspora; that will be enough.* Years ago Herzl[3] developed a formula such as this for membership in the Zionist Organization. We have now reached a new stage which shall be named: gathering the exiles into the State. This formula seems to me to express the full scope of the

---

[2] The Ninth of the Hebrew month Ab is the date traditionally given for the destruction of the First and Second Temple in Jerusalem. (Eds.)

[3] Theodor Herzl was the founder of modern political Zionism. He convened the first Zionist Congress in 1897. (Eds.)

present task of immigration. It is neither maximalism nor minimalism; it is a historic necessity. To all the Jews who consider themselves superfluous in the Diaspora, or whom others consider superfluous, and to all those who wish to contribute their capacities and talents to the building of our country so that the land of their people will become the natural homeland for them, too—our State will be open. That is the oath for Israel's Labor Movement and for the World Zionist Organization: to turn the State of Israel into a state which will gather unto itself the scattered exiles of our people to the last of our brothers yearning for the motherland.

Ours will be the responsibility to arouse in the Jewish masses a thirst for their homeland; to develop in them a sense of need for Jewish life and Jewish creativity, for suitable work and for social justice; to awaken this need and to foster it until it becomes a life's purpose driving them to seek and ultimately to gratify fully and completely this nationalist, human urge within the boundaries of our homeland, in which they too will be efficient and devoted sons and builders, builders of a free State of Israel and of a just and happy human society within the free Jewish State.

THE STATE AND THE WORKERS' SOCIETY

Just as our State is a *sui generis* state inasmuch as it is intended to provide a home not only for its present residents, both Jewish and non-Jewish, but for all Jews the world over who wish to reside in it, dispersed though they be today far and wide in all the foreign lands, so also is our state unique in that it has undertaken to deepen, strengthen and broaden the great social heritage which the Jewish Labor Movement has already deposited deep in the layers of its foundation during its generations of model creative effort. That is the Jewish collective-working-agricultural settlement, whereas the independent forms of settlement in our country—those new cells in our society which our movement's finest men and women have evolved and cultivated, those life-values and human-relations and national concepts upholding the blessings of justice and equality, cooperative work and real comradeship,—all of these together must now be brought to their flowering-stage and growth-perfection in the climate of our political independence.

There is no surer guarantee that our state will indeed be a land of justice and equality for all its residents without distinction of faith or sex, origin or position; and there is no other way of turning our country into a land capable of absorbing a systematic and continuous immigration except through the divine inspiration of creative pioneering applied to all the undertakings of the state-being-built, and through ensuring the encouragement and development of pioneering labor-initiative and injecting it into the general scale of national and State values as a whole,—free of the lust to dominate, or narrow-mindedness, or hatred of ambition but aiming only to enrich the entire state with the tradition, vision and creativeness of the socialist movement and the Jewish pioneering-movement.

OUR ASPIRATIONS FOR PEACE

Even during the crucial test of the ongoing war in our country, our people and our movement aspire most sincerely to peace among nations, to an alliance with our neighbors and to the brotherhood of citizens. It was not we who sought war. We wanted to live, in equality, work and freedom, for us and for all of our neighbors as well. Although we were forced to beat our plowshares into swords and to turn our plowmen into artillery-men, yet our hearts we did not abandon to blind unyielding hatred. Our age has experienced the crucible of war a great many times. But it is doubtful whether it has ever witnessed fighting of such matchless heroism and self-sacrifice as the fighting of our young "sabra" Palestine-born lions, although they were only a few against vast numbers of attackers. Yet it is certain that in all its many battles our generation has never seen a war so desperate and so courageous and at the same time so free of racial hatred for the antagonist and so permeated with readiness to live a long, uninterrupted life of peace with the antagonist, as this war of ours with the Arabs. Let our Labor Movement be a living assurance that, as we managed to overcome our foes in the war, so we shall manage to overcome evil temptations and bitter memories and concentrate on building a life of co-operation, mutual help and brotherhood with all the neighbors among and around us who will wish to build together with us our future and theirs.

THE CURSE OF OUR SOLITARINESS AMONG THE NATIONS

Although countless experiences still await us in our battles both at home and on the international stage, one thing we have already gained: the curse of our frightful solitariness is being removed from us. This state of aloneness was our daily bread throughout these last years of terror. As the extermination of Jews increased in ever-mounting proportion, so also increased the plot of silence which enclosed the people being exterminated. "She is become unclean!" But during the course of our fight for independence this plot began to weaken. And with the establishment of the State the horror began to disintegrate bit by bit. Already at the Lake Success deliberations our representatives no longer encountered a stone wall. This time their empty words did not nullify our words. Their listening ears surprised us. At first only a scattered few responded: the Uruguayan man of spirit and the Guatemalan man of conscience—men who although they themselves and their states were not "directly concerned" were nevertheless outraged by the picture being uncovered before their eyes. Their statements seemingly began to restore the image of man and of mankind around the conference-table of the world's nations. What is more the U.S.S.R.[4] stretched out its brave, confident arm to aid us. What we had vainly hoped to hear from its representatives over a period of decades, we

---

[4] At the time this speech was delivered the USSR was pro-Israel and championed her cause with the Arab nations, whereas the United States was less actively pro-Israel. (Eds.)

heard at this time stated firmly and unequivocally, with all the weighty prestige of a mighty, revolutionary power that knows what it wants, and is prepared to defend it again and again with the full force of its enormous influence. Moreover, at the urging of a number and variety of popular movements and parties, the United States too took its place at our side. More than two thirds of the representatives of the world's nations voted in favor of righting the wrong perpetrated against us for many generations. Then, when we arose and proclaimed our independence, the "recognitions" of nation after nation followed, in theory or in practice, and the chain has not yet ended. It is important to note that today, except for the enemy states, all the countries in which large Jewish communities dwell in their Dispersion, all or nearly all of them— have recognized the State of Israel!

If therefore we succeed—by our spirit, our military arms, our creativity— to stabilize and buttress it and to fill it with independent, constructive, liberating content, then the Jewish State, recognized and protected, will constitute the real, concrete and exalted meaning of the ageless vision for our people and for mankind.

GOLDA MEIR

Golda Meir was born in Kiev, Russia, in 1898 and brought to the United States in 1906, settling in Milwaukee and graduating from the local Teachers' College. In 1921 she came to Palestine and joined Moshav (cooperative) Merhaviah as an agricultural worker. She has held numerous important posts in the *Histadrut* (General Federation of Labor) and the Jewish Agency (since the birth of Israel, an international, non-governmental body coordinating all Jewish efforts on behalf of Israel). In 1948 she was appointed first Israeli Ambassador to the Soviet Union. Later she served as Minister of Labor (1949-56), and Foreign Minister (1956-66). One of her chief achievements in that office was the development of diplomatic, economic and cultural relations with a number of African states.

In 1966 Meir was induced to accept the task of Secretary-General of the faltering *Mapai*, the plurality party in the coalition government. In 1969 she took over the premiership of the country upon the death of Levi Eshkol.

Although a socialist, Meir is a sceptered lady. During her Mapai secretaryship she probably wielded more influence than anyone else in the country. It was against her, and against the then Prime Minister Levi Eshkol, and Pinhas Sapir (who succeeded Meir in the party post) that Ben-Gurion stormed. They, his former disciples—fulminated the *"zaken"* ("grand old man")—were the "Old Guard" who were preserving the East European political structure in which the "party is like a church and the leadership is like the college of cardinals."

But Meir, despite the formidable opposition of Ben-Gurion, General Moshe Dayan and Shimon Peres (Ben-Gurion's erstwhile right hand), had captured the imagination of many Israelis mainly because of her firm stand of not accepting the Arab position of *quid pro nil* and because she was inching towards electoral reform and moving away from the strict party "curia".

What follows is an address by Meir at the inauguration of Professor Abraham I. Katsh as the third president of Dropsie College, now Dropsie University, on November 26, 1967.

The Zionist Purpose

by GOLDA MEIR

IN THIS PLACE OF learning I shall venture to indulge in some thoughts as to what this is all about; by "this" I mean Israel. I think many people in the world—many Jews and certainly non-Jews—wonder at times why there is so much ado about so little a place: little in area, little in population, tucked away in a far part of the earth among large neighbors in a place that connects great continents—and a place too often in the headlines.

I will not go into current history—at any rate, not very much. But as I look back I want to consider the question of what the Jewish pioneers of the last three generations were trying to accomplish. What was the mission they thought was placed on them to execute?

In the first place, these were people—whether we speak of the BILU[1] in the eighties of the last century or of the Second Aliya[2]—who believed that the Jewish people had existed throughout the ages through a specific (probably peculiar) desire to live rather than to perish. This persistent longing was perhaps contrary to all that one would have expected. A people scattered in all corners of the world twice in its history, living as a minority among majorities of different cultures, different religions, different ways of life, and yet remaining a people, was certainly peculiar.

I am now not referring to pogroms, massacres and major discrimination. I only refer to the "nice" disadvantages that Jews have enjoyed, even when at various times in our history Jews lived among people who were not anti-Semitic, where they did not know pogroms, where they were not humiliated as they were in Czarist Russia and other places. But even in comparatively favorable circumstances they were a minority: their religion was different; their day of rest was different. From the beginning the books their children read, as a rule, were in a different language. Yet, despite all handicaps, whether wholly evil or negatively good, here we are.

One asks: How? In my mind there is no doubt that religion, not only general religious concepts but minute and detailed observances, contributed to this endurance. Even those of us who do not observe the rules incumbent upon a pious Jew, must in all objectivity conclude that religious observance has been a major factor in the oneness of the Jewish people. We have seen this to be true in Israel in a dramatic manner, especially after the establishment of the State

---

[1] First modern pioneering movement of Zionists. (Eds.)
[2] Second immigration wave to Palestine, 1904 to end World War I. (Eds.)

when people came to us from the caves of Libya and the hills of Morocco and Yemen. When one saw these immigrants together with European Jews and Israeli-born youngsters, one had to ask himself: What did these various people have in common? Not language; certainly not a way of life; certainly not standards of education; certainly not adjustment to the technology and science of our age.

We had nothing in common except one thing: all of us were Jews. I'll never forget a meeting with a little Yemenite boy of twelve after the mass immigration from Yemen. I saw him in one of the newly-established villages where Yemenites had been settled and I asked him how long he had been here. He said, "Only a few weeks." I asked him how long he had been in Israel and he told me, "Close to a year." And he used very good Hebrew. So I asked him how he knew Hebrew. He looked at me with disdain and said: "Ani yodea torah—ivrit m'hatorah!" (I know Torah—Hebrew comes from the Torah.) Every boy and man that came from Yemen knew how to read because he read his Bible. (No girl or woman knew how to read or write because women did not have to know the Bible.) Yemen was far away. We didn't know the Yemenites; they didn't know us, but the bond between us existed.

The BILU and the people of the Second Aliya were very conscious of the continuity of the Jewish people, of the oneness of the Jewish people. I believe that their interpretation of the concept of "ato b'chartonu" (You have chosen us) meant not that we were chosen as better than other people, nor were we chosen—as some have wished to interpret it, including many Jews—to be dispersed among the peoples in order to teach them moral concepts and other virtues. Our pioneers interpreted ato b'chartonu to mean that when Jews would return to their homeland, and when they alone would be responsible for their home and society, they would make a better society. This is my explanation for their absolute devotion to the concept of Jewish peoplehood and the re-establishment of Jewish independence, combined at the same time with an equal fervor for the nature of the society which would emerge in this independent Jewish state: their desire that it should be something better than what had been known in most parts of the world. These pioneers believed that neither the social nor the national ideal was alien to Jewish thought, Jewish religion, or to the vision of our prophets. Both had to be realized.

Still another significant element marked their attitude. In my forty-six years in Israel I have not known a man or woman in this group who thought of himself as a "giver" to the country or to the people, or who felt that he had sacrificed himself. In Israel, we are much less sentimental and emotional outwardly than we really are within. You probably know that Israeli-born children are called sabras ("prickly pears") because on the outside they are very prickly. Only later did we learn how juicy and sweet they were within. But one usually sees the prickly exterior. Among ourselves we do not usually indulge in long discussions or analyses about why we came and what we did. But if we started probing we would find that nobody considered that he had done something for someone else; rather that he viewed himself as a "chosen" one, or one of the "chosen" generation because he was enabled to do what he did. Generations of Jews throughout the ages had really sacrificed themselves—up to the giving of their lives—for their religion, for their Jewishness, and had accomplished only the strengthening of the obstinacy to carry on among those who were left. At last came generations equally ready for every trial, but who through their endeavor not only endured but accomplished and built for the people. This achievement was granted only to these new generations.

Let me illustrate what I am trying to say by describing three or four types of men and women who came to the land, who achieved something and are responsible for their achievement. Who is more responsible: he who had the idea or those who accept the idea and put life into it? The men of whom I think belonged to both groups.

Aaron David Gordon, for instance, came to Palestine not as a young man; he was not a farmer. He was a Zionist in the sense that he believed that Israel had to be re-established, that it could be done, and that he had to take part in the process, but on one condition: that the building and the re-establishment of the country be done by those who came, not by others. He believed that the Jewish society to emerge in Palestine should be better than those of the contemporary world. But he did not believe in preaching to others. His philosophy held that everyone must live his life so as to influence those about him by example. In 1905, he did not go to a part of Palestine that was already populated or re-claimed; he was among the first who went out to Deganiah.[3]

What did Deganiah symbolize in those days? The settlement was on the other side of the Jordan, in a swampy, deserted section of the country in Lower Galilee where there were no Jewish settlers. The few Arab villages in the vicinity were less than friendly. Yet that abandoned locality was the one that Gordon and his friends chose. And how did they go there? Each one individually? They went as a group. These first nine men and women went as a collective group based on a simple principle—which in spite of its simplicity is so difficult to carry out—namely: from each according to his ability, to each according to his need. Incidentally, this was years before the collectives in Russia; up to this day there is no similarity whatsoever between the voluntary kibbutz and the enforced collective farm of the Soviet state.

Moving stories have been told and written about the difficulties and the tragedies of this lonely kibbutz—difficulties due to the climate, hostile Arabs, the swamps, malaria, and the fact that most of the settlers had never seen a real farm. When the first child was born its mother took care of it. But when a second child was born, to another mother, a new problem arose. Should each mother stay home and take care of her child? How would this affect the work of the group? How would the women do their share in the building of the economy? The first mother that went out to work and left her child in the care of another mother constituted a revolution.

---

[3] "Mother of K'vutzot," pioneer kibbutz, founded in 1908. (Eds.)

Forms of kibbutzim vary and there have been many developments in their structure since then but basically all the kibbutzim in Israel are established on the same principle—that of cooperative labor. As a member of the kibbutz, Gordon never missed a day of work. This is how his example and that of his group influenced the whole country.

Let me mention another type, completely different: Berl Katzenelson, the spiritual giant of Israel's labor movement, a man who asked himself many questions before he gave an answer, and who was never ashamed to admit that he was wrong and to start something else. He came to Palestine in 1906, to the kibbutz of Kinnereth, after he had become disillusioned about other attempted solutions of the Jewish problem. He had become disillusioned that a revolution in Russia would, in its wake, solve the Jewish problem. He had taken part in the revolutionary movement, and decided on the basis of his experience that hope lay elsewhere. He went to Palestine after considering all the difficulties posed by the Arabs and the Turkish regime. He had been earlier attracted by Territorialism.[4] Many of you know that we were offered Uganda.[5] (When several years ago I visited Uganda on an official mission I was happy that we were not there: not because Uganda isn't beautiful but because I couldn't see myself explaining to the local people what Jews were doing there.) Though Katzenelson had been deeply involved in the Russian revolutionary movement and in Territorialism, he was still a young man when he came to Palestine. He had decided that the only meaningful solution for the Jews was to be found in the re-establishment of Jewish independence in Palestine—and in no other place. A Jewish society would have to arise there on a foundation of moral principles, of justice and of human dignity. He brought up two generations of young people in this light.

A brilliant journalist, a brilliant speaker—not an orator—he would never speak at his audience. One always had a feeling that he was discussing something with his audience. Above all, he was an educator. I don't think he would have forgiven us if in his presence we had called him a "leader." That concept was foreign to him as I hope it is foreign to us even today. He was one of us. He could walk for hours if he knew that somewhere there was a young person with whom it was worthwhile to discuss and think. He was a man—like many of his colleagues—who did not think it particularly courageous to attack political enemies, but thought it much more important to criticize, severely if necessary, his own party and his own organization.

Together with Ben-Gurion and others, he was among the founders of the Histadrut, a labor federation unique as a trade union. It had to be. When it was organized in 1920 there were four thousand Jewish workers in the entire country. A big debate was precipitated by a small group who wanted the

---

[4] A movement at the turn of the century dedicated to finding any proper territory for Jewish self-determination. (Eds.)

[5] Actually it was an area in Kenya offered officially to the Zionist organization by the British Colonial Secretary, Joseph Chamberlain. It became popularly known as the Uganda Plan. It was rejected by the Zionists. (Eds.)

"class struggle" to be the main paragraph in the constitution of Histadrut at a time when there was not even a class against whom to struggle—neither a working class nor a capitalist class. The only struggle that had to be waged was against the swamps and deserts and rocks. And against the settlers' ignorance of physical labour. They were not farmers, they were not masons, they were not road-builders. This was the struggle. It required a lot of courage on the part of Katzenelson and Ben-Zvi and Ben-Gurion, who were committed socialists, to realize that the situation in Palestine did not lend itself to dogmatic answers, that we could not with closed eyes passively follow labor movements in other countries and do exactly as they did.

For us it was not a question of fighting against bad conditions, or for more favorable economic conditions. First something had to be built. So Histadrut became not only a labor movement but an organization which to a very large extent was responsible for the fact that, in 1948, there already was an economy in the country, that there were factories, and that there were Jews who knew how to work together. Because there were no capitalists, the Histadrut had to become its own employer and its own investor.

All this was quite different from the practice of other trade union movements in the world. Above all, Histadrut treasured the dignity of the individual. Without the individual nothing could be done; his devotion and his discipline were essential. But the individual was not a tool for something. He was the maker of tools. He was the one who must build. Even for the best purpose it is criminal to turn an individual into simply a means for some ultimate end. A society in which the dignity of the individual is destroyed cannot hope to be a decent society.

Another man, whose name very few in this audience have probably heard, was Shmuel Yavnieli. He came from Eastern Europe like most of the others. Imbued with a labor philosophy, a scholar and a writer, he too became a pioneer. By that time—1908–09—word of the remote Yemenite Jews, almost a lost tribe, had reached Palestine. Yavnieli took it upon himself, after discussions with his colleagues, to bring the great message of the return to Zion to the Jews of Yemen. It was an almost impossible task for a Jew to enter Yemen. By donkey Yavnieli traveled rocky paths and mountain roads for months bringing his tidings. And the Jews in Yemen received him almost like the Messiah, for he came from Jerusalem. He told them of the miracles of rebirth happening in Zion, assuring them: "I have come to tell you that soon our land will be free. Every part of the land of Israel that is worked by Jewish hands is liberated."

The first emigration of Jews from Yemen did not take place after the establishment of the State, as it is generally believed; it took place forty years earlier in the days of Yavnieli. And I must say that Israel would have been a poorer place if we had not had the tribe of Yemen with us throughout the years. When the Yemenites reached Palestine, they realized that Yavnieli was not the Messiah, but they never forgot that he had done something messianic.

I want to mention a woman, too: Rachel Blaustein, a young, delicate girl from Russia who came to Palestine at the beginning of the 20th century. A poet, she came to work on the soil in a new settlement near the Sea of Galilee. Some of her most beautiful poems were written about her work in the fields, though the labor was far beyond her physical capabilities. Throughout her short life, this was her sorrow—that she could not do physical work.

The idea that one must work with his hands was common to all. Some people criticize us even today for supposedly not having enough appreciation for the toil of the mind, the toil of the spirit. However, Jews, wherever they were, always busied themselves with the things of the spirit and studied if only given the chance. What was lacking in Jewish life in the Dispersion were Jews who could work with their hands.

When I was in the Foreign Office of Israel, I went on an official visit to Mexico. At a dinner, my host, the Foreign Minister of Mexico said to me: "I must ask you something. What has happened to your people? You have never been known as farmers. How have you become excellent farmers? Even in Mexico a group of your men is now teaching some of our people various phases of agriculture."

It is easy to explain, but perhaps easy things are difficult to understand. The explanation lies in our history. For centuries the soil was taboo for Jews, especially in Eastern Europe. We could not own land, we could not work in the fields. We were pushed into the ghettos in a few cities. That was the historical background for our insistence on agricultural work. Men and women among the first to come to Palestine—the BILU, the First Aliya, the Second Aliya, and the Third Aliya—understood the basic need for our social re-construction. Had they not, we would never have won independence.

And I believe that if we had not understood this necessity, we would not have merited independence. It would have been too easy for a small number of Jews to come to Palestine, to buy orange groves and let Arabs work them. Arab labor was easier to get along with than Jewish labor. It was cheaper. Arabs had no fancy ideas about an eight-hour day. In many ways it would have been simpler to have Arab workers and Jewish landlords. But if this had been the turn of events, there would have been no room for Jews and no right for us to return to a land reclaimed through the toil of others. The pioneer settlers saved the Jewish people and the opportunity for the re-establishment of Jewish independence, because a simple but basic principle became their Bible: it was called "avodah atzmit"—self-labor.

Jews had to teach themselves to work with their hands. The Third Aliya with its special Hashomer Hatzair group consisted of boys and girls who usually came from the homes of merchants, rabbis, scholars; many were from prosperous assimilated families. Yet they were the ones who built the first road between Tiberias and Nazareth. Labor was their creed. That was the faith each had to accept if he really wanted to build the country. We had to build it. The houses had to be built by us. The roads had to be built by us. The wheat had to be raised by us. The swamps had to be drained by us. This gave us a moral right to the land in addition to the historic right. If there are no more swamps in Palestine it is because we drained them. If there are forests it is because we planted the seedlings. If there are fewer deserts it is because our children went to the arid areas and reclaimed them.

A word or two about another question that my colleague in Mexico posed. It was after the Suez campaign, in 1956, and he asked: "You were never known as experts in the military field. What happened?" I wonder what he would have asked now, after the Six Day War. After I tried to explain why we had become good farmers, I could only tell him that we had been obliged to become good soldiers. But not with joy. We are good farmers with joy. It's a wonderful thing to go down to a kibbutz deep in the Negev and remember what it was twenty-five years ago: sand and sky; maybe a well of brackish water. To go down there now and realize that there is practically no fruit that does not grow there, to see orchards and fields, green and lovely, fills the heart with joy. To be good soldiers is our extreme necessity; but there is no joy in it.

We had to learn lessons from history. We are not the only nation whose fate it was to have its country occupied by foreign powers at some time. But in most instances the people remained in the land; they could at some time revolt, throw out the foreign power and regain independence. Such a situation means fighting, loss of life, and suffering, but the basis for renewal remains. To us, fate was not so kind. Twice in our history, before the State of Israel was reborn, our independence was destroyed by foreign powers who not only occupied the country and put us under their rule; we were twice dispersed and scattered to all corners of the earth.

My friends, if our youngsters fight well, it is because they know both ancient and recent history. They know that the Arab powers who declared war the third time in twenty years, had in mind for us exactly the same fate as that suffered by the Jews of Old Jerusalem when it was conquered by the Jordanian army in 1948, or the fate of the kibbutzim in K'far Etzion. Nobody was left to live in peace. Destruction was the fate that awaited us—in '48, in '56, in '67, not the prospect of a foreign occupation. That the Jewish people survived the two ancient dispersions in our history is something at which the world has marveled. Were the third chance history has offered lost, a fourth chance might perhaps never come.

My friends, let us not forget that the State of Israel was established after six million Jews in Europe had perished. They were the natural reservoir of our religion, of Zionism, of Jewish culture and of Hebrew culture. With that reservoir gone, with three million Jews shut behind the iron curtain, with millions of Jews in the free world who, in addition to enjoying authentic freedom, are also free to assimilate, free not to know Hebrew, free not to go to the synagogue, free not to know the Bible, free from kinship with the Jewish people,—the fear under which we live is that if Israel is annihilated, that fateful historic opportunity will be lost forever.

Several months before that terrible black day when your President was assassinated, I had the great privilege of speaking to him on a security problem in Israel. At one point I said to him: "Mr. President, the Government of Israel, like every other decent government, worries about the welfare of its people and the security of the country. In that, we are no different from other states. But we have an extra responsibility which probably no other government has: that is our long memory of what happened to us twice in the past, and our fear that we may be remembered as the generation which after the annihilation of six million Jews had an opportunity to re-establish Jewish sovereignty and did not know how to hold it. This fear to face history is something additional."

And I had no doubt in my mind that when President Kennedy said, "I understand," he understood.

Maybe this is the second reason why we are good soldiers. We are good farmers because that is the basis, our foundation. Anything built on any other foundation except our own hard physical work would never have prospered. In addition, we are conscious of our responsibility to history; as you go through Israel you cannot help being conscious of history. This is what the present-day Israeli feels. He must protect the future not only for himself and his family, not only for those who are in Israel, today, but for those who could not come and for those who will come.

We are driven by the memory of the past, the responsibility for the future and by the desire to live up to a sense of "chosenness"—not because we are better than others, but because we dream of doing better in building a society in Israel which will be a good society founded on concepts of justice and equality.

LEVI ESHKOL

Levi Eshkol was born in 1895 in the Ukraine. He came to Palestine in 1914 and began his career as a worker and a watchman. He was one of the founders of Kibbutz Degania Bet. His sense of humor and perseverance helped him rise as a leader, first in the agricultural labor councils, then in the *Histadrut*, the General Federation of Jewish Labor, where he later served as Secretary-General. During the Nazi regime he did much to smuggle refugees into Palestine. For a while he was a member of the high command of *Haganah*, the defense forces of the Jewish community. From 1948 to 1963 Eshkol was the director of the Settlement Department of the Jewish Agency. During the same period he served successively as treasurer of the Jewish Agency, Minister of Agriculture and Minister of Finance. The latter office was probably the most impossible assignment in the State. In 1963 he succeeded David Ben-Gurion as Prime Minister.

Autodidactic, he attained the lofty position by his ability to compromise, to see every aspect of a problem, to delay showdowns by using folksy *bon-mots*. A protégé of Ben-Gurion, the iron-willed, fiery prophet and fighter, Eshkol—whose patience, compassion and whimsy served him so well in the most difficult office of Finance Minister—often appeared indecisive and almost helpless, especially when his friend and former chief turned on him, aiming at Eshkol all the barbs in his ample arsenal.

Eshkol died in office in 1969. In reflective aftermath, his achievements, even as Prime Minister, are seen by his countrymen in unexpectedly grand dimensions.

The following excerpts from Eshkol's notes, put down sometime in 1958, were sent to the editors of the anthology on his instructions a short time before his death.

The Initial Step

by LEVI ESHKOL

THE SUN HAD STARTED on its westward descent; dust swirling up from the dirt road covered everything roundabout. We were traveling from Tel Aviv to Jerusalem and decided to take a shortcut through Gezer. In those days all of the Tel Aviv-Jerusalem traffic was routed through Ekron and Huldah.

I cannot remember now why it occurred to me in that twilit hour to make the trip to Jerusalem by a different route. True, I did drive about a great deal in the more remote sections so as to see those parts of the country from which we had been cut off while under foreign rule. Between Ramlah and Gezer we reached a road that was not really a road and the car went bumping and lurching along. I was driving, while my colleague, Ra'anan Weitz, sat beside me.

It was just after the War of Independence. The land and the people had not yet awakened from their astonishment, could not yet fully grasp, or rather sense, that we had indeed won political independence and that henceforward we would be free to choose the way that we should go. The old-time residents were still mourning the war-victims they had but recently buried, and the flood of the great immigration was already in full swing.

This huge wave of immigration had come streaming in before we could even determine what its nature and its dimensions would be, before we could make suitable preparations to absorb and settle the swarm of thousands, occupied as we were with the war. Driven, hurrying, they came, raising the dust in their wake: most of these immigrants were themselves human dust, survivors of concentration camps, shattered remnants of congregations and crushed fragments of communities that were no more. They spread over the country, looking for any crack or crevice to creep into, for all the world like the gushing stream which appears during the rainy season in the *wadi*, when it overflows its banks and seeks a new channel in the fields.

What troubled us at that time was the problem of finding the most practical means of absorbing this enormous flood of humanity, and of directing it into creative, constructive channels, as we have consistently done ever since the days of the Second Aliya (second wave of immigration) as we worked to rebuild this country.

Thorns and nettles covered the open spaces of the country we traversed; thistles and brambles reigned supreme. The field mice and other destructive creatures increased and multiplied. Only the howling of the jackals pierced the dreary stillness of the desolation.

We had already completed a tour of the northern and southern sectors:

it was our custom to go into the abandoned villages, and walk around the narrow, crooked streets trying to evoke the way of life that had been current there until the recent, still fresh past, before the Arabs' panic-stricken flight. I recall a visit to Masmiyeh, which had seemed so large and so frightening in the past, and to blood-soaked Barir, that infamous den of hate-filled robbers and murderers. All of the deserted villages bore mute testimony to the mighty struggle and the cruel vagaries of fate. Their plots to destroy us were frustrated. Now their villages lay desolate, orphaned, silent. From every corner a thousand orbs seemed to stare with a dreadful, hollow emptiness, pleading for new life.

Our eyes were sated with the sight of scorched earth, deserted villages, ruined homes, looted and burned—the remains of all that was and is no more. Here and there a pathetically lonely and frightened dog would come stealing in, faithful to the last, sadly keeping watch over what was gone with the wind and with the stress of war.

This plethora of impressions that we had accumulated, visually and with our very breaths, penetrated our brains, our blood, and our hearts. There they churned in a constant turmoil, never at rest but incessantly, feverishly in motion, crying out for actual deeds.

After achieving our military victory it was incumbent upon us to proceed forthwith to solve the problems of settlement, ingathering of exiles, establishing the masses of our returning brothers securely in the homeland. It was my feeling that the desolation rampant in our country contained the potential solution for the wretched humanity now arriving at our gates from every land throughout the world, speaking every language known to man: the survivors of Hitler's camps and of the vicissitudes of fate, the remnants of our people in its organized widespread dispersal. All of these seemed to be entreating us to open wide the gates of our country and its soil.

It was a dream but we were duty-bound to transform it into reality. If the garden was locked, we needs must open it. With the help of the old-timers and of the young men who soon would be released from the army, we had to alter the reality, which was in fact pregnant with possibilities. It was the will of destiny that we begin the process of carving our unique national entity from the shattered human wreckage of Jewry's communities.

Burdened with worries and sated with sights and impressions, we rode on the highways and byways that lay wide open before us, as if we were seeking physical contact with mother earth, who must surely vouchsafe the elusive answer.

As previously mentioned, we were traveling in the twilight of a late-summer day. A hint of the approaching autumn was already in the air. It was the season for ploughing and preparing the soil for the sowing, but the fields roundabout lay barren and forsaken. It was obvious that they had not been touched since the headlong flight of those who had previously tilled them: orphaned fields of stubble yearning for hands to cultivate them and bring them back to life.

Thus far no one had made a move to subdue all this crying waste and desolation. Mass settlement had not yet been introduced.

We reached the village of Beriyah, a small hamlet perched atop a rocky hill overlooking the Latrun highway and encircled by broad fields. This village was altogether different from all the others we had seen in the south: its houses were built of stone and looked solid. An idea flashed into my mind. Stopping the car, I said to Ra'anan: "Come, let's have a look around this village. I have an idea that may help alleviate our distress." I did not yet know what the actual details would be but I felt a deep conviction that these abandoned stretches of devastated land spelled the answer to the question of ingathering the exiles. I sensed that these open spaces could provide the solution for directing the rushing wave of immigration while simultaneously supplying labor for the forlorn fields. I hoped that inasmuch as there was no alternative, practical means would be devised to remove thousands of immigrant families from the immense camps which had been hastily erected to house them, thereby reducing the tremendous and totally unproductive expenditures which constituted a heavy burden for the Jewish Agency and for the infant government, as well as rescuing the survivors of the European death-camps from the demoralizing life of idleness.

Leaving the car we set out on foot to explore the village and its environs. The houses were solidly built of stone. Traces of the former occupants were in evidence everywhere: mats, cushions, jugs, bits of furniture, water-holes hewn in the rock, some of which still held quantities of water from the preceding winter's rainy season. Scouting the entire area disclosed that the village comprised several dozen houses which could, after the necessary repairs were completed, provide housing for immigrant families, here in the Arab village, amidst the open fields.

We returned to the car. Once again I took the wheel and all the way to Jerusalem we continued to consider and examine this new idea. "Why, there are hundreds of abandoned villages scattered throughout the country. Even excluding villages of clay huts which are not suitable for housing Jews, there remain many dozens and perhaps hundreds of hamlets built of stone, similar to this village of Beriyah. We should take them and get them ready for the approaching winter. Then we'll be able to transfer into every such village dozens of families, accompanied by instructors from the older *kibbutzim* (collectives). We would have to equip each of these groups with work-tools and begin to cultivate the fields. This plan is constructive in every way: the immigrants now live in the camps where their upkeep costs the Jewish Agency vast sums of money. Moreover, these fields should not be left to their devastation. On the other hand, it will require many months to plan permanent forms of settlement, construct the houses, and embark on a planned program of mass settlement.

"The Department of Settlement is small, and not equipped to handle the enormous responsibilities now facing it. It must be expanded, its staff must be substantially enlarged, the tempo of its work must be considerably accelerated. All this will be accomplished in due time, but the process will extend over several months and will certainly not be concluded before next spring. And in the meantime? Why should we not devote the coming winter months to populating a few dozen abandoned empty villages? There are a number of well-built villages whose homes are solidly constructed of stone and need only minor repairs to make them quite suitable for the purpose. Some of the villages are actually located in the midst of fields; one can just go out and get to work at once. Others are situated at some distance from the fields but this poses no problem. Anything is better than adding to the present camps and supporting the immigrants several more months on a dole. Any solution is preferable to that. We must convene the representatives of all of our settlement-oriented movements, demand that they call on their membership for volunteer instructors, alert the engineers of the Technical Department, gather the vital statistics relating to all the villages, meet with contractors, and begin to repair the houses. And should the contractors prove unable to cope with the undertaking or if they have not yet had the time to get themselves organized for work since the War of Independence ended, then we will turn to the army's Engineering Corps and mobilize them for the gigantic task of absorbing the immigrants..."

As the car gulped the kilometres, we exchanged thoughts and ideas at an ever-increasing pace. Suggestions followed one another rapidly all the way from Gezer to Jerusalem. When at nightfall we entered the capital, we already had the structural and practical framework for implementing the entire plan, divided into specific units of responsibility. That same evening I contacted the various movements, summoned the engineers to a meeting, requested counsel and guidance of the army's Engineering Corps, and otherwise started the ball rolling, with the result that in that very winter we succeeded in transforming more than 45 abandoned villages into inhabited settlements bustling with new life

Subsequently events developed as follows: from resettling deserted villages we went on to the establishment of planned immigrant settlements and later of work villages, moved southward to pioneer settlements in the hunger-belt of the Negev, founded the olive-raising settlements, turned northward to settle portions of the Upper Galilee, occupied large tracts in the south, initiated the laying of the water-pipes and others of the impressive achievements attained from that day to the present.

In ten years we completed the first cycle in the establishment of hundreds of settlements, cooperative villages and collectives, model farms and agricultural schools. We benefited from the assistance tendered by the settlement movements, especially that of "Tnuat Hamoshavim" whose hour had come. The history of this portentous decade began in that twilit hour one day at summer's end at the abandoned village perched lonely and sad atop its hill.

We are now entering the second cycle. Who can foretell what form it will assume or foresee how it will end?

BENJAMIN AKZIN

Benjamin Akzin was born in Riga, Latvia, in 1904 and settled in Israel in 1949. He obtained a Ph.D. from the University of Vienna, L.L.D. from the University of Paris, S.J.D. from Harvard University, and held numerous fellowships and visiting professorships at various institutions of higher learning in Europe and in the United States, including New York, Michigan and Heidelberg.

During Akzin's earlier stay in the United States he was senior specialist in international law at the Library of Congress, served on the United States War Refugee Board in the 1940's and was head of the political department of the New Zionist Organization (Revisionists).

In Israel he was appointed the Herbert Samuel Professor of Political Science and Constitutional Law at the Hebrew University and officiated as Dean of the Faculty of Law at the same institution. He also was the president of the Israel Political Science Association. Later, he headed the University of Haifa.

Akzin authored many books and articles in several languages. Among his treatises are *The New States and International Organizations; Principles of Public Administration; Theory of Government; State and Nation.*

Recognized internationally as an authority on constitutional law and political science in general, Akzin has fashioned a thematic curriculum in these areas at the Hebrew University. He succeeded in assembling European and American influences to fit them together in spelling out academically Israel's political democracy. As a meticulous scholar his use of data and assessment of facts enabled him to distinguish between political vogues and organic functions, making his analyses available to various government agencies. Although Israel has no overall written constitution, Akzin contributed a great deal to evolving and crystallizing many organic laws. The following article appeared in *Public Administration*, Vol. VI, Jerusalem, 1966, pp. 9–15.

Introduction to a Project of a Constitution for the State of Israel

by BENJAMIN AKZIN

THE BASIC QUESTIONS which confront us when we deal with the problem of a Constitution are these: Is there need for one? And what is its purpose? Obviously, no Constitution is needed to direct or restrain individuals or groups which wield little or average power in society, or the subordinate and medium layers of public authorities. That task is accomplished by laws, regulations, administrative orders, judicial decisions, and the executive agencies at the disposal of all of these. A Constitution is meant to direct, and especially to restrain, the centres of political power. In terms of Israel realities, these include the majority in the *Knesset,* the Cabinet and its Ministers who enjoy the confidence of that majority and, in fact, are its leaders. They also include the political party or combination of parties, the pressure-group or combination of pressure-groups, which exercise a determining influence on Cabinet and Legislature. One may, of course, believe that in a given country, and, in our case, in Israel, there is no need to restrain those who wield political power; and in that case one would be right in inferring that a Constitution is superfluous. But those who hold that possessors of political power in a State also ought to have their freedom of action limited will wish for a Constitution. And when we talk of a Constitution in this context, we do not refer to a document or a series of documents whose solemn titles carry no special significance (such as the fundamental laws in Israel today) and which in fact depend on the good graces of the centres of political power just as much as do all other laws, regulations and administrative orders in the State. We refer rather to a body of rules so constructed that even these power centres, when faced by them, are expected to halt. By no means should such rules presume to constitute an absolute obstacle to change, for such obstacles would be inconsistent with the dynamic character of contemporary society. What we mean are rules whose change would not be regarded as a matter of routine, readily carried out for no other reason than that it so pleases the rulers at the moment, but would require a special procedure, a more than usually careful consideration, or a measure of consensus greater than that needed for changing other rules of law.

There are three considerations which might justify dispensing with a Constitution. One derives from a tradition of self-restraint in politics generally and among rulers more particularly, a tradition so strong that one may rely on its effect without calling on the artificial restrictive device of a Constitution. The second flows, by contrast, from the suspicion that both the rulers and those who aspire to rule are so contemptuous of legal restraints that the incorporation of these restraints in a Constitution would not hold them either. The third is connected with the possibility that the very regime whose basic ideas the Constitution is meant to express, and to whose stability it is meant to contribute, is resented by influential groups in the State or is sharply opposed by rising currents of opinion. In this case neither judicial verdicts nor administrative regulations, neither ordinary laws nor a Constitution, will be of much avail, for deep-surging revolutionary upheavals will not be arrested by legal documents.

It seems to me that none of these considerations applies to Israel. Only one country in the world—Great Britain—is permeated by so strong a tradition of self-restraint in political life that it sees itself free of the need to add the artificial restraint of a formal Constitution. In so doing, Great Britain has proved successful indeed. No other country (with the exception of New Zealand), not even the countries whose political *mores* and standards of mutual tolerance among political rivals are close to the British—the United States, Canada, Australia, Scandinavia—dared to forgo this device in the long run. Many as the qualities of our people may be, I doubt whether anybody would assert that precisely the qualities of mutual tolerance and self-restraint in public affairs are so pronounced among us that, more than other peoples, we can rely on them without having expressly to formulate limitations which we believe to be desirable. On the other hand, I do not believe that Israel politicians, either of the parties which generally belong to Government coalitions or of the parties whose usual place is in the opposition, could be accused of readiness to overstep the bounds of legality in the way in which it is done by politicians in certain other countries where neither statutes nor Constitutions are taken very seriously. Of Israel, as of most law-minded countries of the world, it can be said that, if the law allows the politicians to change it easily whenever this suits them, they quite possibly will not resist the temptation but will be quick to exploit this legitimate avenue of escape. An unwritten tradition on the British model will hardly suffice to restrain them; but should there exist a Constitution which fastens additional bonds upon them and prohibits them from changing its provisions except by a special, careful procedure, we would be entitled to assume that they will not deliberately violate it, just as we assume that they will not deliberately violate prohibitions laid down by statute. As for the third consideration, while one can never tell whether a far-reaching social revolution might not occur some day and thrust all legal fabrics aside, we may assume that the essentials of the form of government existing in Israel are compatible with the present-day aspirations of the people. If so, any modification that might be found necessary could be introduced by way of orderly procedures prescribed in the Constitution itself.

One question is often heard in our midst: Is it justifiable, and is it consistent with democratic principles, to limit the right of the parliamentary majority to make any decision it wishes? The answer is clearly and unhesitatingly—Yes.

The limitation is not only justified, it is essential. Ours is a generation in which the world has experienced too many cases of majorities proving frivolous and unreasonable, tyrannical and discriminatory, brutal and even inhuman. And though we hope and pray that neither Cabinet nor parliamentary majority nor any other political factor likely to wield determining influence in Israel, either as presently composed or in any other composition, would show itself prone to such failings, we too would be well-advised not to neglect a safety-device which the overwhelming majority of civilised nations has seen fit to adopt. This does not mean that a constitutional safety-device represents an absolute guarantee against the deterioration of a regime, and all of us know of countries where Constitutions have not prevented it. A fence around a pit is no absolute guarantee that people will not fall in, nor are lock and bolt an absolute guarantee against burglary; but that is no reason to renounce the use of fences, locks and bolts. It is interesting, though, that, while politicians express fear lest democracy be affected by provisions that would safeguard the population from action by ordinary parliamentary majorities, their fear does not stop them from entrenching, against such action, an arrangement that is particularly dear to them, namely the electoral system of Israel, which the statute protects from change save by a qualified majority. In view of this contradiction, I make bold to doubt the earnestness of the argument somewhat, and even its sincerity.

The same doubt must be expressed, with all due respect, concerning the argument, so often heard, that we are morally bound to refrain from consolidating the State's image before the process of the 'ingathering of exiles' has been completed. State authorities and political parties incessantly try to change ways of life in which newcomers from many lands had been brought up, and the same authorities and parties are equally intent on instilling or uprooting beliefs and ideas among these newcomers according to the views held by the decision-makers. This being so, there is something odd in the contention that its present population is precluded from determining the country's future image. It strikes one all the more oddly if one considers that the Constitution's main purpose is not to bind the future population—a task which every statute and every regulation accomplishes in any case—but to bind, for the future, the top layer of public authorities and to restrain the centres of political power. I suspect that some of our politicians, while sincerely believing that they oppose the Constitution in the interest of future immigrants, in fact have as their principal concern the safeguarding of their own future freedom of action.

On the other hand, our politicians are quite right in warning us that Constitution-making should be approached carefully. If care is necessary when formulating any legal provision, it is all the more important that special care be observed when drafting a Constitution designed to serve as a framework for the entire political and legal structure. Such a Constitution should unite the nation as far as possible, and may not be used as an instrument of division. This is the reason for the frequent requirement—which I have adopted for the present draft Constitution as well—that neither the original Constitution, nor subsequent amendments, may be adopted except by vote of a qualified majority of the proper representative body. The meaning of this condition is that neither the Constitution nor constitutional amendments become effective if a fairly large majority opposes their current content—a condition which, as we know, the *Knesset* in Israel has already agreed to in a few matters. A number of countries, including countries as enlightened as Denmark, France and Switzerland, hold that the special position of a Constitution warrants its submission in all or some cases to confirmation by popular vote and not only to the decision of the people's representatives. In view of the political realities in Israel, I did not find it opportune to recommend this particular idea with reference to the amending procedure, but I do suggest that it be considered in connection with the adoption of the original constitutional text.

The special standing of a Constitution calls for conclusions that go beyond formal procedures. It calls, notably, for conclusions as regards content. Just because a Constitution is destined to restrain the future leaders of a nation, one may expect its authors themselves to exercise a great deal of self-restraint. It is advisable, more particularly, to avoid inserting provisions in the Constitution which, even though likely to appeal to a large majority, take a stand on matters of sharp ideological controversy or affect the beliefs and opinions of peoples. This is the more so because a Constitution is meant to direct and restrain acts done on behalf of the State rather than to determine beliefs and opinions—a determination which, in a free society, should in any case be left to the individual. In terms of Israel actualities, this means the avoidance of statements of principles bearing on religion and socio-economic goals. Indeed, in my draft I have inserted a minimum of provisions of this kind to the extent only that seemed necessary for the making of policy.

A significant distinction can be observed as regards the form of Constitutions. There are Constitutions consisting of a series of separate documents, each dealing with a different subject-matter, and others formulated as a single comprehensive document. The large majority of contemporary States has adopted the single-document form, and for good reason. Such a Constitution —provided that it has not been rushed through, or drafted negligently, but has been carefully considered—has the advantage of reflecting a unified concept and has a better chance of being more systematic, more comprehensive, and, especially, of being freer from internal contradictions. In Israel, faced with the experiment of fundamental laws enacted in the fifteen years which have elapsed since the *Knesset* authorized that procedure, laws that are few in number, poor in content, and constructed on the piecemeal principle, we should certainly be well advised to learn from our own and other nations' experience and follow the single-document pattern. An added advantage of the single document is that, if it has been written in clear language and is not overly long, it can be a first-class educational instrument, capable of bringing home to the population at large, and to its youth in particular, the essentials of the political structure, *as befits a democracy worthy of the name*. This is much to be preferred to allowing these essentials to be hidden and dispersed in law books and volumes of judicial decisions accessible only to jurists and, in part, to professional politicians. For the same reason, as well as to preserve the elasticity required by legislator and Cabinet for ensuring efficient government, it is better to avoid going into too much detail.

Those who, in the initial stages of the State's existence, have warned us against too precipitate an enactment of the Constitution and pointed to the dangers implicit in too rapid a pace, may have been right. But today, after more than sixteen years of the State, the danger we face is that of too much delay, not of too much speed. The longer we continue to live without a formal Constitution, the more we get used to that condition, and the more we tend to regard it as normal. The population grows accustomed to the idea that there is, indeed, no limit to the authority of the parliamentary majority and of the Cabinet which guides it. As for politicians, the beneficaries of this state of affairs, they are even more inclined to be habituated to it, and, without quite realizing their own promptings are driven to seek rational motives to ensure its continuance. The outcome of it all is that the lack of a Constitution—a condition which, to begin with, was regarded by all of us as a provisional makeshift—increasingly assumes the attributes of permanence. It is a condition in which the individual is restricted—perhaps justly so—at each step, but in which *everything is permitted to the top layer of the State because the law does not curtail its law-making omnipotence.* A stain on our clothing, from force of habit, begins to be taken by us as an ornament, a pimple on our body is mistaken for a beauty-spot. The time has come to take a decisive step in a direction that would radically reverse the trend. And since Cabinet, *Knesset* and political parties, all of them budy with day-to-day problems and some of them plainly opposed to a Constitution that would restrain them, do not show much initiative in the matter, it is well that the initiative be seized by the public at large. For, after all, it is the public, the totality of the citizenry and each individual of it, that, in the final analysis, a Constitution is intended to protect against State authorities.

II
Vessels of Tested Culture

JACOB L. TALMON
SAMUEL H. BERGMAN
ERNST A. SIMON
ELIEZER LIVNEH
MOSHE SILBERG
MOSHE SHAMIR

JACOB L. TALMON

Jacob L. Talmon was born in Poland in 1916 and arrived in Palestine in 1934. He received an M.A. at the Hebrew University and a Ph. D. at London University. For a while he was associated in research and administration with the Board of Deputies of British Jews. Upon his return to Israel he began teaching at the Hebrew University, attaining a professorship in general modern history. He also taught or lectured at Oxford, Sorbonne, Harvard, Cornell, M.I.T. and several other universities.

Recognized as one of the leading contemporary historians, Talmon wrote among others the following books: *The Origins of Totalitarian Democracy* (which won him the Israel Prize), *Political Messianism—the Romantic Phase,* and *The Unique and the Universal* (a collection of essays).

In his life and in his writings Talmon was, as he puts it, in quest of identity, by his "existential situation as a Jew who lived through the traumatic experience of Nazism and Communism, chose Israel as his home, and at the same time feels deeply committed to Western tradition." In his introduction to *The Unique and the Universal* he characteristically points out: "If laying bare concatenation and association is not a solution nor a cure, it does help us, nevertheless, to live with our troubles and adds significance and depth to our lives, even if it does not make us any happier."

A scholar with impeccable credentials, he did not shrink from controversial issues such as tackling the not-so-velvet vetoes, not-so-veiled venalities and not-so-cleverly veneered anti-Semitism of modern times. Some of it is evidenced in his essay, *UNIQUENESS AND UNIVERSALITY OF JEWISH HISTORY* in *The Unique and the Universal,* George Braziller, New York, 1966, pp. 64–90.

Talmon at one time served in Israel's armed forces. Later, a pacifist, he did not hesitate to "take on" the proponents of "greater Israel in its historic boundaries." He firmly advocates increased rapprochement with the Arabs.

Uniqueness and Universality of Jewish History

A mid-century revaluation

by JACOB L. TALMON

THE EPOCH-MAKING changes that have taken place in recent Jewish history have caused more than one Jewish historian to re-examine the basic assumptions of earlier writers. Not only does the extirpation of Jewish civilisation in Eastern and Central Europe mark a decisive shift in the distribution of the Jewish population of the world, it appears to negate Simon Dubnow's* view that the essence of Jewish history lies in the urge for full Jewish self-expression through autonomous institutions.

The Western Jewries that lived most of their lives within non-Jewish patterns seemed to the Dubnowist school a pale reflection and dry limb of the real Jewish existence of Eastern Europe. Today these Jewries may have come to represent a primary datum, a culminating point, rather than a peripheral and secondary manifestation of Jewish life. And in view of the decline of Jewish cohesion and unity that has taken place in both the democratic West and the Communist East, under circumstances of real or merely formal civil equality, it would seem doubtful whether the historian will be entitled to apply the same terms of reference to the diaspora history of the future as he did to Jewish history in the still not too distant past—terms like "the community of a special fate", "identifiable modes of Jewish self-expression", "a corporate Jewish contribution or ingredient".

The emergence of Israel has vindicated the Messianic-nationalist vision and laid for the first time in 2,000 years the foundations for a wholly integrated Jewish life. The fact, however, that the majority of Jews, though powerfully affected by the resurrection of Jewish statehood, show every intention of continuing to live outside Israel is bound to bring about a revision of that strenuously dynamic conception, wholly dominated by the category of "becoming", which treated all of diaspora history as one long preparation for the Zionist consummation, and hardly acknowledged the force of the inertia of mere "being" here and now.

The main question the future historian must resolve for himself is this: Is it right to consider the problem of Jewish nationhood in Israel, and the problem of the Jews living in the diaspora among other nations, as one subject?

---

* Simon Dubnow was a foremost Jewish historian (1860–1941) who advocated Jewish intellectual and spiritual autonomy in the lands of their dispersion. (Eds.)

There are people in the Western dispersion who, afraid of being accused of a dual loyalty, claim that the State of Israel is to them just another little state, the only difference being that most of its inhabitants profess, at least nominally, the Jewish religion. There are some cocksure Israelis who proclaim that the sovereign State of Israel, a country like any other, stands in no special relation to Jews outside its borders. But even if there were no religious or cultural ties between Israel and the diaspora, this attitude would still be completely at variance with reality. It is just not true that Israel and the diaspora are becoming so dissociated in the consciousness of Jews and Gentiles as to do away with the deeply ingrained habit of associating all Jews everywhere in a common responsibility. Should one of those calamities with which Jewish history is punctuated overtake the Western diaspora, above all American Jewry, the State of Israel would be shaken to its foundations. On the other hand, should the Jewish State be engulfed by a catastrophe, the legal status and economic position of Jews elsewhere might not be affected at once, but the blow to their self-confidence, the loss of the vicarious prestige which Israel had bestowed upon them in the eyes of the world, and the general disenchantment would be too great to be sustained for long.

Nor can Israel claim that as "an independent state like any other" she has placed herself beyond the reach of those special laws to which the unique Jewish destiny has been subject for so long. The ultimatum addressed by the Soviet leader at the time of the Suez crisis to Ben-Gurion was an eloquent comment on the fact that the handicaps besetting Israel have a dimension additional to and different from the limitations under which other small states live in our days. In a note to Libya, Sudan, or Haiti, the Soviet leader would never have hinted so darkly yet so directly about their very right to exist as states. The Jewish right to Israel is not taken for granted. One is reminded of the famous words of General Bonaparte about monarchical Europe's non-recognition of the French Republic—"France is like the sun, she needs no one's recognition, she is there in blinding splendour". But Israel needs recognition as no other political entity in a world where the existence of a state is, under international law, proven solely by the fact of its recognition by other states.

Thus, at a deeper level, Israel is still involved in the problematic ambiguity attaching to Jewish existence everywhere and at all times. Abnormality, insecurity, ambiguity, absence of full and unequivocal matter-of-factness and recognition continue to haunt her existence; the refusal of the Arab states to recognise Israel seems a parallel to the European-Christian treatment of Jews as late-comers and aliens. The bitter disillusionment of Israelis with the recent policies of the United States was not a little offset by President Eisenhower's emphatic statement that since 1948 he had never contemplated that Israeli-Arab problems could be dealt with without accepting Israel as a historic fact and as a country whose problems were like those of any other.

Jews of the liberal persuasion were less shaken in their convictions by the Jewish catastrophe under Hitler, in spite of its enormity, than Jews sympathetic to communism have been by Soviet anti-semitism. After all, the Dreyfus affair and the persistence of discrimination amid conditions of legal equality had accustomed Jews to the limitations of their situation even under the most liberal of régimes. It was Communist Messianism that inherited in our time the fervent hopes of the early Jewish liberals that a general cure for the evils of mankind would do away with every vestige of the peculiar Jewish predicament.

Many a non-Communist was prepared to overlook the fact that totalitarian Messianism, insofar as it asserted an exclusive doctrine embracing every aspect of human life and social existence, was an uncongenial setting for Jews, who are nothing if not non-conformists. Even those to whom the unity of the Jewish people was an article of faith were willing to accept the separation of the Soviet Jews from the rest of world Jewry on the grounds that, as a church militant surrounded by the city of the devil, the U.S.S.R. could not permit any part of her population to maintain contact with an international community that had a kind of foreign policy of its own. These "tolerant" Jews knew, of course, that Jewish life shrivels when it is deprived of free channels of communication for ideas, aid, sympathy, and a general sense of kinship, and that it can prosper only in an open society. But the atrophy of Jewish life did not seem to them too high a price to pay for truly equal status.

Events have given the lie to the claim that a Communist régime would do away with the disposition of the non-Jewish world to bracket all Jews in a joint responsibility and guilt by association. The Moscow "doctors' plot", the execution of Jewish writers and artists, and other manifestations of official and social anti-semitism in the Soviet world are, like all other evils, now blamed by the Communists on Stalin or Beria. But this is to evade the fundamental issue.

It used to be confidently said that the triumph of socialism would not only eliminate all the conditions making for social and racial conflict, but that it would inaugurate the reign of fully scientific and deterministic laws of social development under which human arbitrariness and individual or group perversity would be ruled out. If such terrific effectiveness is now ascribed to the personal arbitrariness of one man, surely this is to deny the fool-proof scientific determinism of the Communist system and to open the door to all those psychological and other influences which remain conditioned, but are rarely negated, by social and economic factors. And it is indeed these influences which constitute the core of what has been called the Jewish problem.

Those historians whom faith in dialectical materialism or left-wing sympathies had led to ascribe all anomalies of Jewish existence to its peculiar socio-economic structure, and therefore to hope that these would be conjured away in a classless society, may well now come to see that the top-heavy socio-economic structure of the Jews was ultimately itself an outcome of their initially exceptional character. The Jews were different and were regarded as such, and therefore went—and were driven—into special occupations. In a sense, the experience of the Communist countries goes to confirm a "law" of Jewish history: a new society, régime, or economic system welcomes Jews as pioneers, but thrusts them out unceremoniously as soon as the "natives" are ready to take over the Jewish functions. This was the case in the early days of urban colonisation in Europe, in the first stages of *laissez-faire* capitalism, and the same development appears to have taken place in Russia since the October Revolution.

Under the most dissimilar historical circumstances, the Jewish fate remains very much the same. At the end of World War II the Soviet troops were bound to appear as saviours to Jewish survivors emerging from the forests, bunkers, and caves of Eastern Europe. The Jews had every reason to co-operate with the new régimes, and could offer them cadres of trained personnel and even leadership. But then came the Stalinist drive against "cosmopolitanism", against Jewish intellectuals and Jews in general; and the resurgence of the Poles, the Hungarians, and others under Soviet Russian domination hit Jews from the other side insofar as they were regarded as collaborators of Stalinism. In brief, fate seems always to prove more potent than any human resolve to change things by imposing new, man-willed and man-guided laws.

The historian need not be ashamed to use so heavily charged a word as "fate". The fate of a nation, like that of a person, may be the working out of the traumas of early childhood, the outcome of some basic and decisive experience. The Jewish psyche received a traumatic twist when the Jewish belief in chosenness sustained the terrible shock of national disaster and exile. This made most Jews impervious to the assimilating influences of hellenism and Rome. And they could hardly be absorbed by the amorphous barbarians in whose midst they found themselves in the early Middle Ages. Not only were they the bearers of a higher and more ancient civilisation, by then they were burdened with the charge that they had killed Jesus. Their status as never wholly assimilable strangers in the midst of the European nations was thus determined for centuries to come, and there is little evidence as yet that in the New World, where all are strangers and newcomers, the Jew has ceased to be regarded as more alien and more different than all other newcomers.

What will be the subject matter of the Jewish historian of the diaspora of the future, when Jewish life will have lost its old cohesion and the individual Jew will be living most of his life within non-Jewish patterns; when religious observance will often have been reduced to a minimum or ceased altogether, and Jewish learning will have assumed the character of a philological and antiquarian interest; and when communal activities will not amount to more than care for synagogue and cemetery, charity balls, and youth clubs?

How shall we pick out the slender threads which weave themselves into a Jewish collective pattern distinct from the so much more salient non-Jewish patterns? How shall we detect, in the behaviour and actions of seemingly unconnected individuals, features significantly Jewish? To what extent shall we be justified in pronouncing these a Jewish contribution or ingredient?

We are here confronted with that supreme difficulty which Chaim Weizmann used to call Jewish "ghostliness". The world is scarcely large enough to contain the Jews and they are said to possess all the wealth of the earth, and yet when you strain every nerve to fix them in a definition they elude you like a mirage. It seems impossible to lay a finger on anything tangible and measurable in the Jew's Jewishness; yet an ailing, all-devouring self-consciousness comes like a film between him and the world. Not taken into account when things are normal and prosperous, he is seen as ubiquitous, all-powerful, sinister when there is blame to be apportioned. I believe the links holding Jews together— in the words of Edmund Burke—to be as invisible as air and as strong as the heaviest chains, and the Jewish ingredient to be as imperceptible to the senses yet as effective in results as vital energy itself. Such things, however, are too subtle for the historian's customary crude techniques and his far from subtle instruments.

Jewish impulses and reactions, attitudes and sensitiveness, Jewish modes of feeling and patterns of behaviour call for the intuition of the artist, and indeed can only be intimated by symbols, conjured up by poetic incantation, and communicated by the art of the novelist. In brief, the Jew is part of a collective destiny, even when he does not know it or is unwilling to share in it. To consider as Jews only persons who explicitly affirm their Judaism by positive participation in Jewish activities would be tantamount to approving the statement made in the 1920's by a German Jewish Social-Democratic leader: he maintained that he was no Jew because he had sent a letter of resignation to the Berlin Jewish community—upon which he was asked by a Gentile British friend whether he thought that Jews were a club. Even when they live their entire life in a non-Jewish milieu and have little contact among themselves, Jews still bear within them the imprint of a centuries-old community whose members were regarded by themselves, and by the outside world, as responsible for one another: a community that lived apart, within a hermetically closed framework of laws and regulations, climatic conditions, and economic pursuits, and that was imbued with an intense self-consciousness because it believed in its own special destiny on the one hand, and was discriminated against and persecuted on the other.

Nevertheless, the Jewish historian would be quite mistaken to direct his attention to every single Jew, even one who had never had any ties with Judaism, on the assumption that all the activities and associations engaged in by every person of Jewish extraction came within the purview of Jewish history. Nor should encouragement be given to the presentation of Jewish history as a collection of biographies of persons of Jewish ancestry who made good in the world. History addresses itself to social patterns; the individual—whatever the ultimate uniqueness of every human being—is significant as a representative type. In the absence of an all-embracing Jewish life of the kind that existed in Eastern Europe, the historian's attempt to isolate specifically "Jewish" associations and activities such as attendance at services, charity campaigns, intercession on behalf of suffering brethren abroad, absorption of immigrants, and even Jewish scholarship (of mainly philological or antiquarian character) will prove depressingly unrewarding and jejune.

When the elusive yet extremely potent Jewish patterns of thought, feeling, and behaviour that have crystallised around an extremely tenacious nucleus of race and religion no longer receive—outside Israel—integrated and limpid expression in autonomous and closely knit communities, the nature of these patterns will perhaps best be brought into relief by constant confrontation with general, non-Jewish patterns, and by turning our attention upon the encounter between Jew and Gentile. The earlier historians were naturally inclined to pursue their quest for meaning in Jewish history from within. The future historian of the Jews may prefer to operate from the vantage point of general history. The older historians were impressed by the uniqueness of the history of a people dwelling apart. The newer ones are likely to be struck by the paradox that it is precisely in the uniqueness of a clannish, marginal community dispersed around the world that the secret of the universal significance of Jewish history lies.

An attempt to sort out the elements of an interpretation of Jewish history from the point of view of world history must nowadays take cognisance of two facts. One is of far-reaching significance: the shift of balance which has been taking place between the West and the non-white civilisations. The other is of a more topical and probably ephemeral nature: the treatment of the Jews in Arnold Toynbee's *Study of History,* the most ambitious world-historical synthesis so far undertaken in the twentieth century. The two facts are, in my opinion, closely connected.

I believe that the lack of respect and the air of irritation, if not downright hostility, which mark Professor Toynbee's approach to Jewish history are on a par with his violent reaction against Europe-centrism, and that both are derived from a deep sense of guilt toward the colonial peoples and a corresponding collapse of European self-confidence. What a distance divides Toynbee from Macaulay, who was so cheerfully sure that "a single shelf of a good European library was worth the whole native literature of India and Arabia", and to whom the peoples of the East were simply candidates for admission to Western civilisation!

In Western Christian civilisation's vision of history, the Jew occupied a vital or at least a unique place. To the multitudes of Eastern and South-eastern Asia, Jews are an unknown, incomprehensible, and negligible factor. The Jew in the West might be persecuted, reviled, despised, expelled, and massacred, but he was indissolubly connected with the central event in the history of Christendom. He constituted a terrific problem. He embodied a great mystery. Immense effectiveness was ascribed to him, for good or evil. He appeared to be a factor of significance out of all proportion to his numbers.

The Jews have a long, terrible, and blood-stained account with the Christian West. I venture to suggest, however, that the rise of non-European powers is already beginning to make the record look somewhat different and less straightforward than was the case even in the recent past. For one thing, no Jewish historian, whatever his evaluation of the various factors involved in the restoration of Jewish statehood, can ignore the fact that Zionism would never have had a chance of success if centuries of Christian teaching and worship, liturgy and legend had not conditioned the Western nations to respond almost instinctively to the words "Zion" and "Israel", and thus to see in the Zionist ideal not a romantic chimera or an imperialistic design to wrest a country from its actual inhabitants, but the consummation of an eternal promise and hope. The Far Eastern civilisations, however, show no trace of Jewish associations. Their record is clean of anti-semitism—but it is also empty of Jews.

The whole centuries-long relationship of the West to the East is made to appear by Toynbee as one of sustained aggression, motivated by insatiable avarice against essentially contemplative and pacific civilisations. Church militant, European nationalism and racialism, modern imperialism, acquisitive capitalism, and—in some of its aspects—revolutionary communism are only phases and versions as it were of the sin of self-centred pride and arrogance. Far from having its cause in intellectual or spiritual superiority, the victory of the West over the Eastern and other non-European peoples, Toynbee believes, is due to one single factor—technological mastery. The Western absorption in techniques is evidence that Western man was much less anxious to know the truth than he was eager to turn discoveries and inventions into instruments of self-aggrandisement and dominion. The Chinese fathomed some of the mysteries of science long before the Europeans, but remained indifferent to the possibilities of science's utilitarian application.

The sin of pride has always carried its own punishment with it. *Hubris* prepares its own undoing. Greed expanding and conquering generates irreconcilable social cleavages and antagonisms within the victorious society, and bitter resentment among the conquered. The internal proletariat, alienated from the body politic, feels a common resentment with the external proletariat of the enslaved nations. Together they evolve a system of values—a new religion—to match and oppose the values of the conquerors and to act as a sublimating compensation for the enjoyments from which they are debarred. Dominant society, which has waxed fat and sluggish and succumbed to the malaise of the satiated, is pervaded by the new religion and simultaneously destroyed by the conbined blows administered from within by the internal proletariat, and from without by the external proletariat. Western civilisation— with communism corroding it from within and closing in on it from the outside—having now reached this stage, it can be saved only by a new universal religion based on a synthesis of the four great creeds—Christianity, Islam, Buddhism and Hinduism. Such a universal religion, Toynbee holds, will redeem it from the cancer of aggressive egotism by enabling it to achieve blissful reconciliation with the eternal order of things.

Toynbee[1] appears to trace the original sin of the West, self-idolatry, back to the "arrogant" Judaic idea of a Chosen People. Hebrew society was accor-

---

[1] Arnold J. Tóynbee: *Abridgement of a Study of History* (made by D. C. Somervell), Oxford 1960, pp. 8, 22, 135, 310, 361, 380, 388–9, 509, 640, 729–31, 739, 816.

ding to him only a parochial, marginal community within a much wider Syriac civilisation. Judaic religion evolved in the encounter between the Syriac exiles in Babylon and the proletariat of Mesopotamia, just as Christianity arose out of the meeting between the Jews oppressed by Rome and the proletariat of hellenistic-Roman society.

That the tribal god Yahveh, and not any one of his so much more powerful rivals within "Syriac civilisation", came to be accepted as the One God of the Universe is attributed by Toynbee to the all-devouring jealousy of Yahveh, who would not brook other gods and incited his believers to destroy all idols and images.

Obsessed by its tribal exclusiveness, Judaism failed to seize the chance, offered it by incipient Christianity, of becoming a universal religion, and instead rose against Rome in a nationalist uprising. When the Jewish revolt was crushed, Judaism's role was played out. The subsequent 2,000 years of Jewish history represented the meaningless perdurance of a fossil. The Jews' only response to the challenge of exile and persecution, Toynbee says, was to maintain a hermetically closed, highly intricate ritualistic framework, and to accumulate great financial power.

At the end of this long period of fossilised existence, Zionism marked another outburst of tribal arrogance. Yielding to the essentially Western passion for archaisation, the Jews, instead of keeping their hopes fixed on miraculous Divine deliverance, launched an attack on the Arab inhabitants of Palestine, succeeded in expelling them, and set up a tiny statelet of their own which in its crude aggressiveness combined all the disagreeable features of a military garrison and the Wild West.

Imbibed by the Christian West, the Judaic spirit acted as a potent evil factor in the history of Western civilisation. The intolerant militant exclusiveness of the Church—a primary Judaic legacy—was in due course transformed into the self-idolatry of parochial nationalisms like the English and the French. Taught by the example of Joshua's extermination of the pagan Canaanites, Puritan settlers felt no qualms about annihilating the Red Indians. Believing themselves to be the heirs of the Jews to whom the earth had been promised as an inheritance, European imperialist nations went out to conquer and enslave the non-European races. Having turned their backs on the One God, they abandoned themselves completely to Mammon: all their energies were applied to perfecting the means of accumulating wealth and reaching the highest degree of rational utilitarian efficiency. In brief, the West underwent—in the words of Toynbee—a process of "Judaisation".

At the other end of the scale, socialism and communism were nothing but a version of the Judaic apocalypse, except that the final consummation was again looked for, not in the intervention of the Almighty, but as the result of social cataclysm and a violent uprising of men.

So much for Toynbee's definition of the Jewish ingredient in Western civilisation. How will the Jewish historian, coming from general history, define it?

There is every justification, it seems to me, for the view that finds a distinctive Jewish ingredient at the very core of Western civilisation. This is the measure of the paradox: an essentially marginal group said to be the most clannish of all communities, the Jews have in their tribal seclusion in Palestine as well as in their worldwide dispersion, as spirit and as flesh and blood, played a powerful part in making a collection of tribes, communities, and countries into a civilisation. Needless to add, they were not alone in the field and their influence has not been invariably beneficial.

I shall not labour the obvious: that Judaism was the parent of Christianity, and that therefore almost the whole of Jewish history till Jesus, and on into the first centuries of Christianity—the period in which the latter received its shape either within the Jewish community or in the course of debate with Rabbinic Judaism, and spread through the Jewish communities along the shores of the Mediterranean—it constitutes a vital chapter in world history. One can well imagine a future Israeli historian undertaking to write the history of Western Christian civilisation as the story of the Judaic kernel in its encounter with Greek philosophy and art, the mystery religions of the Orient, the institutions and laws of the Roman Empire, the Germanic traditions, the facts of European economy, etc., etc.

I shall take up only the one idea which Professor Toynbee thinks to be the most distinctive and effective Jewish ingredient in world history—the idea of a Chosen People. I agree as to its paramount importance. But my reasons for thinking that Western civilisation (and consequently universal history) would not have been the same without it are altogether different from his.

To Dr. Toynbee, the whole concept of chosenness signifies mere tribal exclusiveness and a conceited claim to racial superiority. He omits the attributes of a "a holy nation", "a people of priests". I believe that the uniqueness of ancient Judaism did not consist so much in the monotheistic conception, traces of which we can find among neighbouring peoples, or in moral precepts whose similitudes we can find in Greek philosophy and the teachings of the Stoa—it consisted in the idea of a whole people's recognising, as its sovereign, God alone. The laws under which it lives are not dictated by a ruler, are not derived from the will of the people, are not a utilitarian contrivance. Hence what Matthew Arnold called the Hebraic passion for right acting, as distinct from the Greek passion for right seeing and thinking in order to know, experience, and dominate the world around.

Here we have the secret of the victory of parochial Yahveh over Helios, the god of the sun, and all the other pagan deities, and indeed over hellenistic philosophies like the Stoa. The uniqueness of Judaism did not lie, as Toynbee says, in the devouring jealousy of Yahveh, but in the total and one-sided absorption of a whole people—not a sect of the chosen or a monastic order—in the service of an impersonal idea. The teachings of other Near Eastern religions were more tolerant, more open to sweetness and light—and left very many things outside their scope. This is why they failed to revolutionise history. The hellenistic systems are incomparable in their broad humanity, but they were addressed to and absorbed by individuals as counsels of personal perfection. Not conclusions of close discursive reasoning, but the living model and the all-absorbing passion proved so effective in the Jewish case. From that point of view, Toynbee's attempt to dilute the sharp identity of the Judaic source by pointing to a wider Syriac context of ideas and beliefs is hardly relevant.

What distinguishes mature Christian civilisation from other civilisations is to be sought not so much in particular tenets of Christianity, to which parallels of some kind may be found in other religions, but in the fundamentally and peculiarly Western relationship between Church and State. There was no example of it in antiquity, and none to my knowledge in Islam or the Eastern Asiatic civilisations. And this ingredient is substantially Jewish. The Church means in this respect the universality of believers, "the people of priests", and not merely the hierarchy. The members of the *ecclesia* are actuated by consciousness that, as a "holy nation" and a "people of priests", they belong not to the earthly State alone, but to a community of transcendental laws and aims.

The permanent tension between Church and State, as long as neither proved able to absorb the other, is to my mind the source of the essentially Western obsession with the problem of the legitimacy of power. It is not enough that the law is promulgated by the authority which is recognised to have power to legislate. King, Parliament, the sovereign people, even pope and council, must all the time exhibit their credentials in the face of divine or natural law. Natural law, is, of course, of hellenistic and Roman provenance. Yet it is fair to say that without its being amalgamated with divine law, it would have failed to become the great formative influence that it did.

One should not underestimate the other factors which have shaped Western ideas of State, law, and legitimacy, such as the Germanic traditions, feudalism, the guild system, the changes in methods of production. Yet I believe with Lord Acton that none of these was so effective as the tension between Church and State, which was the greatest and most important vehicle of ideas and controversies and which, as it were, enveloped all the others and set the tone. When political theorists of the West spoke of Oriental despotism, what they meant was that the Orient did not know the problem of the legitimacy of power. Power to them was a datum, a fact of nature, an elemental, amoral force to be taken for granted like sunshine and rain, storm and plague. It need not always be tyrannical and malign, it might be as benign as one could wish. But it is given, it is there, and we have to bow to it.

Now it is the tension between Church and State, based on the idea of a chosen holy people, that gave the history of European nations its highly dynamic quality in comparison with the early stagnation of the non-European civilisations. Thanks to the Judaic concept the papacy never could, and perhaps never really wished to, reduce the body of lay believers to mere receivers of grace through the instrumentality of sacramental mystery and miracle. The task of realising the Kingdom of God was never restricted to the *ecclesia docens*. It always continued to rest with the *whole* body of believers. Hence the sense of dignity and awful responsibility of a Christian nation. It could not accept easily an evil king any more than a corrupt pope. For Christianity could never quite be reduced to a matter of personal ascetic discipline and unwordly holiness, and it could not divest itself of all responsibility for this world on the ground that its kingdom was wholly of another. It was thus bound to feel the permanent challenge to realise its high calling here and now. If this be true of the Catholic Church at all times, it is especially true of Calvinism and the Puritans in Britain and America.

There is, I submit with Dr. Toynbee, a direct line from the Church Militant permeated with the Judaic idea of a holy nation of priests, to modern nationalism with its ideology of a chosen people. We are only too painfully aware in the twentieth century of the terrible ravages wrought by nationalism run wild. Yet it would be wrong for the historian to forget that in the first half of the nineteenth century, the national idea in the mouth of a Mazzini, and indeed even of a Fichte, not to speak of the Polish Mickiewicz, was a prophetic clarion call for spiritual regeneration. Far from proclaiming tribal war on neighbours thought inferior, it imposed a special mission, a particularly strenuous obligation on one's own nation within the scheme of mankind's endeavour towards higher things and universal freedom. It is indeed most strange to read today Fichte's boast that the German nation, the *Urvolk* of Europe, would not demean itself by joining the general bloody scramble for territories and colonies, and would take no part in the squalid game of political and mercantilist rivalry. The only truly original nation in Europe, since all others had their thoughts and feelings shaped by an acquired language—whether Latin or German—the Germans were destined to maintain, with brows furrowed and spirits keyed to the highest pitch of concentration, a special communion with eternal values.

Everyone is familiar with the religious, Messianic overtones of Mazzini's philosophy of nationalism, with such slogans as "God and the people", "nationality is a mission", "nation means sacrifice"; with Mazzini's conception of patriotism as a counterpart to selfish utilitarianism and moral self-indulgence; with his vision of a federation of free peoples, each with its own mission, under the inspiring guidance of *Roma Terza*—Rome of the people—the first Rome having been that of the emperors and the second that of the popes. Mickiewicz, like Mazzini, consciously drew on biblical ideas and imagery in describing Poland as the suffering Remnant of Israel, destined to atone for the sins of other nations and redeem them through her self-sacrifice.

Professor Toynbee wrings his hands over the horrors wrought by modern nationalism and its evil offspring imperialism, seeing in them nothing but irredeemable evil, pride, and *hubris*, which stand in such crass contrast to the broad, quietist tolerance of the Eastern religions and civilisations.

It seems to me that in his prostration before the East and self-flagellation as a Westerner, Dr. Toynbee has missed a truth of awful import, a mystery of tragic grandeur—the ambivalence with which the whole of the Western achievement is charged from the start. It is an infinitely tragic fact that great good is somehow always mixed up with terrible evil, that the worst seems always to by the degeneration of the best, that some Hegelian *List der Vernunft,* a trick of Universal Reason, complicates in a sardonic manner the yearning for self-surrender with the craving for self-assertion.

Professor Toynbee is filled with reverence for those Eastern civilisations whose religions are a syncretistic synthesis of various, often heterogeneous, strands, and are ultimately the concern of the individual only, and whose churches know no intolerant militancy. He is attracted by those vast conglomerations of men who are not primarily political animals at all, and whose passion for power is held back by a highly developed capacity for contemplative communion with the invisible world and the attainment of that peace which passeth understanding—a peace for which we all strain in vain, and of which only very few in our midst ever catch a glimpse.

Nearer home Dr. Toynbee selects the Ottoman Empire for special commendation. That was a system in which racial, linguistic, and religious communities lived as *millets* side by side on a completely non-political basis. He is not worried by the fact that the Turkey of the sultans was a byword for despotism, corruption, and bribery, that even the Ulema, the supreme Moslem court of experts in Islam, was most of the time unable to restrain the cruel vagaries of personal despotism; that under such a régime there could be no individual rights and no corporate consciousness or self-respect; that only a palace plot or the assassin's dagger, and at a lower level bribery and flattery, could avert the pure arbitrariness of brute power; and that consequently complete stagnation overcame all cultural endeavour and spiritual vitality under the Ottoman Turks. In the vast empires where there is no political life and no popular passion, the individual may at times attain a very high degree of personal, unwordly perfection. But it is at the cost of the vitality and the moral advancement of the body social.

It is a curious thing that a man so sensitive to any sign of arrogance and pride, and who over acres of self-analysis recording his visitations makes such tremendous efforts to be humble, should at the same time to be so fascinated—as Dr. Toynbee is—by colossal dimensions, the mighty barbarian conquerors wading in blood up to their knees, building sky-high pyramids of the skulls of their slaughtered foes. England and France, on the other hand, Professor Toynbee again and again calls parochial, puffed-up little countries.

The finest flowering of culture never occurred on the vast expanses of steppe and desert but in tiny, overcrowded, noisy, and proud communities such as Athens, Jerusalem, Alexandria, Florence and Amsterdam. Why damn vitality by calling it arrogance? The truth of the matter is that an ambitious undertaking like Toynbee's to embrace all ages and all civilisations in one system, with the help of tidy schemata, sweeping generalisations, and quantitative measurements, can afford little room for the understanding of the unique phenomenon, the local idiom, and the particular concatenation of data and circumstances; little room for the exquisite miniature; and nothing of that feeling for the specific situation, limpid and throbbing with real life, which comes from long meditation and loving immersion in it.

In the last two centuries Western history has indeed become universal history. The non-European civilisations, sunk in languor or atrophy, have had their fate shaped by the expansion of Western capitalism, which turned the whole world into one economic and cultural unit. In our own day the essentially European ideologies of nationalism, democracy, and communism—not the organic growth and inner dialectic of their own heritage—stimulated the Asiatic and African peoples to assert themselves and seek self-determination.

I agree with Dr. Toynbee that in the forging of the various instruments for the unification of the world by the West—or if one prefers, by Western imperialism—the Jewish ingredient played the role of a powerful catalyst. Jews as living men, and not merely the Jewish spiritual legacy, moved on to the centre of the stage of world history in the nineteenth and twentieth centuries. One need not belittle the part Jews played in maintaining international trade almost alone in the early Middle Ages, in interpreting and transmitting for Christian scholarship the classical wisdom preserved in Arab translations, and as a lever in early urban colonisation. Whether you call them rapacious usurers or bankers—as one calls the more respectable because richer Christian Medicis and Fuggers, Lombards and Templars—whether the Jews went into business from their own choice or because all other avenues were closed to them, they kept up through centuries a rudimentary credit system in Europe.

Nevertheless, I hold the somewhat chilling view that the history of most European countries, with the exception perhaps of Spain, Poland and Holland, would not have differed very significantly had there been no Jews—but only the Judaic heritage—in Europe between the end of the Crusades and the eighteenth century. Indeed, for most of that time they had been expelled from a number of the European countries. The living ghetto commanded too little respect to influence directly a society so highly stratified as European society was for centuries.

Only in the last 150 years was it again given to Jews to affect the structural framework of universal history.

I believe it legitimate for the universal historian to call the age ushered in by the French and Industrial Revolutions the "era of industrial civilisation based on contract". This formulation takes account of the two most salient features of the period—industrialism and democratic growth. Furthermore, it implies that capitalism and the various forms of socialism and communism are only two poles of the same development, and not phenomena on different planes. The formulation postulates a type of spiritual-cultural superstructure evolved from the essentially universal and cosmopolitan character of industrial civilisation. The main point to be borne in mind is the transformation of a society based on status and on more or less rigid patterns into a society based on contract—in other words on individual and social mobility. This meant an entirely new situation for Jews, and one of unlimited possibilities.

Nuanced thinking and formulation are required here in order not to overstate our case. None of the early inventors of the industrial revolution was a Jew, and there were to my knowledge hardly any identifiable Jews among the early captains of industry. Werner Sombart's[1] attempt—in imitation of Max Weber's connecting of the Puritans with the rise of capitalism—to make the Jews of the seventeenth century bearers of early capitalism has long been discredited. Yet it is true that in the building of the sinews of the modern international capitalist economy, the part of the Jews, especially on the Continent, was that of pioneers and catalysts *par excellence*. International credit, banking and exchange, joint-stock companies, telegraphic news agencies, railway networks, chain stores, methods of mass production and mass marketing, the media of mass entertainment, experimentation in new techniques—in brief, the lifelines of a universal economy—were in very many cases laid down and set working by Jews, who thus played, in the words of Joseph Addison, the part of "pegs and nails" in the world economy.

The abstract, rational nexus holding together concrete, disparate detail was grasped more quickly by people with a long training in intellectual speculation. Not place-bound, the emancipated and de-tribalised Jew was unhampered by routine and conservative attachments, and his international connections helped him to forge the hinges of new artificial frameworks. It is in the nature of a marginal community, especially one living in metropolitan centres, to acquire the refined sensitivity of an exposed nerve and to be the first to detect the trend and shape of things to come. Hence the disposition and the courage to experiment. Emancipated formally, but not really or fully admitted as equals, lacking the prestige of lineage and long establishment, while eager for a place in the sun, and restless and ill at ease as people in ambiguous situations are, the Jews threw all their pent-up energies into the two avenues of power open to them: economic activity and intellectual prowess. Centuries of disciplined living and sober calculation prevented ambition from dissipating itself in a haphazard, chaotic manner. Vitality turned into a strictly rational instrument of power designed to obtain maximum results at the lowest cost.

As for the Jewish ingredient in revolutionary Messianism, the other pole of industrial civilisation, I have come to the conclusion on somewhat closer study that it was to a large extent the Jewish Messianic vision of history that made the industrial revolution appear not merely as another crisis and another bad spell, but as an apocalyptic hour leading to some preordained final denouement. It was the Jewish Messianic tradition that was responsible for the fact that the social protest of the victims of the industrial revolution did not take the form of another desperate, elemental *jacquerie*, but became part of the preparation for a Day of Judgement, after which justice and peace would reign supreme and history really begin as it were with all conflicts and contradictions resolved.

---

[1] Werner Sombart: *Die Juden und das Wirtschaftsleben*, Munich 1928.

The earliest prophet of socialist transformation in nineteenth-century Europe, Saint-Simon, was quite explicitly linked with the Jewish Messianic expectation. Jews were the leading spirits in his fascinating and influential school, and they emphatically voiced the conviction that they were carrying on the perennial Messianic mission of Judaism. Their future city of universal harmony was to be guided by technicians and bankers who were at the same time artists and priests, and was to rest on a universal religion of humanity, *Nouveau Christianisme*, with the old division into State and Church, matter and spirit, theory and practice done away with forever. It is most significant that Jewish Saint-Simonists, the Rodrigueses, Pereiras, d'Eichthals, should have in the course of time become the architects of France's industrial and financial revolution and of much of Europe's banking and industry.

The deeply ingrained experience of history as the unfolding of a pattern of judgement and deliverance makes it almost impossible for the Jew to take history for granted as an eternal meaningless cycle. Time must have a stop. History must have a denouement. At the same time his lack of roots in a concrete tradition, with its instinctive certainties and the comfort of smooth, almost automatic procedures, combines with the absence of experience of practical government to turn many a Jew into a doctrinaire and impatient addict of schemes of social redemption. When he is of a prophetic temperament, as in the case of a Karl Marx, a torrent of relentless denunciation issues forth. A terrific, fiery oversimplification reduces everything—human laziness and thoughtlessness, the weakness of the flesh and the heterogeneity of impulse, peculiarity of tradition and complexity of situation—to greed, falsehood, and hypocrisy, a kingdom of the Devil that will be overthrown in the imminent future by a kingdom of God. Suspended between heaven and earth, rejected and excluded, tormented by the humiliations, complexities, and ambiguities of his situation, many a young Jew threw himself with the deepest yearning and passion into the arms of the religion of revolution.

We all know the inhumanities practised by capitalism at the height of its imperialistic expansion, and the perverse denial of traditional morality and of man's freedom and dignity which accompanies the attempt to satisfy the Messianic longing for salvation by a totalitarian system. This erosion of ideals has no particular relevance to Judaism as such, for it is rooted in the tragic condition itself of man, in the essential ambivalence of things human and social—as the Christian would say, in original sin. It is at the same time not to be denied that the fact of a surplus of intensity among Jews, such as is peculiar to a marginal minority in constant need to justify its separateness by self-assertion, has its own polar ambivalence: besides idealistic self-dedication to causes and things of the mind, there is a particularly harsh, shrill and unscrupulous style of Jewish self-seeking.

We come now to the Jewish ingredient in the universal or cosmopolitan culture characteristic of an industrial civilisation based on contract instead of status, and sustained by media of mass communication.

It is one of the commonplaces of Jewish apologists to emphasise that Jews have enriched the life and culture of every country in which they have lived. Yet, as I have said, I do not believe that the culture of England, France, Italy, or even of pre-nineteenth-century Germany would have been significantly different if there had been no Jews in those countries. Modern universal civilisation is, however, unthinkable without Marx, Freud, or Einstein, who have moulded the consciousness of modern mankind.

Isaiah Berlin has given an acute explanation of the contrast between the superb achievements of Jews in the sciences and music, and their rather inferior showing in literature. Jewish writers have excelled in biography and the biographical novel (Andre Maurois and Stefan Zweig). They have written in highly stimulating fashion on the complexities and dilemmas of the contemporary human situation (Arthur Koestler, Arthur Miller, and Ilya Ehrenburg). In this they were helped by their psychological acumen, which their race acquired from its agelong need to understand and adjust to others, as well as by their being at the very nerve centre of metropolitan life and at the same time detached and over-sensitive. Yet, while being often stirring and provocative, their writings in no sense represent great literature. It is not enough to be able to penetrate, even lovingly, the inner springs and hidden recesses of men and societies. Vigour and intimacy come to the novel from subtle, almost unconscious and automatic associations, which are not acquired with the algebraic language of science but are imperceptibly experienced within a concrete, long-established tradition. This is why Yiddish literature has such vigour as well as warmth.

The literature produced by Jewish writers in non-Jewish languages in centres like old Vienna—where Jews as producers as well as consumers often formed a nucleus of the most cosmopolitan vanguard—served despite its lack of greatness as a barometer and stimulant of universal significance.

On the political level, the passionate patriotism of a Benjamin Disraeli, a Walter Rathenau, a Leon Blum had perhaps greater intensity and depth than the devotion of an ordinary British, German of French statesman to his country. It was conditioned by an agonised yearning for something romantically idealised which was not a simple datum to be taken for granted. This kind of Jewish patriotism betrayed a deeper and more articulate understanding of the national tradition and its peculiarities than could the patriotism of a "normal" leader, for whom the national tradition was a matter of spontaneous reflexes. And the patriotism of Jews was always more universal) or more imperial, as in the case of Disraeli) in its awareness.

Far from lending support to any doctrine of race in the biological sense, our argument has been concerned, throughout its latter part, with a spiritual legacy and the facts of history and social psychology on the one side, and the individualistic mobility of industrial civilisation on the other.

Indeed, the fate of Jews under Hitler may in this respect be seen as a focal point of twentieth-century history—and not merely because of the enormity of the crime and sufferings inflicted on them with the help of scientific long-term planning and execution, and not only because the mass violation of the sanctity of human life was not calculated to stop with the Jews but was bound to undermine the most vital foundations of our civilisation and initiate general race slaughter. Hitler's racialism signified an attempt to reverse the main trend of modern Western civilisation, and to return from individualistic contract to deterministic patterns of race, caste, and tribe through a denial of the unity of mankind. It is no accident that nazism found it necessary to reinterpret the whole of history as a permanent life-and-death struggle between Nordic Aryanism and the Jewish spirit, attributing to Jews a significance and effectiveness which the most extreme Jewish chauvinist would not dream of claiming.

Some of my readers may have begun to feel a certain surprise that there has been relatively little reference so far to Israel in this survey. Our theme has been Jewish history from the point of view of universal history. Although the Palestine problem has been one of the focal points of international politics, and albeit that little country of such strange destinies is once more a centre of world attention, it is still too early to say whether the return of Jews to Zion (which coincides with the general retreat of Europe from Asia: an extraordinary fact, highly charged with symbolism) will mean more than the establishment of another little state among the dozens of new states which have come into existence in the twentieth century.

In Professor Toynbee's [1] violent condemnation, Zionism figures as an integral part of Western imperialistic rapacity. The music of Messianic hope kept alive for 2,000 years; the saga-like quality of the return of Zion; the historic perspectives and vistas opened by that event; the awful tragedy that the restoration of Jews to Israel had to be effected through a terrible conflict with the Arab world—all this fails to strike a chord. We have instead Dr. Toynbee's nonsense about Jews taking over the Western "heresy of archaisation"; his tasteless, sermonising censure of Jews for not trusting in God's miraculous deliverance, and for demeaning themselves with such unworthy things as a state, a flag, an army, and postage stamps; a selective method of presenting facts which amounts to untruth—as, for instance, the failure to mention the decision of the United Nations, as representative of world conscience, on partition, or to refer by a single word to the invasion of Palestine by five Arab armies. We then get the horrifying comparison of the treatment of the Arab population by the Jews with the extermination of six million Jews by Hitler, and finally the crowning sanctimonious blasphemy: the prophecy that on the Day of Judgement the crime of the Jews shall be judged graver than that of the Nazis.

There are one or two pointers to be borne in mind by the universal historian mediating on the future of Jews within the scheme of world history. There seems to be something almost providential in the way in which the two new centres, Israel and the United States, were as it were prepared just on the eve of the catastrophe which put an end to European Jewry's history of some

---

[1] A.J. Toynbee, *op. cit.*, pp. 735–7.

1,500 to 2,000 years. There is also a striking analogy between the present relations between Israel and the Anglo-Saxon Jewish communities, especially American Jewry, and the relations that obtained at the time of the Second Temple between Jewish Palestine and the Mediterranean Jewish communities of the Roman Empire on one side, and the Jewish conglomeration in Mesopotamia on the other. It is a fact of very great importance that English has come to be the language of the majority of the Jewish people.

The problems that faced that Palestine-Mediterranean axis were very similar to those of the Israel-Anglo-Saxon axis today, including all those needs which had to be met by an annual United Jewish Appeal, the problems of assimilation, mixed loyalties, and so forth. The encounter of Judaism and hellenism, and the synthesis of the two in the Alexandria of Philo, paved the way for the triumph of Christianity. Is it too fanciful to suggest that the New York of today may be destined to play the part of a Jewish Alexandria of the twentieth century? There is much food for speculation in the fact that tiny Israel, on the troubled eastern shore of the Mediterranean, has a kind of counterpart in what is the most vital country in the world today, and the one which seems destined to set the tone in the years to come.

If it was given to the Jews to make some mark on world history, it was not because God, as someone has said, was kind to the Jews, in scattering them among the nations, but because they had fashioned their real contribution—the Judaic heritage—in their own country, and were dispersed only after they had been moulded into a unique phenomenon. . . .

No historian, I believe, can be a complete rationalist. He must be something of a poet, he must have a little of the philosopher, and he must be touched just a bit by some kind of mysticism. The sorting out of evidence, the detective's skill in ferreting out inaccuracy and inconsistency, are of little help when the historian strikes against the hard residue of mystery and enigma, the ultimate causes and the great problems of human life.

The Jewish historian becomes a kind of martyr in his permanent and anguished intimacy with the mystery of Jewish martyrdom and survival. Whether he be Orthodox in belief or has discarded all religious practice, he cannot help but be sustained by a faith which can neither be proved nor disproved.

I believe that notwithstanding all the vexations and entanglements caused by emergency and inescapable necessity—all so reminiscent incidentally of the times of Ezra and Nehemiah—Israel will one day be spiritually significant and, in conjunction with the Jewish disapora, spiritually effective in the world.

History would somehow make no sense otherwise.

SAMUEL HUGO BERGMAN

Samuel Hugo Bergman was born in Prague in 1883 and studied at the Universities of Berlin and Prague. Attaining a Ph. D. degree from the latter, he also served that institution of higher learning as assistant librarian for many years. Bergman settled in Palestine in 1920 as director of the National and University Library in Jerusalem and as lecturer in philosophy, advancing to the rank of professor and achieving the distinction of being the first Rector of the Hebrew University.

A prolific writer, Bergman has enriched Jewish thinking as well as world philosophy with notable works such as *DAS UNENDLICHE UND DIE ZAHL; ARGUMENTE GEGEN DIE RELATIVITAETES-THEORIE; THE PHILOSOPHY OF PHYSICS; HAREALISM V'IDEALISM B'TORAT HAHAKARA*, and works on Kant, Bergson, Shlomo Maimon and others.

Bergman felt an affinity with the ideological elements in the thinking of Ahad Ha'am (a noted Jewish philosopher who conceived of Palestine mainly as a cultural center for Judaism), A.D. Gordon (who pointed out the spiritual qualities of labor) and Martin Buber (who saw in religion a dialogue between man and God). Bergman synthesized these influences in his own capacious mind.

A member of *Brith Shalom* and *Ihud*—in association with Ernst A. Simon, Judah Magnes and Buber, all of the Hebrew University—he originally hoped for Jewish-Arab cooperation either in a bi-national state or in a Middle East confederation.

Deploring doctrinaire society, he envisioned present day Israel as a small land with unlimited horizons.

The following is a chapter entitled, THE PHENOMENON OF ISRAEL from *MID-EAST WORLD-CENTER: YESTERDAY, TODAY AND TOMORROW*, edited by Ruth Manda Anshem, New York, Harper and Brothers, 1956, pp. 336–353.

The Phenomenon of Israel

by SAMUEL HUGO BERGMAN

IN AN ARTICLE entitled "Philosophy at the University and the Jewish Mind,"[1] the philosopher Leon Roth has maintained that it was the task of the Hebrew University in Jerusalem to supply an answer to the question, Is there a Jewish mind? The task to which this chapter addresses itself is far more modest, though it does deal with a segment of the larger problem. Our concern here is with the ideal which constitutes the basis of the latest chapter in Jewish history, the establishment of the State of Israel.

When, in 1910, the distinguished German Jewish philosopher Edmund Husserl founded his "phenomenology" as "the science of all sciences" which, as the "doctrine of phenomena," must claim precedence over all other sciences, he wrote: "Phenomenology is not a science of fact but of essence, a science whole sole object is to establish knowledge of essences, not of facts." Husserl proceeded to say that anyone who wished to investigate the essence of a thing, its "phenomenon," must "cleanse" the facts of all accidents, and that only through such "reduction" is it possible to attain to reality. In this same sense I shall endeavor, in the pages which follow, to enucleate the phenomenon of Israel, the ideal of Israel, the spiritual force which has quickened this state into life and which, in my view, is alone capable of guaranteeing its survival in the future.

1

The Zionist movement and the establishment of the State of Israel are direct consequences of the messianic expectation which the Jewish people cherished deeply and persistently through millenniums. This was a conviction that just as human history took its inception with the expulsion from paradise, so it would have a goal and consummation in the establishment of the Kingdom of God on earth; furthermore, the ingathering of the scattered children of Israel to the home they had lost would mark the inauguration and forward movement of this Kingdom of God. Moreover, the Kingdom of God upon earth would imply a total transformation in nature and in man—"a new heaven and a new earth"; in the language of biology, it would imply the inception of a new and higher species—messianic man. If, guided by "practical intelligence," a man declares that such a fresh creation of heaven and earth is an impossibility, he is incapable of understanding the elemental force out

---

[1] *Hebrew University Garland* (London, 1952).

of which the State of Israel was born. The fact that this messianic ideal is to be found in other places also—in thinkers like the Russian Solovyev and the Indian Aurobindo—by no means diminishes its force but rather enhances it. Peculiar in the Jewish experience is the persistent vitality of the idea over a history of almost three thousand years, of the intimate association of a universal human idea with a national aspiration. Even in the time of Jeremiah, before its first, Babylonian, exile, the Jewish people regarded itself as "the first-fruits of God's harvest," so that it becomes impossible to draw a line between national and universal expectations.

True, the two or three generations of secularized Jews of our day have transformed Zionism into a political ideal, giving it force and actuality, to be sure, but at the same time crippling its transcendental significance; but far more powerful than any political program of conferences and congresses is the myth of the messiah, the archetype of redemption which persists in the collective unconscious of the people and gives shape and meaning to its fate, the fate alike of the community and of the individual. It "possesses" the individual Jew and makes him serviceable to messianic humanity, as prophet, as preacher and agitator, as inventor of a universal language like Zamenhof, or as evangelist of a new social ideal like Popper-Lynkeus. It possesses the entire people so that it strikes its tents and moves on to meet its salvation and realize it in the land of its fathers, in Germany of the seventeenth century as in Yemen of the twentieth. In periods of secularization the eschatological passion is disguised as a struggle for a party program, but the driving force is always the same. It is rooted in the unplumbed depths of the folk soul and is mightier than any rationalistic formulation. At times the archetypal force of the messianic ideal may take on a narrowly nationalist expression, at other times one that is wholly antinational and universal. In itself the force embraces both aspects, national and universal.

"Ye are my witnesses" is God's word (Isaiah 44:8) in the Babylonian captivity. Israel's very existence is what bears testimony. The people style themselves "those that wait for the Lord" and took upon their history of frightful suffering as the history of God's witness to the world: so long as Israel suffers the world is not yet God's, the messiah is not yet come. It is Israel's task to endure suffering and abide faithful to the hope that this chaotic world will still one day become God's world. It is this task which constitutes Israel's "election." The dispersion of Israel is the outward sign that the world is not yet God's world, just as the ingathering of Israel in Zion is the signal for the dawn of a new age.

Even in the Babylonian captivity Isaiah (44:2-3) proclaims the fulfillment of the national hope by an image of the outpouring of the Holy Spirit upon the people: "Thus saith the Lord that made thee and formed thee from the womb, which will help thee; fear not, O Jacob, My servant, and thou, Jeshurun, whom I have chosen, for I will pour water upon him that is thirsty, and floods upon the dry ground; I will pour My spirit upon thy seed, and Mine blessing upon thine offspring."

This is no dreamy fantasy, no abstract "moral ideal," but the genuine dynamism of the archetype of redemption within the range of whose power every Jew stands so long as any Judaism survives. The two redemptions, the messianic redemption of nature and humanity and the redemption of the people of Israel to enable it to discharge its task of bearing testimony upon its own soil and in its own polity, are in the Jewish consciousness a single redemption. Any attempt to dissever these two ideals, tendering nationalism strait and universalism jejune, is either an unreal abstraction or else a falsification.

2

To the question whether a historical event possesses messianic significance and a direct relationship to a valid redemption there can be no "objective" solution. Any answer must be subjective and hazardous. We contemporaries cannot say with certainty whether the establishment of the State of Israel is merely a segment of secular history, a transitory episode which is true today and no longer true tomorrow, or whether it is a direct manifestation of the process of salvation. On the other hand, we are at liberty to form our own judgment of the value we set upon the event and of the point of view from which we approach it.

One thing is certain: the imagination of the Jewish people conceived the establishment of the Jewish state differently from the way it came about in actuality—not as an event in the midst of history, so that an interval of generations might separate the event from messianic fulfillment, but rather as a single and ultimate act. The fact that it did not so transpire, that the establishment of the State of Israel did fall in the midst of history while history proceeds in its customary path, unredeemed and secular as heretofore, is the source of religious and spiritual and even of many political problems in Israel and about it.

The problems may be illustrated, at this point, by the discussion and contention which centered upon two symbols. The proclamation of the State took place on May 14, 1948, or according to Jewish reckoning on 5 Iyar of the year 5708 "after the creation of the world." Since the date of independence was to be fixed for later ages, a choice had to be made between the civil and the religious dating. In Israel as in other countries the international calendar prevails in all concerns of daily life. Fixing a celebration according to a calendar which had only religious significance and was at variance with the customary mode of reckoning involved a considerable inconvenience from the point of view of practical life, even in Israel itself, to say nothing of other countries. Nevertheless the parliamentary decision favored the impractical solution. The dating chosen was the Jewish one of 5 Iyar; the explicit implication was that the commemoration of the establishment of the State was to be regarded as a *religious* event.

But another decision implied the reverse. When the State was proclaimed there was a widespread sentiment in favor of emphasizing the religious character of Independence Day by including in the ritual for that day the reading of the Psalms of Praise *(hallel)*, with appropriate benedictions, as they are read on the pilgrimage festivals—Passover, Pentecost, and Tabernacles. This measure required the approval of the chief rabbinate of Israel. Approval was *not* given. The chief rabbinate was not convinced or felt that there was insufficient justification for declaring that the establishment of the State was part of the *sacred* history of Israel and should receive its permanent place in the cycle of the religious year.

This ambivalent appraisal of transcendent historical consummation which attended the apocalyptic events of World War II and the proclamation of the Jewish state is characteristic of the spiritual predicament of Israel. Born of messianic yearnings, ideally a concomitant of the end of time but in actuality mortised into the midst of history not messianic but secular—that is Israel's quandary.

3

Is Israel to be a wordly or a spiritual state? The answer to this question confronts every citizen of Israel, indeed every Jew in the world, with the gravest and cruelest of dilemmas. Should Israel be a secular polity, with the separation between church and state usual in Western countries? A Jewish state organized permanently as a secular polity with no constitution to bind it to the authentic Judaism of the Torah, a state dependent upon political rivalries and the ephemeral interplay of political parties and their coalitions, a Jewish state whose supreme source of law is a secular parliament, is a logical absurdity. For it is the peculiar character of the Jewish religion that it is not the religion of individuals but the covenant of the *people* as such with God. "Ye shall be unto me a *kingdom* of priests and a holy people." The Jewish religion is a national religion. This character has been misunderstood, and Judaism has been mistakenly regarded as the opposite of universal religion, and the supernational churches, by reason of their universality, as superior to the nationalist synagogue of the Jews.

Its national character does not, however, make Judaism exclusive. The Jewish religion is national in the sense that here the people as such felt itself summoned by God and was given a task which it could discharge only as a people: as a community to labor in its collective life for the realization of the Kingdom of God, and as a people to prepare the way for a messianic humanity. Only by living in its normal condition as a people can Israel fulfill its religious mission—or fall short of fulfilling it. That is why the prayers of the Jews give such manifold expression to petitions for restoration of status as a state. The central Jewish prayer asks for "the trumpets of our redemption," for the "return of our judges," for God's "return to His city Jerusalem," for the advent of the "scion of David." The religious mission which the people received in its encounter with God at Sinai was of such a nature that it could only be discharged by a *people* living upon *its own* soil. That is the decisive import of the "gathering of the scattered" for which the Jew has prayed for two millenniums. And now when the gathering of the scattered has been effected, must state and synagogue be separated, must the religious life of the Israeli be a private affair and not the concern of the community? This is wholly absurd. A *permanently* secular Jewish state is an anomaly.

4

But we are confronted by the second horn of the pitiless dilemma—the establishment of the State of Israel upon a religious basis. This is, in fact, what the partisans of religion have demanded of the political powers. For example, the draft of the constitution which was proposed, shortly before the establishment of the State, by one of the spiritual leaders of orthodox Judaism, the late Dr. Isaak Breuer, begins with the following preamble: "The Torah is the authoritative law of the Israelite people.... The juridical authority of the Torah does not require the consent of individual citizens and the polity.... The Jewish community organized as a state is subject to the discipline of the Torah in all its activities, in legislation, jurisprudence, and administration."

These proposals were not accepted. The State of Israel constituted itself as a secular democracy whose supreme legal authority was not the Torah but acts of parliament. The logical consequence was the recent (1954) declaration of the leader of extreme orthodoxy in Jerusalem that that group recognized the State of Israel only *de facto,* not *de jure.*

This position taken by the right wing cannot be dismissed out of hand. It is a serious attempt to make the principle of *spiritual* authority, hallowed by uninterrupted tradition, sovereign in one's own state. In the spiritual confusion into which mankind has been thrown by a congeries of "modern" movements, the establishment of a vital spiritual authority supported by the tradition of millenniums would be an event of the first spiritual magnitude.

But unfortunately the essential prerequisite, a *living* spiritual authority, is wanting. Orthodox Judaism, alas, is not a living religious force, In Jewish tradition the Torah has been likened to water, but the tradition itself has grown rigid and the Torah has ceased to be a living, ever flowing fountainhead. The commandments of the Torah do not renew themselves from within; in the ever changing conditions of life they maintain themselves only through a huge mass of legal *fictions.* Out of consideration for the dignity of the tradition we shall forbear to marshal a large number of specimens. But one example I shall cite because it exposes the utter absurdity, in view of the establishment of the State, of the subterfuges which must be devised to preserve the letter of the law. The Torah ordains that each seventh year shall be a year of release, when there is to be neither plowing nor sowing, so that the earth may enjoy its rest. Under modern economic conditions it is obvious that the observance of this law must result in ruin for the State of Israel. But there is no authority capable of conceding that a commandment of the Torah must be rescinded. The commandment is therefore formally observed—and circumvented by a fictitious sale of the soil of Israel to a non-Jew. This single example represents many hundreds of cases. The authority of the Torah is maintained even while it is being circumvented, and the circumvention is justified by ingenious juridical fictions. Judaism becomes a religion of quasis.

In the early Christian centuries men of the Talmudic era still possessed the power to accommodate the basic principles of the Torah to altered conditions of contemporary life, so that religious life continued in a constantly fluid state. But little by little this process of self-renewal ceased, and was supplanted by a calcification of ritualism. This is the situation which confronts the State of Israel. The ritualism of orthodoxy is in no position to cope with the suddenly emergent questions posed by a Jewish state. Not courage alone is wanting: there is no supreme religious authority competent to take fateful decisions—no Synedrion such as once existed, for whose reconstitution influential religious circles have hitherto labored in vain.

In large part the tradition was shaped in the Diaspora. As *halakha* (religious law) it regulated the life of Jews in all spheres of activity. But in the Diaspora the Jews had no political responsibility and therefore neither need nor opportunity to construct a *halakha* for spheres of political life, such as distribution of land, foreign policy, police, and the like. As individuals they participated, after the emancipation, in the political development of their environment, but as a religious community they did not. Consequently when the Jewish *state* was proclaimed, Judaism could offer no *halakha* for these decisive spheres of life. Hence for orthodox Jews in particular there was generated a dualism which could not be bridged over—on the one hand a secular state, and on the other an orthodoxy not amenable to the new conditions. In particular the communal settlements *(kibbutzim)* of orthodox persuasion found themselves daily confronted by novel problems growing out of forms of life which the *halakha* had never envisaged.[2]

But the problem is not merely an internal question of orthodoxy—whether orthodoxy can summon the courage and the means to break out of ritualism and accommodate itself to the new situation. The problem cuts much deeper: How and to what degree is it possible for a religion cradled in a *book* with a specific number (no fewer than 613) of specifically formulated commandments and prohibitions to remain faithful to that *book* and at the same time prove vital and creative; how can it remain true to itself as a living faith, confront constantly changing reality, and out of its living faith provide living answers to its demands?

Every religion is comprised of two elements, a direct message and an indirect *tradition*. The message alone constitutes no religious polity; the tradition alone deadens religious life. Constant interplay between the two elements is essential. Ever and again the message, renewal, awakening, must be experienced, in order to break through the crust hardened by tradition; and ever and again the living experience must be molded into fixed forms in order to cement the community. In the religious life of Israel today the element

---

[2] Cf. I. Leibowitz: *Torah umikvot [sic—umitzvot] bazman hazeh*. Jerusalem, 1954.

of "awakening" is almost wholly lacking. Attempts to import reform or liberal or progressive Judaism into the new state from abroad cannot succeed, not only because of the bitter resistance which the established orthodox church will offer, but above all because these movements are themselves alienated from substantive, Israeli, Hebrew Judaism and hardly able to speak its spiritual language.

The need of the State of Israel is a religious awakening from within, a spiritual revolution out of and for the sake of faith, a revolution, to use Meister Eckhart's phrase, which is ready to shatter the shell for the sake of the kernel within, a native *believing* Judaism sprung out of the physical and spiritual soil of Israel and pervading Jewish life out of a desire for truth. It is not a reform Judaism that is wanted, but a Judaism imposing complete reform of life.

It was an act of wise foresight on the part of Dr. Judah L. Magnes that he established a chair for Jewish mysticism at the Hebrew University in Jerusalem, the first such in any Jewish institution of higher learning in the world, and thus paved the way for the scientific investigation of the authentic spiritual forces of Jewish religious feeling. But from the scholarly investigation of the past to renewed vitality in the present is a long road, though formidable obstacles and prejudices have indeed been overcome.

But the current manifestations of what is represented as the official view of religion in Israel are deplorable. A religion like that of Judaism is in its essence a historical religion. The symbols of its revelation are historical events, and hence the Old Testament in its character as a book of history is simultaneously a book of revelation. And now what may well be the greatest event in Jewish history has come about—and the spokesmen for Jewish religion have nothing to say on the subject. We hear their opinion on the question whether meat imported from overseas is or is not kosher, but when decisions are to be taken on central questions of shaping Jewish policy at home and abroad they are silent. The so-called religious parties maintain themselves in power by the usual political devices and exploit parliamentary combinations to enforce this or that concession (as currently the prohibition of swine husbandry in Israel—with the exception of Nazareth). This public display of religious politicizing has contributed largely to the alienation of Jewish youth, even those motivated by a genuine thirst for God, from religious life. The spectator is perforce reminded of the bitter words which the prophet Jeremiah was moved to utter by the religious life of his day: "Is not the Lord in Zion? Is not her king in her? Why have they provoked me to anger with strange vanities?"

So far the youthful state of Israel has proved incapable of taking thought for its spiritual self, for its religious meaning and its religious character. It has pursued vanities, it has aped other states in matters of etiquette and ceremonial, of banners and symbols. So far it has had little conception that its elemental and authentic meaning, its character and its claim to survival, must be anchored in the spiritual powers out of which it was born, the powers of a messianic redemption of humanity; that it must make itself "the beginning of the redemption" (so Ben-Gurion defined it when the State was being founded) —a fresh beginning. This state must be religious through and through, and this implies that at home and abroad, in relation to its own citizens and especially to its Muslim and Christian minorities, in relation to its neighboring states and all the countries of the world, it must at least *attempt* to follow a messianic policy, a policy based on faith in God and His final victory in politics and history. In the Diaspora it has been easy, as it still is, to preach sermons on the ethics of Judaism. But in the State of Israel the issue is *preservation*, preservation of the ethics of Judaism within the so-called realistic politics of the twentieth century, preservation of even a few drops of the ethics of the prophets, whether in domestic concerns or in matters of world interest in which it is the privilege and obligation of the new state to adopt some position. For a messianic policy there is need of a mighty regeneration of the people from within if "sacred" egoism is not to bring all down in ruin. Messianic policy is unpopular; it is risky and it is dangerous. But only messianic policy can be the new tidings which the state can bestow upon the world, only messianic policy can justify its great name Israel (which means "fighter with God and for God"), and only messianic policy can justify the State's existence. Many years ago the Hebrew poet Jacob Steinberg sang: "At the Jordan and in Galilee the plowman saw the brilliance of the divine glory."

5

To make it possible to comprehend the "phenomenon of Israel" in its profoundest sense we have given religion the central place which is its proper due. To ask whether the youthful state will survive is identical with asking whether the scattered members which have streamed in from all parts of the world and are as yet congregated only in a *local* sense can succeed in finding a *spiritual* basis for their congregation, and so in building a people. Grievous as is the state of war with all our neighbors which has now persisted for six years, and onerous as is the political and economic blockade, these hardships have at least produced one benefit: they have hastened and facilitated the formation of a *single* Israeli people out of a hundred disparate splinters. But the process is difficult, and only a living faith can supply the energies requisite for achieving an amalgam. Here people speak of a "second Israel," which designates the immigrants of the past six years, who constitute approximately half the population. Everywhere the question is posed: How will the unification of the "first" and "second" Israel come about?

Mention must be made, however briefly, of the numerous individuals who devote themselves to endeavors, organized or otherwise, to bridge the gap between the old and the new and so to promote the unity of the people. Students of the Hebrew University interrupt their studies to devote a year to teaching in the primitive camps or villages of the new immigrants; teachers spend their vacations there, teaching and helping; an organization of volunteers undertakes services of many kinds. In the immigrant camp at Jerusalem-Talpiot a single teacher, Jakob Maimon, organized a volunteer service which developed into a sort of evening school; here volunteer helpers, high-school students, Boy Scouts, university students, society ladies give instruction to groups large and small. Some teach reading and writing to illiterates, others give instruction in Hebrew conversation, in singing, or in folk dancing. Here the confluence of immigrants from many countries and cultures offers a field for labors of love and sacrifice known to none but God.

The instrument and medium for these heroic efforts is the *Hebrew language*. No one can understand the spiritual visage of Israel without a proper appreciation of the miracle of its burgeoning language. That a language which had for centuries been only the sacred tongue of worship could be quickened into vitality and made sufficiently supple and elastic to serve as the expression for the complicated requirements of modern life in all its ramifications—that is a miracle. I venture to say *the* miracle, of Israel. All "reasonable" considerations opposed the revival of Hebrew. When Herzl wrote his *Judenstaat* at the end of the nineteenth century he remarked, "But we shall not speak Hebrew!" Ahad Ha'am, himself one of the creators of modern Hebrew style, had serious misgivings about the use of Hebrew as the language of instruction in higher education. Einstein advised against it. The revival of Hebrew was promoted by no governmental authority. During the quarter-century of the British mandate in Palestine the enticements of the English language were strong. And yet, despite all misgivings, the Hebrew language did arise out of its enchanted slumber.

The immigration of the "second Israel," of people from North Africa, Iraq, Morocco, Yemen, Persia, Afghanistan, and India, has made the Hebrew language the bearer of a great human task—*the achievement of mutual understanding of East and West in Israel*. What prodigious energies mankind will require for the task can be demonstrated from the experience of Israel; in this respect it has become a universal human laboratory. An excellent characterization of the situation between West and East has recently been offered by Frithjof Schuon in his *Perspectives spirituelles et faits humains*.[3] *Toutes les civilisations sont déchues, mais les modes diffèrent: la déchéance orientale est passive; la déchéance occidentale, active. La faute de l'Orient déchu, c'est qu'il ne pense plus; celle de l'Occident déchu, qu'il pense trop, et mal. L'Orient dort sur des vérités; l'Occident vit dans les erreurs."* Israel shows us both, the errors of the West and the passivity of the East. But here we can also see a thing which Schuon does not mention: the *positive* opportunities afforded by the great and momentous encounter of our age. We can see the activity of the West in its admirable aspects, and we can see the East in its readiness to learn. In all parts of Israel today the draining of swamps, the construction of dams, the transformation of desert into plowland, the afforestation of mountainsides, the channeling of water supply—all illustrate the blessings which the West can contribute. And the Easterners are ready to learn. To be

---

[3] *Cahiers du Sud*, 1953.

sure, there are concomitant dangers, as we ourselves can testify: the activity of the West can easily turn into materialism, and the Easterners are subject to the danger of being uprooted from the spiritual soil of their past, the danger of being hurled into the void of Western nihilism, the danger of "Levantinization," of which there is much talk is Israel. But along with all of these dangers there is a great, an extraordinary, opportunity for a genuine and fertile meeting of West and East in Israel. When people from Yemen and Iraq, from Morocco and Persia, from India and Turkey meet with people from Germany and Russia, from South Africa and the United States, from South America and England and together labor to build up a new state, the enterprise is not merely Jewish and Israeli but concerns humanity at large. Israel today is humanity in miniature, a laboratory for the solution of the gravest problem of modern humanity—the meeting of East and West.

The Quakers in Israel have taken an Arab village near Nazareth under their care in order to introduce the fellahin to Western methods of agriculture. The experiment will serve as a sort of pilot plant for other villages. This endeavor of the Friends is, as it were, a symbol of the service Israel can render humanity: here the West can approach the East in a spirit of brotherhood and *humility,* teaching, but also learning. The West contributes science and techniques, the East a deeply rooted faith. In the act of solving its own problems Israel adjusts itself to the space between West and East which is its geographical position and helps mankind forward on the path of a new unification. Hebrew periodicals habitually use a small boy as the symbol of Israel; the boy is only six years old and still going through the cycle of childhood diseases. But into this small Israel with all its inadequacies and tragic errors there has flowed so much yearning and hope, such deep love and such anguish, so much sweat and blood, and also so much holiness of dedicated men through all the centuries of the Diaspora, that according to all the rules of creation of which we can have any intimation what will grow here must have great stature.

6

From this digression into the universal problem of the union of East and West and its preliminaries in Israel—which can only be a hope and a prayer, not a promise—let us turn once more to the internal Jewish aspect and ask whether any progress has been made toward the solution of the problem of East and West in the domain of Israel. Some light is thrown on the question from certain data which I derive from a study by A.N. Pollak which appeared in 1945, that is, before the State was established.[4] At the time, Pollak reached the following conclusions:

> Despite great difficulties the assimilation of the diverse communities has proceeded to the point where we may speak of a consistent type of Palestinian youth. The administration of Aliyat ha-Noar [the organization for the immi-

---

[4] Excerpts from this work have been reprinted in *Klal Yisrael,* the large anthology of the sociology of the Jewish people published by the Bialik Foundation in Jerusalem.

gration of Jewish youth created at that time by Henrietta Szold], whose work brings it into constant contact with the youth, describes the type in the following terms: All speak Hebrew, though frequently with solecisms. The subject which they know best and to which for the time they are most attached is Bible. Their knowledge of Jewish history is concentrated on certain salient events, without any awareness of continuity in these events. Their knowledge of Hebrew literature is limited; they have a lively knowledge of their homeland. In general geography they have specific information; many are able to speak of various countries and their forms of government, but have no knowledge of the economy of nations and their cultures. The meagerness of their historical knowledge is striking; on the other hand, the boys are interested in general social problems.

This quite critical estimate of Palestinian youth before the foundation of the State is based upon observation of candidates for inclusion in the Youth Aliyah, which implies that they belonged to strata of small means. Critical as these conclusions are, it must be remarked that affiliation with one community or another was not a factor. Pollak cites a report of the youth leaders who state that "in general, membership in a group of common national origin presents no problem among the youth." "It cannot be asserted," the report continues, "that the members of the oriental communities are inferior in capability; sometimes they surpass the others in powers of comprehension." "Accordingly the educators of youth recommend the formation of youth groups on a mixed basis. They advise that the individual groups should contain members of the oriental communities not exceeding a third of their number, so that they might be exposed to the influence of the Western communities. This influence will facilitate their accommodation to life in the village, and will render them less impulsive and inconstant, less susceptible to the impressions of the moment, less oscillating from one extreme to the other."

These observations derive, as has been noted, from a period anterior to the annihilation of European Judaism and before the establishment of the State (1942, 1943, 1945). I cite them because they exhibit the problems which must be surmounted in creating one unified people out of Western and Eastern elements. Since the establishment of the State the numerical proportions have changed markedly in favor of the Oriental element, but on the other hand the State, and in particular the army, has become a powerful force for effecting amalgamation. The problems which we must here wrestle with are problems of a prodigious *reality,* a reality such as Jewish history has not known for millenniums. In this reality Judaism must *preserve* itself. The remarks of Alexandre Safran, the Grand Rabbi of Geneva, in a brochure entitled *Les Rapports Spirituels entre l'Etat d'Israel et la Diaspora*, published in 1954, are pertinent:

Depuis la restauration de l'Etat Juif, le Judaïsme se trouve placé, aux yeux vigilants du monde entier, devant des possibilités de réalisation; et ceci pour la première fois depuis presque deux mille ans. Jusqu'ici, sa position morale fut inattaquable: le peuple juif fut le "Serviteur, maltraité, de Dieu," le Pré-

dicateur de l'Humanité. Le moment est enfin venu pour lui de prouver dans son propre pays, par son propre Etat la possibilité de réaliser ce qu'il a reproché aux autres de ne pas avoir voulu ou su faire. Le Prédicateur d'hier deviendra-t-il, oui ou non, le Réalisateur de demain? Combien grave est la question.

7

The moment of *reality*, the preservation and confirmation of Judaism in concrete manifestation of itself in the state of Israel, in itself constitutes an enormous moral increment, whatever the final outcome may be. In the course of generations, how will Judaism present itself as an actuality before the eyes of the world? Will it be a Judaism of the ghetto, of exclusiveness, of hatred of the stranger, or a Judaism open to the world, drawing upon the sources of its prophetic past and its messianic hopes? A keen opponent of Zionism and Israel, Charles Malik, has called attention[5] to the fearful dangers of an exclusiveness conjured up by the concentration of the three factors of race, language, and religion in a single state. We will grant that these dangers exist, not, however, by reason of the factors which Dr. Malik enumerates, but by the bitter history of the Jews as a persecuted minority, and above all by the frightful experiences of World War II and the horrifying abdication of Western Christian civilization manifested in the destruction of a third of the Jewish people. Small wonder that the myth of the *goy*, of "Amalek," of the hatred of the whole world for the Jews, has received fresh sustenance, and that even a great Hebrew poet of the present day can acclaim this myth. What other people could have emerged from such experiences without injury to its soul? And yet we can console ourselves with the thought that the wound is healing and that it is precisely the establishment of the State of Israel which has largely promoted this convalescence.

The Zionist movement emanated, in its main stream, out of a drive toward *reconciliation with the world,* after the walls of the ghetto, spiritual even more than physical, had been breached. Theodor Herzl wished to combat the "new ghetto" and closed the drama which bears that title with the slogan "Come out of the ghetto!" But what this meant was, Come into the family of humanity, not, however, by way of assimilation and denial of self and sacrifice of self, but by way of a "return to Judaism."

In a subtle study of the nature of the Jewish renaissance, the Hebrew philosopher and sociologist Zvi Vojslavski has shown how strongly the motive of reconciliation with the world and with humanity affected the origins of the Zionist movement and of modern Hebrew literature:

> The Jewish national movement aims to pull down all partitions which separate us from the world. But the most rigid of all partitions is the Diaspora. Generation after generation it has distorted and subverted our picture of the world; through it the fountains of the world have gone dry for us; and it has falsified our relations to heaven, to earth, to God. We yearn for the simplicity of things, for decency

---

[5] *Foreign affairs,* January, 1952.

in relationships between man and man, people and people, civilization and civilization.

The renaissance of Hebrew became the instrument of this reconciliation of the Jew with the world. Wholly oblivious to the spiritual predicament of the Jews, Tolstoy and Ibsen demurred: "Still another little state? Another nationality? Another language to partition man from man?" They did not realize that here partitions were being breached; they did not comprehend that the revival of the Hebrew language is the revival of a civilization, that not only words and sentences quicken into life but also books, thoughts, views of God, world, and man inherited from earlier generations. Above all they did not realize that here was the consummation of a renewed will to culture on the part of a people which, despite its loyalty to its spiritual legacy, had been cut off from the cultural creativity of the world. "When we now assented to the world," Vojslavski writes, "when the deep wounds in our soul began to heal, we assented to human culture in all its properties, we fell in with the cultural creativity of the world."

In the centuries of the ghetto reconciliation with the world was tantamount to defection from Judaism. The narrow bounds of the Jew's own spiritual home and the breadth of the world stood in hostile opposition to each other. Now when Hebrew culture is itself broadening its boundaries and nothing human is longer alien to it, when the people that has become a nation has taken its place in the United Nations, the Jew has freed himself from the mountain of perpetual apologetics which weighed him down, within the ghetto and outside it. Upon principle the Institute for the Science of Judaism in the Hebrew University rejects any apologetic attitude. The process of correction requires time—for example, the Hebrew University still has no institute for the study of Christianity or of Asiatic religions, though it does have one for Islam—but the greatest obstacles on the path of self-liberation have been surmounted.[6]

The flag of Israel before the building of the United Nations in New York stands for a great symbol: the state of Israel symbolizes the Jew at peace with the world and humanity. To abide faithful to self *and* humanity—that is Israel's task.

Some time ago the writer attended one of the beautiful outdoor concerts which the municipality of Haifa presents weekly in the Garden of the Mother, one of the large parks. The program was the *Missa Solemnis* of Beethoven, with Georg Klemperer conducting. About 3000 persons had come; stretched on the greensward in the dark they listened to the church music in breathless silence, under the same starry sky to which the prophet Elijah had looked from Mount Carmel. When the music came to an end and the lights went up, and I saw all the young faces about me entranced by the Christian religious

---

[6] Since this chapter was written, the Board of Governors of the Hebrew University declared that such an Institute will be erected in 1956.

music, I sensed the liberating effect of the establishment of this State of Israel. A gaping, burning ulcer on the body of humanity is beginning to cicatrize, slowly and laboriously after the terrifying experiences of World War II, but the wound is healing; humanity possesses us once more. Perhaps, perhaps, despite all difficulties this is the "beginning of the redemption"—*atkhalta di geula.*

Jerusalem, in the month
of the destruction
of the Temple, 5714 (1954)

ERNST A. SIMON

Ernst Akiva Simon was born in Berlin in 1899 and came to Palestine in 1928. He received his higher education at the Universities of Frankfurt-am-Main, Berlin and Heidelberg, obtaining his Ph. D. degree from the latter in 1923. In Palestine he was in charge of various pedagogic institutions, at one time serving as inspector of secondary and higher education for the Israeli Ministry of Education. In 1940 he joined the faculty of the Hebrew University, bearing the ranks of Professor and Department Chairman.

His contributions to pedagogic literature are many and enduring: *Mishnat Pestalozzi, The Aims of Secondary Education* are among the better known. He also has written extensively in the fields of philosophy, theology and Jewish nationalism: *Revelation and Religious Experience; Are We Still Jews? Bridges* (a collection of essays).

Simon was closely associated with Judah Magnes, first President of the Hebrew University, and with the philosophers Martin Buber and S.H. Bergman. They were the leaders of *Brith Shalom* (Covenant of Peace) and *Ihud* (Unity). In fact, Simon was honorary secretary of the group and chairman of the latter. Both organizations envisioned Jewish-Arab cooperation in Palestine. *Ihud*, organized in 1942 to succeed *Brith Shalom*, worked for a bi-national state in Palestine. After the establishment of Israel, Simon and his followers championed the rights of the Arab minority in the State (whose mobility, for instance, was as a security measure severely restricted during the early days of the State), advocated the return of the Arab refugees (of the 1948 war) to Israel, and territorial concessions, even before 1967, to the Arab neighbors.

Despite the unpopularity of the *Ihud* program, especially its last two points, Simon, as a person and as a scholar, was highly regarded in Israel for his contribution to the system of education and to the moral wealth of his people.

The ensuing article, *VALID AND INVALID QUOTING FROM THE BIBLE*, which deals with Judaic universal humanism, is from *Shdemot*, Summer, 1968, pp. 1–6.

Valid and Invalid Quoting from the Bible
Reflection on the Possibility of a Judaic-Universal Humanism
by ERNST A. SIMON

NOWADAYS EVERYONE CITES biblical quotations in support of the position he takes in politics: believers and non-believers, socialists and capitalists, those who favor and those who oppose our annexation of the occupied areas. On the surface everything can be borne out by the various scriptural writings, which differ from and contradict one another. This arbitrary exploitation of the Holy Scriptures reduces their value to a mere mass of rhetorical embellishments devoid of any real powers of persuasion.

True, the scripture is not all of a piece, as some would have it, and contains many inner contradictions. Small wonder! For the Bible grew over a period of approximately an entire millenium and mirrors all kinds of epochs with their variegated needs and prospects, ambitions and limitations. This fundamental fact provides those who seek it with a highly maneuverable type of material. However, this freedom of movement is not unlimited and is not identical for all the biblical texts. From this standpoint we may distinguish between three main types, as follows:

1–Isolated verses, culled as a rule from the realm of "wisdom", whose definite meaning does not depend on the context and whose content is not *Halakhic;* they are given to almost limitless usage.

2–Halakhic verses which customarily serve as a basis for argumentation among the Sages or the Halakha authorities, reflecting a specific development, in one or another direction. These added portions should be taken into account in any new attempt at Halakhic interpretation, even in the event that the innovator is not in agreement with his predecessors' position. Disregarding a decision without any effort to discuss the reasoning on which it was based would seem a rather arbitrary act.

3–Verses not from the Halakha, whose meaning may be understood primarily from their historic or prophetic context. It is true that at times they are shorn of their original association, as for example: "Thy destroyers and they that made thee waste shall go forth from thee...." (Isaiah, 49:17); employing this verse as a figure of speech has altered it from an expression of consolation to an expression of calamity. In a case such as this, too, the virtue of intellectual integrity should be applied to the essence of the change which took from a text its former simple meaning.

As regards the first group, most of it is given to free usage; in the second group such usage is severely curtailed; the third occupies a midway position between the two extremes.

The following examples will serve to illustrate each of them:

I. We read in the book of Proverbs: "Be not wise in thine own eyes...." (3:7). This is good advice for all persons and all circumstances regardless of almost any religious or moral personal philosophy. In point of fact, however, this universally true beginning shrinks the moment one continues to the end of the verse which reads: "Fear the Lord and depart from evil!" This continuation adds to the first half two restrictions: it defines wisdom as the fear of the Lord, in the sense of: "The fear of the Lord is the beginning of knowledge; But the foolish despise wisdom and discipline." (*Ibid*, 1:7); and it joins this wisdom with the fear of wrongdoing and its opposite, foolishness, with doing evil. It follows therefore that only the first half of this verse applies to everyone, whereas in its entirety it applies only to the person who believes in God and advocates that wisdom and virtue provide mutual nourishment for each other. Nevertheless, there is no objection to anyone's citing, solely and separately, the beginning words: "Be not wise in thine own eyes", as an antidote to arrogance and conceit.

II. Numerous ethical demands have gone beyond the non-mandatory authority of "good advice" and assumed mandatory meaning because they have been declared law. A number of them command a particular interest because they are marked by the addition of the words, "And thou shalt fear thy god" and appear in two portions of the book of Leviticus: *Kedoshim* (ye shall be holy) and *Bahar* (in Mount Sinai). All of them are in the category of *mitzvot* (good deeds) between man and man, as: "Thou shalt not curse the deaf, nor put a stumbling-block before the blind...." (19:14); "Thou shalt rise up before the hoary head and honor the face of the old man...." (19:32); "And ye shall not wrong one another..." (25:17); "And if thy brother be waxen poor, and his means fail with thee; then thou shalt uphold him: as a stranger and a settler shall he live with thee. Take thou no interest of him or increase [usury]...." (25:35–36); "And if thy brother be waxen poor with thee, and sell himself unto thee, thou shalt not make him to serve as a bondservant. As a hired servant, and as a settler, he shall be with thee; he shall serve thee unto the year of jubilee. Then shall he go out from thee, he and his children with him, and shall return unto his own family, and unto the possession of his fathers shall he return. For they are My servants, whom I brought forth out of the land of Egypt; they shall not be sold as bondmen. Thou shalt not rule over him with rigor...." (25:39–43). The common denominator for most—not all—of them is stressed in the Gemara (Sanhedrin, 66:1) as follows: "Of the unfortunates among your people do these verses speak"; they are stated in a generalized form in a portion of the Pentateuch (Leviticus, 25:17, 43), repeated in the Gemara (Kiddushin, 32:2), Baba Metziya, 58:2) and mentioned a third time in a comment by Maimonides with reference to this subject, in these words: "Of everything that pertains to the heart it is said: and thou shalt fear thy God" (Hilkhot Mekhira 14:18).

This reasoning is particularly apt as regards the blind, who does not see the obstacle placed in front of him, and the deaf, who will not be distressed by being cursed, but the Lord who sees all and hears all will demand revenge for them, and for the Jewish slave whose master tyrannizes over him, and similar cases of the poor and deprived. From these verses the Oral Law formulated many interrelated rules of ethical behavior for the purpose of improving the Jewish people and their society. Stress should here be placed on *Jewish* for in juxtaposed chapters it is stated distinctly: "And as for thy bondmen, and thy bondmaids, whom thou mayest have: of the nations that are round about you, of them shall ye buy bondmen and bondmaids. Moreover, of the children of the strangers that do sojourn among you, of them may ye buy, and of their families that are with you, which they have begotten in your land; and they may be your possession. And ye may make them an inheritance for your children after you, to hold for a possession: of them may ye take your bondmen forever; but over your brethren the children of Israel ye shall not rule, one over another, with rigor." (Leviticus, 25:44-46).

For the modern Jew, who cherishes the Torah but strives at the same time to arrive at a kind of religious humanism based on the Jewish sources, this—and many other instances as well—poses a grave problem for which I have not found a full and satisfying explanation. We should of course take into consideration the argument put forth by our apologists that the ethnic segregation implied by the restrictions as expressed in these ethical rules, was necessary at the time they were adopted: for there did not exist then any international law to obligate the neighbors of the Land of Israel to practice reciprocal relations toward it and its inhabitants in accordance with the laws of the Torah.

The real problem however is not, in the main, historical. When we teach our children the Torah as a sacred book, we try to envision it as an everlasting present, possessing eternal values. The very process of the revival of Bible study that we may perhaps be witnessing in its initial stage among a part of the youth now being reared in Israel, brings into sharper relief the conspicuous contradiction between the simple restrictive meaning of certain verses and the general, humane thesis which the innermost instincts of some of us would have us believe is in fact the "true" meaning.

What for example is the connotation of the word "neighbor" in the celebrated verse, frequently quoted only in its latter half: "but thou shalt love thy neighbor as thyself" (Leviticus 19:18)? Does it refer to every human created in God's image or to "your neighbor in the Torah and its precepts" alone? The first part of this verse, "Thou shalt not take vengeance, nor bear any grudge against the children of thy people" does not offer a definitive decision: the parallel phrases may be used to explain either the similarity between the terms employed (neighbor and children of thy people), or the contrast between them, as Rabbi David Zvi Hoffman tried to explain in his "Commentary on Leviticus" (translated from the German by Zvi H. Sheffer and Zvi Aaron Lieberman, Jerusalem, 1954, volume 2, pages 36–37). Let us hope he is right.

But if this excellent commentary had appeared originally in Hebrew and not in a foreign language, my trust in it would have been far greater because in the Diaspora even the fairest of men is occasionally led into apologetic ornamentation. In the language of scholars at least, it seems that "neighbor" means a Jew. (Compare especially Gemara, Baba Kama 4:3 and 37:2).

The Midrash (Shemot Rabba, chapter 1:32) at one point amuses itself with the name Reuel, i.e. Jethro (Exodus, 2:18), saying: "Why was he called Reuel? Because he became the *rea*, friend, of the Lord". In other words, a sincere proselyte. What then of proselytes?

Twice the Torah commands us to love the proselytes, first parallel to and quite close to the love for our neighbor: "The stranger that sojourneth with you shall be unto you as the home-born among you, and thou shalt love him as thyself; for ye were strangers in the land of Egypt; I am the Lord your God." (Leviticus, 19:34). And again: "Love ye therefore the stranger; for ye were strangers in the land of Egypt." (Deuteronomy, 10:19). The allusion to the Israelites' slavery in Egypt, with the aim of learning from it how *not* to behave toward their peers-in-calamity (in the sense of: "Do not reproach your neighbor with a fault which is also your own," Baba Metziyah, 59:2), is also repeated in two other verses in the book of Exodus. One is: "And a stranger shalt thou not wrong, neither shalt thou oppress him; for ye were strangers in the land of Egypt" (22:20). Here Rashi, seemingly without the support of any of the ancient sources, defines the term "stranger" linguistically, as follows: "Every mention of *stranger* refers to a person who was not born in that country but who came from another country to live there." (Compare with the Rashbam interpretation of same). The second one that belongs here is: "And a stranger shalt thou not oppress; for ye know the heart of a stranger, seeing ye were strangers in the land of Egypt" (Exodus, 23:9). Again Rashi contributes an original interpretation, this time a psychological one: "The heart of a stranger ... and how difficult it is for him when he is oppressed."

On the surface it seems that in the above-mentioned four verses the Torah called for complete equality between the two types of people called "strangers" —the non-Jews in the Land of Israel and the non-Egyptians who lived in Egypt. If this interpretation were not only true but also binding from the standpoint of the Halakha, we would be able to claim that we have sought and have indeed found a firm basis for a Judaic-Universal Humanism. There is however a fly in the ointment.

The word "stranger" appears, as already noted, twice in all four of the verses we are considering: first it concerns the foreigner residing in the Land of Israel and then the Jew living in Egypt, whereas a source as ancient as the Unklus Translation transcribes this word *ger* meaning "stranger" in the beginning of all four instances as *giora,* meaning "sincere proselyte", and *gerim* at the end as *dayarim,* or in other words, "residents". The semantics of this translation corresponds to the opinions of the Sages: "He is not a convert until he has undergone circumcision and the ritual bath" (Yevamot, 46:1) and also the Halakha (Rambam, Hilkhot Issurey Biah, 13:4) which

Rashi too did not question. What he remarked in his commentary on the Pentateuch *alone*, expressing a linguistic and psychological point of view, was evidently prompted only by his desire to indicate certain fundamentals in the simple meaning of the verses, but this interpretation is not binding as against the Midrashic law which was subsequently accepted as the final decision.

Furthermore, it is possible that even for Rashi himself his above-mentioned remarks did not exhaust the whole of even the simple meaning. While there is no proof of this there is nevertheless a hint: to the concluding words of the verse, "I am the Lord your God" (Leviticus, 19:34) he adds his own interpretation: "Your God and his God am I"; in other words, that stranger whom we are duty-bound to love was also in his opinion at least a resident stranger, who, abandoning heathen worship, took upon himself the seven universal laws obligatory upon all mankind, and was permitted to dwell in the Land of Israel as a "benign Gentile" [one of the "righteous of the non-Jews"] (Maimonides, Hilkhot Issurey Biah, 14:7).

To summarize: we find here a rejection of racism but thus far no unrestricted religious tolerance. Anyone interested in following the latter's long, tortuous road among us—and not only among us!—should read two illuminating books: *Between Jews and Gentiles,* by Jacob Katz, Mossad Bialik 1961, and *The Problem of Christianity in New Jewish Thinking from Mendelssohn to Rosenzweig,* by Jacob Fleishman, Magnes Publishing Co. 1964.

On the problem of the stranger, the Oral Law is much more severe than the Written Law, as the Talmud itself admits (Yevamot, 46:1-2). The reverse is true as regards other questions which are today far more pertinent. I refer to conquests and destructions. Joshua's conquests are described in the Scripture as the implementation of commands distinctly issued by the Lord, whereas our Sages dared to soften their harshness: "As Shmuel the son Nachman said: three emissaries (or letters) Joshua sent to the Land of Israel before they entered the land, demanding: evacuation, resignation, or war" (Yerushalmi Shviyit, Chapter 6, Halakha 1,36:2 and compare with judgments of Maimonides, Hilkhot Melakhim, 6:5).

We do not find here as yet the perfect international law, but it is a beginning of sorts. Quite right was Hugo Grotius, (1583-1645) the author of the pioneer work in this science: "On the Law of War and Peace" (1625), who as the Christian student of Rabbi Menasseh Ben-Israel of Amsterdam frequently cited our ancient sources as his authority. But anyone who today surmises that by reasoning of this kind he will be able to justify a policy of conquest—and such reasoning has been proffered—is still very far from a modern Jewish humanistic stand.

Now and then a hint is dropped that is even worse. This is done without much publicity but more discreetly, as for example in a "letter to the editor", in which a casual allusion is made to the seven nations whom the Torah ordered to be destroyed. Yet in cases such as these the Law is especially clear and unambiguous.

This question was part of a famous dispute between the rabbis Gamliel and Yehoshua. Rabbi Gamliel forbade a certain Yehuda, an Ammonite convert, "to come into the congregation of the Lord", i.e. to marry an Israelite woman, whereas Yehoshua told him: "You are allowed," and it was the latter who finally won the decision with his argument: "Sancherib the Assyrian king already came and mingled all the nations together" (Yadayim, 4–4, Brakhot, 28–1 and compare with Tosefta Kiddushin, 5–4, Rabbi Akiba). It follows therefore that the seven nations mentioned in the Bible no longer exist, or as Maimonides stated with reference to this subject: "These are other people" who live in the former people's places (Hilkhot Issurei Biah, 12:25 or as expressed in Hilkhot Melakhim, 5:4 "Memory of them is already lost", and compare to Shulkhan Arukh, Even Ha'ezer 4:10).

Anyone who today entertains the thought that the non-Jewish population of Israel in any way resembles the seven nations is in the same category as those who declare the forbidden permissible.

Thus far we have brought a sampling from only two areas: Wisdom and Halakha; it remains but to complement them with examples from the prophetic works.

III. The prophet Amos paid no heed to the orders of Amaziah the priest of Beth-El: "O thou seer, go, flee away into the land of Judah, and there eat bread, and prophesy there" (Amos, 7:12). Is it reasonable to think that this man of God gave advice or even "orders", as some think: "Therefore the prudent doth keep silence in such a time; For it is an evil time" (5:13). It is not so but seems rather a polemical-rhetorical question such as that of Nehemiah in a similar situation, when mercenaries and false prophets approached him and "put him in fear" (Nehemiah, 6:14), and he stood astonished and asked: "Should such a man as I flee?" (*Ibid*, II) and Bialik early brought this into context in the first line of his poem' *O Seer, Go Flee:* "Go flee?— a man like me flees not."

In similar vein Amos' question too may be explained reasonably enough without being removed from its context; the preceding verse speaks of: "Ye that afflict the just, that take a ransom, And that turn aside the needy in the gate" (5:12) and the verse following it (5:14) brings the affirmative closing, saying: "Seek good, and not evil, that ye may live; And so the Lord, the God of hosts, will be with you, *as ye say."* As ye say, as did Amos himself, risking his life facing the tyrannical king Jeroboam—and not keeping silence as did those cowardly men of prudence, who are present in all ages and among all nations including Israel then and now. Obviously, the prophet is displeased with them, and he goes on to demand: "Hate the evil, and love the good, And establish justice in the gate; It may be that the Lord, the God of hosts, Will be gracious unto the remnant of Joseph" (15). With regard to that faith-challenging "it *may* be" (as the late Moshe Klevary put it) compare: Bavli, Khagiga, 4:2.

To summarize: the Bible is not all of a piece by any manner of means. Its words are rich in one place and poor in another and need each other, for what one locks another opens, and occasionally two verses contradict each other until a third verse appears and decides between them, and so on through infinite possibilities. What this proves with regard to drawing on our ancient sources for public debate is that the various parts which comprise the Bible should complement each other like the various voices in a chorus.,

What however is the situation today? We hear the voices of the authors of the Halakha (though they are quite hoarse at times from chronic sclerosis), and the voices of the great scholars, especially of history (though at times they reach us through the excessive din of archaeological enthusiasm), but what will become of the voice of prophecy?

True, since the day the Temple was destroyed prophecy was entrusted to whomever it was entrusted, but an echo remained which issued from the throat of the "sons of the prophets". They are the disciples of the sages and learned men of all generations. Now nearly all of them are silent, and dimmed is the keen cruel light of prophecy that at God's behest served as a criterion for our whole national reality.

God forbid that this voice be stilled in a bad time!

One may ask, why a "bad time"? It was not at all bad in the days of the strong king Jeroboam son of Joash who "restored the border of Israel from the entrance of Hamath unto the sea of the Arabah" (Second Kings, 14:25 and compare with Amos, 6:14), and all the more so in our time—a time of victory and success. Quite right, and yet—a bad time for a prophet such as Amos then, and a bad time for the "enlightened" today.

We must not and cannot be in the position of the defeated in our country and in the world but it is also difficult to be the victor. It behooves us to study this subject which is rather new to us. Nothing but the spirit of the prophets which descended on their sons-and-disciples, as for example, Hillel the Elder, is capable of serving as our model and guide. The ethical and political dispute being waged in our country today reminds us somewhat of the dispute between the Hillel and Shammai schools of thought at about the time of the destruction of the Second Temple. We have not reached a point of spilling blood here at home, and may we never reach such a point, but the students of the two pillars of wisdom of those days did reach such a point: "Says Rabbi Yehoshua . . . the students of the School of Shammai used to stand below [in the House of Study] and kill the students of the School of Hillel . . ." (Yerushalmi, Shabbat, Chapter 1, Halakha 4,3:3 and compare with Tosefta Shabbat, 1:16–17) The Sabbath tractate in the Bavli, 17:1 says, "They thrust a sword in the House of Study, saying: 'He who wishes to enter, may enter but he who wishes to leave, will not leave' (that is to say, the Shammai school quarreled with the Hillel school and kept its majority by means of physical force, while on the same day Hillel (read: the school of Hillel) sat bowed before Shammai (read: the school of Shammai) like a student, and it was as hard for Israel as the day on which the calf was fashioned." In those days too an alliance was formed between the religious and the political zealots. We should not ask for trouble but a hint to the wise is sufficient.

It was Hillel who said to the people of Betheira with regard to the people of Israel: "Let them be, the spirit of God is upon them; if they are not prophets, they are the sons of prophets" (Tosefta Pesachim, 4:2) and it was Hillel of whom the divine voice said: "There is a man here worthy of the spirit of God, but his generation is not worthy of it—and they turned their eyes to the aged Hillel" (Tosefta Sota, 13:3), for indeed he followed in the ways of Aaron, loved peace and sought peace, loved people and brought them closer to the Torah (compare with Abot, 1:12).

The voice of the Almighty was already silent then but an echo still persisted. For us, too, only an echo remains, perhaps the echo of an echo. It is up to us to translate it starting from our Torah and proceeding in two directions: backward to the divine voice itself and forward, to our generation and its needs. Some engage only in translating backward; they are the orthodox-fundamentalists. Others engage only in translating forward; they are the reform-intellectuals. The path of the Jewish-religious-humanist lies between these two poles and he lives their tension hour by hour day in day out. Consequently, he very carefully avoids declaring: this is the opinion of the Torah, or this is the connotation of a verse, this and no other, for he knows what inner contradictions are contained therein, what human and historic forces contend there with one another, what problems exist to no solution. He will on the one hand try to encompass the situation as a whole but will on the other hand state his own convictions fearlessly. While it is true that his stand is selective, his conscience-impelled choice does not silence what he cannot adopt as his own. This essentially is the difference between the Hillel and Shammai schools of thought, today as in the past. Our Sages relate: Rabbi Abba and Rabbi Shmuel said: For three years the dispute between the school of Shammai and the school of Hillel continued unabated; these said: the law is as we say, and these said: the law is as we say, until a divine voice was heard to declare: both these and those are the words of the living God but the law is as the school of Hillel says. Why then, since both these and those are the words of the living God, is the school of Hillel privileged to have the law accepted as they interpret it? Because they were kind and humble and because they studied not only their own but also the arguments of the school of Shammai and what is more, they gave those of the school of Shammai priority over their own arguments (Erubin, 13:2).

May the laws of the State of Israel be determined in the ways of the school of Hillel!

ELIEZER LIVNEH

Eliezer Livneh was born in Lodz, Poland, in 1902 and settled in Palestine in 1920. In his youth he received the traditional Jewish education but later also garnered formidable secular knowledge by attending Oxford University and especially by a great deal of reading in sociology, political science and the humanities in general.

In Palestine Livneh was an agricultural worker, secretary of the Haifa Labor Council, member of Kibbutz Ein Harod, an organizer of illicit Jewish immigration into Palestine, head of the political and education department of the military underground Haganah and editor of the illegal *Eshnav*.

When the State of Israel was founded he continued in a leading role in the Histadrut (General Federation of Labor) and in Mapai, the plurality workers' party, representing the latter in the Knesset (Parliament). In 1957 he parted company with Mapai, founded and edited the non-conformist *B'terem* and free-lanced as a publicist, contributing to journals of various political orientations. Among his books are: *The New Territorialism; Zionism and England; Test of Independence; State and Diaspora; American Jewry: A challenge for Israel.*

As indicated above, Livneh at one time belonged to Mapai's meritocracy, but his social cosmos could not be limited by party discipline. His socialist nations were both pre- and post-Marxist. He developed a distaste for bleeding liberals, lightweight ideologists and crusading reformers. A "loner", he is highly esteemed in the intellectual community of Israel.

In suggesting the following essay *VALUES AND SOCIETY IN ISRAEL* to this anthology, Livneh indicated that some of the points made in it are no longer relevant as a result of the 1967 Six Day War, but nevertheless he felt the article as such represented his major views. The essay appeared in *Judaism,* Summer, 1963, pp. 281–295.

Values and Society in Israel

A Critical Examination

by ELIEZER LIVNEH

THE KEY TERM "scale of values" employed in this essay is to be understood as the totality of aspirations accepted in practice by Israel society today. The stress is on active desire and actual behavior, not on avowed ideology. By "Israel society" we include all socio-economic strata, old and new. For there is no longer any great distinction in the values manifest in ordinary behavior between pre-State inhabitants and immigrants since 1948, between the older generation and the young native population. Within recent years a process of far-reaching cultural-social assimilation has taken place, despite barriers to intercommunal marriage; the Ingathering of the Exiles is progressing apace. A few extreme groups will not be included in this analysis: they are not typical of Israel society, and what is said here has no relevance for them. This applies chiefly to the extreme Orthodox group, whose determining values have not been affected much by modern civilization. In another sense, the same holds true for the remnants of the pioneering generation of the Second and Third *Aliyot* (immigration waves before and after World War I), who are few in number and fast disappearing.

TRANSLATION OF THE AMERICAN INFLUENCE

The influence of the Western way of life and of Western values—especially American—on present Israel society is very strong. American Jewry, by dint of its living example, its financial aid, its steady stream of tourists, constitutes a pipeline exerting enormous pressure. There was a time, in the pioneering period, when *Eretz Yisrael* exerted its profound influence on the Diaspora. At Zionist Congresses and similar meetings, the attempt was made to speak Hebrew, in accord with the *Yishuv's* successful revival of the national tongue; the deliberate simplicity and economic equality of the *halutzic* "way of life" were a matter for praise and emulation (especially in Eastern and Central Europe); the sense of personal fulfillment achieved by the common man in Palestine through his participation in social and communal endeavors was, in the Diaspora, considered the highest ideal to which one could aspire, and not only by Zionists.

Now the reverse has come about. English is the language in which the Israeli attempts to communicate with his fellow Jews abroad. He imitates

American (or Western European) styles of dress and "good times" (cocktail parties, gala dinners, etc.); American prestige symbols (outsize automobiles, for example) are accepted by business magnates and Socialist leaders alike.

However, it would be a fundamental error to view the Israel scale of values and pattern of behavior as a faithful copy of the American way of life. A peculiar distortion has taken place. American concepts are accepted enthusiastically with regard to consumption and service, but not productive aspects. The Israeli wants all the benefits of the affluent society enjoyed by Americans, but he is unwilling to adopt the work pace and competitive effort that this entails. The American attitude to work, especially the intense concentration on efficiency is little known in Israel society, and even less the notion of economic risk. The Israeli's ideal is to avoid any economic risk by putting the entire burden upon the government and its agencies. His ambition is to combine a rising standard of living with total protection: guaranteed wage, guaranteed place of work, guaranteed work procedures, guaranteed profits and, of course, guaranteed property. The capitalist ethos of property as the fruit of risk and daring is not to be found in Israel society; amassing of property is considered basically a function of political effort, of having—and using—the "right contacts" with the powers that be.

In point of fact, the average Israeli desires the economic advantages achieved in the United States and the prosperous Western European countries without putting into effect the methods of productivity and social daring which created the wealth. To be sure, the Israel entrepreneur, private or cooperative, often uses "initiative" and mental effort in running his business. However, it usually means initiative in obtaining favors and exclusive support from the authorities. His time and labors are not directed at reducing production costs but at convincing (or misleading) the authorities that the entrepreneur deserves even broader assistance. The main competition to be found in the upper echelons of the Israel economy is over new kinds of assistance, undreamt of and unanticipated by others. When a particular form of government or public aid becomes the habit of the entire economy or of an entire profession, it begins to be considered ineffectual. Then the entrepreneur tries to invent new forms of assistance—even shady ones—in order to step up his revenue and profits.

The scale values in the general society takes shape accordingly. A man worth imitating (and envying) is not one who knows how to become more efficient, i.e., how to reduce the costs of production or services, but one who can "make out" with the power structure. The quality which insures success is not daring or genuine effort but the cultivation of "connections," putting up a front and currying favors. The industrial and agricultural patterns in Israel are often American, the formal labor-technique, European; but the economic morality is—Levantine.*

---

* In America and Western Europe, firms and trusts also hope to exploit the Treasury by illegitimate means and frequently succeed. However, there is a qualitative difference. There, such intentions are considered undesirable; in the national economic sense they are exceptional,

Levantine concepts in fact are infiltrating the administrative and bureaucratic structures. True, the exterior and formal behavior is Western and up-to-date. There is no other country where social and capital insurance are so all-embracing. Israel ranks highest in the proportion of population employed in public services. From this aspect it is the most "socialist" country in the world. At the same time, it is not strict with its vast bureaucratic organization. The bureaucratic ethic of Western countries, which rigorously limits the civil servant's spending at the public expense and frowns upon his partisan contacts with influence-peddlers is undeveloped in Israel. The prestige value of a civil servant is measured by the size of his expense account and his freedom in using it. On the other hand, Israel has none of the severe selective pressure exerted in Communist countries. The Israel official does not need to fear the professional tests of Western countries, nor the punitive measures of the Soviet societies. He is not confronted by challenge.

There are no proofs that Israel's bureaucracy is any worse than that of Italy or Greece, for example, in the incidence of embezzlements. It is not criminal corruption which typifies it, but recognition by the official that his position is strengthened by favoritism and improved through politico-nepotistic ties. He does not feel dependent on the public but assumes the public must care for his well-being: this is the social significance of his occupation. Hence the tendency—not only in Oriental communities—to prefer bureaucratic status.*

Since we are not concerned here with the country's economic prospects, we shall not investigate whether a society of this kind, whose standard of living is relatively high and whose output low, can persist for long. We also shall not deal with the fundamental problem as to whether technical progress can be combined with "frozen" jobs and social convenience. The average Israeli is well aware of the contradiction, approves of it, and therefore supports the existing regime which tries to perpetuate this state of affairs by means of rather dubious devices. The Israeli, even the educated one, is not interested in drawing conclusions of reproach or of oppositionist activity from his understanding of the sorry situation. This approach is not the result of cultural backwardness. In Israel, alongside Oriental communities which as yet have no civic consciousness, are to be found many who have developed a *post-*

---

i.e., the national economy as a whole exists on what it produces. In Israel, the economy's right, and that of its branches, to receive support from the government's funds—over and above income from its product—is legitimate and accepted. The problem is only the *size* of the subsidy. Public and private branches which do not enjoy this extra "added value" are exceptions to the rule, unworthy of imitation.

* In certain Western countries, especially the United States, a certain type of civil servant is appointed by political or party considerations, but this is not the rule. Mass dismissal of civil servants also takes place, (e.g., by the Labor government in Britain in 1946–49). The situation in Israel is fundamentally different. Here the candidate for a higher position must enjoy political influence, or join a party upon receiving his position. On the other hand, there is no contraction of the total size of the bureaucracy in Israel. The number of bureaucrats—government, municipal and community—grows constantly.

democratic indifference. Formerly accustomed to voluntary political activity, with all its inherent risks, these now hold to the considered opinion that the game is not worth the candle; it is easier to place the responsibility for the way things are developing on the "Establishment" and not force the issue by change. The opposition parties, viewing themselves as candidates for a coalition with the established powers, thus express not only the interests of their leaders in obtaining jobs, honors, favors, etc., but also reflect the unexpressed but agreed tendency of the public not to take responsibility for any change or to draw conclusions from rational or intuitive recognition of the seriousness of the situation. There is a sharp dichotomy between public utterance on political issues and political action; the one does not impinge upon the other. Political discussion has degenerated into sheer gossip. Withdrawal from active citizenship has not come about as the result of primitiveness, external repression, or exhaustion, but out of free choice. It is a sort of political reflection of the joys of economic parasitism.

THE PURSUIT OF THE "GOOD LIFE"

In contradistinction to what obtained in the pre-State years and during the first years of Statehood, the positive value of both labor—in the broad sense of the concept—and of public activity has been distorted. Although certain strata of the population devote much time to work and may even hold two jobs, satisfaction from work itself increasingly diminishes. This applies not only to the proletariat, e.g., unskilled workers and clerks, who in this sense constitute a serious problem in Western society as a whole. The self-employed and the majority of professionals also do not "live" their work. The exaltation of labor in the style of A.D. Gordon would not be understood by the present generation, if it were to read him at all. The balancing and refreshing effects of labor are diminishing. Work is seen only in terms of fatigue, and even this in lessening proportion, with the increase of leisure time, paid vacations, and other fringe benefits.

The intensity of the drive for social justice, as understood by previous generations, has passed. This impulse no longer gives meaning to life nor spiritual satisfaction. Social slogans and formulations serve the present generation as a disguise for a request for discrimination. Equal pay and salaries are justified to insure concealed monetary favors which are not subject to criticism or taxation. The slogan of self-labor in agriculture is exploited to obtain liberal and cheap credit for the acquisition of modern labor-saving means of production. The promise of a "decent" standard of living for wage-earners has become a cliché strengthening political entrenchment or privileged party bosses. These phenomena have hastened the discrediting of social idealism. All agree on a certain "social" minimum, but beyond this there is no belief in anything. Of course, there are conflicts of interest among social strata, professions and temporary groupings (mortgage-holders, for example).

This struggle has, however, no connection with the halo of justice in general, nor with a burning desire for a better society.

The striving for the "good life" is directed very little to satisfaction from work and from civic activity. There is little "class struggle" in Israel, in the accepted sense of the term. Economic and social controversies find expression in attacks by various blocs upon the government, the Jewish Agency treasury, or the Histadrut. Social life is typified by excitability and boiling restlessness. The "good life" consists in pushing up the material standard of living as measured by the amount of income, the emotional stimulation which can be bought by money or by status with a money equivalent. A satisfaction such as more children, is subject to planning; it is given relatively less importance. In this respect, the Oriental communities imitate the veteran inhabitants and Westerners.*

As long as the primary concern was for basic necessities—food, clothing, housing, health—this process did not appear as a spiritual, ethical or aesthetic problem: it was considered normal. By the middle of the second decade of statehood, basic necessities have been assured, more or less. Yet the quest for the "good life" has not slackened at all.

At first glance it would seem that this headlong pursuit is for arrangements which render life more comfortable, such as labor-saving devices in the home, more convenient means of transportation, etc. However, clear-cut standards have been lost. The Sabbath chasing about in cars and motorcycles; the women's devotion to the "beauty cult"; the enjoyment of exhibitionist sport; the constant erotic stimulation—are these the beginning stages of the yearned for apex?

Insofar as one can define or describe the spiritual baggage of the average Israeli, the following are its prominent characteristics: a) enough money to make possible the acquisition of more wealth; b) a minimum of active effort in order to achieve maximum pleasure; c) rapid changes of stimulation and satisfaction; d) innovations in satisfaction; e) fashion. Recreation, the most sought after value, is perceived as pleasure of excitement, supplied externally. For thousands the most pressing weekly—or daily—problem is, "What shall we do tonight?" Travel abroad is highly esteemed. Each man determines what is desirable and valued according to mass snob appeal. The complete relativity of the apparent collective experience is what determines the hierarchy of values.

If the average Israeli does not always know what he wants, he knows full well what he does *not* want: self-control, suspension of satisfaction, moderation in wants, abstention out of choice, conscious inner tension. A selective goal, achieved by personal belief and improvement of the spiritual life, is to him a sealed book. Ethical or aesthetic sublimation—beyond behavior demanded

---

* The annual rate of natural increase of the Jewish population in Israel is less than half that of the Arab population—18.6 births per thousand compared with 42.8 per thousand.

by common propriety—is considered foolishness or hypocrisy (sneeringly labeled "Zionism," "idealism"). This attitude is impressed early upon many, at the age of adolescence, by imponderable influences which outweigh those of the school. The most recent annual report of the Parole Service for Youth states that:

> There has been a rise of 17.5% in youth offenses in 1961 compared to 1960 ... The rise among Jews was 22.5%, while among the minorities there was a 2.3% decline ... Three new groups of offenders have appeared: minors between the ages of 6 and 8; youths from good homes; vagrants ... The second category includes offenses arising out of prosperity. This group is growing. It is not viewed as a serious problem from the criminal point of view, but as a passing stage in the development of young people ... These youths are not destined to become real criminals but are likely to turn into undesirable citizens. (*Ha'aretz*, 11/3/62)

The writers of the report are correct: privileged youths between the ages of 15–18 will not be criminals at 30–40. They will develop into bad citizens, that is, bad neighbors, unfaithful friends, deceivers (within the framework of the law), experts at embezzlement and fraud, masters at wasting public funds and the like. This is not a criminal problem but a social phenomenon. The question, therefore, is not the future percentage of criminals but the level of ordinary citizenship.

The attitudes described above also shape the current response of most of Israel's population to religious experience and faith. Not only is the spiritual content of religious faith incomprehensible to the majority of the population, but also its psychological basis; the *mitzvot*, the religious preference for human equilibrium, contradict the prevalent notions and values. However, the general public longs nostalgically for the traditional folklore and feels that Israel has an obligation to preserve Jewish continuity. There is, therefore, a cleaving to symbols, to holidays, to important national dates. But note the choice of symbols and festivals. For the Orthodox Jew of the past the most important events of the calendar year were Rosh Hashanah, Yom Kippur and the three major festivals (Pesach, Shavuoth, Sukkoth). For the Zionist, the emphasis shifted to Pesach, Hanukkah and Lag B'Omer, holidays of a more pronounced national character. The secular Israeli of today, however, identifies most with one holiday: Purim. The self-forgetting which is the hallmark of the Purim celebration is his delight.

PATRIOTISM AND NATIONALISM

There is no doubting the fervent patriotism of the average Israeli. His social ethic may be murky but not his nationalistic feelings which run higher than among most peoples. It may prove instructive to examine the Israeli's particular concept of patriotism.

The Israeli is not tied to his native land by a special rootedness. The percentage of Italian immigrants, for instance, who return to Italy from the United States after amassing money in the New World is greater than the percentage of Israelis who come back to Israel after having emigrated. Likewise, the Israeli is not especially sensitive to the ethical failures of his country. But in the military-security aspect, the Israeli proves superior. The obvious explanation is the avowed and perhaps real intention of Israel's Arab neighbors to destroy the "intruder" in their midst. The Israeli makes a far-reaching identification between the fate of the State and his personal destiny. This explains the high level of fulfillment of security obligations, in excess of all duties—government, public, social or family. Response to military call-ups is high. Readiness to pay taxes for security reasons is apparent. Although the population has not been tested by full-scale war since 1948,* it would undoubtedly demonstrate disciplined sacrifice in the event of conflict. Military security is an obvious value for Israelis of varying communities and groups.

The average Israeli tends to support his government on all military issues. Not only is he convinced, *a priori*, that his country is justified but he endorses every military action as realistic and right. This quality of Israel patriotism has in it a specific meaning for the nature of the society. The average Israeli does not tend to civic activity but he is sensitive to his freedom of expression. Although he does not insist that his ideas be carried out, he wants to be heard, to demonstrate his freedom of speech. However, the moment the word "security" is uttered from the platform, the public tends to abandon its right to criticize. Nationalism links up with anti-liberal authoritarianism.

What is the spiritual content of the Israel brand of nationalism? For the traditional Jew, the question is non-existent. The body of his values is in Jewish Law, with or without a mystical experience to complete it; the rest is but scaffolding. Does modern Israeli nationalism have its own values, or is it but an instinctive reaction to insure physical survival, which will exist so long as Arab intransigeance continues?

It is not easy to discover a national "ideology" in the secular Israeli's consciousness, that is, a web of values and preferences typical of his positive experience (in contradistinction to a defensive reaction against the enemy). The Bible, apparently, fills this role. The meaning which the Bible has for the present-day Israeli is very different from that which it held for the historic Jew. The latter saw in the Bible an elemental core of Holy Writ to be interpreted by the Oral Law: this view determined the Biblical images and teachings, and the nature of his beliefs. Not so the Israeli. For him the Bible is a sort of autonomous national mythology, a collection of primeval magic symbols which serve to stimulate his faith-lacking soul. A national heritage cannot tolerate a vacuum; "race" serves as a substitute for human values.

---

* Originally written in 1962, this article appeared before the Six Day War.

THE MILITARY ETHOS

The constant external threat to Israel's very existence has had far-reaching consequences on the nature of the military class. In civilian life—economic and social—the average Israeli is not confronted by any serious challenge. If he does not manufacture goods at conditions which meet international competition, subsidies and premiums will compensate him. If his output is low, his standard of living is assured by cost-of-living allowances and extensive social insurance. If his administrative ability is defective, his status is secured by monopolistic prices and a ban on dismissals. An inefficient public servant's position is bolstered by the monies streaming into the political parties and the Histadrut. The absence of challenge, the lack of competition, the general security determine the makeup and concepts of the average citizen.

The situation is otherwise in the military sphere. Here the challenge is ever-present and the competitive pressure of Arab armies unrelenting. Inferiority, professional or moral, cannot be compensated in matters of security by the government "covering up," as in the civilian realm. No subsidy or premium will help if Israel tank crews or jet pilots are found wanting in battle. Here there is no place for juggling or staving off decisions, except at the price of disaster. The Army lives in a constant state of potential war, and the intensity of its imagination determines its capability. The Israel army man is compelled to be better and more efficient than his likely foe, or else he will cease to exist.

Thus an ethos has developed in the Israel Army different from that in civilian life. Selection for jobs is usually based on merit. The efficient and daring officer is preferred over the routine performer. Political nepotism is not apparent. The "real guy" is still the standard for choosing the leadership. Even the manner of speech and type of relationship in the Army is different. Discussions within Army circles are more clear and pointed. The dichotomy between word and intent, between intent and execution is smaller. Sincerity and integrity are regarded as true values.

In other words, the Israel Army, its regular personnel and scientific associates, constitute a sort of Western island of efficiency and competition in Israel society. The man who is considered desirable in the Army differs from the one who knows how to "make out" in civilian life. The Army's scale of values is distinct from that of civilian society, and its advantage over Arab armies is based on that distinction.

However, the question arises: How long can two scales of value exist side by side, one for civilian life and one for the military? It is natural for Army behavior to influence the general society in times of war and emergency. In ordinary circumstances, however, civilian society influences the military. This takes place in various ways. First of all, the career officer is troubled by anxiety over his future civilian occupation since he is entitled to a pension at a relatively early age. He, therefore, must adjust as soon as possible to the ways of favoritism and interparty division of spoils and become "one of the boys." Secondly, the Army is surrounded by the immense civilian establishment of the Ministry of Defense (and a number of officers hope for employment there) which is subject to the same defects of all public organizations. Thirdly, the difficulty of criticizing military actions and doctrines encourages the glossing over of failures. Although there is thorough investigation of every deed and project within the military framework, suitable pressure to cut down errors, to get rid of inferiority and to stimulate progress is created only where professional military discussion combines with general public and intellectual criticism. Military science and military art are no different basically from any other human activity: the more debate widens and is not confined to a closed establishment, the more stimulating its effect and efficient the cure.

The Army has saved Israel in the physical sense. It constitutes a source of encouragement for society. Its nature, characteristics and concepts will be determined in the long run by general sociological processes. The spirit of the people determines the fate of the Army, not the reverse.

ISRAEL AND DIASPORA

Israel society is the fruit of the Zionist movement, in the broad, not the organizational, sense of the word. Expectation of "the next boat" was the standard of behavior of the *Yishuv: aliyah* was considered a value. Tens of thousands of Jews in Mandatory Palestine sacrificed time, money, leisure and personal freedom in order to encourage and make immigration possible. Thousands were imprisoned, injured and even killed in the struggle for "illegal" immigration. This was the essence of the political enthusiasm of the *Yishuv* during the Mandatory period. It was a uniting moral factor, even more than the struggle over the borders of Palestine, for political independence and national pride.

"Immigration" still appears as a slogan from time to time. When the government needs revenue, it introduces a levy under the name of Immigration Tax or Immigration Loan. But the drawing power of such slogans has diminished. In the last election campaign they had no place.

Upheavals in Diaspora lands, however, have not ceased. The Jewry of North Africa is in the process of abandoning its home. The communities of Cuba and several Latin American countries are dwindling. South American Jewry ($\frac{3}{4}$ of a million in number) lives in anticipation of a coming shock. South Africa is losing its Jews. But those hundreds of thousands of Jews leaving their homes in the Dispersion are not coming to Israel; they are exchanging one Diaspora home for another. Exiles of Cuba and Latin America are immigrating to the United States; North African Jews, to France; South African Jews, to the United States and to Commonwealth countries. Relatively few are coming to Israel. Rumanian Jews do arrive but only because they have no possibility of immigrating elsewhere. All of which is clear indication that the appearance of a Jewish problem in a given country does not move the

Jews to immigrate to Israel but to further wandering to a new Exile, as in former days. And this at a time when a Jewish State exists, whose aim is to provide a solution for the Jewish problem (and by virtue of which aim all the difficulties entailed in its founding were justified.)*

Clearly there is something seriously wrong. Continuation of such a situation is likely to weaken the ethico-political position of Israel in the family of nations and in world public opinion. Just as the arrival of the survivors of the concentration camps between 1945–48 helped in the creation of Israel, so the tendency of Diaspora Jewry today to wander all over the map, except to Israel, will have an opposite effect.

How does the Israel public respond to this phenomenon? The average Israeli desires immigration, of course. In his naiveté he thinks that it will bring him material advantage in the future, as it has in the past. However, if the measure of a value is the amount of effort and sacrifice that a man is willing to expend, gaining satisfaction in so doing, then *aliya* has ceased to be a value. It is doubtful whether it occupied an important place in the national consciousness. The socio-economic framework of Israel society does not attract Jews from the free world who are able to come. The eight million Jews of North and South America, Britain, France, and other Western nations prefer a more liberal society, where the success of the individual depends on his talents, initiative and savings, and where the arbitrary power of political authority is not so great. The framework of Israel society does not coincide with their mentality. The Diaspora Jew, therefore, contributes his money to maintain this society but does not look forward to becoming a part of it. There is a debate now current in Israel as to whether the existing socio-economic framework is desirable, but the question is infrequently raised as to whether this coincides with the needs of immigration or the intentions of possible immigrants.

It may be fitting here to introduce another problem, apart from the socio-economic, which, from an historical viewpoint, may be the decisive one. It can be imagined that the pressures typical of Moroccan, Rumanian, and Cuban Jewries will ultimately disappear, and that the conditions of Jewish existence as they are today in the United States, Britain, France, etc. will become universal. These "philo-Semitic" lands will absorb, as they actually do, the Jews from lands of oppression. What then will become of *aliya* to Israel? What factors will move Jews from the stable, successful Diasporas to emigrate to the Jewish State? Will there be reason for *aliya,* at least for a minority?

It seems to me that for certain minorities the spiritual shape of Israel society may be decisive. Western civilization is entering into increasingly direr straits of the spirit in the wake of socio-economic and technological success. A general distress implies emotional confusion for the individual. And so long as the

---

* I shall not touch upon the Jews of the Soviet Union. The size of their immigration, when the gates of the USSR will be opened, is but speculation. The same liberalization, which will open the borders of Russia to free movement, will decrease the pressure to leave. In the long run, what is said of American Jewry applies also to Russian Jewry.

standard of living continues to rise, the inner nausea will deepen; as economic problems are solved, spiritual misgivings will become more pronounced. Secular Western civilization has no way out of its confusion. Its technical achievements have turned into its master; it cannot renounce them, nor put them in their place. The Jews of the West are among the first to be affected, for they are among the successful and progressive: scientists, business leaders, administrators, etc. There is already a large number of Jews seeking spiritual refuge and meaning in a variety of seductive cults. If in the last century Western Jews were prominent in social and political movements, today they fall back on psychological, soteriological and esoteric religious supports.

Some of them will surely turn their eyes to Israel, seeking in historical Judaism, in the place where the ancient tradition confronts the afflictions and doubts of the age, an answer to the modern malaise. As for the level of industrial productivity and political development, the Israel desired by them is a technologically advanced and liberal state. But this alone will not be decisive. They will seek in its spiritual aspect what is lacking in their secular Western society. Israel as a distorted copy of America will arouse disappointment in their hearts. They require an Israel which is different from America in its very nature, which tries to combine technology with a way of life and a scale of values that oppose the empty, fragmented condition of modern society. And only an Israel which constitutes a challenge to the "American" way of life can attract the best among American and Western Jewry.

A SPIRITUAL UNDERGROUND

It would be an unwarranted assertion to state that Israel at present manifests any signs of the sought for spiritual reawakening. Both its secular and religious (i.e. Orthodox) society are far from engendering such revitalization, each for a different reason. Even the forms of mutual discussion have not yet been cast. The only hope therefore lies in such embers as burn secretly among us, in what an American Jewish thinker has called a spiritual underground, whose members are unknown to the multitude but are identified to each other.

We speak of the few. The majority never initiate historical processes or stimulate creativity. Democracy, to be sure, is a relatively efficient system of government for running a nation; it forces political groups to self-restraint, to legal means, and, over the long run, does away with the worst of the political factions. But, as history has amply demonstrated, the masses were never the impelling force in shaping events and altering concepts—at any rate, not by initial choice. They never determined the shape of a people, or carved out the face of a civilization. The Talmudic scholar poring over his tomes in solitude, the Buddhist monk, the learned Confucian, the Western humanist—these and their likes pave the way to the future and create society's values. Can their still, small voices be heard among us?

MOSHE SILBERG

Moshe Silberg was born in Lithuania in 1900 and came to Palestine in 1929. He is the product of the very best in Jewish and Western culture, having studied in foremost Talmudic academies and secular universities. Silberg received his J.D. degree from the University of Frankfurt-am-Main and was admitted to the Palestine bar in 1930.

With the founding of the State of Israel in 1948, Silberg became a district court judge. In 1950 he was raised to the Supreme Court, attaining in time the office of Deputy President of the highest judicial institution in the land. He was also Visiting Professor of Talmudic Law (Personal Status) at the Hebrew University.

Silberg has contributed to many law journals and other publications. Among his books are *Personal Status in Israel* and *Principia Talmudica*.

Universally respected by all elements of the community, Silberg, who is intimately acquainted with the millennial story of Jewish justice, emphasizes the verities and time-honored judicial processes in Judaism. But he also indicates that resenting or resisting orderly change are intolerable paradoxes. The essay cited here is an example of the author's erudition. More significantly, it points to his role as the guardian of the rights of the individual and the purity of judgment in a democratic Jewish society. The article was published in *Molad*, September-October, 1966, pp. 265–274.

The Purity of Judgment in the Hebrew Code

by MOSHE SILBERG

1

IN THE FIRST PART of *That Is the Way of the Talmud* I wrote: "The Hebrew code is—if we may so express it—*a code without judges;* the Hebrew law does not instruct the judge how to *judge*; it teaches the man how to *live*," [1]

The above was stated with a grain of salt—*cum grano salis*. My purpose was to emphasize the claimant's direct relationship to the law without in the least minimizing or rendering superfluous the judicial procedure, not even in civil law. For even if we all were wise and intelligent, learned and versed in the Torah, there would still be room for doubt in the whole range of actual facts. It is all the more so since we lack the above-mentioned virtues and the dispute is likely to extend also to the choice of the Halakha [Jewish religious law].

In the climate of the Hebrew code, however, the factual, partisan argumentation does not necessarily identify itself with the interests of each of the disputants. Sometimes exactly the reverse may occur, for the observance of the "shalt not steal" and "shalt not oppress" precepts is in itself an interest which may at times lead to a plea that negates any material benefit. Such was the case, for example, with a parcel of land disputed by Rav Giddel and Rabbi Abba[2] each of whom argued that it belonged—or by rights should be given—to "the opposite party", until ultimately it became the "realm of the rabbis", the property of the sages.[3]

From this particular standpoint, the standpoint of legal clarification, as opposed to the verdict rendered after trying the case, the importance attaching to the Judge and the Law is stressed in the Hebrew code of Law more than in any other system of law. First of all, there is the judge's "professional integrity". No office in Israel demands a prerequisite of such noble personal qualifications as does the office of judge. To be crowned a king, it is sufficient to establish one's biological kinship with the nation, proving "that his mother is from Israel [Jewish]."[4] To be appointed a judge, even a "municipal" judge

---

[1] *That Is the Way of the Talmud*, published by Mifal Hashikhpul, 1962, p. 52.
[2] Two *Amoraim*, the first a student of Rav and the second, the younger of the two, a student of Rav Houna.
[3] *Kiddushin*, p. 59:71.
[4] *YEVAMOT*, p. 45:72; Maimonides (Rambam), *HILKHOT MELAKHIM*, Chapter 1, Halakha [Law] 4.

(magistrate), one must be endowed not only with wisdom and knowledge but also with many spiritual qualities which are in essence goodness of heart, love of people, and a liberal, down-to-earth approach.[5] The reflection-of-a-reflection of one of the virtues of the Almighty: "I am with him in his distress."[6]

Why and wherefore such exclusiveness for this class? The answer for this is to be found in a certain mighty and exalted concept, namely that in every dispute between man and man, the *Shekhina* [Divine Presence] has, as it were, the rights of a third party—a "concerned" or "interested" party—so that the manner in which the judge discharges the duties of his office may affect, for better or for worse, the "interests" of the Lord. This is a very daring notion, *"and were it not explicitly written in a verse of the Scriptures, it would not be possible to voice it."* The verse does however appear in writing and we therefore have the required authorization. It is written: "The law is the Lord's" and the interpretation of this verse is that the judge is the emissary of the Lord who, by judging justly between fellow-men, sustains the labile balance which the Almighty created in the life of society. If he distorts the law, it follows that he destroys this balance, thereby causing the Divine Presence to be forced to rectify at its own expense the wrong he committed. Here are the words of Rashi [11th century Franco-Jewish scholar] in his commentary on the above-mentioned verse:

"That which you take from someone unlawfully, you *force me* to return to him. It follows then that you pervert the law at my expense...."[7]

2

Among all the terms which the jurist meets along his way, the most difficult to define is "justice" or "justice in law". [7a] As a matter of fact it is not a legal term at all; it is not to be grasped by legal concepts or contained in judicial forms; if it were—it would be not justice but *law*. If at times, from force of habit or routine, or because of practical and methodical considerations, we waive this precise conceptual classification and attempt to assign it a place of its own in the range of judicial concepts, we are obliged to add a post-script to the effect that the proper place of justice in this system is not in the material code but in the procedural code of the State. In other words: *justice is that norm of behavior which the law (maker) has rendered obligatory on the judge in the procedural stage of the case.*

---

[5] Maimonides, *HILKHOT SANHEDRIN*, Chapter II, Halakha 7. For the sources of the Halakha see *LEKHEM MISHNEH* with reference to Maimonides (id).

[6] *PSALMS* 91:15.

[7] *RASHI* on Deuteronomy, 1:17, with the source in *SANHEDRIN*, p. 8:71.

[7a] Only once did the Israeli lawmaker insert into the civil material law dealing with the relationship between man and man the distinct term "justice". I refer to paragraph 37(1) of the Law for the Protection of Tenants, 1955, which says: *"Despite the existence of a pretext for evacuation, the Court has the privilege of refusing to issue an order for evacuation if it is convinced that under the circumstances of the case it would not be just to issue it."* To this day the courts are struggling with the question of what actually was the legislator's intention in using this unusual term. Compare the verdict by Cheshin p. 1,255/57, XIII Verdict 1009 with the verdicts of the presiding judge (Olshan) and judges Silberg and Cohn, p. 1 301/61, XVII Verdict 57.

I will cite as testimony, from the standpoint of modern nomenclature, the report of the committee on the authority vested in the ministers which was appointed by the Lord Chancellor of England. There the committee deals, among others, with the question of what are the principles of natural law, and points out three cases, all of which belong in the realm of procedural or semi-procedural law.[8, 9, 9a]

However, to our great surprise and even greater admiration we find this modern concept clearly expressed by our own most eminent lawgiver of the twelfth century. "The explicit command that the judge should judge with justice as it is written: 'Judge your fellow-man with justice.' What is justice in law? It is equating the two litigants in every respect: the judge should not allow one to speak as much as he needs yet order the other to be brief; he should not address one with friendly courtesy and soft words while showing the other a stern countenance and harsh words; one should not be seated and the other kept standing but both should stand."[10] This comprehensive concept—the master-principle[10a] of equating the litigants—produced a most important "offspring", namely, justice-principle # 2 according to the sequence employed in the report of the above-mentioned committee. I refer to the rule of hearing the *two* disputants, known in the legal world by its Latin name: *audiatur et altera pars* (let the other party also be heard).

This procedural principle, as is quite evident, is not exhausted by the abstract duty of the judge to hear both parties. It was not necessary to trouble justice for this, The significance of this principle lies—if we may express it thus—in its "pedigree". It comes of a noble family, being the "offspring" of the master-principle of equating the two litigants[11]; and in equating there are no degrees It must be complete, decisive, "in every respect" as Maimonides stated *(id)*, and it goes without saying, at all times until the trial comes to its final conclusion, until all arguments and proofs have been fully exhausted. Until that moment the heart of the judge must be—as I expressed it elsewhere in this context[12]—"not confident and sure but alert and open" to every argument, persuasion and proof which are likely to affect the alignment of the scales, tipping the weight to the other side. Furthermore, he may not refuse to hear

---

[8] *Committee on Ministers' Power Report,* April 1932.

[9] For "principles of natural law" in the Palestinian and Israeli connotation of this term, see the verdict of Judge Silberg, Court of Appeals 10/59XIII, Verdict 1182, 1193, and his verdict, Court of Appeals 301/63, XVIII Verdict 598, 622–23.

[9a] See the following paragraph 5.

[10] Maimonides, *HILKHOT SANHEDRIN,* Chapter 21, Halacha 1 and 3. They originate in *BREITA SANHEDRIN* p. 30; 71, and *GEMARA KTUVOT* p. 46:71, but the *definition* for the term "justice in judging" we encounter for the first time in Maimonides as well as the innovated term "equating the litigants".

[10a] "Master-principle" on the model of "master worker".

[11] For it is equating the litigants that constitutes justice in judging according to the definition by Maimonides, and anything that does not fit this does not impair justice.

[12] Court of Appeals 3/58, XII verdict 1493, p. 1511 at the top, opposite margin-letter A.

evidence to the contrary even if he is thoroughly convinced in advance that it will prove to be an absolute failure. Thus Rama (Rabbi Moshe Israelish)[13] in his Responsa:

> "It is impossible to judge a case without hearing the claimant's plea.... Even though this is a simple thing we can learn it from the ways of the Almighty.... It started with His asking Adam: 'Who told thee that thou wast naked?' (Genesis, 3:11), and also Cain, whom He asked: 'Where is Abel thy brother?' *(Ibid, 4:9) in order to hear their arguments*.... Thus the Sages interpreted what was said: *(Ibid 18:21)* 'I will go down and see', i.e. to tell the judges not to pronounce judgment until they *listen and understand,* and from this it follows that even in a case where it is clear to the judge that the accused will prove guilty, he must nevertheless first hear his plea." *(RESPONSA-RAMA,* 108).

What was said above regarding the accused applies in exactly the same measure to the accuser, when the burden of proof pertaining to the testimony given by the accused rests with *him* and the plaintiff's aim is to destroy the evidence presented and win his case. It is therefore possible to express this concept in one general comprehensive formula by saying: the judge must grant the *accused* the opportunity of refuting the *accuser*.

The Rama's "procedural" reference to the dialogue between God and Adam traveled from Poland and about 200 years later reached England where it was absorbed[14] by a Judge Fortescue, a descendant of a distinguished non-Jewish family who—by a very charming remark—used it as the basis for a verdict he rendered in 1723.

The story runs as follows: a certain man named Dr. Richard Bentley, a Fellow at Cambridge University, entered into a controversy with his friend Middleton who claimed the return of a debt in the amount of £4.6s., but to no avail. As was customary in disputes between Fellows of the University, Middleton carried his claim to the Deputy Chancellor in his capacity of the "University Court" by virtue of the authority vested in him by a decree published by Queen Elizabeth in the third year of her reign. A court order was issued and a special messenger was dispatched to Bentley's home to deliver it and to ask him to appear in court. Bentley took the court order, glanced at it, and returned it to the messenger, saying, apparently quite roughly, that there was neither law nor judge nor anything legal in the whole procedure conducted by the Deputy Chancellor, and that he, Bentley, would not appear before the Deputy Chancellor. The day of the hearing came. Middleton appeared and confirmed that his friend Bentley did indeed owe him the sum of £4.6s. The court messenger related all that had happened to him in Bentley's home and the insolent words that the latter had flung at the court. The Deputy Chancellor, who perceived in this a contempt of the court and a desecration of the University's name, convened the authorized statutory assembly, des-

---

[13] Born approximately 1520, died 1572. See Asher Ziv, *ARAMO,* Mosad Harav Kook Publishers, Jerusalem, 1957.

[14] With some light changes which do not alter the main idea.

cribed there Dr. Bentley's actions and asked that they divest Bentley of his academic degrees (Bachelor of Arts and Doctor of Theology). The meeting, conducted without Bentley's being present and without his being invited to appear and plead his case, accepted the Deputy Chancellor's recommendation and divested Bentley of his academic titles.

Bentley then appealed to the Court and asked for an injunction ordering the "Deputy Chancellor, the Masters and Scholars of Cambridge University" to reinvest him with the titles taken from him unlawfully. The arguments brought by the petitioner's representative ranged far and wide but his primary plea—the one that is most relevant to the subject at hand—was that any particular right that a man possesses, be it even of the most negligible significance—as for instance the right of sitting at the same table with his honor, the mayor of the town—may not be taken from the possessor unless he is first granted the opportunity to plead against such divestment. That is precisely what helped Dr. Bentley, at least in the verdict delivered by Judge Fortescue:

> The objection for want of notice can never be got over. The laws of God and man both give the party an opportunity to make his defence, if he has any. I remember to have heard it observed by a very learned man upon some occasion, that even God himself did not pass sentence upon Adam, before he called upon him to make his defence. Adam (says God) where art thou? Hast thou eaten of the tree, whereof I commanded thee that thou shouldst not eat? And the same question was put to Eve also. Per Cur', ulterius concilium.
> .... It was argued a second time ... and without entering much into the debate of the matters, the Court held the whole proceeding to be illegal for want of a summons and so granted a peremptory mandamus."[15]

I enlarged on this tale of Bentley not because of its value as folklore or because of the naiveté or piquancy which characterized Judge Fortescue's verdict, but because this verdict with the three ideas it contains, demonstrated in a very concrete manner the full power and scope of that principle of justice. The English judges in no wise approved of Dr. Bentley's behavior as regards his alma mater and its institutions. "His behavior was crass—declared Chief Justice Ayer—and had he expressed himself in that manner in connection with an order of our court, we would have put him in irons." Even the authority of the Deputy Chancellor and his court (the "congregation" which dealt with the divestiture of his titles) was not seriously questioned by the Court. Nevertheless, the Court approved Bentley's appeal and returned all his titles to him. This shows that if there is anything worse than depriving a man of his material rights it is depriving him of his legal right to protect the right about to be taken from him. This seemingly paradoxical statement contains the logic that without a fair hearing and pure judgement human rights cannot exist altogether. This is an ancient truth.

[15] *The King against the Chancellor,* Masters and Scholars of the University of Cambridge, (1723) 93 E.R. 698, 704.

3

From this derives another "natural-law-principle", a judicial maxim recognized in the courts of nations and even more in the Jewish code, that should also be classified as an offshoot of the principle of equating litigants. I do not presume to state that this maxim is *only* an offshoot of that principle. Undoubtedly it has its own *raison d'etre* and may have appeared by "autogenetic" means. However, inasmuch as this primary principle of equating the litigants does exist, we may be permitted to classify it as one of the offshoots of this primary principle—a fact which adds a new, logical and exhaustive aspect to the uncommonly severe character of this law of justice. I refer to the well-known maxim *ne Judex in re sua*,[16] "an interested party cannot serve as judge".[17] The term "interested party" refers not to the interest of actual ownership but to anything in which the judge has a special interest; this disqualifies him from serving as judge in that case, even if he is convinced that he will not pervert justice. The interests that disqualify a judge from presiding over a case are endless, and mean any benefit whatsoever—or a hint of a benefit, not necessarily monetary—because the slightest benefit he may derive as a result of that case *affects him unconsciously,* dims his sight, stultifies his understanding and concentrates his gaze on one side, rendering him no longer capable of seeing the other side of the dispute.

How severely Jewish law regards a judge who derives a benefit from his judging may be perceived by comparing the Jewish law with the English law. The English doctrine also disqualifies a judge who is interested in the object of the case, but it has a graduated scale that it applies to "judge disqualification" as well as definite restrictions and reservations. Here for example is a fragment from a famous verdict rendered by Judge [Colin] Blackburn from which we receive—once we overcome the awkwardness of the language and its ambiguites—a very clear idea which serves to this very day as a precedent and guide in the interesting discourse on the disqualification of judges.

The story concerns the municipality of Bradford which owned a waterworks. According to an English law the municipality was permitted to draw water from the river without obtaining permission from the neighboring millowners, on condition that it first obtain a document signed by the magistrates stating that a certain water-reservoir, of a certain volume, was completed and filled with water. The request for such a document was duly submitted to the magistrates in Bradford, the millowners objected, the magistrates conducted an investigation, and the document was granted. Then

> "a rule was obtained for a *certiorari* to bring up this certificate to be quashed, on the ground that the justices who granted it were interested. All the objections were disposed of during the argument except the following. On the affidavits on both sides it appeared that a hospital and a friendly society had invested part of their funds in bonds of the Bradford corporation, charging the borough

---

[16] Compare the report of the above-mentioned committee, pp. 76–79. That is justice-principle 1 according to the sequence in the report.
[17] On the model of the saying "A witness does not become a judge" (*SANHEDRIN*, p. 34:72).

fund, and that these bonds were taken in the names of trustees, and that two of the justices in question were, one of them amongst the trustees of the society and the other amongst the trustees of the hospital. Neither of them had, nor by any possibility could have, any pecuniary beneficial interest in these bonds, but no doubt the security of their *cestui qui trusts* would be improved by anything improving the borough fund, and anything improving the waterworks, after they became the property of the corporation, would produce that effect.

The question which we have to determine, was whether this disqualifies the justices from acting in what was certainly a judicial inquiry: and we think it does not. There is no doubt that any direct pecuniary interest, however small, in the subject of inquiry, does disqualify a person from acting as a judge in the matter; and if by any possibility these gentlemen, though mere trustees, could have been liable to costs, or to other pecuniary loss or gain, in consequence of their being so, we should think the question different from what it is: for that might be held an interest. But the only way in which the facts could affect their impartiality, would be that they might have a tendency to favour those for whom they were trustees; and that is an objection not in the nature of interest, but of a challenge to the favour. Wherever there is a real likelihood that the judge would, from kindred or any other cause, have a bias in favour of one of the parties, it would be very wrong in him to act; and we are not to be understood to say, that where there is a real bias of this sort this Court would not interfere; but in the present case there is no ground for doubting that the justices acted perfectly *bona fide;* and the only question is, whether in strict law, under such circumstances, the certificate of such justices is void, as it would be if they had a pecuniary interest; and we think that *Reg. v. Dean of Rochester*[18] is an authority, that circumstances, from which a suspicion of favour may arise, do not produce the same effect as a pecuniary interest.[19] And as the decision in that case was on demurrer to a plea, and might have been taken into error, the authority is one on which we ought to act.

We think, therefore, that the rule should be discharged."[18]

The conclusion reached by Judge Blackburn is briefly as follows: A direct money-interest, however slight, in the result of the trial, unequivocally disqualifies the judge. What is weighed here is not whether the judge is capable of perverting the law on account of his personal interest. On the other hand, the apprehension aroused by another, non-monetary interest, does not disqualify the judge unless there exists an "actual understanding", i.e. a genuine suspicion that because of this non-monetary interest the judge is liable to show preference for one of the parties.

An interesting example of a most negligible money-interest which disqualified the judge may be seen in a verdict rendered in England 100 years ago.[20] It concerns a man who bought a third-class train ticket but traveled in the second-class. He was found guilty, appealed to the "Queen's Bench" for an *order nisi* and the guilt-verdict was rescinded. The reason was as follows:

---

[18] *The Queen against the Dean of Rochester*, (1852), 117 E.R. 1181.
[19] *Reg. v. Rand* (1865), L.R. 1 Q.B. 230, 230–233.
[20] Re Hopkins (1858), 120 E.R. 445.

two judges of the Court of Appeals were shareholders in the railway firm which operated that "deceived" train. Just imagine how much bigger these judges' dividend from the railway company would have been had the man paid the full price for a second-class ticket!

The above-mentioned verdict of Judge Blackburn which consisted of two parts—i.e. that a monetary interest should always disqualify the judge, whereas the fear of perverting justice because of a non-monetary interest should disqualify him only when a real suspicion exists—found support and confirmation in other verdicts. It is worthwhile however to add that in the meantime, while this case was going from one instance to another, there dissolved little by little until it vanished completely the adjective "direct," which was attached in the Rand[21] case to the term "monetary interest". Neither Blackburn himself, repeating the same judgement in the Meyer[22] case, nor Judge Stephen who adopted it in the Farrant[23] case, recalled this epithet any more, and it was forgotten. They apparently gave it up and there is no cause for regret. From the very start I did not understand how a "direct" interest could here be distinguished from an "indirect" interest; is it then important to ask who transmits the monetary benefit to the judge? This merits further consideration.

Such then is the position of the English code with regard to disqualifying an "interested" judge: it is very severe and strict as regards a monetary interest but lenient and restrained when the interest is of any other nature, in which case there has to be very definite cause for suspicion, as was seen in the above example. However—and this is an innovation introduced by the judiciary school which transformed English doctrine with reference to this type of problem from a just to a very unjust one—once a definite suspicion arose with regard to the objectivity of the challenged judge, it seethed like a poison and disqualified the judge's decision even if the suspicion was *proved to be unfounded*. I cannot explain this except by saying that the honor of the Court has in the eyes of the British judges a supreme cultural significance which must be defended even at the cost of a just verdict. Honor must prevail over justice!

This amazing lesson we learn from a verdict handed down in the year 1924[24] and because of its considerable importance we shall relate here in detail the event and its meaning. A man named McCarthy while driving his car, collided with the car of a certain Mr. Whitworth and was criminally charged with dangerous driving. At the close of the hearing the judges retired to their chamber to take counsel together, and were accompanied by the Court Recorder, (or, more accurately, by the man who on that day was substituting for the Court Recorder) and in the end they found the accused McCarthy guilty as charged. It later transpired that the Recorder was a member of a law-firm which was dealing, on behalf of the above-mentioned Whitworth,

---

[21] See note 19.
[22] Reg. v. Meyer (1875), 1 Q.B.D. 173.
[23] Reg. v. Farrant (1887), 20 QBD.
[24] R.v. Sussex Justices; ex parte Mecarthy (1924), 1 K.B. 256.

with a *civil* claim against McCarthy, filed as a result of that collision. This fact—so McCarthy's attorney argued—became know to him only after the judges had retired together with the Recorder to the chamber, and he therefore used it as pretext for a petition to cancel the verdict of guilty rendered against his client. He appealed to the "King's Bench" and obtained an order nisi; the judges replied with a statement that they had not in any way required the Recorder's assistance and had reached their decision independently. The Court expressed full confidence in the judges' statement but nevertheless decreed the order absolute and nullified the guilt-verdict. Judge Heward, the Chief Justice, said:

> "We have been told, and it is doubtless true, that when this gentleman (the Recorder) retired with the judges to their chamber, taking with him the written record of testimonies in case the judges wished to ask his advice, the judges reached their decision without consulting him, and that he himself very carefully avoided making any reference to this case in any manner whatsoever. However, all this notwithstanding, a series of verdicts exists which shows that ... a fundamental importance is ascribed to the fact that justice should not only be done in fact but that it should (also) be clearly manifest and obvious as having been done, beyond any shadow of doubt. The question in this case is therefore not whether the recorder made some remark or voiced some criticism which it was improper for him to remark or express; the question is whether from a civil point of view he was so close to the object of the case that he was not suited to serve as Recorder in this criminal trial. The reply to this depends not on what was actually done but on what appeared to have been done. Nothing may be done which creates even the slightest suspicion that an improper interference occured during the process of the trial...."

We thus see in amazement ... that it was proved that the Recorder had had no part whatsoever in preparing the verdict which found McCarthy guilty and in any event the verdict was without fault or blemish. Justice demanded therefore that McCarthy's appeal be dismissed and that he be compelled to pay the fine (£10) levied by the justices of Sussex. What, however, did the judges of "King's Bench" do? The exact opposite: they canceled the verdict and freed McCarthy of any accusation or fine. Why? Because in the hearts of people who knew of the Recorder's presence among the judges but who did not know of his scrupulosuly correct behavior in the Judge's chambers, lurked the understandable suspicion that the verdict handed down was in part or in whole the work of the Recorder who was an "interested party" in the case, and that it was therefore unjust and unacceptable. In other words: instead of confirming *a just verdict which appeared (erroneously) as unjust*, they themselves rendered an *unjust verdict which to them—to those in error and to them alone—appeared as just*. The honor of the Court was perhaps upheld but justice was certainly impaired.

4.

Altogether different is the attitude of the Jewish law with regard to the "judging-disqualification" of an "interested" judge. First of all and in order to dismiss

The Purity of Judgment in the Hebrew Code

quickly the point we touched at the close of the preceding paragraph, I should like to underline the fact that *in matters of judgement* Jewish law never makes concessions in favor of the Court's honor. Of course one is dutybound to honor the Court[25] but that is not an "asset" which must be safeguarded at the expense of a just trial.[26] However, this does not in itself depict the full difference between the two systems of law contained in the problem at hand pertaining to "judge disqualification." The area disputed is actually much broader and its origin is much deeper, as we shall see later on.

We quoted above (Paragraph 2 of this chapter) from Maimonides, Chapter 21 of Hilkhot Sanhedrin, Halakha one and three, in which he defines the concept of "judicial justice". This, as its formulation testifies ("which is . . . this is . . .") is an exclusive definition which declares the equating of the litigants to be the master-principle from which are derived all those laws and regulations whose aim is to safeguard the purity of jurisdiction. They pointed out that one offspring of this master-principle was the principle-of-natural-law which makes it obligatory to hear both sides, and as an additional offspring we attribute to it the principle-of-natural-law which stipulates that "an interested party cannot serve as judge." This distinction of parentage is not only a family name but—as we stated at the beginning of the preceding paragraph—*"it adds a new, logical and exhaustive aspect to the uncommonly stringent character of this law of justice."*

This judging-disqualification of an "interested" judge is in the Hebrew code a "twin-brother" to the disqualification of the testimony of an "interested" *witness;* but there are one or two types of "interest"[27] in which the law as applied to the judge differs from the law pertaining to the witness, being *more strict and more severe;* this shows that these twins are not "identical" and that one of them possesses components which are not present in the other.

Let us investigate the origin of this double concept and attempt to discover its nature, its reason, its source and its essence.

---

[25] ". . . And I commanded ye in that time, said Rabbi Elazar, in the name of Rabbi Simlai: a warning to the populace to arouse their awe of the law." *(SANHEDRIN,* p. 8:1); "as the judge was instructed to observe this precept, so the populace too was ordered *to show respect to the judge,* as it was said: And I commanded ye—a warning to the populace to arouse their awe of the judge and that he should not make himself ridiculous in front of them *or behave frivolously."* (Maimonides *HILKHOT SANHEDRIN,* Chapter 25, *Halakha* 3). *All the more so, as a court messenger, since whoever dares to belittle him* is banned: "Rav ordered a flogging . . . him who offended a messenger of the rabbis . . . because he dared to challenge a messenger of the court" (Gemara and Rashi *YEVAMOT,* p. 52:1). Compare also Maimonides *HILKHOT TALMUD TORAH,* Chapter 6, *Halakha* 14; *TUR YOREH DEAH* verse 334; *SHULHAN ARUKH, YOREH DEAH,* verse 334, paragraph 43.

[26] "We tied the knot and we dissolved it—people's scorn of the court does not concern us; contempt of court: perhaps people may ridicule the court for contradicting their own law, making a mockery of it" (Gemara and Rashbam *BABA BATRA,* p. 31:2). And so the Halakha was finally accepted by Maimonides, *TUR* and *SHULHAN ARUKH.* (Maimonides *HILKHOT TOEN V'NITAN,* Chapter 15, *Halakha* 5; *TUR KHOSHEN MISHPAT* and *SHULHAN ARUKH HOSHEN MISHPAT,* verse 146, paragraph 2 and 3, see *ibid.)*

[27] See further on.

The *Breita* says:

"If a Torah scroll has been stolen from the people of a certain town, the judges of that town are not to judge this case and evidence is not to be admitted from the people of that town."[28]

If a thief is brought into court for stealing a Torah scroll, which is the public property of the town, and he pleads not guilty or claims to have paid for it, he may not be arraigned in a court presided over by judges of the same town and people of that town may not be brought as witnesses to refute his arguments; because they all share in the ownership of the Torah scroll and are therefore "interested parties" who may not serve either as judges or as witnesses.[29]

The concept deriving from this concrete law became a fundamental basis for two abstract rules, as follows:

"Any case from which the judge stands to receive some benefit he may not preside over as judge; consequently a town whose Torah scroll was stolen, etc., etc."[30] "Any testimony from which one stands to derive benefit is disqualified as testimony; consequently a plot owned by two partners which another came and took from them etc., etc."[31] Heretofore we have dealing with a monetary benefit,[32] but what of *another* type of benefit? This we find in Mishneh Torah.

"These things (referring to "interests" that disqualify the witness) depend only on the knowledge of the judge and the depth of his understanding: he must know the crux of the law and understand the causes and effects of things, as well as penetrate deeply in order to see, and if he finds that this witness derives some benefit from this testimony, however vaguely and remotely, then he is not to testify. *And just as he must not testify because he may be 'interested' in this testimony, so too he must not serve as the judge in this case;* thus too other disqualifications—as witnesses are disqualified so too are judges."[33]

To put it simply the words "he must understand the causes and effects of things" or "if he finds that this witness derives some benefit, however vaguely or remotely" *prove* that not only an actual monetary benefit but also any other benefit such as honor, power, friendship, etc., are liable to disqualify the judge if only there exists a "causative link" (and "he must understand the causes and effects of things") between the benefit and the verdict.[34]

---

[28] *BABA BATRA*, p. 43:1.

[29] See Rashbam *BABA BATRA* (id) halakha 4: do not judge, and 4: proof.

[30] *TUR, SHULHAN ARUKH, HOSHEN MISHPAT*, Verse 7, paragraph 12.

[31] *TUR, SHULHAN ARUKH, HOSHEN MISHPAT*, verse 37, paragraph 1.

[32] Because the classic example of the *Breita* is on monetary benefit.

[33] Maimonides *HILKHOT EDUT* Chapter 17, Halakha 4; brought in quotation from Maimonides' words in *TUR, HOSHEN MISHPAT*, end of verse 37; similarly in *SHULHAN ARUKH, HOSHEN MISHPAT*, verse 37, paragraph 21.

[34] Compare the response of the Ralbah (Rabbi Levi Ben-Habib, 1484–1541) brought in responsa of the Rashdam (Rabbi Shmuel di Modena, 1506–1589) part *HOSHEN MISHPAT*, verse 2,

The Purity of Judgment in the Hebrew Code

"As witnesses are disqualified so also are judges disqualified" is stated there; the reverse however is not stated! This means that there is a category of disqualification-on-account-of-"interest" which does disqualify a judge but does not disqualify a witness. In fact, a bit further in Halakha 6 *(id)* it is said: "Whoever is competent to judge is competent to serve as a witness, whereas some who are competent to serve as witnesses are not competent to judge: those who love, hate, etc.[35] There is an "interest-disqualification" due to love and hate which disqualifies only the judge but not the witness.

We may therefore ask: why this "discrimination" and why should the judge be more suspect than the witness? Two reasons were cited in our sources, both of them psychological, or almost psycho-analytical, and were it not

which reads as follows: "And not only the acceptance (the reference is to the acceptance by the sages of Safed in 1538 in accordance with the efforts of Rabbi Yehuda Birav, to renew the 'ordination' and establish the Sanhedrin, using as their authority the well-known words of Maimonides in his commentary on the *Mishnayot, SANHEDRIN* chapter 1, and *HILKHOT SANHEDRIN* chapter 4, Halakha 14) which they approved in the past is no longer valid . . . but even should they wish to discuss the law again together with us . . . if they continue in their original opinion, their consent is no longer valid for a majority decision *inasmuch as they are now interested in the verdict . . . They are ashamed to retreat from a thing to which they had previously agreed . . . and will not accept any argument to change their minds"*. In another point of the same response, the part not quoted by the Rashdam, after the Ralbah examined, from the standpoint of the Halakha, the question as to whether the judge should be suspected of never retreating from a verdict he rendered even if convinced that it was not correct, he says: "There are some matters on which the law is very clear and on these it is possible for the sage to retreat . . . but on other matters the law is absolutely final and the sage will not retreat from what he already said, *not because he will do this purposely,* but because, having already given his verdict *it will appear to him to be correct as in the past. . . .* Those rabbis would certainly not retreat because it would cause them shame to have decided as they did in the past without going into the law deeply enough, *not because they will now deliberately say anything against a verdict which seemed right in their eyes, but because they had already once passed judgement on this matter and had already* acted (i.e. appointed Rabbi Yehuda Birav), *their hearts will incline to their original opinion. For this same reason it follows that a man who loves or hates someone must be disqualified as judge.* (Responsa of the Ralbah, Venice 1565, p. 279:71, first and second column). This negative benefit of avoiding shame is also termed a benefit which disqualifies him from judging, even though it is not a financial benefit. It should also be noted that even the *Maharit* in his responsa, part *HOSHEN MISHPAT,* verse 80, who believes that a non-monetary benefit does not disqualify the witness, admits that a benefit of that nature does disqualify the judge. For he states *(id)* (published in Tel Aviv, 1919, part 2, p. 318, top of second column):

"But in a case in which there is no monetary benefit but his mind is close you do not say (that the witness is diaqualified), that he is not shown preference over the loved . . . or the hated . . . . The opinion of Rabbi Yehuda is to disqualify him, and our sages have said that Israel [Jews] should not thus be suspected." The judge, as we shall see further, is actually disqualified from sitting in judgement over the loved or hated.

[35] The source of the law as regards the witness' competence is in *SANHEDRIN* p. 27:72: *"Said the sages to Rabbi Yehuda: Israel is not suspected of giving false testimony because of hatred or love" (Mishna* and *Rashi, ibid).* And the source as regards disqualification of the judge: *id,* p. 29:71: Our rabbis taught: if he is not his enemy he may testify . . . one point refers to the judge. As concerns the judge the rabbis agreed that one who hates may not judge *because he will be unable to see anything that is to his credit (Gemara* and *Rashi, id).* The same applies to one who loves as his mind is inclined toward him and he will *not be able to see anything that discredits him.* (See *Gemara, id,* and read carefully.)

for their antiquity I would say that their authors were influenced by the theory of the unconscious which began to flourish at the turn of the twentieth century. The adherents of the first reason were among others Harosh[36] and Smé.[37]

> "For the state of being in favor or against develops within one's being *without malice aforethought* and therefore, with a little love his heart is inclined to favor, and with a little hate it is inclined to oppose."[38]
>
> "As for those who love and hate, who are qualified to testify but disqualified to judge—the reason is that in giving factual testimony, *whatever he experienced he gives as testimony* and we do not suspect him of altering his words in a certain direction because of his love or hatred; whereas it is different in judging, *which depends on logical deduction and thinking and is swayed by love and hate even if not with malice aforethought.*"[39]
>
> The second reason is mentioned by Maimonides himself in his Mishneh Torah and *to me this seems to be the crux of the matter*. "A judge is forbidden to preside over a case of someone he loves even if he is not a close companion and not a dear friend whom he holds in great affection, or if someone he hates even if he is not his enemy and wishes him no harm, *for it is essential that there be two litigants who are equal in the judge's eyes and heart.*"[40]

It is as I noted: *everything derives from the master-principle of equating the litigants*. They should be equal to each other not only in the *eyes* of the judges (i.e. in their *open* attitude), but also in their *hearts,* i.e. in their concealed, *unconscious* attitude.

Obviously if the reason is a discrepancy in the equality between the litigants, then any inclination to either side, even of the slightest, damages the equality and destroys it altogether. For the terms "more" and "less" have no place whatsoever in the concept of equality, and a minute grain disturbs the balance of the scales.

Maimonides' argument, as already noted, seems to me the most important, for two reasons, as follows:

(1) He explains very logically all the great and extreme severity with which the Hebrew code regards the disqualification of judges, whether said disqualification be *post facto* or *a priori* or an act of piety.[41] (2) He and he alone

---

[36] Reb Asher ben Yehiel, 1250–1327.

[37] *SEFER MEIRAT EINAYIM* by Rabbi Yehoshua Walk, 1550–1614.

[38] Harosh on Sanhedrin, Chapter 3, verse 23, after citing Rav Popa, *KTUBOT* p. 105:72: "A man must not judge anyone he likes or dislikes for, in the person he likes he will not be able to see any fault and in the person he dislikes, he will not find anything that is in his favor."

[39] Sme, *HOSHEN MISHPAT,* verse s'k' 1.

[40] Maimonides, *HILKHOT SANHEDRIN,* Chapter 23, Halakha 6.

[41] Compare the comments and events cited in *KTUBOT,* p. 105:71, 106:71, among them the comment of Rav Popa, (*id,* 105:72, which Maimonides considers utterly disqualified, whereas Harosh *(SANHEDRIN* 83, verse 23) and *TOSAFOT (KTUBOT,* p. 105:72, 35) deem it a priori disqualification or a more restrictive measure. See also *TOSEFTA SANHEDRIN* Chapter 5, Halakha 3: "You should not judge one another or with one another or over one another" and also *YERUSHALMI SANHEDRIN,* chapter 3, Halakha 9 (published in Jerusalem, 1949, Vol. 5 p. 18.)

helps us accord to the principle of equating the two litigants the place it deserves as a first and foremost master-basis for all the rules of natural justice. This makes it possible for us to be more "economical" in rules and not split them up too much—an economy to which all scientific research aspires.

If we wish to include in one comprehensive and inclusive formula all of the judge-disqualifications found in the Hebrew code, I think the most apt one would read as follows: A judge is disqualified from trying any case in which he is "interested" either in a "personal" sense, i.e. as a relative, friend, foe and the like, or in a "material" sense, i.e. for a monetary benefit or for any benefit he might gain from a particular result of the trial. In each of these cases "interest" causes the mind of the judge to lean more toward *one* of the litigants, with the result that the principle of equating the litigants and with it the principle of justice will be short-changed.

Among those personally "interested" I included above also relatives. I did this for a calculated reason and after lengthy deliberation. Proof for this may be found in a very old source, the words of Gemara, Sanhedrin, Chapter *Zeh Borer*, the discourse on: his betrothed wife, in which the Talmud distinguishes between the laws of inheritance and impurity in which the betrothed is not considered as her husband, and the laws of testimony in which he is considered as her husband and is disqualified as a witness. There (as regards impurity and inheritance) the emphasis of the Torah is on kinship whereas prior to the marriage he is not yet her kin; *here it is a matter of his being close to her in thought and the fact is that he is already close to her in thought.*[42] From this we learn that the reason for disqualifying witnesses is "personal interest" resulting from being close in thought [42a] and that is the idea we expressed above.[43] Here one may ask: Does this not contradict what is written in the Talmud[44] that the law of disqualifying witnesses due to kinship is a "royal decree" and nothing more?

My reply to this is: It is true that the Torah forbade relatives from testifying for one another even—as in the case of Moses and Aaron vs. their father-in-law—there is not the slightest suspicion that they may lie. But the *internal* reason for this halakha, *the "ratio logis" or rationale* is that the relationship between kin, because of the frequency of their *contacts,* and because of the

---

[42] *SANHEDRIN* p. 28:72.

[42a] See below, note 45.

[43] Other places in which reference is made to judge-disqualification on account of kinship as based on the judge's interest because of the inclination oh his heart toward his kin, are: *PNEY MOSHE COMMENTARY* on the Yerushalmi (by Moshe Margolis, 1715–1781); *YERUSHALMI SANHEDRIN*, Chapter 3, Halakha 9: *"Let not the congregation be relatives of the one who beats or is beaten, as Rav Yossi interprets it ... and now we deduce also that they should not be relatives of the one who beats because it is likely that they will find in his favor, etc.";* COMMENTARY *OF RADBAZ* (Rav David ben Zimra, 1479–1574) on Maimonides, *HILKHOT EDUT*, Chapter 16, Halakha 5: *"Whence* the conclusion that the witnesses should not be relatives of the judge? *Because the judge will not be willing to accept the refutation of his relative's testimony,* thereby making the testimony irrefutable."

[44] BABA BATRA, p. 159:1, *"If you do not say so, then was Moses and Aaron versus their father-in-law because they were not trustworthy? But it was a royal decree."*

recurrent *friction* between them, is highly emotional, or I might say, ambivalent, now close to one another and again distant from one another *and in any event close in particular to the man who is involved in a case with his relative*. For this reason, i.e. because of this "negative" or "positive" interest which the witness or the judge has in the cases of relatives, the Torah disqualified them as witnesses or as judges, both for favorable and unfavorable results.[45] A full explanation, which embraces all the aspects of the problem, smooths over all obstacles and answers all relevant questions, is given by the author of "*Hahinuch*".[46] I am surprised at the authors of the period following the thirteenth century who paid too little attention to his wonderful words. Thus spoke his golden tongue:

> "We were enjoined not to accept testimony of people related to one another with one portion of the group testifying for another portion of the group [of relatives] and concerning this it was said: Fathers should not be put to death because of the sons and sons because of the fathers, which is generally interpreted: Do not kill the fathers due to testimony given by the sons and vice versa; and the same applies to laws pertaining to monies ... for you cannot put credence in relatives, with one group testifying against another ... because man's affairs depend chiefly on the testimony of other people ... and therefore God wished to remove the possibility of doing justice only by giving strong testimony, true testimony, free of all suspicion; and to strengthen this matter He ruled out all testimony by relatives, *even of an incriminating kind*, lest the custom spread to the point of accepting also a relative's favorable testimony ... We also reap another advantage from this: since relatives always live near one another, sit and arise together, it is impossible to prevent their quarreling from time to time, and if we give credence to their testimony for one another, then perhaps in a moment of being at odds with one another they may be angry, come before the judge and incriminate his [adversary's] head to the king [court], and when the anger abates, the incriminating relative will be ready to kill himself with concern for his kinsman and for what he did. All the ways of the Lord are righteous."[47]

The above was stated with regard to disqualifying relatives as witnesses but is of course also valid with regard to disqualifying relatives as judges. For as regards disqualification due to kinship, the same rules apply to both. But as regards the disqualification of judges there is the additional idea that the judge's love or hatred for his relative destroys the equality between the litigants.

---

[45] It is, therefore, possible to combine both examples in one formula and to declare that a relative is disqualified as a witness because of his like-thinking either in the case of his relative or in the case of his relative's adversary.

[46] The author's name is not known; the book was erroneously ascribed to *Haroeh* (Reb Aharon Halevy, died 1293), but modern research tends to disbelieve this and to believe that the author of the book *HAHINUKH* was merely a contemporary of Haroeh. The error was prompted by the fact that the author's preface stated that he was "a Jew of the house of Levy of Barcelona" precisely as Haroeh was.

[47] The book *HAHINUKH* on the 613 precepts, precept 589 (Pardess Publishers, Jerusalem, 1955, together with the *MINHAT HINUKH*, part 3, p. 101).

5

The third rule of the principle of natural-law according to the sequence employed in the report of the above-mentioned Committee,[48] is the obligation of disclosing the reasons for the decision rendered by the judge. It was to this rule I was referring when I said (See part 2 of this chapter) that the three principles of natural law set out in the Committee's report "all belong to the judicial or semi-judicial sphere". A duty which must be executed after the decision has been given is not strictly-speaking a judicial or material one, but from a general intellectual point of view it is closer to the frame of judicial activities, inasmuch as the material right is not affected by it at all.

Hebrew law also recognizes a duty classified in this manner.[49] The accepted name for it is: "The decision rendered and the reason for it." I should actually elaborate on this but inasmuch as it is not relevant to the controversial discussion itself and does not, as is crystal clear, derive from the master-principle of equating the litigants, it does not belong in the frame of our subject, which is the purity of judgment.

---

[48] See above, note 8.
[49] *SANHEDRIN*, p. 31, 72; Maimonides *HILKHOT SANHEDRIN*, Chapter 6, Halakha 6; *SHULHAN ARUKH HOSHEN MISHPAT*, verse 14, paragraphs 1, 4; see also TOS. *SANHEDRIN, ibid*, 45 V'im and TOS. *BABA METZIYA*, p. 69, 72, 45 *ki hai*.

MOSHE SHAMIR

Moshe Shamir was born in 1921 in Safed, Israel (then Palestine). From 1941 to 1947 he was a member of Mishmar Haemek, a kibbutz of *Hashomer Hatzair,* a left-wing socialist movement. During the 1940's he also belonged to *Palmah,* the "shock companies," the commandos of Haganah, which preceded the Defense Army of Israel. He attained the rank of captain.

Novelist, playwright and essayist, he founded and edited *Bamahaneh,* a weekly publication of the army, contributed to the most significant literary journals in Israel and to several dailies writing a weekly column in *Al-Hamishmar,* the organ of Mapam (Marxist-socialist party). He was also a member of the Hebrew Language Academy.

Shamir's literary beginnings immediately established him as a minor Marxist and a major writer. Although in his early works he expressed the "young guard's" iconoclastic tendencies, the "breaking of the tablets," the slighting, if not turning away from the Jewish past and traditions, almost overnight he discovered the nexus between his people's yesterday and today, thus bridging the Israeli "generation gap".

With his *King of Flesh* and *Blood,* and *The War of the Sons of Light,* (each of which was awarded the Bialik Literary Prize). Shamir secured for himself a permanent and respected place in Hebrew belles-lettres—not an easy achievement in the long history of Jewish culture so heavily populated with literary giants.

Shamir was sent on missions to university campuses abroad. He was remarkably successful in unlocking the intellect of the Jewish students in the diaspora.

The excerpts appearing here were, as the author explained, written at different times but combined for this anthology into one cohesive essay.

The Hard Way

by MOSHE SHAMIR

Prefatory Note

THESE FOUR CHAPTERS were written at different times, each as a response or contribution to what then appeared to me a central issue in the life of Israel's society.

The first three are in the nature of *demands* made of that society. The background is the State's existence and the demands have to do with the nature and quality of that existence. The fourth chapter—a kind of summary—is also in the nature of a demand, but against a background that is diametrically different. This was at the time of the Six Day War and its aftermath, when the State's very existence had been cast in doubt, brutally and unequivocally.

The fourth chapter tries to show that the only way of ensuring the State of Israel's continued existence is by fully and faithfully preserving the achievements of the Six Day War. By adding it to the other three I attempt to prove that not only are the principles of morality, of Jewish history and of international politics which underlie the State not impaired by retaining these achievements, but that only under such conditions are these principles—which must continue to guide the State—likely to achieve their full fruition.

THE CHOOSING PEOPLE

The uniqueness of the Jewish people lies not in the idea of being the *chosen* people. There was no nation in ancient times which did not consider itself *chosen*, a characteristic inherited by all nations throughout the ages. In ancient times it was taken literally, with the national mythologies providing the narrative and imaginative material demonstrating the divine origin and messianic destiny of the nations that composed them. In our day this conceit has various trappings and disguises: political, cultural, linguistic, and even Marxist, but it still retains its mythological character.

The uniqueness of the Jewish people lies in the idea of their being the *choosing* people. All the Biblical stories of a covenant, from Abraham on down through the revelation on Mount Sinai, are essentially narratives of a choice, made at the last and most dramatic moment, by a man or by the nation. The Commentaries expound this point at great length, as in the wonderful fable of how the Almighty courted all the nations of the world with his Law, being rejected by each in turn, until finally the people of Israel accepted it.

The Hard Way

God did not choose the people of Israel; it was the people of Israel who chose God. There is an *act* which precedes any acceptance of authority, any system of values, any distinction between right and wrong, and that is the *act of choice*. In this, in the "We will do, and we will be obedient", (the people's response when approached by God) lies the force and validity of all the Biblical commandments, because it is only an act of choice, a decision by the free will, which makes their observance meaningful. The nation that chooses, that is free, is the nation able to fulfill the commandments.

Our lives are fraught with millions of moments of choice, large and small. Our destiny is always a matter of facing crossroads, a giant never-ending roadmap. At every point there is a choice, and that choice is up to us.

"But is not everything predestined?" Yes. The celebrated necessity. Am I to blame because I chose to turn right instead of left, or vice versa? Am I to blame because the instinct of self-preservation as an individual, a family or a nation, leads me by the nose with its exigencies and compulsions? In truth there is no choice. The truth is that cases of pure freedom of choice, with neither benefit on one side nor danger on the other, are few and for the large part theoretical, with the outcome in the great and overwhelming majority of cases preordained by the conditions. Why all this preaching by righteous men since time began about choosing good and forsaking evil? Is that possible? Do I have a choice?

It is quite true that a slave cannot do good. Only a free man has the capacity to do good. Before you come to distinguish between good and evil you have to arrive at freedom of the spirit, at free will. That is the exalted concept of Man: a creature who continually expands his scope of freedom of action; one who takes less and less cognizance of the notion and reality of the absence of choice. On the material plane this is called civilization; on the spiritual plane this is culture, morality.

Hence complete and utter submission to a supreme law handed down from father to son, under the auspices of institutions and organizations, is not the way to the good. Rather it lies in education to freedom of the spirit, to the feeling that each day it is up to me to expand the realm wherein I take it upon myself to make decisions with the maximum freedom possible within the limits of my consciousness. Not to flee to the comfort of objective necessities, but rather to venture and to know. It is up to me; I am free to choose between good and evil.

This is the meaning of the breakdown of authority, any authority—religious, political or pedagogic—in a time of change, revolution, progress. Roads on the map of life are opening up. In every direction, at every crossroads of the journey, Man is encountering more and more pairs of possibilities, more and more choices without restrictions. Authority, the terror of restrictions, holds no water here. What is needed is the determination of a free will; what is needed is freedom of the spirit.

Indeed, the doctrine of "no alternative" is not only not Jewish, it is even anti-Jewish. The history of our nation shows that a great many things are possible for us which are not possible for the nations of the world. No other nation has made so many political "errors", has lost so much and conceded so much as we have. No other nation has accomplished so much that was "impossible". No other nation has survived so long in full consciousness of its unity and destiny.

The Diaspora brought the situation to its ultimate extreme. Of the "chosenness" practically nothing remained. The "chosen people" were chucked out from under Divine Providence and being chosen became contemptible, but it was precisely then that their *choosing* of their God became strengthened and fortified, and being a *chooser* became their chief characteristic. The history of the Jewish rebirth in our generation, with the State of Israel as its climax, is the history of an attempt to regain some of the assets of a "chosen" people, to reassert by right our place among the nations. Our task now is not to forget our true nature. Again we must become a *choosing* people. In the fullest consciousness of time and place we must again assert our place as a nation of obligations.

And first and foremost, then as now, we must recognize, know and believe, with all the force of our iconoclastic history that the choice is up to us.

A MORAL BASIS

Is it true that Israel's military strength is the first and prime condition for its existence? No, this is not so. The first and prime condition for Israel's existence is the moral one. It is recognition of the justice and the right of its existence, by the Jewish people and by all the nations of the world.

This is a tragic and exasperating fact; it costs us our heart's blood, We resist it, but the fact remains that the only political state in the world whose very existence is protested is the State created by the Jewish people. Our supreme and most potent weapon against those who would turn their political and economic protest into a protest by other means—into destruction—is the recognition by us and by all the nations of the world that this protest is unjust, that it lacks any basis, that it is contrary to the principles by which human society lives. In the event of a military attack the Israeli Army will be fighting with all its might for justice. This will always remain the cause of causes of the Army's strength, performance and success.

The existence of the State of Israel rests on the fate of the Jewish people. "There is no State so alone as ours", said Ben-Gurion in one of his great speeches in the Knesset, and in this he saw a source of danger. There is indeed no nation so solitary as ours, no state as alone as ours, and that in my opinion is the source of our strength and the secret of our eternal existence. The State of Israel came into being in a historical process which has no parallel, not only because of what transpired among the people but because of what took place in the country to which they came. We would be foolish and ignoring the truth if we did not admit that the transformation of the nature and character of Palestine from an essentially Arab country to an essentially Jewish one in less than half a century is a phenomenon of significance the likes of which the world has not known in recent generations. Only the special fate of the Jewish people, only an exalted moral right distilled in endless suffering and purified in the agony of generations were able to make it clear to the nations of the world, except unfortunately the Arab nations, that in the mid-twentieth century, at the end of the colonial era and the hegemony of the European nations, in the midst of the generation-of-awakening of the nations of Asia and Africa and the development of the rights of nations on their own land, the Jewish people is entitled and obliged to return to the land of their forefathers and become therein a sovereign nation, depriving the country's former inhabitants of the right of dominion.

It would be a dangerous delusion of conceit to imagine even for one moment that only this strength by virtue of settlement, or only military strength, have endowed us with our existence as a state. Neither the settlement movement nor the army have operated in a vacuum. The contest did not take place in a sports arena. Without the world political setting, which included at all times the indubitable recognition of the special right of the Jewish people to redemption in its historic land, this redemption would not have come about. And there is no need to say that even among the Jewish people all those wellsprings of strength which have made the redemption possible would not have manifested themselves were it not for the full recognition of the justice of the Zionist cause, which is part and parcel of that universal justice shared by all humanity.

In its eleventh year of existence, despite its economic development and military enhancement, the life of our State is still dependent on the strength and vitality of the principles of international morality; it must still be the standard-bearer of morality, peace, brotherly love, mutual understanding, cooperation, support for the weak, freedom for the oppressed, sustenance for the hungry and encouragement for the backward. To ensure its very existence the State of Israel must serve as a model and paragon for the observance of the precepts of human morality in the relations of peoples and states. From this it will derive a twofold benefit: it will help propagate these values and it will gain much valuable political credit.

A RESEARCH CENTER FOR THE FUTURE

For two days we absorbed the scenery, the color, the special atmosphere of Eilat. At the bottom of it all, consciously or unconsciously, was the geological fact: this was land from the days of the Creation, a landscape ancient beyond all antiquity. This was an area that preceded not only man and animal, but even vegetation.

These thoughts might have continued in this vein were it not for my encounter with the people of Eilat, with their work and lives, which, like the landscape, left a strong impression, the conscious or unconscious basis for an unusual train of thought. The conventional viewpoint of most of us shortsighted citizens of the "North" nonchalantly admits the prime importance of Eilat with the formula, "Well, we have no choice, we're a small country and a nation with a lot of problems, we have to invest in wilderness and dead areas because we have nothing better. The whole thing is rather artificial but what can you do, that's the way the country is". This view finds no support among the inhabitants of Eilat and the development areas of the Negev. These people aren't living with the feeling, " Well, we're in Eilat, we're in the Negev, we're in the desert, we have special conditions". They are living in a world, a world complete and varied, one rich in possibilities, harsh but with much beauty and grace, just as man has been living in his world since time began. Their work, their struggle, is not, as far as they are concerned, of a limited nature; it is not, as far as they are concerned, designed to solve the problems of the region. It is designed to solve the problems of the country. It is designed to solve the problems of human life of any nation and of any country.

* * *

The rapid, explosively sudden liberation of all the backward nations of the world, the placing of the question of a billion colored human beings on the agenda of policy, science, transportation, technology, medicine; the shrinkage, sudden as an ax-blow, of the globe to one single continuous inhabited zone, the rapid consumption—rapid as a forest fire—of the resources of nature by a human species whose voracity increases daily like a kind of giant parasite growing by geometric progression, all this reminds us of certain conditions which have for a generation prevailed on a miniature scale in one small country, in one small nation, under the conditions of a test tube or at best of a research center.

Does this not sound familiar to us in Israel? The need to maintain a population with one of the highest standards in a territory whose conditions are among the most rigorous—does this not simultaneously resemble both the history of Zionist settlement in the Land of Israel and the problems of the near future of the entire human race?

The problem of fitting tribes and communities from the lower levels of civilization and from societies lacking civilization all together into the fabric of social, political and cultural life accepted by the Western world—doesn't this remind us at the same time both of our own problems of immigrant absorption and of the problems of the newly emancipated African States, today, especially tomorrow, and for many years to come?

Take a more limited problem, that of water. Until a short time ago we thought that the water shortage problem was a unique Israeli curse, and that solve it we would, even if the cost were to be staggering. But it turned out to be a global problem. Any realistic glance at the future of the human race shows the water problem to be one of the chief obstacles to the continued survival of man on earth. If men do not learn to desalt the water of the oceans they may be able to drink from the Milky Way but not water from Earth.

Thus it seems that the return of the people of Israel to the Land of Israel is not only a return to the past but also a leap up the road into the future.

Of course we do not need this assurance from the Ultimate Purpose to give a basis to our aims here in this country. On the contrary. The more we solve our problems for our own sake the greater the interest in them for others. Israel is eligible to serve as a research center for the future precisely because that is not its aim. Its aim is to correct in the present the wrongs of the past. From this aspect Israel as a whole is like the people of Eilat, who on no account regard themselves as taking part in an experiment but rather as living and settled in their world.

The kibbutz, one of Israel's most important contributions to the future thinking of the human race, owes its entire life and strength to the fact that never once has it regarded itself as a social test tube, but rather as a complete world of human life deriving sustenance from its soil. We will detract nothing from its life-force if we say nevertheless that from the outside one can also observe it as an experiment, perhaps the most encouraging ever made, in bringing together the ideals of freedom on the one hand and equality on the other, fulfilling both without the one contradicting the other.

There were times when, like other undeveloped countries, we struggled with problems which the European nations had long since solved. We were reduced to despair because of a shortage of roads and buildings, meager equipment, low industrial output and the like. Today these have disappeared as primary problems not only for us but also for the other intent states. The problems which have already been solved in the countries of the West no longer cause despair in the undeveloped countries, because nowadays the solution can be brought to the area required in an extremely short time. In any one-day-old state you may find airfields, road building equipment and capital-investments building industry. The various European blocs compete with each other for the right to bestow on the newly emancipated countries the solutions they possess.

Of first rank importance today are the questions for which there is still no solution, either because it has not yet been found, or because such questions have never been asked in the West, or because they have not been asked at all, anywhere. Israel's special position among the states supplying guidance and advice to the undeveloped countries stems not from the inexhaustible supply of solutions at its disposal but rather from the fact that it is a pioneer in solving the historic encounter between the Southeastern problems and the Northwestern problems. The special virtue of Israel in this encounter lies in the fact that its Northwestern problem-solving capacity is not a gift from above, from an alien nation, but comes from within, from among its own people, from among exiles of the West who immigrated East.

The research center of the future called Israel has been and is carrying out an important experiment also in another field, the political field. A burning problem of the present which in my humble opinion will be the gravest, most important and most decisive problem of international politics at least until the end of our century—that of the encounter and dialogue between the world of classical Western culture and that of the cultures of Asia and Africa—this problem too is already being compounded and analyzed in the Israeli melting pot.

Competing with the European nations in achievements already attained by them is a superfluous effort that will bring us no results. Directing our efforts toward the problem, yet unsolved, in ways as yet untried—that is required of us for complete realization of the possibilities granted us with the creation of the State.

AFTER THE WAR—WIDER HORIZONS

The debate between those who call for a greater ("Complete") Land of Israel, including the areas it occupies at present, and those who propose exchanging part of it for some arrangement with the Arab states is daily becoming more and more abstract, more and more theoretical. On the other hand, what is becoming more real from day to day, more urgent and vital, heartening and difficult, is the problem of how to implement, how to give expression to the simple and undisputed fact that indeed this is it, that the State of Israel and the Land of Israel are congruent and identical in every respect in which it is possible for a state and country to be congruent.

The concept of the Complete Land of Israel is today a definition of a situation no less than the expression of the aspiration for historic justice, for a comprehensive conception of a desirable, proper and stable geopolitical arrangement. Without it one cannot have a sober view of reality, especially a new and revolutionary reality.

A new but by no means main ingredient of this reality is the hostility of the Arab states and their rulers toward the State of Israel. We may aspire to peace and must do everything for peace, but we would have to be either blind or suicidal not to introduce into any realistic appraisal of the situation the assumption, which is borne out more and more each day, that the plans and tendencies of the Arab rulers are now not less but more than ever before a *campaign of destruction and extirpation against the State of Israel*. As they did after their previous military defeats, the Arab rulers may again seek other ways and means of accomplishing this objective; they may circumvent an obstacle here and there, formulate one variation or another. Only mystics or dreamers can ignore this basic fact.

For the time being we have not seen attempts at circumvention and have heard no feeble variation at all. For the time being their rigid and standard demand is for us to relinquish our living and security space before they agree to discuss our very life and security.

It seems to me very reasonable and very realistic to assume that the present Arab rulers will persevere in this stand. The change in the Arab states, if and when it occurs, will be in the realm of internal rather than external policy. The real distress of the Arab states is internal, social, governmental, economic and cultural; the key, the fulcrum to any change, any progress, any displacement whatsoever in this area lies in the realm of this internal malaise. Therefore I believe we should be prepared for a long drawn out standstill in the Arab states' foreign relations, particularly in their relation toward us, as long as the great transformation does not take place within them that will create the conditions for a democratic regime, for rational consideration of the good of the masses, for the possibility of liberal, cultural, progressive decisions in other areas as well, including that of foreign relations.

This in my opinion is a realistic situation—appraisal of the kind upon which a nation bases its short and long range course.

There are other ingredients which are not less (and in the long run more) important to this genuine and tangible reality of a Complete Land of Israel. It is an open secret that our presence in the "Territories" is not military alone. Day-to-day facts of living have a tremendous strength of their own. Half a dozen acts of terrorism make the headlines but thousands of acts of building, growth and cooperation are swallowed up in the natural fabric of a country where all that was needed were slight repairs to the asphalt to rejoin roads and send traffic flowing over them East to West, North to South. The proper and natural geopolitical reality—no distortion of which in any period of history has been long-lived—is now materializing before our eyes. There is no scorched earth in the Land of Israel, nor is there any scorched earth policy on either side. In economics, in transportation, in health and in culture, no one loses in the Complete Land of Israel. The beginnings of Jewish settlement in the Golan Heights, Judea and Sinai do not impair the existing fabric of life but rather enhance it. Of course this is not an ideal reality. It is fraught with struggles, which may grow worse. It involves political, administrative and military problems. However, this is not only the best possible reality but the only possible reality.

Good Jews are frightened by the difficulties inherent in this reality, which are liable to increase with its development and implementation. These difficulties run the whole gamut of problems of the history of Jewish rebirth in the Land of Israel, from problems of conscience and humanitarianism at one end to those of foreign relations, economics, finance and international pressures at the other. It seems to me, however, that till now it has been insufficiently stressed that no retreat, no concession, whether territorial, political or otherwise, will exempt us from difficulty in the future. A return to the previous situation means a continuation of the previous situation, its perpetuation. Those who fear the rising and thickening wall of Arab hatred waiting to destroy us will not cause even the slightest crack in that wall by pulling back. Those who fear *political or economic pressure* on the part of the Great Powers must realize that the pressure will be applied tomorrow or the day after in the name and for the sake of a settlement which will be acceptable to no person of sound mind in this country. The semi-official formula of giving back substantial parts of the new territories "in exchange for peace and security" may be sincere and definitive but as we know it insists on keeping within Israel the

Golan Heights, United Jerusalem, considerable parts of the West Bank, the Gaza Strip and parts of Sinai. Tomorrow the entire Israeli nation will be fighting these very same external pressures because their intention will be to have us swallow a "settlement" compared to which the Israeli evacuationists' scheme is the height of imperialism. The maximalists among our friends (are there any?) take it as a foregone conclusion that what Israel stands to contribute to a "solution of the Middle East crisis" is a drastic evacuation of the conquered areas of the Six Day War (including Jerusalem) with the difference between the more pro-Israel and less pro-Israel approach revolving around the Arab contribution to that solution. These do demand more of the Arabs' "recognition" of Israel's existence, direct negotiations, cessation of the state of belligerence and so on; those who demand less—it is too ridiculous to mention. The great disaster, the political blunder inviting pressures is that while the Arab states announce and proclaim that they are prepared to contribute none of these things or even less, their stand being "unconditional withdrawal", official Israeli channels repeatedly declare in one way or another that the Israeli contribution is ready and waiting, lying in the international political bank for someone to come and redeem it, payable to the bearer on demand, with or without guarantors.

In this way it may be proved with regard to all the important problems that relinquishing the borders of victory will not exempt us from the difficulties and problems that will arise (and arise they will) if we hold onto these borders with all our might. But the truth is greater than that: retaining the borders of the Complete Land of Israel will, along with the tension of necessity to overcome difficulties and carry out projects, provide better and broader conditions, laden with more possibilities, to overcome difficulties and implement these projects. It will not be the first, but perhaps the tenth, hundredth or thousandth time in our history and the history of humanity as a whole that we will be both more *compelled* and also more *capable*.

One of the favorite pleas of those who harbor misgivings, those who would contribute a withdrawal for the sake of a settlement, has to do with the "demographic problem". They do not believe in a Complete Land of Israel because they do not believe in a complete people of Israel. To put it simply, they do not believe in aliya [Jewish immigration into Israel].

Here too it should be pointed out first of all that a return to the Israel of the pre Six Day War era will not exempt us from the full brunt of the problem of aliya. The decline in immigration (and the rise in emigration) have only begun to make themselves felt in the full fabric of our lives in the past few years. Let us not forget that aliya exists not merely as a device for solving the problem of demographic balance. It lies at the core of matters far more serious, more far-reaching and more critical than the number of Arab Knesset members. Heading the list is the problem of the stature, and the material, spiritual and military holding power of this nation over the generations. When we referred to the concentration of most of the Jewish people in the Land of Israel we were not amusing ourselves with formulas. Five or six million Jews in the

Land of Israel is still the number one object of the Jewish nation in this generation no matter what borders these millions occupy.

The Greater, Complete Land of Israel will make this aliya not only more necessary, but also more feasible. The necessity itself can either lie dormant in the nation's consciousness (as in the total decline of recent years) or it can be overt, manifest and stimulating even before being joined by new possibilities of implementation. What has happened in the settlement movement, now reawakening due to a combination of need and challenge, even without new sources of manpower, can also happen in aliya. First, the need for aliya has again become painfully real. In May 1967 we were still asking ourselves, "What shall we do if there's a sudden aliya?" Now we're saying, "What shall we do if there is no aliya?" The replacement of the first question by the second is in itself the beginning of aliya.

We have taken a second step in the right direction: we have learned and agreed that we must reorganize in order to cope with the aliya. The new, spacious borders, the shock of the defensive war that produced them and the exuberant joy of deliverance and victory accompanying them are providing us with the strength for this reorganization. On the one hand we are beginning to scrape rust off channels of action and absorption procedures which have deteriorated for want of activity and inspiration; on the other the store of willingness and readiness for sacrifice has been replenished at every level of the people.

The briefing for the main step has been provided by the Jewish nation in the Diaspora. Without preparatory activities, outside of the framework of the various Zionist organizations, the Jewish people have sent us thousands of *young* volunteers. One would have to be blind not to grasp this historic hint—a radical change of direction: from the institutions and their old men to the youth in its masses.

A short time before the May and June crisis, I went on a lecture tour of the United States where I addressed adult and university groups, in the course of which I met our emissaries (*shlihim*) there. In all our talks the recurring feeling was that the bankruptcy of our appeal to American youth stemmed from the fact that the entire cycle of concepts about Israel, Zionism, fundraising, aliya and so on were closely linked with the conformism of a cultivated family life, or satiated and smug petit bourgeoisie, of life in a rut requiring *no* commitments except being a "good boy", listening to Mummy and Daddy and filing away the business about Israel and Judaism in a drawer with the white "yonteff" napkins. The *other* appeal to Jewish youth is possible today thanks to the crisis, the victory and the great challenge entailed in implementing the country's integrity. When this country starts being a land of *opportunities,* a land of strong men confronting spectacular challenges, a land calling for all that is good, brave and noble in man, and no longer a soup kitchen for a handful of welfare cases needing alms—as it has been represented so often with such nagging tearfulness—maybe then it will be able to appeal to young people seeking to live their Jewishness and their humanity differently, willing to this end to join their people in doing the work, and willing to this end even to forgo the charms of American comfort.

This of course is only one area of the complex of aliya problems. Needed is more than a change of style in order to arouse the young Jewish generation of America. On the other hand, there are many more candidates for aliya in the world than there are in the U.S.A. We must appeal to the Jews of spiritual malaise, but at the same time we must not forget the hundreds of thousands of Jews dispersed in smaller communities throughout the world and subjected in some degree or other to material or political hardship. To all of them, in all their diversity of forms and conditions, individually or *en famille*, to the seekers of livelihood and security and to the seekers of spiritual adventure among them, we will be able to appeal differently, by appealing in the name of the Complete Land and its challenges.

III
Mosaic Theophany and Mosaic Secularism

NATHAN ROTENSTREICH
YISRAEL YESHAYAHU
SHULAMIT ALONI
ZURIEL ADMONIT
YITZHAK NISSIM

NATHAN ROTENSTREICH

Nathan Rotenstreich was born in Poland (Galicia) in 1914 and came to Palestine in 1932. He graduated from the Hebrew University where he later taught philosophy, attaining the rank of professor. In 1965 he held the office of University Rector. Among his books are *Between Past and Present, Jewish Thought in Modern Times, Spirit of Man, Philosophical Studies, The Recurring Pattern: Studies in Anti-Judaism in Modern Thought, The Basic Problems of the Philosophy of Marx, The People and the State*, etc. He is the recipient of many awards, including the Israel Prize for his translation into Hebrew of Kant's *The Critique of Pure Reason*.

Rotenstreich has been, despite his occupation with philosophy, a keen observer of the transient realities in Israel, and has a rather firm grip on his country's political pulse. A Ben-Gurion sympathizer, he did not hesitate to admonish Ben-Gurion for bringing up again and again in the 1960's the festering Lavon Affair (a "cloak and dagger" plot for which Rotenstreich felt that Lavon—1955 Defense Minister and heir-apparent to Ben-Gurion—was too severely blamed). In 1965 Rotenstreich organized Israeli intellectuals in support of Prime Minister Levi Eshkol whom Ben-Gurion also attacked.

In the article here cited, SECULARISM AND RELIGION IN ISRAEL, published in *Judaism*, Summer 1966, pp. 259-283, Rotenstreich schematizes the differences and the similarities between Rabbinic Judaism and what he calls "automatic secularism" and their implications for the State of Israel.

Secularism and Religion in Israel

by NATHAN ROTENSTREICH

ONE OF THE MOST urgent problems facing the State of Israel is: What part should religion play in the life of the society and the State? Closely related to this are such questions as: What should be the attitude of religious Jews towards non-religious Jews and (vice versa)? What is the nature of the relationship between the institutions of the state and those of organized religion? These questions are not only a matter of theoretical controversy—where the more ado, the better—but also of every-day, practical life; and on this level the debates tend to muddy rather than clarify the fundamental issues. This essay does not purport to furnish answers to these and related questions; rather, its primary purpose is to define the issues at stake.

THE HISTORICAL BACKGROUND

The religious groups had long had ambivalent feelings toward organized Zionism. In the early days of the movement, they were reluctant to adopt the ideal of modern Zionism and were even inclined to prefer Uganda [Kenya] as a Jewish homeland. Conscious of the religious aura of Palestine, and instinctively foreseeing that this would inevitably create religious conflicts, they sought to avoid an encounter with concrete reality and thus circumvent the problems which a return to Zion would raise. Partly because he took the religious groups into consideration, and partly under the influence of his particular background, Theodor Herzl deliberately excluded the so-called "cultural" questions from the Zionist program. For this he was severely criticized not only by the Russian Zionists, such as Ahad Ha'Am, but also by the Democratic Group which included Chaim Weizmann.

After the First World War, when responsibility for organizing the Jewish settlers in Palestine was shared by the Zionist Organization, the religious question arose again, but under a different guise: How to give structural expression to the part played by religious groups in the upbuilding of a Jewish homeland? The answer was threefold: (1) an autonomous religious sector, the Mizrachi, was included in the (secular) educational system of the Jewish settlement; (2) autonomous religious communities and institutions were set up by the Zionist Organization; and (3) the office of the Chief Rabbinate was, with minor alterations,* perpetuated by the British Mandatory government.

---

* Such as the appointment of two Chief Rabbis, a Sephardi and an Ashkenazi, instead of one, as had been the custom under Ottoman rule.

Although this particular pragmatic solution was challenged, the pragmatic principle itself was not. It prevailed under the Mandate; and it continued after the establishment of the State of Israel. While it left intact the actual threefold solution outlined above, the transition to statehood altered the pragmatic principle and approach in a way which eventually led to the present religious problems.

The pragmatic principle is cast in doubt by the very status of statehood, which carries with it, among other things, the authority of legislation. For legislative authority poses basic problems which do not lend themselves to pragmatic, *ad hoc* solutions—problems such as: What contents will the legislative authority of the state uphold? In matters such as, e.g., marriage, will the laws legislated by the state make Jewish rites binding upon every one, or will they leave room for other types of marriage laws? Or, to take another example, will the laws of the state establish a single judiciary system, sustained exclusively by state courts, or will they leave room for a parallel judiciary system sustained by rabbinical courts? Underlying these is the more fundamental question: From what source will all the judiciary systems in the state derive their authority? From the legislative arm of the state, or from another tribunal, such as the Halakhah? The urgency of this fundamental problem is witnessed, among other things, by the recourse which state courts have to precedents taken from the decisions of rabbinical courts. Nevertheless, no consideration has yet been given to the question of exclusive judiciary sovereignty. Perhaps when that question will be raised, other fundamental implications of the religious problem will also be brought to light.

In the meantime, *ad hoc* solutions based upon the pragmatic principle still prevail*—presumably because it is assumed that religious problems can be solved in no other way. They indicate that there are times when Israelis are capable of making pragmatism the test of pragmatism, so to speak, since in their case the test of a satisfactory solution is whether it works. When a pragmatic solution does not work, problems arise; and such problems cannot be solved by the pragmatic approach. Both religious and non-religious Jews approach the religious problem from a pragmatic point of view. But religious Jews, since they purport to walk by the Halakhah, not by practical considerations, have not mastered pragmatism.

AUTOMATIC SECULARISM

The religious problem arises against a pervasively secular background. Conspicuous by its absence from this background is the militant secularism of the eighteenth and nineteenth centuries. In the twentieth century there are no fighters for secularism, for the right to adopt a secular world-outlook, for the right to walk by that secular view in practice as well as in theory.

---

* This is true in spite of David Ben-Gurion's repeated declarations that Israel is a state of law, not of Halakhah—declarations which clearly are not based upon a pragmatic principle.

What is a secular world outlook? In the present discussion, the term will be used to denote two general views: (1) a moderate view that posits the existence of certain spheres—such as scientific research, hygiene, medicine, economics—over which religion exercises no legitimate control; and (2) a radical view which not only liberates certain spheres from religious control, but also challenges the validity of religious principles eithers as tests of truth or as rules of conduct. With the exception of Soviet secularism with which the present discussion does not propose to deal, there is no major trend toward militant secularism in the modern world. True, there are still individuals and groups that promote the cause of secularism; as a case in point one can cite the humanist circles in England and America. But the point is that there no longer exists a secular movement similar in nature and scope to, say, the Socialist movement or the civil rights movement. The question is: Why is a fighting secularism not a major force in the cultural climate of the West in general, and of Israel in particular? Four major reasons can be suggested in reply:

(1) The primary reason seems to be that the patterns of culture which prevail in our age are secular as a matter of course. Why fight for something that is given, something that exists objectively, even automatically? The factors which shape the image of our age cannot be traced to any historical religion. Today, our cosmic orientation, our understanding of the universe, our grasp of human reality, our notion of man's body and soul—all these are determined by the concepts and methodologies of science. Our astronomical, physical and biological world-picture is painted in colors taken from the palette of science. Here and there we may perceive faint traces of tints from other palettes; but the most vivid impression is made by science.

(2) Another reason why twentieth-century secularism is automatic, and consequently non-combatant, seems to lie in man's technological achievements. The advancement of technology plays a still more prominent role than the concepts of science in shaping the image of modern culture. With instruments made available by technology, man works miracles which he takes for granted: he flies, he intervenes in formations of living organisms, he explores the mysteries of the living cell. Machines produced by technology have altered the organization of man's labor; machines determine the length, the tempo, the schedule of man's work-day; machines even determine the motions made by the man who serves them. Surrounded by his tools, man must serve them that they may serve him; and in serving their maker, machines gain control not only over his physical and economic fate, but even over his contact with his fellow-men and with the events of his world.

(3) The secular origin of many modern movements and social trends constitutes still another reason for the predominance of secularism in the twentieth-century world. The trend toward raising man's standard of living, toward liberating entire nations, the movements which demand equal rights for individuals and for nations—these are all forces which were released when the yoke of tradition, including that of religious tradition, was thrown off. It might perhaps be objected that the regulative ideals by which these forces are

guided can be traced to those historical religions which stressed the dignity of mankind, the worth of individuals, the moral design of the universe, and so on. This objection can be met by observing that to introduce an ideal is one thing, and to transform an ideal into a force which shapes reality is quite another. The ideals may carry a religious birth-certificate; but the forces which transformed them into regulative principles of concrete action transcend the realm of religion. This being the case, religion must find a place for itself in a world shaped by forces over which it has no control.

(4) A less tangible, but no less important, factor shaping the secular image of our age is the generally accepted principle that man has a right to make his own decisions, to walk by his own conscience. This principle apparently originated in the idea of the individual's right to make decisions concerning the nature of political government. But in its broader connotation, it clearly implies the idea of man's right to decide upon his own opinions and beliefs. A religious Jew can claim that we are compelled to walk by the Halakhah. If we ask what compels us, he adduces the authority of his theology. But this theology flagrantly contradicts the principle that no belief has the authority to force itself upon us, because the test of all beliefs and opinions is the decision of man. A man's opinions and beliefs are voluntarily adopted, trimmed and abandoned. Today the burden of proof is upon the believer. Today a non-religious Jew is not obliged to justify the principle on which he bases his opposition to Halakhah-theology; the principle permeates our daily lives to such an extent that walking by it is almost a reflex reaction and does not need reflection. If anyone must reflect and engage in inner conflicts, it is the proponent, not the opponent, of Halakhah-theology. Life today being automatically secular, the only view which calls for justification is that of walking by the Halakhah. This does not imply any logical or theoretical necessity that secularism be automatic. Automatic secularism is a fact, and this fact by itself prevents any attempt to frame an automatic argument in defense of Halakhah-theology. Halakhah-theology must be deliberately adoped and deliberately defended. Whether its proponents can meet this demand remains to be seen.

The foregoing considerations do not purport to have exhausted the factors responsible for the automatic and non-combatant character of twentieth-century secularism. Their purpose was to select the facts which seem most pertinent to an understanding of the religious unrest we are about to examine. The clock cannot be turned backward; the forces at work cannot be arrested. At best, they can be controlled and harnessed to new ends. So inescapable is their impact that even the realm of religion has not remained intact. Thus, for example, one argument which is occasionally put forward in defense of piety maintains that the reward of piety is spiritual tranquillity. But how is spiritual tranquillity represented by this argument? Whereas once it was represented as a gift of God's grace, today it is represented as a product of the believer's confidence in God. Whereas once tranquillity was the effect of faith, today faith is a means of attaining tranquillity. This is only one example of the inroads which secularism has made into the realm of religion.

The repercussions of automatic secularism are not confined to the realm of religion. Secularism itself has been transformed by its own triumph. There is an immediate relation between the non-combatant character of secularism and its automatic operativeness in our daily lives. Non-militant mainly because it has neither slogan nor ideology, wrought into the texture of our daily lives, secularism today is so well understood that it is practically self-evident. The layman who does not understand nuclear physics can perceive the impact of atomic power. Facts, being self-evident, call for no proof.

Secularism is taken for granted, even as the secular image of the modern world is taken for granted. The grave problem which is posed for secularism by its own givenness is one which cannot be solved by appealing to some factor that transcends the secular world. At most, it can be argued that the secular world is not all-embracing, that it must find its complement in a realm which lies beyond it. It, however, is not all-embracing either, but a partial realm. At any rate, it is when secularism becomes automatic that the problem of a secular ideology arises. To become an existing fact is to leave the realm of ideals, the realm of what ought to be but is not bound to be.

THE LIMITED BATTLEFIELD

The fact that secularism exists automatically does not imply that its triumph is complete. Its defeats, no less than its victories, contributed to its non-combatant character. To become practically second nature, secularism had to pay the price of self-limitation. The primary limitation of secularism lies in its failure to furnish a global, all-embracing world-outlook which would not fall short of the religious world-picture in breadth, depth, and insight. Another lies in its failure to furnish regulative principles of conduct which would be no less binding than the commandments of religion. Secularism is neither a gospel nor a system of norms, but a cluster of reflex responses, a conditioned pattern of conduct. We do not subscribe, or fail to subscribe, to the march of technology; we have no choice but to be swept along. We do not even decide whether or not to make decisions; political institutions and electoral procedures have predetermined our decision. Thus, in the very triumph of secularism lies its weakness. And this fortifies the position of religion. For today religion is not a matter of course, but a matter for decision. In itself the theology of the Halakhah does not appeal to the judgment of its proponent, but rather purports to impose itself upon him. But its struggle for survival in a secular world calls for decision, at least as a point of departure.

Still another self-limitation with which secularism pays for its conquests is the confinement of its goals within man's immediate reach. Thus, for example, whereas in the eighteenth and nineteenth centuries the password was human perfectibility, the password today is technological improvement. It is difficult to correlate the goal of technological advancement with the ideal of human progress as conceived by its apostles, Condorcet, Comte or even Marx. It is doubtful whether secularism still constitutes a philosophy of history after it has become an historical force. Once upon a time secularism promised us a passport to a heavenly kingdom on earth; today it offers us earthly rewards only. Once it promised to save man by bridging the gulf between the historical and cosmic orders; today it improves man's condition, offering him more leisure, better health and a longer life. The prominent feature of Marx's teaching lies in the link it forges between the alienated, tension-torn state of society and the laws of history. This link has been severed. We try to improve man's state without pretending that our endeavor pertains to the very essence of history. Bolshevism, *par excellence* a secular ideology, has reached a crisis as a result of severing this link. Secularism having confined man's horizon within his reach, man no longer aspires to transcend that horizon.

The price secularism pays for its victory can be characterized by drawing a distinction between its former status as a *normative* ideology, and its present status as an *operative* ideology. As the constituents of an operative ideology, the contents of secularism no longer inspire the militant spirit which they evoked in our grandfathers and even in our fathers. Secure as a fact, secularism is no longer secure as a value. Religion, by contrast, has gained normative security and lost its operative security. This is another reason why religion is aggressive, whereas secularism is not. As modern psychologists observe, insecurity is the mother of aggression. And the gulf between their normative confidence and their practical insecurity furnishes believers with a strong incentive for aggressiveness. Non-believers, on the other hand, have no such gulf to bridge, and hence no need to be belligerent. Non-believers become belligerent only when they raise to the rank of a normative factor the actual force of technology. The aggressiveness of Bolshevism is a case in point. But recent developments in the Eastern bloc indicate that an increase in the power of technology is attended by a decrease in the appeal of the norm with which it is correlated.

The foregoing remarks should not be understood simply as variations on the theme of "the God that failed." The failure of ideals is due to their deification. The ideals which operate as regulative principles and norms have not failed. Liberty and equality remain valid ideals. Also valid is the Socialist aim of finding social and economic expression for the ideals of liberty and equality in terms of the independence of man from man, or in terms of the non-subordination of man to man. Socialism has failed its ideals, not the other way around, by elevating to their normative status the men who were made responsible for their realization. Men are not ideals. Socialism failed the moment it was raised from the rank of a human ideal to the rank of an almighty judge that could not be questioned without blasphemy. The deified ideal failed the moment a man who dared to question it could be asked, "Where wast thou when I laid the foundations of the earth?" The theodicy we framed for our God spelled His failure. Responsibility for that theodicy rests not with Him but with us, and with the men whose mission was to realize His kingdom on earth, the men who arrogated the right to frame a theodicy. The failure of God is the failure of men to perceive the necessary limitation and partiality of any human answer, their failure to foresee that every realization of an ideal raises new questions for which new answers must be perpetually found. This can be illustrated by the failure of collective economy to do away with specialization, as Marx predicted it would.

The lesson to be learned from the failure of deified ideals is not disillusionment. The conclusion indicated is not that there can be no secular ideology, but that there must be an endless, perpetual examination and reinterpretation of ideals and their practical embodiments. This applies to religious ideology as well, even though a pious person would probably be inclined to disagree. For what is the Halakhah if not a human interpretation of the Word of God? Only in the absence of criticism can the identification of man's interpretation with God's Word hold its ground. Man being a criticizing creature, the identification inevitably collapses. The deification of the Halakhah spelled its petrification. Only by acknowledging that it is merely a human interpretation, no matter how sanctified by the reverence of former generations, can the Halakhah be regenerated. Such an acknowledgement would detract nothing from the Halakhah since its relation to the Word of God pertains to its inner logic. But the implicit distinction between the absolute Word of God and the relative interpretation of man would be rendered explicit. If anything detracts from the authority of the Halakhah, it is precisely the refusal of its votaries to recognize the limits circumscribed by the relative status which it occupies as an interpretation. By representing the subsistence of the Halakhah as contingent upon its transcendence of those limits, Halakhah Judaism becomes as objectionable as fundamentalism. Even as fundamentalists walk exclusively by the letter of the Law, so Halakhah Judaism walks by the letter of Rabbinical interpretations of the Law.

THE CRUX OF THE CONTROVERSY

In Israel, the demand for civil marriage constitutes the only crux of the controversy between religious and non-religious Jews that has aroused widespread public interest. The general interest in this particular issue is due to its bearing upon the immediate concerns of almost everyone, and to its encroachment upon the private sphere of individual integrity. Modern man has been educated by his cultural environment to regard authenticity or sincerity as a cardinal virtue, and hypocrisy or duplicity as a cardinal vice. Measured by the standard of sincerity, a marriage contract sanctioned by an authority which the couple does not respect cannot be acknowledged without compromising one's principles, without practicing some measure of duplicity. How can a marriage contract be represented as authentic when the couple is forced to choose either the frying pan of no social sanction for their bond, or the fire of religious sanction? By leaving people no alternative in this matter, the monopoly of the rabbinate inevitably arouses strong resistance.

The monopoly of the rabbinate creates grave problems not only for non-religious Jews, but also for religious Jews whose interpretation of Judaism differs from that of the rabbinate. By preventing pious Jews from walking by their own lights, the rabbinate undermines the foundations of its own position. For its refusal to recognize any other interpretation but its own could have no other reason than its own interests. One cannot help wondering why less narrow-minded but no less pious Jews do not challenge the policy of the rabbinate. Can it be that they are reluctant to divorce the interpretation from the Word of God?

But whatever the reasons, the fact remains that unlike the marriage question, the problem of rabbinic monopoly in other areas has not aroused widespread public controversy. At present, civil marriage remains the only front on which a major controversy is raging between non-religious Jews and religious Jews.*

What is entailed by the demand of non-religious Jews that religious institutions and state be separated in the sphere circumscribed by the personal concerns of the individual? The demand does not entail state legislation in matters encompassed by this sphere—the state has already made laws pertaining to the personal status of the individual. It does entail that the rabbinate be shorn of the exclusive jurisidiction delegated to it by the state in matters encompassed by the laws of the state; that the state set up state tribunals, provide direct state sanctions, and limit the authority of rabbinical institutions in this sphere.

It is not by the Law of the Halakhah, but by the state, that the authority of rabbinical institutions is sanctioned. Hence Orthodox Judaism must acknowledge—willingly or unwillingly—the supreme authority of the state as a sovereign organ of legislation. Nor is Orthodox Judaism fastidious as to where it gets its power, so long as no substantive conflicts arise between its own institutions and those of the state. It becomes fastidious only when, for example, the Supreme Court hands down a decision which interferes, as it were, in the procedures of the rabbinical courts, or in the activities of the Chief Rabbinate. Thus the theoretical subordination of religious institution to state does not preclude the actual monopolization by these institutions of matters covered by state legislation. The religious institutions are formally divorced from, but substantively wedded to, the state. What people are asking for, then, is substantive separation.

Both the content and the underlying principle of the demand for civil marriage are secular: content, because what is demanded is the substantive manifestation of the sovereignty of the civil-political authorities; secular,

---

* Minor battles are being waged on other fronts of the individual's private domain. Thus the laws which enforce religious dietary laws and religious laws concerning observance of the Sabbath (e.g., prohibition of public and private transportation), have also met with opposition. But the reaction is less violent, because, unlike the rabbinic monopoly over marriage, such laws do not drive a man to renunciation of his integrity by imposing upon him and his loved one an authority which they do not respect. Thus, for example, it was not without a public uproar that the luxury liner *Shalom* was prevented from catering to the tastes of all its passengers by providing two cuisines, one kosher, the other non-kosher. But looking back on the affair from a distance, the issue at stake seems to be of a different order than the civil-marriage issue.

because it upholds the right of man to decide which authority will sanction his marriage bond, and because it undermines the monopoly of rabbinical authority. This principle has far-reaching implications by virtue of its connection with other norms which form the value-framework of secularism, but the content of the demand is moderate, since it does not entail a thoroughgoing denial of religious-rabbinical authority, but merely denies its exclusiveness, i.e., its right to force itself upon everyone. Religious Jews do not regard this as moderate, but to an objective observer the moderation of such a demand is evident.

Underlying the demand for civil marriage is a more general secular claim, which has yet to be stated explicitly: namely, let it be acknowledged by religious Jews that non-religious Jews who submit to the monopoly of rabbinical authority have made a fundamental concession or renunciation. This tacit claim is based upon the valid assumption that even the most pious, Orthodox Jew can reconcile his piety with an acknowledgement of the right of a non-religious Jew to stand upon his own principle. Non-religious Jews are not profligate libertines; they are men of principle who want to walk by their principles. Unfortunately, many religious Jews regard the universal imposition of rabbinical authority as self-evident, and consequently cannot appreciate the concession made by non-religious Jews. If a non-religious Jew submits to rabbinical authority, this in itself does not imply that the authority has been imposed upon him by right. It means that the man thus imposed upon has renounced his right of decision in this particular matter. And his renunciation is itself a manifestation of decision and choice. Religious Jews must admit that their opponent's readiness not to walk by his principles is a form of decision. The imposition of authority is bad enough in itself; why make matters worse by interpreting imposition as abolition of the right to stand upon another principle? Why not recognize that submission to imposition involves renunciation? Why not respect that renunciation?

The answer which religious Jews often offer is that concern for the unity of the Jewish people renders imperative the exclusive authority of the rabbinate. In Israel and in the Diaspora—so their answer runs—the Jewish people is one; which means that it walks by one set of principles only. To the extent that a religious ceremony evidently precludes the possibility of mixed marriage, there may be some justification for objecting to civil marriage, on the grounds that it will either destroy the unity of the Jewish people or encourage assimilation. But the validity of the argument from unity is limited, for the following reasons:

(1) There is practically no danger of falling away from the Jewish people in Israel. The society is Jewish in its majority—so that any "falling away" is into a Jewish society.

(2) Civil marriage would not increase the threat of mixed marriage in Israel. A glance at the situation in European countries where there are Jewish communities, indicates that it is not the availability of civil marriage, but cultural intercourse with the non-Jewish environment that encourages intermarriage.

Civil marriage is the effect, not the cause, of social intercourse and intermarriage between Jews and Gentiles.

(3) Finally, religious marriage—as interpreted by the rabbinate—tends to undermine rather than to uphold the unity of the Jewish people. For by "Jewish" marriage the rabbinate does not a mean a marriage in keeping with the customs of any pattern of the various Jewish communities; it means marriage sanctioned by the authority of the rabbinate in Israel. This wholly unwarranted identification of Judaism with the rabbinate in Israel gives the rabbinate the right to decide whether or not men who have decided to lead religious Jewish lives may indeed be regarded as authentic Jews. This privilege, which the rabbinate arrogates, represents no less, if not more, of a threat to Jewish unity than civil marriage. It is an absurdity not to be tolerated, that the existence of the State of Israel can make it possible for certain Jews to question the Jewishness of other Jews. Religious Jews should be the last to tolerate this absurdity, since it is they who insist that the mere fact of having been born a Jew makes a man Jewish.

The rabbinate has arrogated exclusive jurisdiction not only in Israel but even in the Diaspora. By respecting this privilege of the rabbinate, the State of Israel frustrates its own design of ingathering the exiles. Instead of throwing open its gates to all Jews, Israel has permitted the rabbinate to shut out Jews who cannot be certain that their Jewishness will be recognized. Thus the Jewish homeland not only tolerates anti-Jewish intolerance within its domain, but even encourages Jews to wonder whether they have a right to come home. Responsibility for such subversion of Jewish unity rests with religious Jews, not with secular Jews. For thus far those whose Jewishness has been cast in doubt by the rabbis have been Jews who sincerely desire to lead a religious life, but who sincerely refuse to regulate their Jewish life by the Halakhah. Also subversive of Jewish unity are the threats we occasionally hear, to the effect that the children of Jews who did not marry according to the rabbinate's interpretation of Jewish marriage will not be permitted to marry the children of Jews who did so marry. The resulting possibility of intermarriage between Jew and Jew is an inconceivable absurdity, even if—as certain authorities claim—it is in keeping with the letter of the Halakhah. Non-religious Jews are advised to renounce their principle not in order to express their consideration for the principle of their adversary, but in order to protect their descendants against the possibility of eviction from the Jewish fold. Subscription to the Halakhah becomes an insurance policy which secures for a man's descendants a place in the fold. Such extortion inevitably provokes resistance.

Renunciation, not coercion, is the only plausible argument a religious Jew can use to persuade non-religious Jews not to stand upon their principles. It can be argued that a principle is not necessarily injured in being renounced. It can also be argued that consideration for one's fellow man, as expressed in renunciation, is also a principle, albeit one which clashes with the principle of man's right to make free and sincere decisions, to walk by his conscience. Nor does renunciation necessarily entail violation of one's principles. Even as a republican can pay lip service to the symbols of monarchy which have no concrete bearing upon his every-day life, so a non-religious Jew can pay lip service to the religious wedding ceremony which means nothing to him but so much to his adversary.

This, however, does not mitigate the measure of renunciation involved in showing consideration: non-religious Jews would probably prefer to seal their bond with symbols of their own choosing, more consonant with their general view of life. Nevertheless, renunciation is possible. It is even inevitable, despite the irrefutable argument in favor of civil marriage. But it must be respected and openly acknowledged as such by Jews who have not renounced. Renunciation must secure the abolition of the rabbinate's privilege of examining, questioning, and denying the Jewishness of Jews who do not accept the rabbinate's interpretation of Judaism. Renunciation must guarantee that submission will not be extorted with threats. Only our own decision will make us renounce; threats will not avail. Threats can only provoke rebellion, and can only convince us that all we can expect is belligerence; that our renunciation will not be respected. We expect no more, but no less, than respect in turn for our renunciation.

THE VITALITY OF JUDAISM

Religion is not moribund because God has *not* died. Nietzche missed the mark when he proclaimed the death of God. His shafts misfired for many reasons, but for our immediate purpose it suffices to note that he celebrated the death of God as saving mankind by relieving men of responsibility toward God. But without responsibility, salvation cannot be accomplished; on the contrary, mankind is thus condemned to damnation. Because man is a criticizing creature, he is also a responsible creature, and—in this sense—potentially a religious creature. Religion will live so long as man asks: To whom am I responsible? For whom, or for what, am I responsible? Religion furnishes one possible answer to these questions. That possible answer is perhaps the easiest of all to adopt, because it makes man responsible to a superhuman Judge. The existence of other possible answers may render problematic and questionable the validity of the religious answer. But because man will inevitably face the question of responsibility, the religious answer will inevitably be offered. This applies to Judaism in particular, for Judaism represents man as essentially a responsible creature, that is, as a creature capable of understanding and obeying commandments. The stress it lays upon the responsibility of man is not only the metaphysical root of Judaism, but also the source of its unfailing vitality.

The social orientation of Judaism is another factor that is frequently held to be the source of its vitality. But this factor seems to be a two-edged sword, which undermines the normative status of religion even while fortifying its actual position. In practice, the normative system of Judaism is supported by the role it plays as a force in Jewish society. But in theory, religion should be a force by virtue of being a norm, not a norm by virtue of being a force. In

Judaism, the transition from a normative status to an operative one is facilitated by the central religious role played by society. Yet any human factor, *qua* human, occupies an operative position. And religion—for all its orientation to nonhuman or super-human contents—remains a human force. As a human force, religion carries within itself various means of coercion, such as excommunication or the Index of banned books, in the case of Catholicism, or the refusal to sanction a marriage contract, in the case of Judaism. For these and similar means of coercion religion does not depend upon the state; the very system of religion makes them available. But under the circumstances prevailing in Israel, the ultimate authorization of religious coercion comes from the legislative arm of the state, not from the internal system of Judaism. Here, then, the imminent coerciveness of the religious system is concealed and sustained by the coerciveness of the state.

In all fairness, it should be observed that this marriage of religion and state is not entirely coincidental, nor entirely a matter of political expediency. Because it is oriented to society, and because Israel is the physical concentration and symbolic crystallization of Jewish society, Judaism must face the problem of adapting its role as a society-oriented religion to the reality of a public which is organized politically in a system endowed with sovereign authority.

Religious Jews have solved this problem by demanding state support and protection for the sovereignty of religion. Even as the moral prohibition against stealing is enforced by legal penalties which the state imposes, so the commandments of religion can be enforced by means which the state makes available. The solution sounds simple, but the price of simplicity seems to be an admission that the demands of religion must be sustained by profane sanctions. Morality does not pay so high a price for political protection, because the moral demand and the political sanctions are both human. But the demands of religion are presumably imposed by a super-human or non-human source. Even granting the argument of religious Jews, that the State of Israel occupies a religious status by its very essence, it will still be objected that this religious status cannot cancel the gap between the authority of God and the authority of human lawmakers. Men make laws by making decisions, not by listening to the voice of God. No matter how ideal its composition, the Knesset must make decisions, not listen to the voice of God.

The shift from a normative to an operative status, implicit in the orientation of Judaism toward society, finds explicit expression in the political manoeuvers of the religious parties, which, like all other political parties, constitute a social force that shapes the political system. Even were the members of religious parties, as individuals, to walk only by the Word of God, as participants in the game of politics, they would still have to follow the profane rules of the game. Therefore, truly pious Jews should oppose the use of profane power to impose religious norms. They should be the first to insist that persuasion, not coercion, be the only means of disseminating religious truths. Yet pious Jews do not oppose the marriage of religious institutions and state. Perhaps they are deterred by the tendency to translate into political moulds the social orientation of Judaism. Or perhaps they have unconsciously accepted the logic of secularism, in spite of its incompatibility with religious assumptions. Or perhaps they are afraid that the unaided Word of God lacks adequate persuasive power; perhaps they feel the need to back up the Word of God with the arm of political power, in spite of the wide gap between the divine command and the human sanction. Ironically enough, in using coercion to impose their principles upon their opponents, religious Jews renounce more than non-religious Jews do, in submitting to coercion. As we have seen, non-religious Jews do not necessarily compromise their principle by paying lip service to symbols which their opponents hold sacred. They agree to respect those symbols as an expression of one human view among others. But religious Jews do compromise their principle when they renounce its persuasive radiance in favor of the coercive power of the state. By so doing, religious Jews inadvertently acknowledge that the realm of religious norms is not the only one; that beyond it there lies a realm of power and coercion.

It does the religious community in Israel no credit that no religious movement has recognized the state without seeking to use its coercive power in carrying out the designs of religion. Nor is it to the credit of the religious community in Israel that no religious Jews have joined the campaign against so-called religious coercion. The time has come for religious Jews to wonder. Why is there no nonconformity in the religious camp? Why does the religious community lack the courage of fresh religious reflection?

INTELLECTUAL ISOLATION

In 1904, Solomon Schiller wrote a short article on the relation between Zionism and religion. Schiller observed, among other things, that the development of Orthodox Judaism is governed by the law of inertia. Today, the absence of fresh religious reflection is perhaps the clearest sign that the law of inertia still prevails. In the present context, the terms "religious reflection" and "religious thought" will be used to denote a system of religious principles supported by rational arguments and correlated with specific, concrete, current issues and problems. Jewish thought in this sense has always been characterized by isolationism. Only for polemical purposes has it ever given consideration to matters which have no immediate bearing upon Judaism. Throughout history, the primary concern of Jewish thought has been self-interpretation—interpretation of the heritage of Judaism, interpretation of the relation between Judaism and other religious or philosophical world-outlooks and traditions. In this self-interpretation, Jewish thought was preoccupied almost exclusively with systems of ideas. Hardly any note was taken of living patterns of culture, living problems, concrete circumstances. The image of the modern world, however, is shaped by ideas incarnated in living patterns of culture; by ideas in action, by ideas which play a regulative role in every-day life. This aspect of the modern world has yet to be confronted by modern Jewish thought. To meet the challenge of Christian thought, and to establish Judaism upon a solid theoretical foundation, Jewish thinkers have been forced to deal with the world of non-Jewish ideas. But have they faced the challenge of technology, of science, of social, economic and political development?

When Jewish thinkers make major contributions to our conception of science and its assumptions, they usually are concerned with general problems of philosophy, rather than with specifically Jewish questions. As a striking illustration, one can cite the work of Hermann Cohen. As a philosopher, Cohen analyzed the assumptions of science and of cultural creation in general. As a Jewish philosopher, he rarely dealt either with science or with cultural creativity except for purposes of pointing out the limits of ethics proper. Nowhere did he deal with the impact on Judaism of concrete developments in the modern life of society and the state.

In this respect, Christianity has a decided advantage. Modern developments in the natural and social sciences, in psychology, in technology have all occurred within its realm; hence it was compelled to cope with them, to resist their advance, or to accommodate to them. By turning their back upon all these modern developments, Jewish thinkers fortify the walls of their spiritual self-enclosure and maintain their integrity through isolation rather than through integration. An attempt to integrate the modern secular world into the sacred world of Judaism was made by Rav Abraham Kook. But, like his predecessors, Rav Kook failed to work out the technological, social, political details of the integration.

Jewish thought has not even been refreshed by the comprehensive reality of the State of Israel. Integrity is still maintained through isolationism. The perpetual isolation of Jewish thought seems to be the effect of two causes:

(1) One cause is the prestige of the Halakhah as the crystallized expression of Judaism and as a code of law. Thus far, every Jewish theology has been a Halakhah-theology. Not even the mystical trends in Judaism, as Gershom Scholem demonstrates, managed to break through the limits circumscribed by the Halakhah. As a code of law, the Halakhah crystallizes prevailing conventions and concepts. No innovation can be introduced into the Halakhah without the authority of the Halakhah. Yet only a view which transcends the Halakhah can constitute a foundation for suggested innovation. The Halakhah cannot be the source of such a view, for views, of their very essence, are fluid and uncrystallized; whereas the Halakhah, of its very essence—regarded from the viewpoint of its content—is a fixed crystallization of settled matters.

There have been only a handful of Jewish thinkers, like Maimonides, who were both philosophers and Halakhah authorities; but they flourished long ago. Today, Jewish thought seems to be paralyzed by the long time-span between current questions and past solutions resulting from the occasional meeting, in individual Jewish thinkers of philosophy and the Halakhah. Today, thinkers mistakenly assume that it is the pastness of their predecessors which authorizes the innovations which they introduced. Individuals, like Isaiah Leibowitz, who criticize current interpretation of the Halakhah in Israel, generally base their criticism upon the Halakhah itself, rather than upon a more comprehensive view which transcends it. If, accordingly, the Halakhah is the realm in which Jewish thought is confined, how can the Halakhah itself make available to its inhabitants the means of breaking through its walls?

(2) The isolationism and inertia of religious Judaism is also the effect of the prominent part played by Jewish immigrants from Eastern Europe, and the negligible part played by those from Western Europe and from the Orient, in shaping religious life in Israel. Eastern Jewry has ignored the theoretical and practical reforms which Western Jewry in general, and American Jewry in particular, have introduced into Jewish thought and ritual. In Israel, German and Oriental Jews made no effort to impose upon the immigrants from the East their patterns of religious life. American Jews were still more reluctant to exert pressure upon religious groups in Israel. Thus the immigrants from Eastern Europe were not forced to face the fact that theirs is not the only possible interpretation of Judaism. We have already noted that every religious Jew, regardless of his particular interpretation of what being a religious Jew means, has a right to walk by his own lights. But the fact remains that there is a tendency to identify religious Judaism with Orthodox Judaism. This tendency is so strong that it is usually shared even by non-religious Jews. Thus the pressure of the Orthodox sector, coupled with the passivity of all other sectors—in Israel and in the Diaspora—consciously or unconsciously fortifies the trend toward spiritual isolation of Orthodox Judaism.

Orthodox Jewish thought has yet to face the problem posed by what S. H. Bergman describes as non-Orthodox piety. The stubborn isolationism of Orthodox Jews, who are unable or unwilling to cope with this problem, finds reflection in their refusal to admit its existence. There is no problem of non-Orthodox piety, they protest, because absence of Orthodox is profanity and plagiarism, not piety. Better an atheist than a non-Orthodox Jew! Where non-Orthodox Jews so stand upon their rights as men and as Jews, Orthodox Jewry would be compelled to cope with, and to recognize, the semi-secular principle of man's right to interpret his own faith by his own lights.

Another problem which has yet to be faced not only by Orthodox Jewry, but by all currents of religious Judaism, is the problem posed by non-religious Jews who wish to create a secular Jewish culture. The solution which Orthodox Jewry proposes to this problem consists in what might be called an objective definition of a Jew: he is a Jew who was born a Jew. This definition implies that a Jew has no choice but to be a Jew; willy-nilly, he must remain in the fold. The objective situation of the Jew, so the Orthodox solution runs, carries with it the objective obligation of submitting to the Halakhah—which, of course, has objective authority. Although this solution might perhaps make sense from the point of view of Jews who subscribe to such threefold objectivity, it makes no sense from the point of view of religious Jews who reject the objective approach to begin with.

Furthermore, not even the objectivistic interpretation of Judaism is entitled to ignore the nature of man. It, too, must take into consideration the fact that man is a creature endowed with consciousness and self-consciousness. For even the Jew who is, presumably, inextricably entangled in an objective network does not for that reason cease to be a self-conscious subject. Hence it is incumbent upon Orthodox Jewry to recognize the individual consciousness of the concrete Jewish individual, without assuming *a priori* the existence of a pre-established harmony between his individual consciousness and the objective meaning which the Halakhah assigns to the fact that he is a Jew. The old alternative—either a Jew according to the Halakhah definition or not a Jew at all—is an alternative which cannot bear the brunt of criticism, and which cannot be used to solve the real problem of non-religious Judaism, for the simple reason that it does not recognize the existence of the problem. The problems posed by modern Jewish reality cannot even be clarified, let alone solved, in terms of the assumption that if a man's will does not coincide with the objective fact that he is a Jew, then the will and the consciousness of that man do not count. It is begging the question to insist upon the self-evident advantage which an objective situation and an objective obligation allegedly have over a man's subjective consciousness and desire. The old line of reasoning followed by religious Jewry has not been taken seriously by non-religious Jews who either ignore the problem and do as they please, or else take refuge from the need to create new patterns of Jewish culture by making use of the old customs, holidays, and so on which they find conveniently at hand. In the latter case, a tendency to regard as comfortable the given moulds of Jewish life prompts even non-religious Jews to sustain certain facets of objectivistic Judaism.

The failure of religious Judaism to give this question serious consideration, and the consequences of that failure, can be illustrated by the recent affair of Brother Daniel.* It will be recalled that Brother Daniel, a Polish Jew who had converted to Christianity, claimed that he had the right, as a born Jew, to benefit from the law which grants every Jew automatic Israeli citizenship. According to him, he had this right, even though he refused to abandon Christianity. From the objectivistic point of view of the Halakhah, Brother Daniel represented a perplexing borderline case: it was not clear whether or not he remained a Jew in spite of his conversion to Christianity; nor, consequently, was it clear whether he could with justice be deprived of his right as a Jew to Israeli citizenship. On the basis of objectivistic considerations, a distinction was drawn between the duties which Brother Daniel had as a Jew, and the rights which he did not have as a convert to Christianity. Among the rights Brother Daniel did not have was the privilege of a deed to the land of his forefathers. No such hairsplitting distinction was called for from the subjective viewpoint of non-religious Jewry. The national consciousness of non-religious Jews made it perfectly clear that a man cannot be a Christian and at the same time be regarded as a Jew. What seemed equivocal from the objectivistic standpoint of Halakhah reasoning was not in the least equivocal to the subjectivistic consensus of secular Jews. In this case, then, non-Orthodox Jews guarded

---

* [For a fuller discussion of the Brother Daniel case, see *"Brother Daniel and the Jewish Fraternity,"* by Aharon Lichtenstein, JUDAISM, Summer 1963.—Ed.]

the walls of Judaism more effectively than the Orthodox defenders of the faith. Perhaps Orthodox Jews should admit that here, at least, their objectivistic argument has reached its limit. Perhaps Orthodox Jews should acknowledge that, like any other argument, objectivism is protected by its limit from falling into an abyss of absurd extremism.

JEWISH ECCLESIASTICAL THEORY?

A tendency towards conservatism characterizes the Halakhah by virtue of its very nature as a code of law. In the Halakhah, conservatism and crystallization go hand in hand. But from the viewpoint of a layman, who has not been initiated into the mysteries of its intricate detail, the Halakhah does not appear to be predestined to remain a fossil. If anything, development, growth, evolution would seem to be the law of its nature, since its reason for being is not to codify laws, but to interpret sources—and to interpret is to enlarge. The exegetical procedures employed in the Halakhah always take the interpreter, not the interpreted source, as their starting point. Thus a tension between text and interpretation is the very life of the Halakhah. The fact that this tension is not always sustained is not a necessary consequence of the task and method of the Halakhah; it is, rather, a projection of a particular approach adopted by the proponents of the Halakhah. The fossilization of the Halakhah, in other words, is the fault of its proponents, who project their own image onto it.

One reason for this projection lies in the progressive codification of the Halakhah; for to codify is to embalm, to seal, to arrest. But codification is neither essential to the nature of the Halakhah, nor is it the work of impersonal institutions. The Halakhah was codified, for purposes of convenience, by a number of individuals, by Maimonides, Rabbi Joseph Karo, by Rabbi Moses Isserles. On the other hand, it seems clear that once an exegetical system has been codified, it has less chance of growing than one which has not been codified. For various reasons, religious Jews are evidently reluctant to lay down the law concerning matters which are in a constant state of flux. Hence their aversion to reform; hence also their approval of, and quest for institutional crystallization. Slowly but surely, rabbinical institutions and a rabbinical hierarchy are being solidified into a structure almost as imposing as that of the Catholic Church. For the first time in its history, Judaism is adopting—as it were, inadvertently—a kind of ecclesiology hitherto found only in Catholicism.

About the middle of the fifth century, Dionysus Areopagite gave philosophical expression to the assumption upon which the organized structure of the Church is based. Positing (with Plato and the neo-Platonists) the existence of a cosmic hierarchy, ranging from God to man, Dionysus maintained that this objective structure of the cosmic order finds, or ought to find, reflection in the structure of the Church. Thus the structure of the Church was assigned cosmic-theological value. The deeper implications of the analogy between Church and cosmos were later elaborated by Christian philosophers. It was maintained that the Church constitutes the concrete point of convergence between the visible and invisible worlds, between the material and the spiritual, the historical and the eternal. Still more pertinent for our purposes is the second pillar which supports the sacred status of the Church, namely, the notion that the concrete, visible, structured, hierarchically organized Church inherited the chosen status of the Children of Israel. Further support for the self-consciousness of the structured Church—as the image and agent of heaven on earth—was furnished by the historical tension between the Pope and the Emperor.

In Judaism there is no analogous philosophical support of church structure; nor—until recently—was there an ecclesiastical structure to support. Today, however, we are witnessing the arrogation of an ecclesiastical status by the rabbinate, even though no church theory, or ecclesiology, has been formulated. The process is perceptible in the replacement of rabbis by a rabbinate; in the replacement of great scholars by assemblies; in the replacement of individual decisions by hierarchically structured institutions, by courts and courts of appeal, and by Chief Rabbis. The hierarchical structure, and what might be called team-work, constitute in themselves an obstacle in the way of legislative innovation. As we have seen, ultimate responsibility for this institutionalization rests with the Ottoman regime, which imposed an alien structure upon the Jewish settlement, and with the Mandatory government which transmitted it to the State. The State, however, is now responsible for the ecclesiological trend in Israel's religious institutions, a trend which state legislation authorizes, and state power fortifies.

The organization of religious activity is modeled on the pattern of the secular state. The religious parties, which purport to be responsible for the security of religious life, make urgent demands for a mode of organization that is a faithful copy of political organization. Consequently, the legitimate war of opinions and ideas frequently degenerates into bickering about this imitation-organization of religious institutions. Pious persons are disconcerted by the alteration, and even degradation, of religion effected by the shift from personal faith reflected in pious observance of religious commandments to imitation-organization embodied in institutions. Religious parties are also embarrassed by this shift. From their standpoint, there are two disconcerting discrepancies between their religious ends and their political means. One is the discrepancy between the original structure of the state and the imitation structure of religious parties that fight for a place in the structure, despite the fact that, in theory if not in practice, it transcends the reach of party control. The second is the discrepancy that occasionally emerges between the interests of religion and the interests of the hierarchically structured rabbinical institutions.

Whether this change can be reconciled with the essential spirit of Judaism is doubtful. In Judaism the encounter between divinity and humanity is not relegated to any institution whatever. In so far as an encounter of this kind is represented as occurring, it appears in the words and actions of pious persons, such as the prophet, the scholar, the holy man; and in the conduct of the chosen people. In Judaism, then, the meeting between divinity and humanity is personal and dynamic, not depersonalized and static, as it inevitably becomes when solidified in institutions. Furthermore, the earthly, worldly, practical, interested character of institutions cannot be transformed even in an institution which has been elevated to the status of a concrete meeting-point between the invisible and visible spheres. This is witnessed by the character of the Catholic Church, and by the character of religious life in Israel. Why, then, have religious Jews failed to take into consideration the glaring contradiction between their professed aims and their actual means? Is it due to intellectual surrender through emulation of political organization and recourse to political power for purposes of protecting religious norms? What begins inadvertently and unconsciously eventually develops into a deliberate argument and ideology. In practice, if not yet in theory, there exists a religious ideology of statism. Religious statism underlies the demands that the state solve for religious Jews the problems which they are unable to solve by faith alone. And religious statism underlies the imitation of political patterns by organization in the religious realm.

Perhaps we can make some sense of the religious demands imposed upon the state; for, as we have seen, the state is a comprehensive public domain, and Judaism is oriented to the public. But how can we make sense of the failure of truly pious Jews to notice that without their knowledge or consent they are being swept along by the ecclesiological current? Should not pious persons staunchly resist institutional crystallization and hierarchical organization of their religion, to which these processes are alien? Should they not object, above all, to the institution of the Chief Rabbinate, a foreign branch grafted onto the Jewish stock by an alien régime? This is not to deny that the legitimacy of the rabbinate has been challenged by pious Jews, but to maintain that the challenge is neither sufficiently bold nor based on adequate theological arguments. It is not too late to arrest the ecclesiological advance. From the viewpoint of public psychology, perhaps it is precisely after, rather than before, the introduction of such alien elements as the Chief Rabbinate that the time becomes ripe for protest and resistance. Yet Jewish religious thought remains in stubborn isolation. In this particular case, however, isolationism is unjustified even on its own premises; the rise of ecclesiology in general, and the transfer of authority from individual rabbis to a Chief Rabbinate in particular, present immanent Jewish problems which can be coped with in the traditional Jewish manner of comparison and contrast between Judaism and other religious or philosophical world-outlooks.*

---

* Within the restricted scope of the present discussion, there is no room for a consideration of the thematic demand imposed by the current dialogue between different religions. A reconsideration of Christianity and Islam would be in keeping with the traditional objects of Jewish thought, which has always been obliged to carry on a dialogue with these religions. Although the religions of Asia have never been dealt with by Jewish thought, modern circumstances argue against continued isolationism in this area.

CURRENTS AND CONFLICTS OF OPINION

Currents of opinion always go hand in hand with conflicts of opinion. This is particularly true of the religious area, where opinions are entertained by large groups of individuals and where the issue at stake is not merely a theoretical point of view, but also a practical way of life. Conflict is inevitable when the religious current comes in contact with the secular current, which is likewise more than a merely theoretical point of view and sustained by large groups of individuals. Conflicts of opinions are not to be lamented—provided that the opinions do not vanish in the fray. As a Jewish society organized in a political structure, the State of Israel creates problems and opportunities connected with the shaping of public life. Of its very essence, the state has given the Jewish people an opportunity to maintain public patterns of collective Jewish life. Nothing in the essence of the state requires that those patterns be derived from Jewish tradition in general, let alone from a particular interpretation of Judaism.

Israel has made it possible for Jews to create thematic, ideological, institututional and social forms of collective Jewish life, which they can choose voluntarily. The desire to take advantage of this possibility represents a new, *subjective* trend in Judaism, a trend which makes subjectivity the source of its own objective expressions. Whether the subjective trend will triumph, or whether it will be vanquished, whether it will produce a new objective form of Judaism, or whether it will culminate in indifference to Jewish questions—all these are possibilities which cannot be determined in advance. It is even possible that the subjective trend will ultimately defeat, admit the impossibility of a subjective form of Judaism, and retreat to the position of the objectivistic trend embodied in the Halakhah. But although the direction which the new current will take cannot be foretold, it may at least be urged that it be taken consciously, deliberately, voluntarily. Be the future interpretation of Judaism what it may, let it not be an irresistible current sweeping individuals along automatically. Even if it is doomed to be but a passing, transitional phase, subjectivism must leave its mark on the Jew who passed through its alembic. Subjectivism may be left behind; but let it not be forgotten.

From the viewpoint of the subjective trend, there is some similarity between the situation in Israel and in the Diaspora. Like Jews in Israel, Jews in the Diaspora are moved by a desire to create channels for collective Jewish life. Unlike Jews in Israel, however, Jews in the Diaspora cannot create objective social expression for their subjective desire. The only channels through which that desire can be expressed are the pre-existing religious moulds inherited from past generations and understood by the non-Jewish environment. Conversely, in Israel neither the authority of past generations nor the understanding of a non-Jewish environment are necessary warrants for a particular pattern of collective Jewish life. Religious Jews may not like the opportunity which subjectivism is given in Israel; but they must understand it. Understanding does not presuppose or produce agreement. Understanding means respect, which expresses itself in an acknowledgment that subjectivism is not nihilism. Understanding means an admission that the proponent of subjectivism, like its opponent, is a Jew who adheres to certain principles and who wants to live by his principles. Understanding works both ways; as applied to objectivism, it means an acknowledgment that objectivism in theory is more than mere superstition, and that in practice it is more than a mass of irrational observances fraught with magical elements.

The least one can demand of both camps is that, in waging the war of opinions and beliefs, they treat one another with toleration. The campaign of both camps is characterized by a measure of intolerance. But we learn from experience that the religious camp is less tolerant than the non-religious camp. Tolerance does not mean neutrality. He is tolerant who, in standing upon his own view, at the same time acknowledges the existence of several different points of view and several different ways of life. To treat my opponent with tolerance is to recognize the factual existence of his position and to understand that his position is possible, regardless of whether or not it is in accordance with my own principles.

Mutual tolerance is the only adequate attitude in a situation which lends itself to no tidy, homogeneous, global solution. Beyond this, the only concrete suggestion which it seems possible to make concerns the areas where major battles should be fought. From a strategic point of view, it seems inadvisable to make a major battleground of the civil-marriage issue. Marriage being no less a matter of social taboo than of religious ritual, making an issue of it raises storms in which the fundamental principle being fought for is often forgotten. Non-religious Jews stand to gain more ground by selecting less volcanic territory for the field of battle. Thus, for example, non-religious Jews might win a major victory were they to concentrate their forces upon gaining recognition for their renunciations; were they to force religious Jews to admit that surrender to them involves renunciation of a principle; were they to make religious Jews give up their endeavor to deny, to denigrate, or to explain away the renunciation in their favor. Another area where a major battle should be fought embraces those issues pertaining to the right of every religious Jew to be considered a Jew regardless of whether or not his religious beliefs and practices are in accordance with the prevailing Orthodox interpretation of Judaism. The right of every Jew who regards himself as a religious Jew to be his own priest—so to speak—is a right which every tolerant individual ought to fight for. The violation of this right by the rabbinate must be resisted. The monopoly of the rabbinate must be opposed. State support of that monopoly must be opposed. The use of political coercion for purposes of religious persuasion must be opposed.

Resistance could be rendered more effective were the opponents of Orthodox Judaism in Israel to join forces with kindred currents in American Judaism. For reasons outlined above, modern developments in Judaism have not left their mark on religious life in Israel. Reform and Conservative Jews in America could play a prominent role in the life of Israeli society were they to help non-

Orthodox Jews in Israel. Clearly there can be no simple transplantation of spiritual trends from one part of the world to another. But the impossibility of transplantation does not preclude the possibility of cooperation. On the contrary, there may be more room for cooperation in the religious arena than in any other sphere of interrelations between Jews in Israel and Jews in the Diaspora. Cooperation in itself presupposes dissolution of the ecclesiological structure. Only against the background of a non-ecclesiological organization of Jewish life can reciprocal relations between Jews in Israel and Jews in the Diaspora be established. The first to fight for non-ecclesiasticism should be those pious Jews who are sufficiently secure in their piety to refuse the dubious favor of political protection for religion that political organization of religion is believed to guarantee. Non-religious Jews will, of course, join the anti-ecclesiological campaign; but their motives for doing so will always be suspect. By contrast, anti-ecclesiasticism on the part of pious Jews will be welcomed as an authentic manifestation of religious reflection which promises to culminate in a religious revival.

YISRAEL YESHAYAHU

Yisrael Yeshayahu was born in Sana'a, Yemen in 1910. He arrived in Palestine in 1929. At the age of 24 he headed the Department of Eastern (Oriental) Communities of the Histadrut (General Federation of Jewish Labor). He was one of the implementers of the fabled "Operation Magic Carpet," which in the late 1940's brought out of Yemen some 60,000 to 70,000 Jews—packing them into antiquated aircraft and flying them precariously over belligerent Arab territory into Israel.

Since then Yeshayahu has helped establish scores of cooperatives and other settlements for the Oriental Jews. He did considerable and fruitful research in Yemenite folklore which was published both in article and book form. In time he became Minister of Posts and Telegraph, and Deputy Speaker of the Knesset (parliament). Later he was elected Secretary General of Avodah Party. He is now Speaker of Knesset.

One of the few Oriental Jews to reach the very apex of public life in Israel, Yeshayahu has always been a spokesman for the culturally undernourished in his country and has continually pointed out the sociological malaise of the newcomers from the other Middle East countries and North Africa. Not only has he taken the Western "establishment" to task for its lack of pragmatic approach to the problems besetting the various "tribes of Israel" being forged into one nation; he has also had feuds of various intensity with his own Mapai party and with the religious authorities regarding freedom of speech, freedom of conscience, and perhaps paradoxically with the "unbridled" press. Highly articulate in both the written and the spoken word, he can "take it," as well as "dish it out."

What follows is an address delivered to the Seminar of Conservative-Reconstructionist American Rabbis, conducted by the Histadrut on July 10, 1967.

The Status of Religion in the State of Israel and Among the Jews of Israel

by YISRAEL YESHAYAHU

AFTER THE SIX DAY WAR, after the liberation of Jerusalem and the other holy places, after the moving sight of young Jewish soldiers—most of whom had not the remotest attachment to religion in the true sense—fighting like lions, risking their lives unflinchingly until they reached the Wailing Wall when they burst into tears and hugged the cold stones with an outpouring of love and emotion,—after all that, a problem, even as estimable a problem as the one concerning the status of religion in the state and among the people of Israel, becomes dwarfed and comparatively insignificant. What else can we demand of the sons of our people in this generation?

But deeds are one thing and words another, and just as we were rewarded for our deeds so too we shall be rewarded for our words, in the sense of: *"speak [expound] and receive your reward."* The reward we are seeking in the strengthening of the roots of unity among the Jewish people, in Israel as elsewhere in the world.

Of late this unity was demonstrated by the marvellous solidarity of the dispersed Jews throughout the entire world with the State of Israel, in its war and in the pride of its victory.

The question which presents itself now is: is this solidarity sufficient to sustain the unity of the Jewish people forever? Does it possess the capacity, self-sufficiently to nourish and ensure the continued existence of this unity without any extraneous additions? For wars do not go on forever and not every war is crowned with exciting triumphs.

We are forced therefore to seek additional means of buttressing the unity of the Jewish people. One of these means is to cling to its spiritual heritage which has constituted the corner-stone of its existence hitherto as a nation, of its hopes and desires, above all its hope for redemption and desire for immigration to the Holy Land in order to witness and take part in the rebirth of the Jewish people. One of these means is to cling to its spiritual heritage on the soil of Israel. It is a recognized fact that the spiritual heritage of the Jewish people is identical with the Torah [teaching] of the Jewish people, which in turn is identical with the religion of the Jewish people.

This being so we may take the liberty—or perhaps it is our duty—and inquire into the paths our religion has taken and into its status in Israel. If I had to give a simple reply to this question I should say: the status of religion in Israel is excellent. I should also add: it may well be that the Jewish religion has never before known such good days as it now enjoys in the State of Israel.

Just see how vigorous and full of vitality is religious life in Israel: there are thousands of synagogues, hundreds of religious schools, yeshivas, seminaries and a religion-oriented university. There are hundreds of rabbis, a central rabbinate and local rabbinical institutions everywhere. There is a rabbinate for the military, a Ministry of Religions, a chain of rabbinical courts, religious councils, religious parties, religious newspapers, and religious publishing-firms. Most important of all, there are hundreds of religious cooperative (moshav) and collective (kibbutz) settlements.

All of this religious life is supported, to a greater or lesser degree, by the State and the people. Moreover, it provides a livelihood for tens of thousands of Jewish citizens who perform sacred duties: dayanim, rabbinical judges— whose position and salary is as the position and salary of district judges; rabbis, ritual-slaughterers, kashruth-inspectors, teachers and instructors, yeshiva students whose studying constitutes their occupation, employees of religious institutions, and others.

Even the wealthy and well-established communities in the past never had such unprecedented possibilities with such excellent opportunities for so many religious Jews not only *themselves to identify* with their religion but also *to make religion identify* with their life, their livelihood, and their position to such an extent that they have become one with it.

Furthermore, those religious institutions which provide religious education and religious services, particularly the religious judicial institutions, exist and function with *government recognition*, empowered by State and law, and they are a respected and inseparable part of the comprehensive system of the sovereign authority, both the civil and the military.

But things are not as simple as they appear. The Jewish population of Israel is divided into two camps: the religious and the non-religious, which are given to frequent disputes and altercations that are pursued sometimes calmly and at other times stormily. The main subject of the disputes and altercations is— the status of religion in the State of Israel. From this centerpoint fly sparks of questions and queries: Which has priority and precedence over which: the religion or the State? What is to be the image of this state: shall it be religious or secular? Is religion to be imposed on everything in our life or is it to be a "tree of life to them that cling to it"? Repeatedly the demand is voiced, by certain secular circles and by certain religious circles, to *separate State and religion*.

It is possible to obtain from most of our people the acknowledgment that our religion *preceded* the State, for it was from it and because of it that there grew the roots of our faith and our hope to see the birth of our state. But it is not possible to obtain their assent that our religion has *preference* over the State. Those who do entertain such an opinion appear to attach no value to the State and to be seemingly quite ready to live without it, if only the religion will continue to exist. Their opponents, on the other hand, contradict them, declaring: without the State, the religion too would cease to exist.

As to the question of what shall be the image of the State—on this there are fathomless differences of opinion. Many of those in the religious camp argue that the image of the State should be religious; is it conceivable—they exclaim—that a Jewish state should not be Jewish? As far as they are concerned Judaism has only one meaning—religion. Many however of the non-religious camp insist that it *is* conceivable and possible for a Jewish state to be Jewish without being religious. What is more, a state is basically a *civil, secular entity*, in the literal sense of the term.

Next comes the question of whether religion should be imposed on everything in our lives or whether it should be part of the life of only those who are interested in it. On this score Israel has, with the approval of the majority of the religious camp and a substantial portion of the non-religious camp, taken certain steps whose aim is to strike a balance between the desire to accord the State a religious character and the desire to safeguard civil and secular freedom. I refer to the establishment and existence of the rabbinical institutions and the religious institutions stamped with the seal of sovereign approval; maintenance of religious education; allocation of generous budgets to provide religious services and supply religious needs; and above all, legislation by the Knesset of a number of laws which are fully or partially religious in connotation. At the head of the list is the law which stipulates that the marriage and divorce of Jews in the State of Israel shall be performed *in accordance with the laws of the Torah* and that adjudication in these matters shall be solely in the hands of the rabbinical courts. Similarly, the law concerning rest-days ensures, on the pretense of arranging a rest-day for the workers and the work processes, that on Sabbaths and holidays all trade, industry and public transportation shall cease. To these may be added also the law forbidding hog-raising, though the reasons which led to its enactment were nationalistically and historically oriented. In addition, there is a broad range of municipal ordinances which directly or indirectly accord the State a relatively religious character.

Those who belong to the religious camp are not, however, satisfied with these; they demand the enactment of all sorts of laws which will give the State an unequivocally religious character. When the non-religious camp argues that this would turn Israel into a theocratic state, imposing its will by force and robbing the individual of his freedom—they receive from the people of the religious camp three answers: 1) What if the State should be theocratic? All the better! 2) Every law is imposed by force; what difference does it make whether it is a law which imposes the payment of taxes, or military service, or—observing the Sabbath? 3) There is no intention of robbing the individual of his personal freedom inasmuch as the law refers to the open, public life of the State and its inhabitants whereas the individual in the privacy of his home may do as he likes.

Again the non-religious argue that all public life and the entire populace of the State have a right to be free of all coercion in matters of faith and observance of religious precepts whereas the religious are at liberty, like every other individual, to behave in their homes as they see fit.

The Status of Religion in Israel

The great dispute is being waged therefore around the public side of the life of the State and its populace.

It is my opinion that in this dispute the religionists are not right at all.

First, because the State of Israel cannot be both theocratic and democratic at one and the same time. The citizens of Israel are democratic. The religious-minded citizens are themselves also loyal to Israeli democracy; they lean on it and try to benefit from it. However, whereas democracy's way is to proceed in the direction in which the people—or the majority—wish, theocracy's way is to adhere to: "*A law I have passed, a decree I have decreed*"—and no questions asked. Therefore, anyone who attempts to make use of democracy and its legislative powers in order to institute theocracy, not only makes a mockery of democracy but also enables it to promulgate decrees against religion. *Whoever agrees to have the Knesset enact religious laws cannot ignore the fact that some day the Knesset may decide to enact laws of an anti-religious nature.*

Second, the State is not a *religious personality*. It is under no compulsion to adhere to any precepts whatsoever, from the wearing of the Four Fringes and the Tefillin to observing the Sabbath laws. Observing the precepts is a duty demanded of every Jew *individually,* whereas the duty demanded of *Israel* as a *whole* in keeping the precepts is the *mutual responsibility* for one another. "*All Israel are responsible for one another*" personally, and: "*Persuade your fellow-man, and bear no sin*"—this too is essentially a personal precept. The only religious precept that may conceivably be imposed on the State as a state is in the relam of the observance of the Sabbath. But everyone knows that the State cannot undertake this. The State is duty-bound to maintain the vital services for its citizenry. Granted that there are definite provisions made in the Torah pertaining to ensuring our external security by means of our army. But as regards the *police*, for example—how would it fulfill its responsibility if it should be ordered to keep the Sabbath sedulously? Can the world do without police protection? Will even those who seek to impose Sabbath-observance on our public life succeed in attaining their aim without having at their service a police force to pursue those who desecrate the Sabbath? Also, the services of communication between Israel and the world-at-large must unquestionably be maintained at all times. How can communication-services be maintained while observing the Sabbath-precepts in full? Are we to entrust these and other vital tasks to a "shabbes goy"?* Or consider a Jew who performs such tasks for us on the Sabbath a "shabbes goy"?....

Furthermore, anyone who seeks to impose Sabbath observance on all public life deliberately disregards the necessity of maintaining many essential public services. How are utilities such as electricity and water, or ships at sea, or factories with blast-furnaces which must be operated day and night without pause, to exist on a Sabbath-observance basis?

No rabbi in Israel has troubled to find suitable replies for these questions.

---

* A non-Jew employed by Jews to perform for them on the Sabbaths tasks forbidden to them on the holy day of rest.

Be that as it may, the religionists concentrate the full force of their attack on transportation on the Sabbath. Indeed, our public transportation, buses, trains and planes, are at rest on the Sabbath. There is however private Sabbath-transportation for the public everywhere throughout the country; can that conceivably be forbidden by law? The non-religious populace deeply resents being deprived of the possibility of using public transportation on the Sabbath for it is less costly and more popular than the private, and they term this situation an intolerable restriction. Will anyone then dare to forbid the private transportation as well? I fear he would have to turn the whole State of Israel into a huge prison and even then he would not attain his purpose.

Professor Y. Leibowitz [of the Hebrew University] derides the religious bloc's demands, declaring that they want the buses and cars to observe the Sabbath while the Jews themselves need not bother to do so.

Now we come to the demands to separate the religion from the State. The religious extremists voice this demand because they negate all that the State is doing for religion. As they put it, the little it does means that all the rest is free of any claims and consequently permissible. The non-religious voice this demand because they object to all that the State is doing for religion. As they put it, it is not the business of the State and it constitutes coercion, prejudicial to their freedom.

In my opinion neither side is right.

First because the separation of the State and religion, under the circumstances which characterize the life and existence of the State of Israel, would have no significance other than that of protest and opposition.

Second, the principle of the separation of religion and state came into being in times and under circumstances vastly different from the realities and circumstances in the life of the State of Israel. There simply is nothing to separate. One could perhaps demand the separation of religion from the people of Israel. If anyone wants to challenge this, let him. But what is there to separate between religion and the State? As I have already pointed out, the State is not a religious personality. In point of fact, it is actually not a religious entity, although it is Jewish in essence. Ours is a state whose law and justice are secular. Even the laws it enacted for religious reasons are not a code of Jewish laws but rather secular laws to be enforced as long as we want them, but as liable to repeal as they were to adoption.

However, ours is a state with its own peculiar attitude to religion. Every civilized people respects its religion, and the Jewish state all the more so. We try to respect other faiths as well. We allocate funds in our state budget for the maintenance of religious services. Supposing our State were to clench its fists and declare: I will have nothing to do with religious services or religious education? Would that be behaving decently toward its pious citizens? Would not the religious services in such a situation be defended and assured of their existence by means of donations and voluntary taxes? The difference would then be that they would no longer be under the supervision of the State's institutions—and what advantage would there be in that?

If there is any justification in the principle of the separation of religion from state in Israel, it lies in legislation for religion. The State ought not enact laws of a religious character or implication. This is none of its business. It only irritates both the religious and the non-religious. The religionists argue, and justifiably so, that the *Shulhan Arukh* [code of Orthodox Jewish law] has no need of the Knesset's approval, while the non-religious consider these laws, and justifiably so, as coercion in the realm of faith and conscience.

For these reasons I wonder at the religious parties' ceaseless pressure for the enactment of laws pertaining to religion. Except for the Marriage and Divorce Law—which was passed as a means of protection, in order to safeguard our national unity and prevent our people from being divided into two sects unable to intermarry—every other religious law must perforce connote coercion, resulting in inciting opposition, rebellion and hatred.

The status of religion *among the people* of Israel is another story.

As already noted Israel is composed of a religious camp and a non-religious camp. Each consists of extremists and half-extremists, moderates and half-moderates. However, whereas the religious camp is active and alert, guarding the faith and attempting to transmit it, or to impose it, on others—the non-religious camp is passive and content with: *"a small measure of freedom"*— merely to have nothing demanded of it and have no restrictions placed upon it.

It would, nevertheless, be oversimplifying to state that the non-religious camp is indifferent to religion. We are glad to note that the non-religious bloc has almost no consciously anti-religious individuals, of the so-called heretic type. And what is more, they are not indifferent. There is hardly a Jew in Israel who does not at certain times perform one precept or another. Not only does hardly anyone object to circumcision—and even practicing secularists are happy to have their sons circumcised—but they keep other precepts as well. Marriage and divorce are, as we all know, performed according to Jewish law, whether one does or does not want it so. "Mixed" marriages cause no concern here—inasmuch as we do not have alien faiths to "mix" with—and when they do occasionally arise, they are not a "produced in Israel" variety. The Sabbath-rest in Israel serves as a permanent testimonial to our being a Jewish state despite the fact that the Sabbath is not observed entirely as prescribed. On the High Holy Days nearly every Jew attends synagogue services. When in a referendum the question was asked as to who wanted kosher meat and who did not, 95% chose kosher. In recent years, possibly under American influence, the barmitzva institution has been developing among us, which, while not a precept in its own right, is nevertheless esteemed for bringing the doer "closer to the precepts." I believe that generally speaking the very act of immigrating to Israel and living here is in a sense preserving Judaism no less than keeping the precepts while living abroad. Whoever comes here comes because of his Jewishness. Moreover, here the danger of becoming absorbed and assimilated does not threaten either him or his children. Even if a Jew who lives in Israel should proclaim himself the freest of free-thinkers and categorically refuse to observe any religious precepts whatsoever, it will be of no use. Here it is simply impossible not to be a Jew for the heavens are Jewish, the earth is Jewish, the environment is Jewish. Here the Jew cannot escape his Jewishness and should he try to escape it, he will inevitably reach it again.

This may perhaps be one connotation for the saying of the Sages: *"A Jew even though he commits a sin is still a Jew."* In other words, the inhabitants of Israel, even when guilty of the sin of omission, are Jewish none the less.

Furthermore, very many of those who are in the non-religious category, including urban and kibbutz youth, have recently taken to stressing their interest and desire of understanding the real essence of Judaism! There is a growing thirst within them for the prophetic vision, the divine reality—as it is written: *"My soul thirsteth for God, the living God"*—for the secret of Jewish existence, and the historic heritage of the people of Israel. They ask for guidance; they are eager for knowledge. Whereas the parents broke the chains of religion while under the influence of the revolutions amidst which they spent their youth, their offspring now seek the way back to it.

Unfortunately no one inquires and no one intercedes for them. Were our religious leadership endowed with vision and daring, it would be able to take these young people under its wing, draw them near and warm their souls. But we do not have that kind of leadership.

The rabbis enclose themselves in a frame of what they deem "personal perfection," in the sense of *"My soul have I saved."* They are shackled by an extremist doctrine which demands: all or nothing. They must be either one-hundred-percent religious or not religious at all.

I am cognizant of the fact that the components of religion are: faith, observance of the precepts and guarding the continuity, the tradition. All three bear the stamp of: *"You shall neither add to it nor take away from it."* In other words, they are not to be divided up or changed. Furthermore, our traditionalist *Halakhic* law, exegesis, and religious philosophy developed in the course of thousands of years along paths determined by the general reality and by the circumstances of Jewish destiny. Anyone now wishing, or intending, to blaze new trails will require hundreds of years to do so. Nevertheless, I doubt whether it is possible in this generation of science and knowledge to persuade people to observe the precepts without first laying very firm foundations of deep faith and convictions. To my mind, the Jewish faith is based on conviction and as is known, some of the sages of old went to great lengths to show the reason and logic behind each precept in the Torah.

From what is known of past generations we learn that the continuance of the precepts was zealously guarded either by outstanding scholars or by ordinary ignorant men. Love impelled the former and fear the latter. The middle layer of the people observed the Jewish precepts in middling measure. As the author of *"Hovat Ha'Levavot"* said, quoting a certain philosopher:

> "None will be fit for the sublimest of all worship but he who is by nature a prophet in his generation or a true philosopher who makes use of what he has culled from learning, but all others worship because they do not understand."

Our generation strives to comprehend faith and as already noted there is no contradiction between faith, and comprehension and conviction, particularly as it pertains to men of wisdom and intelligence. But no one helps them. At times they are even repulsed. By "repulsed" I mean not only rejection but also ugly, repulsive behavior. Indeed the behavior of the rabbis in Israel is occasionally repulsive. We do not see any among them with courage enough to arise, shake himself and, throwing off the stultifying bonds of routine, come down from the mountaintop to the people. If any of that caliber do exist they are afraid of their colleagues. Once Rabbi [Yehuda] Maimon [Israel's first Minister of Religion] remarked in jest that only God knew whether the rabbis of our generation feared the Lord but he, Rabbi Maimon, knew they feared one another.

The religious parties and religious workers will not increase in number. They engage in political, coalitional strife;... and when in trouble they suggest and demand the enactment of religious laws. I do not, heaven forbid, make light of what they are doing in general and particularly of their achievements in the religious sphere. Religious education, both government-sponsored and independent, post-elementary schools, teachers'-training schools, the yeshivas and the university, the kibbutz and moshav settlements, the youth movements, and the contemplative religious literature—all these are valuable assets acquired through the efforts of the religious parties. Furthermore, those same parties enlisted the help of the State and of the non-religious parties.

They have however to date revealed no inclination or initiative toward paving new roads for the people who seek self-identification with Jewishness. Between "these" and "those," that is to say among the rabbis and the leaders of the religious parties, there is a thin layer of wise, understanding, religious Jews whose hearts ache because of the profound gap that exists between the religious camp, and the non-religious camp—a gap which at times appears to be growing wider. These good Jews seek for ways to bring the two together. I do not believe they have aleady devised any such ways and I fear they will not, for two reasons: first, because in making the attempt to draw the two closer together, one cannot expect the move to be one-sided, in other words that the others do the approaching while the religious remain where they are. That sort of attempt constitutes missionary-work. A true rapprochement must have the participation of both sides. The question is: will those religious Jews be capable of drawing nearer to the non-religious Jews, that is, take a few steps in their direction so as to bring them closer? And second, if religious Jews will go forward toward the non-religious Jews, and draw nearer to them in order to draw them closer, then the religious camp will consider them no longer religious Jews, including their rabbis and their parties. Since it is crystal-clear that the non-religious camp will not approach religion with eyes shut and accept it as it is, with all its forms and contents and customs, but will wish to choose only that which appeals to its intellect and finds favor in its eyes, as a selective faith—we must conclude that although there are portions of the religious camp and non-religious camp that wish to join forces, there is for the time being no bridge, nor even any plan of erecting a bridge, to span the gap dividing them. The hands are extended; the hearts are open; but the bridge is lacking.

Furthermore, the religious parties together with the rabbinate have in my opinion committed a serious blunder not only by turning the matters of religion and religious services into their exclusive possession which they exploit to obtain status, positions and authority, but also by creating a religious establishment and placing it in an exclusive organizational framework. By doing so they have blocked the way to religion. As a matter of fact, we have in Israel today a very strange situation in which no Jew can be considered religious or perform Jewish precepts without the agreement of the religious authorities. Needless to say, no one can engage in religious matters or act on their behalf unless he has the official approval of the exclusive religious authorities, meaning the religious parties and the rabbinate.

Let me cite an example from what occurs in the Histadrut. Among about a million members who belong to the Histadrut, there are hundreds of thousands who are religious. Their number may be relatively larger than the total number of those who vote for all of the religious parties together. The Histadrut wants them to be completely at home in its midst. Although it provides them with all the services customarily rendered to its membership, it feels that they require certain additional services as well and if it, the Histadrut, will not provide them, then they will seek them from the religious parties, and ultimately they will end by being tossed from pillar to post, between the Histadrut and the religious parties.

The Histadrut tried and continues to try to provide these members with religious services. But the rabbinate and the religious parties not only do not extend their active assistance in this, but even express their antagonism and disrupt it. They prefer to see such an activity, and to grant it their welcome and even their cooperation, only if it is on an altogether secular basis and if all the participants are non-religious. If, however, the Histadrut appoints a staff of kashruth-inspectors for its kitchens, they disqualify it. If the Histadrut wishes to give the children of its members a religious education, they oppose it. And so on . . .

The struggle being waged by the rabbinate and the political parties for a monopoly on religion and its existence affects their equilibrium to the point that they prefer to have the non-religious camp remain as it is. Better do without the religious than to have religious Jews who are not organized within their exclusive organizations!

I for one am sorry that Israel has only one rabbinate to which all are bound. This does not reflect the nature of the Jewish faith. It is not natural for any faith. All that pertains to religion and to the observance of its precepts is as a rule open to shades of opinion, to streams of thought and to a variety of views. Our situation, however, is such that we are told: here is the example; follow it! And none dares to gainsay it with: here is the example: let us modify it!

The Marriage and Divorce Law, which the Knesset enacted, accorded exclusive juridical authority in matrimonial matters to the rabbinical courts. And what did they do? They made the *courts themselves exclusive* so that *"none go out and none come in."* Once we had Ashkenazic courts, Sephardic courts, Yemenite courts and others. Similarily, there were also different rabbinates. But now they have all been combined into one exclusive authority. On the surface this seems very nice and efficient. In fact, however, from the moment the door was closed on a variety of approaches and interpretations, for a lighter or more severe application of Halakhic law, the only door that remained open was to the extremists and their extremism, and whoever surpasses his colleague in severity is to be praised.

We have among us all the Jewish communities from the countries of Asia and Africa which immigrated here together with all their rabbis and judges. Today they constitute about 50% of the total number of Jews in Israel. In their countries of origin they preserved their Jewishness themselves by keeping to their tradition; they preserved it and it preserved them. But they were always tolerant and what is more they inclined toward the more lenient interpretations of the Law. Thus they built for themselves a religious philosophy of life and a religious way of life. . . . It may be that the circumstances under which they lived were a contributing factor. In the Jewish community of Yemen, for instance, which as is well-known strictly guarded its Jewishness and its religion, the Moslems did not eat any meat which had been slaughtered by Jews. As a result the Yemenite rabbis searched assiduously for the lenient interpretations and for all possible leniencies in the realm of Halakhic law with the aim of reducing to the minimum the amount of ritually-slaughtered meat to be disqualified as treyfe [non-kosher]. . . .

But here in the State of Israel all the rabbis and judges who came from the countries of Asia and Africa were pulled, unwillingly and without their agreement, into the vicious circle of over-organization evolved by the Ashkenazic parties and rabbis, and automatically the extremist approach was forced upon them. Had their courts and rabbinates continued to exist, the Yemenites would have continued to live according to the customs of their forefathers and to offer much broader possibilities for religious identification.

If this were so, and if Israel were blessed with religious pluralism, which permits a variety of revered denominational customs and fresh-flowing religious streams, we would be in the position of making it possible for every Jew in Israel to find his place in one of the religious circles. Their competing with each other would attract new members. The competitive spirit would lead to leniency's getting the upper hand and in the final analysis religion as a whole would reap the reward [of unity in diversity].

Let me add just one more point before I conclude. The verse *"This is my God, and I will glorify Him"* was interpreted by our Sages as *"Adorn yourself before Him, by observing his precepts."*

What shall we do, my learned friends, when here in Israel no importance or value is attached to beauty in the practice of the precepts. Most of the synagogues are little *kleizlach* [congregations] on the model of those in the *shtetl*

[East European small town]. Even when the synagogue is architecturally attractive, the manners are of the market-place. Here is neither glory nor grandeur, neither honor nor respect. What wonder then that the youth is not drawn to the synagogues and if they do look in, they are repelled.

This then is the status of religion in Israel, a status not worthy of the name and overrun by a torrent of questions and problems whose replies and solutions remain hidden somewhere in the future.

Remarkably enough, the wonderful and soul-stirring spectacle of the ingathering of the exiles into Israel has revealed to us a very dangerous and serious weakness in the body of the Jewish nation. It has become apparent that the protracted sojourn of different Jewish communities in various countries and among various nations marked them with the stamp of those countries and those nations until they assumed a resemblance to them no less, and sometimes even a great deal more, than to Jewish communities in other countries. For example: Anglo-Saxon Jews resemble the Anglo-Saxon people far more than they do the Jews of Yemen or Babylonia. The State of Israel is now making superhuman efforts to bridge the differences which have been revealed between the exiles returning from one land of the Jewish Dispersion and the other lands of the Diaspora so as to make of them one cohesive unit. We are convinced that in the course of time and as a result of the efforts being invested, there will develop among the exiles returning to Israel processes which will not only give them the *unifying* identification-marks of one nation—in place of the *differentiating* identification-marks of the various sects and tribes—but which will also give that ultimately unified people an image and a look of its own.

SHULAMIT ALONI

Palestine-born *(sabra)* Shulamit Aloni was educated in pedagogics and law at the Hebrew University in Jerusalem. She joined the plurality party Mapai (now a component of *Mifleget Avodah Yisraelit*) only a few years ago and served in the Knesset from 1965 to 1969.

Aloni is not addicted to understatements; to call her iconoclastic would be using a relatively mild term. She hurls her hortatory dicta in all directions and did not spare even her own party colleague Golda Meir, before the latter became Prime Minister in 1969, by suggesting that the then 70 year old iron-willed Secretary-General of Mapai be elected to the largely ceremonial office of President of Israel.

With characteristic curiosity Aloni is not content with occasional factional purrs, but likes to poke once in a while into the political pots of other parties and more often than not she comes up with interesting morsels.

Above all she is seriously and convincingly concerned with the rights of women and with the separation of religion from state. She is the author of a column entitled THE CITIZEN AND THE LAW which appears daily in *Davar*, and books such as *The Citizen and the State*, and *The Rights of the Child in Israel*.

To some Shulamit Aloni may seem God's chosen agnostic in Israel but her presentations are cogent and well-organized, as seen in the following COMMENTS ON MARRIAGE LAW IN ISRAEL, published originally in the literary supplement of *Davar* (and later in *B'ayat Haishah*, October-November, 1964) and in the companion piece, THE ABSURDITY OF RELIGIOUS LEGISLATION, *Ovnayim*, Spring, 1966, pp. 59–64.

The Absurdity of Religious Legislation

by SHULAMIT ALONI

THE ESTABLISHMENT OF ISRAEL as a Jewish state, with all the historic, social and religious connotations its existence implies, has since the day of its inception brought us face to face with the problems of "being" and of "identity" which necessarily and unnecessarily sow discord, confusion and overlapping of authority in our lives. It appears that the longer we delay the basic examination which will make it possible for us to establish definite norms, and continue instead to accept decisions reached under the pressure of this or that case, the more deeply we become involved and the more hybridization do we create in the fundamental rights and basic social concepts of the citizen, until we arrive at absurdities. Thus we see the realities that plague citizens, native-born, whose personal status cannot be recorded in their passports or identity-cards because no decision has as yet been rendered as to who and what being a Jew means: nationality, faith or ties of blood. Moreover, the concept "Israeli," equivalent to the concept "American," "English" or "German," does not even exist in our legal and judicial terminology.

Similarly obscure yet highly significant is the attitude toward *Halakhic* law and its rules, and toward the question of how we may, or should, best express them in our legislation in Israel, especially as certain people perceive in it rules and judgments that are capable of dynamic change, some of which it may be feasible to adopt, some to alter, and the remainder—to reject. There are those who assert that it is perfect as it is and must not undergo fragmentation, whereas others go even further and declare it to be irrefutable Divine Law from which we may not deviate a hairsbreadth, and consequently must accept it in its entirety—just as it is—on behalf of all Israel. Do not therefore inquire into what is beyond your comprehension but obey the precepts and the laws of the Halakha for they and Israel are one: together they preserved each other, together they were preserved, and whoever bans one also, as it were, bans the other.

Another subject currently debated among us is whether it is right for us, the eternal people, to live in accordance with the social and administrative concepts of the twentieth century and of the Western world, or whether it would be better to shun alien cultures and changing times and lead our lives according to the precepts and customs of ancient days, whose quintessence lies in the fact of their antiquity.

Above and beyond all of these looms the gnawing, concrete, fundamental dispute which demands a clear-cut answer: which areas ought to be designated as personal, private matters regarding which one shall have the right and duty of choosing, of one's own volition and responsibility, the path one will follow and the way of life one will practice—and which areas shall be entrusted to the authority, the right and the duty of the State, which shall regulate them and impose them on all Israel by means of laws?

Indeed, whereas in the province of spirit, beliefs, customs and opinions—so long as they remain in the sphere of spirit, ideas and beliefs—we are not permitted, and what is more not able, to impose restrictions such as: STOP, PROCEED NO FURTHER!—in the province of governmental powers it is our distinct duty and obligation to impose restrictions regarding what is "allowed" and what is "forbidden." Contemporary political reasoning has in fact provided the instruments with which we may test and measure the extent of power to be accorded the State. Let us therefore examine the extent of the State's powers in an attempt to assess the interrelationship of religion and state in Israel on the level of legal affirmation and prohibition, without formulating the fundamental question concerning Jewish *being*. For this purpose we will have to examine what in essence is the State's power to impose norms of a religious nature, the imposition of which derives from religion and faith.

2

The State of Israel was established and exists today as a factual socio-political agreement and is no longer a Utopia floating abstractly in the prophets' end-of-days' visions. Whether our sentiments lean in this direction or not, our reason must accept the fact. Furthermore, whereas the Utopia of the prophets developed in a world of the sacred and the secular, of rules and beliefs, of laws of religion and laws of state—which drew their sustenance from one source, the superhuman (this phenomenon applied to Israel as it did to other nations and it was for this reason that Socrates was accused of offending the laws of Athens and its deities)—the State of Israel was born in an age in which sovereignty is the acknowledged form of rule beyond and above which nothing else exists.

It is precisely because the rule of sovereignty is self-sufficient as well as self-sustaining that the doctrine of democracy is so important to us, for the restraint it exercises on the authoritarian powers of the government, restricting it by means of various *thou shalt nots*, establishing well-defined areas of what constitutes public domain and privacy, and obligating the state to protect these areas of demarcation and not to trespass on them. Anyone who forcefully interferes in matters of conscience, religion or spirit; anyone who belies the freedom of the individual and violates the principle of equal rights, is here accused of tyranny, of transgressing the principles of natural justice and man's liberty. For further clarification we need not venture far afield to uncover evidence but need only peruse what has of late been written and spoken with regard to the status of the Jewish religion in Soviet Russia.

In its formal declaration, signed by the representatives of all segments of our population, the State of Israel on the occasion of its establishment, undertook publicly, before the nation and the world-at-large, to: "uphold the full social and political equality of all its citizens without distinction of religion, race, or sex; guarantee freedom of religion, conscience, education and culture; safeguard the holy places of all religions; and loyally preserve the principles of the United Nations Charter."

Here we note another contrast between the factual, existing State of Israel and the Utopian state. Whereas the guarantee of freedom of religion signifies that the State guarantees that every individual will be able to act in accordance with his religion and his customs and that no one will be allowed to impose his religion or faith on anyone who does not want them—nevertheless religion is demanding dominance over the life of the individual and the community, postulating this demand on the existence of an absolute power which is above and beyond the realm of the State's rule. That is why its criteria for what is "allowed" and "forbidden" are not only different from the criteria adopted by the State but even contradictory to them. For example: a sect of *Hassidim*, who look on the biblical injunctions as divine commands and religious verities and who insist, for the purpose of saving the sinful souls of others, on preventing them by force from following the dictates of their own beliefs and conceptions—such as, let us say, riding on the Sabbath—are in the light of the State's laws committing a crime but in the light of their religious doctrines performing a *mitzva*, a good deed. It is the State's responsibility to exercise vigilance so that the "authority" of faith will not enable the believer to trespass on the ground of others, to the detriment of the "authority" of beliefs and ideas. How then can a democratic state adopt the norms of a specific religion as its laws without simultaneously interfering with the freedom of conscience and religion of its citizens?

3

Due to reasons which we shall not specify here, the rabbinical courts of Israel were granted sole powers of judging marriage and divorce cases. By so doing the body politic of Israel committed two grave errors: one was the denial of the freedom and equality deemed inviolable in the Scroll of Independence, and the other—the infringement of its own powers.

The fact that every individual is forced to turn to the rabbinical court of a given denomination—regardless of whether he is a believer or a non-believer, willing or unwilling—signifies not only that coercion implied by the absence of recourse, but that coercion which compels a citizen to declare himself as affiliated with a specific religion even if by conviction he does not believe in any religion whatsoever. What is more, this law tends to erect barriers between citizens who seemingly are equal, for it throws them on the mercies of separate courts and different sets of laws. In the event that they wish to live together, one of them must detach himself from the framework of the sect and religion that the law forces on him (simply because he was born within that framework), and to impose a different code of laws on himself by converting to a different religion.

The Absurdity of Religious Legislation

The second violation implicit in investing the rabbinical courts with this authority lies in enacting a code of laws and regulations over which neither the people nor the indivual has control, not even the Knesset, the legislative body itself—and whose moral foundations and affirmations differ from those of the State's juridical structure.

From this we may conclude that our legislative body relinquished the right accorded it by the people and transmitted it to the clerics, who derive their power and inspiration from a source they believe to be above and beyond anything human. Thus, whereas the Knesset's laws, for instance, incriminate any man who abandons his wife and children, the rabbis exploit the "moral," religious and judicial authority and power vested in them, to induce the man to abandon his wife and children when the discovery has been made that he is descended from "priests" [Kohanim, descendants of Aaron] whereas his wife has been married previously. This is intolerable. For if the man is religious and submits to rabbinical authority voluntarily, and if he is of priestly descent, he certainly will not marry a divorced woman; but as to the man to whom being descended from the priestly line is of little consequence, why should the State designate him and his family as exceptions to the rule? This applies also to the cases of *halitza*,* desertion, children born out of wedlock and other cases of people transmuted by rabbinical jurisdiction into citizens who are forced to suffer shame and anguish needlessly. They are moreover thrust into this plight not because of a religion and faith they themselves espouse but because of a religion and faith others espouse. It is difficult to measure which aspect is the greater: the actual offense or the absurdity of it all. It is obvious that the authority of Knesset legislation pertaining to this law is not essential for religious people for they will in any event obey the relevant precepts without any coercion. This applies all the more to the irreligious: they do not need such legislation for it deprives them and removes them from the fold. Above all, the State itself can unquestionably dispense with it for it contradicts the principles underlying the regime and infringes on the authority of the legislative body inasmuch as notwithstanding its undisputed supremacy, it is prevented from adding or detracting anything because of the fact that divine laws are not made by man.

There are those who argue that the principle of democracy is here outweighed by the historic need for national unity. This has already been refuted by Professor Y. Leibowitz, [of the Hebrew University], who is a religious man and highly competent in the subject of Jewish laws:

> *"The contention that recognition of civil marriage by the State is likely to split the Jewish people into two nations between whom intermarriage will not be possible, is mere prevarication. That such recognition will undermine the sacred institution of marriage is a lie. Those who advance this argument overlook, knowingly or unknowingly, the reality of hundreds of thousands of religious Jews in the western*

---

* A ceremony to release a man from the obligation to marry his brother's childless widow. Without the brother-in-law's consent the widow may not marry. In 1953 Israel legislated imprisonment for the man refusing halitza. (Eds.)

countries who live their married lives in the sanctity and purity of biblical laws, in localities which are under the jurisdiction of state laws that recognize civil marriage and divorce (England, for example), or even demand them (as in imperial Weimar Germany). Observant Jews will continue to marry according to the religious marriage rites and, in the unhappy event of divorce, will obtain it by legal means as dictated by the laws of the Jewish faith. Anti-religionists will merely register their 'marriage' or 'divorce' in a government office in whatever manner the law prescribes. In referring to the latter we enclosed the two all-important terms in quotation marks inasmuch as from a seemingly religious point of view this is not marriage at all but rather cohabitation with an unmarried woman and as a result the problem of divorce does not arise.

Where a marriage did not take place there is no illegitimacy and a child born out of wedlock is not ostracized by the community. We have never known institutions devoted to biblical teaching, to give serious and essential consideration to the Halakhic implications of civil marriage.... This situation, which reduces the problem of illegitimacy to a minimum, would be infinitely better than that produced by the present laws of marriage and divorce which are tantamount to a law aimed at increasing illegitimacy in Israel.... We do not however expect that the rabbinical institutions will deal with this matter objectively inasmuch as they are by way of being vested interests."

4

The marriage and divorce laws are among the most serious examples of religious coercion but by no means the only ones. The dietary laws which give certain large (and highly specific) vested interests full economic control over various branches of our economy, and the Sabbath "blue" laws which serve to highlight a number of "spiritual" attainments by means of legislation, contain unmistakable grains of totalitarianism. A democracy cannot afford to disregard the long slow road of education, information, evolution of a way of life and facing up to spiritual challenge and instead, take a short-cut by imposing molds of "culture," "precepts" and "way of life" by means of legislation that is deeply resented by the majority of the population.

The proliferating appetite of the religious officials on the one hand, and the rigid conservation of the religious institutions (the synagogues and rabbinical courts), has unfortunately given rise to deep-set antagonism on the part of the irreligious people toward anything described as "Judaism." Thus we find that by our numerous "concessions" to the *spirit of the Jewish people*, to *Jewish values* and in the interest of Jewish unity, we have—through this legislation—in effect estranged that self-same spirit and values from our hearts and minds so that the unique values long cherished by our people have consequently been undermined. Unity on the other hand still eludes us. The term "Judaism" has far broader and deeper implications than are contained in a compilation of denomination precepts and laws of matrimony. Even he who cries, *"Let's be like everyone else"* does not have total self-effacement in mind. After all, no nation is a duplicate of any other nation; every people has its own language, its own history, its own customs, its own literature, its own particular way of life. What those who urge "Let's be like everyone else," have in mind is that we live our life simultaneously as Jews and moderns, as Jews whose culture is not rigid but dynamic, preserving itself and at the same time developing further as well as providing every Jew with his individual social and spiritual needs, in accordance with his age. As long as "Judaism" continues to divert us from the state and society, the arts and sciences of our generation—so long will the gap continue to widen and alienate the Jew from his origins, ultimately leading us to the ineluctable result—shattered vessels.

The Sabbath is a unifying force prized by every Jew. That is why it was proclaimed the weekly day of rest in Israel. However, its connotations of the sabbatical spirituality, poetry and way of life can never be implanted by compelling the populace to stay at home in a spirit of dissatisfaction ranging from indifference at best to active resentment. The concepts of work and rest have metamorphosed as their essence too has undergone radical change.

Those who seek to fashion a firm, deep-rooted Jewish culture have abundant possibilities at hand. For one, they may initiate social and cultural activities inspired by tradition and enhanced by their present worth, capable of attracting and gathering together those interested in cultural pastimes, instead of forcing clubs and theatres to be closed on Sabbath Eve, thereby abandoning aimless, idle youth to the emptiness of the streets. It is possible also to combine Jewish law with social and economic legislation appropriate to the needs of the times and even to invest the new laws with a resemblance to their traditional origins, according them the special flavor of our ancient laws. At the same time, however, it would be foolish to deflect and distort matters whose nature and power was not known ten years ago in order to make them fit the mentality and currents of thought that 3000 years ago were considered advanced. It is desirable to broaden the study of Judaism and its traditions, and particularly its lore, in our institutions of learning, but we must guard against imposing on the young a cult likely to create a conflict between children and parents. All the above are bound to lead to closer rapport between people and heighten the mutual sense of unique Jewishness. But they will be possible on condition that one fundamental all-important fact is assured: the acknowledgment that the Bible, the precepts, and Halakhic law on the one hand, and civil and state legislation on the other hand, are separate and different entities. The Knesset is not allowed to enact religious laws and religion cannot use the Knesset to inflict itself on the populace. For believers the Knesset is certainly not the supreme authority in religious matters, whereas the freethinker is unequivocally opposed to its having any such authority.

In the interests of harmony it is time that the clause in our Scroll of Independence which proclaims the *"freedom of conscience and religion"* be transformed into a *"basic law"* that will decorate the walls of all the classrooms and help schoolchildren to learn, together with their a-b-c's, the rules of mutual respect and tolerance, and to realize that people whose beliefs differ are nonetheless people of conscience and understanding, endowed with the same rights and freedoms accruing to all men.

Let everyone among us espouse the thought that being the "chosen people" signifies every indivdual's capacity to be strict with himself and easy-going with others, and to respect all human beings as equally created by God, despite the differences in their faiths and spiritual worlds. This rule of freedom of conscience, religion and thought should be taught to our children concurrently with the teachings of Hillel and Akiba: *"Love thy neighbor as thyself,"* and *"Do not unto others that which is hateful unto you."* As you oppose having anything imposed on you, make sure that you yourself avoid imposing your religion or your views on others.

II

Comments on Marriage Laws in Israel

In Israel, the marriage laws, insofar as they affect Jews, are in the hands of the Rabbinical Courts who judge them on the basis of religious 'halakha' alone. This monopoly right was granted to the Rabbinical Courts by the Knesset in its Law of Rabbinical Courts (Marriage and Divorce) in 1953 and is still in force. In spite of the assumption that the citizen knows the law, it is doubtful whether we all know clearly what 'halakhah' directs in this matter and what its significance is for us in our daily lives.

THE WIFE—HER HUSBAND'S PROPERTY

Many married women will certainly be surprised to hear that from the formal point of view, and not only formal (as we shall explain further) they are the property of their husbands. Members of kibbutzim [collectives] too, who have abolished personal property, will be astonished to learn that all the married men are property owners by being 'legal husbands' or owners, 'baal' of their wives. It is written in the Torah *"For a man shall take a woman"* (Deuteronomy 22, 13) the man takes and the woman is taken. And so, *"I give my daughter to this man"* (Deuteronomy 22, 16). The daughter is given and does not choose to go herself. The law is, however, extremely clear in its Mishnaic form "Seder Nashim Massechet Kedushin," division for women betrothal arrangements, which says: A woman can be bought in three ways and buys herself in two ways. She can be bought for money, with a bill of betrothal and sexual intercourse ... and she can buy herself with a divorce or with the death of her husband. The childless widow of a brother can be bought by the act of consummation (sexual intercourse) and can buy her freedom by 'halitzah' or by the death of her dead husband's brother. (After that there is a Mishna which describes how a slave is bought, followed by directions on how to buy an animal). And so the woman is bought and she becomes her husband's property in one of three ways: a bill of betrothal, money and the act of consummation, of which only purchase for money is accepted today for reasons of modesty, in order that the woman's honour should not be slighted and so that the man should not think that she came to him for nothing (though recognition of the

The Absurdity of Religious Legislation

holiness of intercourse can be one form of legal authorisation of civil marriage, at least amongs Jews). What is the significance of this property? If we just call it a formal matter, this formulation has absolutely nothing to support it for it contradicts the Law of Women's Equality. Let us take a look at reality and examine whether this is really only a formal matter.

1. Sarah married 12 years ago as a young bride of 20. The marriage did not go well and her husband, a young adventurer, deserted her, went overseas and she lost all trace of him. However many enquiries and searches were instituted they could not find out where he was and no Court of Law could loosen the bond between her and the deserter whose wife she was and who was her husband. So long as he could not be found and no Bill of Divorcement was received from him, and so long as there were no witnesses that he was dead, his wife Sarah was not allowed to marry another man.

This means that she is compelled to remain alone all her life. Neither can she become a common law wife of another man since she is a wife and an act of this kind would be an adulterous act. If, heaven forbid, a child should be born it would be a bastard and not allowed to be accepted "as a member of the Jewish community." In other words, this child would be forbidden to marry a Jewess. As for non-Jews, the Law in Israel provides that after 7 years of desertion the woman is free to marry.

2. Esther is today a woman of 35 and has two children. For the last 8 years her husband has been in a mental home and is not even in a condition to divorce and release her. The doctors see no hope of any cure. This means that so long as her husband is alive Esther is condemned to being alone and though everyone pities her and the bitterness of her fate, including those Rabbis to whom she has turned for an annulment of her marriage, no one can help her. She is her husband's property. And since a woman can buy her freedom only in two ways, with a divorce or by the death of her husband, all she can look forward to is her husband's death and to proclaiming to all who may care to listen, that the laws of Israel are worse than those of the Indians who used to bury a living wife with her dead husband, since in that case the agony is not prolonged for years.

3. Miriam has been separated from her husband for 13 years. In the sentence given by the Rabbinical Court 10 years ago it was ruled that the two could not live together and they could not be reconciled with each other. However, since the husband claims that he is ready to take his wife back any time, it was decided that there is not sufficient reason to compel him to give her a divorce and so long as he is not willing to give the divorce Miriam remains his wife and cannot marry another man, and this despite the fact that the Rabbinical Court ruled that the two cannot live together.

4. Shlomit was sold by her family in Yemen to the man who is today her nusband. Since that time 15 years have passed and she consistently escapes from him and refuses to be his wife. She and all her acquaintances, have for years been pleading with the Rabbinical Court to annul the marriage. But nothing helps. Her husband, and he alone can release her if he should wish to.

It would be possible to continue with the stories of countless women bound by a bitter fate, but it seems to me that there is no need to elaborate for everyone here can add cases from his own knowledge.

THE DIFFICULTY OF OBTAINING DIVORCE AND ITS SIGNIFICANCE

Apprehensive of adultery and bastardy, great severity is exercised in the matter of divorce. Laws are laid down, demands are made, and strictness is exercised even in cases of doubt. This has meant that the problem has ceased to be the problem of this, or that, individual and has become the problem of the public as a whole. As we have recently learned, the whole business of 'directives' in the matter of the "Bnei Israel"* was the result of doubt. So far as divorce was concerned, it was said that in that distant country of the dispersion, divorce was not properly practiced, and if divorce is not in order, this means that the woman who is so-called divorced, in fact remains the wife of her first husband and if he has, heaven forbid, married again, hers are children of adultery, bastards, and are not to be accepted as members of the Jewish community and are forbidden to marry a 'kosher' Jewish girl.

They say that in order to avoid discrimination, these directives will now not only fall on "Bnei Israel" but on all Jewry and Heaven preserve us from this 'liberalization'. Only a few months ago a couple immigrated from the United States who wanted to marry and settle in Israel. It turned out that the woman was a divorcee and that her divorce was granted by the Conservative Rabbinical Court. The Israeli Rabbis refused to recognize this divorce in case it was not given according to 'halakha' [Orthodox Jewish law] and insisted that she be divorced from her former husband in a 'halakhic' divorce, according to the demands of our Rabbis. This was impossible and not only for reasons of feeling. The man from whom she was divorced had already married again and if he were to give her a divorce, then he would be regarded as a bigamist. In any case, that couple returned to the United States and married there. If their children should wish to come to Israel these 'directives' will affect them, meaning that they will be forbidden to marry a Jewish girl or boy here and since this disqualification was the rule for Conservative divorce in general, this means that a whole community of American Jewry may face the tragedy which was suffered here by the community of "Bnei Israel". Anyone who anticipates immigration from the U.S.S.R. where divorce was certainly not practiced along 'halakhic' lines for the past 40 years, has reason to be deeply apprehensive. In addition, this strictness in matters of divorce does not only relate to Jews who married and were married by a religious ceremony, but also to those who were married in a civil marriage. Indeed, the Rabbinical Court, that is to say, the 'halakhah' does not recognize the existence of civil marriage, but since it is a matter of two Jews, for fear that these two wished to make a property deal through a marriage contract, they must have a divorce and, of course, a

---

* Jews from India who migrated to Israel.

'halakhic' divorce. Until recently we witnessed the embarrassing results of this system.

A couple who were married in their country of origin by a civil marriage, as is customary there, who lived together for 20 years, set up house and had children, immigrated to Israel. The husband tired of his wife and wanted to marry another woman. The Rabbinical Court ruled that *that marriage was not valid* but in order to avoid any doubt in any matter concerning restriction of the woman, the man was required to deposit a divorce in the Rabbinical Court and was permitted to marry a second wife. This peculiar manner of "a little bit of marriage" which means that the marriage is invalid but a divorce has to be given was also expressed in the sentence of Haklai who was dealing with the marriage of a Cohen and a divorcee.

PROHIBITION OF MARRIAGE BETWEEN A COHEN (PRIEST) AND A DIVORCEE

Though it is the man who buys a woman, not every woman is ritually fit to be his property even if she is free and even if the marriage should not affect the man's rights.

In the Book of Numbers 21, 7 it is written about priests that: *"A desecrated woman and a prostitute shall not be taken for a woman divorced from her husband for he is holy for God."* In the period when the position of the priest was above that of the nation and his post was a holy one, it was regarded as a prohibitive act if he married a woman who was divorced by a bill of divorce for reasons that she was possessed of a "shameful thing" (Deuteronomy 24, 1).

But after all, those days and those occasions were not what should be in force today. Yet the prohibition stands firm today and no man who bears one of the officially accepted names of priests, Cohen, Kagan, Kaganowitz, Adler, Rappaport, Kaplan, Mazeh and other off-spring who Hebraized their names, will receive permission to marry a divorced woman even though this 'no' is not as strict as that which falls upon a woman who was not divorced according to religious practice and the punishment does not fit the "crime". If this couple marries in any case and has children, these children have no disability except in regard to the priesthood. However, the Rabbi, who is a religious man who fears the Torah, cannot disregard this clearly stated prohibition. In spite of the fact that for the needs of marriage according to the Law of Moses and Israel, there is not need for a Rabbi, the presence of a Rabbi is required today by the civil law in order to ensure public order, in the same way as in those states where there is civil marriage, there is an authorized registrar of marriages to whom application has to be made.

In the case of Mr. X, who was interrogated against his will by the Rabbi to whom he applied, it was discovered that he is of priestly origin and married his wife who was a divorcee, in the presence of approved witnesses. The Minister of the Interior refused to register them as a married couple before they brought an official document to testify to their marriage. The two applied to the Rabbinical Court and asked for a proclamatory verdict that this was a religious marriage in order to enable them to register as husband and wife with the registrar of the Minister of the Interior. As a result of this application that peculiar verdict was pronounced (the Haklai judgment) that the two are not married but the wife requires a bill of divorce. This means that the Minister of the Interior refuses to register them as married since the Rabbinical Court ruled that they are not, but that the woman, in any case, is a wife so long as she does not receive a divorce.

There were cases where Rabbis showed greater magnanimity and there is no reason to suppose that they were not God-fearing. There is the case of a Cohen who married a divorcee and appeared before the late Rabbi Kook in 1925, who did *not* refuse to comply with their request. There are also cases today. Not long ago I met a young divorced woman who had married a Cohen 5 years earlier with marriage vows signed by the late Rabbi Shaul Avraham, and when she went to the Ministry of the Interior to correct her identity card they refused to register her as married. She then turned to the Rabbinical Court to request ratification, where they turned her away, she says, as a "cheap and despicable woman." As she did not know the law she was always afraid to have children for fear of their being bastards (which is quite incorrect) and had already had three abortions. A copy of her marriage vows was sent to the head office of the Ministry of the Interior with a request to arrange the registration of the couple in order to save them suffering but they were informed that without a proclamatory ruling of the Rabbinical Court it was impossible to register this couple as married. Obviously, this woman, like her predecessor, is not free to marry anyone else without a divorce. With this, the husband *is* free and can marry another woman for it is not regarded as a proper marriage.

THE LEVIRATE LAW

Prohibition of marriage does not only fall on a deserted woman or on a divorcee to a Cohen, it also falls on a "Yevama", that is to say, a widow without children whose late husband has a brother living. In Deuteronomy 25, verses 5-10, we learn that:

> "If brethren dwell together and one die and leave no male child the widow of the dead man will not be permitted to marry a strange man. Her husband's brother shall go in unto her and shall contract levirate marriage with her.... If the man should not wish to take his sister-in-law the woman shall go up to the elders at the gates and she shall say: My husband's brother refuseth to raise up unto his brother a name in Israel; he will not perform the duty of a husband's brother to me. Then the elders of the city shall call him and speak unto him and he shall say: I like not to take her. Then shall his brother's wife go unto him in the presence of the elders and loose his shoe from off his foot and spit in his face and she shall answer and say: So shall it be done unto the man that doth not build up his brother's house. And his name shall be called in Israel, 'the house of him that hath his shoe loosed'."

The law stands in words and form in this respect and the descriptive implementation of it stands to this day. Except that today the brother-in-law is not compelled to take the widow. And what was in the past regarded as a 'Mitzva' (a pious act) has been ruled by the Rabbis as a prohibition and even if Ruth and Boaz were to come before today's Rabbinical Court they would have been refused marriage and King David would never have been born. The ceremony of "halitza" on the other hand is in full force, compulsory and indispensable today. What was in the past a punishment for the man who refused, expresses itself today in the bonds and threat of living alone for the woman. We shall not describe the shameful ceremony and will go no further than understanding the law. The "Yevama" as alreadynsaid, buys her freedom by "halitza" or through the death of her brother-in-law. "Halitza," in contrast to the divorce, cannot be carried out by proxy. Even though it is written: *"And he give the Bill of Divorce into her hands"* that could be sent by another's hand, but in "halitza" both parties must be present. Similarly, according to the laws of "halakha" the dead husband's brother is his heir and he can refuse to carry out "halitza" until he receives a considerable share of the widow's property, including pension and compensation which she may receive by law as a widow. Indeed, if he demands more than that he may be accused of extortion and he may be compelled to give "halitza" or to pay maintenance, but so long as his financial demands are "reasonable" there is no room, in the opinion of the Rabbis, to regard this as extortion and the money will have to be paid whether she likes it or not. Obviously, a woman who wants to buy her freedom submits of her own free will or by force and pays, but this is not always possible. It may happen that the brother-in-law is a minor and then she may have to wait until he comes of age. If the brother-in-law should be abroad she has to go and ask him, and if he should be in a country where she has no entry, Russia, Egypt, Yemen, she has to remain alone and wait for salvation. That is how a law which in its time was enacted in order to safeguard the woman, has turned against her.

POSSIBLE SOLUTIONS

We have here given only the slightest indications of the marriage laws practiced here which, in order to preserve the family unit, which is being undermined, we have wrapped in a veil of holiness and fear, disregarding how much it undermines the primary right of the citizen, his right to set up a home and family with whomever he wishes and we have denied the woman the rights of a human being with the same legal rights as the man.

These relate to Jews among themselves without touching on the legal standing of couples of mixed marriages and particularly the legal status and fate of children born of these marriages.

This is altogether not a marginal problem in the light of the immigration from countries of East and West Europe and in view of the fact that the population in Israel is not homogeneous from a national, religious standpoint, so that as a state it cannot be run on the lines of a closed congregation in a foreign land.

However, let us leave these questions and remain within the boundaries of relationships between Jews themselves. Is it really necessary so tragically and fatally to bind the freedom of a woman to a man in the steadfastness of his love, in his mental health and in his actual living or disappearing? Is that not too heavy a sacrifice to demand of people who are not religious (since religious people will keep all this even without a law) in order to keep a tradition and even if people say that this sanctified tradition is necessary in order to preserve the unity and wholeness of the nation,—does this really do so? Even if we assume that all the above-mentioned reasons are beyond criticism and that we should not overstep the bounds of "halakha", is this "halakha" so strict and straitlaced or can it have some other interpretation?

Actually, we know, and it has been drummed into us lately even more, that we have no right to tell the Rabbis what to do or how to judge, but the honour of our Rabbis today is not greater than their predecessors', and we could certainly bring to the knowledge of the public the words of others who were also God-fearing but not "rule-fearing" and who dared within the bounds of the "halakha" to lessen the distress of the public and to by-pass the difficult spots of the law. We have already mentioned the permission granted by Rabbi Cook for the marriage of a Cohen and a divorcee and we have many examples of this kind, proving that he was not alone in acting in this way.

As for preventing a state of living alone and of the widow who must obtain "halitza" we have found (Even Haezer 157, 64) *"He who marries a woman and has a converted brother can lay down the double condition that if she should have to turn to the convert for levirate marriage, she should not be regarded as married."* They ruled that the marriage would be completely invalid if this situation were to arise and she would, therefore, not require "halitza". According to the commentators of the "Shulhan Arukh" such a condition may be laid down if the brother is deaf, that is if he is a deaf-mute and the rule is the same for an imbecile or if the brother disappears.

This led to the "halakha" of 'conditional marriage' and was accepted in Israel as "halakha" and which is not practiced (Rabbi Yehezkel Landow, Rabbi of Prague in his book "Known in Judah" and other rabbis have given their opinion on this matter).

Naturally there is no power which obliges the Rabbis in Israel to take this line. But it is a fact that by means of this condition which every bridegroom can put, it is possible to prevent these problems and in order to avoid any fear of a man taking the law into his own hands, this condition should be strengthened by a ruling that every marriage is carried out on the strength of the Rabbi's discretion and he alone can dissolve it. The "halakha" also lays down this rule, though unfortunately it is not done today, neither in the case of a deserted woman whose husband has disappeared, nor where her husband has lost his sanity, nor in cases where the husband refused to give a divorce even if he really should do so. It is said *"To marry according to the law of Moses and of*

Israel". "Israel" for this purpose is the Rabbi at whose discretion the marriage takes place. For those who know "halakha" these matters are not new. In fact, in order to avoid desertion and especially in order to prevent illegitimacy because of divorce which is not according to the "halakha", the Conservative Rabbis in the U.S. suggested as early as in the thirties, to practice 'conditional marriage' but there was a huge outcry and a conflict between various classes with threats of excommunication and the matter was referred. This is not the only possible solution and if only the modern winds of change were to blow through the corridors of the Rabbinate we should then see that even civil marriage is not in contradiction to the bases of "halakha".

PART WEDLOCK AS A POSSIBLE SOLUTION

The "Halakha" recognizes concubines (in the biblical sense) viz. wives in every sense who are not blessed by betrothal (*ketuba*). These relationships are called "Peleg-Ishut" (Questions, Yavetz part 2, chapter 15). Here the bond between the man and the woman and between the parents and the children is recognized without the problem of bastards arising or the other prohibitions which are liable to follow on the couple or on their children (because of a legal wife). Since there is no written marriage contract (ketuba) there is no financial commitment, but this can be fixed by a marriage contract drawn up between the two parties for, after all, the ketuba is also only a bill of commitment.

People who know the law have good reason to wonder why traditionalists oppose a common-law wife. If they were to go into this matter of "Peleg-Ishut", part wedlock, and the marriage contract alongside it, it may well be that there would be no need for a common-law wife and we would be saved from this question of illegitimate children and of prohibitive directives on a priest and a divorcee, of levirate marriage and other legal tortures which have not yet found any solution—and the State, if not the Rabbinate, must be concerned with personal rights.

Many other suggested solutions could be offered but the press is no means for stating these matters and certainly not the way to the hearts of the Rabbis. We have raised these matters in order to arouse an awareness of their existence and of the scope of sacrifice demanded of us, the public which wishes to live a democratic life in the sixties of the twentieth century. We should remember that so far in the State of Israel no serious effort has been made to understand the needs of the nation and the public, in this period of ingathering of the exiles and of renewal of public life, in this whole sphere of marriage laws. The Rabbis in Israel—and there are amongst them those who are great in the Torah and who can overcome great difficulties—are not the spiritual shepherds of the nation, do not feel its needs and fanatically demand that the very letter of the law be carried out.

At the same time, through the legal system of the democratic regime, they want to enforce laws which oppose the very essence of the principles of democratic legislation, which rules that the basic rights of the individual should not be infringed upon. Obviously, we have no right to complain to the Rabbis who go their way according to their own normal line and conceptions and according to their spiritual ability. There is, however, plenty to complain about to the leadership of the State that did not stand guard at the right time over the rights of the citizen and transferred authority to a totalitarian religious body (which is the nature of every factor which has absolute belief) on the basis of principles of "peaceful co-existence" and "status quo". These principles have not been re-examined or re-discussed since the days of the pre-State National Council, Vaad Leumi, and whose real essence has been expanding to the extent that coalitional needs of haggling have made it possible for the convenience of all concerned.

ZURIEL ADMONIT

Born in Germany in 1915, Zuriel Admonit benefited from an excellent secondary and religious school (Yeshiva) education even before he came to Israel in 1937. An attractive personality, he became a leader in the Orthodox youth movement, B'nai Akiva. In Israel he settled in Kibbutz Yavneh and soon gained a reputation as a theoretician of "Hakibbutz Hadati." The latter is a federation of collective settlements founded by the Hapoel Hamizrahi, now affiliated with the National Religious Party of Israel.

As a literary spokesman for his movement, Admonit articulated the socio-economic principles of the kibbutz within the framework of Orthodox Jewry. Of late he and his movement have advocated more pliability in religious ritual, incorporating relevant contemporary expression of nationalism. They have also explored the areas of spiritual affinity with the non-religious elements in the country.

The following exchange of letters seems to point to the contention of some that Judaism is more than a formalistic religion, that it is a culture in which ritual or ceremony is important, but not detrimental. Hence the difficulty of religion and state separation in Israel. Where does religion start and secularism end? Or vice versa.

One Poem and Its Meaning

by ZURIEL ADMONIT

679 WAS THE ESTIMATED initial number of Israeli soldiers killed in the Six Day War of 1967. Reena Barzilai, a member of a leftist free-thinkers' kibbutz, wrote the following poem which loses a great deal in translation because of the specific meaning of its symbolism in the Hebrew language. The poem, first published in *The Week of the Kibbutz Artzi*, the Marxist-socialist federation of collective settlements [September 1967], had tremendous repercussions and was reprinted in the *Soldier's* Page of "Hakibbutz Hadati", the federation of religious collective settlements, (December 1967) where subsequently an exchange of letters between the editor, Zuriel Admonit, and the poetess appeared. [Eds.]

679 AMBASSADORS

Six-hundred-seventy-nine emissaries,
O Master of the Universe, to You,
To the kingdom of the King of all Kings,
To Your holy land we despatched.

For we were abandoned by all. Solitary, alone,
We stayed, facing the threatening foe.
Six-hundred-nine-and-seventy ambassadors
To the Garden of Eden we sent.

With formalities of diplomacy disenchanted,
We'd realized meanwhile beyond doubt
That the people of Israel can rely only
On the best of its sons . . . and on heavenly mercy.

Wounded, ragged they will appear before You,
To intercede for us before the throne of glory,
And in our name present credentials that
With lead were inscribed on their bodies.

Six-hundred-seventy-nine emissaries,
O Master of the Universe, to You we have sent.

Kibbutz Ha'Ogen   REENA BARZILAI

A LIVING, INTENSE RELIGIOUS EXPERIENCE

The Six Day War evoked profound, overpowering experiences which prompted the writing of many poems. What is unique in this poem is that it was written by a member of Kibbutz Ha'Ogen and published in the journal *Shavua Hakibbutz Ha'Artzi* of the Hashomer Hatzair Organization.

Judging this poem from the point of view of *form* we note that it is in the style of Natan Alterman, [a noted contemporary Israeli poet] combining modern terminology with the concepts of ancient Jewish traditions.

However, the documentary importace of this poem lies in its *content*. The Jewish people's aloneness in the battle for its existence awakens in us the realization that we have as a matter of fact no one to lean on except our Father-in-heaven. God's emissaries on earth, who keep His precepts and execute His will, are our sons and brothers who sacrificed their lives to save Israel and liberate the sacred soil.

It is quite significant that our generation discovered this mode of expression and all the more significant that it came from a circle whom we generally designate as "non-religious" and at times even "irreligious". Does not this poem demonstrate that *within* the Jewish heart there throbs even today a living, intense religious faith, concealed though it may be behind an irreligious, secular mask?

We understand how tremendous is the distance between accepting the yoke of the kingdom of God and undertaking the duty of keeping all the precepts, between an expression of faith and a way of life. But it may also happen that one who observes all the laws strictly does not see the hand of God, fails to see the trees for the woods. Consequently it behooves us to cherish such tender shoots of faith, cultivate them cautiously and tenderly, taking care not to crush them with tiresome discussions of questions of a public nature, such as control over the Western Wall.

ZURIEL

To Zuriel,
Shalom!

The last issue of your journal carried my poem "679 Ambassadors". I wrote it on the night of June 6th immediately after the announcement by the spokesman of Zahal [Israel's Army of Defense]—really with my heart's blood. Judging by the abundance of emotional reactions that reached me after it appeared, you might say it was written with the heart's blood of all of us.

It was my privilege to have it published in *Shavua Hakibbutz Ha'Artzi*, from which it was reprinted in other journals. It was gratifying to me to discover that I had succeeded in those difficult moments in expressing the emotions of so many people. If one may mix pleasure with grief for the loss of life, I was proud to have the poem appear in your magazine, too.

Later however came the reactions to the poem. The symbols I employed, which I drew from our age-old traditions, led the letter-writers (and perhaps other readers as well) to the conclusion that this poem was written with a religious approach. This really amazed me: is then the approach to both poetry and religion as superficial as all that?

I do not reject a religious philosophy of life. But I myself am not religious in any way, as anyone who reads my poem thoughtfully must surely sense. Throughout the entire poem *man is consistently placed ahead of God*, preceding and not following God. It is man who acts and activates, whereas the supreme powers constitute background symbols. Is this a religious outlook? In my opinion this is a poem of faith in man, in our kind of man, and not of faith in God.

I might of course have used the names of ancient gods such as the Greek Zeus, or the Roman Jupiter, or the Indian Buddha. Would you then have said that I am a pagan? I did not however use them. Every nation has its own symbols which its indigenous literature ought to use. There is no literature devoid of symbols and the more deeply they are rooted in the national tradition the better.

I believe I have succeeded in my explanations. I thank you none the less for publishing my poem. It is good to see the same identical lines printed in your journal and in ours—together.

Yours,
REENA BARZILAI

Ha'Ogen

To Reena Barzilai,
Shalom!

I read your letter carefully and will try to answer to the best of my ability and understanding, for to my mind fundamental values are involved.

ART AND FAITH

To begin with I wish to assert my doubt that you alone have the sole privilege of interpreting your poem "679 Ambassadors". From the moment the newborn infant comes into the world and takes his place among men, he possesses the unqualified right of independent existence. As the infant's fortunate mother you may have the privilege of choosing where he will experience the first period of his growth—say kindergarten and school—but by the time he has passed this stage and arrived in our midst, his own specific individuality is clearly recognizable and each reader may make his own interpretation, no longer needing the poet's "authentic explanation". We read of great poets whose works were interpreted not by themselves but by poetry critics. This may be painful for you but then birth pangs always are. Moreover, you will surely admit that there is a considerable difference of approach in judging a poem between the moment in which it is composed, giving direct expression to profound emotion while transported by certain fateful events then occurring— and a day some three months later when you examine it anew. Your approach today is affected by all sorts of considerations which are not purely emotional and evanescent. You consider the extent this emotion and expression correspond to a world-outlook; you relate it to earlier and subsequent realities of life; you gauge the effect it may have on people, and so on. As a result *you also interpret it*, precisely as I do. This does not prove that my approach to *poetry* is superficial, as you say! As for my superficial approach to *religion*, I refer you to what follows.

THE WORLD OF OBJECTS AND OF SYMBOLS

You stated that although you used symbols drawn from our national traditions you are not religious in any way. You declared that you might as readily have exchanged these symbols for Greek, Roman or Hindu symbols. Indeed? Try it; let us see whether you really can! The [Hebrew] poet Tchernihovsky tried, and sang to Apollo and Astarte because that was what he wanted to do. No one prevented you from following in his footsteps but you yourself. Do not complain therefore that we are misled when we interpret as we do your perfectly clear symbols ("Master of the Universe", "King of Kings", "your holy land", "heavenly mercy" and "throne of glory"). As a matter of fact, all human language is a langugage of symbols and our actions too contain but little of true reality. Take the flag, for example: if you examine it you find it is only a piece of cloth in two or more colors combined in a more or less attractive design. Yet men literally give their lives for the flag. Or—in a moment of sublime love, the lover slips a ring on his beloved's finger, thereby binding them to each other for life. Indeed? Does that bit of metal actually determine feelings of love, devotion, faithfulness? Of course not! It exists only on the strength of its symbolism.

A similar situation exists in our religious life. We speak of God. Who knows Him? Who is acquainted with Him? Who is even capable of evaluating His influence? They are symbols that represent a world far-removed from us and entirely beyond our control. Before Him we bend our will in the hope that He will relax His will toward us. This brings me to the differences in our approach. You claim that you intended to express faith *in man* (Do you recall Tchernihovsky's poem, "Laught at All My Dreams"?), and you amend this to read: *in our kind of man*, and add that you placed man before God, who serves only as background for him. Here we must pause for a while. Our parents' generation had faith in man, the ordinary man and not necessarily "our kind of man". Enlightened, cultured nations, people of our modern science and civilization, had to become—deliberately or by inertia—mass murderers of our people before we realized how distant is the day when we may put our faith in *man*. In its stead there awoke our faith in *our kind of man*. I don't know whether you have an accurate definition for this term. Who exactly is our kind of man? The Jew? The Israeli? The members of the "Kibbutz Artzi" organization? Probably all of them, for this is what you stated in the language of your symbols:

"For we were abandoned by all. Solitary, alone...
"The people of Israel can rely only
On the best of its sons... and on heavenly mercy."

The traditions of this people, that was abandoned by all the nations of the world and stood solitary and alone before his God, implanted within you the symbolistic world of faith in God.

But the philosophy of our religion enjoins us to obey the precepts—symbolic expressions of our being God's creatures who go before Him. And you want to justify your being a faithful Jewess who believes in her people.

Our illustrious teacher, the late Rabbi A. I. Kook, [chief Rabbi of Palestine, 1921–35] once referred to good souls like yourself as "compulsive saints", who do good but refuse to admit it. As we are aware that in the religious camp there are more than a few who do what is *not good* and refuse to admit it— "compulsive sinners" so to speak—the gap separating us is immediately reduced from that fathomless abyss which the untrained eye conceives it to be. That is why we felt we could publish your poem, just as we noted: as the innocent prayer of a daughter of Israel pouring out her heart before her maker.

With highest esteem,

ZURIEL

YITZHAK NISSIM

Isaac [Yitzhak] Nissim, a native of Baghdad, born in 1896, came to Palestine in 1925. After receiving a thorough religious education in his birthplace, he continued intensive study of the Talmud in his adopted land. He became an eminent authority on *halakha* (Jewish religious law), contributing expository articles on the subject and authoring two books: *Yen Hatov*, and *Kenoga Zedakah*.

Although Nissim did not serve in an official rabbinic capacity, he attained the presidency of the Religious Council of the Israeli Ministry of Religion, and in 1955 was elected one of the two Chief Rabbis, serving the Sephardim, the Oriental Jews, with the traditional title *Rishon L'Zion* (First in Zion). The other Chief Rabbi serves the Ashkenazim, the Western Jews.

Nissim did not belong to the extremist wing of Jewish Orthodoxy. Among the latter were the *Neturei Karta*, who did not even recognize the state of Israel but waited for a messianic theocracy. Nor did he belong to the *Agudat Yisrael*, who recognized the government but cooperated only sparingly with it. Nissim was committed ideologically and theologically to the State. But in his own "moderate" beliefs he was largely uncompromising. He took fierce pride in his office as exemplified by his refusal to leave his Jerusalem residence to meet Pope Paul VI when the latter stopped briefly on the soil of Israel during his visit to the Middle East. Nissim felt that the Pope should have called on the Chief Rabbi first as a matter of courtesy. He criticized the Pope also in a numer of doctrinal and political matters.

Nissim and his colleague, Chief Rabbi I. Y. Unterman were confronted with the dilemma: To submit to the legislative authority of a secular state (as, for instance, the Church of England), or to develop a self-contained, collective existence for the orthodox—a community within a community. The Rabbinate in Israel chose neither. It embarked on a course which would help shape, if not determine, the future of Judaism in Israel. While it attempted—sometimes successfully, sometimes not—to evoke religious self-awareness among the Jews of Israel, it did not entirely close its eyes to the modern world and its problems.

Curiously, Eastern European religious thought, if not all its customs, found a responsive chord among the Oriental Jews; similarly, the secularist Oriental Jews also adopted European lines of argumentation and attack.

One of Nissim's goals was to consolidate the various "tribes of Israel"—Western and Oriental—into one religious community. The other was to retain the Mosaic theophany and its moral and religious imperatives, making them a fundamental part of Israeli society, without impairing the rights of the individual to freedom of conscience and personal behavior.

Nissim's article RELIGION AND THE JEWISH STATE was published in *Jewish Life* March-April, 1956, pp. 6–12.

Religion and the Jewish State

by ISAAC (YITZHAK) NISSIM

THE QUESTION OF "Religion and State," in its application to the State Israel, has not ceased to interest writers and thinkers. Some express their opinion from their view of Judaism and nationalism, while others, through a lack of knowledge and proper understanding of the spirit of Israel, its Torah and history, create a view of Religion and State and the relationship between them that does not always follow from the facts.

With the former it is possible to debate. Such a debate could serve to stimulate thinking and clarify ideas. But debating with the latter can only bring an undesirable result. As our sages tell us, Rabbi Eliezer said, *"Be diligent in your study of Torah, and know what to answer the non-believer."* Rabbi Yohanan explains, *"This refers only to a Gentile non-believer, but a Jewish non-believer would only be further alienated by argument."*

Non-believers have no desire to define the problem or to find a solution. On the contrary, they cling to their ignorance and expound what they please, illogical as it may be. The conclusion is obvious to them even before deliberation. They start with the assumption that Religion and State are separate entities which should have no connection at all. Without a proper grounding in the fundamentals of the problem, they demand of the leaders of the State, both religious and non-religious, that they too conclude that the separation of Religion from the State is good for everybody. Under such circumstances it is obviously impossible to debate, for what could such a debate accomplish?

Before I begin discussing the problem itself I would like to point out that these questions are difficult and to answer them requires a comprehensive knowledge of *Torat Yisrael*, an understanding of its spirit and of the meaning of Nationalism and the State to the Jewish People. One who is not so equipped cannot present an authoritative opinion. It is therefore astonishing to see how many deal with these difficult questions without proper training. They decide Halakhic [religious law] questions, and ascertain what is proper for Judaism and what is not, what should be accepted and what should not, what is humane and what—considering the development of civilization and society—seems, heaven forbid, improper for a "progressive" nation. True, one who has not studied such Torah can be a profound thinker. But this is a far cry from the ability to decide accurately difficult questions of Halakhah. There is much in nature and science that at first glance seems absurd, but when we delve deeper we find the truth hidden there. So it is in the physical sciences and so it is in spiritual matters. There are laws and definitions in the realm of the spirit and they are just as necessary as boundaries between nations or one man's fold and another. Were it not for these spiritual boundaries, who knows where man's way would have led? Just as one who is not a mathematician or a physicist could not express a valid opinion on a problem in these fields, so the authority to deal with the question "Religion and the State" rests with those who are familiar with all aspects of Judaism.

There are three issues that are basic to our discussion: What is Judaism? How was the Jewish nation preserved in exile? What place does Eretz Yisrael [Land of Israel] occupy in Jewish concepts?

The first issue is, in keeping with the concept of other nations, usually associated with religion alone. This concept does not exist in the Jewish nation. If you will search in early Jewish sources you will not find it. The Jewish nation is linked with its Torah and no division between them can be found. Each segment is a part of both Religion and Nation and one who would create divisions must go astray.

The Jewish people have a *Torat Hayim*, a Torah that was created as the path in life. Because it is a Torat Hayim it is always as fresh as the day it was given on Sinai. As our sages put it, *"Each day you should consider it new."* There cannot be found any other system of law that has stood the test of so many generations and the many different circumstances in which the Jews found themselves, as has Torat Yisrael. At the time it was given, in contrast with the other faiths of the period that were not developed at all, our Torah was, then as today, on the highest level of justice and human ethics. This fact attests to the supernatural power embodied in it, which is above time and human comprehension. The Torah is G-d-given and eternal.

The Torah imposes many *Mitzvot* [commandments] upon us, some very difficult. But not all that is difficult is inadvisable nor is all that is easy desirable. There are also many things in the Torah that we mortals cannot comprehend. But has man revealed all the secrets of nature? Indeed, the more science advances, the more we realize how far we are from solving the mystery of existence. Science changes from generation to generation. It develops and advances but nature remains the same. We cannot change nature, we can only study it. So it is with our Torah. It is everlasting and we cannot change it. But we can study it to reach its essence, for in reaching this we arrive at the ultimate good and eternal happiness. Therefore we are not permitted to change the Torah or, heaven forbid, abolish any of its commandments. When we do not understand some segment of the Torah it is because we have not yet reached the substance of knowledge and wisdom. Had we, heaven forbid, adjusted the Torah to the needs of each generation then Torah could not have survived. We adjusted ourselves to the Torah and thereby preserved out national unity and were not assimilated.

Avowed secularists admit that in the course of the generations of exile, the religious tradition was the instrument that preserved the ember of Jewish nationhood. Hence in the view of even the extreme secularists, if not for Torah, Israel would not have been preserved in exile. Religion and nationalism then are linked in our people. This conclusion is very important. For if a *raison d'etre* is found for something under negative circumstances, it necessitates a continuation of it under favorable conditions. If in Exile, when we were subject to the laws and customs of other nations, the Torah was supreme and the laws of the different nations secondary, and we obeyed two sets of laws—no simple matter—in order to preserve our unity and uniqueness, now that we are in our own land and desire to establish our independence not only territorially but spiritually, is it not logical that this Torah should serve as the basis of our spiritual renaissance? If we were able to observe the *mitzvot*, in addition to fulfilling the obligations imposed on us by the states of our dispersion—now when we are in our own land, we should rejoice that we are required to observe only the *Mitzvot Hatorah*.

NUCLEUS CREATED

Now we reach the third issue, the position of Eretz Yisrael in Judaism. On the connection between them we need not waste many words. Many of the Mitzvot Hatorah are observed only in Eretz Yisrael under Jewish rule. In Exile we considered ourselves a torn and oppressed people. We mourned the loss of our independence. When our rule over part of the Land was established our consolation was incomplete, not only because the prophets' vision of a united Eretz Yisrael was not yet realized but also because many Jews remained dispersed in all corners of the world. The Redemption is not complete until all exiles are gathered in the Land.

The Torah commands us to go to Eretz Yisrael, to settle there, work the land, and protect it. The Torah places upon us exalted national duties and when we fulfill them because of faith, we do it joyously and faithfully. What law compelled us to travel to Eretz Yisrael, to bring the memory of Jerusalem to our lips every single day? Was it not by the strength of this faith that our forefathers traveled months and years over seas and deserts to a land ruled by antagonists who squeezed taxes from them, oppressed them and denied them freedom? Thus the nucleus of a society in Eretz Yisrael was created even before the advent of Zionism. Were it not for this nucleus would the issue of a Jewish National Home ever have been revived? This was the conclusion reached by that student of the history of the Yishuv [Jewish Community], President Itzhak Ben-Zvi in his book *"Eretz Yisrael Vyishuvah" ("The Land of Israel and Its Community")*, Jerusalem 1955, p. 15). He writes,

> *"Without the knowledge of this period that lasted exactly four hundred years it is impossible to understand the battle for independence and the victory, nor to evaluate properly the vision of rebirth."* He ends his book with the words, *"The idea expressed one hundred years ago by the great visionaries of Israel led by Rabbi Judah Bibos, that the redemption of the land can be achieved not through entreaties, but with faith in the future of Israel and the visions of the Prophets, that must accompany the power of arms—this idea to return and settle in the land*

of their forefathers was not mere fancy, but was turned into deeds . . . the vision was realized and the State of Israel stands secure at her post" (p. 416).

On what basis, then, can the charge be made that it was religion that prevented the return to Eretz Yisrael lo these many generations? This is a ridiculous libel on Judaism which, with its strength and through its commandments, enabled us to see the establishment of the State of Israel. Who were the first immigrants to Israel before Zionism? They were all devout believers who risked their lives to come to Eretz Yisrael just to fulfill the commandments pertaining to the Land. Only in their footsteps did others come.

When Israel achieved independence, the question arose: What form should we give to the State? All agreed that the religiously observant should be given the right to live their private lives according to their ideals. But is this a gift? How is it possible to supervise someone's private life? This discussion will examine whether religious requirements pertaining to the community as a whole should be preserved.

The commandments of the Torah can be divided into two groups. 1) Mitzvot dealing with man's relation to G-d and to his fellow man. 2) Mitzvot that are in the hands of the State to preserve or abolish.

No one can demand of every citizen of Israel that he fulfill the former. The latter category, however, is in the province of the whole community, and responsibility for them must be placed on the whole community if these commandments are not to be denied to the religious. Let us take vehicular traffic on Shabbat as an example. The automobiles that travel the city's streets on Shabbat disturb the Shabbat of those who observe Shabbat as a commandment of the Torah. This should not be taken lightly.

Restraints are necessary in order to preserve the spiritual form of the State and these are incumbent on the individual. Here we reach the question: How is it possible in a State, most of whose inhabitants vote for secularist parties, for religious laws to be passed?

Had this question pertained not to the field of religion but to another—to taxation, for example—what might the answer be? Is there any doubt that most people would gladly free themselves from taxes? And is not the military draft a heavy yoke? But when the government has the power to collect taxes and draft soldiers the individual accustoms himself to them and accepts the yoke. Therefore, we need not shudder if the observance of the Mitzvot is called "compulsion" because this term does not apply to our discussion. Compulsion is properly such only when the individual, as an individual, is compelled to do something that is related only to him and not to anyone else, something contrary to his will or conscience.

This does not exist in Israel. Has anyone heard of a law or bill requiring every citizen to place a *mezuzah* [tiny encased scroll] on his door? Such a law would mean religious compulsion. The religious Jew strives to see that every Jew understands the necessity for placing a mezuzah on his door, but not every desire is realized by passing a law.

What we ask of the Knesset is not that it fix the religious content of the State but that it do nothing to attack religion. We ask the Knesset to give the Rabbinic Court the authority to implement its decisions, but not that the Knesset formulate the laws of that court. There is then no overlapping between the Knesset and the Rabbinate. The Knesset cannot pass religious laws, but it can authorize the *Bet Din* to implement its decisions. The fear that the anti-religious Jews will organize and appoint their own "Rabbi" is unfounded. For the Knesset, with all its legislative authority, will still abide by the traditional definitions as to what is a Rabbi and what are his duties.

ARE THERE TWO JEWRIES?

I do not believe that "a crisis between religion and the secular population" exists in Israel. It exists only in the imagination of those who strive to make the Holy Land completely secular.

The opposition to "religious laws" that some have lately tried to create is actually an attempt to stir up the community in order to create a problem. The election for the third Knesset shows that the secularist parties—and we will take the three largest parties as an example—know that opposition to religion would affect the outcome. Each in its own way emphasized its regard for religion. This is borne out by the party which claimed that, although it favors certain changes, it is still bound to religion. There is no greater mistake than to think that the number of religious people is proportional to the number of votes received by the "religious parties."

We reject the contention that in Israel there are or can be two Jewries, one religious and the other not. Judaism means following its precepts. Therefore, there is but one Judaism. There are those who discharge their duties to their Creator and faith and those who, from convenience or ignorance, do not fulfill the mitzvot. The latter, however, are also interested in seeing in Israel a life of Torah and authentic Judaism. They endeavor to give their children at least a minimum knowledge of Judaism. Relatively few would remove religion from all areas of life.

Without impressing the form of authentic Judaism upon the life of the State we will not be able to merge all the groups in the State that have drawn from different cultures. We will not be able to preserve our ties with the Diaspora that thirsts to receive from Israel guidance and counsel, to receive spiritual support and a sign of cultural renaissance. For what does the Diaspora need? It is in need of Judaism, the Jewish tradition. If in Israel itself tradition will not be a part of our existence, how will we influence our brothers in the Diaspora? How will we preserve our ties with them?

Therefore there can be no separation between Religion and the State. We should reject any idea of establishing separate sections for the religious and the secular. Such a program would divide our nation far more than it is at present divided into congregations and tribes. We cannot ignore the fact that *"all Jews are responsible for one another."*

OPPOSITION TO REFORM

There is no doubt that Reform will not solve the problem, for in our view Reform is not religion. Religion is not man-made. It is G-dly, higher than man's understanding. A "religion" that is merely in keeping with the ideas of its violators who strive to fix their own way of life is nothing but an "arrangement" that determines the rules to be followed by the members of that sect.

It is then our duty to oppose with all our might the introduction of Reform in Israel. Through the external means of building beautiful edifices, they desire to diminish the authority of Torah and to alienate our youth from Judaism. As the prophet said, *"Israel has forgotten his Maker and has built beautiful buildings."* Reform is a greater danger to Judaism than secularism.

It should not be forgotten what Reform has done to the Jewish people. It has brought confusion and assimilation to the Diaspora. It has erased the name of Jerusalem from its prayer-books and weakened Jewish and national feelings. It has erected a bridge and paved a way from Judaism to Christianity. If under the impact of the miracle of the establishment of the State, Reform has changed and is now more interested in Eretz Yisrael, who can say how long this interest will last?

Does their support of the State give them the right to interfere in the life of the State and split the people in Zion? Did it ever occur to anyone that we should have closer relations with Christianity because there are Christians who support the State? We are obliged to preserve our spiritual unity along with our national and political existence.

Wonderment is widespread in the Jewish State, wonder about the past—the exile and the great catastrophe in Europe; and there is wonderment about the present—the establishment of the State and its spiritual form. We trust that the "secret" which saved our ancient people from the destruction that overtook other nations, which preserved us in exile, even though a nation cannot exist without a State, which let the nation see the establishment of its State in a land that was in strange hands—this "secret", *"the Strength of Israel shall not fail"*, will preserve our nation in the future forever. If we do not learn this we will go from wondering to wandering.

It is advisable then for the non-believing to examine their deeds and realize where their ways can lead Israel: uprooting of faith; alienation from the past; pursuit after material wealth; hate; and a splintering of the nation at a time when the need is for unity to develop our spiritual treasures. Only if we preserve the "secret" that has preserved us in the past can we exist in the future.

May the Lord cause to rest upon us His Spirit from above, and show us the way we should travel and the deeds we should perform, so that the earth may be filled with the knowledge of the Lord and from Zion shall go forth the Torah.

IV
Social Messianism and Unyielding Realities

YIGAL ALLON
YITZHAK TABENKIN
ARYEH L. PINCUS
SHIMON PERES
ISRAEL GOLDSTEIN
HAYIM HAZAZ

YIGAL ALLON

Yigal Allon was born in 1918 in Kfar Tabor, Palestine. He was educated in the Kadury Agricultural School, the Hebrew University and Oxford. Allon is a co-founder and member of Kibbutz Ginossar. During World War II he fought with the allies at the Syrian-Lebanese front. In 1945 he became commander of the celebrated *Palmah*, (the "shock companies") of the *Haganah*, forerunner of Israel's Defense Army. It was under his leadership that the southern Negev and the port city of Eilat were occupied by Israeli forces during the 1948 war of independence. Elements of Allon's Palmah unit inflicted defeat on Lt. Gamal Abdul Nasser and his military unit.

After the establishment of the State. David Ben-Gurion, the first Prime Minister, succeeded — over Allon's objections — in disbanding the Palmah (as well as the more aggressively nationalist *Irgun Zvai Leumi*, commanded by Menahem Begin), claiming that there must be only one army and no elite or ideological division in the defense of Israel. Allon then turned to political activity and helped found *Ahduth Ha'avodah*, a party that stood midway between Mapai, the non-Marxist labor group and Mapam, a Marx- and Moscow-oriented political entity. Allon became Secretary-General of Ahdut Ha'avodah and represented it in the Knesset.

Before the Six Day War in 1967 there was a noticeable rapprochement between Mapai and Ahdut Ha'avodah. Allon, a comparatively young man, became the protege of Mapai's Old Guard against whom Ben-Gurion, Moshe Dayan and Shimon Peres of the right-wing labor party, *Rafi*, fulminated. In the new alignment Allon first became Minister of Labor, then Minister of Immigration and Absorption, and Deputy Prime Minister and Minister of Education and Culture under the premierships of Levi Eshkol and Golda Meir, respectively.

After the 1967 victory an uneasy merger took place of Mapai, Ahdut Ha'avodah and Rafi (Ben-Gurion's faction), resulting in a new party, *Mifleget Avodah Yisraelit*. It was within this party that an intense struggle for leadership developed between Allon and the former Mapai stalwarts on the one hand, and Dayan and Peres of the erstwhile Rafi on the other.

A hero of Israel's war of independence, Allon is also intellectually motile, concerned with the future of democracy and of socialism in Israel. He is troubled by the problem not only of how to make man fit into present society, but also how to make him outgrow it — nurtured by Jewish prophetic ideas and universal socialist values.

The excerpts here cited are from his *MASAKH SHEL HOL* (Curtain of Sand), Hakibbutz Hameuhad, second edition, Tel Aviv, 1960, pp. 208–214; 39–40; 245–248.

The Essence of Democracy

by YIGAL ALLON

POLITICAL DEMOCRACY IS NOT enough. To reach fulfillment democracy must encompass the *social* as well. To ensure Israel's having a just regime, firmly based on its inner assets, it is not enough to provide for freedom of ballot and of legal defense, although in themselves these represent democratic attainments of supreme importance. A society that is truly democratic, in the fullest sense of the term, contains within itself political and social democracy combined. The equal right to vote, free of temptation or pressure on the day of election, if it is not accompanied by the equal right to a decent livelihood, may undermine the foundations of democracy and bring on such degeneration that there will remain only a formal, flimsy shell, incapable of uniting and uplifting a people.

The demand to cultivate democracy in Israel coincides with humanity's most sublime hopes for equality between man and man on the one hand, and with all that is noblest in the visions of our prophets, in Jewish tradition, and in the desire for Jewish national existence on the other hand.

In a state in which there is maximal social democracy, free from class distinctions and class oppression or exploitation, the citizen identifies with the national aims of the state far more than in a state whose people rob or are robbed by one another. The consciousness of equality strengthens the citizen's love and devotion for the society and the state, in ordinary days and in the most trying times alike.

There are many definitions of social democracy. Some call it "social justice" but mean only the recognition of the right of every man who works to a minimum standard of living. Others perceive it as a capitalistic society founded on the sanctity [of the principle] of private property and private exploitation of the workingman's labors, while at the same time recognizing the workers' right to organize themselves by trades and to be assured of a decent standard of living. Such definitions (and others of a similar nature) do not go beyond the limits of the right of maintaining class struggle, and the right of private control of the means of production, and the accumulation of wealth by private individuals through exploitation of others, and fiscal jugglery. A more liberal approach may be noted, as that for example, of a welfare state. The common denominator however for all these forms of democracy lies in the approval that their laws accord to social inequality among members of the human race, and to the right to amass wealth at the expense of others.

Indeed, from a purely moral point of view, the freedom to accumulate wealth and exploit others seems criminal, as is the act of stealing or robbing. The abolishment of private property and of the exploiting classes, and the entrenchment of the principle of political and social equality in the society are therefore legal acts, as the removal of theft, fraud and armed violence from a framework of legitimate tolerance is a lawful act. However, whereas defining theft and robbery as criminal deeds is approved by all classes inasmuch as such acts are harmful to the property-owning class, it is not yet customary to define exploitation as a sin, for this is antagonistic to the selfish interests of the heavily-propertied class. Nevertheless, as long as the workers are granted freedom to organize and fight for satisfactory wages, social rights and a decent standard of living, hand in hand with the freedom inherent in private enterprise—it would be an exaggeration to rank the manifestation of exploitation on a par with the manifestation of robbery. True, from a moral point of view exploitation is in no wise more virtuous than robbery, but from a politically practical point of view they should be quite disparate.

Whereas it is permissible and even essential to employ physical force against violence, the action directed against the manifestation of exploitation should be expressed by the force of legislation. Physical force may and should be directed against it only in the event that the exploiter refuses to abide by the legislation. Forbidding private ownership of the means of production, abolishing the right to exploit and accumulate wealth—all these prohibitive measures, enacted by means of democratic legislation, are not less moral than for example the right of imposing progressive taxation. This applies if the classless society cherishes within its boundaries the freedom of political organization, expression and decision. In other words, a socialist regime free of violence could serve as a cohesive factor to effect a true national unity. If the state of Israel were such, it would indubitably climb to record heights of *moral, national, social and military power*. Such a Utopia, however, all its charm and nobility notwithstanding, is likely to lead statesmen astray. Not only is such a situation not yet reality, but we cannot expect, in the light of Israel's specific historic circumstances, the full implementation of socialism now, without delay. Yet it seems that socialism is destined to reach full implementation in Israel, in *an Israeli fashion*, in accordance with the peculiar historic conditions of the Jewish people in general and of the Jewish state in particular. In fact, even before the society of Israel attains the highest level of social progress, cultural standards and moral values, it is already clear beyond a doubt that as far as all of these are concerned, Israel has not only far outdistanced the Arab countries in the attainment of social concepts but it need not be ashamed of its social achievements even as compared to the developed countries, capitalist and communist alike. We should, however, bear in mind that the Arab world too is undergoing social changes which are likely to lay the foundations for the building of a progressive society, which—*on its way to progress,* before attaining the level of a peace-loving society, may well remain as aggressive as in the past, reinforced by growing qualitative and cultural advancement in addition to its quantitative advantages.

All things considered, a suitable standard of living for the masses is one of the sources from which nations draw their military strength, all the more so a nation small in numbers and subjected to continued threat by nations which are tenfold stronger numerically but greatly inferior in social quality. *The standard of living in its fullest sense is the real source of Israel's military quality.*

From the materialistic point of view this standard of living means among others: a decent wage for every one doing any acceptable kind of work, to enable him and his family to have hygienically suitable living quarters; wholesome food in sufficient quantity to nourish a growing young generation physically healthy and spiritually free of poverty-induced inferiority complexes; and satisfactory medical and social services.

A high standard of health reduces the number of men disqualified for military service and improves the physical qualifications of the young. A decent standard of living increases the relative sense of satisfaction of the workers who constitute the overwhelming majority of the population of our country, and strengthens their spirit to bear with all of our citizenry the burden of our security whether on the field of battle and allied military services, or in accelerated war-production of military supplies.

No greater contributions to benefit our foes can, heaven forbid, be conceived than the manifestation of unemployment or emergency pay for relief work, or severely underpaid wages for farm workers, or a false scale of payment which negatively affects the real earnings of Israel's workers. The reference here is not to absolute (or even relative) economic equality for all citizens of Israel, and certainly not to luxury wages, but to decent wages to prevent hunger, humiliation and depression in our country.

However, man does not live by bread alone. A relatively high standard of living exerts a determining influence on a people's cultural, educational and technical achievements as well as on its spiritual stability. In the face of the scientific and technological developments in the world today, a healthy economy cannot be established by any nation which lags from a scientific and technical point of view in the agricultural, industrial, trade and security services. Military supplies and the various armaments have reached remarkable scientific and technological heights, and the process continues apace.

Clearly then, both the development of the modern economy and the techniques of modern warfare demand of the combatants considerable education and knowledge. Instituting compulsory elementary-school education was indisputably a most significant step toward the complete eradication and prevention of illiteracy and toward the discovery of latent abilities for the higher studies of scientific and technical subjects. The present situation however on the post-elementary-school levels of education—in the secondary and vocational schools and to some extent also in the colleges—does not by any means meet the cultural, economic and security needs of the State. The argument that in Israel the ratio of students who attend vocational and secondary schools and colleges far exceeds that of the Arab countries tends to be misleading. It should be remembered that a high percentage of students in a small population will total a smaller number than a low percentage in a large population.

The real needs of our country—in settlement, industry and labor, and in the military, administrative and cultural services—make *compulsory postelementary education mandatory for all.* Should the State's achievements along these lines be impeded by economic problems or by a temporary shortage of teachers, this program of compulsory education might be implemented by degrees, by adding one year of study every two or three years until the full ceiling of twelve years is attained. Post-elementary school vocational education for all our children will serve as a bridge for the integration of the returning exiles, the layers and sects in our populace, for it is the differences in cultural standards that are the chief factor in splintering our people into ethnic and denominational groups. As concerns university education, unquestionably the state is not able—and it would perhaps not be desirable—to make college education compulsory, or even free of payment. It is, however, highly desirable to encourage by means of propaganda and financial concessions, college study in the subjects essential for the state's welfare.

In encouraging college education for the masses, however, we run the risk of over-exaggeration. Training a surplus number of specialists, in excess of what the State may be capable of absorbing at the crest of its development, is likely to send many our degree-holding university graduates abroad in search of employment in their professional fields. The State needs specialists and professionals not only for our requirements here at home but also to serve as emissaries whom Israel can send to infant states in Asia and Africa to assist and guide them in specific projects. For such a mission the candidate's personality and personal traits are no less important than his professional capacities. Consequently, we must be selective and choose the best quality so as to provide candidates competent to fulfill these highly-portentous, politically sensitive missions.

Higher education need not run counter to the realization of pioneering ideals in a village or kibbutz society. Our agricultural economy is mechanized and operated according to scientific standards which rank with the highest in the world. Most of the kibbutzim have incorporated some form of heavy or light industry. All of them have post-elementary and secondary schools and their own dormitories as well. The work of planning and construction carried out by the kibbutz construction-companies is performed in large measure by kibbutz members who have obtained the necessary training or a wealth of experience. These require a large and ever-growing number of experts: agronomists, engineers and technicians; teachers and instructors; architects, doctors and the like, in far greater proportion than is required by urban society.

Post-elementary and secondary education, of a general and vocational nature, is an inseparable part of the *halutz* [pioneer] philosophy of life which seeks to build an educated, enlightened, progressive society. The more the membership will increase in the workers' settlements, and especially from among the younger generation, the more urgent will be the need to train experts, and the more possibilities will be provided to enable them to complete their higher studies in both general and professional fields.

The rate at which these needs and desires will be attained depends of course on the social concepts and spirit that prevail in the school—beginning on the elementary level, continuing through the secondary and proceeding beyond that to the university level—but it depends also, among others, on the concepts and methods practiced by the entire kibbutz movement, upon whom rests the obligation of assimilating its young people and preparing them to become scientists or practitioners of literature and the arts, in a fashion that will not be at odds with the concepts of a society founded on *self-realization* and *social equality*.

While the problem of preventing illiteracy among the younger generations is being solved with relative success, let us not overlook the fact that recent immigration from certain countries has brought us tens of thousands of adults who cannot read or write. An official estimate states that in 1959 we had approximately *one hundred thousand* adults who could not read or write; many knew very little Hebrew, if any. This number speaks for itself. The danger it spells for the social as well as the defensive strength of our society is perfectly clear. Therefore, a general and Hebrew education for adults, and also training for good citizenship, constitute a national and cultural mission of urgent and vital importance for our government institutions and a great many volunteers.

Furthermore, in the preceding chapters we stressed the need for *nationwide utilization of manpower* for Israel's war-effort in the event hostilities erupt. We underlined the necessity of organizing the entire people, including the women, in an appropriate military framework, to the point of our becoming an armed nation. Reference was made to the Reserve Army as the mainstay of ZAHAL, [Israel's Defense Army], and to the tremendous significance accruing to the network of outer defense which organizes all the many settlements with no discrimination as to world-outlook or political affiliation. We analyzed the social weaknesses and limitations of the regimes currently in power in the Arab countries which prevent their utilizing the full potential of their respective peoples.

Despite all its flaws, *the democratic regime of Israel enables us to entrust the people with arms* and to include the masses-at-large (with only rare exceptions) in assigning special defense-duties throughout the country. Commanding and commissioned officers can be chosen from *all layers of the populace,* without distinction of sect or class, but only in accordance with the individuals' capacities and talents. In Israel no discrimination exists in the selection of the young officers' cadre, or in their appointment and training.

Generally speaking, the standards fostered by a social and political democracy deepen the attachment and responsibility on the part of the whole nation for all that pertains to security, and contributes to the mobilization of its good will in addition to its physical mobilization. Our people's lofty cultural standards and comprehensive military organization will reduce the danger of public panic, the manifestation of mass flight and the formation of Jewish refugee camps, all of which are capable of disrupting the arteries of transportation, the civil defense arrangements, and the battle-array—as actually occurred in the Arab armies in 1948.

Obviously then, the fight for the Israeli standards of democracy in the broader sense is not only a fight for something entirely just, but also a fight for the ability to maintain, develop and strengthen Israel's military prowess.

ABSORPTION OF MIDDLE-EAST JEWS

Courage, loyalty and love of work are not *biological* but *psychological* virtues. There is no connection between the color of a man's skin and the virtues of devotion and diligence. These belong to the sphere of social existence and education. There is no doubt that an effectively assimilative regime and methods of training, tailored to suit the particular mentality of the majority of our immigrants from Eastern lands, will result in good citizens—educated, faithful, hard-working; strong when serving as soldiers, capable of integration with other troops in battalions, and in no wise inferior to the best of fighting men our country has ever known. Such results depend more on the assimilators than on those being assimilated.

But why engage in conjectures when we already have the wealth of decades of tested experience in pioneer settlement, in the *Haganah* [Defense Organization], in struggles and in war. It is an established fact that those who are popularly called "People of the Eastern Communities" [oriental] took an active part in all the stages of our defense—including the organization of self-defense cells in their countries of origin, in our uprisings and in our war of independence, and did not disappoint us. Furthermore, one of the most daring units in the history of the Haganah and later ZAHAL, a special reconnaissance unit of the *Palmah* which relied chiefly on undertakings performed by single individuals, beyond the enemy lines, under conditions of solitude and enormous danger, included in its ranks a number of these sons of the East, some of whom had not been in the country more than a few years, and they attained record achievements of diligence, devotion and self-sacrifice. In field units too these men gained recognition both for the number of participants and the quality of their performance. Those who fought in the southern sector will remember that in one of the decisive night battles in Operation 1948, the battle for the Egyptian posts in Huliakit—or as it is now known in Hebrew, Heletz—which formed the last block on the way to the besieged Negev, it appeared for a long while that these outposts would remain in the enemy's hands. The battle evolved into hand-to-hand fighting, with grenades, bayonets, knives and fingernails directed at the foe. Then, at dawn came the light for ZAHAL's warriors; the siege on the Negev was broken; it was now joined to the rest of the country. Many men of this valiant regiment (of the *"Givati"* Brigade) who won this victory were immigrants from the countries of the East, who had come to Israel but a short time before this, their first experience under fire.

The same applies to the absorption of the immigrants from the countries of the East into social and productive life. Large numbers of them have been assimilated by the workers' settlements of the village and kibbutz types, by industry and by offices, proving thereby that they can be integrated and rooted in our country. This constructive process depends on a sound absorption-policy by the government institutions and the Zionist movement, and on the extent to which the veteran settlers are prepared to absorb the immigrants in their villages and collectives, neighborhoods and housing-projects, even volunteering to go to the new immigrants' settlements wherever they may be, and move in with them—permanently or at least temporarily—in order to guide the newcomers. The fact that there still remain "islands of exile" within our country is proof that, although a great deal has been accomplished in the realm of assimilation, not all possible and essential means have as yet been exhausted for the purpose of removing these immigrants from the loneliness of their ethnic isolation within their separate housing developments and settlements.

* * *

THE KIBBUTZ AS A SECURITY FACTOR

Without detracting in the least from the security value of all the forms of private settlement, it should nevertheless be pointed out that it was the kibbutz way that was, and still is, the most suitable for the task of our country's efforts of defense and conquest. The structure of its economy and subsistence, and the social essence of the kibbutz body (including its political-movement organization) enable it from the start to serve as a more effective social and defensive unit than any other form of settlement.

Even the settlers of our earliest villages and those which were founded later, were forced to lead a cooperative or communal life in the first years of settlement. A fully cooperative mode of life helps overcome damage inflicted by nature, economic want and skirmishes with enemies, all of which await pioneer settlers in the outlying sections. But the advantage inherent in the communes remains even after the passing of the first difficulties which accompany the beginnings of settling on the soil. This applies to the social and economic as well as the military factor. However, here let us consider the military advantages.

The cooperatives are not divided into numerous splintered economic units and are not obliged to locate the farmhouse adjacent to the fields and livestock, as the individual farmers must do. The kibbutz-settlement is flexible in choosing its location; its size and dispersal will render it more suitable for defense purposes than any other form of settlement. The many-sidedness of the large farmstead, the multiplicity of its services, the growth of its mechanization process, of its workshops and occasionally also its industry, place at the service of its inhabitants a high level of technical proficiency and technical means which provide the defending settlers with a superior fighting capacity.

This society's collective ownership of the settlement and its means of production, along with the cooperative allotment of its work, make for a planned and pliable distribution of manpower for its tasks of production, services and warfare, and ensure a higher degree of efficiency and smaller number of mishaps than exists in any other social unit.

Another advantage that the kibbutz possesses is its personal and collective power of endurance under fire. There is at such times a merging of initiative and discipline, of individual action and collective coordination, and also a common sharing in the burdens and sacrifices; volunteer acts and performance of duties; guarding the commonly-owned property from harm as much as possible, and uniform readiness to sacrifice it in case of need. The society and economy of the kibbutz are *from the start* so constructed as to be able, among other things, to carry out all the above. Great similarity is to be found in a kibbutz-settlement and a military unit: both possess a collective character; in both the individual places himself at the service of the whole without any reservations; all properties, installations and accessories are intended to serve the common welfare. In both we see, functioning side by side, the laws of discipline and opportunities for initiative, acts of duty and volunteer acts, together with mutual assistance and other positive features which characterize a fighting unit.

Furthermore, the conscientious kibbutz member is accustomed to a deeply-rooted pioneer and civic sense of responsibility which in no wise reduces the sense of his personal contribution, for he joined the kibbutz of his own free will and not because of the "Law of Compulsory Service", and he lives in the kibbutz without compulsion and with the right to leave it whenever he wishes. He is called upon to demonstrate initiative in the work and in the social life of the kibbutz. The consciousness of public responsibility colors his every deed. While he does not lack all sense of ownership toward the commonly-held properties, he is not enslaved by them as is the private property-owner. What is more, the principles of maximal equality and highest mutual assistance are a source of encouragement to the kibbutz member in the fulfillment of his military duties inasmuch as he is certain that the kibbutz as a whole will bear in full the economic responsibility for his family and himself should he fall in battle or become incapacitated. These facts exercise a profound influence on the spiritual capacity to fight under severe battle conditions. All these factors derive from the collective way of life. To the extent that the social unit and the political framework of the united movement cultivate the kibbutz principles effectively, entrenching them in solid organizational structures, and stabilizing the educational and conceptual ideas of that society, the kibbutz will be able to serve non-urban defense as a coordinated military unit, its virtues outshining those of any other type of settlement.

During the days of the underground and of our struggle against the British, the various types of farm settlements provided the major portion for the skeleton of Haganah command. The agricultural settlements, and particularly those of the kibbutz movement, housed the training courses for officers and specialists as well as bases for the quartering, encampment and actions of the Palmah regiments, taking upon themselves the full measure of the agony contained in the British reprisals for the crimes of smuggling Jews in illegitimately or implementing various acts of sabotage.

In the various stages of the war of independence, when the struggle which at first was relatively limited, became an open clash of opposing powers, our settlements of every form and affiliation, including the towns inhabited by a heterogeneous mixture of ethnic groups, served as a country-wide defense formation and as bases of attack for Israel's military spearheads.

Each and every settlement made its own particular contribution according to its geographic location, social structure, and especial features; the enemy realized that the farm settlements are the basis of our people's existence and the source of its strength, as well as of the State as a whole. For this reason most of the foe's attacks were directed against these settlements, either for the purpose of capturing them for themselves, or to remove them as obstacles which prevented the enemy from advancing toward the heart of our country. Similarly, their assaults on the arteries of transportation, in the first stage of the war, were intended not so much to injure passengers or the means of conveying them, as to separate towns and villages from the country's center, thereby facilitating their conquest. Subsequent events however showed that whenever they directed their attack on a specific place it immediately became a "hedgehog of defense" and caused the attackers heavy losses. Each point became a defensive unit, comprehensive and strong; each group of such points constituted the district's defense; and all of them together formed the lines of total defense for the country as a whole.

Moreover, the populace outside the cities fulfilled not only strictly military tasks. The strategy of advance encirclement of Arab villages by Jewish settlements, decided in advance the fate of whole districts in our country, including some that were inhabited by a dense Arab population.

The fact that centers such as Tiberias, Zemah, Beisan, Acre, Haifa and Jaffa were more or less surrounded by Jewish settlements, determined their destiny from a strategic point of view, and they were "in the hands" of the Haganah and of ZAHAL before the first bullet was fired, even though their final and complete conquest necessitated warfare, with its consequent loss of life.

It is easy to surmise what the fate of the whole of Jerusalem might have been [in 1948] had the Zionist Organization had the foresight to surround our capital in good time with many Jewish settlements, and had the road from Jerusalem to the plain been settled by Jews. It is also easy to conjecture what would have befallen Jewish Jerusalem were it not for those few small agricultural settlements that had managed in good time to put down roots in the vicinity of the capital.

It was these settlements, which were "legitimate" bases during the mandate-period, that in effect determined Israel's territorial dimensions when England relinquished the mandate, and served as springboards for extending the borders. This was of course in addition to their all-important duty of supplying food and also men to serve as well trained soldiers and capable officers in the Haganah and the Israel Defense Forces.

YITZHAK TABENKIN

Yitzhak Tabenkin was born in Russia in 1899. He was one of the founders of Kibbutz Ein Harod in 1921. A member of Mapam, he eventually left the Marxist-Socialist party because it was too doctrinaire, too much concerned with the Soviet Union and too occupied with the Arab minority in Israel. He joined *Ahdut Ha'avodah* (Unity of Labor) to become its acknowledged ideologue. In fact, he was still referred to as the "grand old man" of the labor movement after his party had, in the late sixties, merged with the right-wing Mapai and with Rafi to form Mifleget Avodah Yisraelit.

Tabenkin had a commitment to socialism *per se*. One should keep in mind that the speech presented here was delivered shortly after Israel's independence. It was given at the Seventeenth Conference of *Hakibbutz Hameuhad* (Federation of Ahdut Ha'avodah Collective Settlements), at Givat Brenner in October 1949.

This keynote address also pointed to Tabenkin's view following the Six Day War of 1967 that Israel's rights to all the occupied territories were based not on conquest, but on history, on Jewish identification with the entire area, and—even more significantly—on what she could achieve in this part of the world as a positive social force. Tabenkin died in 1971.

The Kibbutz in an Era of Change

by YITZHAK TABENKIN

THE ANALYTICAL EXAMINATIONS of the Worker's Movement in our country, which were conducted at the convention of the General Federation of Labor and the settlement organizations, should be noted and clarified against the background of the changes that have transpired in the world. We live in a period only a few years following a world war and not many years—we cannot know how many—preceding a world war. We are at a crossroads. In the course of the last hundred years our people were scattered and moved from place to place; centers were destroyed and built up again; and only a small portion of our people, less than one million, was concentrated in the Land of Israel. In the same process our Labor Federation [Histadrut] too was established, the organized portion of the Jewish workers—farmers and laborers, the beginning of a Jewish proletariat, a Jewish agriculture—a phenomenon unknown to our people for two thousand years. At these conventions we question ourselves apprehensively: What lies ahead of us? Where shall we go from here? I do not know whether each and every one of us lives under the same high tension but there is no doubt that objectively speaking the tension is great. Our hope that the second world war would end with the rout of Nazism, the dissolution of Fascism, the abolishment of wars and the signing of a lasting peace between the socialist and the democratic countries, between the countries of the progressive world and those of the social revolution, was in vain.

The recent victory threatens the destruction of all human civilization by means of the atomic bomb; the hope for an end to war is gone. And we, more than others, have already experienced in our own persons during the last war the terror of what is coming.

It was not during this generation that the Jewish people first began to yearn for its country and its independence. Many generations dreamt and longed for the homeland and envisioned its redemption. Our generation's love for the motherland did not exceed that of previous generations and our desire for independence was not greater than theirs; but the vicissitudes and wanderings of our entire people in this generation utterly destroyed the imagined, misleading sense of stability that the Jews had left in the Diaspora. The Diaspora was destroyed, but even prior to its destruction, that partial stability was undermined just as it was undermined throughout the world. Class struggle turned into war—between states, between nations, and within every state. Life was robbed of security; the reaper cut down the feeble. But the feeblest among the nations were we, with our eminently nationalist character, notwithstanding the fact that our nation had no political, territorial or economic independence or fullness of spiritual and cultural life. Ours was the first people to fall victim and it was victimized to the greatest degree.

For forty years we have lived in a continuous state of upheaval which progressively undermined our existence. The stability that we attained here in Israel is functional and merged in the general process of a slowly evolving stability the world over. In the course of the first and also of the second world war, the United Nations Organization (at first it was the League of Nations) stood revealed in its total helplessness to secure peace or the development of humanity, to say nothing of securing our peace and development. Economic, political, social and cultural stability was disrupted in all the lands of the Diaspora. But the significance of the turmoil which struck capitalism throughout the world following the world war, and of the upheavals up to, and following Fascism, did not lie only in the undermining of the existing society. It contained constructive elements as well, a measure of evolving stability.

In the midst of all these upheavals we managed to achieve something here. That is an important attainment, a link in the beginnings of a different life on the face of the whole earth, one brick in the self-advancing world of the creative worker, a link in the alliance of nations and in peace among nations, in the conquest of nature, in the rule of culture, in the cessation of the murder and the slaughter—an alliance of men and nations instead of wars between nations and classes. The emergence of an independent center for the people of Israel, founded on workers in town and village, on a Jewish proletariat and a Jewish peasantry, is the fruit of that process; it determined our destiny, and not only ours.

This process of evolving stability decreed the extinction of national minorities. There was no reason to believe any longer in the continued existence of a national minority unless it could pass on to political and territorial independence. We, however, [until independence] were a national minority without any territory so that togetherness in itself was for us the one primary, essential factor, but we were denied the leverage of negotiation. Due to our situation in the world we always had to be engaged in some sort of negotiation, as in the Diaspora we still are. In the Diaspora we are still on the periphery of the working-classes. For decades masses of our people have been on the move; millions immigrated to America; we experienced the proletarian life only temporarily, as though crossing a corridor, but were shortly removed from it and now our people again are outside the proletarian ranks. Organizationally and ideologically we belong to it but we do not belong to it physically, nor do we belong to it objectively or socially.

This process, which drove Jews from one diaspora to another, is also the process which brought them to Israel where they found the bridge to labor and agriculture, the creation of villages, industry, and a foundation for an independence which fights for its independence. Through this process were discovered, despite tremendous obstacles, tens of thousands of Jews who were not only tossed about, uprooted and plucked up but who also became firmly rooted, building and creating a life of selfhood, an Israeli economic and defensive self-determination, until political independence in a portion of our country was attained. All this they achieved in the process of—becoming. Since the days of the Second Aliyah [the second great wave of immigration, roughly from 1904 to 1920] of workers about forty years ago, and the development here of an economy of workers and working-settlers throughout these forty years, we laid the foundations for independence, building them within the framework of the historic scheme so that today, with the establishment of the State in a portion of our country, we find ourselves once more at a crossroads, asking: What next?

Most of our people still live in the Diaspora; the process of destroying the Diaspora, of undermining our position in the Diaspora, still continues. Considering our situation in our country—and that includes our future, our security, the assurance of our existence—this is no side-issue. We know how sensitive many of us are to all that is transpiring in the various dispersions which comprise the Diaspora. In one area of the dispersion we see backs being turned on Zionism; in another, "normal" conditions are thought to be returning; the result is that aliyah to Israel is frozen.

A world war was waged and one million Jews congregated here. But are we going to be satisfied with only a spiritual center? It is undeniably worthwhile to have a center which is radiant itself and which radiates light to others, which awakens in the Jews of the Diaspora a sense of their own worth through the realization that a state exists in the Land of Israel, that there is a place for its politically independent existence. And certainly the cultural values are particularly vital: for pious Jewry this will be a source of immunity for religious faith while for non-religious Jews it will serve as a firm support in establishing cultural values. There are many diverse and variegated approaches. But as to the continuative process: the urge to immigrate to Israel in order to build it and be rebuilt by it; the need to lay a political and economic foundation for the national existence of our people as a whole—is not this process in danger of being slackened and depleted?

Above all it is important for us to know the truth: there is no stability in the world. No stability is anticipated for capitalism and consequently there is no serene stability in the Soviet Union or in other countries engaged in implementing socialism internally. This explains the lot of our dispersed people.

Of course these remarks can be misused and turned against me: "What are you preaching; do the Jews want war?" The truth of the matter is that no one wants peace as much as the Jews do. But the act of shutting one's eyes to avoid seeing the danger is tantamount to laying down one's arms. Artificially-induced tranquility and unfounded delusions comprise the real danger. From here, from this country, should come forth a troubled warning on behalf of the stability of the world and of our Diaspora as a part of it. For the world is being buffeted; its foundations are being shaken; it is on the brink of another world war, accompanied by the terror of atomic bombardment, and regardless of whether this will culminate in actual war or remain only a war of nerves—all this does not spell stability for minorities among the nations of the world. This is also the background for the increased incitement against our people and of the peril inherent in unrestrained brutality. The Jew is a convenient vehicle for conditioning the masses to hate nations as a preliminary to war among nations.

From here a troubled cry will go forth to the whole Jewish world: don't feel so secure and self-assured. Should another world catastrophe occur, heaven forbid, it is likely again to put the national minority to the self-same test it underwent during the last world war.

What is happening in the world around us does not augur well for the position of the Jews—in Europe, in the Arab-Islamic Middle East, or anywhere else on earth. In such struggles there are never guarantees for the life of a national minority like ours, to say nothing of security. There is not even the consolation of "assimilation or expulsion." Extermination is possible but assimilation is doubtful. In any event, some individuals may save their skins but for the majority a cruel fate has been decreed. Today there are no Jews in the world for whom this is news. Every logically-thinking Jew in the world is aware that for him there is no security anywhere. Yet some whisper: "Tell it not in Gath". Sometimes it is easier to shut one's eyes and sometimes one is afraid "lest it provoke..."

There is no need to worry about Jews' immigrating to Israel. True, there is no way of knowing whether they will be allowed to bring their capital with them. Jewish capital, too, has been through critical times so that it is no longer of the Rothschild variety, that is to say, a wonder-worker. It is now becoming increasingly anonymous. Jewish capital has lost its security so that nowadays the less it can be identified as Jewish the more secure it feels. This is not the time or the place to analyze this particular situation. What we want to know is: Will the Jews come here, along with their possessions, or not? Heretofore the wealthy Jew has put money into our country only as a purely philanthropic act. He has not yet brought his business-money here.

Some among us are of the opinion that we must attract capital here, as though capital could be attracted by propaganda. Money is attracted by profit and security. No one really believes that a rich Jew hesitates to bring his money here because Ben-Gurion said what he said about "socialist experiments". Words do not frighten capital away. Capital has fears of its own. It is not words it fears. It has its own daring too. It dares to go even to dangerous places if there is a good chance of finding there a high rate of interest, additional profit, cheap labor and the assurance that the money will remain safely in the investor's hands.

I am certain that we cannot draw Jewish capital here either by propaganda or by persuasive powers. One thing I am sure of: we will not lack for Jews. All of us are stunned by the sight of thousands of Jews going back to the Diaspora because they were discouraged by the difficulties of adapting themselves here. But this is not the future process for the spot vacated by a Jew is no longer available to him.

Once it used to be said: the European countries will not be built up without Jews. It seemed impossible to imagine that Berlin or Vilna or Warsaw would exist without Jews. Yet Vilna exists without them, Warsaw exists without them, Poland exists without its Jews... Needless to say, Europe experienced a shock. They learned something from Jews and they learned to live without Jews. It was not Jews alone who advanced capitalism; this was not a Jewish invention. The Jew who wandered away does not have his former home waiting for him, and as for Jews who go back, they are not going home. It was not home for them before and it will not be home in the future, and even what they did have there previously is no longer available to them.

It would be sad were many Jews to drag themselves there and back again. But a workers' movement such as ours, a fighting, building, creative movement based on social and economic principles, ought to lean on historic perspectives. The desirable process is: normalizing Jewish life, and doing away with the Diaspora—from both the geographic and the sociological point of view—with its mediation and its easy livelihoods.

There are two aspects to this process. For thousands of years Jews have immigrated here but this time our immigration has been utterly different from that of any preceding age. Our aliyah this time was creative; it put down roots. This process of doing away with the Diaspora will also generate an internal struggle. There is now an ongoing struggle between labor and private capital which is deeper and broader by far than that which its social appearances in their organized, political form, demonstrate.

It is not, heaven forbid, with a sense of joy-at-calamity that we assess these last forty years. But during this period only a very few villages were added. What was added, what came into existence during that period of time, since the beginnings of the workers' aliyah and the start of the Jewish laborer's move to settle the soil and found a collective or cooperative settlement? (The first workers' settlement was a commune, but from it and as part of it sprang the *moshav,* the cooperative settlement which gave its first members their experience and enabled them to plan their way further.) It is thanks to these creative labors that we attained political independence. Was it the number of residents here that brought us our independence? But we are only a small portion of our people. There were cities in the Diaspora, each of which had a much larger Jewish population than we now have in this whole country. Was this a basis for political independence, for independence of any kind? Imagine the Jewish population of this country without the workers' settlements of the various settlement-organizations: without the cooperatives, the collectives, the agricultural villages; and without the cooperative business-concerns: *"Solel-Boneh"* [contracting and industrial cooperative], *"Hamashbir"* [consumer cooperative], and *"Tnuva"* [dairy cooperative]. Would political independence have been possible without them? Could Tel Aviv, or a part of Jerusalem or Haifa, or farm villages, have brought genuine political independence to this whole country? Could even the finest political gifts have transformed these into a state?

Private capital in this country strives to concentrate where no danger threatens. It seeks safety and finds it in concentration. The creative process in our country, was and is to be found in spreading out, in building a workers' economy in all its forms and in all sections of the country. To this day private economy stands helpless and frozen before it. This does not mean that capital is to be disregarded, or that the capitalist did not create anything. One could ask the above question in reverse: Imagine the Jewish population of Israel without all that private capital has created; what would we have gained? We would certainly have lost quite a bit. And yet . . .

My remarks as to what is coming do not imply a prayer for war, or a "prophecy" intent on hastening the coming of war, or a wish to delay even by one moment the war against war. There is no way of knowing when war will erupt but this we know—the world is divided and splintered and we have but a short time left. All that we achieved to date is of value only to the extent that it serves as a basis not only for a historic continuation but for a genuine and timely continuation.

The main question is: What will be the continuation of the process of concentrating the Jews in Israel and of stabilizing our independence? Our political independence, within the boundaries of the split-up country, depends on various factors and on the boundaries themselves. As they are, these boundaries cannot last. Should they be meddled with, they will be moved, and not inward but outward. Should they not be violated, i.e. if peace should reign in Israel—even then they will not remain fixed and we shall arrive at the unification of our country. These borders as they are, with a desolate country beyond them, constitute an ever-present danger. Their weakness—not only is it a catastrophe but it invites catastrophe. This artificial division is a curse inasmuch as it denies us security at any point in the country whether inside the border or across it.

As to the soldiers of our defense army—when they return from these borders to everyday life in the interior, will they be able to settle down quietly in any spot at all knowing that settlements exist there, which number only a handful of members, a few dozen at most? Can we pin all our hopes on the border-patrol alone? It is common knowledge that border-police generally guard against smuggling and also watch over the smuggling. . . . Heaven forbid, not our police! Yet it is not on our border-police that we shall lean for the security of our borders.

Our country was in the gravest peril and we were ready to sacrifice everything for it for there was no alternative, as we did not have a state. It is all the more so now that we do have a state. It obliges us to feel profoundly concerned. It also increases the dangers anticipated. The need of the hour is therefore—settlements on the borders, in the mountains and in the Negev, not for the sake of continuation alone but for the continued existence of the independence we have won. Otherwise what we have won will not be able to exist.

Who will attempt to achieve all this? Will private capital build us new towns and new industries on the borders, in the mountains, and in the Negev? Is it possible to demand that private investors go all the way up to Menara and establish there a factory for milk-cans? Will you demand that of private capital? Why should they not erect this factory in Tel Aviv? Why should they build a milk-can factory in Menara in particular and then have to transport them to other places? But it is in the country's best interests to carry out this undertaking there, in Menara. Not only in the days of the underground did this remote settlement produce arms. Our arms-industry was established by the defense units in the kibbutz-kvutzah-moshav settlements. To this day the people who worked in it have remained anonymous.

What we need is industries not restricted to the cities even though transportation costs will raise the price of their products somewhat. What significance attaches to distances in a divided country such as ours? Developing industry in this fashion is essential for our life here. Will private capital be willing to perform this task? Not only the workers are devoting their attention to our conference. We are not part of a people concerned only with ourselves; we are the sons of a people who are concerned about our entire nation and its future. *Our class-issues do not in any way clash with the needs of our people and its existence.*

As these thoughts are being voiced not just *entre nous,* we must prevent any misunderstandings. We do not negate private capital. Of course we need private capital too, capital with initiative and ability, but first and foremost—capital. Not the desire for capital, or the craving for capital, or pretensions to capital, but real capital which acquires land and is productive. Not capital that obtains land gratis and subsequently receives income from it. What we need is people who will invest their own capital rather than obtain national capital or state capital which will bring them interest. What we need is capital that will build not by exploiting cheap labor but by employing self-respecting labor which assures the workers of a decent standard of living.

I believe in Jewish capital. It is not propaganda that will attract it here. Above all it will be anonymous capital. It will flow to what is promising and sure. It is destined to function in partnership with our cooperative-economy and our state-economy. It will acquire shares offered by the potash company—if this will belong to our country, as it should, and by the oil refineries—if these will be in our hands, as they should be. Shares of enterprises such as these will appeal to buyers with means. We wish and we hope Jewish capital will also come streaming to us. After all, here it is more secure than in any other spot in the world, for no nationalist danger threatens it. As for social danger—this may be anticipated anywhere in the world. It can go on working for years.

But in the Negev, along the shores of the sea, in the mountains, beside the borders, there the new man will be expected to change over to work. There the miracle will be accomplished through the productivization of masses of people who lack capital. And the majority of people lack capital. At this conference and at the workers' conventions in Israel it behooves us to clarify what are our aspirations.

ARYEH L. PINCUS

Aryeh Leib Pincus was born in South Africa in 1912 and came to Israel in 1948. He received the B.A. and L.L.B. degrees from Witwatersrand University in Johannesburg. Before settling in Israel, Pincus practiced law, was chairman of the South African Zionist Federation and chairman of the Zionist Socialist Party. In Israel he made his mark both as an attorney and as a founder and managing director of the national El Al Airlines. A determined and imaginative administrator, he became successively a member, Treasurer, and Chairman of the Executive of the Jewish Agency (which operates, generally speaking, as a non-governmental, international organization to coordinate all Jewish overseas efforts for Israel including education, teacher training, investment guidance, immigration). He later was also elected chairman of the Executive of the World Zionist Organization.

Impelled by a tremendous drive and resourcefulness, Pincus has achieved a rather noteworthy reputation in an arduous and near-impossible undertaking as the head of an agency which has no governmental power, but does have representatives of administrative bodies—frequently dissident, ideologically polarized, quarrelsome political groups.

Pincus' chief and improbable task was to bring about aliyah (immigration) of Jews from the prosperous and free countries to Israel. It is this problem that he discusses in the paper he wrote for this anthology.

The Crux of the Problem—Immigration

by ARYEH L. PINCUS

THE MODERN ZIONIST MOVEMENT began at the end of the nineteenth century, and with it the term "Zionism". However, the aspirations for a return to Zionism and for a renewal of Jewish sovereignty are as old as Jewish history since the destruction of the Second Temple. Although the Jews were dispersed, they were a people united in spirit, in faith and in mode of life, as well as in their desire to return to their homeland and to re-establish an independent Jewish life there.

At all times and in all circumstances the Jewish people felt close to Eretz Yisrael, and made constant efforts to achieve its inspirations. In the last decades of the nineteenth century a Jewish nationalist and political movement began to take shape, the Zionist Movement. In 1897 the first Zionist Congress was convened in Basle, and the World Zionist Organization was established for the purpose of rallying the Jewish people for the establishment of a Jewish State in Eretz Yisrael. The Zionist Movement launched immigration and agricultural settlement activities in Eretz Yisrael. At the same time it undertook intensive political activities to gain political recognition for Zionist goals. In 1917 official recognition was achieved with the Balfour Declaration, by which the British Government stated that it *"looks with favor upon the establishment of a National Home for the Jewish people in Palestine."*

That terse letter from the Foreign Secretary of what was then the most powerful empire in the world with one stroke transformed the Zionist Movement from a band of starry-eyed visionaries into an effective instrument for national revival. For the first time since the fall of Jerusalem almost 2,000 years ago, formal recognition was given to the political relationship between the Jewish people and Eretz Yisrael. Zionism was no longer the expression of an aspiration; it had become a political reality.

For the Jewish people the Balfour Declaration carried a message that stirred dreams which had been dormant for centuries. At the time, the majority of the Jewish people was in East Europe. When news of the Declaration reached the Jewish masses, its effect was electric. To the East-European Jews who were then being buffeted by the forces of war and revolutionary upheavals, the Balfour Declaration stirred Messianic hopes. The British statesman loomed as a kind of modern Cyrus, and the Declaration appeared to be the response to the agonizing yearnings and hopes since the days of the first Zionist Congress in 1897 and the founding of the Zionist Organization. The Balfour Declaration threw open the gates of Eretz Yisrael and presented the Jewish people with an

The Crux of the Problem—Immigration

unprecedented opportunity for the establishment of the Jewish National Home.

In the course of the thirty years between the Balfour Declaration and the final breakdown of the British administration in Eretz Yisrael, the Zionist movement conducted a bitter and protracted struggle with all the ruling British governments to make them adhere to their political commitments. But after twenty years of Israel's existence as an independent Jewish State, the question of "perfidious England" is of less practical importance than the problem of the Jewish people's failure to respond to the initial opportunities offered by the Balfour Declaration. The failure—fifty years ago—to seize this most historic opportunity was tragic enough. That failure is all the more significant because it was by no means exceptional in contemporary Jewish history.

Time and again our people was presented with tremendous opportunities and on each occasion the response of the Jewish diaspora was weak and tardy. For years Chaim Weizmann called to the diaspora: "Jewish people, where art thou?" With the first wave of excitement there could have been set in motion a great movement of aliyah and settlement in Eretz Yisrael. But the response did not measure up to the challenge.

The tragedy was repeated a second time thirty years later when the United Nations Assembly decided upon the establishment of a Jewish State. The 650,000 Jews who lived in Eretz Yisrael responded in full measure to the historic challenge, at the cost of tremendous sacrifices. But the Jews of the Diaspora, most of whom were now in western countries, once again failed to respond in a manner in any way commensurate with the opportunity. Since 1948 one and a quarter million *Olim* [immigrants] have come to Israel, but no more than 5% of them were from the west. The financial aid of Diaspora Jewry to Israel was unprecedented in its generosity, but even this aid never matched the enormous needs of absorbing one and a quarter million Olim dur- during so brief a period in a country that was not yet economically viable.

The sad truth is that the Balfour Declaration of 1917, the United Nations' decision of 1947 and the establishment of Israel in 1948 were landmarks of tragic failures for the majority of the Jewish people and inspiring achievements. for that minority who actually settled in Israel, worked to build it and fought for its security. To the majority, recent Jewish history should be a cause for heart-searching, for spiritual stocktaking, for *Heshbon Hanefesh*—the reckoning of the soul.

This reckoning has now become vitally important, for once again we are in danger of failing to seize a historic opportunity. The massive financial response of Diaspora Jewry following the Six Day War was an expression of the profoundly committed solidarity of Jews the world over with Israel. What we must ask is whether this was a spontaneous but transient reaction provoked by an extreme sense of threat, or whether it marked the beginning of a profound transformation. The Six Day War, when Israel's very existence was in jeopardy, and the magnificent victory which changed the frontiers and the composition of the population, have pointed up as never before the stark fact that Israel still counts only 17% of the Jewish people of the world. From the point of view of the Zionist ideal it was always clear that it was not enough to have a State for the Jewish people but that the Jewish people must build this state and live in it. "Volunteering" for Israel during an extreme crisis certainly expresses a sense of identity with Israel. It is equally clear that volunteering cannot serve as a surrogate for aliyah. What was obvious to Zionists for a long time should now have become crystal-clear to all: if Israel is to exist in peace, thrive economically and become a centre of Jewish life, then more and more Jews, hundreds of thousands of Jews, will have to come to Israel in the next few years as Olim.

The need is all too obvious, and the opportunity exists as never before. And yet, the nagging question is whether this time the tragic failure will be averted. Encouraging signs are everywhere. Jewish organizations in the diaspora that in the past had looked askance at aliyah, or opposed it, now recognize the need for aliyah even from their own countries. Aliyah has become a fashionable topic of discussion for Jewish meetings. All these are heartening winds of change. But the essential and overriding issue is whether Diaspora Jews have a *will for aliyah*. Israel, the ultimate expression of national revival, has survived by swift and dramatic successes against its enemies. It is now obvious that *lasting* success depends upon what the Jewish people can do within itself. Political and military achievements must be followed up by Jews coming in greater numbers on aliyah, to settle and live in Israel.

The issue of aliyah is no longer a matter for committed Zionists only. It must become the concern of every Jewish organization, community and congregation in the Diaspora. But to Zionists everywhere falls the difficult and probably unenviable task to educate and prod, to keep the issue alive, to challenge and arouse. Aid for Israel is no longer the unique preserve of Zionists. The sense of identity with Israel is today shared by most Jews. What will distinguish the Zionist movement will be its role as the spearhead of a massive movement for Aliyah.

Its tremendous achievements are history. The Zionist movement must now go on to make sure that the Jewish people will reap the full benefits of these achievements. In this new era of Jewish identification following the Six Day War, it is up to Zionists to lead the Jewish people in the great movement of aliyah to Israel.

SHIMON PERES

Shimon Peres was born in 1923. He arrived in Palestine in 1934 and received his primary training in the youth village Ben-Shemen. Peres became an active member of *Hanoar Haoved* (Working Youth) and eventually was elected Secretary-General of the organization. He spent some time in the United States, attending Harvard University.

His extraordinary administrative talents attracted the attention of David Ben-Gurion, Israel's first Prime Minister and Minister of Defense. In a relatively short time Peres became Director-General of the Defense Ministry, 1955–59, and then Deputy Defense Minister, 1959–65. As Ben-Gurion's right hand, Peres' achievements in obtaining military equipment in France, the United States, West Germany and other countries were tremendous. He also was instrumental in modernizing and mechanizing the army and the air-force and in the installation of the atomic generator in Dimona. In 1957 the French government awarded him a citation as Commander of the Legion of Honor.

A staunch supporter of his mentór, Peres followed Ben-Gurion when the latter split in 1965 with the ruling party Mapai and with Levi Eshkol, Ben-Gurion's successor as Prime Minister, to form the Rafi party. As Secretary-General of Rafi, Peres fought for electoral reform, restructuring the General Federation of Labor, Westernizing the democratic process in Israel, and dislodging the Old Guard, who had he felt, been passed by the caravan of Jewish history a long time before.

However neither the charisma of Ben-Gurion nor the brilliance of Peres helped Rafi. The new party did not do well in the 1965 elections to the Knesset. After the 1967 Six Day War, Peres and other leaders of Rafi—but not Ben-Gurion—returned to Mapai as it aligned itself with other labor factions to form a new Labor Party *(Mifleget Avodah Yisraelit)*.

An activist by nature, Peres nevertheless devoted much time to observe and analyze the rhythm of the oncoming march of events in Israel and elsewhere.* The following passages were culled from various articles and speeches by Peres and combined by the author into the present form for this anthology.

---

* After the 1969 Knesset elections, Peres was included in the new coalition cabinet of Premier Golda Meir, his erstwhile political adversary, as Minister-without-portfolio. Political vicissitudes and the compulsion for a cooperative approach to external threats have practically eliminated the personal frictions between the Prime Minister and her colleague in the government.

Jacob's New Ladder

by SHIMON PERES

I RECALL THAT DURING his stay in Israel, U Nu—the former Prime Minister of Burma—visited one of our air force bases. When the officers born outside of Israel were presented to him, the birthplace of each of them was mentioned: South Africa, Rumania, United States, Yemen, England, etc. The climax of his visit was a festive dinner at which U Nu spoke. He opened his remarks by saying: "I was glad to note that so many nations sent you their men to help establish your air force . . ."

The Israeli too is sometimes inclined to overestimate the influence that the cultures of the countries of origin exercised on the character of the State of Israel. The Jews came here from variegated realities, prompted by a variety of considerations, united—by a common vision. Our freedom-movement, as one of its leaders has justly pointed out, was motivated not by reality but by vision.

Small wonder therefore that a person coming from afar finds it difficult to comprehend the concept of the ingathering of the exiles. Yet this concept constitutes the very foundation of the State of Israel, and the process of implementing it has not as yet been fully exhausted. The Jewish drama is still unfolding; it will leave its imprint on Israel's future.

A day will come—when the immigrants to Israel will include also distinguished representatives of the Jewries of Soviet Russia and the United States—when Israel will become the leading testing-ground for two confrontations:

1) One will come as a result of comparing the widely divergent cultures which exist in our world. For in Israel you will find persons familiar with the taste of communism and the taste of capitalism; with the culture of the west and the culture of the east; people who know the mountain-paths of Yemen with its life of the Middle Ages, and those who know the mechanism of the newest type of computer; people who admire French culture in its metropolitan as well as its suburban settings and people who studied Shakespeare no less than the Bible. There is no doubt that the society of Israel is potentially capable of evolving into the most interesting society of the twentieth century, presenting as it does the opportunities of summarizing, in a direct manner, a conglomeration of new and diversified experiments and currents of thought.

2) The other will result from a people's identification with its most remote past. The Jews who immigrate to Israel cover not only geographic but also historic distance. Will it prove disillusioning or rewarding to live again in the

ancient bosom of a people so rich in struggles, and to investigate whether the historic genetics of our people has been diminished or increased by the thousands of years of wandering over vast distances?

From another point of view too Israel will be a unique country. The Zionist movement was founded in an era marked by intense suffering for the Jews, most of whom lived in western and central Europe. It still continues its forward march now in these days of remarkable spiritual flowering, the like of which has perhaps never been known in our history.

Toward the close of the twentieth century we find ourselves on spectacular historical and geographical summits, with lights and shadows emanating from our spiritual revival on the one hand, and from our political resurrection on the other hand. Furthermore, as often happens, the enchanting view represents a merging of mountains and sea: the elevation is high and the direction for sailing is open to choice.

2

That the Jewish people have experienced a spiritual revival is no longer doubted. True, this is not a forced revival similar to those that occurred in the past, which were purely introvert in nature. Although the present revival is Jewish in origin, and completely Jewish in character, its end results have not been entirely Jewish.

This process of spiritual rebirth boasts of non-Jewish spectators on the sidelines. It includes a group of subjects which digress from Judaism. Signs of this revival may be detected in numerous, frequently unexpected places ranging from the lists of best-selling books printed every week, to the culmination of long-fermenting thought published years later.

Arthur Miller, Saul Bellow, Israel Bashevis-Singer, Bernard Malamud, Arnold Wesker, Albert Memmi, Bart-Schwartz are all authors of Jewish extraction who deal with Jewish subjects and enjoy a reading-public that is not exclusively Jewish.

All the brilliance attributed to Jews, the searching temperament, the somber intellect, the unacknowledged sentimentalism, the historic skepticism, the veiled solidarity—all of these are articulated in this vague classicism. "*What "What the tongue utters, the tongue is powerless to explain"*, declared Witkenstein. We sense the Jewish expression even before its meaning is explained to us.

However, not only in literature (and its mischievous offspring! Who ever dreamed that Sholem Aleichem's *Tevye*, "Fiddler on the Roof", would be a hit in Tokyo in the Japanese language!), but in the realms of thought too one feels this resurgent intensity. Levi-Strauss searching for a permanent structure in the society of man; Marcuse forecasting the new student-population's adamant refusal to yield to the demands of a consumer-society; Maslow challenging Freud's theory of depth-psychology and arguing that the subconscious also possesses peaks and sides that are positive, creative, and loving—their approach is new, lively, tumultuous and non-conformist all the way!

Moreover, Jews have attained leading positions in the more exact sciences such as physics, chemistry, biology and electronics. From Professor Rabi to Dr. Salk the list is long and variegated.

It is of course not the first time that Jews have excelled in the spheres of scientific and spiritual erudition. This time however one cannot but be impressed by their brilliance as well as by the fact that it also reflects definite mutations which have occurred in the composition and structure of the Jewish people.

A French-Jewish philosopher attempted to sum up this change by means of an example drawn from the field of transportation. For many generations, he declared, the life of the Jews could be likened to a ride on a subway-train; Jewish life flowed beneath, so to speak, the life of other nations. As everyone knows, one cannot see any exterior view from within the subway-train and conversely, one cannot observe from outside the passengers and their behavior inside the subway-train. Today, on the other hand, he added, the life of the Jewish people may be compared to a bus-route: along the earth's surface it wends its way, on the main roads, with windows commanding unobstructed views through which one may look at the general landscape, while from outside one may obtain a reasonably clear impression of the passengers riding within.

But to depart from the language of similes—the parents of the contemporary Jewish generation frequented synagogues a great deal, whereas their progeny of the current generation attend universities in large numbers. In the synagogues there were only Jews; at the universities there are also Jews. In the synagogue people pray a great deal; at the university they study a great deal. The preceding generation was given to yearning; the new generation prefers to make concrete plans.

Jews are progressively becoming a nation of students, instructors, scientists. Eight out of ten Jewish youths in the United States attend universities; four out of ten Jewish youths in the Soviet Union are said to be attending universities. Except for Israel those are the two largest Jewish communities in the world.

This phenomenon is manifested in similar proportions and at an increasing pace in most Jewish communities. Jewry's traditional preference for the career of Talmudic prodigy, merchant, tailor, goldsmith and violinist, has currently been replaced by the more modern ambition to be an engineer, physician, lawyer, scientist or industrialist.

This structural transformation has led to a new rapprochement between Jew and Gentile on the one hand and between Jewry and modern science on the other hand. Like every initial meeting it presents both opportunities and problems which previously did not exist.

The Jewish individual no longer appears inferior (or at least not to the same extent) in other people's eyes (according to New York wits it is "fashionable" nowadays to be Jewish) and on his part the Jew is less apologetic than he used to be. The new Jew devotes more attention to his physical comfort, to aesthetics as such, and even to sports, which had previously been altogether foreign to his way of life.

Contact with the new science has not plunged Jewry into confusion: there was no need to grant rehabilitation to Galileo, for it had never adopted a negativist religious stand against the new sciences except perhaps in the sphere of philosophy.

By nature Judaism actually never was a religion in the accepted sense of the word (the Hebrew word *dat* is not a translation of the word *religion* but is rather synonymous with the word *din,* meaning *judgment* or verdict—as for example, *ahat dato lamoot* ("the only verdict for him is death"), but rather a comprehensive faith, monotheistic, pluralistic and universal. This world-outlook is an outgrowth of our concepts of homeland, language, history, moral values and faith in one God which developed in the innermost depths of one people seeking to excel ("the chosen people"), impelled by its conviction that mankind as a whole is destined ultimately to excel in the practice of moral values.

No religious mediator or ecclesiastical hierarchy stands between the God of the Jews and man. Every man was created in God's image, without being restricted to any one concept of physiognomy, and men's dimensions are indeed as varied as the human race itself is varied. Essentially, therefore, there is no contradiction between Jewish tradition and the new interpretation of the seven pillars of wisdom in modern style.

But as already noted, this double encounter also presents many problems and questions. Juxtaposed to the mountain is the sea. What shall the Jew do with his newly-won circumstances and resources? Whither shall he sail? Toward Jerusalem, toward Babylon, toward Greece?

Will there be a continuation of the concentration of Jews, this time for idealistic reasons, in the State of Israel? Will they embark on an effort to transmute the places in which they now live, in the Dispersion, into a new Jewish ideology? (Rabbi Soloveichik declared in one of his addresses that a youth studying a page of the Talmud in Boston serves his people as well as the youth standing watch on the walls of Jerusalem.) Will they, with terrifying simplicity, sail away toward beckoning horizons that are not at all Jewish, either from the geographic or from the philosophic point of view?

The fact that there is essentially no contradiction between Judaism and the new science does not signify, however, that a part has already been found for Jews to play in modern life. All the immense spiritual strivings of the Jewish people have yet to find the fitting opportunity for renewed expression in our society.

Will the new science devote some time, in the midst of its extraordinary achievements, to a reappraisal of the accepted moral assest and to reflection on their value and ultimate destiny in present-day society?

3

No one will deny that in the imagination of the world Israel occupies considerably more space than it does on the geographic map. Since time immemorial Israel has been richer in drama than in physical dimensions.

Moreover, the independence these twenty years of the State of Israel has from the moment of its inception been characterized by three features which aroused broad repercussions: 1) the structure of its society, particularly the cooperative and collective movement; 2) its security set-up which established new standards in the quality and organization of a people's army; 3) its political activities in the southern half of the earth where most of the underdeveloped countries lie.

Israel dared to pit itself socially against vast ideological empires, repulsed three mighty attacks by military forces numerically far superior and hewed its own particular paths on the continents of Africa and Asia. Thus, the spiritual revival that our people experienced was the faithful companion of its political exertions, and although the return to Israel is ideologically motivated, it is nevertheless difficult to separate the two: it is vision that envelops political activities with a significance that is neither professional nor routine.

But even the establishment of the State of Israel, possibly the greatest achievement in our entire history, did not rid us of fundamental problems. At the very apex of our success it behooves us to formulate historic answers to the penetrating questions that will determine our future: our relations with our Arab neighbors and our relations with our fellow-Jews.

Immediately after the Zionist movement was initiated the confrontation between two movements for national revival began to emerge: the Arab movement, which had a rear guard in Palestine, and the Jewish movement, which had its pioneers in Israel (Palestine). Two of the leaders of these movements, Prof. Weizmann and Emir Feisal*, believed that a clash between their respective movements was not inescapable. It seemed to them that the area available was large enough to make a mutual understanding possible. Subsequent developments however belied the forecast: what followed was conflict and not neighborliness. This is not the place to enumerate the entire store of emotions which tend to overpower logical considerations.

Immediately following the establishment of the State of Israel a heavy curtain descended on communication between Arabs and Jews, a curtain all too frequently punctured by bullets and shells.

Hatred was never an ideal of the Jewish revival movement. What are the prospects of our becoming free of it?

While the movement for *aliyah* (immigration) to Israel contained a few idealistic elements, the vast majority was impelled by the profound sufferings inflicted on the Jewish people in many of the places in which they lived. It is sad to reflect that idealism diminished as suffering was reduced. Now, even though the Jewish people is undergoing a process of recovery, yet the ties between Israel and the Diaspora, characterized as they are by intense feeling and broad financial support, are none the less quite circumscribed: the movement for *aliyah* [immigration to Israel] has been replaced by campaign-

---

* Feisal, later King of Iraq, in 1919 signed an agreement with Dr. Chaim Weizmann, the Zionist leader, for mutual aid in the national aspirations of the Arabs and the Jews. (Eds.)

directing organizations, and spiritual dialogue has been succeeded by the continuously growing schism between the specific world of Israel and the identity-losing world of the Diaspora.

4

Is any solution discernible for all of these fundamental problems? At first glance it seems that just as the character of the Jewish people's questions has undergone a metamorphosis, so must also the character of the answers now be correspondingly different. There is no substitute for the continued concentration of Jews in their own country, or for Israel's efforts to effect a peace with the Arab world. Immigration, however, will in the future not be what it was in the past, and peace will dawn at an altogether different point than was heretofore surmised.

The Zionist movement must move to the universities. That is where most of the new Jews are. It is there you will find young people who have not yet adopted a firm and lasting stand, whose mobility is made easier by being objective. Their aliyah should flow, moreover, from one university directly to the other university (from theirs to ours), and not merely from one country to another.

Israel should become the university-center of the Jewish people, of the students among the Jewish people. One can scarcely envisage a more impressive achievement than the establishment of a series of universities functioning in the State of Israel filled with young Jewish students from Israel, America, England, Argentina, France, South Africa and the like. Arrangements would be made for each group to follow its own curriculum. At the same time however they would benefit from three additional dimensions which they now lack: the dimensions of one people, one country and one language. Such an experience is likely to be profoundly soul-stirring and productive: the young Jews of other countries will bring with them the spirit of the new age and teach their Israel-born peers the elements of conducting a modern economy, while the Israelis will teach their Diaspora-brothers how to live as everyday Jews, free of complexes, with a high potential of creativeness.

Such universities should devote themselves to both the scientific and technological subjects, and the specifically Jewish and philisophical subjects. The typical curriculum should include also their people's historic mission. These should be universities plus an additional something, not universities minus something.

Today the universities teach, among other things, the methods of developing a modern economy and of increasing production. (Doubt no longer exists concerning the direct correlation between the scope and standards of higher education and the scope and standards of the national level of production.) But the universities are not restricted to teaching alone; they are also inhabited by a youthful population, a new addition to our present world. We may be sure that this youthful population will not merely be taught but will also think for itself and strive toward change and progress.

5

All of the Arab states won their independence before Israel did so. When our War of Independence came too close, upon the advice of the Mufti of Jerusalem, most of the Arabs who lived within the political boundaries suggested by the U.N. Assembly, fled across the border. It was only natural for Israel to direct peace-making efforts across the border toward the Arab states. The last twenty years have constituted total failure in the attempts to attain peace and good-neighborliness due to the uncompromising refusal of the Arab countries to respond to these overtures.

The Six Day War altered the situation radically. True, today too the problem of security continues as the chief problem of the Jewish people but it is now mitigated by certain noteworthy and meaningful changes: the present borders are easier to defend and provide a consequently improved balance, in area if not in arms; and significantly, we now live together with most of the one-time Palestinian Arabs, with no hostile authority of any Arab state separating us.

If we succeed in attaining a form of honorable co-existence with these Arabs, we will have paved the right path to lasting peace between the national revival of the Arab world and the national rebirth of the Jewish people. Our foe has never been a nation, race, origin or creed. Our foe is a politically-motivated policy of war. Our foe is—the hostility itself. In the final analysis, hostility is cured by direct contact between the people affected and not merely by diplomatic semantics. There is nothing wrong in choosing to discuss with Palestinian Arabs the future of their country rather than discussing with Hussein the future of the residents of the Western Bank: better talk to the people than to a king.

The most pressing problem now facing us is our policy regarding the occupied territories, as they are popularly called, which actually means determining the relations that shall prevail between us and the 1,300,000 Arabs who live here. A number of fundamental principles are already discernible; others still require a great deal of clarification. It appears that our initial approach, with our positive, responsible attitude, has already gained wide support among the Jewish people. This approach includes—and must, I believe, continue in the future to include—the following guidelines:

1) We must avoid severing the Arab community from the Arab world;

2) Understand that Arabs are members of a specific nation and that they have the full right to maintain their identification with their own people even as a minority;

3) Refrain from government interference in Arab life unless security demands it;

4) Supply the Arab community's religious needs, both Moslem and Christian;

5) Raise the standard of living and improve the services provided to the Arab community;

6) Settle the problem of the refugees living within Israel's borders;

7) Prevent the national differences between the Jewish and Arab communities from evolving into class distinctions between the two. Let each national group attend separately to its own economy and employment on all levels, from the level of physical labor to that of professional academic services;

8) Keep an option open for a lasting settlement of the Jewish-Arab dispute.

Whereas many considered the new areas a real addition to Israel's security, the Arab community, i.e. the addition of people, was seen as a problem which casts a shadow over the future. The difference in proportion between the natural increase common among the Arabs and the natural decrease in the numbers of Jewish immigrants to Israel, constitutes the gravest of all threats to Israel's security in the future. And reversely, a vastly enlarged immigration will constitute the most substantial preparation for lasting peace under satisfactory conditions.

The fate of Jewry and the fate of peace are intertwined from both the conceptual and the political points of view. Jewry now faces a test not of the strength of its demands on other nations, but of the strength of its demands on itself. The challenge exists. Will the challenge be met?

ISRAEL GOLDSTEIN

Israel Goldstein was born in Philadelphia in 1896 and settled in Israel in 1960. Ordained by the Jewish Theological Seminary in New York, he is also a graduate of Pennsylvania and Columbia Universities. In addition, he was the recipient of several honorary doctorates. From 1918 to 1960 he served as rabbi of Bnai Jeshurun in New York. Among the offices he held were the presidencies of the Jewish National Fund, the Zionist Organization of America (centrist in political orientation), the American Jewish Congress, the World Confederation of General Zionists and Brit Ivrit Olamit (World Hebrew Union). He was also one of the founders of Brandeis University and the treasurer of the Jewish Agency. When he settled in Israel he became chairman of Keren Hayesod, the United Israel Appeal, with headquarters in Jerusalem.

Goldstein has written extensively on Jewish and Zionist affairs. Non-controversial, conciliatory, he has the capacity of putting a gentle finger on sore spots in Jewish life and Israeli life in particular. Goldstein has been intellectually significant as a man and as a rabbi who, devoting all his life to the cause of Zion, did not evade the logical conclusion of settling in Zion.

The following is Goldstein's analysis of the current Israeli problems, prepared for this anthology by the author himself.

Israel's Dilemma and Imperative

by ISRAEL GOLDSTEIN

ISRAEL'S NOBLE, TRAGIC DILEMMA is that it must be ceaselessly concerned with its sheer survival and at the same time with being the kind of Israel that will endow its existence with moral justification.

This thesis will probably be repudiated by a large number of Israelis, particularly among its younger constituency. Even though their case can be understood, it cannot be accepted.

It is understandable that the youth of a nation born in blood and obliged thrice within the twenty years of its existence to pay for its life with the blood of its youth, should feel that sheer survival must be its peremptory categorical concern, and that only when its survival will have been assured more enduringly will it be in a position to free its energies and its thoughts for pouring idealistic universal values into its way of life.

Such an attitude, which indeed prevails among large numbers of Israeli youth and among many who are not so young, needs to be resisted and discredited for the sake of Israel's present and future. It violates the historic Jewish concept nurtured by the Hebrew Prophets and enjoined in the Books of Moses. Israel was the only nation in history in whose consciousness the occupancy of a land was made conditional on the observance of a code of moral laws. Indeed, Israel's moral charter, the Torah of Moses, anteceded the conquest of Canaan. Repeatedly, the new Hebrew nation was warned in this Torah that otherwise the land would spew them out as it had spewed out the iniquitous nations who had occupied the land before them.

Herzlian Zionism, [Herzl, 1860–1904, was the founder of political Zionism] which regarded the Jewish National Home primarily as the solution to the problem of Jewish homelessness, also envisioned it as a state which would bring forth ideals of universal import. The Zionist movement kept this twin objective in view and nurtured both parts of it.

Medinat [state of] Yisrael, since its birth twenty years ago, has become home for more than a million of the homeless of our people. At the same time, under the guidance of its leaders who had been cradled in the Zionist movement, it has not overlooked the higher, more universalistic aspects of its national life, endemically and in its stance in the international arena.

The problem which should engage our attention now is, "What of the future?"

The danger exists lest, as leadership passes in the course of time to new and younger hands, the Zionist vision of moral and ethical content and of universalistic idealism may give way to an intense, narrow, self-centred nationalism. There are a few notable exceptions among the relatively younger leadership both in the government and in other influential circles—exceptions which prove the rule. The fact remains that among the Israeli youth as a whole, the sense of identification with Diaspora Jewry is conspicuous by its absence. This danger of exaggerated Israeli nationalism must be decried, resisted and counteracted, for the sake of Israel and for the sake of the Jewish people.

The World Zionist movement and organization have no greater imperative than to prod and spur, so as to prevent Israel from becoming less than Zion.

Israel must be Zionized in the same degree that the Jewish people has been Israelized. Israel's mortal peril immediately preceding and during the Six Day War has dramatically uncovered and demonstrated Diaspora Jewry's deep concern for the fate of Medinat Yisrael. Israel's youth, its soldiers and its civilians, could not but have felt the impact of this phenomenon. It is not as yet sufficiently aware, however, that the extraordinary skill, courage and heroism of Israel's army will not be enough alone to ensure Israel's viability for the long range, and that its long-range future must depend upon the economic and political help of Diaspora Jewry.

Whatever criticism one may level at the inadequacy of world Jewry's support, it would be foolhardy to deny that without this the creation of Medinat Yisrael, its viability and its very survival, would have been incomparably more difficult, if at all possible. American Jewry can be cited as perhaps the foremost example. Its financial contributions have been daubed by some Israeli journalists contemptuously as the "big schnorr", overlooking not only its economic value but its value also as the broadest tangible common denominator of identification with Israel. Investments in Israeli enterprises, so necessary for its economic development, have been made by Jews of the United States and of other countries, not so much because of a desire for profits, since far more tempting profits beckon elsewhere, as by a desire to be constructively helpful. Nor should it be overlooked that the United States' substantial grant-in-aid program to Israel which included also the sales of arms to Israel, would probably not have been available had it not been for the moral weight of American Jewry.

This factor, the value of Diaspora Jewry's support of Israel, can be traced back to the birth of Medinat Yisrael in 1948. It is true that Medinat Yisrael would not have come into being had not the *Yishuv* [Jewish settlement in Palestine] itself sealed the international covenant with its blood. Diaspora Jewry is cognizant and appreciative of that incontrovertible fact. But it is also true that the international charter for the establishment of a Jewish State would not have been forthcoming, had it not been for the intercession of Diaspora Jewry.

Many young chauvinistic Israelis do not like to be reminded of Israel's dependence on factors outside itself. Yet these have been and will continue to be the facts of life. Instead of resisting and rejecting them, Israelis should be proud that Israel has meant and means so much to Diaspora Jewry.

Isolationism, for Israel, would be fatal.

Israel has before it a beehive of problems to solve. Never have so few been under the necessity of solving so much so soon. There is the problem of the uncompleted absorption of the immigration of previous years while courting new immigration. There is the problem of bending economic policy toward the encouragement of more investment capital from abroad without seriously impairing the basic rights of labor. There is the problem of making secondary education free and universal while broadening the accessibility of college and university education to those who are qualified to benefit by it, and of encouraging the arts. There is the problem of welding a diversity of Jewish tribes into one nation. Israel must do all this while maintaining its security posture unimpaired and on the alert.

In all fairness, this unparalleled set of obligations should be borne in mind and should mitigate the harshness of the tone of critical judgment, but it must not be permitted to weaken the substance of the critical judgment of what needs to be corrected in Israel. The point of vantage from which this observer's judgment is exercised is bi-focal, looking at what goes on inside Israel and observing also how the world outside Israel reacts—the Jewish world and the non-Jewish world. Has it not always been the fate of Zion to be under self-scrutiny *sub specie universitatis et aeternitatis?*

Israel's most conspicuous anomaly as a modern, democratic state, is its failure to extend to its Jewish population the democratic dispensation of separation between Church and State. Its non-Jewish population is in a more fortunate position, as the Christian and Muslim communities enjoy religious autonomy, while receiving recognition, help and support from Israel's Ministry of Religions. Jews, however, are under the jurisdiction of the Orthodox establishment even in such vital matters as questions involving personal status, such as marriage, divorce and inheritance.

If it were left as a matter of free choice, there would be, no doubt, many who would urge a respectful attitude toward strict Sabbath observers so as not to offend their sensibilities in their neighborhoods, and who would like to see *"kashrut"* [dietary laws] observed in Jewish public institutions. But the fault in Israel's religious establishment is that for Jews there is no free choice except in the privacy of their homes. The pattern of compulsion in religious matters is inconsistent with the character of an enlightened democracy.

The oft-heard advice that if non-Orthodox Jews would come in sufficient numbers to live in Israel, they could help to bring about a change, is hardly tenable. They should indeed come to live in Israel but for Zionist reasons and for broadly idealistic reasons, unrelated to this particular issue and, indeed, in spite of it.

The above-mentioned advice also evades the political demographic fact that in Israel's present population composition, the non-Orthodox elements already have a substantial political majority. Yet it remains to be seen whether the recently created majority-party will be ready to tackle the Church-State problem.

In the initial years of Medinat Yisrael some of the leading opponents of a theocratic State pleaded that the time was not ripe for a showdown on that issue, that first things must come first, that the newly formed State was in need first of becoming more firmly consolidated before risking controversy and division on the State-Church issue. They were probably right at that time. Is this argument for delay as timely today? Will Israel ever be in a position to afford a showdown on an issue of this character? It would seem that the time is at hand when the Church-State problem needs to be tackled, not precipitously but firmly.

It may sound presumptuous for a non-Orthodox Jew to say it, yet he takes comfort from the fact that it has been said also by more than one exponent of Orthodoxy in Israel—namely, that even from the standpoint of Orthodox Judaism, the separation between Orthodoxy and the State, would result in a net gain for Orthodox Judaism, as many new adherents might be won for Orthodox Judaism on its merit, who now resent it because of its artificial undemocratic advantage. They point to the fact that the experience of Orthodox Judaism in Diaspora Jewish communities indicates that in the "free market" of ideas and ideals, Orthodoxy can compete successfully with other trends in Judaism, even in the appeal to the young. It may be added that in Israel itself, there has been noticeable recently, and increasingly after the Six Day War, a growing trend toward religion among the youth, even in the leftist kibbutzim. This trend is probably far from Orthodox—yet there is in it a more understanding attitude toward Orthodoxy than had existed before. Orthodox Judaism in Israel should be ready to test its intrinsic appeal without leaning so heavily on the crutch of a power position in the State.

Israelis are also subject to criticism on another level, namely, in their relations vis-à-vis the Arab population in Israel. The Arabs in Israel, for the most part, constitute a kind of enclave in the midst of the general population. Much has been done by Israel's powerful Labor Federation, the Histadrut, to bring Arab labor into its membership rolls, to raise their wages, improve their working conditions, and through its auxiliary organizations, extend social services to Arab women and children and to Arab youth. What is lacking, however, is the education of the Israel public to the worthwhileness of cultivating Arab neighborliness and friendship.

And it is especially important to promote Jewish-Arab intercourse on the university level, where Arab cultural and intellectual leadership of the future is being trained. Quite apart from its strategic value, such a program would have a human value. It can be a mutually enriching experience to the Jew as well as to the Arab. It will not happen, however, of its own accord. It needs to be urged, encouraged, stimulated and guided by leaders of public opinion and by national, municipal and township governing bodies. It is a process of education which must begin with the children in the schools. And it must be propagated by all organs of public opinion—press, radio and television, and from the platforms of all the political parties and social organizations. The road ahead is long, but it is absolutely essential.

All of the above-mentioned considerations are desirable in and for themselves. But at the same time they are also relevant to the all-important problem of aliyah.

The more impressive Israel's credentials as a liberal democracy will be, the stronger will be its appeal to idealistic Jewish youth in the Diaspora. This is not to underrate Israel's existing credentials, but rather to plead for adding to an already existing substantial record.

Let us make no mistake about it. After all, due recognition has been given to the power of negative factors in Diaspora lands, such as political oppression, sporadic anti-Semitic outbreaks or general endemic malaise, as potential forces for propelling aliyah. But there will still remain substantial numbers of Jewish youth, fired by a vision of a more just and decent society who can be attracted to Israel if its image will be that of a civilization invested with impressive values of social idealism. These are the best elements which Israel can hope to attract. Opportunities for work and livelihood and a modicum of housing facilities at reasonable rentals will, of course, have to be made available. These, however, will hardly compete in most cases, with corresponding opportunities in the Western countries. Some will be drawn to Israel by the opportunity to experience living in the Jewish National Home, as part of a Jewish majority, and in an historically Jewish milieu. But there will also be not a few for whom the appeal will also have to be the broader one of a civilization characterized by high human values. It is as true today as ever it was, that "not on bread alone doth man subsist."

All the above-mentioned considerations sharpen the relevancy of the question which troubles many in Israel and outside Israel, "Who are to be Israel's leaders in the period ahead?"

Among Israeli youth there is a noticeable trend favoring the men of action, *("bitzuists")*. Other considerations are barely taken into account. In degree, this is a reaction to some of the older political leaders on national and local levels who have not acted swiftly enough or decisively enough in dealing with crises. Youth is impatient. It is also skeptical. Israel's youth, however, must be helped to understand that there are also other criteria for leadership, which are not the unique property of any particular age level. One of the decisive considerations should be, that Israel's leadership must never pander to isolationism, that it must seek the deepest possible ties with world Jewry, that it must throw its weight not only into the challenges of military security, but must concern itself simultaneously with the cultural and spiritual dimensions of its national life, for the sake of Israel's good life at home and good name abroad, and for the sake of enriching the link between Diaspora Jewry and Israel.

HAYIM HAZAZ

Hayim Hazaz was born in the Ukraine in 1898 and came to Palestine in 1931. He lived for short periods of time in Moscow, the Crimea, Istanbul, Berlin, Paris. His early education was in the traditional Jewish academies. His later schooling was sporadic.

In his literary career Hazaz blossomed forth into one of the most prominent novelists in Israel, comparable to S. Y. Agnon, the Nobel Prize laureate. He won nearly all of his country's coveted literary awards: the Bialik Prize for *Cracked Millstones*, the Israel Prize for *Yaish*, the Davar Prize for *Copper Doors*.

The artistic authenticity of Hazaz, whether he is dealing with the era of the Second Temple, the days of the false prophet Shabbetai Zvi, or Jewish life in the Ukraine, in Yemen, Turkey or Israel is astonishing, his realism is overwhelming, his satire demolishing. Hazaz possesses an ebullient and spontaneous mind, evocative, searching—and most of the time locating—the central problems of the times, past or present. This is evident in the following interview published in the widely-read daily, *Ma'ariv*, September 14, 1966.

An Interview With Hayim Hazaz

by RAPHAEL BASHAN

THERE IS HOPE IF THE YOUNG REBEL

A SPECIAL ATMOSPHERE prevails in this house: the rooms are spacious and cool, with high ceilings and softly tinkling chandeliers, a deep sofa and antique chairs with brocade upholstery and curved arms. Bowls of raisins and almonds stand on the table. But Hazaz is bitter.

Question—Such a sense of loss pervades the air these days. People say that Zionism has outlived its usefulness, religion has lost its hold, the sacredness of work is a thing of the past; on what foundations will Jewish culture rest in the coming generation?

Hazaz—(excitedly) That is precisely what I've been talking about here and abroad but (disappointed) nobody listens! Nobody wants to hear these things. Personally I do not think Zionism is outdated; I do not think the Diaspora is lost; I do not think Israel is beyond remedy. (Sorrowfully) Remedies may be administered in many ways but the trouble is that no one bothers. Just think of what went on in the preceding generation and see what is happening now, what a difference between two generations! Society and the individual have always been interchangeable for it is the individual who forms the character of society, but in order to exist society requires certain things (reflectively) that are rather difficult to define because they seem so banal; (defines) let us say, sacred things. In order to exist, society must have ideals. The individual doesn't need ideals; quite the contrary, ideals are an obstacle for the individual! Let us say, self-sacrifice; let's say, manual work; let's say, all kinds of concessions for the benefit of the whole. But society does need them most urgently in order to exist and in order to enable the individual to find his proper place within it.

DEATH WAS NOT FEARED THEN

In the preceding generation this was quite simple and perfectly clear. Life was a serious matter, important. Consequently, the individual could relinquish it without arrogance for the benefit of society. (Draws a broad arc) Life was very, very serious, so serious that it overflowed its narrow confines like a pot boiling over, so that death was not a strictly personal matter; society had a share in it too. (Forcefully) At that time, death did not cast such fear, dying was not a tragedy. Dying for a specific ideal was not considered such a tragic act. That's how socialism was born, how Zionism was established, how revolutionary movements arose. People went to prison, to *katorga* (hard labor), or to be hanged. They sacrificed themselves for ideals in which they really believed and it was not tragic at all. People of the preceding generation considered it natural, realistic. The same applies to the Second Aliyah, [immigration wave] to the Third Aliyah, to the pioneers of the cooperatives and collectives, people who contracted malaria, who went hungry and died. Their ideals lent wings to it all, even to death. (Wrinkles his brow) It seems to have been easier to die then. But when the individual's being became an aim in itself, everything underwent a radical change. Then even death became a matter of personal tragedy, social ideals were crowded aside, and the individual's work for the good of society was discontinued. Each person now believes that actually society exists solely for him and that everything in the whole wide world exists only for his benefit and for his pleasure. (Angrily) And here careerism comes in. That's where we stand today. That's the reason Zionism is outdated or out of fashion. That's the reason for the movement away from the kibbutzim. That is why so few new kibbutzim are being founded. That is the frame for the life which is uniquely Israeli in character. (Bitter) Zionism has lost its flavor, that's true! Not because Zionism has no aim in Jewish life but because we lack people of stature to inspire and guide. (Louder) Inspiration is lacking! We have no truly great men! Why?! Because as soon as the individual's being becomes an aim in itself, he stops being a personality. A man can rise above himself only if his existence is not an aim in itself (raises his arm), only if something lofty and above him is the aim!

WE HAVE NO GREAT MEN TODAY

(Forcefully) We have no great men in Israel today, no great men in the Zionist movement, no great men in the parties! Nor are there any great men in the Jewish Diaspora! (In a dull voice) The Jewish Diaspora is in my opinion in the process of disintegrating. In its present stage it is hovering between life and death. The best of the Diaspora Jews now deny the values that Judaism offers the Diaspora Jew. But we would be both mistaken and extremely naive were we to think that searching for a lost object that has not really been lost will ensure our finding it. Jews can search all day long along Fifth Avenue in New York and not find anything. Old Jewish values no longer satisfy modern men for a variety of reasons. Values are formed, crystallized; they are not found and not invented. Values are created in the course of working, living, as a part of reality and above all of the cultural life. The Diaspora Jew can no longer live an alien cultural life and simultaneously form Jewish values. (Unequivocally) This cannot be allowed! (Angrily) Some Jews have grown up in the Diaspora who are not Jews at all, Jews suspended from a fine thread of doubtful Jewish values which are powerless to keep alive more than a very few coming generations. And that is why (rather ironically) one can discern in the Diaspora a romantic attitude toward Judaism. Romanticism is indigenously something quite concrete which has subsequently been inflated until its volume exceeds its weight. Did you ever see a skinny little horse pulling a wagon full of hay, a wagon stacked as high (demonstrates height) as two storeys? Didn't you wonder how such a feeble creature could pull such a huge wagon? The answer is simple: the wagon has volume, not weight; that wagon is full of romanticism! Romanticism cannot survive more than a generation or two. That is the nature of the neo-religiosity in America and to some extent also here. They are the very thin outer skin of religion. (Severely) And we definitely must not depend on that. Anyone who meditates and is concerned about our national existence is most apprehensive when he sees these transmutations becoming the sole spiritual prop for our existence as a people.

In America today there are groups of placid people, stay-at-homes, some of them eminent scholars who devote themselves to sacred studies, publish antique manuscripts, study the various homiletic writings and write their own interpretations and introductions, assisted by a ramified, well-endowed scientific staff. These scholars are convinced that by their labors they are saving the Jewish people from extinction. The mere sight of it fills one with despair; it is dangerous for people to rely on something that cannot be saved! On the other hand, you have there all kinds of *hassidic rebbes* who do whatever they do and teach in *yeshivas* [theological schools]. Then there are the young people, bereft of anything that is of the heart, seeking Jewish ideals and arriving by chance at the yeshivas, where the observance of the lightest (precepts) is stressed no less than the gravest, where skull-caps must always be worn and the "Four Fringes" must always show beneath one's clothes. (Dramatically) Woe to the generation whose youth dedicates its life and its spirit to the keeping of precepts which actually are already dead. (Sorrowfully) In our days religion has shrunk so much that it is limited only to studying the Scriptures and keeping the precepts. Alone, these two are incapable of enriching man, of nourishing his soul. They represent something static, frozen!

RELIGION NO LONGER SUFFICES

(In the warm tone of personal confession) I am after all a product of religion, of Torah learning, tradition. I come from a pious family. I imbibed that world with all its poetic grandeur, its hopes and yearnings, and I tell you: no, it is not enough! To sustain our people's existence today, religion is not enough! It sufficed in the locked ghetto, in the ghetto that was enclosed by a cultural wall. But today, when the outside world is open and accessible to all, religion occupies but one corner of it. (Categorically) Whoever proposes religion as the sole basis for our people's existence is actually misleading everyone! Religion is capable of nourishing only one more generation; the coming generations (makes incisive gesture) will leave it! Just as we did! But we exchanged it for Jewish culture, for the Hebrew language, for Zionism. Where will they go, those who will now leave the Jewish religion? Where will they go? Those who left it in the past comprised a Jewish intellectual group whose tongues were Hebrew and Yiddish and who devoted themselves to the cultivation of the soul of our people. (With great anxiety) Those who will abandon religion tomorrow and the day after tomorrow, in America and in Europe, where will they turn? What values will appeal to them? In my opinion there is only one thing for them, the one and only sure thing, Israel! The last time I was in America I told them candidly: (sharply) My dear friends and colleagues, in America the Jewish religion has gone into retirement! In other words, it exists but is no longer productive. It lives on its past. It has no youth, no creative powers, except perhaps for the ·few who abide within the narrow confines of the Law, and their meager number cannot sustain the entire generation! (Counts on his fingers) Grace after meals, wearing the skull-cap, laving of hands—these can no longer preserve our nation. (Lowers his voice) I am not against religion. But it is impossible to rely on it alone! Developing in the Dispersion a Hebrew literature and a solid network of Hebrew schools will strengthen Israel's appeal for our dispersed Jews. At present when you come to the Jewish youth in various countries and speak to them of Israel they simply do not know what you want of them. Why should they worry about Israel? Are the Irish immigrants in America so concerned about Ireland? Or the Italians about Italy?

My favorite idea is to bring to Israel every year several thousand university-trained American Jews—we must find the proper contacts and prepare propaganda and also suitable arrangements—to teach in the farthest corner of the State, perhaps the exact sciences that we need so urgently. Why should they join the "Peace Corps" and go off to Ghana or Puerto Rico? Why not teach the a-b-c's to the children of the "ingathered exiles" in Israel"? (Enthused) This wonderful youth goes about with no ideals, and nothing to pour their spirit into. We must go to them with a great demand: come to us in the thousands! Not hundreds but thousands! Let them come, see the country, all of it, study Hebrew in an ulpan, [intensive language course] and—return home. Then, after their return home, they will form the backbone of the Jewish intellectual group in the Diaspora and very likely even alter the image of the Dispersion.

Question—After all you have just said, and after the instruments you have demolished, what remains that may still nourish the spirit and culture of our people?

Hazaz—(Somewhat optimistically) There are still kibbutzim, there are moshav villages, there are young people who go to the farms or down to the Negev, and there is ZAHAL, the army. They are after all living examples for this generation of what it ought to be doing, what its mission is. As you know, while states may be destroyed with relative ease, it is far from easy to destroy a nation. Only when a people identifies completely with one single state, is it likely to be destroyed. (Positive) That's how nations were wiped out! The Jewish people, which did not always live a state-life, must today also rise above present state matters in order to assure its own and the State's existence. (Returns to main subject) The trouble is that this generation is proceeding on its way without a central personality to lead it; let it be a great personality or one not so great, just so it is central (spreads his hands), but there is no such figure today!

Question—Then according to whom and what are we to educate our young people?

YOUTH MUST REBEL AGAINST ELDERS

Hazaz—(Agitated) What do you mean educate youth? That notion is mistaken altogether! You don't educate youth; youth educates itself. When does youth educate itself? (Forcefully) When it rebels! (Runs his hand through his white hair) And if youth fails to rebel, then there's practically no hope! If youth follows placidly in the devious ways of its elders and even adds to them, then there is no hope. Yes, that's what we are waiting for, for youth to rebel against its elders! True, our fathers were innocent and just, and if you like, true idealists. But what is a nation? A nation is the complex relationship that evolves between human beings and their state. In the Diaspora we were in the grip of a situation that was strange and unique among all the nations of the world: we were a nation without a state, a nation which conducted relations with the Almighty alone. For every other people in the world the relations between a man and his God are his own private matter but for us Jews it became a matter of supreme national importance. (Warmly) Actually our forefathers were idealists of the highest order, who conducted relations with the Almighty and lived outside their dwelling place and time! And we, when we entered an era of historic change-of-guard, chose for the sake of our people's existence to rebel against our elders and to go each his own way. Today we are waiting for youth to rebel against their elders and (joyfully) if they do, then there is a great deal of hope.

Question—Nevertheless, in what direction ought we to guide the young? Can you point out some guidelines?

Hazaz—(Rises, walks about the room) In what direction you ask? I want you to know that we live in a highly interesting epoch which is at the same time very complicated: full of danger and deceit, and yet marked by vast, unlimited horizons. We live in an age so materialistic that the materialism of the past generations seems extremely naive by comparison. After all, materialism did not conquer the preceding generation to the point of denying all else; it still retained its morals. If you take Marxism and analyse it in depth, what do you find? Morality. The fulfillment of the prophetic visions of the people of Israel in (actual) practice, a manipulation of our prophets' declarations on justice, truth, decency, equality, prevention of exploitation for all alike. (Frightened) Today's materialism is scientific, cold and rigid; it shows no mercy, does not perceive human matters at all and knows no fear whatsoever. (Quite horrified) This is something terrible, dreadful and horrible in magnitude and in cruelty, something totally unrelated to man and society. (Sighs) Well, such is this generation. And we live in it. We probably are influenced by the whole world in one way or another but in the final analysis we are nothing but a province as far as *place* is concerned. What's more we are something altogether unique in the world: we are also a province in *time*.

Question—Can you elucidate? What do you mean by that?

WE NEED NOT BE A METROPOLIS

What do I mean by that? Most of the countries throughout the world came into existence many generations ago but our state, which came into being only recently, must perforce compete with the full power of this entire materialistic generation, yet at the same time retain a spark of holiness which the other nations are not obliged to do. Therefore I say: the province [the non-urban area] has a right to exist, the real province which fulfills its responsibilities in that it ploughs, sows and reaps. (Shrugs his shoulders) We do not have to be a metropolis! Tel Aviv need not be London or Paris or New York! Quite the contrary, we are duty-bound to safeguard what is specific, unique and implanted in us, that seed which the huge materialistic metropolitan centers yearn for. Those are the ideals that the materialistic world longs for. Not for nought do young people from all the ends of the earth come to us. They come here seeking new ideals. (Ironically) I am not at all sure they always find them. A short while ago I had a visit from several young French intellectuals who were touring Israel and were quite disillusioned. Why? "We expected to find many more kibbutzim, and local color of a specifically Mediterranean character. We didn't come to Israel to look for what we already have in Marseilles!"

We have a great deal to do, not so much for others as first of all for ourselves. (Begins at the beginning) Every people has its own historic road to travel, and its own particular mission. England did not do what France did, France did not do what Russia did. The question is: What is our mission now? Where are we heading? We must decide what is uniquely our way, what is it that today peculiarly and uniquely characterizes us. (Puts his hand on his heart) The first preliminary condition for that is for us to know ourselves. Now mind you, I don't want to play the part of the out-and-out agnostic. I am a Jew and my sole interest lies in the continuity of Jewish existence. Religion is no longer capable of sustaining the life of the Jewish people. Religion, any religion, lacks the capacity of understanding the problems that plague modern man as he abandons values and shatters frames. Religion can no longer nourish the soul of twentieth-century man. (Growing more and more passionate) The assumption that youth will wait for someone to come and show them the way to go is a fatal mistake. Youth does not need anyone to come and show them the way. They will find it themselves. The young will discover unaided how distorted things are; they will look into their hearts and take stock and —rebel. They will be scolded, and admonished, but that will only add fuel to the flames of rebellion. (With satisfaction) When youth rebels, there is no stopping them! I know, at present there is a youth rebellion in progress in China, but that is being directed by a deliberately guiding hand; that is not the kind of rebellion I have in mind. (Trembling) I mean a rebellion from the heart.

WE LACK STYLE
Our youth today is good. Ben-Gurion thinks it is a marvellous youth which has no equal the world over. (Decisively) No such thing! The Jewish youth of days past in the Diaspora were infinitely superior to today's youth in Israel! (With annoyance) Our youth today lacks a distinguishing style, just as our people as a whole lack a distinctive style. In days gone by a Jew possessed a special quality peculiarly his own: the young man had it, the old man had it, and the modern enlightened *maskil* had it; it was evident in the clothes they wore, in their walk, in their speech, in all the little things that are so difficult to define. But today's Israeli traveling abroad is hard to identify; one may easily fail to guess his identity, for he lacks individual style, distinguishing characteristics. Yes, that's it, our people do not as yet have it. What is the result? We imitate others. When young Israelis visit Russia and sing their songs there, they little realize that they are actually singing Russian songs with Hebrew words! That is the general picture but there are also fine delicate nuances almost too elusive to grasp or define. (Angrily) We lack an original distinctive style in poetry, in fiction, in painting. It is just as well that the Gentiles do not read Hebrew literature. They would learn nothing from it of the Israeli people. That our nation is a special kind of people no one will deny, but Israel is also a special kind of country. It has no forests or rivers or cities built on river-banks, only a little soft earth and relatively much rocky soil. It does not have green grass the year round but (looking through the window) it does have limitless, endless sunshine! The eagle does not fear the sun; he flies higher and higher toward it! The Land of Israel was always a land of eagles; the prophets bear this out. In those ancient days, that special something in this country's landscape and climate exerted a powerful influence on the soul and character of our forefathers. (Sadly) We have not yet adapted ourselves to the Land of Israel and there is as yet no originality in us. It is impossible to declare: from tomorrow on I shall be a new, original type of Israeli! It is a gradual process. It may take generations to develop. And only our youth can speed the process.

WE ARE REMNANTS OF A PEOPLE
(Incisively) Why, what have we here actually? One people? Definitely not! We are but remnants of a people! A group of small ethnic communities, crumbs, mosaic pieces not yet fitted together into one integrated whole! (Keenly) We all know this people only slightly; we know ourselves very little! (Apprehensively) We are approaching the edge of an abyss as far as Levantine influences are concerned! We must aim at West-European acculturation of the Eastern communities among us to prevent our being gradually transformed into a people of the East. I feel very strongly about this. For two thousand years we traveled a road which molded us into a European-Jewish cultural unit; we must not now retreat in time and adopt the culture of Iraq, Yemen and Morocco.

Question—Should the Eastern communities among us refuse to adopt Western culture, what then?

Hazaz—They don't say that they refuse! It is our task first of all to turn this nation into a book-reading people. Otherwise it will have no interest in Hebrew culture. I've been told that among the survivors of the Holocaust about 20% are completely illiterate; they simply had not had time to learn to read. I tell you these people will not be properly integrated in the State, or in Hebrew culture, unless they learn to read a Hebrew book or at least a Hebrew newspaper. Ours is a people that always studied: we studied the Talmud, we recited the Psalms; now we must begin to read!

Question—From a practical point of view, how do you go about integrating communities of varying ethnic backgrounds? How is it done?

Hazaz—(Concentrates) It must be a highly intensive process. At this moment we lack the moral and cultural attributes essential to the assimilation of all these groups of returning exiles. (Distressed) At present these exiles are beginning to resemble us in an exterior, superficial manner, and this is catastrophic! For we are bad enough ourselves, but the nature of imitation is such that he who imitates becomes inferior to the original model. A house-maid from an oriental country who apes the ways of a slovenly housewife from a Western country, ultimately becomes far more slovenly than her European prototype. No, at present we do not have the necessary moral and cultural attributes to assimilate all of these exiles. (Deprecatingly) What now goes by the name of integration of exiles is something purely external!

V
Molding a Nation—Ingathering of Exiles and Ingathering of Problems

ANDRE N. CHOURAQUI

NISSIM REJWAN

MOSHE DAVIS

YITZHAK RABIN

ANDRE N. CHOURAQUI

Andre N. Chouraqui was born in Algeria in 1917 and settled in Israel in 1958. He received a thorough Jewish education in North Africa and a Dr. Jur. degree from the University of Paris. During World War II he was active in the French Maquis (underground) movement. After the war he occupied the office of magistrate and headed many Jewish organizations in his native land. A prolific writer in several languages, he published close to twenty volumes—histories of the Jewish people, biographies of Zionist leaders, and law treatises.

In Israel he has concerned himself with the problems of the Middle East and North African Jewry—the "Orientals", the "Eastern communities"—who have not been fully accommodated in their new country, whose problems are different from those who left Europe or South Africa or the United States. Secluded and apart from other Jewries, the Oriental communities have, on the one hand, kept their Judaism more intact, but on the other hand, they have fallen behind in modern socio-cultural behavior. The sudden change of pace for these immigrants in Israel was unsettling to the newcomers from North Africa and other Arab states in the Middle East. In turn, as the number of the "Easterners" grew to equal or surpass the "Westerners", it had a significant impact on the entire population in Israel, on its institutions and goals.

As the problem became more intense, Chouraqui—who had made his presence felt in Israel as a bridge-building personality between East and West—was called by David Ben-Gurion to serve as the then Prime Minister's counsellor on integration. Later Chouraqui became Deputy Mayor of Jerusalem.

The excerpts brought in this anthology are from Chouraqui's book, *Between East and West*, the Jewish Publication Society of America, Philadelphia, 1968, pp. 258-59; 285-315.

Between East and West

By ANDRE N. CHOURAQUI

ZIONISM IN NORTH AFRICA

THE ZIONIST MOVEMENT had had very little success or effect in North Africa, largely because those who headed it were almost exclusively of Eastern European background and had made little effort to understand the specific traditions and attitudes of the Jews of the Maghreb. Even in their choice of emissaries to North Africa the leadership showed a singular lack of understanding, and more than once the persons who had been delegated to address the leaders of the Jewish communities or even the rank and file were unable to communicate with their hearers; few Zionist officials or speakers were able to converse freely in French, none at all in the local dialects, and none of them understood the psychology of the local masses. (The same incidentally, may be said of Zionist endeavors in the other countries of Africa and of Asia.) By not adapting its appeal and its publicity to the local requirements, the Zionist Movement was unable to reach the new group of intellectuals and the new middle classes of North Africa, most especially those of Algeria. Despite this, the three countries regularly sent delegates to every Zionist Congress, and spiritual Zionism, the hope and ideal of an eventual return of the Jewish people to their homeland, was deeply entrenched among the masses where it was nourished by the messianic spirituality of cabalistic traditions.

When the State of Israel was created, the Jews of the Maghreb were seized by a fervid excitement which equalled in many respects the popular reaction, three centuries earlier, to the messianic arousal of Shabbetai Zvi; everywhere in the Maghreb, and especially in Morocco, entire Jewish communities prepared themselves for an early departure for Israel: they sold their property and most of their belongings and waited with their bundled possessions for their return to their ancient homeland. The close links between the Maghreb and the Holy Land that had existed throughout the centuries were loosened somewhat when, following the arrival of the French in North Africa, the traditional association of the area with the vast Moslem world was supplanted by the influence and culture of France and Europe. However, the fact that the Jewish community remained a separate entity and possessed its own schools that disseminated Jewish learning to all, made it impossible for an individual, child or adult, to be unaware of his Jewish identity, even where the superimposed French culture was at its most intense. Their Jewish spiritual heritage always remained close to the Jews of the Maghreb and their yearning for Zion was never extinguished.

North African Jewry had been deeply shaken by the spread of the Nazi terror across Europe and by the sufferings of their fellow Jews there. The period of Nazi domination and the restrictive policies applied to the Jews in the Maghreb itself had opened the eyes of many to their inescapable destiny as Jews. To the rabbis of the distant Sahara the war appeared as the great cataclysmic event that foreshadowed the messianic age and the return of the Jews to Zion. That the end of the war was, in fact, followed by the creation of the State of Israel and, a few years later, by the independence of all three countries in the Maghreb, could not but heighten the dramatic impact of the return of the Jews of North Africa to the Holy Land.

The creation of the State of Israel was accepted by the masses of North African Jewry as an act of messianic fulfillment rather than as the outcome of a political event. In the mystically charged atmosphere engendered by the war and by the interpretations given to these portents by the local rabbis, the night of November 29, 1947, when the United Nations voted in favor of the creation of an independent Jewish state in what was then Palestine, took on the character of a *Lail Shimurim*—Night of Vigil—that according to tradition preceded the Exodus from Egypt. After the centuries of suffering and privation, of fasting and of prayer, the vote at Lake Success was seen throughout North Africa as nothing less than a Divine Judgment, a palpable and visible sign of the final Redemption. If any more impetus was required, it was provided by the massacres perpetrated by the Moslems of Tripolitania on their Jewish neighbors and similar events at Oujda and Djerada in Morocco. These outbreaks were a further reminder to the Jews of the precariousness of their situation as a minority in the Moslem world.

IMMIGRATION

So the mass emigration to Israel got under way. By the end of 1949 close to twenty-five thousand North African Jews had arrived in Israel to take part in the War of Independence and to participate in the resurrection of their ancient homeland. They constituted some 5 per cent of the Jews of the Maghreb, their proportion varying with the size of the respective Jewish communities and reflecting strongly the relative closeness of their ties with Israel. From Algeria, where the Jews had been most fully integrated, and where they felt most secure, only about 750 Jews came to Israel; 6,000 arrived from Tunisia and 18,000 from Morocco during the same period. From other parts of North Africa came over 22,000 Jews, 15,000 of them from Libya and the remainder from Egypt. Within the first fifteen years of the creation of the State of Israel, over half of the Jews of North Africa had migrated to Israel. One-third had migrated to France, the Americas and elsewhere, and the rest—chiefly in Morocco and Tunisia—seemed doomed to disappear within a few years; their communities disorganized and demoralized, dissolved one by one; the individuals who have stayed behind out of loyalty or love for their native countries or out of attachment to their property and their customary way of life remain at the mercy of every unforeseen event that might create a new atmosphere of panic. Their number, however, is dwindling constantly.

The rate of immigration of Jews from the Maghreb to Israel slowed somewhat after 1949. In 1950 and 1951 the annual total reached about 18,000; in 1952 it fell markedly to just over 8,000, while in 1953 it fell to less than half that number, totalling only 3,900. This was due to the severe economic crisis prevailing in Israel at the time and to the difficulties that the new immigrants encountered in their attempts to integrate into the Israel economy.

In 1954 the immigration started a new upward swing under the impetus of local events. Tunisia, engaged in revolutionary war, was about to negotiate its independence, warfare had broken out in Morocco, and Algeria was going through the period of tension that preceded its own war against the French. The uncertainty of the future made many Jews prefer to brave the rigors in Israel. That year there were 11,000 immigrants from the Maghreb. In 1955, as the nationalist movements in the Maghreb achieved new successes, the figure nearly trebled, reaching just on 31,700. In 1956, as the new administrations took over in Tunisia and Morocco, there were 43,850 immigrants from the Maghreb—80 per cent of all immigration to Israel that year—and this despite the tension on Israel's borders and the frequent incursions of Egyptian terrorists that provoked the Suez campaign toward the end of that year.

The year 1956 was the last that free emigration was permitted from Morocco. As the gates clamped shut, only 12,300 North African Jews were able to reach Israel during the next year. In 1958 the number was a quarter of that (3,275) and even less than that in 1953. But, despite the refusal of the Moroccan authorities to issue passports to Jews and the hunting down and persecution of those attempting to flee, the illegal emigration was not without success. There was a slight rise to 3,838 immigrants from North Africa in 1959 and to 4,800 in 1960.

A new period of massive migration started in 1961. One of the factors was the lifting of the restrictions on Jewish emigration by the new ruler of Morocco, King Hassan II. Another was the beginning of massive emigration from Algeria. Hitherto, few Algerian Jews had reached Israel. The highest annual total had been 1,000 in 1956, and in 1953 there were only 81 immigrants. In 1961 the figure suddenly rose to over 4,400. Yet, impressive as this may seem, it was still small compared with the number of Algerian Jews who emigrated that year to France. Of the total Jewish population in Algeria, over 90 per cent in fact had chosen to settle in France by the time Algeria achieved its independence on July 1, 1962.

As was pointed out in the preceding chapter, the Algerian Jews, French citizens, regarded France, not Israel, as their alternative home and, unlike the Moroccan and Tunisian Jews, they were not regarded by the French as foreigners. Economically, too, conditions in France were vastly superior to anything Israel could offer: the country was going through a boom of economic expansion and could provide employment under excellent conditions to all citizens from Algeria—and this in addition to the compensation that all the new arrivals received from the authorities to ease their period of adaptation. Furthermore, the realities of life in Israel discouraged the Algerian refugees from settling there. The difficulties that faced the immigrants from Morocco and Tunisia were even more pronounced for those arriving from Algeria. The Algerian had been used to a fairly easy life in a colonial country under full economic expansion, where he had earned a high salary and where the road to wealth was open to him. To leave such a world, artificial though its structure may have been, and settle for a hard pioneering life in the Negev desert of Israel, could not be achieved without suffering and unhappiness. One-tenth of Algeria's Jews have nevertheless chosen to settle in Israel. This figure is bound to grow, for many of the Algerian Jews consider France to be only a way-station where they complete their education, recover from the shock of their uprooting, acquire new skills, new savings, and new possessions, all of which will facilitate their eventual settlement and integration in Israel. Despite the attractions offered by France, few Algerians have actually re-emigrated there from Israel.

CHARACTERISTICS OF THE NORTH AFRICAN IMMIGRATION

When Israel gained its independence in 1948, the Jews of North Africa formed only a small proportion of its population. Fifteen years later they formed the largest and the most cohesive community in the country. If the *Moghrabim* (the Jews of Maghrebian origin who had been living in the Holy Land for many generations before the State achieved its independence) are included with the more recent immigrants, and the immigrants from Egypt and Libya are added, and if account is taken of the high rate of natural increase among this group which is one of the highest in the world and the highest of all communities in Israel, the Jews of North African origin may now be estimated as making up a quarter of Israel's Jewish population.

Besides being the largest community, the North African is also in aggregate, the youngest, with a median age of 25—as against 31 for immigrants from Asia and 45 for immigrants from Europe. Half of the immigrants from the Maghreb are under 25; the average size of a household is five persons and many families number eight, ten, even fifteen children. A family with only three children is the exception among Jews from North Africa.

Another characteristic that distinguished this mass immigration from that from other countries was the fact that it arrived in Israel lacking its social and economic élite. The well-educated, the affluent, the trained technicians, the intellectuals and the businessmen among them, like their counterparts in other countries, had chosen to make their homes in the West. Israel had drawn those who lacked possessions or resources, those who, more deeply imbued with Judaism and messianic fervor, chose to return to their ancient homeland as if by instinct. This inverse selection naturally aggravated the absorption into Israel of those who did come. The imbalance, however, is slowly being corrected as the better-educated and more substantial type of North African immigrant has been arriving in Israel in increasing numbers, in part attracted by the better economic climate and in part because those factors that had tended up till now to keep him in North Africa have gradually changed and made his situation there untenable.

The masses who came to Israel were the poor, the blind, the paralyzed, the tubercular and the syphilitic. For them the promise of a new future dawned as they saw the coast of Israel.

ENCOUNTER

The sudden and unexpected arrival of nearly 57,000 immigrants from North Africa (including those from Libya and Egypt) between 1947 and 1949 had caught the Israel authorities unprepared. Like Western Jews in general, they had been almost unaware of the existence of what have been referred to as "the forgotten million" Jews of the Orient. In fact one might go so far as to say that except for the work of the *Alliance Israélite Universelle* and the activities of the *Hilfsverein*, the Anglo-Jewish Committee and the Joint Distribution Committee, there had been almost no contact between the Jews of Europe and those living in the Arab world since about the sixteenth century.

During the 1950's, Israel was following a courageous policy of permitting and encouraging free immigration for all Jews from any part of the world. But it lacked the resources to cope with the many problems posed by the arrival of the mass immigration from North Africa, and was seeking formulae for integration. It was a period of experimentation, of trial and error. The unexpectedly long period in which the immigrants were obliged to stay in the transit camps (*ma'abarot*)—immense shantytowns which were hurriedly set up to house them pending their final settlement into proper homes and permanent employment—produced untold social and economic hardship, leaving a canker of bitterness that was not to be eradicated for a long time.

Reversely, the Jews of North Africa had not been prepared for Israel. The World Zionist Organization had never made the effort to draw them into the orbit of active Zionism in which later, as builders of Israel, they were to play such an important part. That which had attracted them to Israel was neither Zionism nor even Jewish nationalism but an uncompromising spiritual tradition based on the Bible, the Talmud, the Cabala, Jewish liturgy and the teaching of the great Jewish philosophers and teachers. These elements played a relatively small part in the Zionist vision and even religious Zionism had never been able to penetrate deeply into the lives of the Jews of the East; the spirit of Orthodox Judaism, such as had developed in Europe after the eighteenth century, was far removed from that of the Sephardi and Oriental Jews.

For the majority of the North African immigrants, then, the adventure of their arrival in Israel was, and for many still is, an event of an essentially religious, messianic, spiritual, almost mystic nature. For many the reality was a sad delusion.

The vision of redemption was dispelled almost on the first contact with the reality of Israel. A typical case was that of a boatload of new immigrants from North Africa who in 1954 had been selected by the immigration department of the Jewish Agency before their departure from the transit camps in France to spearhead a new venture. The immigrants had no doubt dreamed of Israel as a blissful home where they would dwell in eternal tranquillity within the turreted walls of Jerusalem; they were taken by truck straight from the ship to the site that had been chosen as their new home: an isolated spot in the Negev—wilderness, sand and rocks as far as the eye could see and jackals howling in the distance. The immigrants flatly refused to leave their trucks; they demanded to be taken away at once; anywhere at all, just so long as they would not have to remain in this God-forsaken desert. Explanations were of no avail; they bounced off a solid wall of refusal. At last, one of the accompanying officials staged an "incident." Rifles were shot off at random in the dark, the immigrants were told that this was an attack by Arab raiders, and in a second the reluctant immigrants had left their trucks to seek shelter in the huts that had been prepared for them. Today that forsaken site in the desert is Dimona, a modern industrial town of 17,000 inhabitants, most of them immigrants from North Africa. It is a tribute to their courage, hard work and capabilities.

The lack of communication between immigrants of vastly different geographical, social and historical backgrounds did nothing to relieve the disillusionment of the new arrivals. They lacked a common language, were frequently unable to make their needs and fears comprehensible to neighbors and officials. And then, there was the distress that resulted from the break-up of the customary social order into which the Jews of North Africa had been born and under which they had lived. The close, cohesive life of the Maghreb had collapsed with one blow and there was nothing, at first, to replace it. To these was added another problem, that of discrimination, of which virtually all new immigrants from Moslem countries believed themselves to be the victims, especially at the hands of the Jewish Agency. In fact, arrangements for the reception of new immigrants had been made with the needs of European Jews in mind. Housing, for instance, was perfectly adequate for a family that had no more than three children, but for the large families from Moslem countries the resultant overcrowding caused great unhappiness. Neither were salaries and wages scaled to the needs of large families.

The tension that arose from this social and economic maladjustment reached breaking point in the summer of 1959, when a series of incidents forcibly brought the gravity of the problem to the public's attention. The spark was fired in Wadi Salib, a crowded quarter in downtown Haifa near the port. The police tried to arrest a drunkard who was sleeping in a café. In the ensuing altercation a policeman fired a bullet that injured the drunk, who as it turned out was a Jew from North Africa. A crowd of two hundred soon gathered in the streets of the quarter, stoned a police car and roughed up some policemen. Their cries of "assassins" and "exploiters" reflected their conviction that they were the victims of deliberate discrimination and exploitation. At dawn a newly formed organization, "The Union of North Africans," headed by a young, unemployed immigrant from Morocco, David ben Harrosh, incited new demonstrations. Inflammatory leaflets were distributed and a crowd marched out of the lower town headed for the residential and business quarters on the slopes of Mount Carmel, causing a certain amount of damage—and a considerable degree of fear—on its way. The disturbances spread from Wadi Salib and Haifa to other towns where there were large concentrations of dissatisfied immigrants—Tiberias, Beersheba and Migdal Haemek in particular. The North African immigrants there poured into the streets, smashed an occasional shop or office, and roughed up some of their antagonists. There was a feeling of impending revolt in the air that gave rise to fears of a widespread flare-up.

Around the world even the most serious newspapers featured the intercommunal unrest. This new picture of Israel spread consternation wherever concern for the interests of the new State were felt especially among the Jews still living in North Africa. The Israel government immediately set up a commission of inquiry to investigate the matter and to seek the underlying causes of the tension. Its conclusions brought to light the unsolved problems of the integration into Israel life of the immigrants from Oriental countries.

SETTLEMENT AND ABSORPTION

The North African immigration placed an enormous strain on the absorption capacity of Israel and of the Jewish Agency. The inconceivable poverty of the new arrivals from North Africa meant dependence on the Israel authorities for every step of their integration. The number who became social welfare cases surpassed even the most pessimistic estimates. For Israel, itself grappling with problems of national development, its security under constant threat, the attempt to integrate these people so totally unprepared for what was before them, was indeed a courageous undertaking.

1. HEALTH

Immediately upon arrival the North African Jews placed before the Israel health authorities an unprecedented emergency: not only were there hundreds of cases of tuberculosis, trachoma, syphilis, ringworm and other highly infectious diseases that required urgent treatment, but there was also an imminent danger that epidemics would break out in the immigrants' camps and spread throughout the country. The fact that, despite the makeshift medical facilities, no such situation arose is eloquent proof of the efficiency and devotion with which the health services met the crisis. Today, many of the T.B. sanitoriums in Israel have been closed and the eye clinics are relatively deserted in comparison with what they were fifteen years ago. Furthermore, thanks to the nationwide network of mother and child welfare clinics, the infant mortality rate among the North African community is now identical with that of the country as a whole—28 infant deaths per 1,000 live births. (The figure in the United States is 25.) In general, the state of health of this community today is similar to that of Israel's total population.

2. PIONEER SETTLEMENT

The first priority of the State of Israel after its boundaries had been secured was to settle the sparsely populated areas of the country. Those regions most suited for immediate settlement were in the Galilee, certain areas in the center of the country and in the narrow "corridor" of the Judean hills which links Jerusalem with the coastal plain, and then, the northern and western Negev. The departments of Immigration and Settlement of the Jewish Agency were concentrating their efforts on the development of these areas and to them the majority of the new settlers from North Africa were directed. In the eighteen months from October 1956 to April 1958, 66.5 per cent of the North African immigrants who arrived were directed to "development towns"—either those that had been expanded around the nucleus of a small town such as Beersheba and Migdal Ashkelon, or entirely new cities like Dimona and Hatzor: 8.5 per cent settled in the relatively fertile, well-developed and densely populated coastal region; 3 per cent settled in *kibbutzim* (collective villages) some of which, like Regavim and others in the Negev, had been founded originally by immigrants from North Africa; 5 per cent joined *moshavim* (cooperative villages); 14.5 per cent settled in the larger, old-established cities or joined relatives. Over six hundred youngsters (2.5 per cent of the total) were accepted by the agricultural and industrial training centers of Youth Aliyah. Thus, 77 per cent of the immigrants from North Africa in this typical period took to a pioneering life in agricultural settlements and development towns under the harshest conditions that the country could offer. That they tended to resent the hardships is axiomatic. That over three-quarters of a people, so thoroughly unprepared for these new conditions and so recently and brutally uprooted, could succeed in striking new roots despite such difficulties speaks for their stamina and fortitude.

The statistics on agricultural settlement in Israel project a similar picture. Of the 251 new agricultural villages and settlements founded in Israel from 1948 to 1959, 82 were entirely or in large part settled by immigrants from North Africa. The number of villages settled by North Africans has since risen to well over a hundred. The part played by the North Africans in the settlement of new agricultural villages since the independence of Israel is greater than that of any other single group in the country, and it is in this sphere that their success has been most marked. These Jews, whose contact with the soil had been almost non-existent for two thousand years, returned to a soil that had been abandoned for almost as long and, by revitalizing it, were themselves revitalized. "This soil recognizes us and now it is beginning to talk to us," one of them explained graphically. As a 1960 survey of the Jewish Agency stated: "The immigration from North Africa has played a considerable role in the new colonization. . . . The level of development of these settlements inhabited by North Africans is equivalent to the general mean of the other communities." These lines highlight the revolutionary process by which the North Africans, within a few years of their arrival in Israel, have been transformed into a highly productive group, especially as tillers of the soil.

Many young immigrants from the Maghreb joined *kibbutzim*, either as a transitory stage prior to their settlement elsewhere in Israel, or as a permanent way of life. The first group, who migrated from Tunisia with the express purpose of setting up a *kibbutz* in Israel, have been successfully established at Regavim in the Negev for a dozen years and many more *kibbutzim*, especially in the Negev, have since been established primarily with young settlers of North African origin.

3. ECONOMIC INTEGRATION

A fundamental obstacle which hindered the integration of many North African immigrants into Israel's economic life was the fact that 40 per cent of them were illiterate. Among women the rate of illiteracy reached 58 per cent. This was due to the fact that a large proportion of the immigrants came from those regions of Morocco where the scholastic network of the Alliance Israélite Universelle had not penetrated and where, in consequence, schools were virtually nonexistent.

In 1960, the percentage of North African immigrants of working age who were actually employed was the lowest of any group of immigrants at 51.7 per cent—76.2 per cent of men and 26.2 per cent of women. (The low proportion of working women was due both to their lack of education and to their large families.) In the same year, 54.8 per cent of all Israelis over fourteen were employed. However, many of the North Africans registered as employed worked only sporadically. Whereas 80 per cent of Israelis, and 87 per cent of workers of European origin worked throughout the year, only 68 per cent of North Africans were fully employed. Because most marginal benefits such as paid holidays, sick leave and pensions are linked to the number of days worked, these immigrants found themselves at a distinct disadvantage vis-à-vis other Israelis. In addition to the overall low level of employment, the North African immigrants were further disadvantaged by the fact that they were usually employed in the more menial and therefore lower paid jobs in the various spheres. This, coupled with the fact that they had large families to support, further aggravated their economic situation. Among the 24 per cent engaged in the "public services," only about 2,000 were civil servants, half of whom were classified as laborers. The rest held positions in the lowest rungs of the service. Only two were to be found in the highest grades.

Twenty-four per cent of the active North African labor force was employed in public services, 23.4 per cent in agriculture, 18.6 per cent in industry, 14.7 per cent in building and construction, 11.5 per cent in trade and the rest in transport, public utilities and other minor spheres. Thus, well over half were engaged in the three productive fields of agriculture, industry and construction, while only a meager 11.5 per cent were to be found in commerce. This represented a marked transformation in their role in the economy in comparison with that which they had played in their former homes. Some 74 North African immigrants were employed as engineers, technicians, doctors and journalists in 1960—not a large number perhaps but an indication of positions to which others could aspire, given training and opportunity.

The increased facilities for adult education and vocational training which have been set up throughout the country are helping to eradicate illiteracy and to raise the professional and technical capacity of the immigrants of Oriental and North African origin with a view to easing their employment situation. Another powerful factor is the Army which each year equips large numbers of young men with a basic education and a useful trade. However, the absolute improvement in the economic situation of the immigrants, due both to the fact that they have benefited from the general amelioration in Israel's economy and to the improvement in their own skills, has tended to be neutralized by the even greater strides that have been made by the already more advanced sections of Israel's population over the past few years. The fact that the means of production have tended to be concentrated in the hands of those who have been in the country the longest and who have the best skills has further widened the disparity.

There is a difference between being poor and being the most poor. In North Africa the Jews, as a group had been poor but they had not been the most poor. In Israel the North Africans, perhaps because they were the last to arrive, are the poorest, and the least accepted. As such, they feel themselves entrapped with no apparent escape. Israel is not like the Maghreb; the little business deals are out of the question; the pay, as laborer or petty clerk, scarcely suffices to provide food for a large family. Moreover, unless the children are fortunate enough to obtain some kind of scholarship for their post-primary education, the chances that they will enjoy a brighter future than their parents are small.

The immigrant from North Africa below a certain poverty level regards himself as a member of the most unfortunate grouping of any in Israel. He is not a philosopher; the socio-economic reasons for his poverty mean nothing to him. He knows only that he is badly off, that no one seems to take his problem seriously. He believes himself to be the victim of deliberate discrimination. Though this feeling is entirely unjustified, it is widely enough held to constitute a potential danger, the more so because there are irrefutable statistics that can be interpreted in support of this view, even though the real explanations lie elsewhere. When passions run high, there is neither the time nor the inclination to engage in socio-economic analyses. This is a problem which must be eradicated at its source through a thorough modification in Israel's economic, educational and social structure.

4. SOCIAL WELFARE

While waiting for the integration process to take its course, a large proportion of the new immigrants became a charge on the State. One quarter of the 93,300 families who were receiving some form of support from the Ministry of Social Welfare in 1961 were of North African origin. Many other families accepted their misery and adapted themselves to the difficulties. The majority of families receiving assistance had more than six children. The social welfare workers were devoted but hopelessly overburdened. Family benefits as paid under the national welfare scheme for large families were practically meaningless, and a family that might have played a happy and productive role often became transformed into another "welfare case." The 23,100 families receiving various kinds of support, who posed such a severe burden on the State's economy, situated at the lowest point of the social pyramid of the State, clearly demonstrated the condition of the immigration from North Africa; they constituted fully one-third of North African families.

In 1965 the government increased family allowances, and families became eligible for them as from the first child and not from the fourth as hitherto. New legislation regarding assistance for large families is at present under review. Though separate statistics on the number of families of Oriental or North African origin still receiving some form of state aid are no longer available, there is no doubt that the vast drop in the overall figure for the total population during the past five years has been reflected in the situation of Israel's citizens from North Africa.

5. HOUSING

The housing situation in 1960 was not better than that in other fields. Although conditions had improved from the 1957 level, Israelis of Oriental origin, among whom were included the North Africans, were shown to be living under conditions of far more severe overcrowding than the general population. Immigrants from Europe were vastly better housed than those from Africa and Asia whose condition was on the whole similar to that of Jews of Oriental origin who had been established in Israel for some time.

The housing provided by the Jewish Agency for immigrants on arrival was generally one of three standard types: 260–300 square feet; 365–410 square feet or 490 square feet. An average room measured 130 square feet. While adequate for a European family, this bore no relation to the needs of families with five to ten children. In 1961, over a quarter of the immigrants from Oriental countries were living at a density that allowed 32 square feet or less per person. Since then, much larger apartments have been provided—between 500 and 850 square feet in area—but the problem still remains a serious one.

6. CRIME AND DELINQUENCY

The crime rate among North African Jews, which was extremely low in North Africa, has unfortunately grown considerably within this community since its arrival in Israel. The North African community has the largest crime rate of any in the country. During the period 1951 to 1960, there were 20.7 convictions per thousand adults (over 15) among the North African immigrants, 12.7 per thousand among immigrants from Asia and 4.9 per thousand among those from Europe. The results for juvenile delinquency were similar: 13.7 per thousand among North Africans, 9.5 per thousand among immigrants from Asia and 4.1 per thousand for immigrants from Europe.

Social and economic factors are at the heart of these statistics. Where a family is crowded with more than four persons per room and where the monthly income per head is less then the equivalent of twenty dollars, it is only too easy for the weakest to succumb to bad influences and to give way to temptations. As living conditions improve, the rate of delinquency decreases; three-quarters of the offenders proved to have come from the most recent immigrants, those who had not yet managed to find their place in the society or in the economy; for immigrants long established in Israel, who have been integrated into the country's life and have acquired a certain patience to deal with frustrations and aggravations, the tendency is for the crime statistics to taper off and reach a "normal" level.

There is also an important psychological factor in the astonishing crime statistics. The immigrants had lived in their home countries in strict, clearly defined, closely associated, traditional societies where religious and spiritual values reigned supreme. They were uprooted, cast into a harsh adventure for which they were totally unprepared, into a world that rejected their way of life and culture as antiquated and made its youth question not only parental authority and tradition but also the validity of its moral and spiritual values. They found themselves in a bewildering environment they could not understand and, to try and understand it in the light of that which was familiar to them or of that for which they had hoped, only increased their sense of bewilderment to the point of revolt, aggravated by a feeling of isolation that can drive even the strongest to the limits of despair. The isolation was very real; at one blow the immigrant had lost contact with his friends, his relatives, his customs— in brief the whole world to which he had been accustomed. What replaced it was a foreign world. The language spoken was one that he knew, at best, only slightly. When his grasp of it improved he became even more disappointed, for he realized then that he lived in a different society and a special mental universe that went beyond the mere problem of language.

A further complication, one that is a negative by-product of what is in itself a positive phenomenon, is that of the young men who, after being discharged from Army service where they have learned a useful occupation and adjusted to the Israeli way of life, find themselves without employment and with no suitable place in society. Their homes are their homes no longer for they have acquired a totally different outlook and set of values and they no longer have anything in common with the older generation. Unless they are absorbed into the economy immediately upon their release, they create another potential source of maladjustment and crime.

7. EDUCATION

The social and economic position of the Jews of North Africa would be more encouraging if the picture as regards education—which will determine the future of the country—were brighter. Unfortunately, while Israel has made remarkable progress in the fields of agriculture, industry and defense, education still leaves much to be desired. There is a crisis in education at present in even the most developed countries of the West; in Israel, where the population has more than trebled in the past eighteen years, the difficulty of finding teachers and adequate finance has further complicated the issue.

Though primary education from the age of six to fourteen is nominally free, except for various fees and dues, parents must under normal circumstances pay for nursery schools, high schools and university education. Fees are so high for post-primary education that unless scholarships are available, it is entirely beyond the reach of the North African and other Oriental immigrants' children. In 1961, only 12 per cent of secondary school pupils were of Oriental or North African origin. At the university level the Oriental element made up 5 per cent. (It is significant that at that time the total university population was less than one half of one per cent of the population, less than a quarter of what is considered adequate in the West and certainly insufficient for the special requirements of a small developing country like Israel that must maintain the high standards set by its founders.) There were only 29 students from the Maghreb at the Hebrew University in Jerusalem in 1961; 15 were in the faculty of arts and the others were dispersed in the social studies, the natural sciences, the faculty of law, the medical school, the school of agriculture, and the school for social workers. In Algiers, it will be remembered, over a third of the student body was Jewish, and every French university, especially the Sorbonne, was enriched by groups of Jewish students from North Africa who achieved remarkable successes there.

Great efforts have since been deployed to help solve the education problem among the Oriental communities. The budget of the Ministry of Education and Culture has been more than trebled and has risen from 5 per cent to 8.3 per cent of the national budget. Nursery schools have been provided to help close the gap between the elementary knowledge of children from different backgrounds, thus reinforcing the efficacy of the primary schools. The proportion of Oriental secondary school pupils has risen from 12 to 30 per cent thanks to a system of state education grants. At the university level, the proportion has risen from 5 to 13 per cent, also due to an increase in the number of university scholarships. However, the proportion of secondary school and university students who do not complete their studies remains considerable. A special campaign has been launched by the government in cooperation with the ODED (Hebrew for "encourage") organization to promote free university education among students of North African origin and to encourage young Jewish students at present in France to immigrate to Israel. In this way, it is hoped to create the requisite intellectual cadres so lacking among this community.

But there is still an inherent imbalance in educational opportunities and successes and these have tended to create and confirm the notion of the intellectual inferiority of immigrant youth from the Orient. The well-intentioned experiments of fixing a lower passing grade for the admission of these youths to secondary schools, and the provision of two-year vocational high schools for them, have, by creating a double standard, resulted in bitterness and failure at the expense of the children. It would seem to perpetuate the conditions of disparity and make of these children the potentially depressed class of Israel's population. The true reason for the seeming failure of the North Africans in the educational system is to be found not in any intellectual inferiority but in the economic conditions in their homes, in the overcrowding that denies them quiet for study or thinking, in the inability of their parents, by reason of their own poor education, to help their children in their studies. Though

Israel lacks the facilities to compensate for this initial disadvantage, the Ministry of Education and Culture is nevertheless trying to strengthen the influence of the school in the lives of the pupils. Attempts are being made in certain areas to extend the hours of teaching to cover a full day, not as at present only half a day. There is a move to extend preschool education further and to provide one hot meal at school for the pupils. But further assistance must be given to make secondary schooling entirely free, to provide stipends for the specially gifted and to set up a network of residential schools for those who, for one reason or another, cannot make use of the educational facilities available locally. Finally, at the university level, where the number of students must grow, it will be necessary to increase the number and value of scholarships so as to free more students not only from fees but also from material need while studying.

Only a bold and generous policy will enable Israel to correct the defects in its educational system and, as a result, in its social and economic structure. This will impose a serious financial burden on the country but it must be done.

CITIZENS OF ISRAEL

Jews from the Oriented countries today make up just one half of Israel's total population and, given their high birth rate, they are likely to constitute 75 per cent of the country's Jewish population by 1978. No other advanced society has ever been called upon to absorb within fifteen years a group of backward immigrants that outnumbered its own population by two to one; no other society has demonstrated that, with a maximum of willpower and a minimum of resources, such a rapid evolution in the general level of the underdeveloped element can be obtained. Indeed, certain aspects of this social experiment have come to be recognized as workable prototypes for other developing nations.

Though the problems remain vital the generation born and brought up in Israel is palpable proof of the extent to which the community has advanced in less than two decades. The youth of North African origin have become practically indistinguishable from those of European background in their outlook, their way of life and their sense of national and personal responsibility. Over the past few years there has been a sharp drop in intercommunal tension and the number of marriages between youth of different origins is growing slowly but constantly. The process of integration is beginning to work.

Israel's citizens from North Africa have become a feature of the Israel scene. They are dispersed in the north and the south, in towns, villages, moshavim and kibbutzim. Recent years have seen the arrival of an intellectual and technical élite that has enriched the community with doctors, businessmen, engineers and educators. This movement is likely to grow as the élite, whose members were the last to leave North Africa and have tended to tarry in France, arrive in Israel. But even without its élite, the North African community has contributed handsomely to the present and the future of Israel. At least a third of what has been accomplished in the revival of the Galilee can be attributed to the North Africans, over half of what has been accomplished in reclaiming the desert of the Negev is due to their endeavor. A new élite has emerged; a youth that is devoted to communal betterment, that is active in the pioneering youth movements and in political parties. They have made a name for themselves by their dynamism, by their willingness to work hard, by their imagination and by their readiness to take a calculated risk. An outstanding example of their courage was the supreme sacrifice made by Nathan Elbaz, a young soldier from Morocco, who saved the lives of his comrades by absorbing with his own body the explosion of a hand grenade which was accidentally released in the midst of an army camp. Israelis of North African origin are also playing an increasingly important role in public affairs. Four were elected to the Sixth Knesset in 1965, one of whom was appointed Deputy Minister of Agriculture; and over three hundred hold elected office as members of municipal councils, labor councils and representatives of communal and collective agricultural villages.

In Israel's War of Independence, recent arrivals from North Africa played a noticeable part. In the Suez campaign of 1956 they were even more prominent, fighting in the front ranks of battle and giving their lives in defense of their homeland. However, it was the Six Day War which indisputedly revealed their complete integration within Israel society which, during the months of May and June, 1967, proved its real vigor and deep unity both to itself and to the world. At that moment, as every citizen confronted the Arab menace, each felt that Israel was one people and that barriers no longer existed in its midst; no longer were there differences between Easterners and Westerners, rich and poor, old-established citizens and new immigrants. Every individual faced the same danger and fulfilled his duty with the same determination, often with the same heroism. A large number of those who lived in the border areas were Jews who had come from North Africa and Oriental countries. As civilians they carried out their duty to the full. As for the Army, a vast majority of its ranks were filled by youths of African or Asian parentage. Their courage in the hour of trial was eloquently demonstrated. Indeed, in that time of danger, Israel society strikingly proved that it had overcome its inner contradictions. One of the most extraordinary phenomena resulting from the Six Day War was the incontrovertible fact that in only 20 years communities brought together in the crucible of Israel from 102 countries of the world, communities of disparate economic and cultural levels, diverse origins and different patterns of settlement in the country, had become welded into a perfect whole, capable of presenting an indomitable front to the enemy.

But the achievements of the North African immigration and its contribution to Israel's life and development are heroic by other standards too. This young generation, that would have been reduced to a life of futile sterility in North Africa, has been transformed into conquerors of the desert, builders of cities, redeemers devoted to the resurrection of a people and of a land.

They are the heirs and the continuers of the great tradition of Sephardic Judaism, of the poets, philosophers and judges of North Africa who kept the lamp of Judaism alight in the Maghreb in the face of all vicissitudes. This new generation has fulfilled the dreams and aspirations of its ancestors. With its return to Israel, twenty centuries of history have come full circle.

NISSIM REJWAN

Nissim Rejwan was born in Baghdad in 1921 and came to Israel in 1951. He received his Jewish and secular education in his native Iraq and at the Hebrew University in Jerusalem. In Baghdad he was a book and cinema reviewer for the *Iraq Times*. In Israel he became the editor of the Arab daily *Al Yaum* and Middle East expert for the *Jerusalem Post*. He was also a news editor for "Radio Israel" and a contributor to prominent journals in various lands.

A discerning publicist and sociologist, Rejwan has written often about the myopic approach, not disregard, to the problem of Jewish immigrants in Israel from other Middle East countries and from North Africa.

For centuries the *Sephardim* and the *Yemenites* were the "forgotten million" of the Jewish people. Devout and spiritually potent, most of them were culturally and socially undernourished, deprived. The swift transition from the "old ways" in the Arab-speaking countries to the new dynamic European Israel had a traumatic impact on the newcomers as well as on the Western Jews, both immigrants and older settlers.

Rejwan's rare combination of scholarly apparatus and journalistic ability bring to his recitation of facts and analysis of problems a quality of eloquence and urgency. What follows is a good example: THE COMMUNAL FRONT, *The Jewish Frontier* (Supplement), May, 1968, pp. 7–11.

The Communal Front

by NISSIM REJWAN

WHEN MR. LEVI ESHKOL, the Prime Minister, was asked recently in the course of a press interview, what, in his opinion, were the changes brought about by the Six Day War in the various moods of the Israelis, he admitted that it was difficult to answer such questions. "This," he said, "is a matter for the psychologists, for research projects and for questionnaires." On the other hand, a hastily organized, quiz-like inquiry ordered just before the outbreak of hostilities by the Minister of Information, shows that 90 per cent of the 2,500 Israelis who took part in the questionnaire thought that intercommunal relations in the coming years "will be improved," 70 per cent said tensions between the religious and secularists would be eased, and 83 per cent predicted that "there will be more consensus on public and national issues."

However, it seems certain that several years will elapse before anyone can be in a position to say with authority in what spheres, and in what directions, the recent war has left its imprint on the moods and attitudes of the Israelis. In so far as the intercommunal situation is concerned, one therefore can only try to find out in what direction these effects would be felt given certain alternative trends. For there is nothing automatic, inevitable or deterministic about these things.

But before we make such an attempt at re-evaluation, a few words about the nature of the problem under discussion will be in place. Whatever name one gives it—"the Second Israel," the "Ethnic Problem," or "The Communal Controversy"—there is no gainsaying that at the root of our problem lies the socio-economic gap separating the two main ethnic divisions of Israel's Jewish population—Europeans and the Middle Easterners. One way of tracing this gap is to consider the fortunes of the mass immigration which came from countries of the Middle East during the early years of the State and see how the process of their integration worked and in what ways it affected their position, in relation to the veterans on the one hand and, on the other, to those who hailed from European countries.

The story is well-known. The mass immigration which followed the establishment of Israel profoundly changed the face of the Jewish community. Producing a socially-mixed population, this immigration suddenly created an enormous heterogeneity in a society that had formerly been rather selective and more homogeneous. There were two other ways in which this change was expressed: unlike the old settlers, the new immigrants were not grounded in an ideology; and, again unlike the old settlers, the majority of these newcomers hailed from Moslem countries, thus substantially strengthening in the Yishuv the cultural element of the Middle Eastern Jews. The situation was complicated even further by the fact that the Middle Easterners found themselves suddenly plunged into a different technology, new kinds of social and political relations, and a novel system of socio-cultural values. The shock and the estrangement between this type of new immigrant and the European old settler were mutual.

As far as the Middle Easterners were concerned, the main source of frustration for them lay in the prevalent stratification and ranking of ethnic groups. The pattern of this stratification, as well as other aspects of the communal problem in Israel, are briefly and succinctly discussed in Dr. Alex Weingrod's book, *Israel: Group Relations in a New Society* (Praeger, New York, 1966). Dr. Weingrod, a trained anthropologist who worked for some years in Israel, writes as follows about this pattern of ethnic stratification. "Europeans, or to use the more common designation, Ashkenazim, are ranked higher than Middle Easterners or Sephardim. To come from Poland or Britain is, *ipso facto* to be more prestigious than to have one's origin in Egypt or Iraq. The rift is fundamental, and it runs throughout the society."

"This being the case," Dr. Weingrod adds, "it takes little imagination to see that this ranking must lead to resentment on the part of the lower-placed groups—the Middle Easterners. Having immigrated with such high hopes, it is deeply disturbing to discover that being 'Moroccan' or 'Iraqi' automatically sets one low in the social scale. Not only is there resentment, there is an even more powerful sense of discrimination: Middle Easterners are firmly convinced that they are discriminated against. There can be little doubt that these feelings are widespread, and that, whether real or imaginary, Middle Easterners believe that prejudice and discrimination are set against them."

How concertedly the prevalent pattern of social stratification and ranking has affected the actual status of the Middle Easterners we can see from a brief consideration of the long-term trends in these immigrants' social, economic and political mobility. The data are provided by Dr. Weingrod. Concerning the socio-economic mobility, it may be perfectly natural that veterans should earn somewhat more than new immigrants. But what seemed disturbing was that the income gap between veterans and immigrants tended to widen rather than narrow with the passage of years. In 1954, for instance, the ratio of income between pre-1931 veterans and post-1952 immigrants was 109:60. In 1958, it became 106:41.

Another disturbing aspect, supplied by Dr. Weingrod, reveals that a comparison of income according to occupation shows this rank-order: European veterans, European immigrants, Middle Eastern veterans, Middle Eastern immigrants. Thus the incomes of European immigrants have risen far more quickly than those of Middle Eastern immigrants—so that they rank higher than the income of Middle Eastern veterans.

The conclusion is clear: ethnic affiliation is more important than the length of time spent in the country. Thus in Dr. Weingrod's words, "Europeans as a group are more mobile than their Middle Eastern brethren." There is thus no doubt that "subjective variables," such as prejudice and discrimination, are factors blocking the Middle Easterner's path. But what those who study the communal situation in Israeli society found rather surprising was that the ethnic-income split in Israeli society tended to expand rather than recede with the passage of time. In the long run, of course, what all this means is "a joining of ethnicity and class"—a trend which by all accounts is a rather dangerous one.

Not unexpectedly, the same pattern governs the other important sphere of social mobility—education. Here again, there is a joining of ethnicity and lack of achievement. The economic factor is no doubt important here: those who earn less spend less on the education of their children. But, in addition to this factor and probably surpassing it in importance, "cultural differences also select against the Middle Eastern students . . . The school curriculum is heavily slanted towards European traditions; the teachers are also predominantly European, and this too gives advantages to European students." Dr. Weingrod's conclusion is clear: "So long as [Middle Eastern] children are approached as if they were Europeans, the students are unlikely to perform well. . . Similarly, approaching these children as if their own cultural heritage were empty will not lead to the desired results."

What of the future? One key certainly lies with those same "subjective variables" which were at work here all along, namely, prejudice and the discriminatory practices to which prejudice gives rise. If a change is to come, this is where it can come from. Let us start from the meager data we have from the results of the poll conducted by the Ministry of Information and referred to earlier in this article.

There is no doubt that the very fact that as many as 90 per cent of the sample taken by the Information Ministry's research workers should express the belief that intercommunal relations will improve in itself is a sociological factor of significance, even if there is little scientific proof supporting such a claim. It is now considered almost a truism by social scientists that the way human beings appraise a situation is no less crucial in its bearing on that situation than its so-called "objective" nature or "real" attributes. Fifty years ago William I. Thomas, the father of modern American sociology, formulated a well-known social phenomenon when he laid it down that "if men define situations as real, they are real in their consequences."

But if this "theorism" is true of all human situations, it is even more valid where we have to deal with conditions growing out and depending almost exclusively on subjective factors such as prejudices, intergroup hostilities, and the proneness of most human beings to dismiss as "queer," inferior, or just "funny," phenomena to which they are not accustomed. In such cases, the prejudices of the in-group usually help start a pattern of discrimination against the out-group which in turn starts a vicious circle that often seems perpetual and unbreakable. The working of the vicious circle in in-group/out-group relations can be illustrated in innumerable ways and from various fields of social intercourse.

Sociologists have long remarked on the fact that we all acquire our sense of self from the response of others to us. A child who constantly encounters such remarks as "You are inferior, you are bad, you are incompetent," will internalize these attitudes and ultimately conform to them. Likewise, in intergroup relations there are powerful pressures which tend to make members of an out-group into the type of persons the in-group stereotyped image of them makes them out to be. For instance, if, on the basis that its members are "inferior," a group is given poor schools, poor jobs, few opportunities for self-respect and self-appreciation, and little chance of advancement, the dominant in-group soon proves its belief to be correct: it has created the conditions for the confirmation and reinforcement of its own prejudices.

But there is another, "brighter" side to the same coin. For while a pattern of discrimination is a firm structure, with several mutually reinforcing supports, the vicious circle is not always unbreakable. In the case of our child, for instance, a powerful contradicting image supplied by a loving mother, a teacher, a friend, or a successful person from his own group with whom he has identified, can work wonders in restoring to the child his self-respect and a wholly different "looking-glass self." In the case of an out-group the same sort of reverse process, though much slower, is not only capable of taking place but it can do so from ostensibly very modest, almost unnoticeable beginnings.

This point may call for some elucidation. The communal problems of a heterogeneous nation has the manifoldness of human life itself. Some have likened these problems to that of women's place in society. Like it, they touch every other social issue or, rather, they represent an angle of them all. In attempting to analyze a country's communal problem, the student cannot avoid any aspect of that country's life: race, culture, education, breadwinning, economic and social policy, law, crime, class, family, war, politics, attitudes. We have seen how in-group prejudices and out-group standards mutually "cause" each other in an ever-upward spiral we called the vicious circle. In cases where things remain roughly what they are and have been, these two forces can be said to balance each other.

Yet, as Gunnar Myrdal has pointed out in another context, such static "accommodation" is entirely accidental. In actual life one of these two "balancing" factors—namely in-group prejudices and out-group standards—often undertakes certain changes. In this case, says Myrdal, "this will cause a change in the other factor, too, and start a process of interaction where the change in one factor will continuously be supported by the reaction of the other factor." The whole system will thus be moving in the direction of the primary change, but much further.

Drawing further on Myrdal's analysis, we can now give a more concrete illustration of this process of "cumulative causation." If, for example, we assume that for some reason in-group prejudice can be decreased and discrimination accordingly mitigated, this is likely to lead to a rise in out-group standards, which may, in turn, decrease in-group prejudice still a little further—which would again allow out-group standards to rise, and so on and on: the initial change would be supported by consecutive waves of back-effects from the reaction of the other factor.

Moreover, this spiral process of what can be called the vicious-circle-in-reverse can be started not only when one of the factors undertakes change as a whole but also when any one of its components changes. A rise in out-group employment, for instance, or in its health standards, athletic attainments, or its performances in the sphere of the arts or on the battlefields is likely to start the same sort of process by introducing certain changes in the attitudes of the in-group towards its members, allowing for a further rise in its standards and thus affecting still more the attitudes and prejudices of the in-group.

Admittedly, the process described in the preceding passages may, when applied to the situation in Israel, sound somewhat exaggerated. Basically, however, it gives a fairly adequate "ideal type" of what has actually taken place on our communal front. What happened was that some of the immigrants who came to Israel during the first years of the State's existence from countries of the Middle East and North Africa had lower standards of living, a different type and level of education, and widely different customs and mores. Many of them dispossessed and impoverished, their material conditions and their life in shabby and crowded immigrant camps, tended to reinforce the initial impression of their "backwardness," incompetence and sloth. All this was enough to provide a powerful impetus to the workings of the vicious circle described above, and to confirm the Yishuv's European in-group in its stereotyped low opinion of non-Europeans.

That there were other, more deep-seated factors at work here; that the main trouble lay not in the general "low" level of these immigrants but in their being simply different from *us*; that many of them were in fact equipped with a higher level of education and were no less competent than some of those fellow-immigrants who hailed from the "right" backgrounds—all this could not save the newcomers from the Orient as a group from being stereotyped and relegated, again as a group, to a low status in the socio-cultural scale. Thus out-group standards—real and imaginary—led to in-group prejudices and a pattern of "natural" discrimination which caused those standards to fall further downwards and thus reinforce the prejudices and gradually "stabilize" the discrimination pattern.

To reverse this vicious process—or at least to mitigate it—what was needed was a change in either of the two factors involved, namely out-group standards and in-group attitudes, or in one of their components. Such changes were not forthcoming at a sufficient pace or degree. To be sure, as a result of the relative prosperity and the affluence of the first half of the present decade, the general standards of living, housing, health, and, to a lesser extent, education among the "Second Israel" rose considerably during those brief years; but the general standards of the in-group, or the "First Israel" if you will, rose at an even higher rate. The result was that, although the levels of both out-group and in-group rose, the socio-economic gap between them tended to widen rather than narrow. The regime of economic "retrenchment" which followed hard on the heels of the Knesset elections in November, 1965, made things even worse in this respect by hitting the Second Israel the hardest. Not unexpectedly, the economic strains felt by the out-group increased the resentment of its members, who naturally tended to direct it against the "Ashkenazim."

The Six Day War has, even if perhaps only temporarily, put an end to the severe economic retrenchment measures which were in full swing when it broke out. As already indicated, however, it is not by considerations of "bread" alone that intergroup relations are governed. The conviction, for instance, expressed by so overwhelming a majority of the sample used in the Information Ministry's study referred to above, that intercommunal relations in the coming years will improve may be an indication of a change in the in-group attitudes more than one in the out-group standards. Moreover, since the inquiry was made shortly before and in the midst of the war, the note of optimism expressed by the majority has had more to do with a sense of national solidarity and a common fate and purpose than with the actual performance on the battlefield of this or that group.

It is to be supposed that this change in in-group attitudes will be confirmed and reinforced by another, perhaps no less important, process. I refer to the fact that, having fought a war side by side with their comrades from the "First Israel," the sons of the "Second Israel" have rather expectedly acquired a new sense of self-respect, pride, belonging and identification. For, although during the past two decades or so it has been the in-group that has been "defining" the situation—and thus making it real in its results—both for itself and for members of the out-group, this never meant that the latter had not been taking part in that endless process of definition. If what has just been said about the Orientals' newly-acquired sense of pride and identification is correct, then the way in which the "Second Israel" will choose to "define the situation" may henceforth prove as decisive in its consequences as that of the in-group. Needless to say, accompanying changes in the components of the other factor involved, such as a rise in material or educational standards, is likely to enhance these prospects greatly.

But it is possible—rather easy, in fact—to overestimate the importance of these "changes." On the one hand, prejudices die very hard indeed, and even if we are right in discerning the beginnings of a process of change in in-group attitudes, this process is bound to be extremely slow. On the other hand, the greater the expectations, the more cruel the disappointment and the stronger the reaction. There is no doubt that expectations of the "Second Israel" have risen considerably as a result of the recent war, and if no comparative changes in in-group attitudes are forthcoming the disillusion and disappointment may accordingly result in a powerful reaction. In this connection it may be useful to keep in mind that the overwhelming majority of the sons and daughters of Oriental parents in Israel are now either native-born or have lived all their conscious life in Israel, and it is to be supposed that they will not settle for anything less than their full share and full opportunities in the only country they know.

This brings us to the fundamental question: What is the Israeli society's aim in the communal sphere? The answer is not easy. The term *mizug galuyot*, which translated literally means "mixing the exiles," has generally served as an expression of the Israeli ideal in this respect. But it is a problematic term, overcharged with emotion, sociologically devoid of real content, and culturally rather arbitrary and ill-conceived. In actual practice, moreover, it often seemed to denote little more than "remolding" the Oriental immigrant, "bringing him up to our own level," and making of him something that he is not. The result has been *de*-culturation, marginalization and educational and cultural deprivation.

What ought to be the goal in the communal sphere, then? On the face of it, "integration" sounds a far more reasonable, humane and attainable ideal than *mizug galuyot*. However, it too presents certain difficulties. Communal integration can be defined as a situation in which the members of a society, regardless of their color, religion or ethnic origin, move freely among one another, sharing the same opportunities and the same privileges and facilities on an equal basis. Thus defined, the term carries to some degree a connotation of assimilation: the loss of separating group identities, *with differentiation only on an individual basis.**

The main difficulty posed by integration as defined above—which in itself may be taken to be a desirable and attainable ideal for Israeli society—is its seeming emphasis on *individual* absorption. Now the idea of individual absorption, or assimilation, is based on a theory which the sciences of man have long discarded—namely, the theory of "social individualism." This theory teaches, in brief, that society is made up of isolated individuals who depend mainly upon their own talents for the position they achieve in society.

"Individual assimilation," which means the absorption into the prevailing socio-cultural structure individually and one by one, of certain "qualified" members of the out-group, is thus tantamount to a rejection of out-group cultures. It says in effect: "You can be one of us only if (1) you surrender your group affiliation and (2) you become *like* us." This is the surest way to the marginalization of members of the out-group; it has also been a tool for social inequality and discrimination, especially in the case of societies, such as Israel, where the rights, attainments and privileges of an individual rest largely on the status achieved by the group to which he belongs rather than to his purely individual attributes.

---

* For this and a few other technical definitions in this article I am indebted to J. Milton Yinger's excellent survey, *A Minority Group in American Society* (McGraw-Hill, New York, 1965).

Thus, although the ultimate goal of Israeli society may be considered to be integration, this goal cannot be attained by the process of individual assimilation suggested by the ideal itself. Before we can behave as an "integrated society" we must first try to create the framework in which such integration can take place. This may well prove to be a transition period towards full integration, but without it it would be impossible to reach that goal in a healthy, orderly manner.

This framework must be based on tolerance and mutual acceptance and appreciation as between in-groups and out-groups. This is the way of what is called "cultural pluralism," "democratic pluralism," or just plain "pluralism." Now "pluralism" has been defined as a system of society in which membership in distinctive ethnic, religious or cultural groups is accepted and even applauded. Pluralistic societies pride themselves on the freedom granted to diverse groups to preserve different cultural heritages, observe different religions, speak different languages and develop independent associations. This freedom, however, is qualified by one sole requirement, namely loyalty to the prevailing political and economic system.

Besides the richness and variety which it lends to the emerging culture, the ideal of pluralism, with the strong networks of private associations based on it, does not only not weaken the cohesion of a democratic society but actually strengthens it. Professor Yinger, in the work quoted above, asserts that such networks "serve both to relate an individual, through groups that are close and meaningful to him, to the large complex society, and also to protect him from excessive encroachments on his freedom by that society."

The problem of communal integration is not solved by the proclaimed intentions and pious wishes of either the in-group or the out-group; it is solved when conditions are created through which members of the latter group are accepted as full partners by members of the former, while at the same time being allowed to continue to belong to and feel pride in their own group.

MOSHE DAVIS

Moshe Davis was born in Brooklyn, New York, in 1916 and is the product of Jewish general education in the United States and Israel. He received his B.A. degree from Teachers' College, Columbia University, his rabbinic ordination from the Jewish Theological Seminary in New York, and his Ph. D. degree from the Hebrew University in Jerusalem. He served in pedagogic and administrative capacities at the Jewish Theological Seminary—as Provost and as Dean of its Teachers' Institute—and at the same time acted as program director for the "Eternal Light" Series, NBC Radio. Davis has occupied positions of leadership in the *Histadrut Ivrit* (Hebrew Culture and Language Association) of America, Ramah Camps, the American Jewish Historical Society and many other organizations. Since settling in Israel he has headed the Hebrew University's Institute of Contemporary Jewry. He has written extensively on American Jewish life in both English and Hebrew: *Jewish Life and Institutions in America, The Shaping of American Judaism, The Emergence of Conservative Judaism* and several other books, pamphlets and articles.

Davis' major contribution lies in providing a functional nexus between Israel and the United States. While others spoke glibly of the interdependence of the Jewish communities in these countries, he taught courses and administered projects in Israel relating to Jewish experience in the United States. At first very skeptical of the vitality, resourcefulness and promise of American Jewry, in time his Hebrew University students became aware of the turmoil of changing values in the United States. Moreover, *The Study Circle on Diaspora Jewry in the Home of the President of Israel* which Davis directs imaginatively and sedulously, has become an effective medium in the exchange of views and opinions pertaining to Jews and Judaism the world over.

TEACHING AMERICAN JEWISH HISTORY IN ISRAEL, which follows, is an extension of a lecture by Davis under the auspices of the American Jewish Historical Society and the Jewish Museum of the Jewish Theological Seminary of America on March 11, 1959.

Teaching American Jewish History in Israel

by MOSHE DAVIS

TEACHING AMERICAN JEWISH HISTORY begins with America. For the first time in all of Jewish history, continuous and pervasive interaction governs the life of the Jews and the people among whom they dwell. In this country, established by men whose faith was influenced by Hebrew Scriptures, one might say that many basic Jewish concepts had taken root before the Jews arrived. In that sense, the ideas of Judaism welcomed the Jews to America.

If teaching American Jewish history is to teach America, the task is facilitated by America's position in world affairs. In Israel, America is being taught all the time. She is represented first and foremost by what she is and does in the world. For the Israeli, America is part of the day's news. The radio and newspapers report her affairs and her policies, and the national ideals which they embody are subject to continuing discussion and deep interest. Moreover, the ideas of America are available to Israelis through literature and periodicals. The English language is the leading second language in the country. (In the early decades of the century, German and Russian were the dominant foreign languages. For the contemporary generation, English and American literature are more widely read.) The State Department arranged several years ago to export to Israel books and magazines from this country on a free-exchange basis. The result is that the book stores, as numerous in Israel as drug stores in the States, are full of the latest American books and papers. In this way, American thought finds its way into the heart of Israel, and the individual Israeli measures the quality of the American idea by his own insights and background. Furthermore, American public officials, civic leaders, artists, intellectuals, business men and tourists create a human bond with Israel. A list of the eminent American visitors who have worked in the country in its formative years reads like a sampling of *Who's Who in America*. Many of these people correspond with Israeli friends and colleagues in the institutions they served. Many return again and again. Thus Israelis understand America through her deeds, through her creative thought, and through personal contact with excellent representatives of American life.

Israel's best path to understanding America, however, lies through American Jewry. In the experience of Jewish life in America—as in the experience of other religious and ethnic groups—American democracy was transformed from an abstract ideal into the daily opportunity to develop in freedom. The waves of immigration, the attainment of full political rights, the place of Jewish enterprise in the ever-broadening economy, the opportunities in professions and arts—these elements are details in the larger growth of the American nation. At the same time, the inner life of American Jewry, its growth in education and culture, the elevation of the Synagogue to the central place in communal life, the formidable development of the Zionist movement, fraternal orders and mutual aid societies—all these internal concerns were also shaped by the national culture. When Israelis understand the American Jewish saga, they come to know the unique quality of America.

Yet it is commonplace that Israelis know far too little of the history, institutions and aspirations of the American Jewish community. The realities of American Jewish life today are only dimly perceived in the Jewish State. The Israeli student knows more about the Jews in medieval Spain and East-European Jews of the nineteenth century than he does about his contemporaries in America. Even men and women high in government and intellectual life have only the vaguest knowledge of the social and institutional structure of American Jewry. In a lecture at the Hebrew University in 1954, on "American Jewry in the Light of Historical Research," I developed the idea that modern Jewish history cannot be understood without the knowledge of American Jewish history. This was an elementary thesis, and yet the demonstration of the thesis, as I had anticipated, opened a new avenue of thought to the students at the Hebrew University.

In the United States, my academic vocation is to study and teach American Jewish history at The Jewish Theological Seminary. Since my graduate studies at the Hebrew University in 1937, I have also been privileged to teach and lecture on this subject both formally and informally in Israel. During the academic years of 1959–1961 my assignment in Israel is to help establish the Institute of Contemporary Jewry at the Hebrew University, in which American Jewish study is, for the first time, an integral part of the curriculum. Teaching American Jewish life to Israelis has therefore been for me a continuing assignment, and my impressions and observations are cumulative, covering two decades of experience. In this report, I want to describe the insights not so much from what I taught but from what I learned as a student, lecturer, and teacher.

What does this assignment teach? What are the exciting discoveries of Israel about American Jewish life? What are the questions, the misconceptions, the insights learned over these years?

My first discovery was the excitement of Israelis at the importance attached to Hebrew culture in America, and the growing interest in it. Invariably, the story of Hebrew in the American public school system caught the imagination of Israelis. The introduction of the Hebrew language into public secondary education is, to be sure, without precedent in modern education anywhere in the world. Started experimentally in 1923 in New York City, Hebrew is now taught in more than 200 colleges, graduate and professional schools, and in 85 secondary schools in 16 cities; and the movement for instruction in Hebrew as a modern language is increasing steadily. Israelis were struck by the correspondence between the growth of Jewish settlement in Israel and the growth of Hebrew culture in America. Furthermore, they found striking the recognition of Hebrew in American official circles. For example, Lawrence Marwick, Chief of the Hebraic section of the Library of Congress, published in 1957 a *Handbook of Diplomatic Hebrew*, to meet the need for such a text among government agencies, translators, and abstractors. All this was totally foreign to the Jewish experience in Europe and in Arab countries from which most Israelis derive their knowledge of the world. As Europeans, they knew that Hebrew and Bible were studied under Christian auspices, but always as ancient, classical language and text, never as a living tongue of a living culture. Furthermore, Hebrew was always classified under "Semitics" or "Oriental Languages," and it remained the concern of a limited and particular academic group. In America, they learn, Hebrew is taught in tax-supported institutions, to transmit the Hebraic heritage in Western culture and to include it in the formation of the American intellect. Thus it happens that many Jewish children meet Hebrew first in public high school. Furthermore, the part of Hebrew culture in Western tradition, pointed up by Edmund Wilson in an essay in *A Piece of My Mind*,* seems to be emphasized more and more in American universities. Wilson proposed a two-year curriculum in classic Hebrew culture for students in his ideal university. The growing acceptance of these ideas was indicated, among many ways, by Millicent Taylor's article in the *Christian Science Monitor*, "The Study of Classical Hebrew Is Very Much Alive in Schools" (May 10, 1958). This phenomenon of Hebrew's new rooting on American soil, limited though it still is, provided Israelis with a new insight into America and its open-minded civilization.

A second never-ending source of surprise to Israelis is the relation of Christians and Jews in America. Israelis are, of course, deeply impressed and grateful for the many generous acts of Christians to the State of Israel. The deep-rooted love that these Christians have for the sovereign State delighted them and yet puzzled them, too. They would not have been puzzled had they simply seen themselves in perspective. Israelis know only too well that they live in the land of the Bible, but they find it difficult to understand that the western world—and the Jews who live in that world—look upon Israelis as a people dwelling in *The Holy Land*. Most Israelis are not mindful of the fact, even if they know it, that American Christians regard themselves as "children of the Bible," and that their special relationship to Israel flows from their faith.

In a touching memoir about Shalom Aleichem's first visit to the United States in 1914, B. Z. Goldberg recalls his own student days at the University of Iowa several years before:

"There were but three Jewish students—one was preparing for law, the second for medicine, and I was the third, a freshman at the college. Not only was there no sign of anti-Semitism there, but they carried the three of us aloft—we were

---

* Farrar, Straus and Cudahy, New York, 1956.

their darlings—as the children of a people who had given them, these Iowa farmers, the Bible."

In this light, Israelis have come to understand President Truman's insistence, for example, that he is "the modern Cyrus," and the revealing autobiographical statement of Secretary of Agriculture, Ezra Taft Benson:

"My particular interest in Israel goes back a long way—back, in fact to the days of my youth . . . I have long known of God's covenant with Abraham, Isaac and Jacob that their lands could be for them and their seed an everlasting inheritance . . . And so the development of the new nation of Israel was of no real surprise to me . . ."

The Bible as a solid foundation for Christian-Israeli understanding is now well-known in Israel. What the Israelis do not know and have yet to learn is that the relationship of Christian and Jew in America has been translated into a pattern of religious equality amid religious diversity. To explain this idea, which is quite novel to people who grew up in European traditions, I often used Thomas Jefferson's extraordinary statement in response to a Discourse delivered by Dr. de la Motta at the Consecration of the Synagogue at Savannah:
"Monticello, Sept. 1, 1820
Thomas Jefferson returns his thanks to Dr. de la Motta, for the eloquent discourse on the consecration of the synagogue of Savannah which he has been so kind as to send him. It excites in him the gratifying reflection that his own country has been the first to prove to the world two truths, the most salutary to human society, that man can govern himself, and that religious freedom is the most effective anodyne against religious dissension: the maxim of civil government being reversed in that of religion where its true form is 'Divided we stand, united we fall' . . ."

From such a text, I could begin to explain the equality freely given to Judaism to build an indigenous Jewish life in the American social structure.

I also developed the theme of American Jewry as "the spiritual third of the nation," citing the fact that even in the early 1800's, when Jews were a tiny fraction of the population, they were valued as heirs of an ancient *People-Tradition* and not only in accordance with their numbers. This surprised my students. They came to understand, however, that Jews are indeed a "spiritual third" of the American nation, that they are judged by the quality of their ideas rather than the quantity of their adherents and that together with the Protestant and Catholic faiths, they are an organic part of the spiritual life of the country.

A recent example of the Christian love for the Holy Land which illustrated my discussions on the subject in the summer of 1958, was the extraordinary correspondence of Governor Theodore McKeldin of Maryland, and a citizen of Baltimore. This correspondence was published in Israel and elicited widespread response. Governor McKeldin had received the following question:

"Dear Governor McKeldin:

As long as I can remember, I have been taught by my family, by the Maryland public school system . . . that we are Americans. Since this is so, our allegiance is always to our own country—America. We cannot then, it seems, call any other land 'Ours,' and be loyal to the United States. We do not refer to another nation's army as 'our army,' its soldiers as 'our boys' nor the nation itself as 'us.' The officers of the sovereign states of the United States are dedicated to the support of the constitutions of said states and to that of the union . . .

I could not understand from your remarks whether you were an American or an Israelite, a Jew or a Gentile, a Hebrew or a Christian. Which are you, I would like to know?" . . .

Governor McKeldin replied as follows:

"You ask if I am an 'American or an Israelite' (and I shall assume that you meant Israeli).

"You know, of course, that I am an American, because you know that I was the Mayor of an American City and am the Governor of an American State.

"You ask if I am Jew or Gentile, Hebrew or Christian. To the Jew, of course, I am a Gentile. In my faith, I am a Christian.

"Because I am an American, and because of the freedom which is rightfully mine, I can call any man my brother, and when I feel a kinship for his land because it, too, defends the dignity and the liberty of man, I can call it mine—or, in the form to which you specifically object, 'ours.'

"Because I am a Christian, I dare to extend the hand of brotherhood in the full measure, and to identify myself as closely as possible, with a great people who are fighting a gallant fight for that which is right.

"I thus reply to your letter because I, too, was reared in a family with a great and abiding love for America and for the opportunities of America, and I am most grateful for the fruits of the opportunities which I have been permitted to harvest.

"I hope that my gratitude always will be strong enough to keep me from hoarding these fruits to decay in a dark and narrow cellar.

"I hope that its light will be always so bright as to permit me to see the good in other lands and in other peoples, to glory in their struggles for liberty as I glory in ours, and, indeed, even to speak of theirs as 'ours'—because man's fight for freedom is not a thing of isolation. It is a universal and unending battle . . ."

Many Israelis discovered America when they came to understand the foundations upon which so representative an American as Governor McKeldin could say these things:

There were several discoveries about America that dismayed Israelis. One of them is America's passion for change. Invariably, they would question this change and mobility of the American people. When I described America as a land of "inner vibration," they would ask, "Are you not confusing change with growth?" Change for its own sake troubled Israelis, who themselves live in the most fluid of societies.

A second such "negative" discovery is the way the immigrants were absorbed into the American culture. For Israelis, the continuous integration of various groups into the life of the country is a pressing problem. They would like not to learn from America her mistaken idea of a "melting pot." America actually had in its country all of civilization. By the first decade of this century, the whole world was there. Americans felt then that "Americanization" meant to eliminate all differences. In the process of eliminating all differences, children were taught in the schools to repudiate the cultures from which their parents came. Now Americans have to undo the whole process. We will have to train our children to study Italian, Spanish, German, Japanese. We have to undo the long and costly work of "assimilation." Israelis see this and want to learn from our mistakes. In the great process of acculturation in Israel, Israelis are hoping to be able to *preserve* as much as is possible of these cultures.

What are some of the conceptions and misconceptions of the Israelis about the internal structure of American Jewish life? What can they learn about us?

When it comes to the sheer size and intricate network of American Jewish organizations, Israelis are completely baffled. In 1958, the mission of the Council of Jewish Federations and Welfare Funds talked to a cross-section of forty leaders of the Knesset, Jewish Agency, Army and other institutions and held another session with the editors of over twenty leading daily newspapers. The mission reported that even this highly placed and highly responsible group did not know the elementary facts about American Jewish communal life. How, then, could they be expected to grasp the social forces which create our multiple organizations and the variety of cultural forms of American Jewry? One has therefore to explain that the phenomenon of "a nation of joiners" derives from our being a citizen-led nation. Nor do Israelis readily understand the role of laymen in the direction of American religious life. Europeans, generally, do not understand voluntarism in public life as a dynamic of democracy. In a book of mine, translated into Hebrew, I had used the phrase, "the rabbis and the lay leaders." When I got back the proofs, I found that the translator had said: "rabbis and secularists." The idea of a voluntaristic and non-professional society is therefore a real discovery. When one explains this background to the Israelis, they then understand why we do not have in American Jewry a centralized form of *Gemeinde*, similar to the communal pattern in Europe. They see why free enterprise in Jewish organization life was established for the first time in Jewish history in America: it comes as a direct result of voluntarism in American life.

As one continues to describe the internal life of the Jewish community in America, one revelation follows upon another for the Israeli. For example, the re-emergence of the Synagogue as the central unit of Jewish communal life surprises them. The character of the Synagogue as a family institution, filling cultural and social needs, as well as individual religious needs, is almost totally unknown to the Israeli. For Israelis, the choice in religion is between orthodoxy and secularism. They are slowly coming to learn the great strength inherent in American Jewish religious life, in which both adaptation and modification may mean an enlargement of the Tradition.

Another discovery is the nature of the Jewish involvement in *Klal Yisrael*, in the needs and concerns of fellow-Jews. Israelis know this because Americans have taken on themselves a great part of the burden of helping their brethren overseas to rehabilitate themselves in Israel. It surprises Israelis, however, to learn that this was, in fact, a part of American Jewish life from the very beginning. To cite but one example which has contemporary overtones— the Jewish situation in the '70's, of the past century. The following few lines come from a report in the *Cleveland Leader* of May 21, 1877, describing an address of Benjamin F. Peixotto, former consul to Roumania.

"Yesterday afternoon, the Honorable B. F. Peixotto delivered an interesting lecture in the Eagle Street Synagogue on ROUMANIA AND THE ROUMANIAN JEWS. The speaker had lived for 6 years in one of those dark lands where the Son of Israel had suffered so much and had been looked upon as no better than a dog. He took great interest in the terrible massacre of the Jews, which occurred in Roumania in June of 1870, and about that time resolved to do what he could to lighten the burdens of these oppressed people. He then went to Bucharest as the consul of this country to Roumania, and on arriving there found that the Israelites were much alarmed and oppressed in spirit. But as soon as they learned who he was they looked upon him as a new Moses and took courage. They came to him and he assured them that he would do all in his power to protect them. The speaker said, further, that when he first located in Bucharest he advised the Jews to protect themselves and fight in self-defense whenever necessary . . .
"Many of the outrages, which have been perpetrated in the East, the speaker thought, were due to Russian influence—a country which he thought has long been striving to bring about the present state of affairs. . . ."

These discoveries of America through American Jewry have given the Israeli a new respect for the values of the democratic order. It makes him want to come here to study, and to absorb and to apply what he learns here to his own life and institutions. It makes the Israelis feel that in the fraternity of nations, they want to be close to America as, indeed, America wants to be close to them.

No finer summary of the respect that has grown up over the years for the American Jewish community can be given than the remarks of Premier Ben-Gurion at the ceremony of the cornerstone-laying of the American Student Center of the Jewish Theological Seminary in Jerusalem in the summer of 1958.

"This new step is of particularly great importance in that it comes from the United States. Three momentous events have taken place in the history of our people during the first half of the twentieth century: the loss of two thirds of European Jewry, which in recent centuries was the mother of the Jewish people; the growth of the greatest Jewish center that has ever existed in the

Diaspora; and the rise of the State of Israel. These three events may determine our future and the future of the Jewish people all over the world for many decades and even centuries.

"American Jewry, which enjoys full equality of rights and consists of immigrants or the descendants of immigrants like the rest of the Americans (except for the Indian minority), gives outstanding expression to the Jewish individuality, Jewish creativeness and attachment to the Jewish people. There are numerous differences within American Jewry on matters of religion, faith and outlook . . . Yet there is a wonderful unity in American Jewry, in their concern for the fate of Jewry in many countries, and especially in their love and spiritual attachment to Israel.

"This is perhaps one of the most extraordinary phenomena in the life of any people, though it is only one of the expressions of the extraordinary uniqueness that has characterized the Jewish people ever since it came into being . . ."

While the Israelis have indeed come to respect the American Jewish community, as Premier Ben-Gurion's statement reflects, they do put straightforward questions about the character of the community and its future. Can Jews create in America an indigenous Jewish creative community to take its place beside the past diasporic centers of Babylonia, Spain, Russia and Poland? Can America produce a Jewish laity who will practice the *mitzvah* of study and learning so that there may be created in America a distinctive American Jewish culture? Can American Jews join the Israeli Jewish community in shaping a creative Judaism in the modern world? Is the dream of a *Jewish* group future in America dream or mirage?

One question is asked so often in Israel that it is almost a slogan: Can American Jewry be a modern Babylonia? Or, in its literal translation from the Hebrew, the question goes: "Can you produce a Talmud Bavli?"

Addressing the Conference of Historians convened by the American Jewish Historical Society on the occasion of the 7th Tercentenary of the first Jewish settlement on this continent, Professor Ben-Zion Dinur put the question in the form of an historical generalization·

"Wherever you find a Jewish community which exerts great influence on other communities in other countries, you can assume that the history of the Jews in that country gave rise to new elements of Jewish culture which are of vital importance to all Jewish communities of that generation. The place of that Jewish community is determined by the extent to which these principles (taking the heavenly yoke upon themselves jointly, with the will and readiness to work together for the knowledge of Scripture, the service of God, the keeping of the Law and the work of charity and of brotherly assistance) influenced the total community. Only to that extent can we determine whether a community is native and whether it will make its own contribution beside the great contributions of the communities of the past."

From this one question flow many other questions. What is the nature of American Jewish youth? Do the young have a spiritual quality? Do they want to build a Jewish future? And what about the Jewish family? Does it have the solidarity and cohesion of which past generations were so rightfully proud? Where are the real *ideals* of the American Jewish community? Do the synagogues produce people of piety or attendance figures? Do the Jewish schools produce Jewish scholars? Does the Jewish home train character, the love of fellow man?

Out of these questions and the historical generalization comes a valid insight into American Jewry. It is, in a sense, a perception which is the heart of what I learned out of my assignment in Israel. The Israelis recognize and accept the fact that *Jews* can survive in freedom. They know that Jews as a people will continue to live and flourish in America. What they want to know is whether *Judaism* can survive in freedom. Despite the bitterness and horror of the ghetto, Jews and Judaism did survive. They ask whether the faith and heritage of the Jewish people in the Diaspora can endure without the compactness of Jewish group life and its intellectual and spiritual walls. Israelis express sincere doubts. For themselves, they have chosen to live in a majority Jewish culture. They do not believe that American Jews are superhuman. They do not think, on the whole, that American Jews will be able to create a Babylonian Talmud.

Without entering into the realm of "prophecy" or trying to guess what the nature of American Judaism will be in the next generations, it is nevertheless important to indicate that in part, but not entirely, the doubts of the Israelis are based on misconceptions and on a misreading of actual events. Israelis tend to view all diasporic communities from one point of view. They refuse to recognize the differences between them. They generalize on the Jews of South America, of North America, Europe, the Anglo-Saxon countries. This is a profound error. The problems of living in Latin America or in Europe are altogether different from the problems Jews face in America.

Another Israeli misconception is to identify all anti-Jewish acts with racial anti-Semitism. There is virtually not a single major critic of American Jewry in Israel who has not lived through the great sorrows of our times. It is therefore very difficult to explain to them that in America, there are hostilities between various groups, region and region, area and area, Negro and white, industry and labor and so forth. All of this is part of America—problems which Americans are trying to work out. But such conflict, even when Jews are hurt by it, is not to be equated with racial anti-Semitism as Israelis knew it in Europe.

A third misunderstanding is based on the interpretation of American Jewish assimilation. They are aware of the changes that have transformed the Jewish people in America. They know the civilization of Eastern Europe; many of them were born there, many more know the kind of Jews who lived there. They know, too, that American Jews are not identifiably Jewish in ways that they can discern. They see the Jewish community undergoing great inner corrosion. They not only see this, but their press features this process. They are only beginning to learn, however, about the return to Judaism and to the Jewish community of vast numbers of Jews. They do not know about the phenomenon of the third generation. They do not perceive the great positive changes for good in Jewish life here.

Finally, Israelis have yet to explore the potentialities of the State of Israel itself for Jewish life in America. They have been busy building their own State. They do not realize how much American Jewry expects from them and needs of them. They do not know how desperately many American Jews want Torah to come forth from Zion rebuilt. In truth, there has been a great revival of the Jewish spirit in modern Israel and it has transformed Israelis. But the spiritual impact has not yet been felt by American Jewry. Before Israelis can bring religious and cultural assistance to American Jewry, they must come to know and believe in American Jewry in its own terms. The only action that will be successful is inter-action. The more we know about each other, the better the chance to evolve specific ways whereby we can be helpful to one another. To get Israeli Jews to know and believe in American Jewry is my assignment in Israel and, in truth, the assignment of all American Jews, for in that way, we are also building our own community in America.

What are some of the ways in which the cultural bonds between the two communities are being established and strengthened?

The first bridge is human. Until American Jewry is adequately represented in Israel by its spiritual and cultural leaders, Israelis will never fully understand us. Two American Jews who played singular roles in this bridge of human interpretation were Judah Magnes [first president of the Hebrew University] and Henrietta Szold [founder of Hadassah] both of whom, as Americans, already are part of the modern Eretz Yisrael legend. There are important American figures in Israel today who are helping to shape the present generation. The contribution of such men as Reuben Avinoam, Alexander Dushkin, Israel Efros, Simon Halkin and a group of younger American scholars, artists and intellectuals to Israeli education today is unique. These men come to Israel with a love of American life and they are deeply rooted in Hebrew culture and literature. In a sense, they are the best ambassadors of American culture to Israel. For they come as creative forces to a new country in the process of creation. Relating the American and Jewish traditions, they create in the contemporary Hebrew idiom. Thus they add a new dimension to the Israeli amalgam. To cite three examples out of their rich contributions: a recent work of Professor Halkin is an exemplary translation into Hebrew of Walt Whitman's *Leaves of Grass* with an admirable introduction and notes, which, in English, would be a major contribution to American literary criticism; Reuben Avinoam's volume, *Anthology of American Poetry* introduces a new point of view into current Israeli literature; and Professor Dushkin is responsible for the reorganization of the undergraduate division at the Hebrew University, in a way which effectively integrated the University into the educational life of the community.

The profoundest achievement of such men is their presence on the day-to-day scene. Their very personalities exert influence on decisions with regard to standards of study and materials for the curricula of Israeli cultural life outside the formal educational structure. These men serve as consultants to publishing houses, newspaper editors and cultural departments of national organizations. Their counsel is sought and their advice carries a good deal of weight. The Israeli hopes that other individuals of such calibre and background will identify themselves with the cultural enterprises in the new State.

Second, American studies must take a greater part in the training of Israeli scholars. American Jewish history must find its rightful place in all teaching about world Jewry and Judaism. I am gratified to report a developing alertness to this lacuna in historical studies and curricula. Lectures in American Civilization are given from time to time and distinguished American historians like Allan Nevins and Henry Steele Commager have lectured at the Hebrew University and to scholarly gatherings in other institutions. Recently, a documentary history with interesting selections from American Jewish history, was published as a high school text. It was good to see the announcement of the American Jewish Tercentenary theme, in 1954—300 years of American Jewry—posted on the billboards of Tel Aviv, Haifa, Tiberias and Beer Sheba. The comparatively large audience which attended the various lectures given in Israel on this theme was a further indication of awakened interest in American Jewish life. A good deal of the future development of this interest rests with American Jewish scholars and educators.

As I reflect on the overwhelming changes in understanding between these two great Jewish communities which have taken place in a short span of time, I am struck by the significant opportunities that await all of us. These promises for the future are symbolized in the story of a flower described in *Mount Carmel Flowers* published in Israel recently. The flower is the famous *shoshan* (lily), called "the rose" in the Song of Songs, whose white petaled bells open in the spring between Passover and Shavuot. The *shoshan* disappeared from the Land of Israel when the woods in whose shade it had flourished were cut down. It no longer grew wild in the land. For centuries, however, it had been uprooted and exported to other countries because of its religious associations, and it became a garden plant in the West. It was even re-exported to modern Israel and cultivated in gardens there. In our own day, this *shoshan* is once more blossoming, between the rocks of Mount Carmel and in the woods of Galilee. Thus the *shoshan*, born in the soil of the Land of Israel, had to be nurtured abroad and sent back to its native country. Like the *shoshan*, many of the ideas of Judaism, which had been nurtured in the Land of Israel, were sustained in foreign soil, even in America and among its Jewish community. Some of these ideas will be brought back to Israel by way of the American Jew. This return is welcomed by Israelis. In the process of return, American Jewry, too, will gain a greater vision of its own destiny.

YITZHAK RABIN

Yitzhak Rabin was born in Jerusalem in 1922 and educated in the agricultural school of Kfar Tabor and the military Staff College in London from which he was graduated. He was a comrade-in-arms of Moshe Dayan on the Syrian-Lebanese front during World War II. In the struggle for Israeli independence, Rabin rose to become deputy commander of the famed Palmah (commando unit). He also distinguished himself as a general officer in the 1956 Sinai Campaign. During the Six Day War in 1967 he was chief-of-staff of the Defense Army of Israel and formulated the plans for the swift victory over the Arabs. In 1968 he became his country's ambassador to the United States.

Rabin is reputed to be a veritable "think-tank" and to possess a computer mind. His promotions in the tough Israeli army bear testimony to his mental audacity and executive ability. Except for a brief turn at the Rhodes armistice negotiations in 1949 and in several minor political chores, Rabin did not have much experience with diplomacy. His appointment to the very important Washington post was a tribute to his general ability, indicating promise of a significant role in future political activity.

The two speeches printed here tell much of the man and of the army he commanded. The first is an address by General Rabin delivered at a ceremony held on Mount Scopus, in the amphitheater of the Hebrew University on Wednesday, June 28, 1967, at which he received an honorary Doctor of Philosophy degree. The second address was delivered a year later, June 6, 1968, at Dropsie College [now Dropsie University], Philadelphia, also on the occasion of receiving an honorary doctorate.

The People and its Army

by YITZHAK RABIN

I

MR. PRESIDENT, MR. PRIME MINISTER, the President of the Hebrew University, the Rector of the Hebrew University, members of the Board of Governors of the Hebrew University, Ladies and Gentlemen:

I stand in awe before you, leaders of this generation, here in this ancient and magnificent spot overlooking Israel's eternal capital and the birthplace of our nation's earliest history.

Together with several distinguished persons who are without doubt worthy of this honor, you have chosen to do me great honor by conferring upon me the title of Doctor of Philosophy. Permit me to express my feelings on this occasion.

I regard myself here as the representative of the entire Israel Defense Forces, of the thousands of officers and tens of thousands of soldiers who brought victory to the State of Israel in the Six Day War.

It may be asked why the University saw fit to award the title of Honorary Doctor of Philosophy to a soldier in recognition of his military activities. What do soldiers have in common with the academic world, which stands for civilization and culture? What is there in common between those whose profession is violence and those who are concerned with spiritual values? I am, however, honored that you have chosen through me to express your deep appreciation of my comrades-in-arms and of the uniqueness of the Israel Defense Forces, which is no more than an extension of the uniquness of the Jewish people.

The world has recognized that the Israel Army is different from other armies. Although its first task is the military one of maintaining security, it has numerous peacetime roles, not of destruction but of construction and of strengthening the nation's cultural and moral resources.

Our educational work has been widely praised, and it received national recognition in 1966 when the Israel Prize for Education was awarded to the Israel Defense Forces. The *Nahal*, which combines military training and agricultural settlement, also provides teachers for border villages who contribute to their social and cultural development. These are only some examples of the Israel Defense Forces' uniqueness in this sphere.

Today, however, the University is conferring on us an honorary degree in recognition of our Army's spiritual and moral superiority, as revealed precisely in the heat of war. For we are all here in this place only by virtue of the war which, though forced upon us, was forged into a victory that has astounded the world.

War is intrinsically harsh and cruel, and blood and tears are its companions. But this war which we have just waged brought forth rare and magnificent instances of courage and heroism, and at the same time humane expressions of brotherhood, comradeship and even of spiritual greatness.

Anyone who has not seen a tank crew continue its attack after its commander has been killed and its track badly damaged, who has not watched sappers risking their lives to extricate wounded comrades from a minefield, who has not witnessed the concern and the extraordinary efforts made by the entire Air Force to rescue a pilot who has fallen in enemy territory—cannot know the meaning of devotion among comrades-in-arms.

The entire nation was exalted and many wept when they heard of the capture of the Old City [Eastern Jerusalem]. Our sabra [Israel-born] youth, and most certainly our soldiers, do not tend to be sentimental and they shrink from any public show of feeling. But the strain of battle, the anxiety which preceded it, and the sense of salvation and of direct confrontation with Jewish history itself cracked the shell of hardness and shyness and released wellsprings of emotion and stirrings of the spirit. The paratroopers who conquered the Wailing Wall leaned on its stones and wept—in its symbolism an act so rare as to be almost unparalleled in human history. Rhetorical phrases and cliches are not common in our Army, but this scene on the Temple Mount, beyond the power of words to describe, revealed as though by a flash of lightning truths that were deeply hidden.

And there is more to be told. The joy of triumph had seized the entire nation. Nevertheless, a strange phenomenon can be observed among our soldiers. Their joy is incomplete, and their celebrations are marred by sorrow and shock. There are even some who abstain from celebrations entirely. The men in the front lines saw with their own eyes not only the glory of victory, but also the price of victory—their comrades fallen beside them soaked in blood. I know too that the terrible price paid by our enemies also touched the hearts of many of our men. It may be that the Jewish people has never learned and never accustomed itself to feel the triumph of conquest and victory, with the result that these are accepted with mixed feelings.

The Six Day War brought to the fore numerous instances of heroism far beyond the kind manifested in the daring, one-time assault in which the attacker goes unthinkingly forward. In many places there were desperate and lengthy battles. In Rafia, in El-Arish, in Um-Kataf, in Jerusalem, on the Golan Heights and elsewhere, our soldiers displayed spiritual courage as well as bravery and tenacity in a degree to which no one who has witnessed this great and inspiring human phenomenon can remain indifferent. We speak a great deal of the few against the many. In this war, perhaps for the first time since the Arab invasions of the spring of 1948 and the battles of Negba and Degania, units of the Israel

Defense forces stood few against the many in every sector. In other words, relatively small units often entered seemingly endless networks of fortifications, surrounded by hundreds and thousands of enemy troops, and had to force their way, hour after hour, in this veritable sea of dangers. Even after the momentum of the first attack had passed and all that remained was the overwhelming necessity of believing in our strength and in the goal for which the battle was being fought, since there was no alternative, we summoned up every spiritual resource in order to continue the fight to the end.

Thus our armored forces broke through on all fronts, our paratroopers fought their way into Rafia and Jerusalem, and our sappers cleared minefields under enemy fire. The units which penetrated the enemy lines and reached their objectives after hours of struggle, continuing on and on while their comrades fell to the right and left of them, were carried forward by great moral force and by deep spiritual resources far more than by their weapons or the techniques of warfare.

We have always demanded the cream of our youth for the Israel Defense Forces. We coined the slogan *Hatovim l'Tayis* (the best for the Air Force) and this became a meaningful phrase. It referred not only to technical and manual skills. What it meant was that if our airmen were to be capable of defeating the forces of four enemy countries within a few short hours, they had to be imbued with moral values and human values.

Our airmen who struck the enemies' planes so accurately that no one understands how it was done and the world seeks technological explanations in secret weapons; our armored troops who stood their ground and defeated the enemy even when their equipment was inferior to his; our soldiers in all the various branches of the Israel Defense Forces who overcame our enemies everywhere, despite their superior numbers and fortifications—all of them revealed not only coolness and courage in battle but a burning faith in the justice of their cause, and sure knowledge that only their personal stand against the greatest of dangers could bring victory to their country and to their families, and that if the victory were not achieved the alternative was annihilation.

Furthermore, in every sector our commanders, of all ranks, far outshone those of the enemy. Their insight, their understanding, their preparedness, their ability to improvise, their care for their men and, above all, the fact that they went at the head of their troops into battle—all these are not matters of equipment or technique. They have no rational explanation, except in terms of a deep consciousness of the moral justice of their fight.

All this springs from the spirit and leads back to the spirit. Our warriors prevailed not by their weapons but by their sense of mission, by the consciousness of the rightness of their cause, by a deep love for their country and an understanding of the difficult task laid upon them: to ensure the existence of our people in its homeland, to protect, even at the price of their lives, the right of the Jewish people to live in its own state, free, independent and in peace.

This Army, which I had the privilege of commanding through these battles, came from the people and returns to the people—to a people which rises to great heights in times of crisis and prevails over all enemies by virtue of its moral and spiritual strength.

As the representative of the Israel Defense Forces, and on behalf of every one of its soldiers, I accept with pride this token of your appreciation.

II

The period of tension that preceded the Six Day War, and the war itself, emphasized a number of values that are deeply imprinted on the Jewish-Israeli image. These characteristics, shaped and fashioned by traditional Jewish values, and Israel's reality, deserve to be examined at much greater length, at least, mentioned in *this* forum, in which *you* are the participants.

First of all, I want to tell you how the people went forth to war. This war was the war of a people. The Israel Defense Army *is* our people. Over 300,000 men and women served in this war. Every man and woman able to participate in the war effort was transformed overnight from civilian to soldier. When it was over, they returned to their daily lives. You know all this, but most characteristic of our people was how they took it when faced with the war. There was no warmongering, no bellicose or militant speeches. The hysteria and mass demonstrations usually accompanying wars today were entirely missing. All was quiet and anxiety, anxiety for those who would not come back. It was a war of absolutely no other choice or alternative.

Far from any chauvinism, there was deep consciousness of critical national responsibility. I want to read you some lines written by Abba Kovner, one of our poets, a member of Kibbutz Ein Hahoresh who in World War II fought as a Polish partisan. Nothing could better convey to you how we felt on that first day of war.

"I have again seen the people, not only my own (kibbutz) people. There, at home, 125 of our men went to the front, and the women and older folk who stayed behind in the trenches stood the test, as was to be expected of them. But I have also seen the town. It wasn't the biggest of our towns, not the noisiest in its patriotism; it was a town in the Sharon, a small orderly town, with its laborers and shopkeepers, its unemployed and its tradesmen. The morning was pleasant and clear. It was the kind of morning when a man rises and asks himself if war can really break out on a morning like this. Then the radio program was interrupted: the announcer was listing the units called up to report.

"Things of greater moment than these are forgotten as time goes by. Yet this announcer's voice had none of the hysteria that we hear from the Land of the Nile, nor any of the arrogance of the voice of the announcer on the Warsaw radio in September 1939. It wasn't the tragic voice of Prague, nor the pathetic voice of the announcer of Radio Moscow under siege. It was a different voice. It beat out like the stone mason's hammer. It beat out the meaningless code names of the reserve units, plainly and simply; and with that, without comment, it concluded. The town held its breath.

"At that moment I was bending over the newsstand. The rendor was stretching out his hand to pick up a newspaper. His hand stopped, motionless, in mid-air. His eyes opened wide, he looked beyond and through me, and said, with surprise: 'That was my unit they called, too.'

"He covered his newspapers and went off. The storekeeper came out of the store opposite and she stood, uncertain, on the step. She buttoned her blouse nervously, closed her handbag, and went off. The butcher took off his apron, locked the shutters of the store, and he went too. On the grassy edge stood a group of men, glued to a transistor radio. As the code names were read out, one by one the men broke off and away they went. Like a bundle of twigs they fell away, one by one, without a word. A young girl was coming in my direction. The announcer's voice reached her. She stopped, listened for a moment, turned around, and went away. A strange silence fell over the town.

"I have seen cities before, on the day when duty called. I have seen peoples go forth to war. They marched to the sound of noisy strident loudspeakers. I have seen them at railroad stations, the men embracing their weeping wives and mothers. I have seen them being kissed as they march along, and I have seen bayonets decorated with fresh flowers, and nailed boots clattering on the cobbles, as the marching soldiers sang on their way. I have seen them smiling, proud, as the by-standers waved and shouted hurrah. But never have I seen a town rise up to do its duty in silence like this, or people go forth to battle with so heavy a sense of responsibility and such indescribably quiet determination. So it was in Natanya and in Kiryat Shmoneh, in Jerusalem, Tel-Aviv, and Beer-Sheba. This was my people. Never have I known it thus before."

I come now to the second characteristic of our people and our youth going forth to war. There is no hatred. Nor has there ever been, since the time of the earliest settlements in Palestine. For all the long unending tensions, there has never been any hatred for the Arabs, and none for the Arab peoples. Can one fight against enemies without hatred in one's heart? Perhaps in this respect, too, we are different from many other peoples. I do not believe that hatred adds anything to fighting capacity.

On the contrary, the motivation of positive value makes the good fighter. The positive human element is essential for the good soldier. Not a syllable of hatred is to be found in a single Israel Army Training Manual. In this respect, we have our own attitude, a Jewish attitude, to war. We go forth to war when we are forced to, when there is no other choice. We fight for survival, only when the other side makes war absolutely unavoidable. There are lots of stories that our youth have brought home from battle. Despite all the dangers and difficulties, and despite fallen comrades, there is no hatred for Arabs, not even for the enemy soldiers.

The third characteristic is in the victory. I don't know of many wars in which the victory has been so decisive. The few defeated the many. The defenders defeated the aggressors. The threat of destruction had passed. Jerusalem was free. The Western Wall, symbol of Israel's eternity and oneness as a people, was in our hands. What more could have been gained from war? But we didn't celebrate the victory. There were no victory parades. The elation of victory is natural and human. As Jews our celebration was of a different kind. Every one of us in his heart, and all of us together, gave ourselves to thoughts of those who had fallen and those who had been hurt. The ceremony ending the war was quiet and simple. The Commanders of the Israel Defense Forces gathered at the Western Wall and were addressed by the Minister of Defense and the Chief of Staff. Both men spoke of the war, and of the hope and the need of peace.

VI
Securing the Future

MENAHEM BEGIN
URI AVNERY
TAWFIQ TOUBI
SHMUEL MIKUNIS
SHMUEL TAMIR
ARIE ELIAV
DAVID HOROWITZ
ABBA EBAN
MOSHE DAYAN
YITZHAK BEN-AHARON

MENAHEM BEGIN

Menahem Begin was born in Brest-Litovsk, Poland, in 1913 and received his higher education in the faculty of law of Warsaw University. He joined *Betar,* an ultra-nationalist, militant Jewish youth movement, becoming its commander in Poland and eventually emerging as the leader of Betar's parent organization, the Zionist Revisionists, founded by the late Vladimir [Zev] Jabotinsky, who to this day remains the ideological father of a great many Israelis.

During World War II, Begin was arrested by the Russians and sent to a labor camp in Siberia, where he spent two years. Released in 1942, he enlisted in the Polish army, arriving in Palestine with some of its elements that same year. He soon assumed command of the underground *Irgun Zvai Leumi* to lead in the resistance to, and the breakdown of, British rule in Palestine—sometimes clashing and sometimes cooperating with the Haganah, the "official" but less aggressive military underground of the Jewish community.

After the proclamation of the State in 1948, Begin reluctantly acquiesced in the dissolution of the Irgun, founding the *Herut* Movement, a nationalist, right-wing, opposition party to the labor-dominated coalition government. To offer an "alternative" to the labor rule, he helped in 1965 to form a political bloc of the centrist liberal party and *Herut-Gahal.* The new formation did not do very well in that year's elections.

Considering the policies of David Ben-Gurion, Moshe Sharett and Levi Eshkol, the three labor Prime Ministers, too "socialistic" and their foreign policy too moderate, Begin nevertheless cooperated fully with his political antagonists at all times when the State was threatened by its Arab neighbors. In 1967, on the eve of the Six Day War, he agreed to serve as Minister-without-portfolio in the National Coalition Government. Gahal made gains in the 1969 Knesset elections, resulting in larger representation in Golda Meir's Cabinet. Begin continued to serve in the coalition government.

A fluorescent personality, polemical, his speaking style in Hebrew has momentum and color quite lost in translation. His personal sense of outrage at the "mistakes" of the government smolders even when he presents a calm appearance.

The following is an address delivered by Begin at the opening rally of the Ninth Herut Convention, in Jerusalem, May 26, 1968.

An Address at the Herut Party Convention, May, 1968

by MENAHEM BEGIN

EIGHTEEN HUNDRED AND NINETY EIGHT years, nine weeks and four days ago, the Temple Mount, stood in flames. The legions of the mightiest army in the world of those days, the conquering forces of Rome that had carried all before them, made their final assault on the last of the Jewish fighters, breached the first and second wall, reached the Temple, and set it on fire.

The battles fought until that day of bitter sorrow between the Jewish fighters and the Tenth, Fifth and Eighth Legions, under the direct command of Vespasian's son Titus, have been recorded for all eternity by Joseph Ben-Mattityahu, otherwise known as Josephus Flavius, whom Titus had sent to the Jewish commanders to sue for their surrender.

Joseph Ben-Mattityahu tells how the Jewish fighters would attack whole Roman legions without showing any fear of the soldiers of the conquering empire. Thus, for instance, the historian of those days writes:

> "And after the legion that came from Emmaeus joined his forces in the night, Titus Caesar set out from Givat Shaul at dawn and reached a place named Tzofim, from where the city and the Temple in all its greatness revealed themselves to the Romans. As the Romans were making camp, the Tenth Legion also arrived from the Jericho road. This legion was ordered to encamp on a place named the Mount of Olives. The hardships of the war from outside interrupted for the first time—for the first time—the incessant fratricidal strife. In confusion they looked upon the Romans as they entrenched themselves on three sides. 'We are heroes—they cried—only when we fight each other. Shall the Romans benefit from our quarrels and take the town without striking a single blow?' Thus taking counsel together, they picked up their arms and rushed out to attack the Tenth Legion, which would have been lost but for Titus coming to its aid."

That was how our forefathers fought for the Temple Mount, and Titus was forced to send his forces into the fray many more times and to upbraid them for their cowardice in the battle against the Jews, inspired to incredible deeds of valor. Yet, the day came when fire was set to the Temple, and the Jews saw the glory of our nation go up in flames. Their hearts faltered, but they continued the fight—as Joseph Ben-Mattityahu has witnessed for all eternity. Above all, they sought to retain control of the Mount, laid waste and destroyed by fire as it was, of the heart of the nation, the Holiest of Holies; the mighty Temple that was the dwelling-place of the Divine Presence and the fount of all our faith. Then Titus, the victor, offered the Jewish fighters his mercy, saying to them: "If you will lay down your arms and surrender, I will let you escape with your lives." And this was the Jewish fighters' answer: "We cannot conclude a covenant with you, for we have sworn never to do so. Therefore we beseech you to permit us to pass the wall with our women and children and go to the desert." Even on that day, the Jewish fighters did not surrender to Rome, which had vanquished the whole world.

Even more important evidence comes to us from the pen of a historian who was not a Jew, but a Gentile and an early Jew-hater: Cornelius Tacitus. He describes the pagan idols of Rome as "religion" and our belief in one God, invisible and immaterial, as "superstition." This is what he has to say about the subjugation of Judea and the beginning of the siege of Jerusalem—and I quote him in the original: *"Progilgaverat bellum Judaicum Vespasianus obpugnatione Hierolosymorum reliqua, duro magis et arduo opere ob ingenium montis et pervicaciam superstitionis quem quo satis virium obsessis."*

I cannot deny that there is a supreme satisfaction in hearing the ancient tongue of Rome here tonight and then translating it into [Hebrew] our own, even more ancient language. The Roman Legions are no more and their language is dead; we are here, and our language lives.

Tacitus writes that Vespasian was already about to end the war against the Jews, and all that remained was to besiege Jerusalem. This was a hard wearisome task, not so much because of the remaining forces of the enemy, for they were sorely pressed, but because of the nature of the mountain and the Jews' superstitious stubornness. For—he explains—in "the Jewish wars", which began in the days of Cassius (Gaius Longinus), the Jews had roundly defeated the Romans; but the Emporor Nero sent Vespasian, who overcame them and took all the towns except Jerusalem. Meanwhile, civil war broke out in Rome, and the Jews were left to their own devices for a year.

Pace per Italiam parita et externae curae rediere? Augebat iras quod soli Judaei non cessisent. But when Italy was at peace again, the war against the Jews was resumed. After the civil war was over, we began to concern ourselves with foreign affairs; we were greatly incensed because the Jews alone had not surrendered. The whole world had submitted to Rome, and only the Jews did not bow to her.

But as the fire was flung into the Temple and the pure souls of the last defenders rose to heaven with the flames, the Romans coined an expression: *"Hep-hep"*, which became the call of Jew-hatred throughout the ages, until it reached the ears of a young journalist in Vienna and set off a revolution in his mind which brought about a revolution in the history of our people. Theodor Herzl his name was. But "hep-hep" is not just a shout; it stands for the initials of the cry of Vespasian's and Titus' legions: *Hierosolima est Perdita*—Jerusalem is lost. This night, Mr. President, Your Eminence the Chief Rabbi, Ministers of Israel, members of the legislature, we proclaim: Hear, ye peoples, listen, ye nations, *Hierosolima non est perdita; ressurecta est!* [Jerusalem is not lost; it is resurrected!]

Generations passed. We began to return. We were still few and strangers ruled our land, though not our souls.

Twenty-five years ago, on the Day of Atonement, I was praying at the Western Wall. Among the crowd stood a young man of Betar [Militant Zionist Youth Organization] with a *shofar* concealed under his clothes, as had been the custom in the Jabotinsky Movement [ultra-nationalist group] ever since strangers had forbidden the blowing of the *shofar* at the Western Wall. At the end of the *Ne'ilah* [closing Yom Kippur Service], the young man put the shofar to his lips and blew a long, loud blast, and the whole great multitude crowded together in the lane before the Wall cried out: *Leshana ha'baa biYerushalayim habenuya* (next year in Jerusalem the rebuilt)! Suddenly, British policemen ran out and with sticks started to beat men, women, and children in an attempt to find the "criminal" who had blown the shofar. As I stood there and witnessed that sight, I vowed in my innermost heart: If the Almighty grants us life and strength, we will wipe out this shame from our land. Lord God of Israel, shall foreign policemen rule on Israel's holiest day in Israel's holiest place, and prevent us from following what has been our holiest custom ever since we were banished from our land and removed from our soil?

We kept our vow. The very next year, the underground *Irgun Zvai Leumi* warned the British police not to enter the square of the Western Wall on the Day of Atonement; and they knew that when the IZL warned, it was best to pay attention to the warning. On the Day of Atonement of 1944 Jews prayed at the Western Wall. We were in the underground. Some Jews feared that we would keep armed watch to bar the foreign police. We had quite different plans. None of us even dreamt of allowing strangers to touch the hallowed stones. We intended to strike at them elsewhere. But they heeded our warning. The young man blew the Shofar openly, before the Jews and the whole world, and no British police came to beat the Jews. They stayed out of the way. After that, the ram's horn was heard every year at the Western Wall, until twenty years ago.

Twenty years ago, another legion assaulted this city, with tanks and cannon. On the other side were a handful of Jewish soldiers. They fought to the last bullet, to the last breath, but they were overwhelmed by brute strength. The last of the soldiers were buried temporarily in this very square. And after Haganah and IZL commander Gideon—the IZL commander who sits here on the platform with us tonight—was wounded in battle, the Old City fell into the hands of the enemy. We said then: in 1948 a handful of fighters, surrounded and isolated, has held out against enormous forces for months on end. A handful of fighters, starving and thirsty and wounded, has continued to hold out against tanks and cannons. Legendary tales of courage were written on that barricade in the blood of the best of our sons, who stood up till the last moment, in fulfilling a task which concerned the heart of the nation. The fighters, the soldiers of the Haganah and of the IZL, did not surrender. Most of them were wounded or fell in battle. There was no surrender in the Old City, but a war of supreme heroism, which evokes the day when the sons of our people stood heroically on the Temple Mount. May this battle and this heroism give us strength on a day of disaster, confidence that the liberators of Judah and the redeemers of Israel will yet return to the Temple Mount and will yet hoist our flag on David's Tower. In fire and blood the Old City fell, in fire and blood the Old City will rise, and it will be ours forever. Jerusalem, the City of David, will be ours forever. . . .

Therefore, it is our duty and our privilege on this night, in redeemed Jerusalem, that is a city joined together, on the anniversary of its liberation by the heroes of Israel, to render solemn thanks for the miracles and wonders, for the wars and deeds of valor and the salvation which the Almighty has performed for us now, as he performed them for our fathers in those days. Blessed be Thou, Lord our God, King of the Universe, who hast maintained us and sustained us and brought us to this day.

Citizens of Israel, one year ago we were beset by one of the gravest dangers ever, not only to our independence, but to our very existence. All of a sudden, within no more than ten days, we were surrounded by a ring of steel. 1,700 tanks, 1,494 guns, 700 airplanes capable of reaching the centers of our population within three and nine minutes and turn our houses into heaps of ruins, 230,000 professional soldiers bent on war and destruction—that was the danger. Since the re-establishment of our independence there had been none like it. Ever since the smoke had ceased rising from the crematories of Auschwitz and Maidanek, there had been no such determined attempt to exterminate the remnant of Israel.

The first thing we did in the face of this danger was to unite. We had learned the lesson of the fratricidal war of those days of old. Now, for the first time, we were determined to unite the nation, to make long-time opponents stand together. That is a lesson not only for our times, but for generations to come. Let the differences of opinion between us Jews be what they may; there should be differences of opinion; the parties of Israel are free and without them there will be no democracy. The parties are not perfect and the democracy is not perfect; but then, there are no perfect parties and no perfect democracy anywhere in the world. . . There will be parties among us. Let us do all we can to preserve this democracy that is not perfect. But when an enemy rises, when he openly announces that he proposes to destroy Israel, to annihilate men, women and children—set your differences aside, forget your animosities. Unite, join forces, stand together. Then, with the aid of the Almighty, will you overcome your enemies and win. And in the establishment of that national unity, Gahal—the bloc of the Herut Movement and the Liberal Party—played a not insignificant part. To this day, the bloc is one of the great assets of the nation, and we, my friends from the Liberal Party and my friends from Herut, are determined to preserve that asset, for the good of the nation and the country.

When we took the initiative in establishing that National Unity Government, we demanded nothing for ourselves; the one thing we asked for was a government of unity, of national unity, with all elements of importance in Israel combined within one government, in order to make decisions of historic, fateful impact for the salvation of the people and the redemption of the homeland. We demanded that Rafi [right-wing splinter labor party] be included in the national coalition, and that Moshe Dayan [of Rafi] be appointed Minister of Defense. We shall make no calculations of party interest, not even taking into consideration the day which, according to our democratic laws, will come in about 15 months [elections]. Seeing what happened in Israel's history in the Six Days and what happened during the past year, we congratulate ourselves on having demanded that Major-General Moshe Dayan be the Minister of Defense of Israel.

A few months ago I made a tour along the Suez Canal, and at a Cabinet meeting I sent a note to the Minister of Defense saying: "I have been in Sinai and travelled along the Suez Canal. My impression of what I have seen is, in one word, marvellous. Let me only add this: Happy is the nation that has a Minister of Defense like you in charge of the deployment of its armed forces."

The National Unity Government was formed on the first of June last year. Today you have heard the Prime Minister's [Eshkol] cordial message to our Convention. I want to tell him that I agree with his appeal that all of us together should be concerned about the dignity and standing of the National Unity Government, for it is the historic truth that it was, with God's help, united by our fighting sons, to the salvation of Israel; and we are ready to do more. The Prime Minister knows that I will always treat him with respect, whether I am closeted with him or in public. At one of the meetings I told him that in a parliamentary system a Prime Minister is the first among equals: meaning that he should treat his fellow Cabinet members as equals, and they should treat him as the first among equals. That is precisely why, with all due respect, I want to reply to the Prime Minister of the National Unity Cabinet tonight in regard to certain things he made public at that same Cabinet meeting before our Convention met.

The Prime Minister said that there had actually been no need to form a National Unity Government, that we had a beautiful, excellent coalition and that it could have made all the necessary decisions. Ladies and Gentlemen: as for beauty I am no expert, as for excellence, I am no judge, but if that excellent coalition could have made all the decisions, why did it not do so?

According to our calendar, it is the 28th of Iyar today, the anniversary of the liberation of Jerusalem. According to the general calendar, it is the 26th of May. On the 26th of May, Nasser closed the Straits of Tiran, the Gulf of Eilat; and we had always held that this would constitute a hostile act. That was how Israel's representatives and Foreign Ministers regarded it then, and so did the Maritime Powers: the United States, Britain, France and others. True, on that day President Johnson asked us to wait 48 hours, promising he would make up a convoy that would pass through the Gulf of Eilat in defiance of Nasser's ban. About this promise of the President of the United States there were, from

Address at a Herut Party Convention

the first moment, two views: one—that it amounted to a great victory for Israel, the other—that it was an important promise, but nothing would come of it. It is true that we agreed to accept President Johnson's promise. We were not yet in the National Unity Government. We, the representatives of Gahal and what then was Rafi, were invited to the Cabinet Committee on Defense as members of the Knesset Committee on Foreign Affairs and Defense. We were asked whether we agreed to accede to that request. We said yes, and if that was a mistake, then we are as much responsible for it as any member of the Cabinet. But to the best of our understanding it was no mistake. The President of the United States asked for 48 hours' time. We agreed, and it is good that we agreed.

But the night passes and morning comes. The 48 hours passed. On the 25th of May, Nasser stands before the trade unions. Nasser, too, is a socialist and speaks to the trade unions as follows: "When we agreed to the posting of UN forces in Gaza and Sharm El-Sheikh, we were not yet strong enough. That was why we agreed to that arrangement. And we built behind that buffer our strength. We always knew that the day would come when we could demand the removal of the UN force. Now, after we have completed our preparations, that day has come. The war will be total, and our aim is to destroy Israel." That was what Nasser said on the 26th of May, exactly a year ago. And Atassi, [President of Syria] in the North, added: "The whole Arab nation is up in arms and our aim is to wipe Israel off the face of the earth." And Aref, [President of Iraq] who sent an armored division and airplanes to Jordan, added: "This is the day of campaign for revenge. With Allah's aid we shall all meet in Tel-Aviv." Well, with God's help we all met on the banks of the Suez Canal, but that is mere geographical detail. Those were the orders in those days: to destroy Israel, to wipe out Israel, to meet in Tel-Aviv, to beat down, crush—as Radio Damascus said: "Kill, slaughter!" That was on the 26th of May. All the tanks were already drawn up around us, all the guns were trained on us, all the planes stood ready waiting for zero hour, for the three, four,-to nine minutes' flight to Tel-Aviv, Haifa, Jerusalem, Petah-Tikva, Nathanya, all our population centers. Each day increased the danger of bloodshed and unimaginable loss of life which we would have to suffer even if we should win. Our existence was in danger. And there was no decision. The worry in the hearts of our civilians and the minds of our soldiers was great. I speak from my knowledge of the facts. I still can hear in my mind's ear the voices that arose from this small, courageous people, from every tent in the Negev, from every tank beside which the crew was lying ready to move, from every squadron of airplanes: Give us the word; how long must we wait in idleness? How long will we lie on the sand, while the enemy is building up his strength in the East and South and North, day after day, almost hour by hour?—That is the historical truth.

We were beset by danger from outside, but also by a profound crisis at home. We overcame that crisis by establishing the National Unity Government. When Kol Yisrael [Radio Israel] announced that Thursday night that the National Unity Government had been established, cries of relief and joy broke out from the hearts of the thousands of Israeli soldiers everywhere and from the hearts of all Jews in the homeland and abroad, and our repute among the nations increased. On Sunday the National Unity Cabinet held a session. I shall not tell you what we decided or how we decided it. The main thing is that a decision was made. And on Monday morning, following the decision of the National Unity Government, our fighting sons went out to repulse the enemy who was preparing to destroy us in the skies, on land and at sea, and who stood ready in a manner unprecedented in the history of warfare, on three fronts: in the South, in the East and in the North. Our sons went out to defeat the enemy, to save the nation, to redeem the land. The call that has resounded throughout the generations, from Israel's greatest prophet and saviour, from the days of the slavery in Egypt and the wars of David, arose from their mouths: "Rise, O Lord, and Thy enemies shall be scattered, and Thy foes flee before Thee." They fled; and our fighting sons gave us more than a victory: salvation, not for this generation alone, but for generations to come.

Mr. Prime Minister, when you say that the establishment of the National Unity Government brought no change, that there was no need to establish it, you deny your own contribution. True, we all made efforts to establish the National Unity Government, but you were the Prime Minister, and let me say that its establishment depended in a large measure on your consent. It is to your merit that by our joint efforts we succeeded in establishing the National Unity Government, which represents 95% of a free nation united of its own free will. It is your privilege to stand at the head of such a national unity. Therefore, let us say it tonight: The establishment of the National Unity Government was and is one of the factors of Israel's historical victory.

One year after the victory the Security Council adopted a resolution saying that our decision in the matter of Jerusalem is invalid. To that resolution, I think, the whole of this small, valiant nation has one answer: Your resolution about our decision is invalid. Algeria, Senegal, Pakistan—shall they, with the assistance of other votes, dictate to us that Jerusalem does not belong to us, but to Hussein Ibn Talal Ibn Abdallah Ibn Hussein? With all due respect, when Jerusalem was already ours and our kings knelt here, our prophets had their visions and our priests held services here—no one had as yet heard of Algeria, Pakistan or Senegal, or even—of Paris. And if the current President of France [DeGaulle] says, now that we have liberated Jerusalem, we are forced to resort to "oppression" and "repression"—let me ask him now, tonight, from liberated Jerusalem whether in his old age, after slandering us without justification, he himself is not resorting to "oppression and depression"—yes, and "repression" too, against his own people.

Meanwhile, a full year after the liberation of Jerusalem and the redemption of our land a letter has been published by the Egyptian Foreign Minister, Mahmoud Riadh, and a copy of it has been confirmed by Dr. Jahring, [UN Middle East Emissary]. I shall read you the letter:

> "*AFP*. 15.5 *Cairo*. The Government of Israel and Egypt have both indicated to me that they accept the Security Council's Resolution 242–22 November 1967

Address at a Herut Party Convention

for achieving a peaceful and accepted settlement of the Middle East question and intend to devise arrangements, under my auspices for the implementation of the provisions of the Resolution.

"The two governments have expressed their willingness to cooperate with me in my capacity as special Representative of the Secretary General in the discharge of my task of promoting agreement and achieving such a settlement.

"In view of the urgency of the situation and with the view of expediting efforts to reach settlement, I will meet with representatives of Israel and UAR for conference, within the framework of the Security Council Resolution, in New York. I have the pleasure in informing you that the two Governments have responded favourably hereto."

If it were a Zinoviev letter, [an alleged letter to English Communists and a factor in British 1924 elections] I would not read it at all. Out of responsibility towards those whom I represent I must say that this is no second Zinoviev letter, and that is why are so deeply disturbed when we read in this official document that was allegedly issued with the knowledge of the Israeli Government, that we accept the Security Council resolution, that resolution which begins by stating an allegedly great moral principle. We accept this resolution. It does not mention the peace treaties on which the National Unity Government had decided to insist. It does not even mention "peace"—an abstract, but political concept—but, for the first time since we defeated our enemies and they began plotting to deprive us of our victory, it contains the words "peaceful settlement."

There are precedents: the armistice of 1949, or the settlement after the Sinai Campaign with its total withdrawal and the entrance of UN forces into Gaza and Sharm El-Sheikh are perfect examples of what is meant by "peaceful" settlements. It is exactly the peace Nasser needs for he cannot expel us by force of arms.

Also, there is mention of the implementation of provisions. The first speaks of withdrawing from occupied territories. The Government did not decide in favor of the Rhodes formula, [which brought about the 1949 armistice]. It was discussed but not adopted. The Prime Minister has said, and rightly so, that if Jahring wants to bring the parties together, he may preside over one or two sessions, but then the negotiations will be direct, and this time they will not be negotiations about an armistice, but about a peace treaty.

Therefore, it was good news for Israel this week when the Government met and after a long discussion came to a decision—and because the decision has been published, I can quote it—it contains two principal points. First, the letter I read contains statements allegedly made on behalf of the Government of Israel, but those statements are not binding upon the Government of Israel; and second, the Government once more states that it is its policy that the only solution for establishing lasting peace in the Middle East is the signing of a peace treaty between Israel and the Arab States. A peace treaty can only be achieved by direct negotiations between the parties. That is the policy of the National Unity Government, and that will remain its policy. The fact is, that no factor in Israel has accepted the Security Council resolution of November 22. That may be a surprise, but that is how it is. Some in Israel say one thing or another, but all say that we will never agree to return to the lines of the 4th of June; and all want direct talks and a peace treaty. If they are determined never to agree to a return to the lines of the 4th of June, it means that they demand that the Arabs agree in a peace treaty to cede to our sovereignty areas which were not under our control on the 4th of June and confirm that by their signature on a peace treaty. As the Arabs have stated they will never agree to this—it means that those elements themselves prevent a peace settlement with the countries just as they accuse others of doing. But Jewish unilateral or mutual accusations, distinctions between "bad", hawkish Jews who do not want peace and "good", decent, moderate Jews who want peace, have been our share for generations. Shall we level such accusations at each other now, in our own homeland, in our own country, in our own state? No! This, above all, we must avoid and prevent!

Yet if all elements in Israel say: Never back to the 4th of June, then that means that in the peace treaty the Arab states will have to cede to us areas, which they held in the past even if we did not recognize their right to them, and over which our blue-white flag waves now.

However, the resolution of the Security Council of November 22 starts with the pronouncement: "Inadmissibility of acquisitions of territory by war." But then everyone of us here says that in this particular war—a war of self-defense—acquisition of territory is admissible.

We have suggested that Israeli foreign policy pursue the legal and inter-international concept of a peace treaty—and let me say in passing: a few days ago I read something about the "Foreign Minister's policy", but I would like to point out that there is no such thing as the Foreign Minister's foreign policy or—and I say so in his presence—the Defense Minister's defense policy. There is a policy of the Government of Israel. True, any Minister who holds a portfolio, and even a "poor" Minister who has no portfolio, can make proposals to the Government in matters of defense policy, housing or labor, and perhaps it is even his duty to initiate proposals; but when the proposals are adopted, there is no policy of this or that Minister. There is the policy of the Government, and of the Government alone. That is the principle of a Cabinet in a parliamentary democracy.

Well, then, we were the ones who suggested that the foreign policy employ the principle of a peace treaty, but when the Government adopted it, it was no longer the policy of the Gahal Ministers but became Government policy. But since we introduced that principle, we have the responsibility, the opportunity, the right and the duty to explain what a peace treaty means. There is some misunderstanding, some illusion, that if a country which has implemented its right of national self-defense uses the words "peace treaty", it means that it must give up everything for the sake of a peace treaty. Nothing of the kind. Not only does the idea of a peace treaty not require any advance notice of concessions, but a peace treaty may lay down basic territorial changes after the defeat of an aggressor and the repulsion of aggression. There is international precedent for it:

After the first world war, a peace treaty was signed at Versailles and in that peace treaty Germany undertook to give up 60 thousand kilometers in the West, East, South and North. In 1922 a peace treaty was signed with Turkey at Sevres and later Ataturk tore it up, but that same Ataturk, the Father of the Turks, signed a peace treaty at Lausanne in 1923 in which he gave away Turkish claims of sovereignty over Mesopotamia, Syria, Palestine and so on, leaving him in effect with Anatolia and a strip of land beyond the Bosphorus. But why go so far back? After the second world war, only 16 years ago, a peace treaty between the United States and the other Allies and Japan came into effect. What was laid down in this treaty, which the United States signed with the Government of Tokyo?

"*September 8th,* 1951

The Allied Powers and Japan have therefore determined to conclude the present Treaty of Peace, and have accordingly appointed the undersigned Plenipotentiaries, who, after presentation of their full powers, found in good and due form, have agreed to the following provisions:

Chapter 1
Peace
Article 1

a) The state of war between Japan and each of the Allied Powers is terminated.

Chapter 11
Territory
Article 2

a) Japan . . . renounces all right, title, and claim to Korea, including the islands of Quelport, Port Hamilton and Dageled.
b) Japan renounces all right, title, and claim to Formosa and the Pescadores.
c) Japan renounces all right, title and claim to the Kurile islands and to that portion of Sakhalin and the island adjacent to it over which Japan acquired sovereignty as a consequence of the treaty of Portsmouth on September 5, 1905.
d) Japan renounces all right, title and claim in connection with the League of Nations Mandate system.
e) Japan renounces all claim to any right or title to or interest in connection with any part of the Atlantic area . . .
f) Japan renounces all right, title and claim to the Sportly Islands and to the Parceel Islands."

Ladies and Gentlemen, we are of course faced with problems resulting from victory. All of the Western Land of Israel is in our hands, but there is a demographic problem: a comparatively large Arab population. Let me remind you that Herzl, Nordau and Jabotinsky never dreamed we would have a Jewish majority of nearly two thirds in the Land of Israel. If any Zionist had said in the thirties or forties that it would take no more than ten–twenty years to reach a majority of 64% [including the occupied areas], nobody would have taken it seriously. Yet that is the Jewish majority today. We must maintain it and even increase it; we must maintain it for generations to come. But should a people run away from reality already achieved because of demographic problems? Or try to run away? Or think of running away? After all this *is* the Land of Israel!

Everyone says: Jerusalem in its entirety will always be ours. Of course, for it is the holiest part of our history. But when it comes to right, what is the difference between Jerusalem and Bethlehem, between Bethlehem and Hebron, between Hebron and Jericho, between Jericho and Shehem [Nablus]—all in the occupied areas—Shehem was one of the "Cities of Refuge" west of the Jordan. And so one might go on.

We must maintain the majority. First of all by encouraging an increase in the size of families, so that there may be many children in Israel. The Jewish people has a right, in a generation in which a third of its sons were destroyed, to the encouragement of natural growth by available means in order to replace the cruel loss.

There is need for immigration from the prosperous countries. Indeed, this time I fully agree with what David Ben-Gurion says: We must motivate, by all means at our disposal, large vigorous immigration from the prosperous countries, from the free world. To make that possible, it is, according to our conviction, necessary to lay new foundations for our economic and social system. We must give a free hand to free enterprise. Jewish enterprise has built New York, Chicago, Los Angeles, Buenos Aires. It will also build Israel as a flourishing land that can absorb immigrants.

I heard the head of the Histadrut [General Federation of Labor] enterprises speak at the Economic Conference in Jerusalem. I listened very attentively, and I did not feel that Marx was speaking. But what matters are the basics. From this conference I appeal to our friends in the Government and the Knesset: let them hold Socialism as their personal and party faith; we shall respect that even if we do not agree with it; but for the sake of the people and the country, for our future—so that the day may come when we will be able to live by our own toil without dependency on the outside world—give Jewish enterprise a chance to establish industries, to provide sources and places of employment, to build this country, to invest its energy and capital in it. And in no more than ten years, if you stop talking of "Socialism in our time" and if you do not compete through Histadrut enterprises with Jewish private enterprise, you will see this country built up in a way we all can be proud of. And it will be a progressive country with fair living standards for all its residents and citizens. This is our heart-felt call, not as party men, but as Jew to Jew, for the sake of our people, our country and our future. Then there will also be immigration from the prosperous countries. And we believe that one day there will be a large, powerful immigration from Russia as well.

True, relations with the USSR are not good just now, but, ladies and gentlemen, remarkable news is reaching us from Russia. The Jews there are no longer frightened. They know everything that is happening here. They know about the National Unity Government and are glad about it. There is only one solution for the problem of Russian Jewry, which is isolated from us. The Soviet Union has recognized two principles: a Jewish nationality and a Jewish State. And we shall not cease demanding that that mighty country allow its sons of Jewish origin to come and join their brethren in the Jewish State. That is the solution. There is no other.

The day will come, and it is not far off, when Russia will feel that her own interest requires her to allow her Jewish citizens to leave and return home. The day will come, with God's help, when hundreds of thousands of Jews from Russia, like the last thousands of Jews who still remain in Iraq and Egypt and Syria and the other Arab countries, will come.

The idea of the integrity of the homeland has been upheld by the Jabotinsky Movement ever since it was founded, and continued after our independence was re-established in part of the homeland. And the Lord has helped. On that Sabbath night, twenty years ago, when the dawn of independence broke over the Land of Israel, the secret broadcasting station of the IZL said: "The State of Israel has arisen, but we shall remember that the homeland has not yet been liberated. The war goes on."

As you see, our fighters did not speak vainly. The homeland cannot be other than entire and cannot be dismembered, for it is an eternal law that a state and a nation cannot be separated.

Later, there were many who told us that the idea of the intergrity of the homeland prevented us from getting votes. Every party wants votes; the more, the better. But when we had to choose between the votes of the people and the voice of national conscience, we followed the voice. In its platform for the Constituent Assembly, called the First Knesset, the Herut Movement said: The main tasks of Hebrew foreign policy are to bring about peace and the integrity of the homeland. In its platform for the Second Knesset it said: The aim of our foreign policy is a temporary one—to abolish the artificial partition of the eternal homeland and to reunite its occupied parts with the part that is under sovereign Israeli rule. Our platform for the Third Knesset said, in the field of foreign policy and defense—to reunite the whole Land of Israel, and its eternal capital Jerusalem, under the Hebrew flag. An end to bloodshed. Peace with the Arab States. The platform for the Fourth Knesset stated that: The right of the Jewish people to Eretz Yisrael in its historic entirety is eternal. A peace treaty between Israel and the Arab peoples is possible on the inalienable principle of reuniting the whole Land of Israel, with all its inhabitants, without distinction of religion or community, enjoying equal rights as free citizens. . . . No peace treaty has been achieved and signed, yet peaceful relations are possible . . .

At the time of the elections for the Fifth Knesset, Herut said: The right of the Jewish people to the entire Land of Israel is an eternal right. We also said: Peace is no abstract concept. We give it its concrete legal meaning, while making clear distinction between a peace treaty and peaceful relations.

And before the elections to the Sixth Knesset, Herut and the Liberal Party in Israel, agreed to declare: The Herut Movement and the Liberal Party in

Israel have decided to form a joint bloc in order to replace the present system and create a national-liberal regime. And then: the Herut Movement will continue to cleave to the principle of the territorial integrity of our homeland, namely the right of the Jewish people to Eretz Yisrael, in its historic entirety, is eternal and inalienable.

By virtue of our having upheld this idea and this flag, we may, after the mighty changes that have altered the history of the Jewish people, declare:

> "We, the disciples of Zev Jabotinsky, directing our hearts towards his grave on Mount Herzl, in agreement with all his disciples in the homeland and in the Diaspora, inform him tonight: "Sir, Rosh Betar [Commander of Betar], we have upheld your will during your life and after your death. When the flag was taken from your hand after you fell, while the people to whom you had addressed your warning that 'If you will not liquidate the Diaspora, the Diaspora will liquidate you', were utterly destroyed, we, your disciples, took up the flag, carried it high and rejected the evil counsel that we abandon the idea, the vision of giving the homeland back to the people and the people to the homeland. We have done your will. We have taught your teachings. We have carried the flag."

On this night, on the slopes of the Temple Mount, before the remains of our glory in redeemed Jerusalem, after the great salvation to which we have contributed our share, we can say: Happy the disciples whose teacher implants the faith in redemption in their hearts; and happy the teacher whose disciples uphold his teaching and his banner in faith.

We are told that to-day many accept the idea of the integrity of the homeland. I want to welcome them, all of them, whatever their party.

May the Lord grant that all His people stand for the integrity of the homeland, the eternal heritage of our fathers. In this spirit, I have the honor to propose to the Ninth Convention, with the consent of my friends and colleagues of the Herut Movement, that it adopt the following Declaration of the Rights of the Jewish People to its homeland, to liberty, security and peace.

DECLARATION

OF THE RIGHTS OF THE JEWISH PEOPLE TO ITS HOMELAND, TO LIBERTY, SECURITY AND PEACE

1. The right of the Jewish people to the Land of Israel in its historic entirety is eternal and inalienable. In this country our people established its kingdom, sanctified its faith, created its culture and brought forth the prophets' vision, which have enlightened the path of many nations from ancient times to this very day. Imbued with love of freedom, the Jews stood up against mighty enemies, resisted oppression, rose against enslavement, never surrendered. Profound as was their love for their country, so exalted were the courage and self-sacrifice with which they defended it and fought for it. Eighteen hundred and ninety-eight years ago, the sheer physical force of an all-conquering empire overpowered

Address at a Herut Party Convention

them; eighteen hundred and thirty-five years ago, the same empire suppressed their revolt. Thus Judea was subjugated, the Temple razed, Massada destroyed, Betar reduced, and the Jewish people exiled from its country and dispersed among the nations.

2. Ever since the Jewish People was expelled from its land, its history has been one of persecution, discrimination, humiliation, expulsion, wanderings and massacres. It never forgot its homeland, sanctified it for all generations, every single day. At all times, from the farthest corners of the earth, its soul clung to the land of its forbears. Such fidelity of a people to its homeland in the face of centuries of enforced separation, has no parallel in the annals of mankind.

3. The right of our People to the land of its forefathers was also recognized by other nations which affirmed the historic link between the Jewish People and the Land of Israel. The partitions of the Land of Israel were never founded on law. They were the result of colonial plots, arbitrariness, or aggression. These partitions never could or will annul our right.

4. By virtue of this right, *per se,* the national sovereignty of the re-established State of Israel applies *de facto* to every part of the Land of Israel that is liberated from unlawful foreign rule. It should also be applied *de jure.*

5. The Jewish People was exposed not only to persecution but also to physical destruction. Throughout generations its blood was shed by its enemies and in the last generation, one third of its sons were annihilated by the Germans, while the other nations in the East and West, alike, with few exceptions, did nothing to halt the systematic campaign of extermination. No people has ever lost so many lives in any war.

6. The enemies of the Jewish State who surround it on all sides seek to destroy those who were saved from German extermination and returned to Zion. That was what the Arab rulers announced in 1948, in 1956 and again on the brink of the Six Day War of Redemption, in May and June of 1967. In the light of those proven facts, in view of the repeated threats and actual dangers, the right of our people to the Land of its fathers and its right to the freedom, security and peace of its sons, can no longer be separated. All these rights have become one.

7. The people of Israel strives for peace with the Arab peoples. Peace, after war, means conclusion of peace treaties, which in the nature of things can only be achieved through direct negotiations between the belligerents. Once aggression has been defeated there can be no distinction between peace treaties and security conditions, if the renewal of the threat to the existence of the State and the life of the nation is to be prevented. According to our national experience and to international law, these security conditions are linked to our control over the areas which have served our enemies as bases for aggression.

8. Large-scale Jewish settlement in the areas of Judea, Samaria and Gaza, on the Golan Heights and in Sinai is urgent and essential for the maintenance of our nation's security.

9. The people of Israel believe in the sacred principle of equal rights for all citizens, without distinction of origin, nationality or religion. An Arab resident of the Land of Israel who applies for citizenship of the Jewish State and undertakes to be loyal to it—such loyalty is the condition for granting citizenship to any person in any State—shall receive it. The Jewish majority in the Land of Israel will be maintained mainly through the Return to Zion.

10. In accordance with the teachings of the standard-bearer of the idea of Hebrew statehood in our generation, Zev Jabotinsky, we shall lay the foundation for a new life in the territory under our sovereignty and control, on the principles of liberty, equality and justice.

So be it, with God's will.

URI AVNERY

Uri Avnery was born in Germany in 1923 and came to Palestine in 1934. Active in the underground *Irgun Zvai Leumi* (National Military Organization) during the war of independence, 1948, he was a member of "Samson's Foxes" of the famed *Givati* commando unit and was wounded in battle.

Returning to civilian life, Avnery joined the daily *Ha'aretz*, an independent centrist and staid newspaper. But in 1950 he founded *Haolam Hazeh* which quickly became a mass-circulation, exposé-type weekly. The mass appeal of this publication inspired Avnery to found the "Haolam Hazeh—New Force Movement," which elected him to the Knesset in 1965 and again in 1969. Avnery is the author of books in several languages: *War and Peace in the Semitic Region, Our Struggle, Total War, Israel Without Zionists* and others.

Although chronologically he has passed that age, Avnery is still the *enfant terrible* of Israeli public life. Described by many as a sycophant, his feuilletonistic verve and journalistic audacity make him a factor in the politics of his country. Deemed a professional collector of injustices, he has championed the cause of the Jewish "Orientals" (those who came from Middle East or North African countries) and of the Arab minority in Israel. His ideological outlook is somewhat ambivalent, with a leftist slant. At times he fights dogmas with stigmas.

Avnery's central theme is the "Semitic Idea". Believing that neither Arab nationalism nor Israeli nationalism can under the circumstances prevail in the Middle East, he supports "combining the two nationalisms, an ideal with which nationalists on both sides can identify." His views differ from some other bi-nationalists in the country in that he thinks that Israel should abandon, or at least weaken, its identification with Zionism, the Jewish religion and the West, and become a part of the Middle East "region" as a Semitic state in a new regional union or confederation of Arabs and Jews.

The following are two chapters from Avnery's book, *Israel Without Zionists*, The Macmillan Co., New York, 1968, pp. 153–165; 180–191.

The Mistake of Columbus

by URI AVNERY

ON OCTOBER 12, 1492, Columbus landed on a Bahama island called Guanahani by the Indians—and discovered the New World.

But Columbus did not have the slightest idea what he'd done. It was the oldest of worlds he was looking for—India and the spice islands.

.... Using only the crudest of instruments, knowing very little about geography, his head crammed with false ideas, Columbus bravely sailed forth into the unknown and inadvertently changed the shape of the world.

Something like this happened to Zionism, and therein lie the causes of all its inner conflicts, as well as the solutions to its problems.

Zionism set out with the idea that the Jews of the world constitute a nation—a nation in the European sense, a group of people who identify themselves with a political state, either an existing one or one to be established. Starting from this assumption, the problem was one of transportation, in the widest sense: once a Jewish homeland in Palestine was created, all Jews, or at least most of them would go there to live in Herzl's *Judenstaat*. [Theodor Herzl (1860–1904) was the founder of political Zionism.]

History has proved this theory false. A Jewish state was indeed set up in Palestine, but the great majority of Jews has not shown any undue inclination to go there. Two and a half million, most acting under diverse forms of duress, have indeed settled in what is now Israel. But several million others, who were not subject to physical persecution, stayed where they were. Immigration is near a standstill, with only the wish of Soviet Jewry, not allowed to leave its closed society, still in doubt.

It seems, therefore, that world Jewry is not a nation, in the Zionist sense. This would have spelled the failure of the Zionist experiment, if something quite unforeseen had not happened in the meantime: A new nation was, indeed, born in Palestine.

Looking back today, this seems to have been as inevitable as the discovery of the New World, once Columbus and his little fleet left the shores of Europe on a westward course. If you transfer hundreds of thousands of people to a foreign land—a new climate and landscape—in which they speak a newly resurrected language and respond to different physical and political challenges, the stage is set for the emergence of a new society. If this society has a sense of political destiny and unity, it becomes a new nation. This has happened in the United States, in Australia, in Brazil, in many other countries. It happened in Palestine.

We, the sons and daughters of Zionism, are indeed a new nation, not just another part of world Jewry that happens to live in Palestine. This is the central fact of our life, obscured by obsolete ideas and slogans, a truth that must be grasped if anything about our existence, our problems, and our future is to be understood.

What is a nation? Many answers have been given to this question, each influenced by the particular ideology of its proponent. Some put the emphasis on a common territory, others on a common culture or economy. I don't believe in abstract formulas to which life has to be somehow adapted. To me the answer seems simple and pragmatic: A nation is a group of people who believe that they are a nation, who want to live as a nation, have a common political destiny, identify themselves with a political state, pay its taxes, serve in its army, work for its future, share its fate—and, if necessary, die for it.

In this sense, we in Israel are a nation, unmistakably and irrevocably, for better or for worse. Our nation comprises all of us, from Dan to Eilat, but it does not include a Jew in Brooklyn, Paris or Bucharest, much as he may sympathize with our country and feel an affinity for it.

The difference between Jewish fathers anywhere in the world and Israeli sons is much more than the usual contradiction between generations; it is a mutation. A different mode of life, nutrition, climate, political reality and social environment could not but make the Palestinian-born son vastly unlike his ghetto-born father. It is not uncommon for a young Israeli in the United States or Europe to be told: "But you don't look like a Jew!" This dubious "compliment" carries a grain of truth. The robust, tall, often dark-blond and blue-eyed *sabra,* is, indeed, even externally different from his Jewish ancestors, much as the average Australian or American differs from his English great-grandfather. Jewish culture, created in the Diaspora by a persecuted, religious-minded minority, does not appeal to an Israeli generation which has a somewhat exaggerated sense of freedom. That part of the Jewish religion based on the Talmud and the Halakha, both products of the Diaspora, has in Israel generated into party slogans; the Bible, however, the most powerful book in Hebrew literature, is immensely popular, and archeology has become a national fad. In day-to-day modern Hebrew usage Israelis have unconsciously come to use the term *Jewish* when they mean foreign Jews or religion and to call *Hebrew* everything connected with themselves. We never speak about the Jewish army, Jewish nation, Jewish settlement or Jewish labor, but the Hebrew army, Hebrew nation, Hebrew settlement and Hebrew labor. Thus, long before the *idea* of a new *Hebrew* nation had evolved, it had become an unconsciously accepted fact.

We are a new nation, the Hebrew nation, whose homeland is Palestine (which we call Eretz Yisrael) and whose political creation is the State of Israel.

This does not mean, except for a small lunatic fringe, that we want to turn our backs on world Jewry and cut ourselves off from it. As the period of the Six Day War has clearly demonstrated, there is a very real and profound feeling of solidarity between Jews all over the world and Israel. We are grateful for this and reciprocate it. Solidarity there is. Affinity there is. But world Jewry is not a nation while the Hebrew Israelis are . . . .

Thus Zionism created something which it never consciously intended, a new nation. And by its very success, Zionism has become obsolete; by attaining its goals, Zionism provided for its own negation.

The existence of a new nation, Middle Eastern by birth, makes an entirely different approach to the Israeli-Arab problem possible. Unfortunately, this has yet to become clear to both Arab and Israeli. It is a common historical phenomenon that the ideological superstructure of a society, what the French call *mystique,* may linger on long after the reality upon which it was based has disappeared and made a new approach necessary.

An ideology is not just a set of ideas which can be changed easily. It is bound up with vested interests on many different levels. It exists in the textbooks of schools, in the mental set of teachers molding the minds of boys and girls, and in social institutions, with their hosts of functionaries and economic enterprises. Political parties fighting for political power perpetuate the philosophies imprinted on them since their inception; this is particularly true in Israel, all of whose political parties were founded in Europe before their leaders even came to the country. It is natural that a political regime which led Zionism to its heroic period is not one to relinquish power voluntarily and easily. The Zionist ideological and political superstructure, therefore, still exerts an immense influence in Israel. The establishment of the State has not changed this. Therefore it is very difficult to answer a question like: "Is Israel a Zionist state?"

For many young people in Israel, "to talk Zionism" means to use "highfaluting" slogans devoid of concrete meaning. To the practical *sabra* mind, pragmatic by nature, it has long been obvious that some fundamental tenets of Zionism have not stood the test of time; yet they unconsciously cling to them. . . .

The fundamental tenets of Zionism can be defined as follows: (a) all the Jews in the world are one nation; (b) Israel is a Jewish state, created by the Jews and for the Jews all over the world; (c) the Jewish dispersal is a temporary situation, and sooner or later all Jews will have to come to Israel, driven, if by nothing else, by inevitable anti-Semitic persecution; (d) the Ingathering of these Exiles is the *raison d'etre* of Israel, the primary purpose to which all other aims have to be subservient. This line is taught in Israeli schools, propounded in political speeches, written in the press. It is the essence of the existing regime.

Yet nothing could be further from what young Israelis believe in. Theirs is a different outlook, an Israeli nationalism pure and simple, bound up with the fortunes of the State of Israel, its territory, language, culture and army.

The two different sets of ideals can co-exist only because the gap between them seldom becomes obvious. Yet it is real and has a profound, if hidden, influence on the day-to-day conduct of affairs.

Let's take, for example, the question of religion.

Few people are as non-religious, even anti-religious, as the great majority of Israelis, but in few countries has organized religion such a stranglehold on life. While Jews in America are the most extreme defenders of the principle of the separation of church and state, this idea is considered heresy in Israel, for a very elementary reason: The Declaration of Independence, promulgated on May 14, 1948, proclaims Israel to be a Jewish state, and this is embedded in the legal structure of Israel. The Law of Return gives every Jew the automatic right to come and settle in Israel. A second law confers Israeli citizenship upon every Jewish immigrant the minute he enters the country, unless he waives his right.

. . . . Yet what is a Jew? Who is a Jew? No clear-cut legal definition exists. Nor can any definition exist but a religious one. Throughout the ages, Jews were a religious community. In fact, the courts of Israel have decided that a person ceases to be a Jew if he adopts another religion—a decision which makes it clear that being Jewish is basically a religious thing. If so, the argument runs, how can there be a separation between synagogue and state? If Israel exists for world Jewry, if its main aim is to ingather those Jews who are organized as a religious community, how can the concept of a Jewish nation be separated from the Jewish religion? Indeed, those of us in Israel who fight for the separation of synagogue and state are constantly accused of trying to sever Israel from world Jewry, turning it into just another small Levantine state. Thus, not one of the big, old Zionist parties advocates such a separation. All of them declare that state and religion, nation and religion, are one in the unique case of the Jews.

The minority in Israel who are religious, therefore, have a power quite disproportionate to their numerical strength. Only about fifteen per cent of the population voted for the three religious parties represented in the *Knesset*, giving them seventeen out of 120 seats in the 1965 elections. But by Israeli law there is neither civil marriage nor civil divorce, these affairs being within the sole dominion of the Rabbinate. A Jew cannot marry a Christian or a Moslem, nor can a Jew named Cohen marry a divorced woman. . . . Cohens or those with similar names are assumed to belong to the ancient families of priests, who are forbidden by Jewish law to marry anyone but a virgin: in theory, they might be called upon someday to officiate again in a new Temple. One cannot abdicate this right even if one wishes to: once a Cohen, always a Cohen. . . Neither busses nor the railway operate in Israel from sundown Friday until the first three stars appear on Saturday evening . . . .

It is a situation of many paradoxes, with controversy and clashes, extremely irritating to the vast majority of the people. Yet these same people accept the situation as natural and inevitable, forced to this conclusion by the concept of oneness of religion and nation. Only the repudiation of this concept by Israeli nationalism, an ever growing factor in Israeli life, will eventually lead to Israel's becoming a normal secular state.

Religion also plays a great role—even if a largely unconscious one—in the demographic dynamism of Israel. Any foreigner coming to Israel is immediately struck by the incredible variety of racial types in the streets. There are Jews of many colors, all the way from Nordic white to Ethiopian black, with many shades of brown in between. Ours is obviously a very non-racial kind of society.

Anyone considered a Jew is easily absorbed in Israel. While it is quite true that much hidden, often unconscious, discrimination exists between the communities, one should not exaggerate its importance. Jews of European descent, called *Ashkenazim,* may look with condescension upon Jews of Mediterranean and Eastern descent, generally called *Sephardim* who are considered culturally inferior and educationally backward, and Ashkenazi parents will often object to their offspring marrying Sephardim. Yet discrimination like this exists in many countries. The essential facts are that no Israeli, with the possible exception of a handful of crackpots, will consciously justify such discrimination and that it disappears in times of national stress, such as the recent war. For Zionists, a Jew is a Jew, wherever he comes from and whatever his mother-tongue. . . . It seems virtually certain that this kind of discrimination will disappear in time and constitute no real danger to the State, irksome as it may be right now.

A different situation prevails, however, as far as non-Jews are concerned. The idea of a homogeneous Jewish state is inherent in Zionism. A state which exists for the solution of the Jewish problem should be populated, so the Zionists feel, by Jews. Any non-Jew is really a foreign element in the present Israeli regime. Non-Jewish immigrants, even non-Jewish spouses of Jewish immigrants, find great obstacles to their absorption into Israeli society. Here, Zionist religionism and Israeli nationalism part. In modern times it should be easy to join a nation, the average Israeli feels: if you want to be a part of Hebrew society, speak its language, bring up your children in its culture, support its state, and serve in its army, you should be welcome. For a Zionist, this idea is unacceptable. You can become a Jew only by undergoing a religious ritual—circumcision for men, immersion in water in a religious bathhouse for women, with all the accompanying religious ritual.

While this question may only be important to the few non-Jewish immigrants, the idea of a homogeneous Jewish state has grave consequences for Arabs. It was not only a question of security and political allegiance which made it impossible for Israel to integrate the 300,000 Arabs living in it before the 1967 war. Far more operative, though seldom mentioned, was the instinctive conviction of old-time Zionists that Arabs could never really be a part of a state which was Jewish. For anyone entertaining this conviction, the idea of repatriating Arab refugees and increasing the Arab minority was positively obnoxious.

Prior to the 1967 war, Ben-Gurion's closest adherents started an outcry against the possibility that the Arab minority—then less than twelve per cent—would eventually become a majority in Israel by natural increase. . . . But it is not only the fear of an Arab majority which set Zionists against any idea of refugee repatriation, but the deeply felt, if quite often unconscious, conviction that Jews should be alone in their state, that Israel should remain homogeneously Jewish, that the Arab minority, if inevitable, should at least be kept as small as possible.

Before June 1967, the Arab minority, while constituting nearly twelve per cent of the population, held only two per cent of the posts in the government administration, with not one single Arab among the top-ranking officials, judges or cabinet ministers. Among the 120 members of the *Knesset,* only seven are Arabs, not one of whom occupies an important position in the House.

.... It is, in truth, while exploring the wider problem of Israeli-Arab relations that the gap between the Zionist philosophy and a normal healthy Hebrew nationalism becomes apparent.

Nothing frightens the Arabs more than the idea of the Ingathering of the Exiles. There arises before Arab eyes the spectre of a wave of Jewish immigration, bringing to Israel another ten million Jews, overflowing its narrow frontiers and conquering Arab states, evicting the inhabitants and grabbing land for innumerable new *kibbutzim.* There is something ludicrous in the present situation. Zionists leaders make visionary speeches about millions of Jews who will soon arrive on the shores of Israel. This is the sort of wishful thinking by which an antiquated regime tries desperately to preserve its obsolete slogans. Yet, to millions of Arabs these speeches sound like definite threats to Arab existence.

Thus an empty slogan can become a political factor in the most negative sense.

But the Zionist philosophy has a more destructive influence on Israel's own mentality. Because a Zionist considers Israel the beachhead of world Jewry, world Jewry is seen as an inexhaustible reservoir of manpower and money; thus, the relationship between Israel and the Jews, mainly in the West, seems of primary importance, while that between Israel and the Arab world automatically, therefore, takes a back seat. The location of Israel in the Middle East seems a geographical accident, to be disregarded whenever possible.

.... How else can one explain the most astonishing fact in Israeli public life? After a Zionist-Arab conflict which has gone on for three generations, and the actual state of war between Israel and the Arab states which is now entering its twentieth year, there does not exist an effective government department for Arab affairs. While we have a Ministry for Posts and a Ministry for Transportation, to say nothing of a Ministry for Tourism and a Ministry for Police, we do not and we don't have a Ministry for Middle Eastern Affairs. These are relegated to the Foreign Ministry, whose primary job is to defend Israel in the international arena from the political onslaught of the Arabs and, therefore, has nothing much to do with making contact with the Arab world and creating an atmosphere of peace. Indeed, such a task requires quite different approaches and talents. All the dealings between Israel and the Arab countries, all political initiatives from Israel toward the Arab world, are the proper province of the department for Middle Eastern affairs in the Foreign Ministry. But this department employs only thirty out of 900 officials in the Foreign Office, out of a total number of government employees well over 50,000, excluding policemen and teachers. Even this figure of thirty is misleading. If we deduct from it the personnel dealing with non-Arab Middle Eastern countries, such as Iran, and the purely clerical jobs, there are but three or four officials left to deal with what obviously is the main problem of Israel.

The 1967–68 budget of the government of Israel exceeds five billion Israeli pounds. Of this sum, less than 0.05 per cent—or less than three per cent of the expenditure of the Foreign Office—is devoted to Middle Eastern affairs. This sum again includes the Israeli activities in Iran, which are extensive, as well as clerical expenses.

Such a neglect of Israeli-Arab affairs would be impossible, after all that has happened, were it not for the Zionist image of an Israel oriented toward Western Jewry and the West in general. Of all the legacies Zionism bequeathed to the State of Israel, this is perhaps the most dangerous.

The new Hebrew generation has necessarily a different view of its place in the world. It has grown up in Palestine. It knows that it belongs to a new nation born in Palestine. It does not look at the Middle East from the outside, but from the inside. In fact, it has abolished the term Middle East in Hebrew usage. Middle East is a European term, assuming the center of the world to be somewhere in the West, but it is ridiculous for an Israeli to talk about the Middle East when he means, for example, countries like Algeria or even Egypt, which lie to our west. Therefore, when we started to talk about a Hebrew nation instead of a Jewish nation, we also started to talk about the Semitic region, or simply The Region *(ha-merkhav)* instead of the Middle East.

Belonging to The Region means dealing with the central problem of our existence—the Arabs—either by military or by political means, either through war or through peace. We Israelis, who have been born into this problem, know that we must solve it.... We don't wrack our brains trying to find a solution to the Jewish Question, real or imaginary; the central task of our generation is to integrate our nation into the framework of our region.

We are nationalists.... Nationalism means that in the world of today, individuals, except for perhaps a handful of universal geniuses, function within national political frameworks and national cultures. In the best sense, nationalism, defending its own national rights, recognizes the national rights of others. It is only in its exaggerations, in its imperialist or fascist forms which try to suppress other nations, that nationalism becomes a destructive force.

Even extreme nationalists, such as Dayan, recognize the national aspirations of the Arabs, something our Zionist fathers were unable or unwilling to take into account.

The emergence, then, of a young nationalist generation, superseding Zionism, creates the psychological basis for a solution.

The Federation of Palestine

THE WAR BETWEEN Israel and the Arab world is not an ordinary one between states. In an ordinary war states clash over some grievance, a piece of land or economic advantages. After the war, some kind of peace arrangements are made, tracing new boundaries or allocating rights, sometimes by agreement, sometimes by dictate of the victor. Our is a different war, a clash between two great national movements going on now for three generations. It cannot be ended by a peace settlement of the classic type, with representatives of the two sides assembling in conference around a green table, each party stating its demands, a compromise hammered out and embodied in a solemn peace treaty.

Many concrete problems are bones of contention between Israel and the Arabs, yet not one of them constitutes the real cause of the war. While solutions to these problems must be found, as we shall endeavor to do, one must realize that no solution will be practical unless the genuine causes of the war are removed. Quite simply Israel must recognize that it belongs to the Region and must take a positive attitude toward the national aspirations of the Arab peoples. The Arab world must recognize that Israel exists and has become a legal and permanent part of the Region.

This mutual recognition is the focal point of the problem. Without it, all talks about a Regional peace settlement are nonsense. Without it, all foreign intervention and attempts at mediation, well intentioned or otherwise, will be of no avail. Mediators, go-betweens, peace brokers may be important as messengers in certain phases, but they are no substitute for direct confrontation between Israel and the Arabs.

Which Arabs?

This important question is often overlooked. The answer, to my mind, is, first of all, the Arab-Palestinian nation.

One unresolved question in the Middle East is whether the Arabs constitute one nation or a group of nations. In other words, whether all the Arabs can or should unite in one big Arab state, stretching from the shores of Morocco to the boundaries of Iran, or whether they should retain the separate existing states. The idea of unity is inherent in the Arab national movement. Arabs look back with longing at the time, glorious but short-lived, when the whole Arab world, indeed all of Islam, was united under the caliph. In modern times both the *Baath* ("resurrection") party, centered in Syria, and Abd-el-Nasser have been spokesmen for the idea of the great unitary Arab state. Yet it seems this idea has failed. As in Europe and Africa, and even in the Soviet bloc, smaller states stick to their own political existence and interests, even while recognizing a broader, unifying regional idea.

Each Arab people has its own state, save one: the people of Palestine. This people was the great loser of the 1948 war. According to the original United Nations partition resolution of November 29, 1947, an independent Arab state was to be set up in those parts of Palestine which were not allocated to the Jewish state. Such an Arab state never came about. The war, which the Arabs of Palestine themselves started in order to prevent the partition of the country and the establishment of Israel, created new realities. During the war, which Israel did not want, Israel conquered part of the areas originally allocated to the Arabs. The neighboring Arab states, which sent their armies into Palestine in order to help their brethren, ultimately annexed the remaining parts of Palestine. At the end of the war Palestine had ceased to exist as a political entity; it was divided among Israel, Egypt and Jordan. Yet Palestine remained a mental reality. The Palestinians never resigned themselves to a fate which meant that they had ceased to exist as a nation. In Jordan, in the Gaza Strip, in refugee camps dispersed all over the Region, the idea of Palestine lived on. It was exploited by the Arab states in their fight against Israel and among themselves, each of several states trying to usurp the role of the patron of the Palestinian nation. Egypt installed a shadowy adventurer, Ahmed Shukairy, a refugee from Haifa, as the chief of the Palestine Liberation Organization, a post he was forced to relinquish in December 1967. Hussein pretended that his shaky kingdom was the true personification of Palestine. The Syrians supported the Palestinian *el Fatah* ("conquest") organization, whose acts of sabotage led directly to the crisis of the 1967 war.

The official Israeli attitude has fluctuated between diametrically opposed poles, according to expediency. Until the 1948 war, the Zionist leadership insisted that its conflict was solely with the Palestinian Arabs. It objected vigorously to the official invitation extended by the British government to the Arab states to take part in discussing the Palestine problem. This was believed to be a typical trick of perfidious Albion, an attempt to cheat us out of our rights and annul the Balfour Declaration. After the 1948 war, the government of Israel maintained that Palestine had ceased to exist, together with any imaginary Palestinian nation, and that its conflict was now solely with the Arab states. This stand was taken because any recognition of the existence of a Palestinian nation might raise questions about boundaries and refugees which the government was anxious to avoid. Now, after the 1967 war, the situation has changed again. Except for some hundreds of thousands of former and new refugees, all Arab Palestinians live in the territories occupied by the Israeli Army during this war, and these territories include all the area of Palestine as it existed under the British Mandate until 1948.

The question of what to do with these territories is, therefore, bound up with the question whether to recognize the Palestinian-Arab nation and deal with it or disregard its existence.

Today the Israeli government insists that the present situation—the precarious cease-fire—can be changed only if the Arab governments start direct and open negotiations with Israel. Moreover, the Israeli government refuses to state, or even to hint, what its condition for peace may be. It says that only during the official, direct negotiations with the Arab governments will it state these conditions.

This very comfortable and expedient stand relieves the Israeli government of the necessity to decide upon peace-conditions, a task quite beyond the present Great Coalition, some of whose members could not agree to anything but full and outright annexation, while some of its other members could not tolerate annexation. Premier Eshkol who, like President Johnson, wants to be the personification of a great consensus, would like to keep this coalition intact until the elections of 1969, thereby postponing a move in any direction.

For the Arab states, direct negotiations as a *first* step are impossible. Such a repudiation of all the slogans which dominated the Arab world for fifty years cannot be the beginning of the road to peace, but rather the end of it. Many things—the solution of the Palestinian refugee problem, the neutralization of many other factors which poison the region—must come first.

Moreover, the Arab governments suspect that the call for direct negotiations is a trap. As a high-ranking Egyptian official put it to me: "What does Israel want from us? Only recognition of its lawful existence. We, on our part, have many concrete demands—retreat from the cease-fire lines, repatriation of refugees, and so forth. If we agree to direct peace negotiations, we already do accord Israel recognition. In other words, we are giving you *in advance* what you want, without receiving anything in return. After making such a mistake, Israel could say, at the negotiating table, that it does not want to concede anything. Therefore, secret negotiations by mediators must come first. We must know what Israel wants to give up in return for recognition, before any leader can make any open move."

Thus a new vicious circle is formed—one which allows the Israeli and Arab governments to postpone everything.

This postponement is also freezing debate in Israel itself, with the unfortunate result that no one knows where public opinion really stands. The struggle between the adherents of annexation and federation cuts across nearly all the parties. The propagandists for a Greater Israel are more vociferous, and command much more support in the mass-circulation press, but the adherents of a Palestinian federation are far more numerous and influential than would seem at first glance. Significantly, many of them belong to the higher echelons of the Israeli Army which, quite unlike most armies, is one of the least chauvinistic and most sober factors on the Israeli scene. The military governors who administer the occupied territories of Palestine, as well as many higher civilian government officials, in general advocate a more liberal and far-sighted policy than many politicians and publicists.

A few weeks ago, I proposed in the *Knesset* a resolution calling for immediate steps to create a Palestinian Republic. The first paragraph read: "The whole of

Palestine is the homeland of two nations—the Hebrew nation and the Arab-Palestinian nation." I proposed that two states embodying the two nations—Israel and the Republic of Palestine—should form a federation.

Only one other member voted for this resolution. But after the vote, twelve members, ranging from the right-wing *Herut* to the left-wing *Mapam,* and including a cabinet minister, approached me privately in the lobby, expressing their private support, adding wistfully: "I wish I could have voted for this resolution." By Israeli standards of party discipline, this was, of course, impossible, as all the great parties support the government policy of waiting for direct negotiations with the Arab states.

In a famous remark, Moshe Dayan has said that he is "waiting for the Arab leaders to ring his telephone." This is now official Israeli policy. The point is that this policy is aimed only at negotiations with *existing* Arab governments—and thus excludes automatically the one Arab people which has as yet no government, but who is the most directly concerned—the Palestinian people, with whom a solution can be worked out and implemented at once.

In fact, three alternatives face Israel today, after the 1967 war.

The first is to give the occupied territories back to the neighboring Arab states. Very few Israelis think that that is either practical or desirable. At worst, it would mean that hostile Arab armies would appear again sooner or later in their old positions, ten miles from the seashore of Netanya, fifteen miles from the heart of Tel Aviv, with future wars virtually inevitable. At best, if the Arab states do agree to some kind of peaceful settlement, it would mean that Israel would still be surrounded by the dispossessed Palestinian Arabs, longing for their own national identity, a cause for further trouble. The question of Jerusalem, now unified and annexed by Israel and the focus of intense emotions on both sides, makes such a solution even more unlikely.

The second, opposite proposal, shrilly demanded by a coalition of all the more extreme elements in Israel, would be the annexation of all or most of the occupied territories. Here, two inherent traits of Zionism clash. As a colonizing movement, Zionism is expansionist by nature, at least within the historical boundaries of Palestine. It is, therefore, quite natural for an old-time Zionist to advocate the "liberation" of all of Palestine, opening up new areas for Jewish settlement. Yet this instinctive demand, quite natural after a victorious war, clashes with another inherent trait of Zionism: the idea of a homogeneous Jewish state. Israel has not succeeded in integrating 300,000 Israeli Arabs into its psychological structure: how, then, could it absorb nearly a million and a half? The annexation of the territories and their inhabitants would turn Israel into a bi-national state, an idea detested by most Israelis. Worse, the natural increase of Palestinian Arabs being more than two times greater than that of Hebrew Israelis (45 as against 22 per thousand) and no significant Jewish immigration in sight, it seems virtually certain that the Arabs would be the majority in Greater Israel within less than a generation, thereby achieving the very aim they set themselves before the creation of Israel—a Palestinian state ruled by an Arab majority, who could stop immigration. There may be some on the lunatic fringe of the annexation idea who believe the Arabs should and could be evicted in due course from the country, enabling all of Palestine to become a homogeneous state. Others advocate that these Arabs should not be given citizenship rights after annexation, thus turning Israel into a new South Africa or Rhodesia, with the Hebrew citizens exercising political power over a native population in the minority today but perhaps the majority tomorrow. Several politicians of the old parties have advocated a policy to "help and encourage" Arabs to emigrate from Palestine.

Annexation means turning Israel into a Hebrew empire, with a colonial regime controlling the Arab inhabitants. No one can believe that within such an empire, plagued with an ever-growing problem of inner security and armed resistance, democracy could be preserved even for Hebrew citizens—emergency laws and arbitrary rule have a way of expanding, once applied on a large scale. One way or another, annexation would be the end of Israel as we know it, the end of any hope for peaceful integration in the Region, the final turning of Israel into an armed Crusader state.

This is not only true about outright official annexation. The status quo may generate another kind of annexation—a creeping, unannounced, factual annexation, brought about by hundreds of little acts and omissions. Here a Hebrew settlement is set up, temporarily, to support the army of occupation, there an abandoned Arab village is razed to the ground for "security and sanitary reasons" (as Moshe Dayan said the other day in the *Knesset*, in answer to my question). If such acts accumulate, a point of no return may be reached, which will have the same results as an official annexation. Practical annexation might become the continuation of old-time "practical" Zionism.

The third alternative is to encourage the setting up of an Arab republic of Palestine. My friends and I have advocated this plan for Israel's integration into the Semitic Region since 1948, long before the Six Day War and the occupation of the West Bank and the Gaza Strip.

In the present circumstances, it would mean that the government of Israel would offer the Palestinian Arabs assistance in setting up a national republic of their own, this offer being conditional upon a federal agreement between such a Palestine and Israel. The Palestinian Republic would comprise the west bank of the Jordan and the Gaza Strip. Transjordan could join it if its inhabitants were able and willing so to decide.

Jerusalem as a unified city would become the federal capital, as well as the capital of both states, thus finding a solution—the only practical one, I believe —to an issue charged with emotions, both religious and nationalist, which make retreat for either side impossible.

The federal agreement should be preceded by an economic, political and military pact. It should safeguard the military security of Israel by forbidding foreign armies to enter the territory of Palestine, guaranteeing this in a practical way by a system of military coordination between the armies of Israel and the Arab republic of Palestine on the lines of NATO or the Warsaw Pact. It should unify the economy of the area, which had been one economic entity from the dawn of history to 1948, including the two hundred years of the Crusader State. It should establish some form of political coordination, providing, for example, that neither Israel nor Palestine should enter any foreign alliance without the agreement of the other. This is the bare minimum, which could be expanded, gradually and by mutual consent, into a deeper and more significant federation, once Arab Palestine catches up, economically and socially, with Israel.

Such, then, is the plan which the government of Israel should offer the Palestinian-Arab nation, those residing in the territories now occupied by the Israeli Army and those outside, who must be allowed to return.

Many doubts and objections have been raised to this plan. Some of my Arab friends fear that such a Palestinian republic would be free in name only, becoming in reality a kind of Bantustan, like the so-called "autonomous" Negro reservations set up by the racist white regime in South Africa. This danger would exist if the plan were used by an anti-Arab regime in Israel as a camouflage for what would really be colonialist expansion. But every plan can be perverted, and this possibility is no argument against it. The plan as such, executed in the same spirit in which it is offered, should be the subject of debate. The real question is: Can the Palestinian republic become a living organism, a more or less equal partner with Israel?

I answer the question in the affirmative. True, after twenty years of Jordanian and Egyptian rule, both the Gaza Strip and the West Bank are devoid of any industry. Just now, they are no match for Israel in this sphere. But things have to be viewed in a more dynamic context. The settlement of the refugees and the restoration of the Arab territories to their natural place in a unified country will give their economy a boost on the road to economic prosperity. Politically, the very fact that this will be an Arab republic, a part of the Arab world with which Israel has to deal, will give the Palestinian republic a status of importance beyond its own resources. It will become the natural bridge between Israel and the Arab world.

This idea of a bridge is central to our concept. We don't want a quisling state, serving Israel and considered as treasonous by the other Arab peoples. On the contrary, the Republic of Palestine, in order to fulfill its natural function as a bridge of peace, must be a true expression of the Palestinian nationality, led by true leaders, and acceptable to the Arab world.

We do not conceive the Palestinian solution as opposed to a regional settlement—but rather as a step toward it, and eventually as a part of it. Even today, the products of the West Bank, mainly agricultural, daily cross the Jordan bridges and fords, on their way to Transjordan, Kuwait, even Iraq and Saudi Arabia. Many Palestinians travel from the occupied territory to Transjordan and back, to conduct their business. Thus, owing to the situation of the Palestinian Arabs, the cease-fire lines are not as hermetically closed as the old armistice lines, which were crossed only by terrorists, soldiers and smugglers. Palestine already serves as a bridge.

If Israel offers the Palestinian nation assistance in setting up their republic, and if this offer is accepted by a responsible Palestinian leadership, one of the first moves should be for these leaders to go to Cairo and other Arab capitals, in order to canvass overall Arab support for this solution. My judgment is that Egypt and its allies—while not openly welcoming this plan—will make it clear that they do not object to it. Indeed, in one of his most extreme anti-Israeli speeches at the end of 1967, Nasser still emphasized that the Palestinian question is a matter for the Palestinians themselves to solve, and that from them must come the initiative for a settlement. This was interpreted by many Palestinian leaders as a green light to go ahead—cautiously.

But—some Zionists ask—are the Palestinians a nation? After all, there never existed an independent Arab state of Palestine. What right have the Palestinians to a state of their own?

There is a certain irony in the fact that these questions are raised by Zionists—for not long ago these same arguments were thrown into their own faces. Were the Jews a nation? Was even the Hebrew community in Palestine a real nation, deserving statehood? . . . .

The answer is: people who believe that they are a nation, thereby do become a nation. This is the only valid criterion. Once a people aspires to statehood, longs for it and strives for it, they deserve it. Whether this state ever existed before, whether it has a history or not, is quite immaterial. Even today the Palestinian nation is stronger than many of the nations in the United Nations.

The merits of Palestinian-Arab statehood are not a debating point in New York or Paris. It is in Nablus, Ramallah and Gaza that it has to stand its test. No one who visits these towns, who speaks freely with their inhabitants, can fail to be impressed by the intensity of Palestinian nationalism, by the deep conviction of people of all ages who answer clearly: We are not Jordanians, nor Egyptians. We are Palestinians. *Falasteen* is our country. As Palestinians we are part of the Arab world.

I believe in the force of nationalism as a prime mover in contemporary history. Try to combat nationalism and you are bound to lose. Harness nationalism to concrete solutions of problems and you have a chance to put an end to war. If we try to suppress this nationalism, we only create a vacuum which will be filled by adventurers like the detested Shukairy or by terrorists like the *el Fatah,* who are trying to start a genuine war of liberation against Israel. Nature abhors a vacuum. Wishing Palestine away will not make it disappear; it will haunt the Region and Israel, creating new dangers and miseries.

But once a provisional Palestinian Government is formed, a real revolution will be set in motion, a revolution, which will change the climate of the whole Region.

For Israel it will mean the beginning of peace, actual cooperation between it and an authentic Arab state. For the Palestinian nation it will mean a place on the map, the restoration of its national identity, a safeguard to its territorial integrity, and last but not least, an end to the misery of the refugees.

TAWFIQ TOUBI

Tawfiq Toubi was born in Haifa in 1922 and educated in the Bishop Gobat School. He received the Palestine matriculation certificate. In his political activities Toubi has been a member of the World Peace Council and the Politburo of *Rekah (Reshimah Kommunistit Hadasha)*, a rival of the Communist Party of Israel *(Maki)*, from which it split in 1967 on the issue of war and peace with the Arab neighbouring countries, the treatment of the Arab minority in Israel and other ideological matters. Several Jewish members of the parent party, led by Meir Wilner, joined Toubi in the new organization. He was also the editor of *Ittihad* (a twice-weekly Arabic newspaper), and a member of the Knesset (Parliament)—one of several Arabs in that legislative body.

A polemicist of no mean ability, Toubi identifies himself with the Kremlin, accusing Israel of a conspiracy against a just future for both Arabs and Jews. He visits his wrath on capitalism in Israel and moralizes against the evils of bourgeois institutions and the "pseudo socialist" government which—he claims—brought about an imperialist-colonial confrontation with the Arab countries, especially with the U.A.R. (Egypt) and Syria, which in his opinion were on the road to revolutionary socio-economics.

Toubi is less concerned with causes and situation-ethics attending the 1967 events than with the problem of a just and equitable world. Although some of his statements sound like tired international communist phraseology, they are meaningful in Israel because they are freely uttered by him both there and abroad. They provide the Arabs of Israel with the opportunity to break out of their parochialism and make contact with the outside world. Toubi seems to be cognizant of this fact and, one suspects, also appreciative of his state in which he can function more freely (not completely, to be sure, because of Israeli security measures) than in most other states in the world—East, West or non-aligned.

The following is a speech by Toubi at the session of the Praesidium of the World Peace Council, Nicosia, June 8, 1968.

An Address at the World Peace Council

by TAWFIQ TOUBI

I would like to deal in my word [speech] with the present crisis of the Middle East resulting from the war launched a year ago by the Israeli ruling circles against the neighboring Arab countries. This crisis continues to be a most serious threat to peace and security in the Middle East and the world over.

We, the anti-imperialist and peace forces in Israel, who have opposed and condemned the aggression launched by the ruling circles of our country in the interests of U.S. and other imperialist designs against the Arab peoples and in pursuance of territorial conquests, would like to stress the following points:

More and more people now realize out of experience and as a result of the policy of the Israeli ruling circles the falsehood of the pretext of "self-defense in the face of danger of annihilation" presented by the Israeli ruling circles and their imperialist supporters for initiating the war in June [1967].

The development of events proved to many who believed this claim, that the real aim of the war was to strike a blow at the Arab anti-imperialist national movement, impose USA imperialist domination on the Arab countries and impose on the Arab countries a settlement which would deprive the Palestine Arab people of their just rights and bring the Israeli ruling circles territorial gains.

Opposing and condemning the war of last June, we told our people, the people of Israel—and in the face of wild chauvinist incitement against us—that under the deceptive slogan of self-defense, they are being led to an unjust war. We defend, of course, the just rights of the people of Israel, the right of Israel's existence which was formed as an expression of self-determination and in accordance with the decisions of the UNO 1947 resolution which called for the formation of two independent states—an Arab and a Jewish state—as a means of throwing out the British colonial rule. While upholding and defending this right of the people of Israel, we told them, however, the truth that the war had nothing to do with defending this right, but it is an adventure against the neighboring Arab countries which can never bring any real benefit to the people of Israel and would never bring Israel and her people nearer to security and peace. It would never solve problems, but on the contrary it can only complicate relations, deepen the trenches between Israel and Arab countries and create new dangers to the security of the people of Israel.

The intoxication of military victory by which the ruling circles of Israel tried to blind the clear sight of the mass of the people in our country, is giving way under the hard facts of life. More people in our country are starting now to doubt the "wisdom" of the Israeli official policy and look towards an outlet from the impasse.

Moshe Dayan, in an interview to the Army Journal last week, had to confess that it was a mistake on his part to believe that the military victory will bring with it solutions.

The war certainly brought difficulties and tragedies to all peoples of the region, and, paradoxical as it seems to be, the military success of the Israeli ruling circles brought difficulties to Israel and to the people of Israel as well. This is explained, of course, by the failure of the war to realize the main desired aims of the USA imperialists of imposing their sway and upsetting the anti-imperialist Arab regimes. This was possible thanks to the act of stopping the war, itself before achieving these aims, thanks to the real world balance of forces in favor of the forces of peace, anti-imperialism and socialism, and to the detriment of the imperialists, their proteges, and of aggression.

All this has also upset the schemes of the rulers of our country and is behind the awkward situation into which they pushed Israel and its people.

What is the situation now faced by the people of our country?

Having failed to dictate their scheming upon the Arab peoples, the Israeli ruling circles faced the people of our country with the burden of continuous mobilization to the armed forces in order to maintain the present situation with an ever increasing military budget which now reaches 43% of the whole state budget, and the military yearly expenditure nears now the 800 million dollars mark and continues to increase at the expense of diminishing social services and economic difficulties.

In the occupied territories, popular resistance is widening and deepening. The latest mass demonstrations during a whole week in the Gaza Strip, yesterday's general strike and demonstrations in the West Bank in occupied Jerusalem are also expressions of the failure of the Israeli authorities to impose on the population of the occupied territories separate capitulatory settlements which would legalize the occupation.

The growing popular resistance to the occupation coupled with the daily loss of life paid by Arabs and Jews alike makes the situation grave and creates doubts in the minds of the people about the perspective that lies ahead.

The Israeli people feel the impact of the growing international isolation of Israel engraved by the continued aggression of its ruling circles and by acts of annexation as in Jerusalem, defying various resolutions of the UNO and the Security council. Even previous allies to the official Israeli line are showing opposition. All this leads many people in our country to think anew and the forces in Israel who opposed and condemned the war of June are not alone in demanding a withdrawal from the policy of occupation and the sincere acceptance by the Israeli government of the UN Security Council resolution of November 11, 1967.

Voices heard lately amongst Israeli youth, students and intellectuals, preferring peace to annexation of territories as advocated by the extremists, is an expression of the growing disagreement with the government policy.

Interesting, for instance, is an interview by Professor Yeshayahu Leibovitz, a religious professor at the Hebrew University in Jerusalem, given to *Yediot Aharonot* evening daily on 12 April last. He said:

"Annexation is a tragedy, destruction of the state, annihilation of the people, break-up of the social structure, and the demoralizing of men. It will be a secret police state, it will formulate the whole atmosphere with several influences on the basic freedoms, on the freedom of speech, expression, organization... corruption will rise high. After spiritual demoralization there will come physical destruction. What is then the alternative? To get out from ruling one and a half million arabs, to return to the status-quo of June 5th... I do not see in the territorial gains of the Six Day War any lever for positive development. Some speak about federation: federation is imposing colonialism, imposing a rule of quislings; this is worse than annexation—this is occupation with hypocrisy."

Important was the appeal by the ninety personalities of various shades of life who, at the beginning of the year, published an appeal calling to put an end to the policy of repressive measures against the Arab people in the occupied areas and against the infringement of democratic rights in Israel itself. Many of these personalities are now being subjected to a witch-hunt and public terror. There is also strong opposition to Jewish settlement in Arab occupied areas by various intellectuals, even amongst circles who supported the war.

We attach great importance to these manifestations of opposition to the policy of occupation and oppression expressed under a suffocating arrogance coupled with repressive measures, and act to widen the front opposing aggression and occupation and struggle for the implementation of the UN resolution.

The increasing and widening international isolation of the Israeli government and the set-backs falling on the policy of its U.S. imperialist allies in Vietnam, in other parts of the world and in the Middle East as a result of the continued isolation of aggression and the strength of anti-imperialist forces, is imposing on the Israeli government the necessity of manouvering when dealing with the present crisis.

Under such international pressure, and placed in an awkward position by the acceptance of the UAR and Jordan to the peaceful settlement of the Palestine problem and the Middle East crisis, by the acceptance of these two Arab countries in full without any reservations of the UN Security Council resolution, under the pressure of such a situation, the Israeli official position moved from a policy of non-cooperation with Jahring immediately adopted after his nomination, to a position where the Israeli UNO representative Tekoah had to declare, in the middle of May, Israel's acceptance of the UN Security Council resolution of 22 November 1967 as a basis for reaching peace. Even this step, which was called by Mr. Eshkol, Israel's Prime Minister as a tactical step, raised a crisis within the Israeli ruling circles. Under pressure of the most extreme militant and chauvinistic circles, the Israeli government retreated even from this tactical step. Under the demagogic slogan of direct negotiations, the real position of the Israeli government is, in fact, to sabotage the carrying out of the UN Security Council resolution which lays internationally recognized steps for the peaceful settlement of the crisis to the advantage of all states of the region and safeguarding the just rights of all people concerned.

I would like to stress here the positive importance of the clear and unambiguous declarations made by the Foreign Minister of the UAR concerning the readiness of his government to implement in the full the UN Security Council resolution and to adhere to a prescribed time-table for the implementation of all its parts. This step is a contribution to the just and peaceful settlement of the Middle East crisis and the Palestine problem.

Such clear-cut positions in favor of a peaceful and just settlement emanating from responsible Arab leaders, such positions in favor of a peaceful settlement of the Palestine problem based on respect of the just rights of all peoples of the region including the Arabs of Palestine and the people of Israel, such peace seeking positions are not only just and correct; at the same time they isolate and weaken the policy of force, occupation and aggression held by the Israeli rulers under cover of direct negotiations, and serve best the interests of all peoples concerned.

While always opposing and struggling against the pro-imperialist, predatory and militarist policy of the Israeli ruling circles who refused to recognize any right of the Palestine Arab people and thus blocked the way to a settlement, we, at the same time, opposed adventurous and reactionary nationalist Arab positions heard in the past and still being heard in certain circles, falsely interpreting the just right of the Palestine Arab people as meaning the liquidation of the state of Israel. Such adventurous positions still find expression in the refusal of certain circles to cooperate with the UN for the implementation of the UN Security Council resolution, to the detriment of the cause of struggle for eliminating the consequences of the last June war and of peace.

Experience shows that the more clear and striking the position of the anti-imperialist forces in the Arab countries in favor of a just and peaceful settlement to the Palestine problem based on the mutual recognition of the rights of both peoples, the Arab peoples and the people of Israel—the more difficult it will be for the imperialist and reactionary forces to exploit the Israeli-Arab dispute against the interests of all peoples of the region and against the anti-imperialist Arab national movement, and the easier it will be to mobilize forces in the world and even in Israel itself for the peaceful and just settlement of the present crisis, for the liquidation of aggression and for ensuring the just rights of all peoples concerned.

Dear friends, the continuation of the present unsolved crisis is a source of permanent danger to peace and that is why we have to exert great efforts for its speedy settlement. The development of events proved the possibility of a just and peaceful settlement which will safeguard the interests of all peoples of the region.

The axis of the struggle for a peaceful settlement of the Middle East crisis and for the elimination of the consequences of the war last June and for safeguarding the interests of the Arab and Israeli peoples, is now the world wide struggle for implementing in full the UN Security Council resolution. This resolution which condemns territorial gains as a result of military conquests calls for:

> The withdrawal of Israeli forces from occupied territories for the relinquishing of the state of war among countries of the region and for recognition of the right of every state to a sovereign existence. It also calls for the ensuring of freedom of navigation in international waters and the just solution of the Palestine refugee problem.

The full implementation of such a resolution by all sides concerned would advance the region on the path of peace and prosperity.

We, in Israel, small as our forces are and hard as our conditions are, will continue our struggle against the pro-imperialist policy of the Israeli government for the withdrawal of the Israeli forces from occupied Arab territories, against acts of oppression and trampling on the just rights of the Arab people in the occupied areas and against discrimination toward the Arab population in Israel itself. We shall continue to struggle so that the Israeli government will accept fully, as a last resort, the UN Security Council resolution and, through this, arrive at a peaceful settlement.

This struggle of ours is first and foremost in the interest of our people—the people of Israel whose future relies on cooperation and friendship with the Arab peoples whose interest is not in being in the imperialist front against the Arab peoples but with the Arab peoples against imperialism.

In this struggle of ours, we draw strength from your support to us, from your struggle for peace and a just settlement of the crisis.

One last word I would like to say to our Vietnamese friends. We follow your heroic struggle daily, we are joyous at every success of yours, every blow you strike at the U.S. imperialists is a help towards a just and peaceful settlement in our region as well. Your successes, dear friends, are our successes, and peace in Vietnam will strengthen the cause of peace in our region.

We wish this session of the Presidential Committee of the World Council of Peace every success in its work for the cause of peace, freedom and independence.

SHMUEL MIKUNIS

Shmuel Mikunis was born in Russia in 1903 and came to Palestine in 1921. Later, pursuing his higher education in France, he became a civil engineer. During the late 1940's, he worked in the communist countries of Eastern Europe to procure help for the emergence of Israel. He was a member of the Provisional State Council in 1948–49 and has been a member of the Knesset (Parliament) since its inception.

Mikunis was one of the organizers of the Communist Party of Israel, *Maki (Miflagah Kommunistit Yisraelit)*, and became its secretary-general and the chairman of its Politburo. The party, which includes both Arabs and Jews, was fragmented along both ideological (Peking vs. Moscow) and ethnic lines for many years. The Six Day War of 1967 finally brought about a split in the organization and a legal struggle over the name of the party. In January, 1969, the courts ruled that the Mikunis group had the right to the original name. The rival faction, with most of the Arab and some of the Jewish followership, assumed the name *Rekah (Reshimah Kommunistit Hadashah)*, under the leadership of Tawfiq Toubi and Meir Wilner.

Mikunis' ideological diction is clearer than that of his comrade and co-worker, Dr. Moshe Sneh. The latter is sometimes accused of political solecism, having traveled from the centrist General Zionists of *Mapam* (Marxist-socialists) and from there to *Maki*. Mikunis throughout the years evinced intellectual determinism until his ideological landscape—not principles—shifted from Moscow as a result of the Kremlin's adamant stand in the Arab-Israeli struggle, the Czechoslovak occupation and the hardening of the USSR's doctrinal arteries.

The "theses" for the Sixteenth Congress of the Communist Party of Israel appeared in Maki's *Information Bulletin,* October, 1968, pp. 5–42.

In the Battle for Peace

by SHMUEL MIKUNIS

1. BETWEEN CONGRESSES

THE YEARS AFTER THE Fifteenth Congress [of the Communist Party in Israel] held in 1965, were characterized by the extreme intensification of the Israeli-Arab conflict that reached its climax in the Six Day War of June, 1967, and continued in different forms and other conditions to the present day. On this background we waged our struggle to prevent war and save the peace, defend Israeli rights without jeopardizing the rights of the Palestinian Arab people, defend the rights of the working people and democracy, for a foreign policy of independence and non-alignment and against the policy of encouraging the big capitalists in Israel. Our party, armed with the resolutions of the Fifteenth Congress that were inspired by Marxist-Leninist theory, the sources of Israeli patriotism and proletarian internationalism as well as the party's experience of many years—with its positive and negative aspects—waged the struggle in every sector of life internally and externally from positions of faithfulness to the interests of the working class and the masses of the people as well as faithfulness to the vital national interests of our people and our country.

The extreme intensification of the Israeli-Arab conflict, that became the focus of dangers to peace from the local and international standpoint, demanded of our party an even greater and unprecedented struggle for the defense of Israel's right to exist in theory and practice. No other communist party in the world had experienced such a struggle. The proclaimed refusal of the Arab rulers to reconcile themselves to the existence of Israel while laying a "progressive-theoretical" basis for the unconcealed racial-extermination of Israel, caused us to intensify the struggle for a just and lasting peace between Israel and the Arab countries, for the good of peace in general and both sides in the dispute in particular, and foil the imperialist plots which fed on the Israeli-Arab conflict. The surrender to the anti-Israeli Arab chauvinist approach on the part of a considerable portion of the socialist and anti-imperialist camp in the world caused our party to engage in a searching ideological and political argument with them. This argument had—and will continue to have—strong reverberations in our country and in the communist and anti-imperialist movement in general, since it concerns not only the problem of the existence and future of Israel which is very important to us, and not only the problem of the means and ways to struggle against imperialism and neo-colonialism in the Near East, but also the basis for true understanding of the theory and practice of Marxist-Leninism, the principles of proletarian internationalism and socialist foreign policy. The success or failure in removing the hindrances and obstacles from the path of the struggle to settle the Israeli-Arab conflict on the basis of the mutual recognition of the just national rights of both sides and opening a high road to peace, independence, social and cultural progress of the nations of the region, is in a large measure dependent on the outcome of this argument. All the development that Israel and her neighbors have experienced since our Fifteenth Congress prove the correctness of the position we adopted at the time of the crisis in our party, when the Toubi-Wilner group left the Israeli Communist Party. Their point of departure was—and remains—Arab chauvinism and Jewish national nihilism wrapped in the cloak of dogmatism and factionalism which changes its colors like a chameleon in accordance with the measures of the Arab leaders and their supporters. The entire course of events until after the Six Day War proved the correctness of the analysis, evaluations, conclusions and prognoses of our communist party which stemmed from our serious attachment to communist principles and our responsible approach to concrete truths of reality. Our communist party refused to become an instrument of anti-Israeli Arab chauvinism by ignoring its dangers and even justifying it, refused to reconcile to submission to it by certain socialist states and important communist parties, to their unbridled accusations against Israel. *This refusal is the cause of the Soviet and other communist parties' anger and their boycott of the Israeli Communist Party.* Our independent and principled positions which are compatible with the best interests of the working class and the masses of the people in Israel, and with our finest internationalist obligations, has inspired respect for our party in the Israeli workers' movement and given it an important place in the renewal process of the international communist movement.

2. FROM WAR TO A JUST AND LASTING PEACE BETWEEN ISRAEL AND HER ARAB NEIGHBORS

The struggle of our party in the sphere of Israeli-Arab relations since the Fifteenth Congress can be divided into two periods: to the time of the Six Day War and after it. What is common to both periods was—and remains—the struggle for peace between Israel and the Arab countries, the relaxation of nationalist tension and hatred, the prevention of the exploitation of the conflict by imperialism—especially the American, and the raising of principles and concrete policy beyond enmity to Jewish-Arab understanding and *reciprocal* recognition of the just national rights of both sides—especially those of the Israeli and the Palestinian Arab peoples. The common denominator was—and is—the defense of Israel's right to exist, and the struggle for a just and lasting peace for the good of both the Israeli and Arab peoples without dictation on one side and surrender on the other; the elimination of the focus of war which is rooted in this national conflict, that by its very existence feeds the ground for imperialist and neo-colonialist intrigues in our region. The common denominator was and remains the struggle—while approving the necessary defense means—against the militarist and chauvinist forces in the government that see the solution to the problem in repetitive military "solutions" of the conflict and against the reluctance of more realistic forces in the government to integrate defense preparations with concrete and reasonable peace initiative to eliminate the conflict in a vigorous and systematic way; consistent opposition to the policy of hatred and refusal to accept the existence of Israel on the part of the Arab rulers; efforts to mobilize help from the socialist countries that have some influence on the neighboring countries to relax the tension and dangers and promote peaceful co-existence and co-operation between the peoples in their struggle for their complete liberation from imperialism.

UNTIL THE SIX DAY WAR

Up to the Six Day War we fought to prevent border incidents, clashes and military reprisals, advocated the resort to static and mobile means of defense in border regions and opposed the penetration of Arab saboteurs and murderers beyond the armistice lines and similar activities in violation of the armistice agreements. We approved Israeli-Arab participation in all the armistice committees and the solution of border quarrels by that means. We demanded that the government support political activity among all the international factors for the cessation of terrorist activities and the promotion of a just, peaceful settlement of the Israeli-Arab conflict. We demanded an agreement between the world powers to check the arms race in our region and systematically struggled for the prohibition of the use of atomic weapons in the Near East. We opposed militaristic declarations and onesided activities to the detriment of others—from any side. With this campaign we combined our struggle for the immediate abolition of the military rule, the complete stoppage of the policy of national discrimination and the guarantee of completely equal rights to the national Arab minority in our country.

In accordance with the resolution of the Fifteenth Congress our party proposed until the Six Day War a peace program based on the principle of an agreed-upon solution to the problem of Palestine on the basis of the right of self-determination of both the Jewish and Arab peoples which provided that:
a) Israel needs to recognize the right of the Arab refugees to return to their homeland or receive commensurate indemnity.
b) Both sides need to reveal a willingness to solve the territorial problem justly and peacefully by a mutual agreement between the authoritative representatives of the Israelis and Arabs who will jointly determine the permanent agreed-upon boundaries, the boundaries of peace.
c) The Arab states need to recognize the existence of the state of Israel and its legal rights including her right of free navigation in the Suez Canal and the

Straits of Tiran, abolish the Arab boycott of Israel and reach an agreed-upon settlement of the partition of sources of shared water, etc.

We warned that the lack of *mutual* recognition of the legal rights of both sides would continue to nourish animosity and chauvinism which bear the danger of a military confrontation that will aid imperialism, the main source of the danger of war.

Faithfulness to Leninism on the national question as on all others guided our party to the integration of Israeli patriotism and proletarian internationalism, support of the rights of the discriminated Arab people of Palestine with opposition to the nationalistic approach of its spokesmen who intend to infringe upon the rights of the Israeli people. Our responsibility to the Israel working class and the entire Israeli people was and is inseparable from our internationalist responsibilities. *Thus, in spite of the hostile approach of the rulers of the Arab countries and the regressive tendencies of the Arab national movement that denies Israel's right to exist, which we have rejected in the past and will continue to reject in the future, we have not abandoned our positive attitude from the working-class standpoint to the process of anti-imperialist development in some Arab countries, and expressed our solidarity with it.*

While rejecting the chauvinist anti-Israeli approach of the leaders of the Arab national movement, whose most extreme and adventuristic expression was "The Organization for the Liberation of Palestine" and *"El Fatah"*, we welcomed every step of the Arab national movement that contributed towards strengthening economic and political independence and advancing the economic and social interests of the Arab peoples in one country or another whether it be Egypt, Syria or Yemen. We hoped that the strengthening of ties between a number of Arab countries and the U.S.S.R. as well as other socialist countries would have a favorable effect in this respect and promote the chances of Israeli-Arab peace. We judged, and events have proved this judgement to be a mistake —that the restraining and balancing influence on anti-Israeli Arab chauvinism on the part of the socialist countries would be stronger than any attempt by Arab rulers to put the stamp of their chauvinist approach on socialist and democratic factors. In our contacts with the communist parties of socialist and capitalist countries we toiled incessantly for such an exertion of a restraining and moderating influence of socialist factors in a number of Arab countries. We expected this to find expression in public criticism of Arab anti-Israeli chauvinism in the Soviet Union and other socialist countries because of the importance of this matter for the cause of peace and the anti-imperialist struggle, and because of its importance in improving the conditions for the struggle of our party on behalf of a change of Israeli policy in respect to the Arab-Israeli problem and the recognition of the just national rights of the Palestinian Arab people by official government policy.

The twelfth meeting of our Central Committee which was held October 27—28, 1966, convened under increasing tension along Israel's borders due to the laying of mines by "El Fatah" and other terrorist organizations and their subsequent detonation. We strongly demanded that the government should despite these provocations abstain from any measure that might increase the tension which would help the imperialists' designs of intervention and domination. This meeting which condemned all manifestations of militarism and anti-Arab chauvinism in Israel, directed the attention of all the peace-loving factors to the repetitive declarations of the representatives of the Syrian government about guerilla warfare in the "Vietnam style" and obliteration of Israel as the only solution to the Palestinian problem—declarations which endangered peace in the Near East and aided imperialist intrigue.

This question came up again and was discussed in the fourteenth meeting of the party Central Committee on March 17th and 18th, 1967, when tension on the borders mounted daily and threatened to explode. The Near Eastern war crisis soon followed when Egyptian military units entered the Sinai Desert in the middle of May 1967. This action was preceded by Syrian provocations and Israeli reprisals as well as *the deliberate lie* that Israel—as it were—had deployed its best as well as most of its divisions on the Syrian border with the intention of launching an attack against her. The United Nations forces were driven out of their positions at the command of the Egyptian president, a naval blockade of the Straits of Tiran was instigated and a military alliance was concluded between Egypt, Syria, Jordan and Iraq. These aggressive acts were accompanied by official declarations by the Presidents of Egypt and Syria, King Hussein of Jordan and the President of Iraq, that the Arabs were ready for a military showdown with Israel. The emergency session (the sixteenth) of the Central Committee which convened in the hours of the evening and night of May 25–26, 1967, made an appeal to the people in Israel, the Arab peoples and all the forces of peace in the world in order to remove the danger of war and save peace in a joint effort, and decided to send urgent letters to the central committee of the C.P.S.U. and the central committees of the communist parties in a number of other countries, which expressed the views of the Israeli Communist Party on the Near Eastern crisis and the means to solve it and prevent war. To our regret, we didn't receive replies to these urgent appeals.

These aggressive acts of the United Arab Republic and her Arab allies prepared the ground for the Six Day War of June, 1967. Twenty years in which the Arab countries had refused to reconcile themselves to the existence of Israel—and likewise twenty years in which Israel ignored the problem of the Arab refugees, nourished the seeds of dissension and enmity between the two sides. The hatred of Israel overcame all realistic considerations even among the Arab anti-imperialist forces and they played the main role in the deterioration of the situation to war which they called "war in the services of imperialism".

Thus, another Marxist-Leninist assumption of the Israeli Communist Party which had been opposed by all the pseudo-scientific considerations in the journals of certain communist parties was verified. It maintained that although imperialism is the *main* source of the danger of war, it isn't the *only* one since nationalist hatred as such also endangers the peace.

In the entire period preceding the Six Day War our party made unprecedented efforts in the Communist movement to implement the principle of peaceful co-existence between Israel and the Arabs as a way of solving the disputed problems between them peacefully on the basis of respect for the legitimate rights of both sides. While struggling to alter Israeli policy toward the Palestinian problem, we consistently opposed the outbreak of war which would only serve the interests of external factors but not those of the peoples of the region.

After hostilities between the Arab armies and Israel commenced on the morning of June 5, 1967, the special seventeenth meeting of the Central Committee which convened that same morning set forth the Israel Communist Party's attitude towards this war, according to the political aims of the belligerents—a war for the destruction of the state of Israel by the governments of the United Arab Republic and the other Arab countries, and war to preserve the existence, security and sovereign rights of the state of Israel by Israel. *The meeting decided in favour of the participation of the Israeli Communist Party in this battle together with the entire people.*

We learned from Leninism the difference between "the defense of the homeland" as a hypocritical slogan in the service of imperialism abroad and bourgeois reaction at home, and a true, sincere national defense. Therefore, our party participated in the War of Independence of 1948 and opposed the Sinai War of 1956. That is also the reason why we wholeheartedly supported the defense efforts of the entire people in the Six Day War.

That same morning we decided to appeal to the great powers not to intervene in the armed conflict in favor of this or that side, but to make a concerted and agreed-upon effort in the United Nations and outside it to reach an armistice agreement and settle the problem peacefully on the basis of respect for the legal rights of both sides; to call upon all the political factors concerned to urgently convene an international conference to bring peace to the Near East and replace the armistice agreements of 1949 between the Arab states and Israel with a lasting peace agreement.

Thus began the second and graver period in the Near Eastern crisis, and the second and graver period in the struggle of the Israeli Communist Party for peace.

FROM THE SIX DAY WAR TO THE PRESENT

The Six Day War was a war of national defense for the physical existence of the people and the sovereign existence of the state of Israel against a pan-Arabic plan whose professed goal was the destruction of Israel. This struggle in which the United Arab Republic, Syria and Jordan suffered a military rout ended with cease fire lines on the Suez Canal, the Jordan River and the Golan Heights. The Israeli army fought alone without cooperation or assistance from any foreign power. The brilliant victory of the Israeli army saved the existence, security and independence of the state of Israel.

Our party immediately appeared with a demand to convert the military victory into a lever of struggle for a just and lasting peace and opposed territorial annexation. We rejected both the demand from outside that Israeli troops retreat unconditionally to the lines of June 4th as well as the tendencies to make the territorial conquests permanent, which might provide the conditions for a new war. Instead we favored the struggle for peace agreements and security arrangements which would determine permanent agreed-upon boundaries and abolish the territorial conquests, and proposed that all issues connected with the Israeli-Arab dispute should be settled peacefully by both sides for their mutual benefit.

The peace program that our party suggested in public and in the Knesset at the end of the war included the following general points:

a) Self-determination of the Palestinian Arab people in the occupied territories. Their democratic representatives elected in completely free elections will engage in negotiations with the government of Israel for peace agreements that include permanent boundaries, the rehabilitation of refugees, reciprocally friendly economic and other relations as agreed upon.

b) The replacement of the armistice agreements with Egypt, Syria, Jordan and Lebanon by permanent peace agreements on the basis of the international boundaries, freedom of navigation and access over land.

c) A joint regional economic development program to utilize the water of the rivers to irrigate arid areas, produce electricity and extract natural resources.

d) An international agreement of the four great powers to neutralize the region, limit conventional arms, demilitarize the area in respect to atomic weapons and help regional development financially and technically.

Our program which was also proposed in the Knesset on June 21, 1967 met with a very favorable response in an appreciable part of Israeli public opinion.

The battle for peace has become the decisive battle for the masses of the Israeli people, for the majority of the organized Israeli society.

The new problems we encountered on the Israeli-Arab plane affected Israel in general and the Israeli Communist Party in particular—both internally and externally. One of them, the most fundamental, was the problem of defining the nature of the Six Day War.

Not only the Arab camp which was a direct participant in the war, but also the convention of the socialist countries in Moscow on June 9, 1967, defined it as a war of aggression in the service of imperialism and demanded the unconditional withdrawal of Israeli forces to the lines of June 4th while consciously and completely ignoring the basic facts that precipitated this war and forced it upon Israel. Except for socialist Roumania that opposed this spurious evaluation and the definition of Israel as an "aggressor", coupled the Israeli withdrawal with the question of peace and a mutual agreement between Israel and the Arabs, and did not break off diplomatic relations with Israel; and except for socialist Cuba which supported the Arab cause but didn't sever her diplomatic relations with Israel—all the other countries that participated in that convention in Moscow broke off their diplomatic relations with Israel. The communist parties of those countries—and also a number of communist parties in the capitalist countries that followed in their footsteps broke off relations with the Israel Communist Party for the "sin" of considering the Six Day War as a war of national defense of the Israeli people.

The government of the Soviet Union and the governments of a number of other socialist countries one-sidedly favored the pan-Arab front against Israel, thereby continuing their long standing surrender to Arab anti-Israeli chauvinist extortion.

Our party was of the opinion that in the Israeli-Arab conflict, which is a national conflict between neighboring countries exploited by imperialism, the principle of peaceful coexistence obligates the communist movement and the socialist states not to support one belligerent against another, but to favor peace and the attempt to bring the warring sides to negotiation, mutual agreement and peace in order also to undermine imperialist intrigue. The deformation of the one-sided position assumed by certain socialist states caused an entire series of additional deformations that didn't serve the cause of peace, the anti-imperialist struggle, progress or the prestige of the Soviet Union and a number of other socialist states. These distortions added oil to the anti-Israeli Arab chauvinist blaze and the fire of anti-Arab Israeli chauvinism.

In order to justify the distortion of one-sidedness in the Israeli-Arab crisis, the Soviet leaders imposed on the Israeli-Arab armed conflict an arbitrary "theoretical equation" which declared that this conflict was not a clash of conflicting national interests that can be *exploited* by the imperialists, but one of the links in the chain of strategical plans of imperialism against the anti-imperialist Arab front. "Thus"—the lack of willingness to act to localize the conflict and the constant attempt to give it a global, international character is only "logical", and we may add—to the detriment of the cause of peace and the benefit of imperialism. The fate of the Israeli people and the fate of the Palestinian Arab people were, in effect, sunk in the waters of this distorted theoretical conception in the service of the one-sided position of socialist foreign policy. The political tactics of the U.S.S.R. and other socialist countries in connection with the Six Day War presented a contradiction to their recognition of Israel's right to exist and their interest in extinguishing the foci of local wars.

There are those in the communist camp who argue, and not accidentally, that the armed Israeli-Arab conflict was of a *social* rather than of a *national* nature in order to "establish" the assumption of "Israeli aggression". Marxism, as we know, rejected and rejects most correctly the notion that war is a "normal" or inevitable phenomenon in the life of human society. Marxism considers war as a historical phenomenon which is rooted only in certain social relations that cause conflicting class and national interests. When these causes are abolished, the conditions will be created for removing war from the areas of human life.

To our sorrow, in the specific social relations existing in Israel and the Arab countries, including the advanced ones, there still exist the objective and subjective conditions for animosity and national Israeli-Arab conflicts. This national conflict is, of course, the direct result of the existing social relations both in the Israeli society and in the Arab society, and the efforts made to cultivate them by imperialism. But even when we reveal the basic factor in the conflicts between peoples it would be incorrect to make the abolition of these conflicts and the achieving of peace dependent upon the change in the social relations in the Israeli and Arab societies, taking also into consideration the relation of world forces in our time. The national character of the Israeli-Arab dispute can't be denied if one recognizes Israel as a legal, independent and sovereign state, if one negates the arbitrary and chauvinistic criteria of the Arab leaders that Israel is an "artifical creation of imperialism" that doesn't have the right to exist and a colonial "alien sapling" that must be uprooted.

The fear of calling a spade a spade and the refusal to see the national background of the armed Arab-Israeli conflict, are the result of a justified suspicion that in such a case the fact that the Soviet Union and her other partners supported the side of Arab nationalism whose motto was—and remains—the extermination of Israel, will be revealed to everyone.

The facts speak for themselves. If imperialism pursues a policy of encouraging "local wars", which is a fact, the aggressive steps of the rulers of the Arab countries against Israel since the middle of May, 1967 created that opportunity for it. *The common denominator of the Arab anti-Israeli front including anti-imperialistic, monarchal-feudalistic and reactionary elements, was not anti-imperialism, but the openly declared chauvinistic and adventuristic design to exterminate Israel.* Israel's true motive was not an "imperialist mission" or the "downfall of progressive regimes" in Egypt and Syria, but self-defense and the removal of the threat to destroy Israel. The international significance of this armed conflict and the danger that it would be exploited by imperialism, which our party saw and warned against in time, obligated the socialist and anti-imperialist forces to act here as they did in the Pakistani-Indian conflict or the India-Chinese one even before the Six Day War began and especially afterwards. This had to be the line in spite of the pro-western policy of the rulers of Israel and in spite of the policy of war as the only policy against Israel adopted by the rulers of Syria and Algeria who are considered to be the most "progressive". Since the leaders of socialist policy and the anti-imperialist movements did not act in this way in the conflict under discussion, they diminished the prospects of peace between Israel and the Arabs—which would have been a serious blow to imperialism and its global strategy—and were responsible for the failure of their stragegical and tactical measures as well as the cause itself, as the long political struggle over the Near East crisis proves.

The Israeli victory in the Six Day War is not proof that Israel did not face a grave danger, nor does it prove that the expressed threats of extermination uttered by Arab leaders with official authority weren't serious, as people are forever trying to convince us, to lull us into a false sense of security.

AGAINST AN ORIENTATION ON IMPERIALISM

The continuation of the mistaken position that the U.S.S.R. is at odds with political reality, damaging the interests of Israel and the Arabs and being harmful to the growth and unification of the anti-imperialist and democratic peace forces in Israel and the Arab countries, should not diminish our concern over imperialist activity in this region of the Middle East.

De Gaulle's reversal of policy toward Israel—from friendship to demonstrative hostility, his support of the Arab front against Israel, after he received an oil and sulphur concession in Iraq for the French monopolies, revealed once more the nature of imperialist hypocrisy and treason with which we were familiar from past experience with the strategy and tactics of British imperialism toward us. This was an additional instructive fact that should guide Israel not to rely on imperialism.

More and more people in Israel are learning—and will continue to learn—that they can't rely on American imperialism either. It is impossible to equate Israel's national interests with imperialist interests in the Middle East. It is a fact that the American and British oil companies have vital interests in the Arab east and exert tremendous and constant pressure on the American government against Israel and in favor of a policy of appeasement toward the rulers of the Arab countries. These concerns regard Israel as a *nuisance* that obstructs normal relations between them and the Arab countries who have rich oil fields in this region. These facts belie one of the falsehoods of anti-Israeli propaganda, namely, that Israel is a "fortress" for the defense of the interests of the Anglo-American oil magnates and it is for their sake that Israel entered the Six Day War.

American imperialism endeavors to strengthen its economic and strategic positions in the Middle East, enhance its influence in the Arab countries and mainly in Egypt. In accordance with these goals the United States courts Nasser, supplies fighter planes and tanks to Jordan in broad daylight, intrigues in various Arab countries, strengthens the reactionary regimes hostile to Israel no less than the "progressive" ones, and unites forces against all anti-imperialist development in our region and against the Soviet Union.

In contrast to these wayward goals, the goal of Israeli national policy should be genuine peace with the Arab peoples that will pave the road to good neighborliness and fruitful cooperation, strengthen economic and political independence and insure conditions for social and cultural progress.

From the beginning of the Middle East crisis our party warned that American policy would exert pressure on Israel in accordance with American interests, moving from positions of temporary support to a compromise position and attempts to make Israel surrender, in order to prove to the Arab rulers that concessions from Israel could only be obtained by Washington. The best and only choice that Israel has is a policy of non-alignment, an independent, dynamic national policy that will prove to Israel's Arab neighbors and the entire world that Israel doesn't desire to perpetuate the territorial conquests;

that—on the contrary—*Israel desires a just and lasting peace, based on the resolution of the Security Council of November* 22, 1967. Such a policy will help Israel win true friends and strengthen her international position.

IN THE POLITICAL BATTLE FOR PEACE

In all the stages of the political battle since the end of the Six Day War our party had a clear, continuous principled position: Defense of Israel's right to existence and all other legal rights without infringing upon the legal rights of the Arab side and especially—of the Palestinian Arab people; opposition to partial or complete annexation tendencies favored by part of the government of "national unity" and Israeli public opinion; struggle to settle the Israeli-Arab conflict and bring about a just and lasting peace that can be maintained between Israel and the Arabs on the basis of *mutual* recognition of the just national rights of both sides.

The political battle against Israel in the United Nations since the end of the Six Day War ended in failure. The demand of the Arab-Soviet front to reprimand Israel as an aggressor, order her to withdraw unconditionally to the pre-war lines and require her to pay reparations for war damages to the Arab countries failed. The Security Council's resolution of November 22, 1967 put an end to the unjust presumption of the Arab-Soviet front in an international extent and created a logical and reasonable basis for a just and lasting peace in the Middle East which links the evacuation of conquered territories with the recognition of the sovereignty of all the nations in the area, their right to peace and security within recognized and secure boundaries, as well as freedom of navigation in international waterways, a just settlement of the refugee problem, guarantees of the territorial integrity and political independence of every state in the region. The resolutions of the Arab Summit Conference in Khartum in August, 1967 that basically boil down to four negations—no recognition of Israel, no negotiations with Israel, no peace with Israel and no settlement of the Palestine problem—completely contradict the unanimous resolution of the Security Council of November 22, 1967.

In the present circumstances our party takes the formal agreement of the governments of Israel, Egypt and Jordan, to the Security Council resolution as a point of departure and struggles so that the government of Israel will pursue an unequivocable and clear policy based on that resolution. Such a a policy would be a contribution to the prospects of peace and would lower the wave of annexationist tendencies which demoralize our youth, distort the image of Israel in the world and blemish the purity of the defensive Six Day War.

The struggle for a just and lasting peace is the basic assumption of this Security Council resolution and that should be the goal of national Israel policy. We appeared and shall continue to appear in favor of flexibility about the form of the negotiations in their first stages in spite of our objective conviction that the demand for direct negotiations is completely just and pertinent.

Those in the government and among the people, who favor territorial annexations and want to convert the cease-fire lines into permanent boundaries of Israel—whatever the reason—know or should know that the objective significance of this wish is the encouragement of the tendency of a large-scale war of revenge against Israel on the part of the Arab world on a scale that can't be imagined today and in circumstances that can't be foreseen. On the other hand, the political realists—who are proportionately more numerous among the masses of the people than among the members of the government—want to struggle for peace and demand in effect secure and recognized boundaries in the framework of peace agreements and security arrangements in accordance with the resolution of the Security Council that stipulates the conditions for Israeli withdrawal. The annexationists either don't believe in peace or don't want it; the others believe in peace and want it. Our party is struggling against the adventuristic annexationist policy and strengthening the realistic and peace-promoting policy. Such a policy can exert a positive and moderating influence on realistic circles in the Arab society. *In the name of this policy we point to the need of disbanding the government of national unity and establishing a peace government based on a firm majority in the Knesset.*

Today our party is more convinced than ever that the position it adopted in June, 1967 that the government should make it possible for the Palestinian Arab people in the occupied territories to implement their right to self-determination is most vital. The Palestinian Arab people should determine its democratic and peace-loving representation to conduct negotiations with the Israel government on all problems requiring a solution, including the settlement of the Arab refugee problem. This would create the conditions for new relations between Israel and the Arab people—not the relations of conquerors and conquered but the relations of equals, and contribute to the solution of the entire Israeli-Arab dispute.

Our party suggests at this time the same principled basis that guided us in the Fifteenth Congress: mutual recognition; agreement and equality; peace and security; and the solution of all disputed problems between Israel and the Arabs, in the framework of peace and security agreements.

The struggle of our party for a responsible, national policy of this kind is linked with our appeal to the Soviet Union and other socialist countries to renew their diplomatic relations with Israel and shift from their one-sided positions to a policy of bringing the parties closer to negotiations and peace.

Although our communist party has its own program for the solution of the Israeli-Arab dispute it will be ready to support any peaceful solution that will take the legal rights of both sides into consideration.

Our party sees a contradiction between the Soviet Union's desire to avoid another war in the Middle East and her constant and considerable support of the policy of the Arab leaders who refuse to make peace with Israel as a sovereign, independent state. It is our expectation that in the light of the dangers inherent in a situation of no war and no peace, the Soviet Union will finally abandon her anti-Israeli approach and adopt a policy of bringing the parties to the controversy closer together and of consideration for the just rights of all the peoples in the Middle East, including Israel.

The separate principled position of socialist Roumania on the question of the Israel-Arab dispute and the present crisis; the new development in Czechoslovakia which among other things, includes the demand by popular opinion for a change in the direction of a balanced relationship to Israel and the Arab countries; the sober voices heard more frequently from the Yugoslav press,— all these facts show that there is a reasonable prospect for a change. The "eclipse" in our movement will pass and give way to the purity of the noblest principles of Marxism-Leninism and proletarian internationalism. *Our party will continue to fight for peace, justice for the Israeli and Arab peoples, mutual understanding and the complete settlement of the Israeli-Arab conflict.*

3. FROM A POLICY OF DEPENDENCE ON IMPERIALISM—TO A POLICY OF PEACE AND NON-ALIGNMENT; FROM A POLICY OF ENCOURAGING CAPITAL—TO A POLICY OF ENCOURAGING LABOR

In the time between the Fifteenth and Sixteenth Congresses our party engaged in a continuous and consistent struggle for a basic change of government policy at home and abroad, both before and after the establishment of the government of "national unity". The events of the past year in the realms of the Israeli-Arab crisis, of social and economic life, completely justified both our opposition to the establishment of the "government of national unity" and our systematic struggle to disband it and replace it with a government of peace and social progress based on a solid majority in the Knesset.

The Eshkol government tried to change its foreign policy to some extent but didn't do so consistently. This found expression in a number of attempts to improve relations with the Soviet Union and other socialist countries, while strengthening relations of dependence with the United States and Western Germany, which sometimes bordered on open or concealed identification with them.

These efforts, that provoked the wrath of the bourgeois right and the adventuristic "guardians" of security at that time, did not succeed because of the attachment to the imperialist west that dominates Israeli foreign policy and also due to the unwillingness of the U.S.S.R., which relied more and more on its influence on the rulers of the Arab countries. The facts prove that when socialist Roumania showed a readiness to maintain and expand cultural and economic relations with Israel, the government replied willingly.

Our party is struggling for an independent, peace-seeking Israeli foreign policy that isn't identified with either of the rival blocs in the world. This struggle proceeds from the experience and the objective assumption that imperialism and neo-colonialism, that promote wars and the enslavement of peoples to their strategic and rapacious interests, are not a support for Israel as for all nations in general . . . .

Bankrupt in Vietnam, American imperialism faces the same certain prospect also in the Mid-East. The goal of American imperialism is not to help Israel but to exploit her for its own interests in the Middle East. A genuine national and responsible far-seeing Israel policy cannot rely on the temporary presence of the United States in our region.

The pragmatic, unserious considerations are also operative in Israeli foreign policy toward militaristic Germany. They also imply a lack of national pride as the neo-Nazi rulers themselves expressed a certain "uneasiness" about the rising strength of the avowedly Nazi party in the recent elections.

4. JOINT FORCES FOR THE CREATION OF A PROGRESSIVE ISRAELI SOCIETY

Our party devotes a great deal of attention to the problem of creating an Israeli society to influence, in a progressive spirit, the solution of the basic problems: peace, democracy and workers' rights. We are struggling for profound democratic changes in Israeli foreign and internal policy, Israeli-Arab relations, questions of the Arab national minority in Israel, Israeli economy and culture. Our struggle to defend, widen and deepen democracy is inseparable from our struggle for a fundamental change in Israeli policy. Our struggle for necessary reforms in existing capitalist relations of production by democracy and democratic means is not our party's basic goal; it is a lever to guarantee conditions for such democratic changes as will help future socialist transformations in Israeli society. This struggle is especially vital for Israeli youth, which has been hit hard by the existing regime in which monopoly foreign and local capital dictate policy to the government.

The defense of democracy and the basic interests of the Israeli people and especially of the working class is the point of departure for the struggle which our Communist Party is waging—and will continue to wage—against national discrimination and unfair treatment of the Arab minority in Israel in every sphere of life, for the struggle against misery and any prejudicial treatment of the working and poverty stricken strata of Israelis of Asian and African origin in every respect, against militant religious compulsion making use of governmental authority, adversely affecting the masses and severely infringing on the the democratic principles of freedom of conscience, guaranteed in the "Charter of Independence". This struggle is being waged also in favor of the annulment of the "Emergency Defense Regulations" inherited from the days of British rule, because they contradict the very basis of democratic statehood, the democratic liberties of society and of the individual; in favor of the enactment of a democratic and secular constitution for the State of Israel. We oppose the designs for the abolition of the country-wide proportional-representation system of election or for the raise of the minimum vote required for appearing on the ballot in the parliamentary elections. Our Communist Party favors the defense of democratic freedoms and rights of the trade unions, of the workers and all the wage-earners in their places of work, and the prevention of any economic, political and/or police pressure on workers. We favor transmitting the human and national progressive cultural values to Israeli youth as a firm foundation in the educational, cultural and artistic life of our country, thus counteracting the negative, harmful influences of contemporary, decadent capitalist culture and the various deformations in Israeli society which in combination produce the moral-spiritual crisis befalling certain circles of Israel youth.

SHMUEL TAMIR

Shmuel Tamir was born in Jerusalem in 1923. An advocate, he received his legal training in the city of his birth, which he also served as deputy regional commander of the *Irgun Zvai Leumi* (National Military Organization, an underground group dedicated to the eviction of the British from Palestine). For these activities the English deported him to Kenya. After the State of Israel was created, he was one of the founders of *Herut,* an ultra-nationalist party under the leadership of Menahem Begin.

Herut's alignment in 1965 with the centrist liberal party to form the *Gahal* Bloc as an alternative to the labor coalition government was not much to Tamir's liking. That year the new coalition lost ground in the elections to the Knesset, capturing only 21 per cent of the vote, less than the total percentage of the two parties in the previous election. Tamir and his followers broke away from Herut to form a new party: The Free Center.

Tamir's indictments are all-embracing, sounding caveats in all directions. Paradoxically, like former labor leader David Ben-Gurion, Tamir wants to do away with the "old fashioned" electoral system and to curb party power. No political party, he insists, should be allowed to maintain private enterprises in industry or agriculture as this makes many voters depend economically on the party. Even more zealously than Begin, he urges Israel to keep all areas she occupied in 1967. Thus in the political spectrum of the country Tamir has emerged as a leader of the right-wing opposition to the labor party and to Gahal. In the 1969 Knesset elections the splinter party lost ground.

The following is a resume of some of Tamir's views, gathered from speeches and articles and sent to the anthology by their author.

After the Victory—Dangers and Prospects

by SHMUEL TAMIR

THE SENSE OF MAGNIFICENT military victory, the spiritual exaltation of our entire people, the whole-hearted identification on the part of the Jews in other countries and the feelings of esteem shown Israel throughout the free world, may possibly deflect our attention from certain vital political lessons.

The First Lesson: The declarations voiced by the color-bearers of Arab imperialism, with Abdul Nasser at their head, regarding the destruction of Israel as their central and supreme aim, are true and unequivocal. We should hope and strive for peace with an Arab state or states, but with the domineering Arab imperialism real peace is inconceivable.

The Second Lesson: Any war between Egypt or Syria and Israel automatically becomes a three-front war, whatever the underlying reasons for this may be. Thus it was in the time of our "friend" Abdullah, and thus events repeat themselves with his grandson, Hussein.

The Third Lesson: The paltry and at times non-existent significance of international guarantees, especially those not based on specific and immediate interests. The frightened collapse of the United Nations troops, the unrestrained, openly proclaimed violation of distinct commitments by France and Great Britain, and the endless hesitations on the part of the great sea-powers in the face of the blocking of the Straits of Tiran, should destroy the illusions of even the staunchest Utopian.

The Fourth Lesson: This one should have been impressed on us also in the Sinai Battle: breaking the Egyptian army is in itself, despite its breath-taking consequences, only a temporary solution. A people which numbers 27 million souls and is aided by world powers can, notwithstanding its profound fundamental weaknesses, rehabilitate its army in several years' time.

The Fifth Lesson: Israel's previous borders constitute a direct, tempting and continuous invitation to attack and to calculated annihilation. The Golan Heights as a base for Syrian artillery, the hilltops of Ephraim and Judea in Jordanian hands, and the Gaza Strip and northern Sinai under Egyptian authority, place Jerusalem, Tel Aviv, the valleys, the Sharon, the south, and all the other centers of our population on the front-line, turning every battle into a fight for life or death for the State and for its inhabitants. At best these borders make the life and very existence of Israel and its inhabitants dependent on a total, well-nigh inhuman preparedness, permanently attached to the second-hand of the clock, for the purpose of trying to ensure for us the first sixty seconds' initiative and surprise.

The Sixth Lesson: The Palestinian Arab population beyond Israel's borders is the center and forefront of the hostility directed against us, while the Arab population within the scope of Israel's authority did not cause us any damage whatsoever, not even in war-time.

These indisputable facts point to the first inference: the necessity of exploiting to the full every advantage we gained in order to guarantee the new borders. Only rarely does so firm a moral and political basis present itself for keeping captured, liberated areas in the hands of the victor-state as it does in our case. Even the individual who belittles ancient historic rights and ignores the mandate of the 1920's, cannot deny the fact that Trans-Jordan was never granted any rights in western Palestine, not even in the United Nations Resolution of 1947. It was the Palestinian Arabs—who according to the U.N. resolution were directed to join together as an independent state—who caused its defeat. By placing his army in Abdul Nasser's hands, Hussein voluntarily or involuntarily launched an all-out attack on Israel, turning all territories in western Palestine under his rule into bases of attack, thereby further justifying Israel's maintaining its control in those areas. The same judgment applies to the Gaza Strip and also to northern and western Sinai, which three times served as bases for Egyptian assaults in the plan to defeat and exterminate Israel. Therefore, not only is Israel's right to occupy Nablus, Hebron and Gaza not inferior to its right to Lydda and Western Galilee (which are outside the original dividing boundaries) but the recent military and political realities reinforce the validity of these rights. As to our holding the Golan Heights, El-Arish, Abu-Aweigila, and the Bay of Solomon—this is certainly more justified from an international point of view than was Egypt's control of Palestinian Gaza or Jordan's seizure of the Western Wall or of the Latrun Road, both of which were, according to the United Nations resolution, to remain open and accessible to Israel.

It is evident however that Israel's political reasoning lags considerably behind the operational speed of its military forces. While the Israel army's mark of identification is its initiative of attack, Israel's political stand is marked by apologetic defense.

When the fighting erupted on the morning of June 5th, Israel had no well-defined aims for war or peace. The goal of disrupting the threatening Egyptian forces, or of breaking the blockade imposed on the Tiran Straits, even though attained by means of a matchless military offensive, was nevertheless, from a political point of view, defensive. Such too was the reaction to the Jordanian and Syrian attacks.

When, at the conclusion of the first four days of fighting, our Chief of Staff informed the world via the press that the Israel Defense Forces had fulfilled the mission assigned to them and that our army had reached the Suez and the Jordan, our Air Force was in almost absolute command of the entire expanse of the heavens, and our troops were arrayed 70 kilometres from Cairo and 50 kilometres from Amman (as well as 10 kilometres from Aqaba, Jordan's sole outlet to the sea). Two days later our forces were 60 kilometres from Damascus.

The time has not yet come to consider the question of whether the government then in command could have ordered our victorious armies to attempt to dictate peace terms inside the capital city of one of the enemy countries in order to end the military campaign with a political solution, to prevent this third round from being merely a phenomenal triumph which brought us magnificent achievements but which basically may be in danger of ending in a blind alley. What is quite clear is that once the fighting was over, Egypt and her allies, large and small, immediately renewed their propaganda and their political onslaughts, whereas Israel began to lose its initiative. The government of Israel waived the opportunity of retaliating with a political counter-attack; failed to raise the elementary demand that the United Nations oust any state which threatened to destroy a U.N. member-state; failed to denounce in a world-wide program of information the murderous plans of the new war-criminals; did not categorically demand the immediate opening of the Suez Canal while stressing the fact that Egypt's continued blocking would justify other powers' guaranteeing free passage; and did not even take from our foes their chief political and propagandistic weapon by refraining from an explicit declaration to the effect that the problem of the Arab refugees was now solved and that we would, with international assistance, see to their rehabilitation in the liberated areas of Palestine and the territory we occupied in Sinai.

Instead of all the above, what most of the official speakers articulated was an apologetic version which takes withdrawal for granted, adding only the reservation: "We shall not withdraw until . . ." The inescapable result has been that even the friendliest nations undertook only to define the conditions and the time-table for the withdrawal. Due to Israel's silence not one voice was raised in the United Nations to warn against rewarding the aggressor and to demand that he be prevented from returning to the bases from which he might be tempted to test his luck again and again toward the possibility of crowning one of his criminal attempts with success.

Our failure with regard to the political and propagandistic aspects directed outside was soon followed by voices inside calling for withdrawal. These strange, numerous voices are prompted by a variety of factors. The inhabitants of the central portion of our country are not fully conscious of the military significance of the Golan Heights and of the areas of western and northern Sinai; the brief hours of shelling experienced by the communities of the coastal plains, the swift destruction of the Jordanian artillery posts, and our army's lightning attack on the Jordanian armored units bent on advancing to the sea— all of these dimmed or even destroyed the sensitivity of many people to the severe danger which threatened the heart of our country as long as the hilltops of Ephraim and Judea were occupied by other than our own forces; the rapid and decisive victory and the losses described as relatively light were woven into a rather mystic belief that in any contest, under any conditions whatsoever, between us and all of the Arab countries, we would always emerge triumphant. Let us not forget moreover that for the great majority of Israel's residents the Western Bank was unfamiliar ground, and aside from the tie, admittedly important, of blind yearning and faith, they had none of the direct attachment which binds our country's old-timers to the long-familiar, well-loved landscapes of the liberated areas. Above all, there are the deep and understandable misgivings regarding the million Arabs, misgivings born of a life-long tradition of fear of strangers, introversion, isolationism and *ghetto* in all its manifestations.

This readiness to relinquish almost voluntarily vital Palestine territory because of the apprehension regarding the absorption of its inhabitants, was at the core of the withdrawal from the Gaza Strip after Operation Sinai [1957]. Several weeks ago we were on the verge of being forced to pay a tragic price for this act. The meaning of this state of mind—which has prompted most of the proposals for establishing a Palestine state or granting autonomy to the Arab Triangle—is in fact a confession of the failure of the original Zionist program. The great Zionism, that of Herzl, Nordau and Jabotinsky, whose aim was not the establishment of a new ghetto on the shores of the Mediterranean Sea but of a modern state that would become a weighty political, economic and social factor abroad—always accepted in advance the existence of an Arab minority within the sovereign Jewish state, despite all the complicated problems this implied. In the early thirties the Jewish community of Eretz Yisrael numbered four hundred thousand; later it grew to six hundred thousand, while the number of Arabs in Eretz Yisrael totalled 900,000. The demand for a Jewish state to be established at once was voiced on the basis of these figures. No one anticipated the Arabs' flight; everyone expected them to remain in our midst.

Now for some reason we seem to be afraid, so that many prefer that we sentence ourselves to suffocation rather than accept a supreme challenge.

Anyone who means to return us to the narrow bottle-neck of the 11 kilometres that stretch from Kalkliyeh to Herzliyah's seashore, or the 14 kilometres between Tul-Karm and Netanya, or even to widen these suffocating strips by a few kilometres, sentences our future life, at best, to a ghetto in the shadow of constant threat.

Of all the Arabs in this region, the Palestinian Arabs are the only ones with whom our historic clash occurred and they alone have concrete claims against us. They are also the most advanced of all the Arabs in the region. Precisely for this reason and in the light of our experience with the Arabs living among us, it behooves us to include them within the bounds of our state and not to fall into the trap of establishing a new political framework for them. We should rehabilitate the Arabs who were uprooted from their homes, inside the enlarged Israel, in a sincere and thorough fashion. We would solve thereby a real and painful human problem fraught with great suffering, and simultaneously free ourselves of the severe, malignant political weapon which has been aimed at us these twenty years, and which is now once again being directed at us from all the capitals of the world.

Anyone who is prepared to erect for the Palestine Arabs a new political framework, whether independent or autonomous, builds with his own hands the political structure which will by degrees eventually become the most aggressive anti-Israeli factor in the entire area. No matter what military controls are imposed on it, any such framework will by degrees evolve into a state of Ahmed Shukairy [a former commander of Arab guerillas]. Similarly, autonomy, under Israel's supervision cannot escape such a fate. In recent times all the autonomous structures were rapidly transformed into independent states in the fullest sense, especially when sovereign national factors with a close ethnic basis existed on the other side of the border.

Admittedly, in order to tackle the new problems and digest the fruits of victory, we shall be forced to undertake a thorough-going re-evaluation of Israel's economic structure, society, and internal authorities. We shall have to assert once again that mass immigration to Israel is now the supreme mandatory requirement, completely outweighing all other accounts and considerations. We shall have to develop a new program of settlement the like of which we did not know even in the first years following the establishment of the State. We shall have to amend the law of citizenship to incorporate realistic yet decent changes which the new facts dictate. Substituting the district system for the present system of elections will become imperative. What is more, we shall be duty-bound to exert the utmost effort and draw up from our innermost beings that balanced combination of human tolerance and national aggressiveness that is indispensable for vanquishing the ocean of problems we now face.

Whereas in the days preceding May 1967 the State had in certain aspects arrived at a cul-de-sac, the people in their hour of destiny rose to sublime heights. Once again we saw demonstrated that, when pressed into a narrow frame our people tends toward disintegration, discovering untold reservoirs of strength within itself only as a great nation engaged in a contest worthy of its greatness.

Its spectacular military feats opened before Israel horizons and expanses rich in promise and pregnant with danger. Only political enterprise and spiritual daring, matching the military sweep and incomparable courage of ZAHAL, our army, can subdue them.

The decisions we make now will affect the future destiny of our people and our country. Even though considerable importance accrues to the position maintained by outside factors, in the final analysis it is our own will that will determine the results.

ARIE ELIAV

Arie L. Eliav was born in 1921 in Moscow and was brought at the age of three to Palestine. Educated at the Hebrew University and at agricultural schools in England, he was one of the most effective leaders of *Aliyah Beth* (illegal immigration to Palestine under the British regime). His exploits were legendary. During the war of independence he attained the rank of Lt. Colonel. Later he served successively as Deputy Minister of Industry and Commerce; Agriculture; Finance; Immigration and Absorption. In 1969 he was elected secretary-general of the Labor Party *(Avodah)*; Israel's plurality party. In 1971 he resigned from his post, devoting his time to research.

Eliav's extraordinary skills were evidenced as director of the settlement projects Lahish and Arad in the Negev desert. He also had diplomatic service as First Secretary in Israel's embassy in Moscow. For a time he was the late Prime Minister Eshkol's special adviser.

Affectionately known as "Lyova", Eliav is a "comer" in Israeli politics, one of the younger people associated with the Old Guard. But he is also trusted and respected by the opponents of the Old Guard. His charisma, as well as his ability to synthesize various points of view, make him very effective. Thus he had a great deal to do with getting Prime Minister Eshkol and political rival Moshe Dayan together on the eve of the Six Day War—no mean achievement.

A man of vision, Eliav foresaw Israel as the culturo-scientific center of the Middle East. Unlike many other leaders in the country he anticipated sizeable immigration from the "lands of prosperity"—United States, England, France—as well as from the countries behind the Iron Curtain. These people with their skills in modern technology, he believes, could easily establish Israel as the focal point for the medical, engineering and computer sciences.

In the following article, ISRAEL AND PALESTINIANS, *National Jewish Monthly*, July-August, 1969, pp. 11, 26–27, Eliav offers a solution to the problem of the Palestinian Arabs on the basis of his idea of socio-economic and culturo-scientific planning.

Israel and Palestinians

by ARIE L. ELIAV

Zionism set itself three targets:

1. Establishing a Jewish State in the Land of Israel.
2. Providing a refuge in this State for any Jew who wished or needed one.
3. Creating in this State a new society based on justice, equality, and freedom of man, on the heritage of the Prophets of Israel and the Jewish moral law, and on the social teachings of the world's great thinkers: a developing society which would create fresh values and become a symbol to all Jews and a model to the world.

Only one of these aims was fully realized: the State of Israel came into being. The other two are, however, an integral part of the national movement of renaissance and it might even be said that the state was created in order to attain them. Yet we are far from having done so.

We have this on the credit side: under conditions of continuous siege by the Arabs, generations of thinkers, workers, and fighters established the State, where one-fifth of the Jewish people live and where new and unique patterns of life have emerged. The Jews of Israel have given to the Jews of the world a glorious symbol and an unceasing source of national Jewish pride. Israel's creativity in the social field has been a model to other nations.

HOSTILITY SLOWS PROGRESS

But there is another side. The realization of the Zionist dream has led to a bitter and terrible dispute between us and the Arabs, particularly the Palestinian Arabs. The central question is how to realize the aims of bringing many more Jews to Israel and creating a progressive society in the face of this terrible Arab hostility, which is a tremendous obstacle to our progress.

Historically, Zionism was born at about the same time as the Arab nationalist movement. Emerging from national struggles against the Turks, the British, and the French, the Arabs realized the greater part of their political aspirations, and set up over a dozen independent states which are now in various stages of political and economic development. The Arabs set themselves also to—wipe Israel off the map. This aim was not realized, nor is it possible.

But in the course of this struggle there emerged a twin to the Jewish nation in the Land of Israel: the Arab-Palestinian nation. Perhaps it is a paradox of history that Zionism was a contributing cause of its creation.

The Palestinian nation is identifiable by a national consciousness, by continuous territory where most of the Palestinians live, by a history of several decades replete with battles and wars, and a diaspora which maintains a link with the Palestinian homeland. At the same time it is conscious of a common national catastrophe, sacrifice, suffering, and heroes. It has dreams and the start of a national literature.

Palestinians number some $2\frac{1}{2}$ million, about a million living in the Israeli-administered territories of the West Bank and the Gaza Strip, another million on the east bank of the Jordan, while the remainder are dispersed throughout the Arab world. Our relations with them constitute the most important element of our relations with the Arab world as a whole, and the two are inseparably linked. Herein lies the key to the solution of the over-all problem.

Prior to the Six Day War, the vast majority of the Palestinian Arabs lived in Jordan, where they developed their national consciousness and tools of government. The Six Day War cut Jordan and the Palestinian Arab nation in two. When conditions of peace arrive we must take into account the possibility that the two parts of the Palestinian nation will be reunited.

Now let us consider the roots of the problem of the Israeli-occupied territories. The armistice lines were fixed by the sword in 1948, after a battle of life and death forced on Israel by the Arabs. That war fixed the borders of Israel and its demographic composition. Hundreds of thousands of Arabs fled across the borders. In its 21 years of existence, Israel has taken in hundreds of thousands of immigrants and developed its own way of life and culture, to realize the Zionist dream—a Jewish State with the aims of taking in more Jews and building a progressive society. We said that to realize these aims we wished for peace with the Arab nations and that we had no expansionist aims.

But the Palestinians sought revenge. And the Arab States exploited the refugees and their misery as a weapon against Israel. In May, 1967 it appeared to the Arab leaders that the time had come to annihilate Israel. In six days the Israel Army reached new borders, broader and safer. But it was a desire for neither conquest nor "liberation" that propelled the troops forward. The strength of the Army and of the nation derived from its determination to defend its country. And in defending it the Army reached Suez, Tiran, the Jordan, and the Hermon.

PEACE WOULD RELEASE LAND

We must prove to ourselves, to the Arabs, and to the world that we are holding territories only as a surety for security and peace, and not as objects of annexation. Let our neighbor-enemies know that if they talk peace and not war, and if they are prepared to sign peace treaties containing suitable guarantees, we will be prepared to give up "territories". Let the Arab states know that we shall never deny the Palestinians' right to self-determination and that we are ready to help them set up the State in which they will find fulfillment of their national aspirations.

A declaration to this effect by the State of Israel would bring about a radical change in our international position. It is very doubtful whether any serious power could then threaten to remove us from territories without peace in exchange. Friends and enemies alike will understand that until peace is achieved we stand fast at the borders of June 11, 1967.

As for Jerusalem, it is Zion, the focus of Jewish yearning for the Land of Israel. It is the capital of Israel. Everyone understands that our capital city cannot again be divided. But at the same time we must understand the special status of the Old City for the Moslem and Christian worlds. We must find a way of satisfying the feelings of these two world religions regarding their holy places. We must come to an arrangement with the Moslem and Arab world permitting free and honorable access to the Moslem religious sites which would be turned over to the jurisdiction of Moslem institutions. These arrangements, too, would be subject to general peace accords.

A solution to the tragic problem of the Arab refugees, awaits an atmosphere of peace. Agriculture will not play a large role. The West Bank and the Gaza Strip are settled to a high degree of density by Arab farmers, and it will eventually become necessary to engage in more intensive farming and reduce the number of farmers. The solution for the hundreds of thousands of refugees lies essentially in urbanization and industrialization. It will mean building new cities and expanding existing ones on the west and east banks, establishing industrial and tourist enterprises, and increasing the proportion of workers in the services and trade. This program, which can be carried out with the assistance of international funds and with the aid of Israel and the Arab states, also depends on a peace agreement. But until then Israel must not sit with folded hands.

It must start laying the foundations for a solution, or for a number of integrated solutions, to the refugee problem. We must set our most capable men to work to determine means and methods, to fix priorities, and estimate costs. We must draft an over-all plan. By its very existence such a blueprint would be of inestimable value for us, the Arabs, and the world. Even with peace far distant we must begin acting on the general lines of the plan and, so far as possible, start setting up enterprises in the territories we control today. Most important of all is the establishment of a vocational education network for refugee children. But thought must also be given to the start of urbanization, mechanization, and industrialization.

With peace and normal relations with our neighbors—first of all with the Palestinian Arabs—Israel's Arab minority will achieve greater ease. They will be loyal citizens of Israel without the terrible pull of dual loyalties, and find greater scope of action as trade and service develop between Israel and the Arab States. Israelis will be able to travel west and east of the Jordan. Perhaps also—with the agreement of the Arabs—there will be Jewish settlements west and east of the Jordan. A policy of this kind is consistent with the true aims of Zionism and of Israel.

The danger to Israel's existence is no less now than in the period that preceded the Six Day War. Peace is still not on the horizon. Israel must maintain a strong, modern standing army. It is a people's army; the nation's sons and daughters all pass through it. The army will be called upon to carry out a total war against Arab terrorists and at the same time serve as a modern deterrent instrument.

DAVID HOROWITZ

Born in Poland in 1899, David Horowitz was educated in the Universities of Lwow and Vienna. Arriving in Palestine in 1920, he served the Jewish community in that country and later the State of Israel in many capacities: as Secretary of the American Economic Committee for Palestine (which encouraged and directed the flow of American investments into Palestine); Director of the Economic Department of the Jewish Agency for Palestine; expert in economics for the Israeli delegation to the U.N. General Assembly. Later he held the posts of Director-General of the Ministry of Finance and of chairman of the Board of Directors of the Eliezer Kaplan School of Economics and Social Sciences of the Hebrew University.

It was Horowitz who helped negotiate the claims and counterclaims of the United Kingdom and Israel at the termination of the British mandate and who assisted in formulating Israel's indemnity claims from Germany. In recognition of his broad economic knowledge and administrative skills, he was chosen Governor of the Bank of Israel and also Governor for Israel of the International Bank of Reconstruction and Development. He has written many articles and treatises in his field.

Probably the most esteemed financial expert in Israel, Horowitz believes in a pluralistic, mixed economy. His contributions to a new state, struggling for its existence—in the face of the Arab boycott and oscillating from one economic theory to another—were near miraculous. In 1968 he was awarded the Israel Prize, for translating messianic dreams into charts, graphs and statistics.

The following brief statement sent to the anthology is a summation by the author of his basic ideas regarding Israel's economy.

The Economics of Israel

by DAVID HOROWITZ

IN ANY ANALYSIS OF the situation of Israel today, we have first of all to clarify what is the objective of the economic activity of our nation. Admittedly, this is an unusual procedure. In the ordinary way of business, the objective of economic activity in a country is to maintain and support its population. However, in this respect Israel is different. It is an economy with a purpose far beyond the support of the population and connected with the absorption and integration of immigration, its occupational reshuffle and the reconstruction of the country as a whole.

The elements of that wide pattern of objectives can be summarized in one sentence: the economic objective of Israel is to telescope an economic development, which should normally take half a century, into one decade, and thus win the race against time.

Many difficulties and contradictions are involved in this task. The economic policy will have to provide for a rapid growth of the Gross National Product, so as to substitute the country's production for foreign assistance, which may dwindle into insignificance in the not too distant future. This has to be done under conditions of full employment and is to be dovetailed with the integration of immigration. The performance of this task without falling into the trap of inflation which would anyhow defeat the purpose of development is fraught with difficulties, dangers and internal contradictions.

The economic forecast in Israel is based on the assumption that import of capital will gradually decrease and taper off because of the cessation of reparations, personal restitution and other sources of influx of capital, while the amounts necessary for the debt service of the State on account of the Development and Independence Bonds, etc. will increase substantially.

Therefore, rapid development is imperative with a view to bridging the gap in the balance of payments in the face of decreasing assistance from abroad.

With this objective in view, it is essential to expand the capacity of production while the economy of the country has to provide sources of living for the population which has more than quadrupled within the last 20 years.

This is a dual task: the transformation of the economic structure of the State and the transformation of its growing population. These two transformations represent the core of Israel's economic and social problem.

Israel is a country with scarce natural resources and against this background the country has to be transformed by large-scale development of such scarce natural resources as are available, with the help of influx of capital from abroad and accumulation of capital and savings in the country. Investment has to comprise not only capital but simultaneously, skills, exploration of natural resources, research and know-how. As in other small countries, foreign trade must play an important role in the development of the country.

The transformation of the population is most important. Hundreds of thousands of new immigrants who were merchants, peddlers and clerks in their country of origin, had to be absorbed in two decades in agriculture, in industry, in the army and in shipping. Within a short period of time they had to be taught to till the ground, turn a lathe, guard the frontiers, sail the seas. This transformation has not been confined to the occupational reshuffle. These newcomers had to be imbued with the civic spirit and heroic tradition and with the social, economic and political values already created and crystalized in this country.

The geographical transplantation of various segments of the population from over 70 countries is a one-time act. But their social and economic integration is a protracted process; while the first is a logistic task requiring transport and housing, the latter represents the core of the economic problem of Israel.

The fact that a rapid economic development was achieved under a democratic and stable regime was the result of several factors: the particular political conditions and the large scale of import of capital, the quality of human material, the tension in which the tremendous effort was rooted, the security conditions—all of them created a set of circumstances unique in character.

Import of capital did not, of course, entirely eliminate the need for policies which must have been unpopular; for a period, a regime of austerity had to be maintained, heavy taxation and the diversion of resources from consumption to investment imposed on the population. Evidently, however, the financing of development on the scale accomplished in Israel by internal capital formation, even if at all possible, would have resulted in stresses and strains on the the social and political structure of the country which have no precedent in history and were well-nigh impossible, and thus the import of capital played a most important role in the development of this country.

At the present juncture it is obvious that after the establishment of the physical framework of the economy in the first two decades of the State it will be possible subsequently to utilize the productive capacity of the country for the solution of the problem of economic emancipation. It is intended that the increase of exports, slowing up of imports and increased saving for investment should gradually reduce the gap in the balance of payments so that at the end of the third decade the economy should become self-supporting and the import of capital serve only for its further expansion. The result of this venture in the first two decades is the more conclusive as it was carried into effect under the most difficult conditions:

First—demographic growth, by far exceeding the pace in underdeveloped countries. The population increased within 20 years by 260 per cent or by more than 4 times;

Second—the geo-political and military background were adverse to development. Boycott and blockade were a serious handicap to the economic development of the country and the geo-political situation involved a heavy expenditure for arms;

Third—the experiment was conducted in a small and arid country, with scarce natural resources, with no coal, iron deposits or substantial oil wells;

Fourth—part of the population brought into the country was accustomed to the European standard of life and that standard had to be maintained within the framework of a poor and underdeveloped country;

Fifth—the occupational structure of a part of the population and its cultural background were unadapted to the exigencies and needs of the country. An occupational reshuffle of most of the population became imperative;

Sixth—people coming from 70 countries, with nearly as many languages, sometimes centuries apart in their development, had to be wielded into one ethnic and national entity.

Under these difficult conditions, a sustained growth was achieved, reflected in the annual average increase of the Gross National Product of some 9 to 10 per cent in real terms, an increase of national income of 10–11 per cent in real terms, from IL 1,096 million in 1950 to IL 5,720 million in 1967, an increase in exports within this period from $46 million to $532 million. While in 1949 only 14 per cent of imports were covered by income from exports, in 1967 the proportion was 68 per cent. In 1949 a population of one million was supplied with foodstuffs from local production up to 50 per cent; in 1967 a population of 2.75 million was supplied from domestic production at the rate of over 80 per cent. While in 1949 import of capital represented some 40 to 50 per cent of the total resources of the country, this proportion was reduced to about 16 per cent in 1967.

This progress was not only quantitative but caused also a fundamental change in the economic structure of the country.

In the future the Gross National Product will have to increase at the rate of at least 8 per cent per annum in order to secure full employment and to increase the production of goods and services for the increasing population.

The decrease of the gap in the balance of payments will necessitate the rapid increase of exports at the rate of some 15–20 per cent per annum, mainly of industrial products.

Further, production for substitution for imports will have to be increased. In this field also, industry will have to play a predominant role.

Consequently in the next decade a larger proportion of the Gross National Product will have to be directed to exports and serve as a substitute for imports. Mining, international transportation and the chemical industries will have to reach a pace of accelerated growth.

Three main factors will play a decisive role in this qualitative and quantitative transformation of Israel's economy: 1) skill, know-how and initiative; 2) import

---

* Constant prices of 1955

of capital; 3) imponderabilia involved in the historical, national and social background of economic activity.

1) One of the serious obstacles in the way of development in underdeveloped countries is the scarcity of know-how and skill on all levels of development of production and lack of entrepreneurial initiative. Israel is fortunate in having a fairly substantial reserve of experts in many important fields of economic enterprise.

Scientific institutes such as the Hebrew University, the Weizmann Institute and the Technion in Haifa, provide a basis for scientific research and education of experts.

The resources of skill and know-how which are in such short supply in other underdeveloped countries but available in Israel are the result of immigration under the pressure of persecution, or motivated by a positive desire to participate in the reconstruction work in the country.

2) Import of capital into the country in the first 20 years of Israel's existence as a State was very substantial. Its continuation is indispensable for the further development of the country, particularly in view of the renewed immigration.

3) The imponderabilia and enthusiastic dedication to the cause and initiative, resulting from aspirations deeply rooted in the soul of the nation, are most important factors, although they do not lend themselves to quantitative evaluation. This view was strikingly expressed by an outside observer, the former Ambassador of the U.S.A. to India, Professor Galbraith, who sums up this development as follows:

> "One country that has shown great advance since the war, including great capacity to make effective use of aid, has been Israel. It is singularly unendowed with natural resources. It has no oil wells, few minerals, insufficient water and not much space. But all the four elements mentioned—high literacy and a highly educated élite, the sense and the reality of social justice, an effective government and a strong sense of purpose are all present. So there is a rapid progress. The Israelis, were they forced to it, would better do without their aid than without their education, their sense of shared responsibility and shared gain, their public administration and their clear view of their destiny."

It is our hope that the tremendous forces inherent in our movement of national renascence which were effective in Israel till now, will help us to overcome the difficulties in the coming decade, until the task of economic emancipation will be accomplished in this period.

ABBA EBAN

Born in 1915 in Capetown, South Africa, Abba (Aubrey) Eban was educated at Cambridge where he later served as research fellow and lecturer in Arabic and Oriental languages. He came to Israel in 1940 and was appointed chief instructor and vice-president of the Middle East Arab Center in Jerusalem. He was also drawn into the work of the Political Department of the Jewish Agency for Palestine. In 1947, at the time of the U.N. Palestine partition debates, he was first a member of the delegation and then permanent representative of Israel at the U.N. from 1950 to 1959. He served simultaneously as Ambassador to the U.N. and Ambassador in Washington.

Surmising that he had been absent too long from the state he represented and feeling the necessity of identifying more closely with the people of his country, he returned to Israel, where he has held successively the posts of Minister of Education, 1960–63; Deputy Prime Minister, 1964–65; Foreign Minister since 1965. Until the burdens of his diplomatic responsibilities became too heavy, Eban also was president of the Weizmann Institute of Science and helped make it a world-renowned research center.

Eban has written several books and contributed articles to some of the most prestigious journals. He is the author of the *Modern Literary Movement in Egypt, Zionism and the Arab World, Voice of Israel, Tide of Nationalism,* and *My People.*

Eban was the anointed spokesman of Israel at the United Nations and the world at large. An address of his at the U.N. was a "happening", a special event. Admirers and detractors alike stood in awe of his verbal virtuosity and extemporaneous mind.

Permeated by optimism and faith in the Western countries, Eban is less idolized by the Israelis than by the outside world; for them he seems too much of an exotic bloom. Although a specialist in Islamic and Arab culture, he is deemed too steeped in Western civilization, especially by Israelis who want their country to become a part of the Middle East, not merely an extension of Europe in Asia Minor. Moreover, he is one of the very few members of *Mapai* (the plurality party now merged into *Mifleget Avodah Yisraelit)* who has ascended to the near top without having trod the Histadrut (General Federation of Labor) road.

Nevertheless, Eban has left large footprints on the pages of Israel's history, especially in her diplomacy. Following is his June 19, 1967 speech at the United Nations.

An Address at the General Assembly of the United Nations, June, 1967

by ABBA EBAN

THE SUBJECT OF OUR discussion is the Middle East; its past agony and its future hope. We speak of a region whose destiny has profoundly affected the entire human experience. In the heart of that region, at the very centre of its geography and history, lives a very small nation called Israel. This nation gave birth to the currents of thought which have fashioned the life of the Mediterranean world and of vast regions beyond. It has now been re-established as the home and sanctuary of a people which has seen six million of its sons exterminated in the greatest catastrophe ever endured by a family of the human race.

THE TRUE ORIGINS OF THE MID-EAST CRISIS

In recent weeks the Middle East has passed through a crisis whose shadows darken the world. This crisis has many consequences but only one cause. Israel's right to peace, security, sovereignty, economic development and maritime freedom—indeed its very right to exist—has been forcibly denied and aggressively attacked. This is the true origin of the tension which torments the Middle East. All the other elements of the conflict are the consequences of this single cause. There has been danger, there is still peril in the Middle East because Israel's existence, sovereignty and vital interests have been and are violently assailed.

The threat to Israel's existence, its peace, security, sovereignty and development has been directed against her in the first instance by the neighboring Arab States. But all the conditions of tension, all the temptations to aggression in the Middle East have, to our deep regret, been aggravated by the one-sided policy of one of the Great Powers which under our Charter bear primary responsibility for the maintenance of international peace and security. I shall show how the Soviet Union has, for 15 years, been unfaithful to that trust. The burden of responsibility lies heavy upon her. Today's intemperate utterance illustrates the lack of equilibrium and objectivity which has contributed so much to the tension and agonies.

I come to this rostrum to speak for a united people which, having faced danger to the national survival, is unshakeably resolved to resist any course which would renew the perils from which it has emerged.

The General Assembly is chiefly preoccupied by the situation against which Israel defended itself on the morning of June 5. I shall invite every peace-loving state represented here to ask itself how it would have acted on that day if it faced similar dangers. But if our discussion is to have any weight or depth, we must understand that great events are not born in a single instant of time. It is beyond all honest doubt that between May 14 and June 5, Arab governments, led and directed by President Nasser, methodically prepared and mounted an aggressive assault designed to bring about Israel's immediate and total destruction. My authority for that conviction rests on the statements and actions of Arab governments themselves. There is every reason to believe what they say and to observe what they do.

THE PATTERN OF AGGRESSION—1957–1967

During Israel's first decade the intention to work for her destruction by physical violence had always been part of the official doctrine and policy of Arab States. But many members of the United Nations hoped and some believed that relative stability would ensue from the arrangements discussed in the General Assembly in March 1957. An attempt was then made to inaugurate a period of non-belligerency and co-existence in the relations between Egypt and Israel. A United Nations Emergency Force was to separate the armies in Sinai and Gaza. The maritime powers were to exercise free and innocent passage in the Gulf of Aqaba and the Straits of Tiran. Terrorist attacks against Israel were to cease. The Suez Canal was to be opened to Israel shipping, as the Security Council had decided six years before.

In March, 1957, these hopes and expectations were endorsed in the General Assembly by the United States, France, the United Kingdom, Canada, and other states in Europe, the Americas, Africa, Asia and Australasia. These assurances, expressed with special solemnity by the four governments which I have mentioned, induced Israel to give up positions which she then held at Gaza and at the entrance to the Straits of Tiran and in Sinai. Non-belligerency, maritime freedom and immunity from terrorist attack were henceforth to be secured, not by Israel's own pressure but by the concerted will of the international community. Egypt expressed no opposition to these arrangements. Bright hopes for the future illuminated this hall ten years ago.

BREATHING SPACE FOR LATER ASSAULT

There were times during the past decade when it really seemed that a certain stability had been achieved. As we look back it becomes plain that the Arab governments regarded the 1957 arrangements merely as a breathing space enabling them to gather strength for a later assault. At the end of 1962, President Nasser began to prepare Arab opinion for an armed attack that was to take place within a few brief years. As his armaments grew his aggressive designs came more blatantly to light. On 23 December 1962, Nasser said:

> "We feel that the soil of Palestine is the soil of Egypt, and of the whole Arab world. Why do we all mobilize? Because we feel that the land of Palestine is part of our land, and are ready to sacrifice ourselves for it."

The present Foreign Minister of Egypt, Mahmoud Riad, echoed his master's voice:

> "The sacred Arab struggle will not come to an end until Palestine is restored to its owners."

In March 1963, the official Cairo radio continued the campaign of menace:

> "Arab unity is taking shape towards the great goal—i.e. the triumphant return to Palestine with the banner of unity flying high in front of the holy Arab march."

The newspaper *Al-Gumhuriya* published an official announcement on the same day:

> "The noose around Israel's neck is tightening gradually ... Israel is no mightier than the empires which were vanquished by the Arab east and west ... The Arab people will take possession of their full rights in their united homeland."

Egypt is not a country in which the press utters views and opinions independently of the official will. There is thus much significance in the statement of *Al-Akhbar* on 4 April, 1963:

> "The liquidation of Israel will not be realized through a declaration of war against Israel by Arab States, *but Arab unity and inter-Arab understanding will serve as a hangman's rope for Israel.*"

The Assembly will note that the imagery of a hangman's rope or of a tightening noose occurs frequently in the macabre vocabulary of Nasserism. He sees himself perpetually presiding over a scaffold. In June 1967, in Israel's hour of solitude and danger, the metaphor of encirclement and strangulation was to come vividly to life.

In February, 1964, Nasser enunciated in simple terms what was to become his country's policy during the period of preparation:

> "The noose around Israel's neck is tightening gradually ... Israel is no nightier the time; it is we who will dictate the place."

SYRIA'S "POPULAR WAR" AGAINST ISRAEL

A similar chorus of threats arose during this period from other Arab capitals. President Aref of Iraq and President Ben-Bella of Algeria were especially emphatic and repetitive in their threat to liquidate Israel. They were then far away. The Syrian attitude was more ominous because it affected a neighbouring frontier. Syrian war propaganda has been particularly intense in the past few years. In 1964, the Syrian Defense Minister, General Abdulla Ziada announced:

> "The Syrian army stands as a mountain to crush Israel and demolish her. This army knows how to crush its enemies . . ."

Early last year Syria began to proclaim and carry out what it called a "popular war" against Israel. This was a terrorist campaign which expressed itself in the dispatch of trained terrorist groups into Israel territory to blow up installations and communications centers and to kill, maim, cripple and terrorize civilians in peaceful homes and farms. Often the terrorists, trained in Syria, were dispatched through Jordan or Lebanon. The terrorist war was formally declared by President Al-Atassi on 22 May, 1966, when he addressed soldiers on the Israel-Syrian front:

> "We raise the slogan of the people's liberation war. We want total war with no limits, a war that will destroy the Zionist base."

It is a strange experience in this hall of peace to be sitting with a delegate whose philosophy is: "We want total war with no limits."

The Syrian Defense Minister, Hafiz Asad, said two days later:

> "We say: We shall never call for, nor accept peace. We shall only accept war and the restoration of the usurped land. We have resolved to drench this land with our blood, to oust you, aggressors, and throw you into the sea for good.
>
> "We must meet as soon as possible and fight a single liberation war on the level of the whole area against Israel, imperialism and all the enemies of the people."

From that day to this not a week has passed without Syrian officials adding to this turgid stream of invective and hate. From that day to this, there has not been a single month without terrorist acts, offensive to every impulse of human compassion and international civility, being directed from Syria against Israeli citizens and territory. I would have no difficulty in swelling the General Assembly's records with a thousand official statements by Arab leaders in the past two years announcing their intention to destroy Israel by diverse forms of organized physical violence. The Arab populations have been conditioned by their leaders to the anticipation of a total war, preceded by the constant harassment of the prospective victim.

ISRAEL'S POLICY 1957–1967

From 1948 to this very day there has not been one statement by any Arab representative of a neighbouring Arab State indicating readiness to respect existing agreements on the permanent renunciation of force; to recognize Israel's sovereign right to existence or to apply to Israel any of the central provisions of the United Nations Charter.

For some time Israel showed a stoic patience in her reaction to these words of menace. This was because the threats were not accompanied by a capacity to carry them into effect. But the inevitable result of this campaign of menace was the burden of a heavy race in arms. We strove to maintain an adequate deterrent strength; and the decade beginning in March 1957 was not monopolized by security considerations alone. Behind the wall of a strong defense, with eyes vigilantly fixed on dangerous borders, we embarked on a constructive era in the national enterprise. These were years of swift expansion in our agriculture and industry; of intensive progress in the sciences and arts; of a widening international vocation, symbolized in the growth of strong links with the developing world. At the end of her first decade Israel had established relations of diplomacy, commerce and culture with all the Americas, and with most of the countries of Western, Central and Eastern Europe. In her second decade she was to build constructive links with the emerging countries of the developing world with whom we are tied by a common aspiration to translate national freedom into creative economic growth and progress.

Fortified by friendships in all five continents; inspired by its role in the great drama of development; intensely preoccupied by tasks of spiritual cooperation with kindred communities in various parts of the world, and in the effort to assure the Jewish survival after the disastrous blows of Nazi oppression; tenaciously involved in the development of original social ideas, Israel went on with its work. We could not concern ourselves exclusively with the torrent of hatred pouring in upon us from Arab governments. In the era of modern communications a nation is not entirely dependent on its regional context. The wide world is open to the voice of friendship. Arab hostility towards Israel became increasingly isolated, while our position in the international family became more deeply entrenched. Many in the world drew confidence from the fact that a very small nation could, by its exertion and example, rise to respected levels in social progress, scientific research and the humane arts. And so our policy was to deter the aggression of our neighbours so long as it was endurable; to resist it only when failure to resist would have invited its intensified renewal; to withstand Arab violence without being obsessed by it; and even to search patiently here and there for any glimmer of moderation and realism in the Arab mind. We also pursued the hope of bringing all the Great Powers to a harmonious policy in support of the security and sovereignty of Middle Eastern States.

CUMULATIVE EFFECTS OF ARAB VIOLENCE

It was not easy to take this course. The sacrifice imposed upon our population by Arab violence was cumulative in its effects. But as it piled up month by month the toll of death and bereavement was heavy. And in the last few years it was evident that this organized murder was directed by a central hand.

We were able to limit our response to this aggression so long as its own scope appeared to be limited. President Nasser seemed for some years to be accumulating inflammable material without an immediate desire to set it alight. He was heavily engaged in domination and conquest elsewhere. His speeches were strong against Israel. But his bullets, guns and poison gases were for the time being used to intimidate other Arab States and to maintain a colonial war against the villagers of the Yemen and the peoples of the Arabian Peninsula.

But Israel's danger was great. The military build-up in Egypt proceeded at an intensive rate. It was designed to enable Egypt to press its war plans against Israel while maintaining its violent adventures elsewhere. In the face of these developments Israel was forced to devote an increasing part of its resources to self-defense. With the declaration by Syria early in 1965 of the doctrine of a "day by day military confrontation" the situation in the Middle East grew darker. The Palestine Liberation Organization, the Palestine Liberation Army, the Unified Arab Command, the intensified expansion of military forces and equipment in Egypt, Syria, Lebanon, Jordan and more remote parts of the Arab continent—these were the signals of a growing danger to which we sought to alert the mind and conscience of the world.

ARABS SOUGHT PRETEXT FOR WAR

In three tense weeks between 14 May and 5 June, Egypt, Syria and Jordan, assisted and incited by more distant Arab States, embarked on a policy of immediate and total aggression.

June 1967 was to be the month of decision. The "final solution" was at hand.

There was no convincing motive for the aggressive design which was now unfolded. Egyptian and Soviet sources have claimed that a concentrated Israeli invasion of Syria was expected during the second or third week in May. No claim could be more frivolous or far-fetched. It is true that Syria was sending terrorists into Israel to lay mines on public roads and, on one occasion, to bombard the Israeli settlement at Manara from the Lebanese border. The accumulation of such actions had sometimes evoked Israeli responses limited in scope and time. All that Syria had to do to ensure perfect tranquility on her frontier with Israel was to discourage the terrorist war. Not only did she not discourage these actions; she encouraged them. She gave them every moral and practical support. But the picture of Israeli troop concentrations in strength for an invasion of Syria was a monstrous fiction. Twice Syria refused to cooperate with suggestions made by the UN authorities and accepted by Israel for a simultaneous and reciprocal inspection of the Israeli-Syrian frontier. On one occasion the Soviet Ambassador complained to my Prime Minister of heavy troop concentrations in the north of Israel. When invited to join the Prime Minister that very moment in a visit to any part of Israel which he would like to see the distinguished envoy brusquely refused. The prospect of finding out the truth at first hand seemed to fill him with a profound disquiet. But by 9 May the Secretary General of the United Nations from his own sources on the ground had ascertained that no Israeli troop concentrations existed. This fact had been directly communicated to the Syrian and Egyptian governments. The excuse had been shattered, but the allegations still remained. The steps which I now describe could not possibly have any motive or justification in an Israeli troop concentration which both Egypt and Syria knew did not exist. Indeed the Egyptian build-up ceased to be described by its authors as the result of any threat to Syria.

THE PLAN OF WAR

On 14 May Egyptian forces began to move into Sinai.

On 16 May the Egyptian Command ordered the United Nations Emergency Force to leave the border. The following morning the reason became clear. For on 17 May, 1967, at 6 in the morning, Radio Cairo broadcast that Field Marshal Amer had issued alert orders to the Egyptian armed forces. Nor did he mention Syria as the excuse.

This announcement reads:

> "1. The state of preparedness of the Egyptian Armed Forces will increase to the full level of preparedness for war, beginning 14.30 hours last Sunday.
> "2. Formations and units allocated in accordance with the operational plans will advance from their present locations to the designated positions.
> "3. The armed forces are to be in full preparedness to carry out any combat tasks on the Israel front in accordance with developments."

On 18 May, Egypt called for the total removal of the United Nations Emergency Force. The Secretary-General of the United Nations acceded to this request and moved to carry it out, without reference to the Security Council or the General Assembly; without carrying out the procedures indicated by Secretary Hammarskjold in the event of a request for a withdrawal being made; without heeding the protesting voices of some of the permanent members of the Security Council and of the Government at whose initiative the Force had been established; without consulting Israel on the consequent prejudice to her military security and her vital maritime freedom; and without seeking such delay as would enable alternative measures to be concerted for preventing belligerency by sea and a dangerous confrontation of forces by land.

It is often said that United Nations procedures are painfully slow. This decision was, in our view, disastrously swift. Its effect was to make Sinai safe for belligerency from north and to south; to create a sudden disruption of the local security balance; and to leave an international maritime interest exposed to almost certain threat. I have already said that Israel's attitude to the peacekeeping functions of the United Nations has been traumatically affected by this experience. What is the use of a fire brigade which vanishes from the scene as soon as the first smoke and flames appear? Is it surprising that we are firmly resolved never again to allow a vital Israeli interest and our very security to rest on such a fragile foundation?

EGYPT BENT ON EARLY ASSAULT

The clouds now gathered thick and fast. Between 14 May and 23 May, Egyptian concentrations in Sinai increased day by day. Israel took corresponding precautionary measures. In the absence of an agreement to the contrary, it is legal for any state to place its armies wherever it chooses in its territory. It is equally true that nothing could be more uncongenial to the prospect of peace than to have large armies facing each other across a narrow space, with one of them clearly bent on an early assault. For the purpose of the concentration was not in doubt. On 18 May, at 24 hours, the Cairo Radio *Saut El Arab* published the following Order of the Day by Abdul Muhsin Murtagi, the General then Commanding Sinai:

> "Egyptian forces have taken up positions in accordance with a definite plan.
> "Our forces are definitely ready to carry the battle beyond the borders of Egypt.
> "Morale is very high among the members of our armed forces because this is the day for which they have been waiting—to make a holy war in order to return the plundered land to its owners.
> "In many meetings with army personnel they asked when the holy war will begin—the time has come to give them their wish."

On 21 May General Amer gave the order to mobilize reserves.

Now came the decisive step. All doubt that Egypt had decided upon immediate or early war was now dispelled. Appearing at an air force base at 6 o'clock in the morning, President Nasser announced that he would blockade the Gulf of Aqaba to Israeli ships, adding: "The Jews threaten war and we say by all means we are ready for war."

On 25 May, Cairo Radio announced:

> "The Arab people is firmly resolved to wipe Israel off the map and to restore the honor of the Arabs of Palestine."

On the following day, 26 May, Nasser spoke again:

> "The Arab people want to fight. We have been waiting for the right time when we will be completely ready. Recently we have felt that our strength has been sufficient and that if we make battle with Israel we shall be able, with the help of God, to conquer. Sharm-el-Sheikh implies a confrontation with Israel. Taking this step makes it imperative that we be ready to undertake a total war with Israel."

Writing in *Al Ahram,* on 26 May, Nasser's mouthpiece Hasanein Heykal, wrote, with engaging realism:

> "I consider that there is no alternative to armed conflict between the United Arab Republic and the Israeli enemy. This is the first time that the Arab challenge

to Israel attempts to change an existing fact in order to impose a different fact in its place."

On 28 May, Nasser had a press conference. He was having them every day. He said:

"We will not accept any posibility of co-existence with Israel."

And on the following day:

"If we have succeeded to restore the situation to what it was before 1956, there is no doubt that God will help us and will inspire us to restore the situation to what it was prior to 1948."

There are various ways of threatening Israel's liquidation. Few ways could be clearer than to ask to move the clock of history back to 1948.

THE RING CLOSES AROUND ISRAEL

The troop concentrations and blockade were now to be accompanied by encirclement. The noose was to be fitted around the victim's neck. Other Arab States were closing the ring. On 30 May, Nasser signed the defense agreement with Jordan; and described its purpose in these terms:

"The armies of Egypt, Jordan, Syria and Lebanon are stationed on the borders of Israel in order to face the challenge. Behind them stand the armies of Iraq, Algeria, Kuwait, Sudan and the whole of the Arab nation.
"This deed will astound the world. Today they will know that the Arabs are ready for the fray. The hour of decision has arrived."

On 4 June Nasser made a statement on Cairo Radio after signing the Protocol associating Iraq with the Egyptian-Jordanian Defense Pact. Here are his words:

". . . We are facing you in the battle and are burning with desire for it to start, in order to obtain revenge. This will make the world realize what the Arabs are and what Israel is. . ."

Nothing has been more startling in recent weeks than to read discussions about who planned, who organized, who initiated, who wanted and who launched this war. Here we have a series of statements, mounting in crescendo from vague warning through open threat to precise intention.

GREATEST CONCENTRATION IN HISTORY OF SINAI

Here we have the vast mass of the Egyptian armies in Sinai with seven infantry and two armored divisions, the greatest force ever assembled in that peninsula in all its history. Here we have 40,000 regular Syrian troops poised to strike at the Jordan Valley from advantageous positions in the hills. Here we have the mobilized forces of Jordan with their artillery and mortars trained on Israel's population centers in Jerusalem and along the vulnerable narrow coastal plain. Troops from Iraq, Kuwait and Algeria converge towards the battlefront at Egypt's behest. 900 tanks face Israel on the Sinai border, while 200 more are poised to strike the isolated town of Elath at Israel's southern tip. The military dispositions tell their own story. The Southern Negev was to be sundered in a swift decisive blow. The Northern Negev was to be invaded by armour and bombarded from the Gaza Strip. From May 27 onward Egyptian air squadrons in Sinai were equipped with operation orders, now in our hands, instructing them in detail on the manner in which Israeli airfields, pathetically few in number, were to be bombarded, thus exposing Israel's crowded cities to easy and merciless assault. Egyptian air sorties came in and out of Israel's southern desert to reconnoitre, inspect and prepare for the attack. An illicit blockade had cut Israel off from all her commerce with the eastern half of the world.

THE BLOCKADE OF THE TIRAN STRAITS

Now those who write this story in years to come will give a special place in their narrative to the blatant decision to close the Straits of Tiran in Israel's face. It is not difficult to understand why this outrage had such a drastic impact. In 1957 the maritime nations, within the framework of the United Nations General Assembly, correctly enunciated the doctrine of free and innocent passage through the Straits. Now, when that doctrine was proclaimed—and incidentally, not challenged at the time by the Egyptian representative—it was little more than an abstract principle for the maritime world. For Israel it was a great but still unfulfilled prospect; it was not yet a reality. But during the ten years in which we and the other States of the maritime community have relied upon that doctrine and upon established usage, principle has become a reality consecrated by hundreds of sailings under dozens of flags and the establishment of a whole complex of commerce and industry and communication. A new dimension has been added to the map of the world's communications, and on that dimension we have constructed Israel's bridge towards the friendly States of Asia and Africa, a network of relationships which is the chief pride of Israel in the second decade of its independence and on which its economic future depends.

All this, then, had grown up as an effective usage under the United Nations flag. Does Mr. Nasser really think that he can come upon the scene in ten minutes and cancel the established legal usage and interests of ten years?

There was in this wanton act a quality of malice. For surely the closing of the Straits of Tiran gave no benefit whatever to Egypt except the perverse joy of inflicting injury on others. It was an anarchic act, because it showed a total disregard for the law of nations, the application of which in this specific case had not been challenged for ten years. And it was, in the literal sense, an act of arrogance, because there are other nations in Asia and East Africa that trade with the Port of Elath, as they have every right to do, through the Straits of Tiran and across the Gulf of Aqaba. Other sovereign States from Japan to Ethiopia, from Thailand to Uganda, from Cambodia to Madagascar, have a sovereign right to decide for themselves whether they wish or do not wish to trade with Israel. These countries are not colonies of Cairo. They can trade with Israel or not trade with Israel as they wish, and President Nasser is not the policeman of other African and Asian States.

BLOCKADES ARE ACTS OF WAR

When we examine, then, the implications of this act, we have no cause to wonder that the international shock was great. There was another reason too for that shock. Blockades have traditionally been regarded, in the pre-Charter parlance, as acts of war. To blockade, after all, is to attempt strangulation—and sovereign States are entitled not to have their trade strangled.

The blockade is by definition an act of war, imposed and enforced through armed violence. Never in history have blockade and peace existed side by side. From May 24 onward, the question who started the war or who fired the first shot became momentously irrelevant. There is no difference in civil law between murdering a man by slow strangulation or killing him by a shot in the head. From the moment at which the blockade was imposed, active hostilities had commenced and Israel owed Egypt nothing of her Charter rights. If a foreign power sought to close Odessa, or Copenhagen or Marseilles or New York harbor by the use of force, what would happen? Would there be any discussion about who had fired the first shot? Would anyone ask whether aggression had begun? Less than a decade ago the Soviet Union proposed a draft resolution in the General wssembly on the question of defining aggression. The resolution reads:

"In an international conflict that state shall be declared an attacker which first commits one of the following acts:

(a) Naval blockade of the coasts or ports of another State."

This act constituted in the Soviet view direct aggression as distinguished from other specified acts designated in the Soviet draft as indirect aggression. In this particular case the consequences of Nasser's action had been fully announced in advance. On March 1, 1957, my predecessor announced that:

"Interference, by armed force, with ships of Israel flag exercising free and innocent passage in the Gulf of Aqaba and through the Straits of Tiran, will be regarded by Israel as an attack entitling it to exercise its inherent rights of self-defense under Article 51 of the United Nations Charter and to take all such measures as are necessary to ensure the free and innocent passage of its ships in the Gulf and in the Straits."

The representative of France, declared that any obstruction of free passage in the Straits or Gulf was contrary to international law "entailing a possible resort to the measures authorized by Article 51 of the Charter."

The United States, inside and outside of the United Nations gave specific endorsement to Israel's right to invoke her inherent right of self-defense against any attempt to blockade the Gulf. Nasser was speaking with acute precision, therefore, when he stated that Israel now faced the choice of either to be choked to death in her southern maritime approaches or to await the death blow from northern Sinai.

ISRAEL FACED PERIL ON EVERY SIDE

Nobody who lived those days in Israel between May 23 and June 5 will ever forget the air of heavy foreboding that hovered over our country. Hemmed in by hostile armies ready to strike, affronted and beset by a flagrant act of war, bombarded day and night by predictions of our approaching extinction, forced into a total mobilization of all her manpower, her economy and commerce beating with feeble pulse, her main supplies of vital fuel choked by a belligerent act, Israel faced the greatest peril to her existence that she had known since her resistance against aggression nineteen years before, at the hour of her birth. There was peril wherever she looked and she faced it in deepening solitude. On May 24 and on succeeding days, the Security Council conducted a desultory debate which sometimes reached a point of levity. Russian and Oriental proverbs were wittily exchanged. The Soviet representative asserted that he saw no reason for discussing the Middle Eastern situation at all. The distinguished Bulgarian Delegate uttered these unbelievable words:

> "At the present moment there is really no need for an urgent meeting of the Security Council."

This was the day after the imposition of the blockade!

A crushing siege bore down upon us. Multitudes throughout the world began to tremble for Israel's fate. The single consolation lay in the surge of public opinion which rose up in Israel's defense. From Paris to Montevideo, from New York to Amsterdam, tens of thousands of people of all ages, parties and affiliations marched in horrified protest at the approaching stage of politicide —the murder of a State. Writers and scientists, religious leaders, trade union movements and even the Communist parties in France, Holland, Switzerland, Norway, Austria and Finland asserted their view that Israel was a peace-loving State, whose peace was being wantonly denied. In the history of our generation it is difficult to think of any other hour in which progressive world opinion has rallied in such tension and agony of spirit to any cause.

ISRAEL'S CHOICE—TO LIVE OR PERISH

To understand the full depth of pain and shock, it is necessary to grasp the full significance of what Israel's danger meant. A small sovereign state had its existence threatened by lawless violence. The threat to Israel was a menace to the very foundations of the international order. The state thus threatened bore a name which stirred the deepest memories of civilized mankind, and the people of the threatened state were the surviving remnant of millions, who in living memory had been wiped out by a dictatorship more powerful, though scarcely more malicious, than Nasser's Egypt. What Nasser had worked for with undeflecting purpose had come to pass—the noose was tightly drawn.

On the fateful morning of June 5, when Egyptian forces moved by air and land against Israel's western coast and southern territory, our country's choice was plain. The choice was to live or perish, to defend the national existence or to forfeit it for all time.

From these dire moments Israel emerged in five heroic days from awful peril to successful and glorious resistance. Alone, unaided, neither seeking nor receiving help, our nation rose in self-defense. So long as men cherish freedom, so long as small states strive for the dignity of survival, the exploits of Israel's armies will be told from one generation to another with the deepest pride. The Soviet Union has described our resistance as aggression and sought to have it condemned. We reject this accusation with all our might. Here was armed force employed in a just and righteous cause; as righteous as the defense of freedom at Valley Forge; as just as the expulsion of Hitler's bombers from the British skies; as noble as the protection of Stalingrad against the Nazi hordes, so was the defense of Israel's security and existence against those who sought our nation's destruction. What should be condemned is not Israel's action, but the attempt to condemn it. Never have freedom, honor, justice, national interest and international morality been so righteously protected.

MESSAGE TO JORDANIAN KING

While fighting raged on the Egyptian-Israel frontier and on the Syrian front, we still hoped to contain the conflict. Jordan was given every chance to remain outside the struggle. Even after Jordan had bombarded and bombed Israel territory at several points we still proposed to the Jordanian monarch that he abstain from general hostilities. A message to this effect reached him several hours after the outbreak of hostilities on the southern front on June 5. Jordan answered tragically not with words but with shells. Artillery opened fire fiercely along the whole front with special emphasis on the Jerusalem area. Thus, Jordan's responsibility for the second phase of the concerted aggression is established beyond doubt. This responsibility cannot fail to have its consequences in the peace settlement. As death and injury rained on the city, Jordan had become the source and origin of Jerusalem's fierce ordeal. The inhabitants of the city can never forget this fact, or fail to draw its conclusions.

Address at U.N. June, 1967

THE SOVIET ROLE IN THE MIDDLE EAST CRISIS

I have spoken of Israel's defense against the assault of neighboring states. This is not the entire story. Whatever happens in the Middle East for good or ill, for peace or conflict, is powerfully affected by what the Great Powers do or omit to do. When the Soviet Union initiates a discussion here our gaze is inexorably drawn to the story of its role in recent Middle Eastern history. It is a sad and shocking story; it must be frankly told.

There was in Soviet policy a brief but important episode of balanced friendship. In 1948, the USSR condemned what she called "Arab aggression."

Since 1955 the Soviet Union has supplied the Arab States with 2,000 tanks, of which more than 1,000 have gone to Egypt. The Soviet Union has supplied the Arab States with 700 modern fighter aircraft and bombers; more recently with ground missiles, and Egypt alone has received from the USSR 540 field guns, 130 medium guns, 200 120 mm. mortars, 695 anti-aircraft guns, 175 rocket launchers, 650 anti-tank guns, 7 destroyers; a number of Luna M and Sopka 2 ground to ground missiles, 14 submarines and 46 torpedo boats of various types including missile carrying boats. The Egyptian army has been trained by Soviet experts. This has been attested by Egyptian officers captured by Israel. Most of this equipment was supplied to the Arab States after the Cairo Summit Conference of Arab leaders in January 1964 had agreed on a specific program for the destruction of Israel; after they had announced and hastened to fulfil this plan by accelerating their arms purchases from the Soviet Union. The proportions of Soviet assistance are attested to by the startling fact that in Sinai alone the Egyptians abandoned equipment and offensive weapons of Soviet manufacture whose value is estimated at two billion dollars.

Together with the supply of offensive weapons the Soviet Union has encouraged the military preparations of the Arab States.

Since 1961, the Soviet armaments have assisted Egypt in its desire to conquer Israel. The great amount of offensive equipment supplied to the Arab States strengthens this assessment.

Thus, a Great Power which professes its devotion to peaceful settlement and the rights of States has for fourteen years afflicted the Middle East with a headlong armaments race; with the paralysis of the United Nations as an instrument of security; and with an attitude of blind identification with those who threaten peace against those who defend it.

EFFORTS TO CURTAIL ARMS RACE

The constant increase and escalation of Soviet armament in Arab countries has driven Israel to a corresponding though far smaller procurement program. Israel's arms purchases were precisely geared to the successive phases of Arab, and especially Egyptian rearmament. On many occasions in recent months we and others have vainly sought to secure Soviet agreement for a reciprocal reduction of arms supplies in our region. These efforts have borne no fruit. The expenditure on social and economic progress of one half of what has been put into the purchase of Soviet arms would have been sufficient to redeem Egypt from its social and economic ills. A corresponding diversion of resources from military to social expenditure would have taken place in Israel. A viable balance of forces could have been achieved at a lower level of armaments, while our region could have moved forward to higher standards of human and social welfare. For Israel's attitude is clear. We should like to see the arms race slowed down. But if the race is joined, we are determined not to lose it. A fearful waste of economic energy in the Middle East is the direct result of the Soviet role in the constant stimulation of the race in arms.

INCENDIARY REPORTS SPREAD BY SOVIET UNION

It is clear from Arab sources that the Soviet Union has played a provocative role in spreading alarmist and incendiary reports of Israel intentions amongst Arab governments.

On 9 June President Nasser said:

> "Our friends in the USSR warned the visiting parliamentary delegation in Moscow at the beginning of last month, that there exists a plan of attack against Syria."

Similarly an announcement by TASS of 23 May states:

> "The Foreign Affairs and Security Committee of the Knesset have accorded the Cabinet on 9 May, special powers to carry out war operations against Syria. Israeli forces concentrating on the Syrian border have been put in a state of alert for war. General mobilization has also been proclaimed in the country..."

There was not one word of truth in this story. But its diffusion in the Arab countries could only have an incendiary result.

Cairo Radio broadcast on 28 May (0500 hours) an address by Marshal Gretchko at a farewell party in honour of the former Egyptian Minister of Defense Shams ed-Din Badran:

> "The USSR, her armed forces, her people and government will stand by the Arabs and will continue to encourage and support them. We are your faithful friends and we shall continue aiding you because this is the policy of the Soviet nation, its party and government. On behalf of the Ministry of Defense and in the name of the Soviet nation we wish you success and victory."

This promise of military support came less than a week after the illicit closing of the Tiran Straits, an act which the USSR has done nothing to condemn.

USSR ATTITUDES ON ARAB-ISRAEL QUESTION IN THE UN

The USSR has exercised her veto right in the Security Council five times. Each time a just and constructive judgment has been frustrated. On 22 January 1954 France, the United Kingdom and the United States presented a draft resolution to facilitate work on the West Bank of the River Jordan in the Bnot Yaakov Canal project. The Soviet veto paralyzed regional water development for several years. On 29 March 1954, a New Zealand resolution simply reiterating U.N. policy on blockade on the Suez Canal was frustrated by Soviet dissent. On 19 August 1963, a United Kingdom and United States resolution on the murder of two Israelis at Almagor was denied adoption by Soviet opposition. On 21 December 1964 the USSR vetoed a United Kingdom and United States resolution on incidents at Tel Dan, including the shelling of Dan, Dafne, Shaar Yishuv. On 2 November 1966, Argentina, Japan, Netherlands, New Zealand, Nigeria joined to express regret at "infiltration from Syria and loss of human life caused by the incident in October, November 1966." This was one of the few resolutions sponsored by member States from five continents.

The Soviet use of the veto has had a dual effect. First, it prevented any resolution to which an Arab State was opposed from being adopted by the Council. Secondly, it has inhibited the Security Council from taking constructive action in disputes between an Arab State and Israel because of the certain knowledge that the veto would be applied in what was deemed to be the Arab interest. The consequences of the Soviet veto policy have been to deny Israel any possibility of just and equitable treatment in the Security Council, and to nullify the Council as a constructive factor in the affairs of the Middle East.

ISRAEL OBJECT OF UNBRIDLED INVECTIVE

Does all this really add up to a constructive intervention by the USSR in the Arab-Israel tension? The position becomes graver when we recall the unbridled invective against the Permanent Representative of Israel in the Security Council. In its words and in a letter to the Israel Government the USSR has formulated an obscene comparison between the Israel Defense Forces and the Hitlerite hordes which overran Europe in the Second World War. There is a flagrant breach of international morality and human decency in this comparison. Our nation never compromised with Hitler Germany. It never signed a pact with it as did the USSR in 1939. To associate the name of Israel with the accursed tyrant who engulfed the Jewish people in a tidal wave of slaughter is to violate every canon of elementary taste and fundamental truth.

In the light of this history, the General Assembly will easily understand Israel's reaction to the Soviet initiative in convening this special session for the purpose of condemning our country and recommending a withdrawal to the position that existed before June 5.

In respect to the request for a condemnation, I give a simple answer to the

Soviet Representative. Your Government's record in the stimulation of the arms race, in the encouragement throughout the Arab world of unfounded suspicion concerning Israel's intentions, your constant refusal to say a single word of criticism at any time of declarations threatening the violent overthrow of Israel's sovereignty and existence—all this gravely undermines your claims to objectivity. You come here in our eyes not as a judge or as a prosecutor, but rather as a legitimate object of international criticism for the part that you have played in the somber events which have brought our region to a point of explosive tension. If the Soviet Union had made an equal distribution of its friendship amongst the peoples of the Middle East, if it had refrained from exploiting regional rancors and tensions for the purposes of its own global policy, if it had stood in evenhanded devotion to the legitimate interests of all states, the crisis which now commands our attention and anxiety would never have occurred. To the charge of aggression I answer that Israel's resistance at the lowest ebb of its fortunes will resound across history, together with the uprising of our battered remnants in the Warsaw Ghetto as a triumphant assertion of human freedom. From the dawn of its history the people now rebuilding a state in Israel has struggled often in desperate conditions against tyranny and aggression. Our action on the 5th of June falls nobly within that tradition. We have tried to show that even a small state and a small people have the right to live. I believe that we shall not be found alone in the assertion of that right which is the very essence of the Charter of the United Nations.

CALL FOR DIRECT NEGOTIATIONS

Similarly, the suggestion that everything goes back to where it was before the 5th of June is totally unacceptable. The General Assembly cannot ignore the fact that the Security Council, where the primary responsibility lies, has emphatically rejected such a course. It was not Israel, but Syria, Egypt and Jordan, who violently shattered the whole fabric and texture of interstate relations which existed for a decade since 1957. That situation has been shattered to smithereens. It cannot be recaptured. It is a fact of technology that it is easier to fly to the moon than to reconstruct a broken egg. The Security Council acted wisely in rejecting the backward step, now advocated by the Soviet Union. To go back to the situation out of which the conflict arose would mean that all the conditions for renewed hostilities would be brought together again. I repeat what I said to the Security Council: Our watchword is not backward to belligerency—but forward to peace.

What the Assembly should prescribe is not a formula for renewed hostilities, but a series of principles for the construction of a new future in the Middle East. With the cease-fire established, our progress must be not backward to an armistice regime which has collapsed under the weight of years and the brunt of hostility. History summons us forward to permanent peace and the peace that we envisage can only be elaborated in frank and lucid dialogue between Israel and each of the States which have participated in the attempt to overthrow her sovereignty and undermine her existence. We dare not be satisfied with intermediate arrangements which are neither war nor peace. Such patchwork ideas carry within themselves the seeds of future tragedy. Free from external pressures and interventions, imbued with a common love for a region which they are destined to share, the Arab and Jewish nations must now transcend their conflicts in dedication to a new Mediterranean future in concert with a renascent Europe and an Africa and Asia which have emerged at last to their independent role on the stage of history.

THE VISION OF PEACE

In free negotiation with each of our neighbours we shall offer durable and just solutions redounding to our mutual advantage and honour. The Arab States can no longer be permitted to recognize Israel's existence only for the purpose of plotting its elimination. They have come face to face with us in conflict. Let them now come face to face with us in peace.

In peaceful conditions we could imagine communications running from Haifa to Beirut and Damascus in the North; to Amman and beyond in the East; and to Cairo in the South. The opening of these blocked arteries would stimulate the life, thought and commerce of the region beyond any level otherwise conceivable. Across the Southern Negev communication between the Nile Valley and the Fertile Crescent could be resumed without any change in political jurisdiction. What is now often described as a wedge between Arab lands would become a bridge. The Kingdom of Jordan, now cut off from its natural maritime outlet, could freely import and export its goods on the Israeli coast. On the Red Sea, cooperative action could expedite the port developments at Elath and Aqaba which give Israel and Jordan their contact with a resurgent East Africa and a developing Asia.

The Middle East, lying athwart three continents, could become a busy center of air communications, which are now impeded by boycotts and the necessity to take circuitous routes. Radio, telephone and postal communications which now end abruptly in mid-air would unite a divided region. The Middle East with its historic monuments and scenic beauty could attract a vast movement of travellers and pilgrims if existing impediments were removed. The minerals of the Dead Sea and the phosphates of the Negev and the Araba—could be developed in mutual interchange of technical knowledge.

Economic cooperation in agricultural and industrial development could lead to supranational arrangements like those which mark the European Community. The United Nations could establish an Economic Commission for the Middle East, similar to the Commissions now at work in Europe, Latin America and the Far East. The specialized agencies could intensify their support of health and educational development with greater efficiency if a regional harmony were attained. The development of arid zones, the desalination of water and the conquest of tropical disease are common interests of the entire region, congenial to a sharing of knowledge and experience.

In the institutions of scientific research and higher education on both sides of the frontiers, young Israelis and Arabs could join in a mutual discourse of learning. The old prejudices could be replaced by a new comprehension and respect, born of a reciprocal dialogue in the intellectual domain. In such a Middle East, excessive sums deveoted to security could be diverted to development projects.

Thus, in full respect of the region's diversity, an entirely new story, never known or told before, would unfold across the Eastern Mediterranean. For the first time in history, no Mediterranean nation is in subjection. All are endowed with sovereign freedom. The challenge now is to use this freedom for creative growth. There is only one road to that end. It is the road of recognition, of direct contact, of true cooperation. It is the road of peaceful co-existence. This road, as the ancient Prophets of Israel foretold, leads to Jerusalem.

FREE ACCESS TO ALL FAITHS

Jerusalem, now united after her tragic division, is no longer an arena for gun emplacements and barbed wire. In our nation's long history there have been few hours more intensely moving than the hour of our reunion with the Western Wall. A people had come back to the cradle of its birth. It has renewed its link with the mystery of its origin and continuity. How long and deep are the memories which that reunion evokes!

For twenty years there has not been free access by men of all faiths to the shrines which they hold in unique reverence. This access now exists. Israel is resolved to give effective expression, in cooperation with the world's great religions, to the immunity and sanctity of all the Holy Places.

The prospect of a negotiated peace is less remote than it may seem. Israel waged her defensive struggle in pursuit of two objectives—security and peace. Peace and security, with their juridical, territorial, economic and social implications, can only be built by the free negotiation which is the true essence of sovereign responsibility. A call to the recent combatants to negotiate the conditions of their future co-existence is the only constructive course which this Assembly could take.

We ask the Great Powers to remove our tormented region from the scope of global rivalries; to summon its governments to build their common future themselves; to assist it, if they will, to develop social and cultural levels worthy of its past.

We ask the developing countries to support a dynamic and forward-looking policy and not to drag the new future back into the outworn past.

To the small nations which form the bulk of the international family we offer the experience which teaches us that small communities can best secure their interests by maximal self-reliance. Nobody will help those who will not help themselves. We ask the small nations, in the solidarity of our smallness, to help us stand firm against intimidation and threat such as those by which we are now assailed.

Address at U.N. June, 1967

We ask world opinion which rallied to us in our plight to accompany us faithfully in our new opportunity.

APPEAL TO UNITED NATIONS

We ask the United Nations which was prevented from offering us security in our recent peril, to respect our independent quest for the peace and security which are the Charter's higher ends. We shall do what the Security Council decided should be done—and reject the course which the Security Council emphatically and wisely rejected.

It may seem that Israel stands alone against numerous and powerful adversaries. But we appeal to the undying forces in our nation's history which have so often given the final victory to spirit over matter, to inner truth over quantity. We believe in the vigilance of history which has guarded our steps.

The Middle East, tired of wars, is ripe for a new emergence of human vitality. Let the opportunity not fall again from our hands.

MOSHE DAYAN

Moshe Dayan was born in Kibbutz Degania Aleph, Palestine, in 1915. He is a graduate of the Senior Officers' School in England and of the School of Law and Economics in Tel Aviv. He also studied three years at the Hebrew University in Jerusalem.

Working as a farmer in the cooperative settlement, Nahalal, Dayan at the same time enlisted in the *Haganah*, the underground military arm of the Jewish community in Palestine. In 1937, he joined the illicit "night squads" of Orde Wingate, the pro-Zionist British commander, becoming one of his deputies. From 1939 to 1940 he was imprisoned by the British government of Palestine in the Acre prison, but upon his release he fought alongside the English on the Syrian-Lebanese front against the Vichy French. It was during one of these battles that he lost an eye.

Rising rapidly from one military rank to the next due to his audacious exploits, Dayan served as commander of various fronts during the Israeli War of Independence in 1948. In 1953 he was appointed Chief-of-Staff of the Defense Army of Israel, occupying that post until 1958. It was during his tenure of that office and as a result of his brilliant planning, that the Israelis won the spectacular Sinai victory in 1956, reaching the Suez Canal "in 100 hours."

In 1959, Dayan figuratively beat his sword into a plowshare, becoming Minister of Agriculture in Prime Minister David Gurion's government, where again he demonstrated extraordinary administrative ability.

When Ben-Gurion became disenchanted with his party's leadership and broke away from *Mapai*, Dayan, a Ben-Gurion protégé, hesitated before joining the new *Rafi* party. Somehow he managed to stay away at the time from the various political squabbles. During the critical days of May, 1967, public opinion literally forced the then Prime Minister Levi Eshkol to appoint Dayan Minister of Defense. Many credit Dayan's appointment with the psychological uplift of the people that led to the Napoleonic victory, although obviously the architect of the military plans for the Six Day War was the then Chief of Staff, Yitzhak Rabin. Dayan continues to serve as Defense Minister in the cabinet of Eshkol's successor, Golda Meir.

Dayan was not born to oblivion. He is a strikingly evocative personality—although essentially a "loner"—rebelling against like-minded leaders who created party machinery for members to remain like-minded. In a way he is Samsonian both militarily and politically. He has the uncanny capacity to identify issues and even an uncannier capacity to stay away from some of them.

Immensely popular in Israel, paradoxically he was also liked and respected by many of the Arabs in the occupied areas after the 1967 war. Recognizing that belief and reality in the Arab world are deserts apart, Dayan envisioned a solution to the Arab-Israeli impasse by demonstrating that Arabs and Jews could live together as the Israeli Jews and the Israeli Arabs (a minority of about 300,000 in Israel proper) have lived together ever since the establishment of the State in 1948. He advocates socio-cultural and especially economic and technological help to the occupied areas and a two-way "open-door" policy, leaving political autonomy to local authorities, except in Jerusalem, the Golan Heights and several other strategic points which he feels should be annexed to Israel.

Dayan's approach to the problem is described in the speech he delivered at a student meeting in Haifa on March 19, 1969, as it appeared in *Midstream,* June-July, 1969, pp. 26–39.

Jewish-Arab Coexistence

by MOSHE DAYAN

WHAT I INTEND TO SAY in my introduction falls into three parts: first—a description of our situation today or at least a stressing of its main aspects; I will refer mainly to the security situation, but not exclusively to it; second—what I call the costs of the situation: how much it costs us and the diffculties it entails; and third—what we now must do in this situation.

We are reviewing our present situation at the end of two years and as the third year begins. Two things should be emphasized: the fact that after two years, we are at all able to sum up the situation in several specific areas (*Fatah*, the cease-fire lines, the international political configuration), and two years is not a short time; and secondly, the fact that the two years that will end in May will usher in a third, and this requires a special perspective. Not necessarily as it is a third year, but as it constitutes a dividing line between the first period which followed immediately upon the war and a subsequent, protracted period, which must be measured not in weeks or months, but in years.

When one year after another passes and a third year is already upon us we must begin asking ourselves questions of a sort we did not have to ask at the outset.

My first subject is the front line with Egypt. It should not be compared with the other fronts—neither with the Jordanian nor with the Syrian. What was true in the past—that Egypt was the foremost Arab country from the military standpoint and because of its position of leadership in the Arab world—continues to be true today. There is also an additional factor: Soviet assistance to Egypt in the form of arms supplies is immeasurably greater, more developed and more effective than that which the Jordanians and even the Syrians are receiving. And this is true not only in arms. The planning by the Soviet experts along the Suez Canal line, the facilities which the Soviets have installed and whose use they are directing there—the radar installations and others which I will not name—are clearly what contribute to making this the toughest line of fire confronting us today, and, to the extent that I can assess, the toughest that the Israel Defense Forces have ever had to confront. I cannot remember a time when we faced as tough a line of fire as we confront at the Suez Canal today.

This line erupts from time to time, and I am not speaking figuratively. The Suez line is afire for the third time already. The petroleum, the installations and the cities along the line are igniting and burning. The narrow 200 meters that separate our men from the Egyptian soldiers; our resolve not to move back even one meter, even for operational purposes of increasing the range in our favor; and the direct, almost palpable view, without even any need of binoculars, which every Egyptian and Algerian soldier has of our men who are there stringing barbed wire fences and pouring concrete—all these certainly have their consequences. These are the eruptions of fire we have been witnessing, with all the costs that are entailed for the Egyptians. But we too have been compelled to pay a price, from the sinking of the destroyer *Eilat* to the events of yesterday and today. However, Egypt is the one bearing the brunt—and at great cost—of any attempt to open fire across the Suez Canal.

At the end of two years, it can be said that this line is neither easier nor quieter than it was during the war. On the contrary, tension along the Suez Canal line has grown, most recently in particular, but this has been a steady process.

There is also the eastern front, which is the important front from the Arabs' point of view. If they are planning a war against us—and they *are* planning such a war—they are undoubtedly greatly interested that we should be attacked along two fronts: the western front with Egypt, and the eastern front with Jordan, which would be manned by Syrian, Iraqi and Jordanian troops, and perhaps by others too, from Lebanon . . .

I do not believe that during these two years (actually it is somewhat less than two years, for el Fatah did not begin operating immediately following the war) there has been, from the military standpoint, any appreciable improvement in the terrorists' capability, organization, achievements or competence. Militarily speaking, they are little more than a shaky body, devoid of any significant achievements, and moreover, showing no signs whatever of progress in their development.

But there are other aspects of el Fatah to which we should address ourselves. One is their effect on the Arab world; and the other, the response they have succeeded in eliciting throughout the world to their claim of being a liberation movement. (When I speak of el Fatah, I am also referring to all the terrorist organizations. As I will not deal here with the organizational divisions among the terrorists, I will continue to use the one name—el Fatah.)

El Fatah enjoys great influence on the Arab man in the street, and therefore on the Arab states. Its influence has also grown among the Arabs in the occupied territories, in Judea, Samaria and Gaza and even the Israeli Arabs have been somewhat affected by it. But this influence has grown especially within the Arab states. It is not mere chance that Nasser, in a programmatic address before the conference of terrorist organizations in Cairo, felt constrained to make statements completely at variance with the political stand expressed by his Foreign Minister, Mahmoud Riad, only a few months earlier.

Nasser said: Egypt accepts the Security Council resolution demanding (according to his interpretation) Israel's withdrawal to the armistice lines. But he cannot, and indeed, does not want to prevent the terrorist organizations from continuing their war against Israel, for their aim is not simply to return to the armistice lines but to undermine Israel's very existence. And Egypt—according to Nasser's announcement—not only will not object to this or prevent them from carrying on their war, but will place all her resources at their disposal to enable them to carry on this war.

That statement, and that particular political formulation, are the outgrowth of the feeling among average Arabs—in Jordan, in Egypt, in Syria and to some extent in Lebanon, too—that el Fatah should be aided. It is bitter and galling, from the Arab viewpoint, that the Arab armies cannot expel the Israelis from the territories they occupied, but if there are irregular Arab forces ready to fight one should give them all the help possible. There are youngsters in el Fatah who are prepared to risk their lives in an attempt to penetrate into Israel to fight the Jews. And there is not an Arab who would want to stint his help to these youths unless he is under Israel rule and the authorities prevent him from extending such help. But in Egypt and in Jordan and among the Arab populations in Judea, Samaria and the Gaza Strip the influence and significance of the terrorist organizations on Arab consciousness has grown— not their military significance, but the nationalistic significance of the war (and I am not calling it a war of liberation) which the Arabs are waging against Israel in their fashion . . .

I do not agree with those who feel that el Fatah is succeeding in building up an image as a "liberating force." It may be that when el Fatah first appeared on the scene it enjoyed the benefit of many feature articles and television interviews. But I hope, and believe, that the more intelligent public in the world is aware of two basic elements which distinguish el Fatah operations. One is the nature of the warfare which the terrorist organizations are conducting: shooting at civilian planes, placing explosive charges in supermarkets and in bus terminals. I hope that world public opinion is not particularly enthusiastic about this type of warfare, and if el Fatah continues with operations of this sort, I doubt whether they will be helping the image of an Arab warrior and of an Arab war. It is not enough for them to call themselves "freedom-fighters." There is also the question of what they are doing—in Zurich and in Athens and here at home. I believe that in the long run these murderous anti-civilian operations will not serve the aims of Arab propaganda or their desire to obtain world sympathy for the Arab cause.

Of not lesser importance are the political objectives declared by el Fatah. It does not speak of the implementation of the Security Council resolution but of the elimination of the State of Israel. Here too, I believe that this stand of the terrorist organizations is detrimental to the Arab states who demand that we withdraw to the armistice lines. For when the Arab states join with el Fatah in dividing the war against us into phases—first we should retreat to the 1967 borders and then el Fatah will continue its war against us with all the resources of Egypt and the other Arab states at its disposal in order to "liberate" not only Shehem, Hebron and Gaza, but also Jaffa, Acre and other places inside Israel—then I seriously doubt that el Fatah is building up political sympathy or support for the Arab war against us.

But as I said before, this has nothing to do with the positive reaction to the terrorist actions on the part of the Arab populations, for among the Arabs these problems do not give rise to any internal conflicts. They are fully prepared to murder our citizens and to destroy the State of Israel. The Arabs of Egypt and of Jordan and perhaps even those of Judea, Samaria and Gaza are not shocked either by the nature of the terrorist fighting or by its political goals.

A third aspect in a description of the situation must concern the Arab inhabitants of the occupied territories. Their opposition to our presence there has increased. Partly this is because they have overcome the initial shock of the war and its immediate aftermath; to an even greater extent it derives from their reaction to the decisions of the Security Council and other international bodies, over which we Israelis can hardly rejoice, and which the Arabs interpret as support for their demands that we withdraw from these territories; and finally, el Fatah and the radio and television broadcasts from the Arab states have also had their effect.

Perhaps I should also emphasize two additional points which I am passing on as I heard them from Arab leaders in the occupied territories, who voiced them not as propaganda, nor out of hypocrisy or a desire to flatter us. One point they make is that if it were not for outside interference of el Fatah, of Arab leaders such as Nasser, Hussein and others, they are convinced that the Arabs of Judea, Samaria and Gaza could live with us in peace and harmony. This is not to say that they would want to do so—they want us to get out of there—but in the context of the needs of daily life, they are fully aware that they can live with us in peace while conducting orderly lives, to the extent that any foreign government (and for them we are a foreign government) is capable of maintaining an orderly way of life there.

They cannot do this because of the strong outside pressures which range from the dispatch of terrorists, through the payment of salaries to local notables by the Jordanian government, to the Egyptian, Syrian and Jordanian appeals to the nationalist sensibilities of the Arabs of the occupied territories that they too contribute their part to the resistance to Israel.

And one more thing: the authority and influence of the indigenous leadership —of the families, the clans, the town councils and the school authorities—have been nearly completely undermined. Children on the street and in school wield more influence than do their teachers. The "street"—in the most negative sense of this word—is master. The children stone storefronts. If the schools are closed, they stone the schools. And I'm speaking not only of children but of all sorts of hooligans. A few days ago, in Gaza, a grenade was thrown into a group of children on their way to school, and eighteen were wounded. Arab children are made the target of attack so that they should not study, so that the schools should be forced to close down. Every now and then the Arab leaders, the community and town council heads, issue proclamations calling for the resumption of studies, but the "street" simply disregards these.

I should add another two points in describing our situation. One is known—

the French embargo, which has closed to us our main source of arms, especially in regard to air power.

The other point concerns the policies of the big powers and the consultations of the U.S., the Soviet Union, France and Britain. Somewhat simplistically it can be put as follows: After two years in which no settlement has been reached in the region itself, the big powers have decided to take matters into their own hands—at least by adding their weight and influence—to consult among themselves, in order to lend their full assistance (and perhaps even pressure) to the attainment of such a settlement...

In this situation we have not only held our own but we are now entering the third year with a greater sense of confidence and fewer anxieties (though not completely without any anxieties) than I had thought possible immediately following the war. We have not squandered the time. Not in regard to fortifications along the Suez Canal, nor in regard to caring for the inhabitants of the occupied territories, nor in regard to fighting el Fatah. At the end of two years we can say that we are living with the situation and making a go of it.

Certainly there are many difficulties, and the brunt is being borne by the border settlements. The families and the children who have been sleeping for two years in shelters are not army men who come and go.

But we are paying a price for the situaion in which we find ourselves. We are capable of mastering the situation, of persisting in it, but we are paying the price for it. Foremost are our losses in life. Our casualties in the Six Day War, in killed and wounded among soldiers and civilians, came to about 3,800. Most of these, of course, were wounded, not killed. Since the end of the war, as of today, we have suffered an additional 1,600 casualties, that is, about half the number of our wartime casualties. I am not including the crew of the *Dakar* (an Israel submarine mysteriously lost in the Mediterranean last year. Eds.) but I am including those lost on the destroyer *Eilat*. That is, all the losses connected with war activities. That has been the cost. A high cost.

The security budget for next year will require $2\frac{3}{4}$ billion Israel pounds. This is a lot of money and it distorts the national economy and hamstrings it. It is nearly two and a half times—230 per cent—as large as the last pre-war security budget. Such a budgetary load, year after year, cannot but have its effect for many years to come.

Let me say that the price we are paying for this war, both for the Six Day War and for the period following it, is not higher than that paid by other states when they go to war or when war is declared against them and they refuse to capitulate. I state this here because I am speaking to young people, who personally are called upon to pay this price. Young men and women in Britain, France, Holland, or any other country, when they are called upon to fight for their homeland or to protect their freedom, pay no less than we are paying. The goals for which we are fighting are no less noble, no less important, than the goals for which other nations fight...

I am not underestimating the importance of 1,600 casualties since the end of the war. And I am not ignoring the children who have been sleeping in shelters in Gesher and in other settlements in the Jordan Valley. But we must see the goals for which we are fighting and realize that this price too is part of the war.

The third point I would like to touch on is an answer to the question, "What must we do?" The situation is a fact; we are meeting it as best we can; we do not see imminent peace; we are paying the daily price in blood, financial resources, toil, economic problems and suffering. And we must ask ourselves, are we simply paying the price without attempting to bring about the basic changes which we need and aspire to, and for which the war was and is being waged?

I will begin answering this question by touching on its technological aspect. We must develop and produce arms by ourselves in order to reduce our dependence on foreign suppliers. This problem has become particularly aggravated in the wake of the French embargo. And we can do it. Not completely. We cannot be completely independent in this field, but in this twentieth year of our independence there is much more that we can do toward becoming substantially independent in regard to arms supplies.

In order to attain this objective we will need years. And we will need know-how, above and beyond the know-how that we have in Israel today, but which exists among the Jewish people, particularly among the Jews in the U.S., but in other countries too. We must bring these Jews to us. We will need much money in order to develop our industry and its production so that we can reduce our dependence on other countries for arms.

At the same time we must prepare for the possibility of the Arabs renewing their war against us. This means not only that we have to manufacture arms, or buy them abroad, or develop our military industries, but also that we must invest extensively in preparations on the ground: more and better fortifications, additional airfields, roads, water and telephone lines. We must mobilize ourselves to meet the threat of a renewed war, on the fullest scale, on all fronts. We must be ready for such an eventuality if we do not want to lose such a war.

We must continue to fight el Fatah, and to conceive of this fight in three aspects. One is defensive—those fences and mines which make it difficult for the terrorists to cross the Jordan River and to reach their targets. But we require not only defensive measures. We must hit at el Fatah camps and bases, not in retaliation for their own raids, not in a spirit of bookkeeping in which we total up their attack and finally hit back when they reach a certain number, but on the principle of hitting them wherever we know them to be, whether it is at a training camp, a bivouac or in a unit approaching our borders; we must hit at them without waiting for them to strike first, in order to prevent them from acting; hit them from the air and on the ground . . .

And not only this. We cannot and should not absolve the Arab states of responsibility for el Fatah raids which originate in their territories. We should not create or condone a situation in which any Arab state—Jordan or Egypt, Syria or Lebanon—can wash its hands of the problem and say to us: "O.K. We have el Fatah. You conduct your war against them; that's between you and them. We aren't doing anything except providing them with a territorial base, equipment, money, assistance in crossing the border and artillery cover. Why blame us?"

What do we want from these Arab states? They are our neighbors and we have cease-fire agreements with them. These agreements do not permit any Arab state to employ terrorist groups against us or allow such groups to operate from its territory.

Our agreements are between states—between us and our neighboring states. And these states must be held responsible for what happens on their soil. We have no intention of keeping accounts with groups of private residents of Jordan, Egypt, Syria or Lebanon.

Operations against targets in these neighboring states serve as signals to their governments that we hold them responsible for el Fatah activities which originate in their territories. We took such actions against Egypt when we struck their electrical transformer stations and their Nile bridge; against Jordan when we struck at her bridges; and also against Lebanon in our raid on the Beirut airfield. We should not abandon this principle of holding the neighboring Arab states responsible for the Fatah actions emanating from within their borders. They should not be absolved of this responsibility. We cannot search for the Fatah marauders in the hills everywhere. We have a cease-fire agreement with a neighboring state, and this state is expected to make sure that the agreement is observed. And if it does not: if Egypt dispatches commando units across the Canal; if Jordan permits el Fatah to continue operating; if Lebanon permits terrorist units to train on its territory and then set off for Zurich, we will hold them responsible for such terrorist incursions, and remind them that we, too, can penetrate into the interior of that Arab state which permits such activities and can strike at targets within these states.

Therefore in our fight against el Fatah we must do the following three things: adopt defensive measures to make it more difficult for them to reach us; hit at el Fatah wherever they may be found even before they have an opportunity to attack us; and employ military operations against any Arab state or states which assist the Fatah and permit them to operate against us from within their borders.

In regard to the Arab population: the most important element that I see in the web of relations between us and them is that we Jews must recognize the fact that we must establish a reality of coexistence between Israel and the Arab population even in the midst of conflict and in the absence of peace. This means that even when a mine goes off in the Hebrew University cafeteria or in a supermarket, we must not turn the matter into a generalized attack against all Arabs. We must punish those among the perpetrators who are caught, and blow up their homes. But the other Arabs in Jerusalem must be enabled to go about their daily lives unmolested. At present we cannot completely prevent occasional acts of terror. But these should not be permitted to escalate into a full-fledged crisis between us and the Arab population. This would ill-serve us and our cause. We must not permit terrorist acts to completely disrupt the as yet limited web of relationships which we have barely managed to establish.

This is certainly not "peaceful co-existence"; it is coexistence in war, but coexistence nonetheless. Today, close to 15,000 Arabs from the occupied territories are employed in Israel, both in organized and unorganized labor. Even after an explosion has taken place in West Jerusalem, these Arab workers leave their homes in the morning to make their way to work in the Jewish sector: and Israelis go on foot and by vehicle to East Jerusalem. It might well be that those who planted the explosive charge and set it off made their way through East Jerusalem, even if they came from Ramallah. But we should not permit the acts of terror to undo our developing joint existence.

But even when we feel constrained to blow up the homes of saboteurs in Jerusalem, Ramallah or Shehem, we must adopt and pursue a policy that will permit the other Arabs, the ones who did not engage in terrorist acts, to continue their evolving relationships with us. So that they should not feel compelled to say that since Israel has blown up homes, they are severing all contacts with us. For this can lead to crises between the two peoples and we should do our best to avoid such situations.

This might well prove to be the most difficult test for us: to live together with the Arab population in the midst of conflict, in the midst of occasional terrorist actions against us, and in the midst of the blowing up of homes among them. We must try to maintain our common existence above these events and within such a situation. We have no other way. If we could stop the terror completely, we would of course have done so. But the question, rather, is whether, when it is impossible to stop the terror completely, it is necessary to disrupt our common framework of existence. In my opinion, it is not.

We must regard the Arabs of the occupied territories, in Judea and Samaria and Gaza as citizens and not as enemies. There are enemies among them, and they would all like to get us out of there. But if we do not want that there should be another government in those territories we will have to be the government there. And if we are the government, we must provide employment and services, and grant everyone his due civil rights rather than viewing him, *a priori,* as an enemy. One who is caught perpetrating a hostile act should be treated as an enemy. But we are today the government in Shehem and they our, our citizens.

True, they do not act that way toward us. They view us as alien conquerors and do not want to be Israeli citizens. That being so, we should enable them to maintain their contacts with the Arab world, to cross the bridges over the Jordan and drive to Amman. One or the other: either we annex the territories and turn them all into Israel citizens or, if we do not, we should permit them to continue their contacts with Jordan as Jordanian citizens. I, personally, am against granting Israel citizenship to the inhabitants of the occupied territories and I am for enabling them to maintain their contacts with Jordan. To give them neither one nor the other—that is impossible.

I am speaking about what we should do in the third year, what common framework we should encourage, what resources we should devote, and which policy we should pursue in order to attain, or even partially advance, our objectives. We must act as a government there to reduce their dependence on the Arab states, and to increase their dependence on us. If we are not annexing these territories—and I do not suggest that we annex them at present—and we are not imposing Israel citizenship on their inhabitants, we must grant them a substantial degree of freedom, both communal and municipal, to conduct their lives as they see fit in Shehem, Hebron and Gaza and in their villages. And we should enable them to maintain their contacts with the Arab world, not sever them.

But the main emphasis in the question of what we must do lies not in the sphere of our relations with the Arab population but, rather, in the area of our relationship with ourselves. We must try out policies, especially at present, that could partially, if not completely, change the fundamental situation. We should not resign ourselves to saying: "The Arabs don't want peace, therefore we remain in the front lines." Such a freezing of the situation, by itself, is not good enough. Such a freeze, and the price we are forced to pay to maintain it, is far from making use of our full resources and capabilities.

For we are also capable of bringing about a change in the fundamental situation to some extent, even a structural change.

First and foremost, in the relations between the two peoples: between us and the Arabs of Judea, Samaria, and Gaza, 15,000 of whom work in our midst daily. I am wholeheartedly in favor of our mingling with them as much as possible in order to create a common framework of life. Certainly we will not become one people, or one culture, or members of one community. They live in Hebron and we in the Etzion Bloc. But let there be no barriers to our meeting one another, working with one another, intermingling, and then each going his own way to live his life according to his own lights. I do not believe that we can or should encourage Arab emigration from Judea and Samaria into Israel. But when there is unemployment in the occupied areas and work is available in Israel, we should enable them to work. We should not only provide them with jobs. We should create an interlocking economy with common power lines, and to the extent possible, a common network of water pipes.

We should view this country as one, economically speaking: common framework for a joint tourist industry to encompass Jerusalem, Bethlehem and Ramallah, joint transportation companies, economic assimilation and amalgamation of Gaza, Judea and Samaria with Israel.

If we do this, the situation will change in its human aspects, too. If we will live with them, and bind the two parts of this country together economically, it will no longer be the same country it was before, when the Green Line divided the two parts and anyone who crossed it invited and received a bullet.

We should also try to change the basic situation by weakening the formal and informal affiliation and identification of the Arab population in the occupied territories with the Arab countries, and reducing their dependence on them. Immediately following the war it seemed only natural that the mayor of Shehem be a Jordanian appointee and the mayor of Gaza an Egyptian one. The question now is whether, three years later, it is still natural that the Jordanian and Egyptian appointment systems continue to exist, and whether these should still determine who are to be the mayors, the judges and the other officials. In this, the third year, we must re-examine whether or not this formal connection should be maintained. Just as we have abolished the Egyptian pound as legal tender in the Gaza Strip, so must we re-examine the question whether the Jordanian dinar shall continue to serve as legal currency in Judea and Samaria. Maybe it should; maybe it shouldn't. But we should examine the matter and ask ourselves what measures we should take to weaken the formal ties of the inhabitants with, and their dependence on the Arab states and what we should do to enhance their ties with us.

And, of course, we must establish Jewish-Israeli settlements in the occupied territories, not only in the Golan, and not with the intention of later abandoning them. Not just tent encampments which can be put up and taken down in a day. We should set up such settlements only in areas from which we are convinced that we shall not withdraw, in accordance with what we consider a suitable future map. But we have to get going and do it.

All these things—the establishment of economic ties, the human contacts that will result from their working in our midst and our presence in their midst, the establishment of Jewish settlements and army bases in the territories, will eventually result in the creation of a new land. It will no longer be the same map, or the same structure, or the same situation.

At a time when we have been in the territories for two years and still do not see peace in the offing, when we are daily forced to pay the price along the Suez and in the Jordan Valley, we must try again and again, every day, to alter the basic situation so that it becomes easier for us to attain our desired objectives.

And finally, a word concerning the proposal that a solution be found by the four powers. In my opinion we should unequivocally reject such an approach and refuse to have anything to do with it. We must refuse to become the partners of the big powers in their desire to set themselves up as our guardians who will try to determine what will be in the Middle East.

We adopted two political principles in the aftermath of the Six Day War: one, we want new borders and refuse to return to the old ones; and two, we want a new relationship with the Arabs, a relationship of peace, normal peace such as exists between any other country in the world and its neighbors. A peace that will be achieved through negotiations around a table. We must adhere to and guard these principles. We don't need the Soviet Union's guarantees, nor those of the U.S. We don't want anyone else to guarantee anything for us. They did not fight us, or break the blockade of the Straits of Tiran.

We do not need guarantees—neither from four powers, nor from two powers, nor even from one power. We don't need U.N. forces to come, ostensibly to ensure free navigation, the free flow of oil and peace. And we don't need demilitarization of areas, or any similar arrangement. We live here with the Arabs; it is with them that we want to conclude peace and to establish new boundaries for our state.

We must obstinately insist on these two principles and reject any alternatives to a network of direct relationships of peace between Israel and the Arabs.

QUESTIONS AND ANSWERS

(following the speech)

QUESTION: Recently we have witnessed the intensification of Arab attacks against Israeli civilians and soldiers, especially in Gaza. Would it be at all practical to think in terms of transferring the Gaza population to other areas as a solution?

DAYAN: I think that the questioner is perfectly correct in distinguishing the factors which make Gaza different and cause the situation there to be more serious than in other places. The reason, of course, is the presence of the refugee camps in Gaza and its vicinity. This undermines the orderly course and structure of life there . . . I do not know to what extent we will be able to transfer part of the population—from among the indigenous population and from the refugees—to other locations. We certainly will not be able to do it without their consent. Today, any resident Arab or refugee is free to move to Judea or to Samaria and settle there—not to Israel though—and in general he also finds there better work, and better conditions than in the Gaza Strip. As far as I know, the authority in charge of the refugees—U.N.R.W.A.—does not deny refugee status to anyone moving from Gaza to, say, the Bethlehem or Shehem areas. That is to say that he continues to receive his allotted food rations in his new location too. This may eventually lead to some population shift. I do not believe that this can be effectuated forcibly, that these people can simply be loaded onto trucks and deposited someplace else. If they would want such a transfer I would certainly see it as a favorable development, and it is not impossible that such a development may occur, not involving large numbers, but some such movement may take place.

QUESTION: . . . Don't you agree that the growing seriousness of the situation and the resistance to us in the occupied territories two years after the war, would indicate that there is little chance of this changing unless the government changes its present policy in these territories?

DAYAN: . . . It's possible that if we had adopted a different policy it might have led to a certain change in the attitude of the Arabs there toward us, and to a lessening in their resistance. Theoretically, if we could have—and I do not believe that we could—attained a situation during these two years in which Jewish settlements would have been intermingled with Arab population concentrations so that there would not exist a solid concentration of Arabs in Shehem, Tubas, Ramallah and other places, there might have been a change for the better. This is a highly hypothetical conjecture, and I doubt whether it could have been carried out. Certainly not in two years.

But it seems to me that the questioner meant to ask whether we should not have adopted a more stringent policy in the territories and have had recourse to more severe measures. One of the possibilities, for example, is sentencing convicted terrorists to death. I am ready to assume that if every terrorist who was caught had been hanged this would have given the others pause and might perhaps have served to discourage some of them from further terrorist acts. But I must add that if I were called upon, today, to decide whether to recommend a policy of death sentences, I would decide against recommending it.

... I do not believe that such executions would do away with the acts of terrorism, or that they would create a better basis, in the long run, for a stable relationship between us and the Arabs ... At the moment, I believe that we should continue our war on the terrorists without hangings.

In regard to severer measures, we have been resorting to quite severe measures against the terrorists, and against those who have been collaborating with them or otherwise helping them. Besides bringing them to trial we have also been blowing up their homes. The question is whether we should view the Arabs in any locality as a collectivity, and say: "Stones were thrown there, or some other act was perpetrated, therefore let's clamp down a curfew on the entire community." I am against this. Even after two years I believe that we are correct in our policy of not treating the Arabs collectively, of distinguishing between the Arab who continues to live his life peacefully, who goes to work, opens his store or goes to school, and the others who abet the terror. This is to be preferred to the punishment of Shehem as a whole because it is Shehem and thereby setting Shehem against Tel Aviv, the Jews against the Arabs, us against them ...

Furthermore, we have not taken any steps to prevent expression of opposition, as long as they do not constitute a call to violence. I am very happy that an Arab paper is being published, and I know that the paper is not pro-Israel. If it would be pro-Israel it would be a Quisling paper. I believe that we should enable the Arab population of close to a million to have its own media of expression. If we want to attain some measure of normalization, if we want to be able to live together with them, we cannot write their newspapers for them. Let them write their own papers. We will not forbid them to listen to the radio or to watch television. Which means that they will be tuning in to Damascus or Cairo. So what? They are part of the Arab world.

I do not even know ... whether it is desirable to prevent the five thousand students in Judea and Samaria from studying at the universities of Cairo and Damascus, for we have no Arab universities of our own. And I am fully aware that while there, they not only receive an anti-Israel education, but some of them are given Fatah training and are inducted into el Fatah. I know this. But the alternative is to say to them: "There is Israel rule here. Therefore you will not be permitted to go to Cairo or to Damascus, for there you will be indoctrinated against us, and you will be enlisted in the Fatah. You stay here." And what will such a student do here? He'll stay here and say to himself: "This is how it is under Israel rule. I've been graduated from high school, but I can't study a profession and I can't study at all." Won't he then want to enlist in el Fatah? And can't he be trained by them here?

If our purpose is, at some time in the future, to arrive at a situation in which we can declare: We *can* live together, then we must find a way to enable the high school graduate to go on to a university, even to an Arab university. That he is indoctrinated there against us, and conscripted to fight us, is regrettable. If caught as a Fatah he will have to deal with the Israel Defense Forces, or rather, they will deal with him. But to establish a completely impossible framework from the outset is to give up on the possibility of any framework for a common existence.

Are we to become an occupying power and keep the Arabs as a suppressed population with second- and third-class rights? Are we to tell them: This you may not study, and that you may not do, and if something happens we will declare a curfew?

The question is, what are we aspiring to attain? If we want to achieve a capacity for joint existence, then we cannot be simply occupiers. We must also be neighbors . . .

QUESTION: Why shouldn't we deport any persons convicted of illegal activities in Judea and Samaria to Jordan? In this way we could get rid of extremist elements. If there is widespread opposition you'll be able to eliminate all extremist elements.

DAYAN: . . . I persist in my view that Israel's problem is how to live with the Arabs, not how to expel them . . .

Now after twenty years of statehood there was a war. We have a contiguous settlement of two and a quarter million Jews. We are confronted with three quarters of a million Arabs in Gaza and in the hill area. Do you want to tell me today that the solution to our problems is to throw them out across the bridges into Trans-Jordan? I believe that in the present situation we must seek ways to live together with them.

Let me take Hebron and the Cave of Machpela (the Patriarch's place) as an example. I have read all about it, and I know that Abraham bought the Cave of Machpela, etc. etc. Fine. In the meantime a mosque was built there, and it's been standing there for hundreds of years. Whether that is really the site of the original Cave of Machpela, I couldn't say. But I do know that there is a mosque standing there. At first they didn't let us get closer than the seventh step outside the mosque. Now that there's Israel rule there, we said: "This is both the Machpela and a mosque." We sat down together with the Moslem religious leaders and sought a way out of the problem. And I must say to the credit of the Hebronites that they, too, sought a solution which would enable both Jews and Moslems to worship in one place, for the place is holy both to us and to them. And that is because Abraham is a holy man both to us and to them. Their tradition, like ours, speaks of Abraham, Isaac, the Matriarchs, etc.

I know there are other Jews among those who were involved with this problem who believe otherwise (in general, everything I have said and am saying tonight is, of course, an expression of my personal opinion only). There are some who feel: We captured the place—to hell with everything, let's get rid of the mosque. This is our Cave of Machpela. There are all sorts of deeds from Abraham's days, and this place will belong to us alone. When the Arabs conquered it they made it like this. Now, we have conquered it and we will turn it into what we want.

I can't agree with this viewpoint. What do we want there? Do I need deeds to the Cave of Machpela to enable me to live there? I want to make it possible for Jews to come there to pray. Whoever wants to kiss the curtain on the graves, let him kiss them. And if the Arab on the other side of the partition is praying, let him pray. He isn't disturbing me. The question is whether I want to *prevent him* from doing something, or whether I want to *enable us* to do something. This, in a nutshell perhaps, is what the entire question concerning our relations with the Arabs is all about.

I repeat: is that what we want? To dispossess them? To expel them? Or is what we want, rather, to enable us to visit, settle, and maintain our forces there? If we are able to achieve all the positive things I believe Israel requires, we will do it without depriving them of anything—certainly not by dispossessing or expelling them. They will continue to live in Shehem and we will occupy the hill nearby, because we require it for security purposes. And we will settle near Hebron, in the Etzion Bloc, or somewhere else. And we will settle other places when we need them for our security or for other purposes.

This is the watershed between the two approaches. My approach is not to build a bridge and to expel as many as we can. The objective is to seek all possible ways to achieve agreement on living together. And I am happy about the Cave of Machpela, where this has somehow been achieved. It may not be a big thing but I prefer it that way, to be able to say: "Look, here is one place we are together."

I am also very happy about the situation in Jerusalem. I know that explosions and sabotage also occur in Jerusalem, more so than in other places. But within an hour you can go to the shops and the Arabs will be selling everything. We manage to live together. We will build alongside the university (on Mt. Scopus) and the city will no longer be divided. We will live alongside each other.

We need to live together. This is how I see the problem of Jerusalem. Not how to get rid of the seventy thousand Arabs there, but how to live with the seventy thousand Arabs. How to live with the Western Wall when it is adjacent to the Mosque of Omar...

QUESTION: Your motto throughout your lecture tonight has been, "How to live together with the Arabs in the hope that it will work out in the long run." With this in mind, don't you agree that Israel's failure to resettle the refugees is a serious omission on our part and that we should at least make an effort in this direction to prove to the Arabs that our image is not what they thought it was?

DAYAN: No. I don't agree that it is an omission because I don't believe that Israel can resettle the refugees . . . The question is whether there is an objective possibility in the areas under our control of resettling 200,000, 300,000 or 400,000 refugees and providing them with adequate sources of livelihood. These refugees formerly lived in what is today the State of Israel, and Israel has brought other inhabitants in their place, from Arab countries and from other places.

If Israel were to take back the refugees, in keeping with recent proposals that every Arab refugee be given the choice between returning or not, and assuming that they would say that they wanted to return (depend on the Arab states not to let any Arab indicate that he would prefer not to return) to Acre, Jaffa, Ashdod, Ashkelon, etc., we would no longer have a Jewish state. It may well be that our image among the Arabs would improve tremendously, but we would be left without the State of Israel.

I am opposed to taking back the Arab refugees into the territory of the State of Israel. They have been in the Gaza Strip for 20 years and they could not be absorbed there. That leaves Judea and Samaria . . . I believe that I am quite familiar with whatever concerns the problems of land, water and agriculture there. I do not believe that it will be possible to resettle the refugees there, certainly not without the cooperation and aid of Jordan, since all water development projects in the area . . . must be based on an assumption of regional cooperation, at least of cooperation with Jordan. Without such cooperation I simply do not see how one could take 200,000 refugees from the Gaza Strip and resettle them in Judea and Samaria. I don't see how it's possible, either from the economic or from the agricultural point of view. It is not a matter of establishing a model of how it could be done; it is, rather, a question of finding a solution to the problem, which is extremely difficult. I do not want to provide the solution within the State of Israel, because this would destroy the state; I do not believe that it's possible to achieve a solution in Judea and Samaria; and there is simply no room for one in the Gaza Strip.

It would be possible to truly resettle the refugees if there were only a little bit more cooperation; and not even on the part of all of the Arab states, but at least on the part of Jordan and of the international agencies. Without the cooperation of Jordan and of the international agencies (and the latter will not cooperate today as long as the Security Council resolution exists) it would be impossible to resettle not only all, but even a large part of the refugees in the areas under our control. "Well," you may ask, "what about resettling a small number?" This could be done, but in my opinion it will not lead to anything.

QUESTION: I would like to hear from you, as a prospective candidate for the premiership, what would be the basic lines of your policy for attaining peace?

DAYAN: I do not believe that we could do more to bring about a peace than we are doing today. In this connection I have only this to say to the Arabs: "Let's sit down together around the table and talk." They do not come; and we cannot make peace without them.

From the economic point of view, which is part of the larger picture I described above, I believe that we shall be able to hold out like this for many years. If we were only two and a quarter million Jews here, perhaps it would become impossible to hold out for that long. But there is world Jewry, especially the Jewish community of the U.S. and its material, technological and scientific assistance. If we have to remain along the Suez Canal, the Jordan and Golan, without attaining peace, and the Arabs persist in their refusal to make peace, I do not believe that we will weaken and break for economic reasons. We may have to pull in our belts, make do with less, adopt certain measures. But we will be able to carry on like this even if peace does not come . . .

YITZHAK BEN-AHARON

Yitzhak Ben-Aharon was born in Austria (Roumania) in 1906. He came to Palestine in 1928. The year before that he attended the School of Political and Economic Sciences in Berlin. Ben-Aharon was one of the founders of the *Hashomer Hatzair* (Marxist Socialists) in Roumania, pursuing his movement's ideological lines in Palestine as well but gradually moving towards a less rigid orientation and ultimately rising to leadership of the more moderate *Ahdut Ha'avodah*.

A captain in the Jewish Brigade of the British Army in World War II, he later joined the struggle to evict the English from Palestine. For a while he was secretary of the Tel Aviv Labor Council. Later he represented his party Ahdut Ha'avodah in the Knesset and in the Cabinet as Minister of Communications and Transport. In 1969 he was elected Secretary-General of the Histadrut, the immensely powerful General Federation of Labor.

Ben-Aharon has written a great deal on socio-political problems. His books include *Listen, Gentiles; Letters To My Son; On the Eve of Change*. He contributes regularly to the press.

Sometimes referred to as the "conscience" of the labor movement in Israel, Ben-Aharon is also regarded as the "guardian" of the political hygiene of his movement. Highly respected by his countrymen, he is the most articulate advocate of labor unity in Israel, which was in fact achieved partially by the merging of various parties into *Mifleget Avodah Yisraelit* and partially by an alignment with several other labor groups. His notions of justice are Sinaic first and Marxist second, although he strongly believes that the social future is not ordained but manipulative, but as Secretary General of the Histadrut he has had his problems.

THE JUST SOCIETY IN ISRAEL appeared in the *Jewish Frontier*, June, 1969, pp. 4—8, as part of a symposium, "The Jewish Conditions Today."

The Just Society in Israel

by ITZHAK BEN-AHARON

THE TITLE WHICH you chose for this morning's session is a sort of enigma, not only for you, but also for the Israelis. We have no clear-cut answers to that question and, before sticking any labels on ourselves and our society, I should like to be pragmatic and see what kind of yardstick we can use in order to get a fair notion about the make-up of Israeli society and economy.

I speak about society and economy, not because of my Marxist training, but because the interrelation between the two has a major bearing on the development of Israel as a society and as a nation. To make use of one single generalization as the key to an understanding: we are a developing society made up of immigration waves which began on a major scale about fifty years ago. If we take the Balfour Declaration as a starting point, fifty years ago there were about 60–80,000 Jews in the country and today we are close to $2\frac{1}{2}$ million. We must consider the whole chain of developments in Israel, in the world in general, and in the Jewish world throughout that time with particular stress on the last twenty years. We started with over 650,000 Jews at the establishment of the State and we cannot yet speak of any fixed economy or society because ours is still a developing society. Although all of us are Jews, or generally agree to call ourselves Jews, we are nevertheless made up of many cultures and origins. We are being amalgamated into a new type of Jewish entity.

Certainly, the development of such an entity is preceded first of all by the efforts to create an economy. The influx of immigrants whom we call, in our Zionist self-congratulatory style, *olim* ("ascenders"), are from the point of view of sociology just immigrants. This influx of hundreds of thousands of Jews into the country could not be absorbed by a simple natural process. There was nothing in the country prepared and set up which could, by its very nature, have absorbed those waves of immigrants. The Arab economy had its own character; the Turkish, and later the British-Arab regime, had nothing to offer to this type of immigrant, neither ideologically nor politically and, above all, not economically. The new immigrants just could not penetrate into the setup.

The Jewish immigration had therefore to create its own environment in all respects. And this process is still going on by different means, different set-ups and techniques. This very fact is probably one of the decisive issues in the understanding of the whole Israeli "miracle" as it was called by many tourists and scientific observers. The environment had to be created and the people had to create a country and an economy "in their own image." This need is also their ideology and their way of life.

Naturally, such a beginning is always a *halutzic,* a pioneering beginning. This was not only an ideological choice; above all, it was a must. There was just no other way, and for every *halutzic* pioneer attempt there had to be a plan of procedure for absorbing immigrants, because there were no latent powerful traditional forces inherent in the existing economy. Here the process of creation was natural. Australia, Canada, and America each in its time began a similar dialogue between the cultural and ideological notions of the immigrant and the objective conditions of the country. But in each of these lands the resulting developments were naturally different. In Palestine the first need was—co-operation; this is a fairly familiar feature in all new immigration waves. Co-operation was for the early immigrants, as it is to this day, one of the preconditions for survival. It was not merely a matter of using an efficient, organized way of carrying on, of working, of making a living—it was also the only way to survive. Very few individuals could survive in mass immigration unless they co-operated in many different ways and by many methods.

Secondly, they had to turn to the soil. I speak now from the point of view of Israel. The creation of industry, of communications, of all those upper storeys of an economy is of course preconditioned by certain developments of infrastructures that were non-existent in this country. The most elementary, immediate possibility for making a living in the existing national conditions left little choice but to go to the land. Land was always a basis for the shaping of a community.

Thirdly, whatever we did, we always had to defend ourselves. I am not going to continue with this historical analysis, but I mention these three basic elements in order to make clear that the ensuing processes in the development of the country and its society were basically predestined by that beginning. The objective conditions in the country and the consequent creation of a communal collective organization of rural communities was dictated by the need for self-defense. The ensuing tremendous consequences—their imprint on the character of the whole society which grew up in Israel—stems from these basic pioneer elements. Every country has a birth certificate whose imprint is powerful and maintains itself for ages. It also takes ages to get rid of it, if you so desire, but it certainly puts its stamp on the development of the community. In Israel its stamp is upon the society to be found here.

Another element was the fact that the Jewish people as such organized themselves for development, for settlement. These terms are inescapable in Israel. A basic element was a Jewish organization, the Zionist organization as founded by Herzl, which organized a section of the Jewish people with the sympathy of the vast masses of the people. It created implements, concrete state implements or quasi-state implements, development funds, investment funds for the reclamation of land, for irrigation, training centers, vocational schools and so on. In other words, we had here an enterprise of an international nature. We had a body of people with funds and some political status, which took it upon itself to accomplish certain tasks in this country. This sort of co-operation between local immigrants and an internationally-recognized world Jewish organization created the particular stress toward further development. And this form is with us to this day, with all its blessings and failings.

Now this concentration of Jewish strength—economic, cultural, even military under certain historical circumstances, brought about the establishment of the Jewish State. Naturally, with the establishment of the State we start a new chapter, because until the establishment of the State, we dealt with a semi-state organization. It should be remembered that throughout these years preceding the establishment of the State the people here and abroad felt that they were dealing with an independent Jewish community—the *Yishuv*, we called it. The *Yishuv* had its own quasi-government, a sort of state-on-the-way and its para-military organization—features which did not always correspond to the actual condition. They were in some sense propagandistic, educational, ideological and superimposed on actual fact.

The establishment of the State with its own government and all the apparatus of a state changed the position thoroughly. Yet to this day we cannot be sure whether the real conditions of Israel—notions, ideologies, organizations—have completely submitted to the fact of the State. In other words, the State itself is still a young offshoot of pre-state conditions, and in coolly assessing conditions, we must assume that the adaptation of the people to statehood is a prolonged process moving in a geometrical escalation. Each year, the generation growing up makes this process faster and more decisive.

What then is the society and the economy of Israel? Let's again consider a few facts. As far as I know, Israel is the only democratic, parliamentary state in the world which has, by law and tradition, nationalized its whole land. Nationalization, except for certain sectors owned by private individuals, is roughly in a ratio of 9 to 1. As far as I know, we are the only democratic, parliamentary state in the world which has nationalized all its natural resources by democratic means—by ballot, by parliament. It is the only democratic country in the world in which the labor organization, in our case Histadrut, is a body of organized labor representing almost the totality of the labor force. (Upon reaching 80–85% you can speak about a totality.) And this labor force maintains freely, without compulsion, a large slice of the economy of the country, a labor economy employing anywhere between a quarter to a third of the whole labor force. We are in this respect the only country in the whole world, both Soviet and free, where the co-operation of free people has created communal settlements and co-operative settlements which are, in fact, the dominant basis of its agriculture. And over the past ten years it has been edging into the industrial field as well. Already 15% of Israel's total industrial production is a part of our co-operative society.

In other words, in the nation, predominance lies strongly with an independent, free labor movement. This is a structural phenomenon of Israel and its society. Whatever people may think today about ideologies, whether to have socialism or not, co-operation is today an irrevocable characteristic of Israel's economy and society with all its consequences for the culture, organization, human relationships and other values of social life.

Many people have some difficulty in understanding the working of our economy—so have our economists—but some lines for its understanding may be found in two or three guideposts. First of all, the decisive weight of development funds and capital in this country is in the hands of the nation, no matter how these funds are obtained. It is a free country, of course, with free influx of private capital, private investment, and no objective limitation by law or policy exists. Still, the basic illuminating issue is that development of this country is being carried on by public funds in the hands of the state, the whole society. This is, of course, a most powerful element in any development scheme. It came about not by ideological choice—although ideologies were also involved. You need only remember those controversies at Zionist congresses: Berl Katzenelson versus Brandeis, Silver, Neumann, and many others. But the victory of the labor ideology in this field was not the outcome of a power struggle; it was the outcome of the objective conditions of the country. There was no other practical method.

Secondly, in spite of statehood, laws, or police, the development of such a a state as Israel can be carried out basically only by voluntary means. In our time, many countries in the world have reached unprecedented heights of development by dictatorial means. There are many sociologists, anti-socialists, and anti-Communists who believe that development projects on a vast scale, molding a new economy, a new nation in transition from medieval to modern times, cannot be done except by the power of the state, coercion, and regimentation. In Israel we could not act this way. We have had some ideologists quite capable of establishing a dictatorial regime, and within their own framework they did what they could in this respect. But the development of the country in the past and today could only be achieved by a free people. That is why the State had to adopt a policy of free enterprise, and to assist any kind of initiative, any kind of productive effort. Therefore there grew up in this country, during the past 40–50 years, a pluralistic form of economic enterprise and a variety of social forms and ways of life.

Nevertheless it must be stated that there is a dominant guiding influence—the hegemony of the public sector, Governmental and Histadrut. This is not a result of a power struggle but a result of prevailing motivation among the people. There are many discussions in this country today about where we are going. The economy and the way of life of the people is of course a market economy, and the economic process is based on profit. Its principles have evolved ideologically, politically and pragmatically. Ours is a free market economy based on the principle of profit. But if I stop here, I will have stated something worse than a lie: I will have stated a half-truth. In fact, the economy is based on general state insurance for all. You might call it a soft economy: here nobody falls on his head; here all of us fall like cats on our feet—from whatever story we drop! The Government, at this stage of development, must function as a developing unit, as an immigration and immigrant society, creating many things, including the immigrant! To guide the new immigrants, to keep them alive and to keep them above water, such insurance was inescapable.

From the point of view of the annual balance sheet and economics, this is, of course, an impossible procedure which makes nonsense of the basic prerequisites and postulates of the economy. This is one thing overlooked by many young economists in this country, and by many more outside it. We are still engaged and will continue to be engaged in an historical enterprise which is not be be judged by annual balance sheets. This applies not only to the State of Israel but to many formidable economic enterprises all over the world. Take, for instance, the atomic effort in the modern world. Is there a natural annual balance sheet for it? Can there be? Nor was there in the past for the building of railways. All those development schemes wherever they were, eventually brought with them profit for the individual, profit based on historic effort and historic investment and the sweat and blood of the nation. Not all of the people of the United States got the benefit out of the conquest of the West: the historical investment was that of the nation, the immediate profits and benefits were not divided appropriately between the nation and the individual.

In our case, if you project this further, we are still engaged, and will be for many years to come, in an historical investment scheme of the creation of land. Mark you, we are the only country in the world that I know of engaged in the creation of land. We had no land here to be handed on. Creation of land, water resources, communications, development of natural resources, development of the immigrant and his education, adaptation and integration, all of this had to be done *de novo*. At the same time we had to provide the major defense expenditure and defense efforts which are a basic integral part of our lives.

This has, of course, tremendous side benefits. The topic of our talk includes the problem of the military in our social set-up. You will realize readily that defense is not a separate arm. There is no such thing in Israel as a military establishment on its own. It is economically, humanly, not feasible. It is always very good if ideology goes hand in hand with objective conditions and one more or less determines the strength and the limits of the other. In Israel the military establishment is one of the basic features of the economy, of education, settlement, co-operative organization and the shaping of the unity of a nation. It is completely within the heart of the society and the nation and not a side issue, and not an off-shoot of the society with its own life and its own goals. Today, if you follow our development after the Six Day War, we have undertaken to make ourselves, as far as possible, independent in the manufacture of military equipment. We are also attempting independence in creating the most advanced aircraft. Naturally we are not asleep in the modern fields of atomics and electronics for peace. From the point of view of static economics, this is of course, absolute madness. But if you look at us, a small country, a small people in this "nice" geo-political set-up, defense is economics and economics is defense—and not only for us. I challenge you to investigate what defense is now in the whole make-up of the American economy.

Looked upon in a cold-blooded way that has no particular respect for economics as a science, a historic fight is going on in Israel between old-fashioned labor ideology and modern thought. I believe that this old-fashioned labor notion is going to be the last cry of modernism. About two years ago at a Berkeley seminar, I asked: "What are economics for and why can't you make of economics an exact science? After all, the ultimate object is man; man as an individual and man as society. It does not matter very much which way money and efforts are exchanged or ruled. The question is, what kind of control has man over his own creation?"

All we attempt in Israel is done as much by necessity as by ideology: our faithful battlefield ally, *ain breyra* ("no choice"), shapes the integrity of our national effort and national development. People are afraid of capitalistic development in this country. We have capitalists here and huge profits are made in this country. There are indecent standards of living, speculation, embezzlement—all properly 100% Jewish. However, just two preconditions are missing in this country which are required by such individualism. First of all, Moses did not put us into Iraq or even Kuwait. Israel is a poor strip of land, whatever may lie hidden within it. We are still looking for oil here, or for some such treasure. We may find it some day, or may not, but there is little in this country which can create for a fair section of the population a pseudo-American standard of living, a sort of American society. The preconditions for such a development are simply not here. In addition, consider labor. An efficient organization for extracting the last ounce of sweat from labor and then dividing national income arbitrarily in one way or another is just not available here.

This country, for a long time to come, if not forever, will not be a basis for the creation of vast private fortunes. Even if we had a fascist regime to extract from working people and from everyone else the last drop of sweat, it would still not be possible to achieve an American standard of living even for the Jew.

It is also a fact that countries of small population under democratic institutions cannot be turned toward a colonial status. The human values and the human shape developed in this country do not provide materials for colonialism. The Jewish man and woman of Israel with their particular background are just not the human material for a colonial experiment.

In conclusion, I would like to sum up with a few general observations. First, Israel's society is a workingman's society and cannot be altered. All modern industrialized societies are becoming workingmen's societies, whatever their concentration of power and money and wealth. In Israel, out of a population of approximately $2\frac{1}{2}$ million, there are about 800,000 men and women who get up at dawn and come home late. It is a workingman's society. The only basis for its existence is work and more work! This is one of the great victories of Zionism and one of the great victories of Socialist Zionism.

Second, the maintenance of a decent standard of living coupled with all other obligations dictated by the environment and by defense needs, presupposes the most highly qualified technological development and organization. There is no limit to the objective need for technological development in this country. In terms of politics this means the preponderance of social organization, planned and controlled by the society.

Third, for many years, I suppose for decades to come, the basic issue will remain new immigration. Without going deeply into this field I will point out only that I don't foresee any major changes in the development of Jewish history. Ups and downs, prosperity and crisis will follow each other in Jewish life all over the world. Those laws which worked in past Jewish history are still operative because the society of the gentile world is also still following in the same ways—and will continue until the Messiah comes. Until that time, crises in Jewish life in the Diaspora will continue. They may be different in nature. They may differ from the physical destruction under Hitler. It is just nonsense to maintain that Jews, or any other nationalities or sects, move only under the pressure of economic crisis or of danger to their very physical existence. The critical developments, the limits to Jewish adaptation to their environment, and the limits in the progress of mankind to absolute freedom and equality, these are the determining elements in Jewish life. And they are the background for further Jewish immigration to Israel, plus the tremendous, new, unprecedented fact of a new Jewish nation, society and state. For the first time in our history we have no yardstick for judgment. It is a matter for speculation, since we have never experienced the effect of a Jewish state on the spirit and soul of the Jewish people.

The critical development of Jewish life abroad in the world, in view of this new fact, is still not yet analyzed—or perhaps beyond analysis at present. The future developments of a new Jewish entity with all its bearings on man as man, and people as people, remains the third factor which is going to determine developments in Israel.

Fourth, and not last, certainly not least, is our position in the immediate Arab world in which there exists just one Jewish state. We don't know as yet all the implications of this fact. We had a little realistic flash in this position after the Sir Day War—a flash and smash! Many people are worried that our propaganda is not in good order. It is not our propaganda which is not in order—our victory is not in order for the world!

The problem of our standing in the world is a tremendous challenge for Jewish society here. We are like the one Jewish boy in a gentile college. We are sitting in a class of about one hundred and fifty nations in the world with a single Jewish member whom we call the State of Israel. This is a tremendous challenge to be met for the sake of existence as well as for ideological reasons. It must be met by a tremendous effort in the field of values—in depth, not in the superficial sense which can, of course, be attained. And we have attained it. To overtake the Americans and the Dutch in the output of milk per cow is not a simple task, but we have done it. (It is also difficult in basketball: we have got to bring in American immigrants if only because they come over two meters tall.) We are a state, a society, and an economy under permanent challenge. This has produced the need for judging things by historically unprecedented criteria, things that are in any case beyond rational measure. These *imponderabilia* must be taken as part and parcel of the understanding of Jewish society throughout the ages, and the more so for the realistic interpretation of Israel.